T0336731

Delivery and Adoption of Cloud Computing Services in Contemporary Organizations

Victor Chang
Computing, Creative Technologies and Engineering, Leeds Beckett University, UK

Robert John Walters
Electronics and Computer Science, University of Southampton, UK

Gary Wills
Electronics and Computer Science, University of Southampton, UK

A volume in the Advances in Systems Analysis, Software Engineering, and High Performance Computing (ASASEHPC) Book Series

An Imprint of IGI Global

Managing Director:	Lindsay Johnston
Managing Editor:	Austin DeMarco
Director of Intellectual Property & Contracts:	Jan Travers
Acquisitions Editor:	Kayla Wolfe
Production Editor:	Christina Henning
Typesetter:	Amanda Smith
Cover Design:	Jason Mull

Published in the United States of America by
    Information Science Reference (an imprint of IGI Global)
    701 E. Chocolate Avenue
    Hershey PA, USA 17033
    Tel: 717-533-8845
    Fax: 717-533-8661
    E-mail: cust@igi-global.com
    Web site: http://www.igi-global.com

Copyright © 2015 by IGI Global. All rights reserved. No part of this publication may be reproduced, stored or distributed in any form or by any means, electronic or mechanical, including photocopying, without written permission from the publisher. Product or company names used in this set are for identification purposes only. Inclusion of the names of the products or companies does not indicate a claim of ownership by IGI Global of the trademark or registered trademark.

    Library of Congress Cataloging-in-Publication Data

Delivery and adoption of cloud computing services in contemporary organizations / Victor Chang, Robert John Walters, and Gary Wills, editors.
    pages cm
 Includes bibliographical references and index.
  ISBN 978-1-4666-8210-8 (hardcover) -- ISBN 978-1-4666-8211-5 (ebook) 1. Organizational change. 2. Information technology--Management. 3. Cloud computing. I. Chang, Victor, 1976- editor. II. Walters, Robert John, 1958- editor. III. Wills, Gary, 1962- editor.
  HD58.8.D443 2015
  658'.0546782--dc23
                    2015003295

This book is published in the IGI Global book series Advances in Systems Analysis, Software Engineering, and High Performance Computing (ASASEHPC) (ISSN: 2327-3453; eISSN: 2327-3461)

British Cataloguing in Publication Data
A Cataloguing in Publication record for this book is available from the British Library.

All work contributed to this book is new, previously-unpublished material. The views expressed in this book are those of the authors, but not necessarily of the publisher.

For electronic access to this publication, please contact: eresources@igi-global.com.

Advances in Systems Analysis, Software Engineering, and High Performance Computing (ASASEHPC) Book Series

Vijayan Sugumaran
Oakland University, USA

ISSN: 2327-3453
EISSN: 2327-3461

MISSION

The theory and practice of computing applications and distributed systems has emerged as one of the key areas of research driving innovations in business, engineering, and science. The fields of software engineering, systems analysis, and high performance computing offer a wide range of applications and solutions in solving computational problems for any modern organization.

The **Advances in Systems Analysis, Software Engineering, and High Performance Computing (ASASEHPC) Book Series** brings together research in the areas of distributed computing, systems and software engineering, high performance computing, and service science. This collection of publications is useful for academics, researchers, and practitioners seeking the latest practices and knowledge in this field.

COVERAGE

- Computer System Analysis
- Performance Modelling
- Computer Networking
- Virtual Data Systems
- Metadata and Semantic Web
- Computer Graphics
- Engineering Environments
- Storage Systems
- Human-Computer Interaction
- Software engineering

IGI Global is currently accepting manuscripts for publication within this series. To submit a proposal for a volume in this series, please contact our Acquisition Editors at Acquisitions@igi-global.com or visit: http://www.igi-global.com/publish/.

The Advances in Systems Analysis, Software Engineering, and High Performance Computing (ASASEHPC) Book Series (ISSN 2327-3453) is published by IGI Global, 701 E. Chocolate Avenue, Hershey, PA 17033-1240, USA, www.igi-global.com. This series is composed of titles available for purchase individually; each title is edited to be contextually exclusive from any other title within the series. For pricing and ordering information please visit http://www.igi-global.com/book-series/advances-systems-analysis-software-engineering/73689. Postmaster: Send all address changes to above address. Copyright © 2015 IGI Global. All rights, including translation in other languages reserved by the publisher. No part of this series may be reproduced or used in any form or by any means – graphics, electronic, or mechanical, including photocopying, recording, taping, or information and retrieval systems – without written permission from the publisher, except for non commercial, educational use, including classroom teaching purposes. The views expressed in this series are those of the authors, but not necessarily of IGI Global.

Titles in this Series

For a list of additional titles in this series, please visit: www.igi-global.com

Emerging Research in Cloud Distributed Computing Systems
Susmit Bagchi (Gyeongsang National University, South Korea)
Information Science Reference • copyright 2015 • 370pp • H/C (ISBN: 9781466682139) • US $200.00 (our price)

Resource Management of Mobile Cloud Computing Networks and Environments
George Mastorakis (Technological Educational Institute of Crete, Greece) Constandinos X. Mavromoustakis (University of Nicosia, Cyprus) and Evangelos Pallis (Technological Educational Institute of Crete, Greece)
Information Science Reference • copyright 2015 • 432pp • H/C (ISBN: 9781466682252) • US $215.00 (our price)

Research and Applications in Global Supercomputing
Richard S. Segall (Arkansas State University, USA) Jeffrey S. Cook (Independent Researcher, USA) and Qingyu Zhang (Shenzhen University, China)
Information Science Reference • copyright 2015 • 672pp • H/C (ISBN: 9781466674615) • US $265.00 (our price)

Challenges, Opportunities, and Dimensions of Cyber-Physical Systems
P. Venkata Krishna (VIT University, India) V. Saritha (VIT University, India) and H. P. Sultana (VIT University, India)
Information Science Reference • copyright 2015 • 328pp • H/C (ISBN: 9781466673120) • US $200.00 (our price)

Human Factors in Software Development and Design
Saqib Saeed (University of Dammam, Saudi Arabia) Imran Sarwar Bajwa (The Islamia University of Bahawalpur, Pakistan) and Zaigham Mahmood (University of Derby, UK & North West University, South Africa)
Information Science Reference • copyright 2015 • 354pp • H/C (ISBN: 9781466664852) • US $195.00 (our price)

Handbook of Research on Innovations in Systems and Software Engineering
Vicente García Díaz (University of Oviedo, Spain) Juan Manuel Cueva Lovelle (University of Oviedo, Spain) and B. Cristina Pelayo García-Bustelo (University of Oviedo, Spain)
Information Science Reference • copyright 2015 • 745pp • H/C (ISBN: 9781466663596) • US $515.00 (our price)

Handbook of Research on Architectural Trends in Service-Driven Computing
Raja Ramanathan (Independent Researcher, USA) and Kirtana Raja (IBM, USA)
Information Science Reference • copyright 2014 • 759pp • H/C (ISBN: 9781466661783) • US $515.00 (our price)

Handbook of Research on Embedded Systems Design
Alessandra Bagnato (Softeam R&D, France) Leandro Soares Indrusiak (University of York, UK) Imran Rafiq Quadri (Softeam R&D, France) and Matteo Rossi (Politecnico di Milano, Italy)

www.igi-global.com

701 E. Chocolate Ave., Hershey, PA 17033
Order online at www.igi-global.com or call 717-533-8845 x100
To place a standing order for titles released in this series, contact: cust@igi-global.com
Mon-Fri 8:00 am - 5:00 pm (est) or fax 24 hours a day 717-533-8661

Table of Contents

Section 3
Current Cloud Advances

Section 4
Proofs-of-Concept and Demonstrations

Konstantinos Koumaditis, University of Piraeus, Greece
George Pittas, University of Piraeus, Greece
Marinos Themistocleous, University of Piraeus, Greece
George Vassilacopoulos, University of Piraeus, Greece
Andriana Prentza, University of Piraeus, Greece
Dimosthenis Kyriazis, University of Piraeus, Greece
Flora Malamateniou, University of Piraeus, Greece

Wei Chen, The University of Texas MD Anderson Cancer Center, USA
Yun Wan, School of Arts & Science, University of Houston - Victoria, USA
Bo Peng, The University of Texas MD Anderson Cancer Center, USA
Christopher I Amos, Geisel School of Medicine, Dartmouth College, USA

Kiran Voderhobli, Leeds Beckett University, UK

ChandraMani Sharma, Institute of Technology and Science, Ghaziabad, India
Deepika Sharma, Govindam Business School, India
Harish Kumar, Institute of Technology and Science, India

Section 5
Security

Pasquale Puzio, SecludIT, France & EURECOM, France
Refik Molva, EURECOM, France
Melek Önen, EURECOM, France
Sergio Loureiro, SecludIT, France

Deniz Tuncalp, Istanbul Technical University, Turkey

Chapter 18

Detailed Table of Contents

Section 1
Cloud Fundamentals and Surveys

    Victor Chang, Computing, Creative Technologies and Engineering, Leeds Beckett University,
       UK
    Robert John Walters, Electronics and Computer Science, University of Southampton, UK
    Gary B. Wills, Electronics and Computer Science, University of Southampton, UK

This chapter presents a selected review for Cloud Computing and explains the issues and risks of adopting Cloud Computing in a business environment. Although all the risks identified may be associated with two major Cloud adoption challenges, a framework is required to support organisations as they begin to use Cloud and minimise risks of Cloud adoption. Eleven Cloud Computing frameworks are investigated and a comparison of their strengths and limitations is made. The result of the comparison is that none of them can deal with all the Cloud adoption challenges thoroughly and a new, comprehensive framework is required if organisations are to overcome these challenges. This proposed framework would ensure that benefits of Cloud adoption are maximised whilst minimising the risks of Cloud adoption and can integrate existing and new projects with Leeds Beckett Cloud.

    Kijpokin Kasemsap, Suan Sunandha Rajabhat University, Thailand

This chapter introduces the role of cloud computing adoption in global business, thus explaining the application overview of cloud computing, the adoption of Information and Communication Technology (ICT), and the Technology, Organization, and Environment (TOE) framework related to technological context, organizational context, and environmental context. In addition, technological context includes the relative advantage, uncertainty, compatibility, and trialability. Organizational context includes the size, top management support, innovation, and prior technology experience. Environmental context includes competitive pressure, industry, market scope, and supplier computing support. Adopting cloud computing in global business will significantly enhance organizational performance and achieve business goals in the digital age.

Chapter 3

Morgan Eldred, University of Portsmouth, UK
Carl Adams, University of Portsmouth, UK
Alice Good, University of Portsmouth, UK

The global nature of cloud computing has resulted in emerging challenges, such as clashes between legal systems, cultural differences, and business practice norms: cloud-computing is at the forefront of recognising, and "smoothing over," emergent differences between nation states as we move towards a more globally connected world. This chapter uses the emergent differences over regulation governing data protection; as the world becomes more interconnected, we are likely to see more examples of technology practices and models sweeping around the globe, and raising further areas for clashes between nations and regions, much like the fault lines between tectonic plates. This chapter provides contribution by capturing some emergent "fault lines" in an in-depth case study comparing the evolving EU directives covering data protection and how they relate to non-EU data protection legal systems. This provides the foundations to consider cloud-computing challenges, inform policymakers in measures to resolve "clashes," and in informing researchers investigating other global technology phenomena.

Section 2
Cloud Adoption Issues and Cases

Chapter 4

Victor Chang, Computing, Creative Technologies and Engineering, Leeds Beckett University,
UK

This chapter explains the use of Organizational Sustainability Modeling (OSM), a model to evaluate the status of risk and return for Cloud Computing including Mobile Cloud, where the customer satisfaction rate is an important indicator. The authors describe how to use OSM to collect and analyze French and Italian 2011 data, in which the iPhone 4S Cloud service is used as the representation for Mobile Cloud industry. OSM data analysis shows that French and Italian data have declined customer satisfaction, being affected by the economic downturn. There are medium-high uncontrolled risks and good data consistencies in both countries. The use of 3D Visualization helps further data analysis and interpretation. Comparisons between French and Italian data are presented, and rationale for their similarities and differences are explained in detail. Additionally, OSM and other similar methods are compared. Due to the capabilities to support both quantitative and qualitative approaches with support from real case studies, OSM is a better method to analyze customer satisfaction in Mobile Cloud.

Chapter 5

Cloud Computing is an increasingly important worldwide development in business service provision. The business benefits of Cloud Computing usage include reduced IT overhead costs, greater flexibility of services, reduced TCO (Total Cost of Ownership), on-demand services, and improved productivity. As a result, Small and Medium-Sized Enterprises (SMEs) are increasingly adopting Cloud Computing technology because of these perceived benefits. The most economical deployment model in Cloud Computing is called the Public Cloud, which is especially suitable for SMEs because it provides almost immediate access to hardware resources and reduces their need to purchase an array of advanced hardware and software applications. The changes experienced in Cloud Computing adoption over the past decade are unprecedented and have raised important issues with regard to privacy, security, trust, and reliability. This chapter presents a conceptual model for Cloud Computing adoption by SMEs in Australia.

Chapter 6

Nowadays, cloud computing is becoming popular within the business environment. Cloud services is not new, but the evolution of mobility, connectivity, and computing hardware has made it interesting for the business. Cloud services provides a way to increase the capacity or add capabilities dynamically without investing in new IT infrastructure, training new personnel, or licensing new software. Focusing on the consumer product goods (CPG) market with its mainly small and medium-sized companies, we see dramatic changes from the market demands, logistic challenges and price competition. The purpose of this chapter is therefore to present the positioning of cloud services in the CPG industry and to outline an approach that enables a typical company in the CPG industry to link the current capabilities of cloud services this to a business-process-driven evaluation approach to provide a transparency for the decision towards cloud services. The result of the business process investigation underlies assumptions and inductive conclusions.

Chapter 7

Half of the world's population live in rural areas and majority of them are in developing countries. The rural population face many challenges in their life compared to their urban counterparts. Some of these challenges include high unemployment rate, limited employment opportunities in their areas, high brain drain to more developed cities, lack of access to education and healthcare facilities. Information and communication technology has been identified as the enabling technology that can be used to overcome the present day problems. There are several ICT projects implemented across the world with the objective of helping these rural masses. But many of these projects face sustainability challenges due to lack of resources. In this chapter, the author takes an in depth look at how cloud computing can be leveraged successfully to address the sustainability problem of current rural ICT implementation.

Section 3
Current Cloud Advances

Chapter 8

Abdulelah Alwabel, University of Southampton, UK

Robert John Walters, University of Southampton, UK

Gary B. Wills, University of Southampton, UK

Cloud computing is a new paradigm that promises to move IT a step further towards utility computing, in which computing services are delivered as a utility service. Traditionally, Cloud employs dedicated resources located in one or more data centres in order to provide services to clients. Desktop Cloud computing is a new type of Cloud computing that aims at providing Cloud capabilities at low or no cost. Desktop Clouds harness non dedicated and idle resources in order to provide Cloud services. However, the nature of such resources can be problematic because they are prone to failure at any time without prior notice. This research focuses on the resource allocation mechanism in Desktop Clouds. The contributions of this chapter are threefold. Firstly, it defines and explains Desktop Clouds by comparing them with both Traditional Clouds and Desktop Grids. Secondly, the paper discusses various research issues in Desktop Clouds. Thirdly, it proposes a resource allocation model that is able to handle node failures.

Chapter 9

Norhazlina Hamid, University of Southampton, UK

Robert John Walters, University of Southampton, UK

Gary B. Wills, University of Southampton, UK

A multi-core cluster is a cluster composed of numbers of nodes where each node has a number of processors, each with more than one core within each single chip. Cluster nodes are connected via an interconnection network. Multi-cored processors are able to achieve higher performance without driving up power consumption and heat, which is the main concern in a single-core processor. A general problem in the network arises from the fact that multiple messages can be in transit at the same time on the same network links. This chapter considers the communication latencies of a multi core multi cluster architecture, investigated using simulation experiments and measurements under various working conditions.

Chapter 10

Zakaria Benzadri, University of Constantine 2, Algeria

Chafia Bouanaka, University of Constantine 2, Algeria

Faïza Belala, University of Constantine 2, Algeria

Cloud Computing is an emerging topic with high potentials in the IT industry. Its offered services need to be adapted to deal with variations caused by hostile environment, such as the Internet. Hence, a challenging issue in Cloud systems architecture is to model and analyze cloud-based services. However, few work has been dedicated to guarantee safe and secure adaptable services. The main objective of this chapter is to propose a formal framework for specifying cloud systems and offering analysis support to model-check their inherent properties. Based on Bigraphical Reactive Systems, the formalization process is achieved via the definition of the BiCloud-Arch model. Then, cloud architecture dynamics is formalized by a set of generic reaction rules to be applied on the obtained bigraphical model. This chapter also addresses a mapping from the proposed model (BiCloud-Arch) to a Maude-based formal executable specification (BiCloud-2M). On this basis, the proposed BiCloud Maude-based Model Checker (BMMC) is used to formally verify some Cloud system properties.

Chapter 11

Leonard Heilig, University of Hamburg, Germany
Stefan Voß, University of Hamburg, Germany
Lars Wulfken, Amazon Web Services, Germany

The highly automated and scalable nature of cloud computing encourages practitioners and scholars to reconsider software delivery processes. To efficiently leverage the benefits of elastic clouds, applications are typically provisioned and deployed several times a day in different environments and regions. Related procedures must support agile development and deployment of software components as well as the associated management of different versions and configurations. To efficiently utilize auto-scaling mechanisms, the latency produced by provisioning and deployment activities needs to be reduced while ensuring consistency, repeatability and reliability. In this chapter, an integrative process-oriented approach to improve the overall quality and performance of deployment processes is presented. Based on a comprehensive analysis of requirements, the proposed process considers the link between deployment and configuration management as well as tools and organizational aspects. Further, related research challenges and a case study focusing on the Adobe Shared Cloud are presented.

Section 4
Proofs-of-Concept and Demonstrations

Chapter 12

Konstantinos Koumaditis, University of Piraeus, Greece
George Pittas, University of Piraeus, Greece
Marinos Themistocleous, University of Piraeus, Greece
George Vassilacopoulos, University of Piraeus, Greece
Andriana Prentza, University of Piraeus, Greece
Dimosthenis Kyriazis, University of Piraeus, Greece
Flora Malamateniou, University of Piraeus, Greece

Healthcare organisations are forced to reconsider their current business practices and embark on a cloud adoption journey. Cloud-Computing offers important benefits that make it attractive for healthcare (e.g. cost effective model, big data management etc.). Large Information Technology (IT) companies are investing big sums in building infrastructure, services, tools and applications to facilitate Cloud-Computing for healthcare organisations, practitioners and patients. Yet, many challenges that such integration projects contain are still in the e-health research agenda like design and technology requirements to handle big volume of data, ensure scalability and user satisfaction to name a few. The purpose of this chapter is (a) to address the Cloud-Computing services for healthcare in the form of a Personal Healthcare record (PHR) and (b) demonstrate a multidisciplinary project. In doing so, the authors aim at increasing the awareness of this important endeavour and provide insights on Cloud-Computing e-health services for healthcare organisations.

This chapter discussed the latest development of using cloud-computing technology for genome sequencing in bioinformatics field. It introduced the definition of genome sequencing and cloud computing, discussed the current status of NGS in cloud with the example of Nimbix. It also provided a rich source of cloud computing related service providers and technologies for references. Finally, it discussed the challenges of conducting NGS in a cloud environment.

This chapter describes a novel approach to study network patterns in a data centre with the aim of reducing power consumed. Cloud infrastructures rely on numerous networked devices in data-centers to provide virtualization and sharing of resources. Network traffic is one of the key contributors to power consumption. Numerous techniques to develop power-aware data-centers have been proposed in the recent years. Virtualization management is based on many critical decisions including work-load, utilization, location of physical resources etc. This chapter takes a unique network management angle to greening a data center. It describes how Simple Network Management Protocol (SNMP) has a great potential to characterize traffic which can then feed into decisions for management of virtualized entities.

Massive military manpower is deployed on borders to keep a vigilant eye on possible infiltration from neighboring countries. This traditional approach is prone to errors because of human factors. To make border surveillance more effective, countries have installed CCTV cameras on borders but generally such systems are passive in nature and require human operators to keep an eye on the captured video footage. This chapter describes a cloud based approach for infiltration detection in border defense environments. The processing of video data, in cloud, and the real-time response are the factors that make system suitable for military purposes. As far as affordability is concerned, the governments can easily bear expense of establishing a private cloud for implementing visual surveillance. This chapter represents pertinent research of authors in the field of visual surveillance as well as other state-of-the-art breakthroughs in this area. The chapter is of multi-disciplinary significance in the field of cloud computing, video & image processing, behavioral sciences, and defense studies.

Section 5
Security

Pasquale Puzio, SecludIT, France & EURECOM, France

Refik Molva, EURECOM, France

Melek Önen, EURECOM, France

Sergio Loureiro, SecludIT, France

With the continuous increase of the number of users and the size of their data, data deduplication becomes a necessity for cloud storage providers. By storing a unique copy of duplicate data, cloud providers greatly reduce their storage and data transfer costs. The advantages of deduplication unfortunately come with a high cost in terms of new security and privacy challenges. In this chapter we propose ClouDedup, a secure and efficient storage service which assures block-level deduplication and data confidentiality at the same time. Although ClouDedup is based on convergent encryption, it remains secure thanks to the definition of a component that implements an additional encryption operation. Furthermore, as the requirement for deduplication at block-level raises an issue with respect to key management, we suggest to include a new component in order to implement the key management for each block together with the actual deduplication operation. In this chapter we show how we have implemented the proposed architecture, the challenges we have met and our solutions to these challenges.

Deniz Tuncalp, Istanbul Technical University, Turkey

There are a number of risk domains that are relevant for information privacy and security in cloud-based scenarios and alternative deployment models, which require implementation of a number of controls. However, cloud service providers often take a one-size-fits-all approach and want all their customers to accept the same standardized contract, regardless of their particular information security and legal compliance needs. Taking ISO 27001 Information Security Management standard as a guide, we have employed the Delphi method with a group of cloud computing experts from around the world who are subscribed to the "Cloud Computing" group on LinkedIN to identify the most applicable controls in a generic cloud service provider – customer context. Based on these results, we use a sample of cloud computing customer service agreement as a case study to further discuss related contingencies. As a result, this chapter argues that a more balanced approach is needed in service contracts to ensure the maintenance of necessary service levels and the protection of cloud users.

Enterprise security is the key to achieve global information security in business and organisations. Enterprise Cloud computing is a new paradigm for that enterprise where businesses need to be secured. However, this new trend needs to be more systematic with respect to Enterprise Cloud security. This chapter has developed a framework for enterprise security to analyze and model Enterprise Cloud organisational security of the Enterprise Cloud and its data. In particular, Enterprise Cloud data & Enterprise Cloud storage technologies (Amazon s3, Drop Box, Google Drive, etc.) have now become a normal practice for almost every computing user's. Therefore, building trust for Enterprise Cloud users should be the one of the main focuses of Enterprise Cloud computing research. This chapter has developed a framework for enterprises which comprises of two models of businesses: Enterprise Cloud provider enterprise model and Enterprise Cloud consumer enterprise model.

Preface

In its origins, computing and computer services were confined to a small number of people with specialized knowledge and needs, but this is no longer the case. In recent years, computer services have grown up to become a widespread general resource of interest and has a major impact on our everyday work and lives. In the commercial context, organizations are finding they need to process and store ever-increasing quantities of data and manage constantly evolving technology, although this work is not their core business in most cases. Many, especially small and medium organizations, are looking to Cloud Computing for help with these difficulties. Cloud Computing can offer a ready-made solution which does not require major investment in hardware, infrastructure and expertise, and is also able to expand and contract according to demand whilst the costs incurred reflect only the resources actually used.

This notion of ready access to computing services as and when we need or want them, utility computing, is not new. It represents a vision which was proposed as long ago as the 1960s when John McCarthy suggested that in the future people and organisations would simply plug in to a computing facility for computational resources rather than using their own. His vision was of a pattern of use just like connecting to an electrical outlet for power with fees charged based on what is used. Cloud Computing may be thought of as a logical evolution of these envisioned computing concepts which uses modern techniques to provide an elastic, self-managed, cost- and energy-effective computing environment. Cloud Computing is a new business model that delivers computing capabilities at different levels, ranging from computing infrastructure to high-end applications for a fee according to any agreed service level agreements and usage.

This book looks at a variety of issues and factors which may affect an organization considering; as such, it will be of interest to professionals and researchers working in the field of Cloud Computing in various disciplines such as computer science, consulting, information technology, information and communication sciences, healthcare, and finance. The book also provides insights and support for executives concerned with the management of expertise, knowledge, information, and organizational development of different types of Cloud implementations.

The book is organized into five sections as follows:

CLOUD FUNDAMENTALS AND SURVEYS

The first section includes three chapters, each of which considers fundamental aspects of Cloud adoption, frameworks to assist organizations considering Cloud, and factors which may affect their decision to go ahead.

The first chapter, "Cloud Computing and Frameworks for Organisational Cloud Adoption," describes existing work to develop frameworks for Cloud adoption. It looks at 11 published frameworks for Cloud adoption, compares and contrasts these various frameworks, and identifies weaknesses within them. The chapter includes a technical review of Cloud Computing and considers how organizations adopt Cloud Computing, business models they use, and risks associated with the adoption. The chapter then proposes a new framework for Cloud adoption that addresses the weaknesses identified in existing work.

The second chapter considers the role of Cloud Computing adoption in global business and how the flexibility offered by Cloud Computing permits small and medium sized enterprises to compete with larger competitors. This is possible because, where in the past these smaller organizations have been unable to afford or justify the costs of traditional IT implementations where the software, hardware and networking, Cloud Computing permits them to gain access to these facilities by buying-in what they need as a service from a Cloud service provider. The chapter considers the implications for global business and proposes a framework for adoption of Cloud computing in this context.

The third chapter considers the implications of another consequence for organizations of adopting Cloud-based storage solutions which is that, whilst remaining readily available, data stored "in the Cloud" is not normally held at the organization's own premises. A number of consequences follow from this movement of data from the owner's premises. The most obvious concern is security: loss or unauthorized disclosure of this data. Such events are nearly always embarrassing and may even destroy and organization. Another concerns the necessity for organizations to comply with data protection laws and related regulations. Ideally, these would be the same, or at least compatible, throughout the world, but unfortunately, this is not the case, which can cause difficulties for organizations storing data "in the Cloud" where the service provider operates in more than one country. The chapter focuses on the present regulatory position in Europe and also examines the differences between EU and non-EU regulations. It then discusses have how binding corporate rules might be used to resolve some of the difficulties.

CLOUD ADOPTION ISSUES AND CASES

The second section of the book comprises four chapters that examine Cloud adoption issues in four specific situations.

Chapter 4 looks at how to model the risks associated with adoption of Cloud Computing. The chapter presents a method for the analysis of risk that highlights the importance of differentiating between risks which can be controlled and those which cannot. The first category of risks relate to events such as hardware failures which are in the control of the operator and may be controlled and ameliorated in contrast with the other category, such as a general downturn in economic activity. The chapter shows the proposed modeling technique being applied to a studies of Mobile Cloud systems in France and Italy.

The next chapter in this section looks at the adoption of Cloud Computing by small- and medium-sized enterprises in Australia where there is growing interest in Cloud adoption. The authors carried on out a survey of thirty such enterprises with the aim of discovering enabling and inhibiting factors for adoption of Cloud Computing. They use their results in the development of a conceptual model for Cloud Computing adoption by small and medium sized enterprises in Australia.

Chapter 6 provides an analysis of Cloud Computing in the consumer products industry, starting with the observation that improvements to IT technology mean services previously limited to large enterprises are now available to all by using Cloud Computing to rent necessary computing resources on demand; Cloud Computing provides a means for enterprises to adjust capacity and capabilities rapidly without investing in new infrastructure and personnel. The chapter presents the position of Cloud services in the consumer products market and outlines an approach to a business process driven evaluation of Cloud Services.

The final chapter in this section looks at the use of Cloud Computing in the delivery of Information and Communications Technologies (ICT) to rural populations located far from urban centres who have traditionally faced a lack of access to infrastructures and services readily available in urban areas. The chapter examines the shortcomings of traditional approaches to ICT implementations for such populations which are unable to afford to buy computing hardware and then looks at how Cloud Computing projects can overcome these issues.

CURRENT CLOUD ADVANCES

The four chapters in this section describe work to develop new Cloud implementations and improvements to existing systems. The first two chapters describe approaches to the construction of Cloud Computing systems; the third describes a novel approach to the construction of a computing cloud whilst the final chapter looks at the communication networks connecting the nodes within computing clusters or Clouds.

The first chapter of this section notes that errors in any distributed system are difficult to locate and correct and this problem is exacerbated by the complexity of modern Cloud implementations. It is therefore proposed that a formal approach be adopted to development of Cloud systems leading to an executable specification which may be subjected to evaluation using model checking software and a framework to support this approach is described.

Automated deployment of resources is a necessary feature of any Cloud Computing environment. It is this property of elasticity whereby resources are allocated to and removed from users as their needs rise and fall that sets it apart from other approaches. This chapter examines work to improve auto-scaling mechanisms and presents an approach to solving the problem.

The third chapter of this section considers a problem in the management of Desktop Clouds. In common with Volunteer Grids, a Desktop Cloud uses spare capacity available in the many personal computers running in offices and homes in place the traditional approach of using dedicated hardware located in purpose-built datacenters. A particular problem for this approach is that individual machines may be withdrawn from the Cloud at any time. This chapter examines this problem and proposes a resource allocation approach able to cope with such failures.

Based on the conjecture that efficient communications between the nodes is a key requirement for good performance of any example of distributed computing whether it be Cluster, GRID, or Cloud, the final chapter in this section looks at a model of the communications between the nodes of a distributed system. It presents a new model of this communications that addresses the particular issues that arise when the nodes of such systems use modern, multi-cored processors.

PROOFS-OF-CONCEPT AND DEMONSTRATIONS

The four chapters in this section describe studies of particular applications of Cloud Computing: ihealthcare, genome sequencing, "green-aware" networks, and intrusion detection systems.

The first chapter in this section identifies that Large IT businesses are investing heavily to facilitate the implementation of Cloud Computing-based solutions for healthcare organizations but that many challenges remain, including ensuring scalability and user satisfaction. It looks in particular at the implementation of a Personal Healthcare Record system as a demonstration of a multidisciplinary project that combines healthcare services.

Bioinformatics is the subject of the second chapter in this section. As an activity that entails storage and analysis of mass data, this is an obvious application for Cloud Computing, yet presently there is little software available that is able to handle such large volumes of data. The chapter looks at options available to researchers and considers future developments and challenges.

The third chapter in this section describes a novel use of SNMP. SNMP or Simple Network Management Protocol is a standard for use with network-attached devices which was developed to enable managers to discern faults or other conditions and events which require administrative attention. It is widely available in routers, switches, servers, workstations, printers and similar hardware. The chapter describes a practical application of this protocol to monitor network traffic and make energy savings by using facilities of the protocol identify devices that may be placed into low energy states without undue adverse effects on network performance.

The final chapter of this section investigates using Cloud Computing in the monitoring and securing of national borders. With increasing numbers of incidents, it is important for countries to support their border personnel with automated systems to assist with the task of identifying and locating intruders. Despite being an application that might appear to be an obvious application for it, current visual surveillance systems make little use of Cloud Computing.

SECURITY

The final section of the book looks at three aspects of security, which is an important consideration in Cloud Computing.

The first security chapter identifies that, if it is to be effective, security needs to be a prime consideration throughout the development of an Enterprise system. A framework is presented for the construction of secure Enterprise systems in which security and trust are important considerations throughout the development.

The next chapter looks at contractual aspects of managing privacy and security, and the individuals' right to keep personal (and other) information private. It concludes that without adequate information privacy and security control, public and commercial trust in online services cannot be sustained.

The final chapter looks at one particular implication for Cloud providers of encryption of data. It has been established that there is considerable duplication in the files held by a Cloud service provider providing storage for many individuals, and when working with unencrypted data, the service provider can save considerable resources by noting this duplication and only storing a single copy of files, or file fragments concerned. If users encrypt their data, the similarities are lost and this optimization can no longer be applied. This chapter examines how this problem may be overcome without compromising users' security.

This collection of publications is useful for academics, researchers, and practitioners seeking the latest practices and knowledge in the field of Cloud Computing, which has transformed the way many organizations work and offers added value for operation management and service computing.

Victor Chang
Computing, Creative Technologies and Engineering, Leeds Beckett University, UK

Robert J. Walters
Electronics and Computer Science, University of Southampton, UK

Gary B. Wills
Electronics and Computer Science, University of Southampton, UK

Acknowledgment

Our review and selection process would not have happened without the efforts of our reviewers, who helped us to maintain a high academic standard. We kindly appreciate the time, assistance, and advice given by our reviewers.

Victor Chang
Computing, Creative Technologies and Engineering, Leeds Beckett University, UK

Robert John Walters
Electronics and Computer Science, University of Southampton, UK

Gary Wills
Electronics and Computer Science, University of Southampton, UK

Section 1
Cloud Fundamentals and Surveys

Chapter 1
Cloud Computing and Frameworks for Organisational Cloud Adoption

Victor Chang
Computing, Creative Technologies and Engineering, Leeds Beckett University, UK

Robert John Walters
Electronics and Computer Science, University of Southampton, UK

Gary B. Wills
Electronics and Computer Science, University of Southampton, UK

ABSTRACT

This chapter presents a selected review for Cloud Computing and explains the issues and risks of adopting Cloud Computing in a business environment. Although all the risks identified may be associated with two major Cloud adoption challenges, a framework is required to support organisations as they begin to use Cloud and minimise risks of Cloud adoption. Eleven Cloud Computing frameworks are investigated and a comparison of their strengths and limitations is made. The result of the comparison is that none of them can deal with all the Cloud adoption challenges thoroughly and a new, comprehensive framework is required if organisations are to overcome these challenges. This proposed framework would ensure that benefits of Cloud adoption are maximised whilst minimising the risks of Cloud adoption and can integrate existing and new projects with Leeds Beckett Cloud.

1. INTRODUCTION

Cloud Computing has transformed the way many organisations work and offers added value for operation management and service computing. Researchers have demonstrated the positive impacts Cloud can offer for business engineering and service level management (Ambrust et al., 2009; Brandic et al., 2009; Buyya et al, 2009). Ambrust et al. (2009) identified cost reduction in IT services from using Cloud Computing. They also presented their Cloud Computing economics and ten major challenges for Cloud Computing. They emphasise a shift of risk from maintaining

DOI: 10.4018/978-1-4666-8210-8.ch001

Copyright © 2015, IGI Global. Copying or distributing in print or electronic forms without written permission of IGI Global is prohibited.

data centres and the capital costs of running them to the loss of data while managing Clouds in a demand-based model. Buyya et al. (2009) assert that Cloud Computing offers billing-based Service Level Agreements (SLA) which can be used for operational management offering cost savings and streamlining business activities and processes. In addition, Cloud Computing offers a variety of other benefits including agility, resource consolidation, business opportunities and green IT (Foster et al; 2008; Weinhardt et al. 2009 a; 2009 b; Schubert, Jeffery and Neidecker-Lutz, 2010; Kagermann et al., 2011; Khajeh-Hosseini et al., 2010 a; 2010 b; Chang et al., 2010 a; 2010 b; 2011 b; 2011 c; 2013 a; 2014).

There is an increasing number of organisations offering Cloud Computing products and services in industry. Salesforce.com is a pioneer in Cloud Computing and offers their Customer Relation Management (CRM) applications to a large number of their users. Amazon is the market leader in Public Cloud Computing and offers Elastic Compute Cloud (EC2) for computing capacity and Simple Storage Service (S3) for storage capacity. Microsoft provides Windows Azure services for developers to store their code and develop new applications for their clients or companies. IBM and Oracle (following their acquisition of Sun Microsystems) both offer products and services ranging from hardware to application services. In addition, there are many more Small and Medium Enterprises (SMEs), who can offer different types of business models and perspective (Marston, et al., 2010), developing and selling Cloud Computing services and products.

Computing Clouds are commonly classified into Public Clouds, Private Clouds and Hybrid Clouds (Ahronovitz et al., 2010; Boss et al., 2007; Marston et al., 2011). Cloud adoption is dependent on the type of Clouds and the intended use for the deployment. For small organisations that aim to save cost and test their software products before release, using public clouds is a good option (Khajeh-Hosseini et al., 2010 a;

2010 b). For organisations that have sensitive data and have data ownership and privacy concern, hosting private clouds is more suitable. Chang et al (2011 a; 2013 a; 2013 b) demonstrate the use of private clouds designed and adopted in finance and healthcare sectors. Hybrid clouds may be used for large-scale simulations and experiments, since they allow scientists at different sites to work and collaborate with one another (Ahronovitz et al., 2010; Khajeh-Hosseini et al., 2010 a; 2010 b).

The majority of Cloud literature defines a Cloud Computing Framework as a Service Oriented Architecture (SOA) (Foster et al; 2008; IBM, 2008; Dillion et al. 2010; Chang et al., 2010 a; 2010 b; 2013 a; Schubert, Jeffery and Neidecker-Lutz, 2010) offering one of three types of service: Infrastructure as a Service (IaaS); Platform as a Service (PaaS) and Software as a Service (SaaS).

Lin et al. (2009) provide an overview of industrial solutions for Cloud Computing, and summarise the list of challenges for the enterprise. They state that adoption benefits of cost and flexibility are enterprise-ready, but security, performance and interoperability need significant improvement. There are two issues to be resolved for each of security, performance and interoperability.

The remainder of this article is structured as follows. Section 2 presents motivation for organisations adopt Cloud Computing and Section 3 describes technical review for Cloud Computing. Section 4 explains Cloud business models and Section 5 lists risk factors and categorises them into Cloud adoption challenges from stakeholders' points of views, which leads to Section 6 that a framework for Cloud Computing is necessary. Section 7 evaluates a shortlist of eleven frameworks for Cloud Computing and concludes that none of them addresses all Cloud adoption challenges fully so that a new framework is required. Sections 7 and 8 explain our proposal for the framework. Section 8 discusses two topics related to the proposed framework and Section 9 sums up Conclusion and Future Work.

2. WHAT DRIVES ORGANISATIONS ADOPTING CLOUD COMPUTING?

There are several explanations for the rise of Cloud Computing. Firstly, many technologies in Grid Computing and Web 2.0 are mature enough and able to simplify the complex process while maintaining high performance capability and web-interfaced environments. The fusion between Grid and Web 2.0 allows ease of use for business processes and technical resolutions (Hunter, Little and Schroeter, 2008). Secondly, the economic downturn makes many organisations want to consolidate their data centre deployment. Reduction in servers, server maintenance and staffing costs by virtualisation make this attractive (Gillen, Grieser and Perry, 2008). Electricity and operational costs can be saved as shown by the CA Technologies case (Dunn, 2010) which highlighted savings of US $6.5 million for labour costs; and US $2.4 millions of operational costs in 5 years through the closure of 19 server sites.

The type of Cloud an organisation adopts will depend on the organisation's needs and the volumes, types of services and data the organisation plans to have and use. Cost-saving offered by Cloud Computing is a key benefit acknowledged by academia (Buyya et al., 2009; 2010 b; Celik; Holliday and Hurst; 2009; Khajeh-Hosseini et al., 2010 a; Schubert, Jeffery and Neidecker-Lutz 2010) and industrialists (Creeger, 2009; Dunn 2010; Oracle, 2009 a; 2009 b; 2010). It is one of the reasons for its popularity and organisational adoption in the economic downturn.

Achieving long-term organisational sustainability is an important success factor for organisations particularly in an economic downturn. Chang, Mills and Newhouse, (2007) present case studies of organisations which achieve more than ten years of organisational sustainability and conclude that their success factors include cost-saving methodology. Creeger (2009) and Dunn (2010) demonstrate their cost-saving methodology and conclude that it helps their organisations to do well in an economic downturn. This explains why cost-saving is a common organisational goal of technology adoption.

From the academic point of view, Buyya et al. (2009) introduced Service Level Agreement (SLA) led cost-saving models and explained how to calculate savings in detail. Buyya et al. (2010 a) also demonstrate applications and services developed for Cloud Computing, and these services are helpful for start-up firms generate additional revenues. Further to their work, Buyya et al. (2010 b) introduced a Return on Investment (ROI) power model which can calculate power cost-saving and present it using 3D visualisation. Celik, Holliday and Hurst (2009) introduce their Broadcast Clouds technique which allows communications and cost-savings. They use simulations to support their proposal. Khajeh-Hosseini et al. (2010 a; 2010b) use qualitative research methods to explain how industry can save costs. They present case studies of two companies and demonstrate cost-saving in infrastructure costs, and support and maintenance costs. Schubert, Jeffery and Neidecker-Lutz (2010) present an overview and opportunities including cost-saving as an added value offered by Cloud Computing.

In industry, CA Technologies (a global IT firm) use Cloud Computing for cost-saving including: US $6.5 million for labour costs; and US $2.4 millions of operational costs in 5 years; and closure of 19 server sites. This allows CA Technologies to consolidate their infrastructure and remove maintenance costs such as staffing and resource expenses (Dunn, 2010). In addition, Oracle who faced a similar challenge after acquiring Sun Microsystems, consolidated their infrastructure and resources using Cloud Computing. After spending a six month transition period, Oracle is able to share and use a similar level of IT resources and data centres to before acquisition, instead of doubling its size. This is largely due to virtualisation. Many of their servers and services are in clusters of virtual machine (VM) farms, facilitating effective management from architects and management (Oracle 2009 a, 2009 b, 2010).

2.1 Surveys for Cloud Computing Adoption

There are different factors for organisations to adopt or consider adoption. Khajeh-Hosseini et al (2011 a) assert that organisational adoption for Cloud computing is an emerging challenge due to factors such as cost, deployment and organisational change. They also explain that understanding the benefits and drawbacks is not straight forward because the suitability of the cloud for different systems is unknown; cost calculations are complicated; the adoption results in a considerable amount of organisational change that will affect the way employees work and corporate governance issues are not well understood. However, there are benefits of adopting Cloud such as consolidation of resources, green IT, cost-saving and new business opportunities which make adoption attractive (Buyya et al., 2009; 2010 b; Celik; Holliday and Hurst; 2009; Khajeh-Hosseini et al. 2010 a; Schubert, Jeffery and Neidecker-Lutz 2010; Creeger, 2009; Dunn 2010; Oracle, 2009 a; 2009 b, 2010).

Khajeh-Hosseini et al. (2010 a) also conduct a large number of interviews with stakeholders who decide in favour of organisational Cloud adoption. They perform stakeholder analysis and summarise benefits and risks arriving at top ranking factors as follows.

- **Benefits:**
  - Improve satisfaction of work;
  - Opportunity to develop new skills;
  - Opportunity for organisational growth;
  - Opportunity to offer new products/ services;
  - Improved status;
  - Opportunity to manage income and outgoings.
- **Risks:**
  - Lack of supporting resources;
  - Lack of understanding of the Cloud;
  - Departmental downsizing;
  - Uncertainty with new technology;
  - Deterioration of customer care and service quality;
  - Increased dependence on third parties;
  - Decrease of satisfying work.

Khajeh-Hosseini et al. explain their rationale for each top-ranked factor. Interestingly, the top ranked-factors for benefits are different from the researchers' views which include factors such as availability, agility, scalability and elasticity (Armbrust et al. 2009; Buyya et al, 2009). Those top ranked factors for benefits indicate the outcome of adopting Cloud from the perspective of organisations. Employees can learn new skills. They will enjoy their work more if they find those skills are useful and interesting. This is particularly true for technical developers. If their work can be completed while maintaining the quality of their service, they can have better satisfaction of work. In addition, Cloud computing can offer the organisations new products and services, which then offer opportunity for organisational growth with potentially more customers, cost-saving and revenues involved. On the other hand, the top-ranked risks factors suggest that organisations are concerned about lack of supporting resources and understanding of the Cloud. Stakeholders are uncertain whether Cloud adoption can provide the long-term benefits they look for. The risk-level increases when there is a temporary upsizing in the IT department or a surge in demands for services. Those factors need to be clarified and explained intelligently by a framework and model that can provide guidance to the organisation as to whether they should adopt Cloud computing or use another alternative.

According to Dillion et al (2011), IDC conducted a survey in 2008 (sample size = 244) to investigate what type of IT systems or applications migrated to Cloud. Their results indicate as follows: IT Management applications (26.2%), Collaborative applications (25.4%); Personal Applications (25%); Business Applications (23.4%); Application Development and Deployment (16.8%); Server Capacity (15.6%) and Storage Capacity (15.5%). Those results show that some organisations which have migrated to the Cloud have several different types of applications and also suggest organisations deploy more SaaS than IaaS to Cloud because core activities are kept in house with additional software outsourced to Cloud.

IT outsourcing is an alternative to Cloud migration and adoption and there are researchers investigating the implications of IT outsourcing. Dibbern et al. (2004) studied the impacts of outsourcing and found that although it was beneficial to the organisation at the beginning, outsourcing projects performed unsatisfactorily after going through several rounds of contracts. This led some organisations to take previously outsourced IT systems and services back in house as a result of unsatisfactory service levels, change in strategic direction or cost-saving failure (Overby, 2003). Some organisations use Cloud as an alternative to outsourcing their resources. However, Khajeh-Hosseini et al (2011 a) explain there is a key difference between Cloud Computing and IT outsourcing: Self-service, scalability and pay-as-you-go model give clients more flexibility and control than traditional IT outsourcing.

3. TECHNICAL REVIEW FOR CLOUD COMPUTING

Chen et al. (2010) define Cloud Computing as a tower architecture where the virtualisation layer sits directly on top of hardware resources and sustains high-level cloud services. It goes onto the IaaS, PaaS and SaaS layers. The IaaS layer provides an infrastructural abstraction for self-provisioning, controlling and management of virtualised resources. In PaaS, consumers may leverage the development platform to design, develop, build, and deploy cloud applications. The SaaS layer is the top of the cloud architectural tower and

delivers specific applications as a service to end users. There is a self-managing cloud system for dynamic capacity planning which is underpinned by monitoring and accounting services. Capacity planning hides complex infrastructural management tasks from users by automatically scaling in and out virtualised resource instances in order to enforce established SLA commitments. Security applies at each of the service delivery layers to ensure authenticated and authorised cloud services and features include identity management, access control, single sign-on and auditing. Chen et al. (2010) also identify CC for research challenges and classify this as Research Clouds. They have presented six user cases as below:

- **Cloud Sourcing:** Researchers using cloud capabilities (compute, storage, platform) provided by public Cloud Service Providers (CSPs) to develop, test or run research applications.
- **Cloud Bursting:** HEIs own research computing services while bursting and offloading to public cloud services due to fluctuating demands. Cloud bursting is commonly used to improve demand management.
- **Private Clouds:** HEIs own research cloud computing services shared inside an institution only.
- **Hybrid Clouds:** Cases involving both private cloud and public cloud.
- **Community Clouds:** Multiple private clouds with shared requirements and interfaces. This includes federations of multiple private clouds.
- **Cloud Tool/Services Provisioning:** Provisioning of self-management facilities, programming abstraction tools, debugging tools, and other platform services to public and/or private clouds.

Use cases are useful to support technical Cloud projects and support the validity of Cloud technical review.

Rozsnyai et al. (2007) propose an Event Cloud, where they use XML and AJAX technologies to implement a Cloud Search platform and they explain how their Cloud Architecture works. Their Event Cloud also provides ranking of search outcomes. Hammond et al. (2010) provide an overview of Cloud Computing for research and classify Political, Social, Economic, Societal, Technological and Legal issues to be resolved while adopting Cloud Computing. They have presented research use cases in storage, Monte Carlo simulations, bioinformatics and SLA.

There are additional technical reviews for Cloud Computing, which are essential for organisations to adopt Cloud. These technical reviews present current literature and state-of-art solutions for Cloud implementations, which allow stakeholders and management need to know limitations and challenges as a result of Cloud adoption.

3.1 Security for Cloud Computing

Security is always a popular topic and there are the following areas of specialisations for Clouds: identity management, access control, single sign-on and auditing (Chen et al., 2010; Martino and Bertino, 2009). In Chen et al. (2010) context, auditing means intrusion and detection mechanisms as well as policy-related security. The Hwang et al. (2009) proposal for cloud security relates to intrusion and detection despite having identity management enforced. Yee and Korba (2008) identify that personalising a security policy to a particular customer is needed. Therefore, Yee and Korba (2008) propose a flexible security personalisation approach that aims to allow an Internet or Web service provider and customer to negotiate an agreed-upon personalised security policy. They also present two application examples of security policy personalisation. The proposal from Paci et al. (2008) is for access control where they explain and demonstrate their Access-Control Framework for WS-BPEL, so that WS-BPEL not only has high performance but also maintains a high level

of security for Web Services and interoperability. Kangasharju et al. (2008) investigate mobile WS security and focus on XML security with binary XML.

Security is a concern for some organisations to adopt Cloud, since privacy and data ownership are amongst key factors for organisations that decide not to move to Cloud Computing. Chang et al (2011 a) introduce "Fined Grained Security Framework" (FGSF) for Cloud security. In the most recent work, Chang and Ramachandran (2014) demonstrate the prototype as follows. There are three layers of security mechanisms in place to protect the data and access. The first layer of defence is Access Control and firewalls, which only allow restricted members to access. The second layer consists of Intrusion Detection System (IDS) and Prevent System (IPS), which detect attack, intrusion and penetration, and also provide up-to-date technologies to prevent attack such as Denial of Service (DoS), anti-spoofing, port scanning, known vulnerabilities, pattern-based attacks, parameter tampering, cross site scripting, SQL injection and cookie poisoning. The third layer is the isolation management: It enforces top down policy based security management; integrity management – which monitors and provides early warning as soon as the behaviour of the fine-grained entity starts to behave abnormally. It offers both weak and strong isolations. Weak isolation focuses more on monitoring and captures end-to-end provenance. Strong isolation can fully isolate malicious hosts and cut all attacking connections to ensure that existing services are not affected by the attacks or unauthorised intrusion.

3.2 Portability for Cloud Computing

Ambrust et al. (2009) state Cloud portability is one of the challenges in Cloud deployment. Ahmed (2010) identifies data risk mitigation to Cloud as an adoption challenge where the portability is important in ensuring data risk mitigation to Cloud over different Clouds. Ahronovitz et al. (2010)

identify applications portability as a challenge and classify it as a Cloud bursting, a desirable characteristic for Cloud Computing. Friedman and West (2010) focus on privacy and security of Cloud Computing as a focus in Cloud risk mitigation to Cloud which they explain as adoption challenges. They make these recommendations:

- **Transparency:** This allows users to understand the security precautions taken by a particular provider and have enough information to make an informed choice between two alternatives about their risk exposure.

- **Competition:** Cloud infrastructure is a competitive marketplace in which the service provider must improve the extent of security functionality and services. Providers must be large enough to leverage economies of security investment, information sharing and usable interfaces.

- **Legal Clarifications:** The first issue is the privacy rights of all users should be protected. The second issue is that the law must reflect how Cloud-based data and systems will become a new target for online criminals.

3.3 Business Integration

In their pioneering paper on business integration (BI) for Cloud Computing, Service Oriented Architecture (SOA) is a common approach. Chrisdutas (2008) presents SOA Java business integration (JBI), and he explains the operation of JBI including each individual component and the interactions between different JBI containers. This work is based on SOA architecture which either focuses on JBI or semantic approaches. The first 'pure' Cloud approach is designed by Papazoglou and van den Heuvel (2011), who present two models related to BI. The first is a cloud delivery model in which they explain interactions between virtualised applications, clients and a stack comprising IaaS,

PaaS and SaaS suitable for Business Process as a Service (BPaaS). Their second model, the blueprint model, is proposed to allow BPaaS or SaaS applications to run dynamically on virtualised clouds to enable service virtualisation. There are three components to the model:

1. Blueprint definition language (BDL);
2. Blueprint constraint language (BCL); and
3. Blueprint manipulation language (BML).

They also explain an architectural scenario showing how blueprint support for the cloud service life cycle can work. However, their approach is at the system design level without details of implementation, testing or use cases. Moran et al (2011) present Rule Interchange Format (RIF), RIF Mapping, RIF-expressed rules and a use case. They explain how semantic based integration can be achieved on IaaS level. However, their notion of BI is not the same as ours for the following reasons. Firstly, their integration is based on data exchange between different VMs to update the RIF status in the Cloud. Secondly, it is not clear whether their use case only works for IaaS, although they seem to imply this approach may work on PaaS and SaaS level in future work.

Understanding how to integrate different Cloud services is important, since this is also a Cloud adoption challenge, where Buyya et al (2010 a) propose a Federated Clouds to provide work-around and solutions for service integrations. Integrations between different services can offer benefits including improvement in efficiency and collaboration while bringing down the costs of deployment and maintenance. Chang et al. (2012 b) present the concepts of Business Integration as a Service (BIaaS), which includes the architecture, implementation and discussions. There are two case studies involved. Firstly, the University of Southampton has adopted BIaaS to allow different departments to work on business analytics projects, which can compute both of cost-saving and risk modelling calculations in one go without using two different services. Secondly, the Vodafone case study allows the computations of profitability and risk modelling to be performed simultaneously. This allows the investors and stakeholders to understand the pricing and risks associated with their investment at any time.

4. CLOUD COMPUTING FOR BUSINESS USE

Our previous work (Chang et al., 2010 a; 2010 b; 2011 b; 2011 c) explain the importance of Cloud Computing business models and their relevance to orgasnisations that adopt Cloud. There are eight Cloud business models are classified by Chang et al. (2010 a; 2010 b; 2013 a), who explain the background, literature and rationale of Cloud business models categorisation and benefits of using multiple business models. This information is highly relevant to stakeholders who need to decide the best strategies for operating their Cloud business model and computing. These eight business models with supporting case studies and examples are as follows:

- Service Provider and Service Orientation;
- Support and Services Contracts;
- In-House Private Clouds;
- All-In-One Enterprise;
- One-Stop Resources and Services;
- Government Funding;
- Venture Capital;
- Entertainment and Social Networking.

To classify the business models and processes, Chang et al. (2010 a; 2010 b) classify all Cloud business models into eight types and they use Cloud Cube Model (CCM) to represent the good practices in Cloud businesses supported by case studies. They also explain strengths and weaknesses in each business model which collaborators and investors have found useful. Table 1 shows advantages and disadvantages of eight Cloud business models (Chang et al., 2010 a).

Having the winning strategies also greatly influences decision-makers from traditionally non-cloud organisations. Wolfram is a computational firm providing software and services for education and publishing, and apart from using CCM, it has considered adopting the second business model. Upon seeing revenues in iPhone and iPad, they added a new model, the eighth model, by porting their applications onto iPhone and iPad. Similarly MATLAB, adopted the first and second model, and began the eighth model by porting their application to iPhone and iPad in order to acquire more income and customers. There were start-ups such as Parascale using the seventh model to secure their funding, and they adopted the first model by being an IaaS provider. They moved into the second model to generate more revenues. The National Grid Service (NGS) has used the sixth model to secure funding, and their strategy is to adopt the fifth model by becoming the central point to provide IaaS cloud services for the UK academic community. Facebook has used multiple business models; the first, seventh and eighth model to assist their rapid user growth and business expansion.

Guy's and St Thomas' NHS Trust (GSTT) and Kings College London (KCL) spent their funding on infrastructure and resources to deliver a PaaS project. Knowing that outsourcing would cost more than they could afford financially together with the possibility in project time delays, they decided to use the third business model, "In-House Private Clouds", which matched to cost-saving, a characteristic of Cloud. They divided this project into several stages and tried to meet each target on time. In contrast, other NHS projects with more resources and funding, have opted for vendors providing the second and forth business models, "Support and Service Contract" and "All-in-One Enterprise Cloud".

Table 1. Advantages and disadvantages of each of eight business models

No.	Business Models	Advantages	Disadvantages
1	Service Providers and Service Orientation	This is a main stream business model, and demands and requests are guaranteed. There are still unexploited areas for offering services and making profits.	Competitions can be very stiff in all of infrastructure, platform and software as a service. Data privacy is a concern for some clients.
2	Support and Service Contracts	Suitable for small and medium enterprises who can make extra profits and expand their levels of services.	Some firms may experience a period without contracts, and they must change their strategies quickly enough.
3	In-House Private Clouds	Best suited for organisations developing their own private clouds which will not have data security and (permanent) data loss concerns.	Projects can be complicated and time consuming.
4	All-In-One Enterprise	Can be the ultimate business model for big players Consolidating different business activities and strategies, including an ecosystem approach or comprehensive SaaS.	Small and medium enterprises are not suitable for this, unless they join part of an ecosystem.
5	One-Stop Resources and Services	A suitable model for business partnership and academic community. Can get mutual benefits through collaboration.	All participating organisations or individuals should contribute. If not managed well, it may end up in other business models or a community breaking apart.
6	Government Funding	Government can invest a massive amount, and this is beneficial for projects requiring extensive R&D, resources and highly trained staff.	Only affluent governments can afford that, and also top-class firms and universities tend to be selected.
7	Venture Capital	Can receive a surplus that is essential for sustainability. Useful for start-ups, or organisations nearly running out of cash.	It can be a prolonged process without a guarantee to get anything.
8	Entertainment and Social Networking	If successful, this model tends to dash into a storm of popularity and money in a short time.	Teenage social problems and a few extreme cases seen in the media.

(Chang et al., 2010 a; 2010 b).

5. STAKEHOLDERS' POINTS OF VIEW: RISKS FOR ORGANISATIONAL ADOPTION AND HOW RISKS ARE RELATED TO CLOUD ADOPTION CHALLENGES

Before considering or deploying organisational adoption, different types of benefits and risks should be identified so that mitigation approaches can be proposed. This is useful for project management to maximise the extent of benefits and to minimise the risks. There are two steps involved. The first step is to tabulate the types of risks and determine their impact, with the ones with high impact factors being classified as adoption challenges. The second step is to analyse the benefits of adoption and explain how these benefits can address those challenges. Khajeh-Hosseini et al (2011 a) performed a similar survey on Cloud users and clients. Based on their analysis, they tabulate different types of risks while adopting or outsourcing to Cloud presented in Table 2. Related details will be presented in Section 8.2.

Table 2. Different types of risks for organisational adoption of Cloud

ID	Risks	Mitigation Approaches and Potential Indicators	References
R1	Organisational: Loss of governance and control over resources which might lead to unclear roles and responsibilities.	Clarify roles and responsibilities before cloud adoption.	Catteddu, and Hogben (2009); Dibbern et al. (2004); Khajeh-Hosseini et al (2010 a, 2010 b); Jurison (1995).
R2	Organisational: Reduced staff productivity during the migration as changes to staff work and job uncertainty lead to low staff morale and anxiety spreading in the organisation.	Involve experts in the migration project so that they have a sense of ownership.	Khajeh-Hosseini et al (2010 a); Grudin (1994).
R3	Organisational: Managing a system deployed on several clouds can make extra management effort compared to deploying systems in-house.	Make management aware of the extra effort that might be required.	Aubert, et al. (2005); Dibbern et al. (2004); Buyya et al (2010 b)
R4	Organisational: Changes to cloud providers' services or acquisitions by another company that changes/terminates services.	Use multiple providers.	Catteddu, and Hogben (2009)
R5	Technical: Performance is worse than expected. It might be difficult to prove to the cloud provider that their system performance is not as good as they promised in their SLA as the workload of servers and network can be variable in a cloud.	Use benchmark tools to investigate the performance of the cloud under investigation before decision making. Use monitoring tools to independently verify the system performance.	Aubert, et al. (2005); Armbrust et al. (2009); Durkee (2010); Jurison, J. (1995).
R6	Technical: Interoperability issues between clouds as there are incompatibilities between cloud providers' platforms.	Use cloud middleware to ease interoperability issues.	Catteddu, and Hogben (2009)
R7	Financial: Actual costs may be different from estimates, this can be caused by inaccurate resource estimates, changing prices or inferior performance resulting in more results to be required than expected.	Monitor existing resource usage and use estimation tools to obtain accurate cost estimates of deploying IT systems on the cloud. Check results of performance benchmark.	Aubert, et al. (2005); Khajeh-Hosseini et al., (2011 b); Dillion et al. (2010)
R8	Financial: Increased costs due to complex integrations. Inability to reduce costs due to unrealisable reductions in system/support staff.	Investigate system integration issues upfront, avoid migrating highly interconnected systems initially.	Dillion et al. (2010); Herbert and Erickson (2011); Kotsovinos (2010).

(Catteddu and Hogben, 2009; Khajeh-Hosseini et al, 2010 a, 2010b; 2011a).

5.1 How Those Risks Relate to Cloud Adoption Challenges

All these risks present a number of adoption challenges, although some can be overlapped or related to one another. For example, both financial risks (R7 and R8) can be classified as cost estimate risks for which a prediction model can be used to calculate business performance including the return on investment (ROI) as accurately as possible.

Rosenthal (2009) report that Cloud Computing offers a new business paradigm for biomedical sharing and the impacts of such adoption have a significant effect on the way biomedical research can go forward. The added value is regarded as 'risk and return analysis', in which Youseff et al (2008), Weinhardt et al (2009 a) and Hugos and Hulitzky (2010) acknowledge the importance of measuring return and risk with their rationale presented. However, their approaches do not include key metrics for a systematic calculation. They do not demonstrate a process and methodology which can be reproduced by the commercial and research communities. This presents the first challenge as "model and analyse risk and return on adoption of a large computer system systematically and coherently".

Organisational risks (R1, R2 and R3) and technical risk (R5) present problems related to people, system and policy as a result of service migration to Cloud. Those risks are directly involved with migration, since a change in service model has implications in terms of lack of control, staff morale, system management, service availability and benchmarking. All these terms can be summarised as "risk mitigation for migrating to a new system including Cloud", as those problems arise due to service migration to Cloud. Services should be delivered efficiently after migration. To ensure organizations have a smooth transition to system adoption including Cloud adoption, it will be useful to provide detailed descriptions about how to mitigate risks of migrating to Cloud.

Organisational risk (R4) and technical risk (R6) present an interesting case that different services and clouds should work together. This can ensure different clouds can communicate. However, current deployment is a challenge as integrations are not straightforward. An easy-to-use and innovative approach for cloud and service integration needs to be considered.

There are additional risks such as legal and security risks but neither is dealt with here since additional resources would be required. In addition, the current focus for organisations that are adopting Cloud such as University of Southampton, NHS, IBM and Commonwealth Bank of Australia (CBA) is to address technical, financial and organisational issues and related adoption challenges.

The high-level question is how organisations should adopt or consider adopting Cloud Computing. If they decide to adopt Cloud, "how stakeholders can understand the benefits and risks for Cloud adoption easily" is the question stakeholders ask (Information Week Survey, 2010). This

needs to include risk analysis as a critical factor (Misra and Mondal, 2011) as it brings significant impacts to the adopting organisations including organisational and technical risks (R1, R2, R3, R4, R5 and R6) as a consequence of adoption. Meeting the stakeholders' expectations and the evidence of worthiness of adoption is an important agenda for stakeholders (Khajeh-Hosseini et al, 2010 a, 2010b; 2011a). This means return and risk calculation needs to take technical and organisational factors into consideration and is not limited to financial factors. Presenting results of return and risk allows stakeholders to understand the status of benefits and risks, which also fulfil the strategic goal for organisational adoption.

5.2 Additional Cloud Adoption Challenges

There are researchers investigating adoption challenges such as Service Level Agreements (SLA) in Clouds (Brandic et al., 2009; Buyya et al., 2009) and Business Models and Classification (Chou, 2009; Weinhardt et al., 2009 a). SLA focuses on billing models and has direct implications on prices, but they focus on the prices paid for the duration of using Cloud. Business models and classifications tend to focus on the way organisations can obtain the profitability not limited to SLA. There are initiatives explaining how SLA can demonstrate cloud business models (Brandic et al., 2009; Buyya et al., 2009). A limitation about SLA is they only focus on operational levels and are not directly connected to strategic levels. Other aspects for successful Cloud delivery have to be investigated at a wider scale, particularly the alignment between the strategic and operational focus of Cloud adoption. There are good examples for how dominant Cloud vendors focus on strategic levels for Cloud adoption to get a greater share of benefits. These organisations include Microsoft, Google, Oracle, IBM and Facebook, all of which obtain more revenue through other forms of services.

To help organisations designing, deploying and supporting clouds, especially private clouds, considering both strategic and operational approaches for Cloud adoption is recommended. Armbrust et al. (2009) describe Cloud Computing technical adoption challenges and considered vendors' lock-in, data privacy, security and interoperability as the most important challenges. Khajeh-Hosseini et al (2010 a; 2011 a) identify human-social issues in Cloud adoption to be resolved and explain their importance using case studies. This means adoption challenges need to take technical, financial and organisational issues into strategic consideration before adoption and implementation take place. Based on the discussion above, the most influential adoption challenges are summed up in Table 3 with their justification provided.

6. MOTIVATION OF USING A FRAMEWORK AND IDENTIFIED PROBLEMS WITH EXISTING FRAMEWORKS

Although there are existing work from researchers (Armbrist et al., 2009; Buyya et al., 2009; Weinhardt et al., 2009), recommendation has to be easy to used by organisations adopting Cloud Computing. The feedback from industrialists (Financial Times Book, 2009; Chee, Wong and Jin, interviews, 2009; Chou, 2009; Information Week Survey, 2010) is that the CBMs proposed by Buyya et al. (2008, 2009) and Armbrust et al. (2009) are too complicated to understand and as a result, these models cannot be used and applied easily and effectively in real-time cloud computing businesses and organisational Cloud adoption. In addition, there are few Cloud Business Frameworks that can accommodate different types of technical solution in relation to their businesses (Klems, Nimis and Tsai, 2008). Although IaaS, PaaS and SaaS are generally classified as three business models, there is no definite guideline for running successful and sustainable cloud businesses. Proposing a suitable framework is useful for Cloud Computing adoption.

Our previous work (Chang, 2013 c) define the importance of a proposed framework to addresss Cloud Computing adoption by rganisations. We also investigate a number of frameworks and study the suitability of using any of them for organisational adoption. Each of the Cloud Computing frameworks presented has some drawbacks such as insufficient detail of how organisations should adopt Cloud Computing; and if they adopt, what are the issues and priorities they should be aware of for delivery of Cloud deployment and services. Limitations of existing good frameworks are presented in Table 4, with the proposal for the development of a new framework to address those issues.

Table 3. Summary of Cloud adoption challenges

Adoption Challenges	How Do They Relate to Table 2	Justification	Types of Focus
Model and analyse risk and return on adoption of a large computer system systematically and coherently	R7 and R8 Additional literature: Youseff et al (2008) Rosenthal (2009) Weinhardt et al (2009 a) Hugos and Hulitzky (2010)	Useful for stakeholders to understand whether they should adopt Cloud and calculate their business performance after adoption to prove its worthiness.	Strategic
Risk mitigation to system adoption including Cloud	R1, R2, R3 and R5	Detailed descriptions about how to compute and reduce risk of system adoption including Cloud will be demonstrated to help organisations have a good management and control of Cloud projects.	Operational

Table 4. What a proposed framework can offer for limitations of existing frameworks

Existing Frameworks	Limitations of Existing Frameworks	What a Proposed Framework Should Offer
Cloud Business Model Framework (CBMF; Weinhardt et al., 2009 a; 2009b)	CBMF assumes that each layer is independent, and only connects directly to Business Model layer. CBMF does not provide any details about how their framework can help organisations to adopt Cloud Computing, and does not have any recommendations about how to run and maintain Cloud services.	A proposed framework will allow different service layers connecting to each other. For example, work developed for PaaS can be further improved to SaaS. The proposed framework has included case studies for how organisations adopt Cloud and sums up key lessons learned.
Linthicum Cloud Computing Framework (LCCF; Linthicum, 2009)	There are not enough use cases/case studies, as Linthicum appears to generalise his architectural framework based on his own experience. There are not enough details about whether organisations should continue adopting more Cloud resources and services, or simply run one service without opening new services or expanding existing services.	A proposed framework should include several case studies, which are used to show how organisations can calculate their Risk and return analysis and discussions about benefits of Cloud adoption supported by results. Examples can allow the finance industry to adopt Cloud and to perform multiple workloads such as calculating risks and pricing, achieving good accuracy without sacrificing performance, and also to perform large-scale simulations in a short period of time.
Return on Investment (ROI) for Cloud Computing (ROICC; Skilton, 2010)	ROICC does not show any details about how to calculate ROI (or return) and how to perform cost-benefit analysis. By stating KPIs without showing how to calculate ROI, it does not help stakeholders to understand whether they should adopt Cloud Computing or expand existing services.	A proposed framework can calculate risk and return analysis to Cloud for technical, cost and user focused projects for Cloud adoption for organisations that adopt Cloud. Results should be supported by case studies.
Performance metrics framework (PMF; (Assuncao, Costanzo and Buyya, 2010)	They only focus on one aspect of risk and return analysis, particularly SLA. There are other types of risk and return analysis they should look at. PMF does not measure other services such as PaaS and SaaS, and does not deal with challenges in Cloud adoption such as risk mitigation to Cloud.	A proposed framework can calculate risk and return analysis for three types of Cloud adoption, which include technical, cost and user aspects of risk and return analysis. It can calculate for IaaS, PaaS and SaaS.
IBM Framework for Cloud adoption (IFCA; IBM, 2010)	IFCA tries to provide a generic solution for all types of industries and all types of Clouds. However, there are no use cases or case studies at all since it has been available for more than 2 years.	A proposed framework has detailed case studies to explain the benefits of Cloud adoption. Stakeholders can understand the extent of return and risks for their Cloud adoption easily. A proposed framework can be fully adopted by non-IT sectors such as Healthcare and Finance to demonstrate that it is a generic solution working across sectors.
Oracle Consulting Cloud Computing Services Framework (OCCCSF; Oracle, 2011)	It is difficult to see how OCCCSF can be fully adopted and applied by non-Oracle customers. A robust and valid framework should allow customers to choose any technologies and vendors which can work under different types and conditions for Cloud implementation.	A proposed framework allows customers to choose their hardware and software technologies. The proposed framework focuses on the delivery of their Cloud adoption and allows flexibility for adoption. The key focus can model risk and return analysis and demonstrate risk mitigation for Cloud adoption.
CloudSim (Calheiros et al., 2009)	Key variables and values must be defined before the use of CloudSim. Not all organisations that adopt Cloud should always need these variables. There are insufficient examples that CloudSim can be fully delivered for private clouds and hybrid clouds, as the challenges for Cloud adoption should be resolved. Their proposal of InterCloud may resolve some of these issues.	A proposed framework can allow any Cloud services working on public, private and hybrid Clouds, which are supported by publications and framework adopting-organisations.

continued on following page

Table 4. Continued

Existing Frameworks	Limitations of Existing Frameworks	What a Proposed Framework Should Offer
BlueSky Cloud Framework for e-Learning (BCF; Dong et al., 2009)	BCF is a conceptual framework, as there are insufficient evidences to justify it has real implementations and case studies. There are no descriptions about the validation methods. There are no follow-up journal articles to explain the current status of their framework project.	A proposed framework will have real implementations and case studies to support its validity. There will be papers published each year to ensure the improvement of the framework is helpful to organisations that adopt Cloud.
Hybrid ITIL V3 Cloud (Heininger, 2012)	ITIL V3 does not provide specific solutions for any types of Cloud adoption problems and expects organisations to resolve problems themselves. There are no any guidelines and recommendations for specific types of emerging Cloud adoption such as Mobile Clouds.	A proposed framework should have details of how to help Cloud-adopting organisations to resolve adoption challenges and have hand-on experiences for implementations. Organisations can reproduce recommendation and steps proposed by the framework, which keeps up-to-date with the latest technological offers such as Mobile Clouds.
DAvinCi (Arumugam et al., 2010)	The project does not have any publication updates since 2010. A working framework should have updates to present its most up-to-date results and improvements over existing adoption challenges. In addition, a framework should also work for other domains and not just for robots.	A proposed framework has regular updates to report its progress and most up-to-date results, case studies and successful Cloud deliveries. It can work in a number of domains and organisations, and has a continuous life cycle after Cloud adoption.
Cloud Computing Business Framework (CCBF; Chang et al., (2011 b; 2011 c; 2012; 2013 a)	The framework focuses more on the literature, process and methodology that leads to the development of the conceptual framework and how it can be useful for organisations and businesses with selected case studies. More case studies and recommendations should be focused on Cloud adoption challenges and issues to resolve.	A proposed framework needs to offer more industrial feedback, case studies and demonstrations of proof-of-concept than CCBF. The proposed framework should offer more technical implementations for Cloud Computing, and recommendations to make good practices into repeatable steps for Cloud-adopting organisations. The proposed framework has more up-to-date summary of lessons learned from case studies and the process of Cloud development.

Table 5. How a proposed framework can meet the criteria to be a Cloud adoption framework

Criteria for a Cloud Adoption Framework	How to Meet the Criteria
Align technical activities with business models and strategies	Business model is at the top of a proposed conceptual framework to apply strategies and case studies approach. The Business process is on the strategic layer of the proposed framework. The objective is to align IT and business requirements and to fully translate the stakeholders' demands to design, deployment, data collection and analysis for Cloud adoption.
Be easily adopted by the industry or any organisations	There are several organisations that have used the proposed framework.
Integrate fully with activities of organisations that adopt Cloud	A proposed framework can demonstrate different levels of Cloud framework adoption. The level-four and level-three adoption are the highest, which are organisations that design the Cloud service from the beginning to the implementation and to the service delivery and support.
Compile all key lessons learned and recommendations which can be influential to academia and industry	All key lessons can contribute to recommendations which can be influential in academia and industry. There are organisations which have used CCAF to report contributions to their Cloud adoption. There are good-quality journals to be published.

The eleven different Cloud Computing frameworks presented here have their own drawbacks such as insufficient details of how organisations should adopt Cloud Computing; and if they adopt, what are the issues and priorities they should be aware of. Since adoption is an important organisational decision and process, a relevant and valid framework should address those issues and adoption challenges.

8. DISCUSSION

Section 5 identified and discussed Cloud adoption challenges, and explained how work for these two adoption challenges can provide recommendations and workarounds for Cloud adoption. Two key areas for these research questions are identified which correspond to "calculate risk and return analysis of a large computing system adoption including Cloud adoption" and "risk mitigation to Cloud". Section 6 explains why it is better to have a framework approach to deal with Cloud adoption and also describes selected frameworks and highlights the limitations of each. It becomes apparent that there is a need for a new framework to address limitations of the existing frameworks.

8.1 Desired Characteristics for a Proposed Framework

The new framework needs to overcome limitations from other frameworks presented in Table 4. It can be validated by quantitative methods including simulations, modelling and experiments, and also supported by qualitative methods that contain feedback from surveys and selective interviews. According to Chang (2013 c), a good framework should have the following characteristics:

- Align technical activities with business models and strategies.
- Be easily adopted by the industry or any organisations.

- Integrate fully with activities of organisations that adopt Cloud.
- Compile all key lessons learned and recommendations which can be influential to academia and industry.

Table 5 presents how a proposed framework can meet each of these criteria.

8.2 Future Challenges for Risk and Return Analysis

Risk and return analysis is a major challenge identified in Section 5 from the stakeholders' points of view. There are three types of risk and return analysis required: technical, costs and users (Chang et al; 2011 b; 2011 c; Chang 2013 c). These are future challenges for a proposed framework to resolve.

8.2.1 Costs (Financial) Measurement for Risk and Return Analysis

There is a need to measure risk and return analysis in terms of its business benefits to aid the strategic decision of Cloud adoption. This will address the key financial risk that needs to be addressed when adopting cloud: R7 the risk of the actual costs being different from the estimates, this can be caused by inaccurate resource estimates, changing prices or inferior performance resulting in more resources spent than expected. This is mitigated by monitoring existing resource usage and using estimation tools to obtain accurate cost estimates of deploying IT systems on the cloud. (Aubert, et al., 2005; Khajeh-Hosseini et al., 2011b; Dillion et al., 2010). The type of risk and return analysis is focused on cost-saving and profitability. Inaccurate resource estimates can be reduced using precise cost calculations and consolidated resources to reduce operational costs. Precise and accurate calculations of profitability enable stakeholders to understand benefits due to Cloud adoption.

8.2.2 Technical Measurement for Risk and Return Analysis

Technical performance (R5) considers whether Cloud adoption can provide better performance such as completing requests more quickly or whether more work can be done in the same period of time. This relates to efficiency, and this type of risk and return analysis is focused on improvements in efficiency. The same number of jobs/requests can be completed quicker, or more jobs/requests can be done in the same time frame for Cloud systems comparing to non-Cloud systems.

8.2.3 Users (or Organisations) Measurement for Risk and Return Analysis

Organisational issues identified (R2 and R3) are concerned with adoption challenges which include whether the internal feedback is positive and the extent of user satisfaction rating. This is a measurement to reflect users and clients' rating about Cloud adoption, which is an important aspect to confirm the added values of using a new Cloud platform or application. This type of risk and return analysis is focused on User satisfaction ratings. An increased percentage of users (or clients) feel there is an improvement to the quality of products and services such as having a quicker response time, a higher proportion of jobs completed at the same time and a more efficient system/application to get their work completed, which results in a higher positive rating for Cloud adoption. In general, this is summed up as user satisfaction rating.

The proposed framework should be able to meet all these three requirements and allow stakeholders to understand the extent of return and risk of their Cloud adoption, regardless of whether they adopt a technical, costs or users focus.

8.3 The Desirable Features in the Improved Framework

Since there is a need for redevelopment of the framework, the improved version, Cloud Computing Adoptiopn Framework (CCAF), should have the desirable features for future development presented as follows.

- **Integration:** Integrations with different services are crucial to the organisations in their enterprise activities. The advantages of doing so allow them to improve efficiency and need not spend multiple resources to do multiple tasks. Instead, one single service can deliver requests for two services. Chang et al (2011 d) firstly made a pioneering proof-of-concepts, Business Integration as a Service (BIaaS), to demonstrate how different services can work together as a single service. They expand their work by demonstrating architecture, computational analysis and methodology (Chang et al., 2012 b). Further to this, Chang (2013 a) demonstrate his BIaaS work for small and medium enterprises that adopt SAP. Those results can help organisations to analyse return and risk in one go, instead of inputting different data for each service and get two separate results which are not connected together. Integrations between services can reduce time, effort and funding to manage Cloud services.

- **Big Data:** The return and risk analysis is essential to Big Data research, which needs algorithms to process datasets, calculate complex modelling and present them in a way that can be understood easily by researchers and stakeholders. Some of the work has been demonstrated by Chang et al (2012 c; 2013 b) to manage and analyse medical data including images, datasets and experimental results. A platform is required to help scientists analyse Big Data, process results quickly and accurately and present the results which can be interpreted easily. The use of BIaaS can help achieve these goals.

- **Specialised Disciplines for Cloud Adoption:** Some disciplines require highly sophisticated tools and services for Cloud adoption. Medical informatics is one of such area that needs integrations of different expertise and technologies. Chang (2013 b; 2013 d; 2014 e) demonstrate that Cloud Computing can be used in brain segmentation technology to understand the brain cell activities while relearning a skill such as dance. Advanced techniques can be applied to analyse thousands of datasets and process them at once between four and ten seconds.

CCAF will aim to develop new case studies for Cloud Computing adoption and demonstrations in healthcare, finance, education and natural science.

8.4 The Development of Leeds Beckett Cloud

This section describes the development of Leeds Beckkett Cloud, which follows the recommendations from our previous work (Chang et al., 2011 a; 2011 b; 2011 c; 2012 a; 2012 b; 2013 a; 2013 b; Chang, 2013 a; 2013 b; 2013 c; 2013 d; 2014 a; 2014 b; 2014 c; 2014 d; 2014 f; 2014 g; Chang and Ramachandran, 2014; Ramachandran and Chang, 2014 a; 2014 b) and the essence of this paper. All the Cloud projects are presented as follows:

- **Cloud Security:** As explained in Section 3.1, innovative approaches in the use of Fined Grained Security Framework has been developed with three layers of security. The techncial design, implementation and experiments have been demonstrated (Chang and Ramachandran, 2014; Ramachandran and Chang, 2014 a).

- **Cloud Computing Quality of Experience (QoE):** The majority of Cloud services follow the SLA models and do not entirely take users' experience into consideration in Cloud adoption (Ambrust et al., 2009; Buyya et al., 2009). The latest theories and empirical studies have been presented (Safdari and Chang, 2014).

- **Analysing Customer Satisfaction in Mobile Cloud Services:** Chang (2013 a, 2014 a) develop the Organisational Sustainability Modelling (OSM) to analyze the status of risk and return of Cloud projects or organisations that Cloud Computing. OSM has been used for mobile phone industry (Chang et al., 2011 b). The most recent work include analysing the German customer satisfaction of using iPhone 4S Mobile Cloud service in 2011.

- **Risk Visualisation as a Service (RVaaS) and Financial Software as a Service (FSaaS):** Chang (2014 b) demonstrate the latest development of his proposed RVaaS with the improved version of Black Scholes Model. Experiments and simulations have been used to support his work. Ramachandran and Chang (2014 b; 2014 d; 2014 f) illustrate their latest FSaaS prototype and demonstrate their research contributions to the community.

Additionally, there are other Cloud Computing and Big Data project lead by Chang (2014 a; 2014 b) and new projects such as weather science, social network analysis and business intelligence systems. The next stage is to integrate all these projects altogether under the development and careful implementation of CCAF. All the demonstrations will ensure that CCAf is a dynamic and useful framework for organisations to adopt Cloud Computing. Eventually, all the proof-of-concepts, services, case studies and demonstrations will get to the highest level in Cloud Computing adoption, Consulting as a

Service, in which Chang (2014 c) also illustrate his previous experience while working in China for a short period of time.

9. CONCLUSION

This paper presents a review related to Cloud Computing focusing on the benefits of adoption and background to Cloud Computing. This is highly relevant to industry and academia as there are growing numbers of organisations adopting or actively using Cloud. Understanding Cloud usage and adoption is highly relevant, as it helps stakeholders to understand their risk and return analysis and the extent of added values (such as efficiency, cost-saving, profitability and user satisfactions) offered by Cloud adoption. Adoption challenges including risk and return analysis and risk mitigation to Cloud arise for organisations that adopt Cloud, particularly private clouds. The use of a framework can help to manage Cloud design, deployment and services much better. Existing frameworks all have their limitations and cannot meet requirements for Cloud adoption challenges fully. A new framework is required to deal with adoption challenges and offer solutions and recommendations in the shortcoming of other frameworks. This framework is Cloud Computing Adoption Framework (CCAF), which will fully integrate with existing and new projects togehte rwith Leeds Beckett Cloud.

Technical, financial and user requirements and complexity in handling Cloud adoption challenges need a structured and well-organised framework to deal with emerging issues and provide solutions for others. A proposed framework needs to be dynamic and structured to help different types of Cloud services, whether risk and return analysis and risk mitigation to Cloud. Future directions are discussed, and innovative ways for integrations, Big Data and specialised disciplines for Cloud adoption will be the focus of the next-generation of Cloud adoption.

REFERENCES

Ahronovitz, M. (2009). *Cloud computing use cases white paper, version 4.0*. National Institute of Standards and Technology.

Anstett, T., Leymann, F., Mietzner, R., & Strauch, S. (2009). Towards BPEL in the Cloud: Exploiting Different Delivery Models for the Execution of Business Processes, 2009 World Congress on Services, I, 6-10 July, Los Angeles, CA, USA.

Armbrust, M., Fox, A., Griffith, R., Joseph, A. D., Katz, R. H., Konwinski, A., … Zaharia, M. (2009). *Above the clouds: A Berkeley view of cloud computing* (Technical Report, No. UCB/EECS-2009-28). UC Berkeley.

Arumugam, R., Enti, V. R., Liu, B., Wu, X., Baskaran, K., Kong, F. F., . . . Goh, W. K. (2010). A cloud computing framework for service robots. In *Proceedings of 2010 IEEE International Conference on Robotics and Automation* (ICRA). Singapore: IEEE. doi:10.1109/ROBOT.2010.5509469

Assuncao, M. D. D., Costanzo, A. D., & Buyya, R. (2010). A cost-benefit analysis of using cloud computing to extend the capacity of clusters. *Journal of Cluster Compute*, *13*(3), 335–347. doi:10.1007/s10586-010-0131-x

Aubert, B. A., Patry, M., & Rivard, S. (2005). A framework for information technology outsourcing risk management. *ACM SIGMIS Database*, *36*(Oct), 9–28. doi:10.1145/1104004.1104007

Boss, G., Malladi, P., Quan, D., Legregni, L., & Hall, H. (2007). *Cloud computing* (IBM white paper, Version 1.0). IBM.

Brandic, I., Music, D., Leitner, P., & Dustdar, S. (2009). *VieSLAF framework: Enabling adaptive and versatile SLA-management*. Paper presented at the 6th International Workshop on Grid Economics and Business Models 2009 (Gecon09), Delft, The Netherlands.

Briscoe, G., & Marinos, A. (2009). Digital ecosystems in the clouds: Towards community cloud computing. In *Proceedings of the 3rd IEEE International Conference on Digital Ecosystems and Technologies* (pp. 103-108). IEEE.

Buyya, R., Beloglazov1, A., & Abawajy, J. (2010b). *Energy-efficient management of data center resources for cloud computing: A vision, architectural elements, and open challenges.* Paper presented at PDPTA'10 - The International Conference on Parallel and Distributed Processing Techniques and Applications, Las Vegas, NV.

Buyya, R., Ranjan, R., & Calheiros, R. N. (2010 a). *InterCloud: Utility-oriented federation of cloud computing environments for scaling of application services, algorithm and architectures for parallel processing.* Lecture Notes in Computer Science, 6081, 13–31.

Buyya, R., Yeo, C. S., & Venugopal, S. (2008). *Market-oriented cloud computing: Vision, hype, and reality for delivering IT services as computing utilities.* Paper presented at HPCC 2008 Cloud Computing.

Buyya, R., Yeo, C. S., Venugopal, S., Broberg, J., & Brandic, I. (2009). Cloud computing and emerging IT platforms: Vision, hype, and reality for delivering computing as the 5th utility. *Journal of Future Generation Computer Systems, 25*(6), 559–616. doi:10.1016/j.future.2008.12.001

Calheiros, R. N., Ranjan, R., De Rose, C. A. F., & Buyya, R. (2009). *CloudSim: A novel framework for modeling and simulation of cloud computing infrastructures and services, technical report.* Grid Computing and Distributed Systems Laboratory, The University of Melbourne.

Catteddu, D., & Hogben, G. (2009). *Cloud computing: Benefits, risks and recommendations for information security.* Technical Report, European Network and Information Security Agency.

Celik, A., Holliday, J., & Hurst, Z. (2006). *Data dissemination to a large mobile network: Simulation of broadcast clouds.* Paper presented at the 7th International Conference on Mobile Data Management (MDM) 2006, Santa Clara, CA.

Chang, V. (2013a). Business integration as a service: Computational risk analysis for small and medium enterprises adopting SAP. *International Journal of Next-Generation Computing, 4*(3).

Chang, V. (2013b). Brain segmentation – A case study of biomedical cloud computing for education and research. In *Proceedings of Learning Technologies Workshop, Higher Education Academy (HEA).* University of Greenwich.

Chang, V. (2013c). *A proposed model to analyse risk and return for a large computing system adoption.* (PhD thesis). University of Southampton.

Chang, V. (2013d). Cloud computing for brain segmentation technology. Paper presented at IEEE CloudCom 2013, Bristol, UK. doi:10.1109/CloudCom.2013.110

Chang, V. (2014a). *The big data analysis for measuring popularity in the mobile cloud.* Paper presented at the First International Workshop on Emerging Software as a Service and Analytics, Barcelona, Spain.

Chang, V. (2014b). *Introduction to the risk visualization as a service.* Paper presented at the First International Workshop on Emerging Software as a Service and Analytics, Barcelona, Spain.

Chang, V. (2014c). Consulting as a service – Demonstrated by cloud computing consultancy projects in the greater China. In *Advances in cloud computing research.* Nova Publishers.

Chang, V. (2014d). The business intelligence as a service in the cloud. *Future Generation Computer Systems, 37*(1), 512–534. doi:10.1016/j.future.2013.12.028

Chang, V. (2014e). Cloud computing for brain segmentation – A perspective from the technology and evaluations. *International Journal of Big Data Intelligence*, 7(2).

Chang, V. (2014f). An introductory approach to risk visualization as a service. *Open Journal of Cloud Computing*, 1(1), 1–9.

Chang, V. (2014g). Measuring and analyzing German and Spanish customer satisfaction of using the iPhone 4S mobile cloud service. *Open Journal of Cloud Computing*, 1(1), 19–26.

Chang, V., Bacigalupo, D., Wills, G., De Roure, D. (2010a). *A categorisation of cloud computing business models*. Paper presented at the CCGrid 2010 IEEE Conference, Melbourne, Australia.

Chang, V., De Roure, D., Walters, R. J., & Wills, G. (2011b). Organisational sustainability modelling for return on investment: Case studies presented by a national health service (NHS) trust UK. *Journal of Computing and Information Technology*, 19(3). doi:10.2498/cit.1001951

Chang, V., De Roure, D., Wills, G., & Walters, R. (2011c). Case studies and organisational sustainability modelling presented by cloud computing business framework. *International Journal of Web Services Research*, 8(3), 26–53. doi:10.4018/JWSR.2011070102

Chang, V., Li, C. S., De Roure, D., Wills, G., Walters, R., & Chee, C. (2011a), The financial clouds review. *International Journal of Cloud Applications and Computing*, 1(2), 41-63.

Chang, V., Mills, H., & Newhouse, S. (2007). *From open source to long-term sustainability: Review of business models and case studies*. Paper presented at the UK e-Science All Hands Meeting, Nottingham, UK.

Chang, V., Walters, R. J., & Wills, G. (2012b). Business integration as a service. *International Journal of Cloud Applications and Computing*, 2(1), 16–40. doi:10.4018/ijcac.2012010102

Chang, V., Walters, R. J., & Wills, G. (2012c). *Cloud storage in a private cloud deployment: Lessons for data intensive research*. Paper presented at the Second International Conference on Cloud Computing and Service Sciences (CLOSER 2012), Porto, Portugal.

Chang, V., Walters, R. J., & Wills, G. (2013a). The development that leads to the cloud computing business framework. *International Journal of Information Management*, 33(3), 524–538. doi:10.1016/j.ijinfomgt.2013.01.005

Chang, V., Walters, R. J., & Wills, G. (2013b). Cloud storage and bioinformatics in a private cloud deployment: Lessons for data intensive research. In *Cloud computing and service science*. Springer Lecture Notes Series, Springer Book. doi:10.1007/978-3-319-04519-1_16

Chang, V., Walters, R. J., & Wills, G. (2014). Monte Carlo risk assessment as a service in the cloud. *International Journal of Business Integration and Management*, 7(2), 1–16.

Chang, V., Wills, G., & De Roure, D. (2010b). *A review of cloud business models and sustainability*. Paper presented at the IEEE Cloud 2010, the third International Conference on Cloud Computing, Miami, FL.

Chang, V., Wills, G., Walters, R., & Currie, W. (2012a). Towards a structured cloud ROI: The University of Southampton cost-saving and user satisfaction case studies. In *Sustainable ICTs and management systems for green computing* (pp. 179–200). IGI Global. doi:10.4018/978-1-4666-1839-8.ch008

Chang, V., Wills, G., & Walters, R. J. (2011d). *Towards business integration as a service 2.0*. Paper presented at the IEEE International Conference on e-Business Engineering, the 3rd International Workshop on Cloud Services - Platform Accelerating e-Business, Beijing, China.

Chen, X., Wills, G. B., Gilbert, L., & Bacigalupo, D. (2010). *Using cloud for research: A technical review*. TesciRes Report for JISC.

Chang, V., & Ramachandran, M. (2014). *A proposed case for the cloud software engineering in security*. Paper presented at the First International Workshop on Emerging Software as a Service and Analytics, Barcelona, Spain.

Chard, K., Caton, S., Rana, O., & Bubendorfer, K. (2010). Social cloud: Cloud computing in social networks. In *Proceedings of 2010 IEEE 3rd International Conference on Cloud Computing* (pp. 99-106). IEEE.

Chou, T. (2009). Seven clear business models. Active Book Press.

Christudas, B. D. (2008). *Service oriented java business integration*. Packt.

Creeger, M. (2009). CTO roundtable: Cloud computing, special article. *Communications of the ACM, 52*(8), 50. doi:10.1145/1536616.1536633

Dibbern, J., Goles, T., Hirschheim, R., & Jayatilaka, B. (2004). Information systems outsourcing: A survey and analysis of the literature. *ACM SIGMIS Database, 35*(Nov), 6–102. doi:10.1145/1035233.1035236

Dillon, T., Wu, C., & Chang, E. (2010). *Cloud computing: Issues and challenges*. Paper presented at the 2010 24th IEEE International Conference on Advanced Information Networking and Applications, Perth, Australia.

Dong, B., Zheng, Q., Qiao, M., Shu, J., & Yang, J. (2009). BlueSky cloud framework: An e-learning framework embracing cloud computing. *Lecture Notes in Computer Science, 5931*, 577–582. doi:10.1007/978-3-642-10665-1_55

Dunn, T. (2010). *Identity management: Cloud and virtualisation, keynote*. Munich Cloud.

Durkee, D. (2010). Why cloud computing will never be free. *Communications of the ACM, 53*(May), 62. doi:10.1145/1735223.1735242

Educause. (2008). *The tower and the cloud: Higher education in the age of cloud computing*. Author.

Financial Times Book. (2009). Managing in a downturn: Leading business thinkers on how to grow when markets don't. *Financial Times*.

Foster, I., Zhao, Y., Raicu, I., & Lu, S. Y. (2008). Cloud computing and grid computing 360-degree compared. Paper presented at IEEE Grid Computing Environments (GCE08), Austin, TX.

Friedman, A. A., & West, D. M. (2010). Privacy and security in cloud computing. *Issues in Technology Innovation, 3*.

Gillen, A., Grieser, T., & Perry, R. (2008). *Business value of virtualization: Realizing the benefits of integrated solutions* (White Paper). IDC.

Gillett, F. E. (2009). *The personal cloud – How individual computing will shift from being device-centric to information-centric*. Forrester Research White Paper.

Heininger, R. (2012). *IT service management in a cloud environment: A literature review* (working paper). Social Science Research Network.

Herbert, L., & Erickson, J. (2011). The ROI of cloud apps. In *A total economic impact™ analysis uncovers long-term value in cloud apps*. Forrester.

Hobona, G., Fairbairn, D., & James, P. (2010). Orchestration of grid-enabled geospatial web services in geoscientific workflows. *IEEE Transactions on Automation Science and Engineering, 7*(2), 407-411.

Hosono, S., Kuno, A., Hasegawa, M., Hara, T., Shimomura, Y., & Arai, T. (2009). A framework of co-creating business values for IT services. In *Proceedings of 2009 IEEE International Conference on Cloud Computing*. Bangalore, India: IEEE. doi:10.1109/CLOUD.2009.57

Hugos, M. H., & Hulitzky, D. (2010). *Business in the cloud: What every business needs to know about cloud computing*. Wiley Publishing.

Hull, J. C. (2009). *Options, futures, and other derivatives* (7th ed.). Pearson, Prentice Hall.

Hunter, J., Little, S., & Schroeter, R. (2008). The application of semantic web technologies to multimedia data fusion within e-science. In Semantic multimedia and ontologies (pp. 207-226). Academic Press.

Hwang, K., Kulkarni, S., & Hu, Y. (2009). *Cloud security with virtualized defense and reputation-based trust management*. Paper presented at the 2009 Eighth IEEE International Conference on Dependable, Autonomic and Secure Computing, Chengdu, China.

IBM. (2010). *Defining a framework for cloud adoption* (technical paper). IBM.

Information Week Survey. (2009). *Why do you use SaaS and private clouds, results based on interview and surveys 250 managers and directors*. Author.

Jurison, J. (1995). The role of risk and return in information technology outsourcing decisions. *Journal of Information Technology, 10*(Dec), 239–247. doi:10.1057/jit.1995.27

Kagermann, H., Österle, H., & Jordan, J. M. (2011). *IT-driven business models: Global case studies in transformation*. John Wiley & Sons.

Kangasharju, J., Lindholm, T., & Tarkoma, S. (2008). XML security with binary XML for mobile web services. *International Journal of Web Services Research, 5*(3), 1-19.

Khajeh-Hosseini, A., Greenwood, D., Smith, J. W., & Sommerville, I. (2011 b). The cloud adoption toolkit: Supporting cloud adoption decisions in the enterprise, software. *Practice*.

Khajeh-Hosseini, A., Greenwood, D., & Sommerville, I. (2010a). *Cloud migration: A case study of migrating an enterprise IT system to IaaS*. Paper presented at the 3rd IEEE International conference on Cloud Computing, Miami, FL.

Khajeh-Hosseini, A., Sommerville, I., Bogaerts, J., & Teregowda, P. (2011). *Decision support tools for cloud migration in the enterprise*. Paper presented at the IEEE 4th Int. Conf. on Cloud Computing (CLOUD 2011), Washington, DC. doi:10.1109/CLOUD.2011.59

Khajeh-Hosseini, A., Sommerville, I., & Sriram, I. (2010b). *Research challenges for enterprise cloud computing* (LSCITS Technical Report). Academic Press.

Klems, M., Nimis, J., & Tai, S. (2009). Do cloud compute? A framework for estimating the value of cloud computing. *Journal of Designing E-Business Systems – Market Services and Network, 22*(4), 110–123.

Lin, G., Fu, D., Zhu, J., & Dasmalchi, G. (2009, March/April). Cloud computing: IT as a service. IT Pro.

Linthicum, D. (2009, January). Defining the cloud computing framework. *Cloud Computing Journal*.

Marston, S., Li, Z., Bandyopadhyay, S., Zhang, J., & Ghalsasi, A. (2011). Cloud computing - The business perspective. *Decision Support Systems, 51*(1), 176-189.

Martino, L.D., & Bertino, E. (2009). Security for web services: Standards and research issues. *International Journal of Web Services Research, 6*(4), 48-74.

Moran, D., Vaquero, L. M., & Galan, F. (2011). *Elastically ruling the cloud: Specifying application's behavior in federated clouds.* Paper presented at the 2011 IEEE International Conference on Cloud Computing, Washington DC.

Oracle White Paper. (2009a). *Architectural strategies for cloud computing.* Oracle.

Oracle White Paper. (2009b). *Platform-as-a-service private cloud with Oracle fusion middleware.* Oracle.

Oracle White Paper. (2010). *Oracle cloud computing.* Oracle.

Oracle White Paper. (2011). *Oracle consulting cloud services framework.* Oracle.

Overby, S. (2003). *The hidden costs of offshore outsourcing, keynote and technical report.* CIO.com.

Paci, F., Bertino, E., & Crampton, J. (2008). An access-control framework for WS-BPEL. *International Journal of Web Services Research, 5*(3), 20-43.

Papazoglou, M. P., & van den Heuvel, W.-J. (2011). Blueprinting the cloud. *IEEE Internet Computing, 15*(6), 74–79. doi:10.1109/MIC.2011.147

Ramachandran, M., & Chang, V. (2014a). *Cloud security proposed and demonstrated by cloud computing adoption framework.* Paper presented at the first international workshop on Emerging Software as a Service and Analytics, Barcelona, Spain.

Ramachandran, M., & Chang, V. (2014b). *Modelling financial SaaS as service components.* Paper presented at the First International Workshop on Emerging Software as a Service and Analytics, Barcelona, Spain.

Rosenthal, A., Mork, P., Li, M. H., Stanford, J., Koester, D., & Reynolds, P. (2010). Cloud computing: A new business paradigm for biomedical information sharing. *Journal of Biomedical Informatics, 43*(2), 342–353. doi:10.1016/j.jbi.2009.08.014 PMID:19715773

Schubert, L., Jeffery, K. & Neidecker-Lutz, B. (2010). *The future for cloud computing: Opportunities for European cloud computing beyond.* Expert Group report, public version 1.0, January.

Skilton, M. (2010). *Building return on investment from cloud computing* (White Paper). The Open Group.

Sobel, W., Subramanyam, S., Sucharitakul, A., Nguyen, J., Wong, H., Klepchukov, A., . . . Patterson, D. (2008). Cloudstone: Multi-platform, multi-language benchmark and measurement tools for web 2.0. In Proceeding of Cloud Computing and its Applications (CCA 2008). Academic Press.

Tian, Y., Song, B., & Huh, E. N. (2011). *Towards the development of personal cloud computing for mobile thin-clients.* Paper presented at the IEEE International Conference on Information Science and Applications (ICISA), Jeju Island, South Korea.

Weinhardt, C., Anandasivam, A., Blau, B., & StoBer, J. (2009). *Business models in the service world.* IEEE Computer Society.

Weinhardt, C., Anandasivam, A., Blau, B., Borissov, N., Meinl, T., Michalk, W., & Stober, J. (2009). Cloud computing – A classification, business models, and research directions. *Journal of Business and Information Systems Engineering.*

White Paper, I. B. M. (2008). *IT service management to enable the fulfilment of your SOA strategy.* IBM Global Services.

Yee, G. O. M., & Korba, L. (2008). Security personalization for internet and web services. *International Journal of Web Services Research, 5*(1), 1-22.

Youseff, L., Butrico, M., & Da Silva, D. (2008). *Toward a unified ontology of cloud computing.* Paper presented at the Grid Computing Environments Workshop, Austin, TX.

KEY TERMS AND DEFINITIONS

Business Models for Cloud Computing Adoption: The establishment of new business models pose a main factor for organisational Cloud computing adoption. Table 1 of this chapter has explained there are eight identified types of business models based on literature review and our previous research. Successful businesses should adopt multiple types ofm business modesl to ensure their businesses are competitive in the market.

Cloud Computing Adoption Challenges from the Stakeholders' Perspective: Amongst the eight identified risks, some can be categorised together. Based on our analysis, literature review and our previous studies, we identify two major risks for Cloud Computing adoption in the eye of the stakeholders since they influence the way that organisations go forward and they are the main decision-makers. Many papers focus much more in the eye of service providers or technical specialists who only focus on the "service level agreement" and "security" respectively. In the eye of the stakeholders, they highly regard anything that can prevent their success or return on investment. Thus, each adoption challenge consists of the combination of technical, financial and organisational challenges.

Cloud Computing Adoption for Organisations: This is an area to investigate why organisations adopt Cloud Computing and use it dauily for their work. As closely related to the benefits of Cloud Computing adoption, some businesses use it to reduce the operational costs like CA technologies. Some organisations use it to allow the businesses to be more competitive since they can create virtual hardware much quicker, they can offer more types of services to customers, and they can integrate different types of services together. This area can also provide an in-depth study, since adoption depends on various factors apart from technical reasons. Organisational and financial reasons can motivate organisations for adoption. However, there are technical, financial and organisational risks which pose challenges for Cloud Computing adoption.

Cloud Computing: It consists of three major services: Infrastructure as a Service, Platform as a Service and Software as a Service and four main types of Clouds: Public Cloud, Private Cloud, Hybrid Cloud and Community Cloud. Cloud Computing is a technology-based (normally internet based) service that allows organisations to offer service delivery that supports the organisational IT strategy, design, transition, operation and continuous service improvement. Organisations need to buy servers and hardware equipment since the resources are outsourced to the Cloud, normally Public Cloud. Private Cloud are the internal clouds implemented and used by the employees of the same organisation. Virtualisation is the main technology behind Cloud Computing that allows rapid scaling up and down of resources and creation of virtual hardware in the Cloud to improve on the work efficiency. Cloud Computing can work with Green IT to reduce electricity consumption due to consolidation of data centres and business models to provide additional revenues and opportunities for the service providers.

Frameworks for Cloud Computing Adoption: Frameworks are commonly used in IT to recommend the best practices and encourage the organisations to follow the successful deliveries illustrated in the past. Often frameworks are designed and implemented by experienced researchers and practitioners who have extensive level of experience of successful deliveries based on their own experiences. However, most of the frameworks are not particularly designed for Cloud Computing and there are limitations that can prevent organisations from successful Cloud adoption. Some frameworks have been designed for Cloud Computing but they are generic and do not provide detailed solutions for adoption challenges. As a result, adopters may experience problems during or after the migration to Cloud computing. Revuiews have been explained in Section 6 and Table 4. Table 5 then explains how a proposed framework can meet the criteria to be a Cloud adoption framework, which will be presented in our future work.

Risks for Cloud Computing Adoption: They are classified as technical, financial and organisational risks. It is important for organisations to know their impacts and the recommendations overcoming these risks. However, the first step before Cloud adoption is to understand eight major types of common risks as presented by Table 8. Rationale and supporting literature have been provided.

Two Major Challenges: Continued from the previous point, organisations should know the most two important challenges in order to set the required targets and milestones for successful deliveries of Cloud Computing services and projects. This can also directly affect the successful rate of cloud Computing adoption and let the organisations to know how well they perform as a result of cloud computing adoption. Hence, we identify two issues to resolve. First, it is about "a model and analyse risk and return on adoption of a large computer system systematically and coherently". Second, it is about "risk mitigation to system adoption including Cloud". Table 3 has explained the rationale and supporting literature.

Chapter 2
The Role of Cloud Computing Adoption in Global Business

Kijpokin Kasemsap
Suan Sunandha Rajabhat University, Thailand

ABSTRACT

This chapter introduces the role of cloud computing adoption in global business, thus explaining the application overview of cloud computing, the adoption of Information and Communication Technology (ICT), and the Technology, Organization, and Environment (TOE) framework related to technological context, organizational context, and environmental context. In addition, technological context includes the relative advantage, uncertainty, compatibility, and trialability. Organizational context includes the size, top management support, innovation, and prior technology experience. Environmental context includes competitive pressure, industry, market scope, and supplier computing support. Adopting cloud computing in global business will significantly enhance organizational performance and achieve business goals in the digital age.

INTRODUCTION

Cloud computing is a technological innovation that has adapted the utilization of information systems from traditional physical computers to virtual technology services (Ratten, 2014). The rapid emergence of cloud computing usage has occurred because of its dynamic and innovative nature (Stein, Ware, Laboy, & Schaffer, 2013). The use of ICT can improve business competitiveness, and has provided genuine advantages for small and medium-sized enterprises (SMEs), enabling them to compete with large firms (Bayo-Moriones & Lera-Lopez, 2007). Cloud-based end-user services, such as e-mail or office applications, find their ways into daily business practices, offering new opportunities and capabilities, but equally creating new challenges for stakeholders (Alshamaila, Papagiannidis, & Li, 2013). Cloud computing services are helpful to consumers because of the reliability and flexible access they provide to data on hosting devices (Gray, 2013).

Cloud technology allows an organization to scale its business operations easily (Berman, Kesterson-Townes, Marshall, & Srivathsa, 2012). Sultan (2013) stated that cloud computing makes economic sense in the digital age. Cloud computing represents a fundamental shift in the delivery

DOI: 10.4018/978-1-4666-8210-8.ch002

Copyright © 2015, IGI Global. Copying or distributing in print or electronic forms without written permission of IGI Global is prohibited.

of IT services that has permanently changed the computing landscape (Srinivasan & Getov, 2011). Organizations can use cloud computing to be more flexible and cost effective so that people working for them can have better scalability of information systems (Ratten, 2012). Cloud computing services save consumers money by handling information maintenance needs and by facilitating quick technology applications without the high upfront costs of purchasing hardware or software resources (Karakas & Manisaligil, 2012).

The strength of this chapter is on the thorough literature consolidation of cloud computing. The extant literature of cloud computing adoption provides a contribution to practitioners and researchers by describing a comprehensive view of the functional applications of cloud computing to appeal to different segments of cloud computing in order to maximize the business impact of cloud computing adoption. In this chapter, the TOE framework is explained and leads the practitioners and researchers in the area of innovative business management regarding technological context, organizational context, and environmental context systematically utilized to gain sustainable competitive advantage in modern organizations.

Background

In computer networking, cloud computing involves a large number of computers connected through a communication network such as the Internet, similar to utility computing (Carroll, Kotze, & van der Merwe, 2010). Cloud computing is a synonym for distributed computing over a network, and means the ability to run a program or application on many connected computers at the same time. Cloud computing reshapes the IT sector and the IT marketplace in modern business (Prasad, Gyani, & Murti, 2012). In traditional IT environments, the software, hardware, and networking equipment require specialists for implementing and maintaining IT services (Thinkstrategies, 2002).

Cloud computing is defined as a new style of computing in which virtualized resources are provided as services over the Internet. Cloud computing economically moderates the requirement of advanced handsets for running mobile applications (Prasad et al., 2012). Mell and Grance (2010) defined cloud computing as a model for enabling ubiquitous, convenient, on-demand network access to a shared pool of configurable computing resources that can be rapidly provisioned and released with minimal management effort or service provider interaction. Cloud computing is considered as a collection of disembodied services accessible from anywhere using any mobile device with an Internet-based connection (Erdogmus, 2009; Gartner, 2009; Misra & Mondal, 2010; Sultan, 2010). Cloud computing is viewed as a type of parallel and distributed system consisting of a collection of interconnected and virtualized computers that are dynamically provisioned and presented as one or more unified computing resources based on service-level agreements established through negotiation between service provider and consumers (Buyya, Chee Shin, & Venugopal, 2008).

Cloud computing includes network access to storage, processing power, development platforms, and software. Cloud computing has been in use for years. In 1990s, cloud computing is developed by major IT providers such as Sun, Microsoft, Google, and Amazon. Different products come into use for different levels of users. The most popular services for end users include web-based email systems (e.g., AOL, Gmail, Hotmail, and Yahoo Mail), and office applications (e.g., Google Docs and Microsoft Office Online). Developers can run their programs on the cloud like Google App Engine, Windows Azure, and Force.com. Organizations store their large data on remote servers such as Rackspace, Microsoft Azure, Animoto, Jungle Disk, Amazon's EC2, and S3 servers (Liu & Cai, 2013).

ROLE OF CLOUD COMPUTING ADOPTION

This section introduces the application overview of cloud computing, the adoption of ICT, and the TOE framework concerning technological context, organizational context, and environmental context.

Application Overview of Cloud Computing

In common usage, the term "the cloud" is essentially a metaphor for the Internet. Marketers have further popularized the phrase "in the cloud" to refer to software, platforms, and infrastructure that are sold as a service through the Internet. The seller has the actual energy-consuming servers which host products and services from a remote location, so that end-users do not have to; they can simply log on to the network without installing anything. Cloud computing is a style of computing in which resources scalable on demand are provided "as a service (aaS)" over the Internet to users who need not have knowledge of, expertise in, or control over the cloud infrastructure that supports them.

The network-based services, provided by real server hardware and served by virtual hardware, are called cloud computing. Such virtual servers do not physically exist and can be moved around and scaled up or down on the fly without affecting the end user, somewhat like a cloud becoming larger or smaller without being a physical object. The provision of cloud computing services can occur at the infrastructural level (IaaS), platform level (PaaS), and software level (SaaS). Google, Amazon, IBM, Oracle Cloud, Salesforce, Zoho, and Microsoft Azure are the well-known cloud computing vendors.

Organizations have to adapt to changes quickly, explore innovations, and be flexible in order to remain competitive in modern business (Carroll et al., 2010). The IT landscape has evolved to allow organizations to develop a competitive advantage and to meet business targets such as reduced costs, scalability, flexibility, capacity utilization, higher efficiency, and mobility. Many benefits are achieved through the utilization of technologies such as cloud computing and virtualization. In many instances, cloud computing builds on the capabilities of a virtualized computing infrastructure to facilitate multi-tenancy, scalability, and a highly abstracted cloud computing model.

The Internet, built upon ubiquitous connectivity, low-cost processing capacity, open standards and loosely coupled IT infrastructure, has been widely recognized as a tremendous enabler for business collaboration (Chen, Zhang, & Zhou, 2007). In the global marketplace, the Internet is a tool by which businesses may uncover additional opportunities and is viewed as a requirement to develop a technology-driven competitive advantage. The Internet-based cloud computing model, while intangible in context, offers a means by which technologically savvy organizations may leverage previously unavailable tangible IT capacity for a fraction of the traditional resource commitment (Cegielski, Jones-Farmer, Wu, & Hazen, 2012). Synthesizing from several sources, cloud computing may be defined as a connectivity-facilitated virtualized resource (i.e., software, infrastructure, or platforms) that is dynamically reconfigurable to support various degrees of organizational need, which allows for optimized systems utilization (Vaquero, Rodero-Merino, Caceres, & Lindner, 2008).

Buyya et al. (2008) defined cloud computing as a type of parallel and distributed system consisting of a collection of interconnected and virtualized computers that are dynamically provisioned and present as the unified computing resources based on service-level agreements (SLAs) established through negotiation between service provider and customer. Wang, Von Laszewski, Younge, He, Kunze, Tao, and Fu (2010) defined cloud computing as a set of network enabled services, providing scalable, normally personalized, and inexpensive computing platforms on demand, which could be accessed in a simple and pervasive way. The scalable IT-related capabilities are provided as a service using Internet technologies to multiple external customers (Plummer, Bittman, Austin, Cearley, & Smith 2008). Cloud deployment models are classified according to type of exclusive and non-exclusive method of providing cloud services to the clients (i.e., public cloud, private cloud, hybrid cloud, and community clouds) (Mell & Grance, 2010).

Cloud computing is considered as the technology of changing how the Internet and information systems are presently operated and used (Sharif, 2010). Cloud computing is recognized as an important area for IT innovation and investment (Armbrust, Fox, Griffith, Joseph, Katz, Konwinski, Lee, Patterson, Rabkin, Stoica, & Zaharia, 2010; Goscinski & Brock, 2010; Tuncay, 2010). A user on the Internet can communicate with many servers at the same time, and these servers exchange information among themselves (Hayes, 2008). Cloud computing has spread out through the main areas related to information systems and technologies, such as operating system (OS), application software, and technological solutions for organizations (Armbrust et al., 2010). Adoption of various levels of cloud computing technology has moved into the mainstream and become a major topic of discussion and debate about technologies (Liu & Cai, 2013). Cloud computing mainly forwards the utility computing model, where consumers pay on the basis of their usage. Cloud computing promises the availability of virtually infinite resources.

Cloud computing is a kind of the application service that is like email, office software, and enterprise resource planning (ERP) and uses ubiquitous resources that can be shared by the business employee or trading partners (Hayes, 2008). To enhance competitive advantage, developing cloud computing capability is an important undertaking because it is not only rapidly changing the way that enterprises buy, sell, and deal with customers, but it becomes a more integral part of enterprises' business tactics (Pyke, 2009). Cloud

computing is an innovative technology that is changing how ICTs are accessed and used (Ross & Blumenstein, 2013). Cloud computing introduces strategic options and business challenges (Rader, 2012). Cloud computing offers ubiquitous access to applications for interacting with all parts of an organization's value chain and it connects an organization with the rich learning opportunities percolating in communities formed by the users of the service.

The resources of cloud computing are acquired as a service rather than deployed locally. Cloud computing relies on sharing of resources to achieve coherence and economy of scale similar to a utility (like the electricity grid) over a network (NIST, 2011). The foundation of cloud computing is the broader concept of converged infrastructure and shared services. Cloud computing also focuses on maximizing the effectiveness of the shared resources (NIST, 2011). Cloud computing resources are usually not only shared by multiple users but as dynamically re-allocated per demand. Cloud computing allows organizations to avoid upfront infrastructure costs, to focus on projects that differentiate their businesses instead of infrastructure, to get their applications up and running faster, with improved manageability and less maintenance, and to adjust resources of cloud computing for reaching the unpredictable business demand (NIST, 2011).

Cloud computing offers the potential to do more with less, thus benefiting an agile, strategic adopter of its rapidly evolving technology and service (Rader, 2012). Cloud computing provides an infrastructure (resembling a pool) for resources to be virtually accessible and easily usable. These resources (i.e., hardware, development platforms, and services) are adjustable and scalable in order to fit the changing load (Patel, Seyfi, Tew, & Jaradat, 2011). Moreover, this dynamic nature makes possible the reconfiguration and optimum utilization of such resources. The infrastructure provider of this pool of resources also guarantees the utilization of these resources by employing customized SLAs (Patel et al., 2011). A pay-per-use model is typically used to exploit the resources. Shifting the location of the computing infrastructure in the network in order to balance the load and reduce the management costs of resources hardware/software is the basic idea of this new paradigm.

Cloud computing has been widely recognized as the next generation's computing infrastructure. Cloud computing offers some advantages by allowing users to use infrastructure (i.e., servers, networks, and storages), platforms (i.e., middleware services and operating systems), and software (i.e. application program) provided by cloud providers (e.g., Google and Amazon) at low cost. In addition, cloud computing enables users to utilize resources elastically in an on-demand fashion. Such resources of cloud computing are virtually interconnected and dynamically provisioned to resemble the unified resources of computing. These provisions and presentations follow the mentioned SLAs that are initiated between consumers and service (or infrastructure) providers (Hayes, 2008; Vaquero et al., 2008).

The impact of cloud computing technologies on management practices and business strategies is not only a topical area for investigation, but little research has been conducted into the extent to which human resource management (HRM) should be involved in the planning and introduction of ICTs (Ross & Blumenstein, 2013). The diffusion of cloud computing becomes a significant research topic because it enables organizations to execute data transactions along value chain activities (i.e., manufacturing, finance, distribution, sales, customer service, information sharing, and collaboration with trading partners) (Gartner, 2009; Pyke, 2009). While cloud computing has been discussed as a new technology develop that can provide several advantages, both strategic and operational, to its adopters, the cloud computing adoption rate is not growing as fast as expected (Banerjee, 2009; Buyya, Yeo, Venugopa, Broberg, & Brandic, 2009; Goscinski & Brock, 2010).

The Internet-based cloud computing model, while intangible in context, offers a means by which technologically savvy organizations may leverage previously unavailable tangible IT capacity for a fraction of the traditional resource commitment. Synthesizing from several sources, cloud computing may be defined as a connectivity-facilitated virtualized resource (i.e., software, infrastructure, and platforms) that is dynamically reconfigurable to support various degrees of organizational need, which allows for optimized systems utilization (Vaquero et al., 2008; IBM, 2009; IBM Global Technology Services, 2010). Cloud computing facilitates scalable on-demand computing power, rapid deployment, and reduced support infrastructure, all while facilitating lower cost of ownership (Aymerich, Fenu, & Surcis, 2008; IBM Global Technology Services, 2010).

Cloud computing is utilized in many different forms by various members of different organizations, which can make the technology even more useful in the context of collaborative supply chain (IBM Global Technology Services, 2011). Sclater (2009) surveyed different firms from different industries that have built custom applications in the cloud and analyzed how cloud computing affected the companies' operations in security integration areas The future of computing lies in cloud computing, whose major goal is reducing the cost of IT services while increasing processing throughput, reliability, availability, flexibility, and decreasing processing time (Hayes, 2008). Telecommunication and network technology have been progressing fast, thus containing 3G, FTTH, and WiMAX, so that the high-speed infrastructures are integrated strongly. Cloud computing services can provide the user seamlessly, the convenience, and the quality-stable technological support that can develop the enormous potential demand (Buyya et al., 2009).

Cloud computing provides the opportunity of flexibility and adaptability to attract the market on demand (Buyya et al., 2009). Several computing paradigms have promised to deliver a utility computing vision, and these involve cluster computing, grid computing, and more recently, cloud computing (Buyya et al., 2009; Armbrust et al., 2010). A review of the published research on cloud computing reveals that most studies either focus on exploring the architectures and applications of the cloud environment or propose lists of opportunities and obstacles for firms considering cloud computing (Buyya et al., 2009; Armbrust et al., 2010). Saya, Pee, and Kankanhalli (2010) stated that while extant research has studied cloud computing architecture, potential applications (Liu & Orban, 2008), costs, and benefits (Assuncao, Costanzo, & Buyya, 2009), the decision making on the adoption of cloud computing has not been empirically examined. Cloud computing is attractive for organizations, and can maximize the return on investment in an ever-demanding business environment.

Well-known cloud computing services include SaaS, PaaS, and IaaS (NIST, 2011). Gartner (2009) defined a style of cloud computing as a service to external customers using Internet technologies. Gartner (2009) indicated that cloud computing is used in the areas of business when compared to other fields. Pyke (2009) described the following benefits of cloud computing: scalability, ease of implementation, using skilled practitioners, freeing up of internal resources, and quality of service. Erdogmus (2009) considered cloud computing a pool of highly scalable, abstracted infrastructure capable of hosting end-customer applications that are billed by consumption. Sultan (2010) defined IT capabilities that are requested, provisioned, delivered, and consumed in real time over the Internet. Organizations can leverage cloud-based IT services from providers like Amazon Web Services, Google, and IBM to scale systems quickly to meet their respective organizational needs for capacity, collaboration, and coordination without sacrificing any control, and perhaps most advantageously, pay for only the capacity that they actually utilize (Lohr, 2007). Cloud computing is a paradigm in which computing resources are not locally stored on end-user devices but accessed through a network (Hayes, 2008).

The advantages of cloud computing, which include ubiquitous access to online resources and cost savings by reducing investments in local computing equipment (Vaquero et al., 2008), are in part achieved through the principle of multi-tenancy, an approach where multiple customers share a large resource pool, while individual users perceive the resources as being dedicated to them. Patel et al. (2011) stated that the advantages of cloud computing include initial cost saving, data security, scalability, pay as you go, device and location independence, and efficiency. Cloud computing also focuses on maximizing the effectiveness of the shared resources. Cloud resources are normally not only shared by multiple users but are also actively reallocated per demand. This can work for allocating resources to users. For example, a cloud computer facility that serves European users during European business hours with a specific application, such as email, may reallocate the similar resources to serve North American users during North America's business hours with a different application (e.g., a web server). With cloud computing, multiple users can access a single server to retrieve and update their data without purchasing licenses for various applications. However, the disadvantages of cloud computing involve the following aspects: lack of open standards between cloud computing providers; it cannot be clearly measured how much it will cost to change the technology if the organization discontinues the service; security of the provider is not well guaranteed; freedom of users is limited, meaning that they become dependent on the cloud providers; and loss of control from the users' perspective of the ICT resources and services (Patel et al., 2011).

Cloud computing is the result of evolution and adoption of existing technologies and paradigms. Buyya et al. (2008) defined cloud computing as a type of parallel and distributed system consisting of a collection of interconnected and virtualized computers that are dynamically provisioned and present as one or more unified computing resources based on service-level agreements established through negotiation between service provider and customer. Wang et al. (2010) defined cloud computing as a set of network enabled services, providing scalable, quality of service guaranteed, normally personalized, inexpensive computing platforms on demand, which could be accessed in a simple and pervasive way. Plummer et al. (2008) defined cloud computing as a style of computing where massively scalable IT-related capabilities are provided as a service using IT to multiple external customers. For cloud computing service providers, multi-tenancy offers the benefits of increased resource utilization and economies of scale. Idle resources are available to serve any customer when required and are balanced in real-time among active and idle consumers (Bezemer, Zaidman, Platzbeecker, Hurkmans, & Hart, 2010). For consumers, this provides the appearance of near-infinite computing resources that are available on demand (Armbrust et al., 2010).

The main enabling technology for cloud computing is virtualization. Virtualization abstracts the physical infrastructure, which is the most rigid component, and makes it available as a soft component that is easy to use and manage. Virtualization provides the agility required to speed up IT operations, and reduces cost by increasing infrastructure utilization. Autonomic computing automates the process through which the user can provision resources on demand. By minimizing user involvement, automation speeds up the process and reduces the possibility of human errors (Hamdaqa & Tahvildari, 2012). Cloud computing users face difficult business problems every day. Cloud computing adopts concepts from service-oriented architecture (SOA) that can assist the cloud users break these problems into services that can be integrated to provide a solution of cloud computing.

Cloud computing offers access to applications for interacting with the value chain. Cloud computing connects an organization with the rich learning opportunities percolating in communi-

ties formed by the users of the service (Rader, 2012). Cloud computing allows users to choose from a pool of hardware, software, and networking infrastructure individually managed within an organization or externally by a vendor (Joint, Baker, & Eccles, 2009; Armbrust et al., 2010). Cloud computing has been linked to entrepreneurship and innovation with its pay-on-demand model making it easier and cheaper than ever for anyone anywhere to be an entrepreneur and to have access to the best infrastructure of innovation (Ross & Blumenstein, 2013), thus leading to innovative business models as organizations leverage the opportunities provided by the cloud computing (Baker, 2007). Cloud computing, an innovative technology with dynamic scalability and usage of virtualized resources as a service through the Internet, is regarded as a potential solution to advancing modern organizations' IT competitiveness and performance (Ercan, 2010; Goscinski & Brock, 2010; Thomas, 2011; Wu, 2011; Ross & Blumenstein, 2013).

Cloud computing is a model for provisioning and consuming IT capabilities on a need and pay by use basis (Dhar, 2012). Cloud computing helps in shifting the cost structure from capital expenditure to operating expenditure and also helps the IT systems to be more agile (Dhar, 2012). Various researchers (Lyer & Henderson, 2010), defined cloud computing as a new paradigm and emerging technology while Dillon, Chen, and Chang (2010) stated that cloud computing is not really a new concept, as it uses traditional computing technologies. The general view of cloud computing is that it is a set of computer resources that are offered as scalable, on-demand services through the Internet (Ratten, 2012). For organizations, cloud computing offers reduced IT costs in terms of electricity and hardware purchase and maintenance while increasing the availability of real time data that enables employees to have flexible access to information from any geographic location (Ratten, 2012). Commercial and individual cloud computing services are already available from Amazon, Yahoo, Salesforce, Desktop Two, Zimdesk, and Sun Secure Global Desktop, while Google's efforts in cloud computing have attracted a great deal of interest (Delaney & Vara, 2007; Naone, 2007).

Cloud computing provides all of its resources as services, and makes use of the well-established standards and best practices gained in the domain of SOA and mobile cloud to allow global and easy access to cloud services in a normalized way. As an emerging service, mobile clouds have become influential to the European market, whereby Chang (2014 a) described the research method, data collection process and analysis of results in Germany and Spain.

Cloud computing also leverages concepts from utility computing in order to provide metrics for the services used. Measured services are essential parts of the feedback loop in autonomic computing, allowing services to scale on-demand and to perform automatic failure recovery. Cloud computing is a kind of grid computing; it has evolved by addressing the quality of service and reliability problems. Cloud computing provides the tools and technologies to build data applications with much more reasonable prices compared to conventional computing techniques (Hamdaqa & Tahvildari, 2012). Cloud computing shares characteristics (Hamdaqa & Tahvildari, 2012) as follows:

1. **Client-Server Model:** Client–server computing refers largely to any distributed application that distinguishes between service providers (servers) and service requestors (clients).
2. **Grid Computing:** A form of distributed and parallel computing, whereby a super and virtual computer is composed of cluster of networked, generally coupled computers acting in concert to manage very large tasks.
3. **Mainframe Computer:** Powerful computers used primarily by large organizations for critical applications, commonly bulk data processing such as census; industry

and consumer statistics; police and secret intelligence services; ERP; and financial transaction processing.

4. **Utility Computing:** The packaging of computing resources, such as computation and storage, as a metered service similar to a conventional public utility, such as electricity.
5. **Peer-to-Peer:** A distributed architecture without the requirement for central coordination. Participants are both suppliers and consumers of resources (in contrast to the conventional client–server model).
6. **Cloud Gaming:** Also known as on-demand gaming, is a process of delivering games to computers. Gaming data is collected in the provider's server, so that gaming is independent of client computers effectively used to play the game.

Cloud computing is a model for facilitating ubiquitous, convenient, on-demand network access to a shared pool of configurable computing resources (i.e., networks, servers, storage, applications, and services) that can be quickly provisioned and released with minimal management effort or service provider interaction. This cloud model is composed of five major characteristics, three service models, and four deployment models (NIST, 2011).

Below are the five characteristics of cloud computing.

1. **On-Demand Self-Service:** A consumer can arrange computing capabilities, such as server time and network storage, as needed automatically without requiring human interaction with each service provider.
2. **Broad Network Access:** Capabilities are available over the network and accessed through standard mechanisms that enhance use by heterogeneous thin or thick client platforms (i.e., mobile phones, tablets, laptops, and workstations).

3. **Resource Pooling:** The provider's computing resources are pooled to serve multiple consumers using a multi-tenant model, with different physical and virtual resources dynamically assigned and reassigned according to consumer demand. There is an aspect of location independence in that the customer has practically no control or knowledge of the actual location of the provided resources but may be able to indicate location at a higher level of abstraction (e.g., country, state, or datacenter). Examples of resources include storage, processing, memory, and network bandwidth.

4. **Rapid Elasticity:** Capabilities can be provisioned and released, in some cases regularly, to scale quickly outward and inward commensurate with demand. To the consumer, the capabilities available for provisioning often appear to be unlimited, and can be appropriated in any quantity at any time.

5. **Measured Service:** Cloud systems naturally control and optimize resource use by leveraging a metering capability at some level of abstraction appropriate to the type of service (e.g., storage, processing, bandwidth, and active user accounts). Resource usage can be monitored, managed, and reported, providing transparency for both the provider and consumer of the utilized service.

Below are the four service models of cloud computing:

1. **Software as a Service (SaaS):** The capability provided to the consumer is to use the provider's applications running on a cloud infrastructure. The applications are available from different client devices through either a thin client interface, such as a web browser (e.g., web-based email), or a program interface (NIST, 2011). The consumer does not manage the basic cloud infrastructure, including network, servers, operating sys-

tems, storage, or even individual application capabilities, with the possible exception of limited user-specific application configuration settings. In the business model using SaaS, users are provided access to application software and databases. Cloud providers manage the infrastructure and platforms that run the applications. SaaS is consistently referred to as "on-demand software" and is commonly priced on a pay-per-use basis. SaaS providers normally price applications using a subscription fee. In the SaaS model, cloud providers install and operate application software in the cloud, and cloud users access the software from cloud clients. Cloud users do not manage the cloud infrastructure and platform where the application runs. This eliminates the requirement to install and run the application on the cloud user's own computers, which simplifies maintenance and support. Cloud applications are different from other applications in their scalability which can be achieved by cloning tasks onto multiple virtual machines at run-time to meet changing work demand (Hamdaqa, Livogiannisand, & Tahvildari, 2011).

2. **Platform as a Service (PaaS):** The capability provided to the consumer is to expand onto the cloud infrastructure consumer-created or acquired applications developed using programming languages, libraries, services, and tools supported by the provider (NIST, 2011). The consumer does not manage the fundamental cloud infrastructure, including network, servers, operating systems, or storage, but has control over the deployed applications and probably configuration settings for the application-hosting environment. In the PaaS model, cloud providers distribute a computing platform, normally including operating system, programming language execution environment, database, and web server. Application developers can promote and manage their software solu-

tions on a cloud platform without the cost and complication of buying and managing the fundamental hardware and software layers. With some PaaS offers like Windows Azure, the basic computer and storage resources scale generally to match application demand so that the cloud user does not have to manually allocate resources. The latter has also been proposed by an architecture aiming to enhance real-time in cloud computing environments (Boniface, Nasser, Papay, Phillips, Servin, Zlatev, Yang, Katsaros, Konstanteli, Kousiouris, Menychtas, Kyriazis, & Gogouvitis, 2010). Zhang, Zhang, Fiaidhi, and Chang (2010) stated that PaaS focuses on the middleware and design tools as services, while SaaS deals with traditional applications.

3. **Infrastructure as a Service (IaaS):** The capability provided to the consumer is to arrange processing, storage, networks, and other fundamental computing resources where the consumer is able to deploy and run arbitrary software, which can involve operating systems and applications (NIST, 2011). The consumer does not manage the primary cloud infrastructure, but has control over operating systems, storage, and deployed applications; and possibly limited control of select networking components (e.g., host firewalls). In the most basic cloud-service model, providers of IaaS offer computers physical and virtual machines (A hypervisor, such as OpenStack, Xen, KVM, VMware ESX/ESXi, or Hyper-V runs the virtual machines as guests. Pools of hypervisors within the cloud operational support-system can promote large numbers of virtual machines and the potential to scale services up and down regarding customers' varying requirements). IaaS clouds frequently propose additional resources such as a virtual-machine disk image library, raw (block) and file-based storage, firewalls, load balancers, IP addresses,

virtual local area networks (VLANs), and software bundles (Amies, Sluiman, Tong, & Liu, 2012). IaaS-cloud providers provide these resources on-demand from their large pools installed in data centers. For wide-area connectivity, customers can use either the Internet or carrier clouds (dedicated virtual private networks). To expand their applications, cloud users install operating-system images and their application software on the cloud infrastructure. In addition, the cloud user sustains the operating systems and the application software. Cloud providers routinely bill IaaS services on a use computing basis.

4. **Knowledge Management as a Service (KMaaS):** KM practices that promote efficiency, effectiveness and innovation are becoming a source of competitiveness (Kridan & Goulding, 2006; Sharma, Hui, & Tan, 2007; Mohamed, Ribie`Re, O'sullivan, & Mohamed, 2008). Kasemsap (2013a) indicated that KM is favorably related to job performance. The relationship between knowledge-sharing behavior and team performance are functionally positive in global business (Kasemsap, 2013b). Kasemsap (2014a) suggested that knowledge-sharing behavior is effectively correlated with organizational innovation in the digital age. Dai and Zhang (2013) stated that KM in a cloud computing platform consists of three core management technologies: KM, node management, virtual machine management. Langenberg and Welker (2011) recognized the cluster of KM applications in the cloud (also known as the Knowledge Cloud) as example of the SaaS solution. Dave, Dave, and Shishodia (2013) stated that most of KM workflow and search capabilities are generic in nature and SaaS application is suitable for KM purposes. Baqir and Kathawala (2004) stated that the right combination of different technologies is essential to manage knowl-

edge sources of a learning organization. The dynamic cycle of value creation through KM and cloud computing is changing the rules of the game through disruptions of business models.

Lamont (2011) stated that cloud computing can benefit many applications, but it is particularly helpful to KM solutions in which agility is a valued quality. Kambil (2009) indicated that centralized KM outlived its appropriateness and must shift to "knowledge clouds" in which social media, learning, decision support and everybody plays an important role in managing knowledge as an infinitely valuable resource. Cloud computing forms a fundamental transformation in internal, external fluid collaboration and reduces platform-incompatibility problems (Doelitzscher, Sulistio, Reich, Kuijs, & Wolf, 2011; Lloyd & Sloan, 2011; Jung, Chang, & Chao-Chinwu, 2012). Al-Masud (2012) explained that cloud computing mobility will force organizations to reconsider their current business model. Lin and Chen (2012) stated that cloud computing will radically change the thinking in all domains of organic organization by building collaborative competencies through distributed cognition processes. Dave et al. (2013) stated that the low cost of implementation and maintenance play a major role in the acceptability of cloud computing usage for KM. Velev and Zlateva (2012) explained that the use of cloud computing technology is a natural extension to Enterprise 2.0 KM, which is based on Web 2.0 and form speedy enhancement to KM effectiveness.

Below are the four deployment models of cloud computing.

1. **Private Cloud:** Private cloud is cloud infrastructure completely operated for a single organization, whether managed internally or by a third-party and internally or externally hosted (NIST, 2011). Undertaking a private cloud project requires an important level and degree of obligation to virtualize

the business environment, and requires the organization to reconsider decisions about existing resources. When done right, it can develop business, but every step in the project raises security issues that must be presented to prevent severe vulnerabilities. The infrastructure of private cloud is managed for exclusive use by a single organization comprising numerous consumers (i.e., business units and business structures). Private cloud may be owned, managed, and operated by the organization, a third party, or some combination of them.

2. **Community Cloud:** The infrastructure of community cloud is managed for exclusive use by a specific community of consumers from organizations that have shared concerns (e.g., mission, security requirements, policy, and compliance considerations). Community clouds may be owned, managed, and operated by one or more of the organizations in the community, a third party, or some collection of them.

3. **Public Cloud:** A cloud is called a "public cloud" when the services are distributed over a network that is open for public use. There may be little or no difference between public and private cloud architecture, however, security considerations may be extensively varied for services (i.e., applications, storage, and other resources) that are made available by a service provider for a public audience, and when communication is effected over a non-trusted network. Public cloud service providers (e.g., Amazon AWS, Microsoft, and Google) operate the infrastructure and offer access only via Internet. The infrastructure of public cloud is managed for open use by the general public. Public clouds may be owned, managed, and operated by a business, academic, or government organization, or some collection of them. They exist on the assumptions of the cloud provider. Companies using public clouds do not have ownership of

the equipment hosting the cloud computing environment, and because the environment is not incorporated within their own networks, public cloud customers do not have entire visibility.

4. **Hybrid Cloud:** The infrastructure of hybrid cloud is a configuration of two or more specific cloud infrastructures (i.e., private, community, or public) that remain unique entities, but are bound together by standardized or proprietary technology that enables data and application portability (e.g., cloud bursting for load balancing between clouds).

Chang, Walters, and Wills (2013) proposed Cloud Computing Business Framework (CCBF) describing four major areas for organizations adopting cloud computing services: categorization of business models to offer cloud-adopting organizations the optimum business strategies and business cases; offer a systematic framework to correctly review cloud computing business performance; to deal with application portability from desktops to cloud computing offered by various vendors; and to supply the relationship between different cloud computing research methodologies and between IaaS, PaaS, SaaS, and Business Models.

Chang et al. (2013) stated that there are five key groups involved with CCBF:

1. **Financial Services:** Applications are created to imitate and model financial assets involving pricing calculations and risk analysis (Chang, 2014 b). CCBF can help to measure risks and demonstrate them in visualization so that stakeholders can simply understand.

2. Researchers and practitioners working in cloud business, PaaS, SaaS, health research, financial services, and consultancy. One collaborator is IBM US where the Director of Cloud Initiatives has worked together on this aspect.

3. Participating organizations for organizational sustainability. Sustainability measurement is a specific area of interest and demand in electronic research, and the CCBF can offer and explain research methodologies for organisational sustainability modelling (OSM). OSM supplies an orderly and methodical process to measure return on investment in technical aspects or user aspects of cloud computing adoption (Chang et al., 2013). Organizations with data and 3D analysis include NHS UK (Chang, De Roure, Wills, & Walters, 2011a), SAP (Chang, Wills, & De Roure, 2011b), and Vodafone/Apple (Chang et al., 2011b; 2012).

4. Directors and investors seeking to develop business models. Cloud computing business models are progressing, and are not limited to the pay-as-you-go or SLA billing systems, but require a well-organized business approach.

5. Organizations which plan to design, arrange, move to cloud computing platforms and services.

Cloud computing is suitable for business scenarios as follows:

1. **IT Green Services:** Most organizations roll out new services and offerings to their customers with innovative solutions for higher customer satisfaction and to gain market share. With limited IT budgets, it is always difficult to make investments on such initiatives. By choosing cloud services for these new initiatives, the up-front investment to get started becomes minimal, and there are no penalties due to infrastructure failures. In addition, cloud services allow rapid infrastructure deployment and use of services on demand. Innovative pilot projects can easily take advantage of cloud services and deploy them with minimal risk (Buyya et al., 2009; Armbrust et al., 2010). Chowdhury (2012)

stated that this is required for developing new information services in response to climate change.

2. **IT Operation and System Management:** When IT operations and systems management is complex, and costs are high, cloud computing offers low cost easy to manage operational solutions and minimizes capital expenditure. Some cloud service providers offer automatic failover systems and monitoring services that reduce overall management and operational costs (Catteddu & Hogben, 2009; Weinhardt, Anandasivam, Blau, Borissov, Meinl, Michalk, & Stoßer, 2009; Armbrust et al., 2010).

3. **Business Operation:** Cloud computing systems are engineered to handle large-scale operations while in reality the demand of such computing needs seldom reaches its peak. Computing demand varies over time and hence many systems are underutilized and computing recourses are wasted. This leads to inefficient use of infrastructure (both hardware and software) and poor capacity planning. Cloud computing addresses these issues with on demand elastic services which can be easily scalable as computing need grow (Buyya et al., 2009; Catteddu & Hogben, 2009; Weinhardt et al., 2009). The business benefit of cloud computing has been validated by many investigators in different areas such as the IaaS (Jensen, Schwenk, Gruschka, & Lo Iacono, 2009), reducing economic risk (Li, Li, Liu, Qiu, & Wang, 2009), resource provision (Jung et al., 2012), promotion of business (Etro, 2011), collaboration (Lloyd & Sloan, 2011), democratization and monetization of software services (Katzan, 2009).

Cloud computing contributes to the global economy through the promotion of organizational innovation (Kshetri, 2010; Chesbrough, 2011; Kushida, Murray, & Zysman, 2011). Or-

ganizational innovation leads to organizational performance in modern organizations (Kasemsap, 2013c, 2014b). Kasemsap (2013d) suggested that organizations aiming to enhance workgroup performance and reach strategic goals should focus on developing human resource practices, organizational innovation, and customer value in the global business environment.

Economics of cloud computing is indicated as follows:

1. **Multi-Tenancy Drives Value:** Multi-tenancy means that a single instance of the particular software runs on a server, and it can serve multiple clients concurrently. By implementing a multi-tenant architecture, each software application is configured to partition its data virtually and each client works with a customized pre-configured virtual application instance. This kind of architecture has many advantages – for example, a single instance to maintain including troubleshooting, fixing, and upgrading. In addition, the cloud service provider is able to manage its resources efficiently. Designing the multi-tenant architecture may be more expensive to begin with but the long-term benefits outweigh the up-front costs (Weinhardt et al., 2009).

2. **Faster Time-to-Market:** Cloud computing lowers IT expenditure in two fundamental ways – it leverages a virtual suite of pre-integrated cloud-based applications and infrastructure and simplifies the complexity of traditional IT services. Cloud computing also reduces infrastructure management and monitoring costs and optimizes resource utilization by provision on demand (Buyya et al., 2009).

3. **Reduced Total Cost of Ownership (TCO) Through Shared Infrastructure:** Cloud computing depends on service providers also known as cloud providers for various low level management and service levels of their

multi-tenant applications, platforms, and infrastructures. This also leads to minimal capital expenditure through pay-as-you-use-model (Buyya et al., 2009; Weinhardt et al., 2009; Armbrust et al., 2010).

The evolution of cloud computing-related IT services can be summarized as follows:

1. **Growing Acceptance of Global Delivery:** Regional boundaries are diminishing and global delivery model is becoming a standard practice. This success may be attributed to efficient communication, lower costs along with value-added services (Lee, Huynh, Kwok, & Pi, 2003; Buyya et al., 2009; Catteddu & Hogben, 2009; Weinhardt et al., 2009).

2. **Increasing Client Sophistication:** Organizations are becoming more educated buyers of IT services. Because of their past experience of working with outsourcing vendors, they are effective in vendor management. They clearly understand the complexities and challenges of outsourcing, and are clear about their requirements and expectations. This has resulted in timely outcome of the projects and value-based pricing along with formation of long-term strategic relationships (Nam, Rajagopalan, Rao, & Chaudhury, 1996; Hall & Liedtka, 2007; Buyya et al., 2009; Joint et al., 2009).

3. **Adoption of Multi-Sourcing and Higher Vendor Accountability:** As a result of a large number of poor executions and failure of traditional IT outsourcing projects, many organizations are shying away from large, multi-year commitments for outsourcing projects. They are opting for short-term projects, which involve allocating separate IT functions to different vendors. In addition, they are leveraging skills and value propositions of each vendor, thus reducing risk and increasing efficiency (Nam et al., 1996; Dhar & Balakrishnan, 2006; Goo & Nam, 2007).

4. **Increased Scale and Breadth of Cloud Computing Service Providers:** The leading vendors are expanding their cloud operations on a global scale along with a wide range of services (Lee et al., 2003). These factors coupled with a number of cloud services make them serious contenders for larger deals and acquisitions in modern business. The vendors of cloud computing deliver a wealth of program management expertise and governance and help their clients achieve success for their outsourcing projects.

5. **Increasing Use of Cloud Computing Services and Virtualization:** To meet the specific requirements of clients and forge long-term relationships with them, outsourcing vendors are embracing emerging delivery models including cloud-based services (Lee et al., 2003; Buyya et al., 2009). For example, SaaS is a preferred delivery model for on-demand services. It provides low-cost access to various applications across a global network. It provides greater flexibility and allows customers to focus on core business processes rather than developing and managing IT infrastructure. This results in faster payback on investment, timely deployment of various services and excellence in service delivery and minimization of risk.

The new paradigm of cloud computing provides a collection of advantages over the past computing paradigms, and many organizations are migrating and adopting it. However, there are still a number of challenges, which are currently being addressed by researchers, academicians, and practitioners in the field of cloud computing. Below are the challenges of cloud computing (Chang et al., 2013; Chang, 2014 b; Chang & Ramachandran, 2014).

1. **Performance:** The major issue in performance is intensive transaction-oriented and other data intensive applications, in which cloud computing may lack sufficient per-

formance. Users who are at a long distance from cloud providers may experience high latency and delays.

2. **Security and Privacy:** Organizations are still concerned about security when using cloud computing. Users are concerned about the vulnerability to attacks, when information and critical IT resources are outside their firewall.

3. **Control:** A number of IT wings or departments are concerned because cloud computing providers have control of the platforms. Cloud computing providers do not design platforms for specific companies and business practices.

4. **Bandwidth Costs:** Organizations can save money on hardware and software; however they can suffer higher network bandwidth charges. Bandwidth cost may be low for smaller Internet-based applications, which are not data intensive, but can grow significantly for data-intensive applications.

5. **Reliability:** Cloud computing still does not always offer round the clock reliability. There are cases where cloud computing services suffer outages of several hours.

Adoption of ICT Innovation

Innovation is defined as the generation, development, and adaptation of new ideas on the part of the firms (Damanpour, 1991). This type of innovation, from an IT perspective, refers to a new practice or operational idea (Annukka, 2008). ICT can affect organizational productivity (Caldeira & Ward, 2003; Oliveira & Martins, 2011). In addition, there is a large number of published studies which have considered the adoption and diffusion of ICT-based innovations (Alshamaila et al., 2013). Numerous theoretical and empirical studies have examined ICT innovation adoption, and many theories have been examined by researchers (Rui, 2007; Oliveira & Martins, 2011). For user adoption,

a number of models have been proposed in information systems research. The main aim for these models is to determine which factors influence users' adoption within organizations (Ndubisi & Jantan, 2003). Examples of major theories applied to study the adoption of ICT innovation and adoption in past research include theory of planned behavior (Harrison, Mykytyn, & Riemenschneider, 1997), innovation diffusion theory (IDT) (Cragg & King, 1993), theory of reasoned action (Elena et al., 1999), and technology acceptance model (Grandon & Pearson, 2004). Many ICT-related theories consider various units of analysis, generally the user (micro-level), the firm (meso-level), or the market innovation (macro-level) (Alshamaila et al., 2013). At the organizational level, ICT-related theories such as diffusion of innovation (Rogers, 2003) have been widely applied.

The TOE Framework

The TOE is a multi-perspective framework (DePietro, Wiarda, & Fleischer, 1990). The TOE framework is an organization-level theory. The TOE framework represents one segment of the innovation process, i.e., how the organizational context influences the adoption and implementation of innovations (Baker, 2011). Regarding TOE framework, the technology innovation adoption process is influenced by three main aspects of an enterprise's context:

1. **Technological Context:** Represents the internal and external technologies related to the organization. Both internal and external technologies are already in use in the organization, available in the marketplace, but not currently in use (Baker, 2011). These internal and external technologies may involve either equipment or practice.

2. **Organizational Context:** Related to the resources and the characteristics of the organization (e.g., size and managerial structure).

3. **Environmental Context:** Refers to the arena in which the organization conducts its business. Environmental context can be related to the surrounding elements such as industry, competitors, and the presence of technology service providers.

These three contexts present both constraints and opportunities for technological innovation (Tornatzky & Fleischer, 1990). These three main elements influence the firm's level of technological innovation (Alshamaila et al., 2013).

Technological Context

In the original TOE framework, the technological context described both the internal and external technologies relevant to the firm (Rui, 2007; Oliveira & Martins, 2011). Premkumar (2003) stated that there are not enough studies that have investigated the impact of technological characteristics.

- **Relative Advantage:** It is taken as a central indicator to adoption of new information system innovation. The impact of relative advantage on technology adoption is broadly explored in previous studies (i.e., Gibbs & Kraemer, 2004; Lee, 2004; Ramdani & Kawalek, 2008). The probability of the adoption will increase when businesses perceive a relative advantage in innovation (Thong, Yap, & Raman, 1994; Thong, 1999; Lee, 2004).
- **Uncertainty:** The short lifetime of an innovation may regularly lead to some degree of uncertainty (Jalonen & Lehtonen, 2011). Uncertainty may indicate that lack of knowledge about a specific innovation and can lead to less expected results (Alshamaila et al., 2013).
- **Compatibility:** There is a large volume of published studies describing the role of compatibility. Compatibility is defined as

an essential determinant of IT innovation adoption (Ching & Ellis, 2004; Daylami, Ryan, Olfman, & Shayo, 2005; Zhu, Dong, Xu, & Kraemer, 2006).

- **Trialability:** Trialability is one of the most important components in the process of adopting a new technology (Rogers, 2003; Martins, Steil, & Todesco, 2004; Ramdani & Kawalek, 2008). Trialability influences the adoption of Internet and new online technology in education (Jeyaraj, Rottman, & Lacity, 2006; Hsbollah & Idris, 2009).

Organizational Context

- **Size:** According to Rogers (2003), size is one of the most critical determinants of the innovator profile. Organizational size is considered as an important predictor of ICT innovation adoption (Jeyaraj et al., 2006; Lee & Xia, 2006).
- **Top Management Support:** Technology innovation adoption is influenced by top management support and attitudes toward change (Eder & Igbaria, 2001; Daylami et al., 2005). Jeyaraj et al. (2006) stated that top management support is the major link between individual and organizational ICT innovation adoption.
- **Innovation:** Innovation is the idea, product, program or technology, which is new to the adopter (Hameed, Counsell, & Swift, 2012). Innovation encompasses improved service performance expectations by consumers (Gnyawali & Srivastava, 2013). Innovation is linked to the human characteristics of the decision maker (cognitive style). Innovation relates to the openness to follow new ways, and the methods by which clients process information, take decisions and solve problems (Kirton, 2003; Marcati, Guido, & Peluso, 2008). Cloud computing for consumers provides the benefit of better storage and capacity

utilization made possible by technological innovation (Karakas & Manisaligil, 2012). It also encourages technological innovation through the comprehensive computing platform that can be used by consumers that encourages multiple usages (Vouk, 2008).

- **Prior Technology Experience:** Users' recognition of prior technology experience is viewed on a continuum that describes the degree of linkages between present practice and past experience (Lippert & Forman, 2005). A relationship exists between a user's prior knowledge and their understanding of a new context or situation (Bandura, 1977).

Environmental Context

- **Competitive Pressure:** The external environment has a direct effect on organization's decisions. The competitive pressure faced by the organization is a strong incentive to adopt relevant new technologies. The importance of competitive pressure is a driver of cloud computing adoption (Iacovou, Benbasat, & Dexter, 1995; Crook & Kumar, 1998).
- **Industry:** According to Levenburg, Magal, and Kosalge (2006), the adoption of IS innovation by the organization can be influenced by the industry in which the organization operates. The industry may have an effect on the organization's adoption of new technology (Goode & Stevens, 2000).
- **Market Scope:** Market scope is defined as the horizontal extent of the organization's operations (Zhu, Kraemer, & Xu, 2003). Chopra and Meindl (2001) stated that when organizations increase their market scope, they acquire inventory holding costs and search costs (e.g., searching for consumers, trading partners and distributors).

- **Supplier Computing Support:** Marketing activities, that suppliers execute, can greatly influence SMEs adoption decisions. Supplier computing support may affect the diffusion process of a specia innovation. Previous researches (e.g., Frambach, Barkema, Nooteboom, & Wedel, 1998; Woodside & Biemans, 2005) have attempted to draw a connection between supplier marketing efforts and the client's adoption decision.

FUTURE RESEARCH DIRECTIONS

The strength of this chapter is on the thorough literature consolidation of cloud computing. The extant literature of cloud computing adoption provides a contribution to practitioners and researchers by describing a comprehensive view of the functional applications of cloud computing to appeal to different segments of cloud computing in order to maximize the business impact of cloud computing adoption.

Future research should conduct quantitative research to examine the antecedents of cloud computing adoption further by surveying a large group of people and using a structured questionnaire with a specific set of research questions to fulfill the research contribution.

The classification of the extant literature in the domain of cloud computing adoption will provide the potential opportunities for future research. Future research should broaden the perspectives in the adoption of cloud computing in knowledge-based organizations. Researchers should also consider the applicability of a more multidisciplinary approach toward research activities in adopting cloud computing with KM-related variables (i.e., knowledge-sharing behavior, knowledge creation, organizational learning, learning orientation, and motivation to learn). It will be useful to bring additional disciplines together (e.g., strategic management, marketing, finance, and human resources) to support a more holistic examination of cloud computing adoption and to combine or transfer existing theories and approaches to inquiry in this area. An examination of linkages between cloud computing adoption and business management would seem to be viable for future research efforts.

Emerging technologies and services may play a center of attention. For example, Financial Software as a Service (Ramachandran & Chang, 2014) can perform large-scale simulations of risk and price in one go to allow the stakeholders to keep track of risk and understand the associated prices. Business Intelligence as a Service (Chang, 2014 b) can compute complex risk and pricing options within seconds and provide the investors the real-time information to help them make better judgment in the decision-making processes. On the other hand, the entertainment industry can increase their revenues and level of influence. For example, Yao and Chang (2014) reported the Cloud gaming, including the revenue, trust building, their data collection process and analysis of their results. Emerging services and entertainment industry blended with the TOE framework can play influential roles in the future Cloud Computing adoption.

CONCLUSION

This chapter introduced the role of cloud computing adoption in global business, thus explaining the application overview of cloud computing, the adoption of ICT, and the TOE framework (in terms of technological context, organizational context, and environmental context). In addition, technological context includes the relative advantage, uncertainty, compatibility, and trialability. Organizational context includes the size, top management support, innovation, and prior technology experience. Environmental context includes the competitive pressure, industry, market scope, and supplier

computing support. This chapter has important implications and great value to the research community, managers and ICT providers, in terms of formulating better strategies for cloud computing adoption.

Using cloud computing services providers may need to improve their interaction in organizations who are involved in the cloud computing experience, in an effort to create an effective environment for cloud computing adoption, and to remove any vagueness surrounding this type of technology. Providers may need to clarify their position and viewpoint when it comes to offering in-house services versus cloud computing services, which can affect clients' confidence. Prospective users appear to be willing to adopt cloud computing services despite security concerns, as they rely on the element of trust. Adopting cloud computing in global business will greatly improve organizational performance and reach business goals in modern organizations.

REFERENCES

Al-Masud, S. M. R. (2012). Extended and granular classification of cloud's taxonomy and services. *International Journal of Soft Computing and Engineering*, 2(2), 278–286.

Alshamaila, Y., Papagiannidis, S., & Li, F. (2013). Cloud computing adoption by SMEs in the north east of England: A multi-perspective framework. *Journal of Enterprise Information Management*, 26(3), 250–275. doi:10.1108/17410391311325225

Amies, A., Sluiman, H., Tong, Q. G., & Liu, G. N. (2012). *Developing and hosting applications on the cloud*. Indianapolis, IN: IBM Press.

Annukka, V. (2008). *Organisational factors affecting IT innovation adoption in the Finnish early childhood education*. Paper presented at the 16th European Conference on Information Systems (ECIS 2008), Galway, Ireland.

Armbrust, M., Fox, A., Griffith, R., Joseph, A. D., Katz, R., Konwinski, A., & Zaharia, M. et al. (2010). A view of cloud computing. *Communications of the ACM, 53*(4), 50–58. doi:10.1145/1721654.1721672

Assuncao, M., Costanzo, A., & Buyya, R. (2009). *Evaluating the cost-benefit of using cloud computing to extend the capacity of clusters.* Paper presented at the 18th ACM International Symposium on High Performance Distributed Computing, Garching, Germany.

Aymerich, F. M., Fenu, G., & Surcis, S. (2008). *An approach to a cloud computing network.* Paper presented at the First International Conference on the Applications of Digital Information and Web Technologies, Ostrava, Czech Republic. doi:10.1109/ICADIWT.2008.4664329

Baker, J. (2011). The technology-organization-environment framework. In Y. Dwivedi, M. Wade, & S. Schneberger (Eds.), *Information systems theory: Explaining and predicting our digital society* (pp. 231–246). New York, NY: Springer-Verlag.

Baker, S. (2007). Google and the wisdom of clouds: A lofty new strategy aims to put incredible computing power in the hands of many. *Bloomberg Business Week.* Retrieved August 12, 2014, from http://www.businessweek.com/magazine/content/07_52/b4064048925836.htm

Bandura, A. (1977). *Social learning theory.* New York, NY: Prentice-Hall.

Banerjee, P. (2009). *An intelligent IT infrastructure for the future.* Paper presented at the 15th International Symposium on High-performance Computer Architecture, Raleigh, NC. doi:10.1109/HPCA.2009.4798230

Baqir, M. N., & Kathawala, Y. (2004). Ba for knowledge cities: A futuristic technology model. *Journal of Knowledge Management, 8*(5), 83–95. doi:10.1108/13673270410558828

Bayo-Moriones, A., & Lera-Lopez, F. (2007). A firm-level analysis of determinants of ICT adoption in Spain. *Technovation, 27*(6-7), 352–366. doi:10.1016/j.technovation.2007.01.003

Berman, S. J., Kesterson-Townes, L., Marshall, A., & Srivathsa, R. (2012). How cloud computing enables process and business model innovation. *Strategy and Leadership, 40*(4), 27–35. doi:10.1108/10878571211242920

Bezemer, C. P., Zaidman, A., Platzbeecker, B., Hurkmans, T., & Hart, A. (2010). *Enabling multi-tenancy: An industrial experience report.* Paper presented at the 2010 IEEE International Conference on Software Maintenance, Timisoara, Romania. doi:10.1109/ICSM.2010.5609735

Boniface, M., Nasser, B., Papay, J., Phillips, S., Servin, A., Zlatev, Z., . . . Gogouvitis, S. (2010). *Platform-as-a-Service architecture for real-time quality of service management in clouds.* Paper presented at the 5th International Conference on Internet and Web Applications and Services (ICIW 2010), Barcelona, Spain. doi:10.1109/ICIW.2010.91

Buyya, R., Chee Shin, Y., & Venugopal, S. (2008). *High performance computing and communications.* Paper presented at the 10th IEEE International Conference, Dalian, China.

Buyya, R., Yeo, C. S., Venugopa, S., Broberg, J., & Brandic, I. (2009). Cloud computing and emerging it platforms: Vision, hype, and reality for delivering computing as the 5th utility. *Future Generation Computer Systems, 25*(6), 599–616. doi:10.1016/j.future.2008.12.001

Caldeira, M. M., & Ward, J. M. (2003). Using resource-based theory to interpret the successful adoption and use of information systems and technology in manufacturing small and medium-sized enterprises. *European Journal of Information Systems, 12*(2), 127–141. doi:10.1057/palgrave.ejis.3000454

Carroll, M., Kotze, P., & van der Merwe, A. (2010). Securing virtual and cloud environments. In I. Ivanov, M. van Sinderen, & B. Shishkov (Eds.), *Cloud computing and services science* (pp. 73–90). Berlin, Germany: Springer-Verlag.

Catteddu, D., & Hogben, G. (2009). *Cloud computing: Benefits, risks and recommendations for information security.* European Network and Information Security Agency. Retrieved August 12, 2014, from http://www.enisa.europa.eu/act/rm/files/deliverables/Cloud-computing-risk-assessment

Cegielski, C. G., Jones-Farmer, L. A., Wu, Y., & Hazen, B. T. (2012). Adoption of cloud computing technologies in supply chains: An organizational information processing theory approach. *International Journal of Logistics Management*, *23*(2), 184–211. doi:10.1108/09574091211265350

Chang, V. (2014 a). Measuring and analyzing German and Spanish customer satisfaction of using the iPhone 4S mobile cloud service. *Open Journal of Cloud Computing*, *1*(1), 19–26.

Chang, V. (2014 b). The business intelligence as a service in the cloud. *Future Generation Computer Systems*, *37*, 512–534. doi:10.1016/j.future.2013.12.028

Chang, V., De Roure, D., Wills, G., Walters, R., & Barry, T. (2011a). Organisational sustainability modelling for return on investment: Case studies presented by a National Health Service (NHS) trust UK. *Journal of Computing and Information Technology*, *19*(3), 177–192. doi:10.2498/cit.1001951

Chang, V., & Ramachandran, M. (2014). A proposed case for the cloud software engineering in security. In *Proceedings of the First International Workshop on Emerging Software as a Service ESaaSA*. Academic Press.

Chang, V., Walters, R., & Wills, G. (2012). Business integration as a service. *International Journal of Cloud Applications and Computing*, *2*(1), 16–40. doi:10.4018/ijcac.2012010102

Chang, V., Walters, R. J., & Wills, G. (2013). The development that leads to the cloud computing business framework. *International Journal of Information Management*, *33*(3), 524–538. doi:10.1016/j.ijinfomgt.2013.01.005

Chang, V., Wills, G., & De Roure, D. (2011b). Case studies and organisational sustainability modelling presented by cloud computing business framework. *International Journal of Web Services Research*, *8*(3), 26–53. doi:10.4018/JWSR.2011070102

Chen, M., Zhang, D., & Zhou, L. (2007). Empowering collaborative commerce with web services enabled business process management systems. *Decision Support Systems*, *43*(2), 530–546. doi:10.1016/j.dss.2005.05.014

Chesbrough, H. (2011). Bringing open innovation to services. *MIT Sloan Management Review*, *52*(2), 85–90.

Ching, H. L., & Ellis, P. (2004). Marketing in cyberspace: What factors drive e-commerce adoption? *Journal of Marketing Management*, *20*(3-4), 409–429. doi:10.1362/026725704323080470

Chopra, S., & Meindl, P. (2001). *E-business and the supply chain.* Upper Saddle River, NJ: Prentice-Hall.

Chowdhury, G. (2012). Building environmentally sustainable information services: A green IS research agenda. *Journal of the American Society for Information Science and Technology*, *63*(4), 633–647. doi:10.1002/asi.21703

Cragg, P., & King, M. (1993). Small-firm computing: Motivators and inhibitors. *Management Information Systems Quarterly*, *17*(1), 47–59. doi:10.2307/249509

Crook, C., & Kumar, R. (1998). Electronic data interchange: A multi-industry investigation using grounded theory. *Information & Management, 34*(2), 75–89. doi:10.1016/S0378-7206(98)00040-8

Dai, J., & Zhang, L. (2013). Trusted cloud platform oriented to knowledge management. *Journal of Computer Information Systems, 9*(12), 4997–5004.

Damanpour, F. (1991). Organizational innovation: A meta-analysis of effects of determinants and moderators. *Academy of Management Journal, 34*(3), 555–590. doi:10.2307/256406

Dave, M., Dave, M., & Shishodia, Y. S. (2013). Cloud computing and knowledge management as a service: A collaborative approach to harness and manage the plethora of knowledge. *International Journal of Information Technology, 5*(2), 619–622.

Daylami, N., Ryan, T., Olfman, L., & Shayo, C. (2005). *Determinants of a aaAAa pplication service provider (ASP) adoption as an innovation.* Paper presented at the 38th Annual Hawaii International Conference on System Sciences, Hawaii, HI. doi:10.1109/HICSS.2005.193

Delaney, K. J., & Vara, V. (2007). Google plans services to store users' data. *Wall Street Journal.* Retrieved August 12, 2014, from http://online.wsj.com/article/SB119612660573504716.html?modhps_us_whats_news

DePietro, R., Wiarda, E., & Fleischer, M. (1990). The context for change: Organization, technology and environment. In L. G. Tornatzky & M. Fleischer (Eds.), *The process of technological innovation* (pp. 151–175). Lexington, MA: Lexington Books.

Dhar, S. (2012). From outsourcing to cloud computing: Evolution of IT services. *Management Research Review, 35*(8), 664–675. doi:10.1108/01409171211247677

Dhar, S., & Balakrishnan, B. (2006). Risks, benefits and challenges in global IT outsourcing: Perspectives and practices. *Journal of Global Information Management, 14*(3), 59–89. doi:10.4018/jgim.2006070104

Dillon, T., Chen, W., & Chang, E. (2010). *Cloud computing: Issues and challenges.* Paper presented at the 24th IEEE International Conference on Advanced Information Networking and Applications (AINA 2010), Perth, Australia. doi:10.1109/AINA.2010.187

Doelitzscher, F., Sulistio, A., Reich, C., Kuijs, H., & Wolf, D. (2011). Private cloud for collaboration and e-learning services: From IaaS to SaaS. *Computing, 91*(1), 23–42. doi:10.1007/s00607-010-0106-z

Eder, L., & Igbaria, M. (2001). Determinants of intranet diffusion and infusion. *Omega, 29*(3), 233–242. doi:10.1016/S0305-0483(00)00044-X

Elena, K., Detmar, W. S., & Norman, L. C. (1999). Information technology adoption across time: A cross sectional comparison of pre-adoption and post-adoption beliefs. *Management Information Systems Quarterly, 23*(2), 183–213. doi:10.2307/249751

Ercan, T. (2010). Effective use of cloud computing in educational institutions. *Procedia: Social and Behavioral Sciences, 2*(2), 938–942. doi:10.1016/j.sbspro.2010.03.130

Erdogmus, H. (2009). Cloud computing: Does nirvana hide behind the nebula? *IEEE Software, 26*(2), 4–6. doi:10.1109/MS.2009.31

Etro, F. (2011). The economics of cloud computing. *The IUP Journal of Managerial Economics, 9*(2), 7–22.

Frambach, R., Barkema, H., Nooteboom, B., & Wedel, M. (1998). Adoption of a service innovation in the business market: An empirical test of supply-side variables. *Journal of Business Research, 41*(2), 161–174. doi:10.1016/S0148-2963(97)00005-2

Gartner. (2009). *Cloud computing inquiries at Gartner*. Retrieved August 12, 2014, from http://blogs.gartner.com/thomas_bittman/2009/10/29/cloud-computing-inquiries-at-gartner

Gibbs, J., & Kraemer, K. (2004). A cross-country investigation of the determinants of scope of e-commerce use: An institutional approach. *Electronic Markets, 14*(2), 124–137. doi:10.1080/10196780410001675077

Goo, J., & Nam, K. (2007). *Contract as a source of trust – Commitment in successful IT outsourcing relationship: An empirical study*. Paper presented at the 40th Annual Hawaii International Conference on System Sciences (HICSS 2007), Waikoloa, HI. doi:10.1109/HICSS.2007.148

Goode, S., & Stevens, K. (2000). An analysis of the business characteristics of adopters and non-adopters of world wide web technology. *Information Technology Management, 11*(2), 129–154. doi:10.1023/A:1019112722593

Goscinski, A., & Brock, M. (2010). Toward dynamic and attribute based publication, discovery and selection for cloud computing. *Future Generation Computer Systems, 26*(7), 947–970. doi:10.1016/j.future.2010.03.009

Grandon, E., & Pearson, M. (2004). Electronic commerce adoption: An empirical study of small and medium US businesses. *Information & Management, 42*(1), 197–216. doi:10.1016/j.im.2003.12.010

Gray, A. (2013). Conflict of laws and the cloud. *Computer Law & Security Report, 29*(1), 58–65. doi:10.1016/j.clsr.2012.11.004

Hall, J. A., & Liedtka, S. L. (2007). The Sarbanes-Oxley Act: Implications for large-scale IT outsourcing. *Communications of the ACM, 50*(3), 95–100. doi:10.1145/1226736.1226742

Hamdaqa, M., Livogiannisand, T., & Tahvildari, L. (2011). *A reference model for developing cloud applications*. Paper presented at the 1st International Conference on Cloud Computing and Services Science, Noordwijkerhout, The Netherlands.

Hamdaqa, M., & Tahvildari, L. (2012). Cloud computing uncovered: A research landscape. *Advances in Computers, 86*, 41–85. doi:10.1016/B978-0-12-396535-6.00002-8

Hameed, M. A., Counsell, S., & Swift, S. (2012). A conceptual model for the process of IT innovation adoption in organizations. *Journal of Engineering and Technology Management, 29*(3), 358–390. doi:10.1016/j.jengtecman.2012.03.007

Harrison, D., Mykytyn, P. Jr, & Riemenschneider, C. (1997). Executive decision about adoption of information technology in small business: Theory and empirical tests. *Information Systems Research, 8*(2), 171–195. doi:10.1287/isre.8.2.171

Hayes, B. (2008). Cloud computing. *Communications of the ACM, 51*(7), 9–11. doi:10.1145/1364782.1364786

Hsbollah, H. M., & Idris, M. (2009). E-learning adoption: The role of relative advantages, trialability and academic specialization. *Campus-Wide Information Systems, 26*(1), 54–70. doi:10.1108/10650740910921564

Iacovou, C., Benbasat, I., & Dexter, A. (1995). Electronic data interchange and small organizations: Adoption and impact of technology. *Management Information Systems Quarterly, 19*(4), 465–485. doi:10.2307/249629

IBM. (2009). *The benefits of cloud computing.* Retrieved August 12, 2014 from http://public.dhe. ibm.com/common/ssi/ecm/en/diw03004usen/ DIW03004USEN.PDF

IBM Global Technology Services. (2010). *Getting cloud computing right.* Retrieved August 12, 2014, from http://public.dhe.ibm.com/common/ ssi/ecm/en/ciw03078usen/CIW03078USEN.PDF

IBM Global Technology Services. (2011). *Strategies for assessing cloud security.* Retrieved August 12, 2014, from http://public.dhe.ibm.com/common/ssi/ecm/en/sew03022usen/SEW03022U-SEN.PDF

Jalonen, H., & Lehtonen, A. (2011). *Uncertainty in the innovation process.* Paper presented at the European Conference on Innovation and Entrepreneurship, Aberdeen, Scotland.

Jensen, M., Schwenk, J. O., Gruschka, N., & Lo Iacono, L. (2009). *On technical security issues in cloud computing.* Paper presented at the 2009 IEEE International Conference on Cloud Computing, Los Angeles, CA. doi:10.1109/CLOUD.2009.60

Jeyaraj, A., Rottman, J. W., & Lacity, M. C. (2006). A review of the predictors, linkages, and biases in IT innovation adoption research. *Journal of Information Technology, 21*(1), 1–23. doi:10.1057/ palgrave.jit.2000056

Joint, A., Baker, E., & Eccles, E. (2009). Hey, you, get off of that Cloud? *Computer Law & Security Report, 25*(3), 270–274. doi:10.1016/j. clsr.2009.03.001

Jung, J. J., Chang, Y. S., & Chao-Chinwu, Y. L. (2012). Advances in intelligent grid and cloud computing. *Information Systems Frontiers, 14*(4), 823–825. doi:10.1007/s10796-012-9349-x

Kambil, A. (2009). Obliterate knowledge management: Everyone is a knowledge manager. *The Journal of Business Strategy, 30*(6), 66–68. doi:10.1108/02756660911003149

Karakas, F., & Manisaligil, A. (2012). Reorienting self-directed learning for the creative digital era. *European Journal of Training and Development, 36*(7), 712–731. doi:10.1108/03090591211255557

Kasemsap, K. (2013a). Innovative framework: Formation of causal model of organizational culture, organizational climate, knowledge management, and job performance. *Journal of International Business Management & Research, 4*(12), 21–32.

Kasemsap, K. (2013b). Strategic business management: A practical framework and causal model of empowering leadership, team cohesion, knowledge-sharing behavior, and team performance. *Journal of Social and Development Sciences, 4*(3), 100–106.

Kasemsap, K. (2013c). Unified framework: Constructing a causal model of Six Sigma, organizational learning, organizational innovation, and organizational performance. *The Journal of Interdisciplinary Networks, 2*(1), 268–273.

Kasemsap, K. (2013d). Innovative human resource practices: An integrative framework and causal model of human resource practices, innovation, customer value, and workgroup performance. *International Journal of Business, Management &. Social Sciences, 2*(7), 44–48.

Kasemsap, K. (2014a). The role of knowledge sharing on organisational innovation: An integrated framework. In L. Al-Hakim & C. Jin (Eds.), *Quality innovation: Knowledge, theory, and practices* (pp. 247–271). Hershey, PA: IGI Global. doi:10.4018/978-1-4666-4769-5.ch012

Kasemsap, K. (2014b). Strategic innovation management: An integrative framework and causal model of knowledge management, strategic orientation, organizational innovation, and organizational performance. In P. Ordóñez de Pablos & R. D. Tennyson (Eds.), *Strategic approaches for human capital management and development in a turbulent economy* (pp. 102–116). Hershey, PA: IGI Global. doi:10.4018/978-1-4666-4530-1.ch007

Katzan, H. J. (2009). Cloud computing economics: Democratization and monetization of services. *Journal of Business & Economics Research*, *7*(6), 1–12.

Kirto, M. J. (2003). *Adaption-innovation: In the context of diversity and change*. London, UK: Routledge.

Kridan, A. B., & Goulding, J. S. (2006). A case study on knowledge management implementation in the banking sector. *VINE: The Journal of Information and Knowledge Management Systems*, *36*(2), 211–222. doi:10.1108/03055720610683013

Kshetri, N. (2010). Cloud computing in developing economies. *IEEE Computer*, *43*(10), 47–55. doi:10.1109/MC.2010.212

Kushida, K. E., Murray, J., & Zysman, J. (2011). Diffusing the cloud: Cloud computing and implications for public policy. *Journal of Industry, Competition and Trade*, *11*(3), 209–237. doi:10.1007/s10842-011-0106-5

Langenberg, D., & Welker, M. (2011). Knowledge management in virtual communities. *Open Journal of Knowledge Management*, *16*(3), 13–19.

Lee, G., & Xia, W. (2006). Organizational size and IT innovation adoption: A meta-analysis. *Information & Management*, *43*(8), 975–985. doi:10.1016/j.im.2006.09.003

Lee, J. (2004). Discriminant analysis of technology adoption behavior: A case of Internet technologies in small businesses. *Journal of Computer Information Systems*, *44*(4), 57–66.

Lee, J., Huynh, M. Q., Kwok, R. C., & Pi, S. (2003). IT outsourcing evolution: Past, present, and future. *Communications of the ACM*, *46*(5), 84–89. doi:10.1145/769800.769807

Levenburg, N., Magal, S. R., & Kosalge, P. (2006). An exploratory investigation of organizational factors and e-business motivations among SMFOEs in the US. *Electronic Markets*, *16*(1), 70–84. doi:10.1080/10196780500491402

Li, X., Li, Y., Liu, T., Qiu, J., & Wang, F. (2009). *The method and tool of cost analysis for cloud computing*. Paper presented at the 2009 IEEE International Conference on Cloud Computing, Bangalore, India. doi:10.1109/CLOUD.2009.84

Lin, A., & Chen, N. C. (2012). Cloud computing as an innovation: Perception, attitude, and adoption. *International Journal of Information Management*, *32*(6), 533–540. doi:10.1016/j.ijinfomgt.2012.04.001

Lippert, S., & Forman, H. (2005). Utilization of information technology: Examining cognitive and experiential factors of post-adoption behavior. *IEEE Transactions on Engineering Management*, *52*(3), 363–381. doi:10.1109/TEM.2005.851273

Liu, H., & Orban, D. (2008). *GridBatch: Cloud computing for large-scale data-intensive batch applications*. Paper presented at the 8th IEEE International Symposium on Cluster Computing and the Grid, Lyon, France. doi:10.1109/CCGRID.2008.30

Liu, W., & Cai, H. (2013). Embracing the shift to cloud computing: Knowledge and skills for systems librarians. *Perspectives*, *29*(1), 22–29.

Lloyd, A. D., & Sloan, T. M. (2011). Intercontinental grids: An infrastructure for demand-driven innovation. *Journal of Grid Computing*, *9*(2), 185–200. doi:10.1007/s10723-011-9190-3

Lohr, S. (2007). Google and I.B.M. join in "cloud computing" research. *New York Times*. Retrieved August 12, 2014, from http://www.csun.edu/pubrels/clips/Oct07/10-08-07E.pdf

Lyer, B., & Henderson, J. (2010). Preparing for the future: Understanding the seven capabilities of cloud computing. *Management Information Systems Quarterly Executive, 9*(2), 117–131.

Marcati, A., Guido, G., & Peluso, A. (2008). The role of SME entrepreneurs' innovativeness and personality in the adoption of innovations. *Research Policy, 37*(9), 1579–1590. doi:10.1016/j.respol.2008.06.004

Martins, C., Steil, A., & Todesco, J. (2004). Factors influencing the adoption of the internet as a teaching tool at foreign language schools. *Computers & Education, 42*(4), 353–374. doi:10.1016/j.compedu.2003.08.007

Mell, P., & Grance, T. (2010). *The NIST definition of cloud computing*. Retrieved August 12, 2014, from http://www.newinnovationsguide.com/NIST_Cloud_Definition.pdf

Misra, S. C., & Mondal, A. (2010). Identification of a company's suitability for the adoption of cloud computing and modelling its corresponding return on investment. *Mathematical and Computer Modelling, 53*(3-4), 504–521. doi:10.1016/j.mcm.2010.03.037

Mohamed, M. S., Ribie`Re, V. M., O'sullivan, K. J., & Mohamed, M. A. (2008). The re-structuring of the information technology infrastructure library (ITIL) implementation using knowledge management framework. *VINE: The Journal of Information and Knowledge Management Systems, 38*(3), 315–333. doi:10.1108/03055720810904835

Nam, K., Rajagopalan, S., Rao, H. R., & Chaudhury, A. (1996). A two-level investigation of information systems outsourcing. *Communications of the ACM, 39*(7), 37–44. doi:10.1145/233977.233989

Naone, E. (2007). Computer in the cloud. *Technology Review*. Retrieved August 12, 2014, from http://www.technologyreview.com/Infotech/19397/?af

Ndubisi, N. O., & Jantan, M. (2003). Evaluating IS usage in Malaysian small and medium-sized firms using the technology acceptance model. *Logistics Information Management, 16*(6), 440–450. doi:10.1108/09576050310503411

NIST. (2011). *The NIST definition of cloud computing*. National Institute of Standards and Technology. Retrieved August 12, 2014, from http://csrc.nist.gov/publications/drafts/800-145/Draft-SP-800-145_cloud-definition.pdf

Oliveira, T., & Martins, M. (2011). Literature review of information technology adoption models at firm level. *The Electronic Journal Information Systems Evaluation, 14*(1), 110–121.

Patel, A., Seyfi, A., Tew, Y., & Jaradat, A. (2011). Comparative study and review of grid, cloud, utility computing and software as a service for use by libraries. *Library Hi Tech News, 3*(3), 25–32. doi:10.1108/07419051111145145

Plummer, D., Bittman, T., Austin, T., Cearley, D., & Smith, D. (2008). *Cloud computing: Defining and describing an emerging phenomenon*. Stamford, CT: Gartner.

Prasad, M. R., Gyani, J., & Murti, P. R. K. (2012). Mobile cloud computing: Implications and challenges. *Journal of Information Engineering and Applications, 2*(7), 7–16.

Premkumar, P. (2003). Meta-analysis of research on information technology implementation in small business. *Journal of Organizational Computing and Electronic Commerce, 13*(2), 91–121. doi:10.1207/S15327744JOCE1302_2

Pyke, J. (2009). *Now is the time to take the cloud seriously*. Retrieved August 12, 2014, from http://www.cordys.com/cordyscms_sites/objects/bb1a-0bd7f47b1c91ddf36ba7db88241d/time_to_take_the_cloud_seroiusly_online_1_.pdf

Rader, D. (2012). Case - How cloud computing maximizes growth opportunities for a firm challenging established rivals. *Strategy and Leadership*, *40*(3), 36–43. doi:10.1108/10878571211221202

Ramachandran, M., & Chang, V. (2014). Financial Software as a Service–A Paradigm for Risk Modelling and Analytics. *International Journal of Organizational and Collective Intelligence*, *4*(3), 65–89. doi:10.4018/ijoci.2014070104

Ramdani, B., & Kawalek, P. (2008). SMEs & IS innovations adoption: A review & assessment of previous research. *Academia Revista Latinoamericana de Administracioen*, *39*(1), 47–70.

Ratten, V. (2012). Does the sky have to be the limit? Utilizing cloud-based learning in the workplace. *Development and Learning in Organizations*, *26*(5), 21–23. doi:10.1108/14777281211258662

Ratten, V. (2014). Indian and US consumer purchase intentions of cloud computing services. *Journal of Indian Business Research*, *6*(2), 170–188. doi:10.1108/JIBR-07-2013-0068

Rogers, E. (2003). *Diffusion of innovations*. New York, NY: Free Press.

Ross, P., & Blumenstein, M. (2013). Cloud computing: The nexus of strategy and technology. *The Journal of Business Strategy*, *34*(4), 39–47. doi:10.1108/JBS-10-2012-0061

Rui, G. (2007). *Information systems innovation adoption among organizations a match-based framework and empirical studies*. Singapore: National University of Singapore.

Saya, S., Pee, L., & Kankanhalli, A. (2010). *The impact of institutional influences on perceived technological characteristics and real options in cloud computing adoption*. Paper presented at the 31st International Conference on Information Systems (ICIS 2010), St. Louis, MO.

Sclater, N. (2009). *Cloudworks: eLearning in the cloud*. Retrieved August 12, 2014, from http://cloudworks.ac.uk/cloud/view/2430

Sharif, A. M. (2010). It's written in the cloud: The hype and promise of cloud computing. *Journal of Enterprise Information Management*, *23*(2), 131–134. doi:10.1108/17410391011019732

Sharma, R. S., Hui, P. T. Y., & Tan, M. W. (2007). Value-added knowledge management for financial performance: The case of an East Asian conglomerate. *VINE: The Journal of Information and Knowledge Management Systems*, *37*(4), 484–501. doi:10.1108/03055720710838542

Srinivasan, S., & Getov, V. (2011). Navigating the cloud computing landscape: Technologies, services, and adopters. *Computer*, *44*(3), 22–23. doi:10.1109/MC.2011.91

Stein, S., Ware, J., Laboy, J., & Schaffer, H. E. (2013). Improving K-12 pedagogy via a cloud designed for education. *International Journal of Information Management*, *33*(1), 235–241. doi:10.1016/j.ijinfomgt.2012.07.009

Sultan, N. (2010). Cloud computing for education: A new dawn? *International Journal of Information Management*, *30*(2), 109–116. doi:10.1016/j.ijinfomgt.2009.09.004

Sultan, N. (2013). Knowledge management in the age of cloud computing and Web 2.0: Experiencing the power of disruptive innovations. *International Journal of Information Management*, *33*(1), 160–165. doi:10.1016/j.ijinfomgt.2012.08.006

Thinkstrategies. (2002). *Solving the IT challenges of small and mid-size organizations via "utility computing"*. Retrieved August 12, 2014, from http://www.thinkstrategies.com/images/CBE_Whitepaper_110602.pdf

Thomas, P. Y. (2011). Cloud computing: A potential paradigm for practicing the scholarship of teaching and learning. *The Electronic Library, 29*(2), 214–224. doi:10.1108/02640471111125177

Thong, J. (1999). An integrated model of information systems adoption in small businesses. *Journal of Management Information Systems, 15*(4), 187–214.

Thong, J., Yap, C., & Raman, K. (1994). Engagement of external expertise in information systems implementation. *Journal of Management Information Systems, 11*(2), 209–231.

Tornatzky, L., & Fleischer, M. (1990). *The process of technology innovation.* Lexington, MA: Lexington Books.

Tuncay, E. (2010). Effective use of cloud computing in educational institutions. *Procedia: Social and Behavioral Sciences, 2*(1), 938–942.

Vaquero, L. M., Rodero-Merino, L., Caceres, J., & Lindner, M. (2008). A break in the clouds: Towards a cloud definition. *Computer Communication Review, 39*(1), 50–55. doi:10.1145/1496091.1496100

Velev, D., & Zlateva, P. (2012). *Enterprise 2.0 knowledge management development trends.* Paper presented at the International Conference on Economics, Business Innovation (ICEBI 2012), Singapore.

Vouk, M. A. (2008). Cloud computing-issues, research and implementations. *Journal of Computing and Information Technology, 16*(4), 235–246.

Wang, L., Von Laszewski, G., Younge, A., He, X., Kunze, M., Tao, J., & Fu, C. (2010). Cloud computing: A perspective study. *New Generation Computing, 28*(2), 137–146. doi:10.1007/s00354-008-0081-5

Weinhardt, C., Anandasivam, A., Blau, B., Borissov, N., Meinl, T., Michalk, W., & Stoßer, J. (2009). Cloud computing: A classification, business models, and research directions. *Business & Information Systems Engineering, 1*(5), 391–399. doi:10.1007/s12599-009-0071-2

Woodside, A. G., & Biemans, W. G. (2005). Modeling innovation, manufacturing, diffusion and adoption/rejection processes. *Journal of Business and Industrial Marketing, 20*(7), 380–393. doi:10.1108/08858620510628614

Wu, W. W. (2011). Mining significant factors affecting the adoption of SaaS using the rough set approach. *Journal of Systems and Software, 84*(3), 435–441. doi:10.1016/j.jss.2010.11.890

Yao, Y., & Chang, V. (2014). Towards trust and trust building in a selected Cloud gaming virtual community. *International Journal of Organizational and Collective Intelligence, 4*(2), 64–86. doi:10.4018/ijoci.2014040104

Zhang, L. J., Zhang, J., Fiaidhi, J., & Chang, J. M. (2010). Hot topics in cloud computing. *Computer, 12*(5), 17–19.

Zhu, K., Dong, S., Xu, S., & Kraemer, K. (2006). Innovation diffusion in global contexts: Determinants of post-adoption digital transformation of European companies. *European Journal of Information Systems, 15*(6), 601–616. doi:10.1057/palgrave.ejis.3000650

Zhu, K., Kraemer, K., & Xu, S. (2003). Electronic business adoption by European firms: A cross-country assessment of the facilitators and inhibitors. *European Journal of Information Systems, 12*(4), 251–268. doi:10.1057/palgrave.ejis.3000475

ADDITIONAL READING

Armbrust, M., Stoica, I., Zaharia, M., Fox, A., Griffith, R., Joseph, A. D., & Rabkin, A. et al. (2010). A view of cloud computing. *Communications of the ACM, 53*(4), 50–58. doi:10.1145/1721654.1721672

Aziz, N. (2010). *French higher education in the cloud.* Grenoble, France: Grenoble Ecole de Management.

Badger, L., Grance, T., Patt-Corner, P., & Voas, J. (2011). *Draft-cloud computing synopsis and recommendations.* Gaithersburg, MD: National Institute of Standards and Technology.

Bias, R. (2010). The Cloud is not outsourcing. *Cloudbook Journal, 1*(2), 11–13.

Breeding, M. (2012). *Cloud computing for libraries.* Chicago, IL: American Library Association.

Buchinger, S., Kriglstein, S., Brandt, S., & Hlavacs, H. (2011). A survey on user studies and technical aspects of mobile multimedia applications. *Entertainment Computing, 2*(3), 175–190. doi:10.1016/j.entcom.2011.02.001

Cervone, H. F. (2010). An overview of virtual and cloud computing. *OCLC Systems & Services, 26*(3), 162–165. doi:10.1108/10650751011073607

Chaisiri, S., Lee, B. S., & Niyato, D. (2012). Optimization of resource provisioning cost in cloud computing. *Computer, 5*(2), 1–32.

Chang, V., Li, C. S., De Roure, D., Wills, G., Walters, R., & Chee, C. (2011). The financial clouds review. *International Journal of Cloud Applications and Computing, 1*(2), 41–63. doi:10.4018/ijcac.2011040104

Dwivedi, Y. K., & Mustafee, N. (2010). It's unwritten in the Cloud: The technology enablers for realizing the promise of Cloud Computing. *Journal of Enterprise Information Management, 23*(6), 673–679. doi:10.1108/17410391011088583

Goldner, M. (2011). Winds of change: Libraries and cloud computing. *Multimedia Information & Technology, 37*(3), 24–28.

Goldner, M., & Birch, K. (2012). Resource sharing in a cloud computing age. *Interlending & Document Supply, 40*(1), 4–11. doi:10.1108/02641611211214224

Guinard, D., Trifa, V., Karnouskos, S., Spiess, P., & Savio, D. (2010). Interacting with the SOA-based Internet of things: Discovery, query, selection, and on-demand provisioning of web services. *IEEE Transactions on Services Computing, 3*(3), 223–235. doi:10.1109/TSC.2010.3

Han, Y. (2013). IaaS cloud computing services for libraries: Cloud storage and virtual machines. *OCLC Systems & Services: International digital library. Perspectives, 29*(2), 87–100.

Heinle, C., & Strebel, J. (2010). *IaaS adoption determinants in enterprises. Economics of grids clouds systems and services.* Berlin, Germany: Springer-Verlag.

Jain, L., & Bhardwaj, S. (2010). Enterprise cloud computing: Key considerations for adoption. *International Journal of Engineering and Information Technology, 2*(2), 113–117.

Krikos, A. (2011). Cloud computing as a disruptive technology. *Cloudbook Journal, 2*(2), 13–18.

Low, C., Chen, Y., & Wu, M. (2011). Understanding the determinants of cloud computing adoption. *Industrial Management & Data Systems, 111*(7), 1006–1023. doi:10.1108/02635571111161262

Marston, S., Li, Z., Bandyopadhyay, S., Zhang, J., & Ghalsasi, A. (2011). Cloud computing: The business perspective. *Decision Support Systems, 51*(1), 176–189. doi:10.1016/j.dss.2010.12.006

Mavodza, J. (2013). The impact of cloud computing on the future of academic library practices and services. *New Library World, 114*(3-4), 132–141. doi:10.1108/03074801311304041

Mimecast (2010). *Cloud computing adoption survey*. London, UK: Mimecast.

Mitchell, E. T. (2010). Cloud computing and your library. *Journal of Web Librarianship*, *4*(1), 83–86. doi:10.1080/19322900903565259

Mulholland, A. (2010). *Enterprise cloud computing. A strategy guide for business and technology leaders*. Tampa, FL: Meghan-Kiffer Press.

Ojala, A., & Tyrvainen, P. (2011). Value networks in cloud computing. *The Journal of Business Strategy*, *32*(6), 40–49. doi:10.1108/02756661111180122

Ratten, V. (2012). Implementing cloud learning in an organization: A training perspective. *Industrial and Commercial Training*, *44*(6), 334–336. doi:10.1108/00197851211254761

Rochwerger, B., Breitgand, D., Levy, E., Galis, A., Nagin, K., Llorente, I., & Galan, F. et al. (2009). The Reservoir model and architecture for open federated cloud computing. *IBM Journal of Research and Development*, *53*(4), 535–545. doi:10.1147/JRD.2009.5429058

Ross, P. K. (2011). How to keep your head above the clouds: Changing ICT worker skill sets in a cloud computing environment. *The Employment Relations Record*, *11*(1), 62–74.

Ryan, W. M., & Loeffler, C. M. (2010). Insights into cloud computing. *Intellectual Property & Technology Law Journal*, *22*(11), 22–28.

Shroff, G. (2010). *Enterprise cloud computing: Technology, application, and architecture*. Cambridge, UK: Cambridge University Press. doi:10.1017/CBO9780511778476

Silic, M., & Back, A. (2013). Factors impacting information governance in the mobile device dual-use context. *Records Management Journal*, *23*(2), 73–89. doi:10.1108/RMJ-11-2012-0033

Truong, H. L., & Dustdar, S. (2012). A survey on cloud-based sustainability governance systems. *International Journal of Web Information Systems*, *8*(3), 278–295. doi:10.1108/17440081211258178

Uchibayashi, T., Apduhan, B., & Shiratori, N. (2013). An ontology update mechanism in IaaS service discovery system. *International Journal of Web Information Systems*, *9*(4), 330–343. doi:10.1108/IJWIS-10-2013-0025

Unhelkar, B., & Murugesan, S. (2010). The enterprise mobile applications development framework. *IEEE IT Professional*, *12*(3), 33–39. doi:10.1109/MITP.2010.45

Walterbusch, M., Martens, B., & Teuteberg, F. (2013). Evaluating cloud computing services from a total cost of ownership perspective. *Management Research Review*, *36*(6), 613–638. doi:10.1108/01409171311325769

Wu, W. W., Lan, L. W., & Lee, Y. T. (2013). Factors hindering acceptance of using cloud services in university: A case study. *The Electronic Library*, *31*(1), 84–98. doi:10.1108/02640471311299155

Zhang, Q., Cheng, L., & Boutaba, R. (2010). Cloud computing: State-of-the-art and research challenges. *Journal of Internet Services and Applications*, *1*(1), 7–18. doi:10.1007/s13174-010-0007-6

KEY TERMS AND DEFINITIONS

Application Software: The complete, self-contained computer program that performs a specific useful task.

Cloud Computing: The process where a task is solved by using a wide variety of technologies, including computers, networks, servers, and the Internet.

Information Technology: A set of tools, processes, and associated equipment employed to collect, process, and present information.

Internet: A means of connecting a computer to any other computer anywhere in the world via routers and servers.

Knowledge Management: The strategies and processes designed to identify, capture, structure, value, leverage, and share an organization's intellectual assets to enhance its performance and competitiveness.

Network: The operating system that enables users of data communications lines to exchange information over long distances by connecting with each other through a system of routers, servers, switches, and the like.

Operating System: The master control program that automatically runs first when a computer is switched on, and remains in the background until the computer is turned off.

Platform: The operating system that is the technological foundation on which the application software runs.

Software: The organized information in the form of operating systems, utilities, programs, and applications that enable computers to work.

Chapter 3
Impact of EU Data Protection Laws on Cloud Computing:
Capturing Cloud–Computing Challenges and Fault Lines

Morgan Eldred
University of Portsmouth, UK

Carl Adams
University of Portsmouth, UK

Alice Good
University of Portsmouth, UK

ABSTRACT

The global nature of cloud computing has resulted in emerging challenges, such as clashes between legal systems, cultural differences, and business practice norms: cloud-computing is at the forefront of recognising, and "smoothing over," emergent differences between nation states as we move towards a more globally connected world. This chapter uses the emergent differences over regulation governing data protection; as the world becomes more interconnected, we are likely to see more examples of technology practices and models sweeping around the globe, and raising further areas for clashes between nations and regions, much like the fault lines between tectonic plates. This chapter provides contribution by capturing some emergent "fault lines" in an in-depth case study comparing the evolving EU directives covering data protection and how they relate to non-EU data protection legal systems. This provides the foundations to consider cloud-computing challenges, inform policymakers in measures to resolve "clashes," and in informing researchers investigating other global technology phenomena.

INTRODUCTION

Cloud computing is not viewed as a new technology, but more as a new way of delivering computing resources. Several types of cloud computing platforms exist, of which the main types are public, private and hybrid. Public clouds are normally offered by commercial organisations that provide access for a fee. Private clouds exist within a specific organisation and typically are not available for outside use.

DOI: 10.4018/978-1-4666-8210-8.ch003

Copyright © 2015, IGI Global. Copying or distributing in print or electronic forms without written permission of IGI Global is prohibited.

Hybrid clouds are a mixture of private and public clouds with the typical setup being that of a private cloud that has the ability to call upon additional resources from a public cloud. (Chang, 2014)

The mainstream cloud computing frameworks are infrastructure as a service (Iaas), platform as a service (Paas) and software as a service (SaaS). Infrastructure as a service is divided into compute clouds and resource clouds, with the compute cloud providing access to computational resources such as CPU's, while resource clouds contain managed and scalable resources as services to users. Platform as a service provides computational resources via a platform upon which application and services can be developed and hosted. Software as a service often referred to as application clouds, provide applications/or services using a cloud infrastructure or platform, rather than providing cloud features themselves (Chang, 2013).

The main advantage of cloud computing is the ability of equilibrating the access to computing resources for all types of businesses, regardless their dimensions and investment capabilities. These advantages include cost efficiency, scalability, concentration, security and accessibility with a further list below.

- Productivity gains supported by economies of scale for all enterprises.
- Data centers that provide cost-effective, secure and sustainable computing power.
- Increased accessibility for SMEs to computing resources coupled by a standardized interface usage.
- Efficient scaling of resources.
- Resources concentration.
- Timely access to updates and defaults.
- Effective audit and evidence gathering useful in forensic analysis.

An independent research from Vanson Bourn reveals that 70 percent of the interviewed CIOs considered that "cloud computing and virtualization technologies had the biggest positive impact on business in 2011".

Cloud computing is on the rise all over the globe. Research conducted by IDC in 2011 revealed that $8.2 billion is expected to be spent by European companies on cloud professional services in 2015 compared to only $560 million in 2010. Private cloud facilities in the EU are becoming more prevalent; however organisations still resist public cloud services, mainly due to concerns over security and last-mile connectivity issues. Europe is also in the incipient stages when it comes to hybrid cloud and best practices development. It is expected that the mass adoption of cloud computing will emerge in parallel with the development of best practices and regulations (IDC, 2012).

In an ideal cloud-computing world the global landscape would be developed by homogenous countries that offer a consistent and complementary set of regulations. This is not the case today, as studies reveal the disparities between groups of countries where developed countries are considered to be more cloud-ready than developing countries. However, developed countries are still plagued by an improper alignment of their legal aspects, while developing countries are faced with a long way to go until being cloud prepared. This is one of the main concerns, as developing countries are also the countries that managed to obtain positive economical results in a very turbulent period, bringing great prospects for the cloud-computing industry, if handled efficiently (BSA, 2012).

This chapter will look at data protection concerns with cloud computing and limitations in terms of their applicability with cloud computing. It will specifically focus upon the current regulatory directive in Europe- Directive 95/46/EC and the draft European General Data Protection Regulation, which will supersede Directive 95/46/EC, which is aimed for adoption in 2015. The chapter will also briefly touch upon differences between EU & non-EU data protection legal systems and how binding corporate rules could be used to mitigate certain gaps.

Given the vast range of data protection regulations, the focus of the analysis will be placed upon international data transfers that imply a European Member State and outside EU states. Three main hypotheses are launched from the beginning as a support for the chapter's announced objective:

- The outdated character of the current European Directive;
- The confusion generated by the differentiated implementation of the Directive at the level of each Member State;
- The difficulties incurred by third party countries transfers that bear the obligation to offer an adequate level of protection.

As such, the chapter captures a picture of the cloud computing global phenomenon resulting in emerging clashes, or fault lines, between differences over regulation governing data protection. The chapter also identifies how these fault lines can be addressed from practical perspective as well as raising further emergent issues. The paper can also be considered as providing a strong case study of global technology adoption phenomena within a globally interconnected and reliant world and the emergent issues that arise from such technology adoption processes.

The rest of the chapter is structured as follows:

- Data protection concerns with cloud computing and the impact on jurisdiction reach.
- The current state of affairs of data protection in Europe, looking at the thinking process and issues around cloud computing before an expected major change in EU legislation.
- Differences in data protection laws between EU and non-EU countries.
- Binding corporate rules, what they are and how they can be used to mitigate risk.
- Global cloud technology adoption and tectonic plates.
- Conclusion.

DATA PROTECTION CONCERNS WITH CLOUD COMPUTING

When personal details are given to an organisation or individual, they have a legal duty to keep these details private and safe. This process is known as data protection, as opposed to 'data controllers' which are those who control the contents and use of personal details. There is a direct link between data protection and the growth of cloud computing as numerous hypotheses have indicated that the scale of cloud computing implementations may be affected in the short to medium term due to identified data protection risks as listed below.

- **Data Security:** The cloud customer is under the obligation to ensure that the cloud provider takes adequate technical and organisational security measures and that it will provide contractual warranties regarding the security of data processes. Data security is affected by shared technology vulnerabilities, data loss and data leakage, hijacking of traffic, malicious insiders or insecure APIs, and the reverse threat model where by malicious customers are able to undermine cloud services (Cloud Security Alliance, 2012).

- **Lawfulness in Data Processing:** It will be difficult for customers to assess the lawfulness in data processing carried out by the provider. Given the fact that the customer (data controller) is the person responsible to safeguard the lawful processing of personal data this risk can lead to administrative, civil or criminal sanctions. For example, under the United Kingdom's Data Protection Act 1998, in case of data security breaches the cloud customer and not the cloud provider, would be fined up to the prescribed amount of £500,000 by the Information commissioner's office (U.K. Information Commissioner's Office, 2010).

Table 1. Data protection impact on reach of jurisdictions

Critical Impact	• Data security breaches in federated clouds. • Lawful usage of data in federated clouds. • Multiple jurisdictions emergence.
Medium Impact	• Data security breaches in single based environments. • Lawful usage of data in single based environments. • The cloud provider's risk of handling unlawfully collected data. • Confidentiality breaches.
Low Impact	• Data integrity issues. • Business discontinuities.

- **Data Security Breaches:** That may or may not be notified to the data controller.

- **Unlawfully Obtained Data:** Exposure of the cloud provider to the risk of handling unlawfully obtained data by the data controller.

- **Multiple Jurisdiction Storage:** When data is moved to the cloud, the loss of control may translate into the storage of data in multiple jurisdictions. Although this action minimises the effects of concentrating risks into one "basket", other compliance issues arise, mainly generated by the differentiated status of countries in owning adequate levels of protection. The main concerns are related to personal data, which can be excluded from the cloud transfer or can be replaced with anonymous features before compliance issues are resolved.

- **Confidentiality Issues:** Due to possible data exposure and leakage that may lead to confidentiality breaches.

- **Data Integrity Issues:** Given the loss of control of data processes, the data controller might be faced with data compromise.

- **Business Continuity:** Customer may suffer from business discontinuities and concerns related to the reliability of cloud services. The data controller needs to make sure that proper storage, backup, and disaster recovery systems are in place at the cloud provider premises (Lambo, 2012).

- **Federated Clouds:** The above mentioned risks are heightened when using federated clouds that call for multiple data transfers and thus generate a higher loss of control for the data controller.

There is an inherent need to understand the impact of these risks when an organisation is looking to move its data into a public cloud. The European Network and Information Security Agency has identified risk ratings for information security on the cloud (Enisa, 2009). Table 1 categorises a simple impact matrix on these risks into the impact level they have on data protection and the on the level of jurisdiction reach, with multiple jurisdictions and data transfers being considered as having a critical impact, while data integrity and/or business continuity are rated in the lowest impact category.

Privacy concerns are amongst the main topics within the risks of cloud computing (ITU-T Technology Watch Report, 2012). Cloud computing providers should be able to guarantee that there is no potential third party access to cloud facilities, revealing thus the two dimensions of privacy protection, the ability of the cloud provider to transfer and store private information and the ability to maintain privacy in future conditions (IA Newsletter, 2010). The privacy notion is complex in nature, especially in the world of cloud computing in which users have various expectations of confidentiality, control and service responsiveness when defining their privacy requirements

(Creese, et al, 2009). This concern for privacy is highlighted within the World Economic Survey dated 2010 which indicates that 90 percent of Europeans rate privacy as a very serious constraint on adopting cloud computing (World Economic Forum, 2010). Similarly the U.S. Department of Commerce declared that the ability to "safely use services such as cloud-based email and file storage to their full potential depends on privacy protections that are consistent with other computing models" (U.S. Department of Commerce Internet Task Force, 2010).

The following is a set of questions that should be considered prior to the setup of any cloud service (Wessing, 2010):

- How will data be stored by the cloud provider? (e.g. co-mingled with other customer data)
- What assurances will the provider offer, ensuring that any personal data will only be processed in accordance with the customer instructions? (e.g. will it be deleted upon request)
- Will encryption be used or in certain cases be permitted?
- Does the provider have any relevant industry accreditations, such as ISO27001-2005?
- What are the provider's security measures and do they maintain a security plan?
- How will security breaches be monitored and reported?
- How will the provider respond to security breaches?
- Do customers have access to security audit reports or other evidence of the provider's security track record?

Many US companies, who are interested in the concern European companies, have to keep their data inside Europe due to data protection and security issues and will have already placed part of their infrastructure in Europe. For example: Microsoft in Amsterdam and Dublin, Rackspace in UK, and Amazon in Dublin (European Parliament, 2012). The need to have data stored as close to the home country as possible is not just a European view with 86 percent of US end users wanting to keep their data stored within North America, with only 9 percent of the respondents including Europe on their list of acceptable storage locations (Cloud Industry Forum, 2012).

EU DIRECTIVE 95/46/EC AND CLOUD COMPUTING

The current guiding European directive on the protection of individuals with regard to the processing of personal data and its free movement is Directive 95/46/EC dated the 24th of October 1995. A basic protection level of personal data is explicitly included in the EU's Charter of Fundamental Rights (Article 8), and in the Treaty on the Functioning of the European Union (Article 16) (European Commission, 2012). According to Directive 95/46/EC the meaning of personal data is "any information relating to an identified natural person (data subject)." Viviane Reding, Vice-President of the European Commission in charge of Justice, Fundamental Rights and Citizenship, referred to personal data as "the currency of the digital market, and like any currency it has to be stable and trustworthy" (Reding, 2012).

When it comes to the processing of personal data, Directive 95/46/EC points to "any operation or set of operations which is performed upon personal data, whether or not by automatic means, such as collection, recording, organisation, storage, adaption or alteration, retrieval, consultation, use, disclosure by transmission, dissemination or otherwise making available, alignment or combination, blocking, erasure or destruction".

The Directive identifies the subjects involved in the processing of personal data as the controller, processor, third party and the recipient. All subjects refer to a natural or legal person, public authority, agency or any other body, with the controller determining the purpose and means of the processing, the processor being the one that processes the personal data on behalf of the controller, while the recipient is the one to whom data is disclosed. The third party refers to any other subject that is authorised to process the personal data.

Data protection is enforced within the European Union through the principle of applicable national law. Under Article 4, Directive 95/46/EC specifies that each Member State shall apply the national provisions defined to the Directive for any controller that has activities of an establishment set on the territory of the Member State. If multiple European establishments exist, the controller must comply with local requirements put forth by each Member State. The provisions of the Directive also apply to controllers that are not established on the Member State's territory, but are located in a place that falls under the provisions of international public law. The object of the Directive extends further to controllers that are not established on Community territory, but make use of equipment, automated or not, situated in the territory of a Member State, excluding transit only activities.

Article 4 opened the gateway to the creation and implementation of diverse national regulations that complicated data protection activities for international businesses. One of the main issues declared by the cloud industry as hampering its development beyond Member State borders is the diversity of Member State transpositions. Around 50 percent of cloud-computing providers consider that the Member State diversity raises barriers for cloud computing. There are still many cloud providers that have not settled on giving a definitive answer to this topic. This has created a consensus between companies and individuals who find that "the extent of regulation in Europe and the variations of the rules in different EU Member States have created some confusion and misperceptions, often leading to exaggeration of the scope and intentions of such rules". (European Commission, 2011) Diversity also leads to contradictory regulations for companies when they need to comply with data protection requirements (Reding, 2012).

Data management that takes place within the European Union and its Member States may become a concern for some stakeholders, while others may have issues when it comes to the risk of having their data exposed outside European borders. A recent example of this is how in December 2011, BAE Systems, a British defence company, dropped its plans to use a Microsoft cloud service, because of the provider's inability to guarantee that the data will not leave the European Union (Vogel, 2012). The transfer of personal data is protected by the provisions found at chapter IV of the Directive 95/46/EC which states in its opening article 25 that the transfer may take place only if "the third country in question ensures an adequate level of protection". However, so far the European Commission has only assessed the adequacy of the protection level for a limited number of countries, giving positive determinations for Andorra, Argentina, Canada (regarding the transfers made to recipients subject to the Canadian Personal Information Protection and Electronic Documents Act), Faeroe Islands, Guernsey, Isle of Man, Israel, Jersey, the Safe Harbor Privacy Principles of the United States Department of Commerce and Switzerland (European Commission, 2011).

Apart from the European Commission's Directorates that are in charge of data protection and digital agenda, other national data-protection bodies or high-level representatives instate cloud computing as a priority area on their agendas. An example on this regard is the interest shown on cloud computing by Peter Hustinx, the European data protection supervisor, and by German and French regulatory bodies (Vogel, 2012). The German Federal Commissioner for Data Protection and Freedom of Information (FfDF) which was adopted in September 2011 put forward a resolution on using cloud computing services in compliance with data protection regulations, while directing customers to verify the existence of information security systems before closing a cloud services contract (Moos, 2012).

In France, CNIL (Commission Nationale de l'Informatique et des Libertés) launched in October 2011 a public consultation on cloud computing, the results of which clearly indicate the need to define technical guidance on personal data protection and cloud computing (CNIL, 2012). The interest for data protection within cloud computing is perceived as an expected trend in the light of the November – December 2010 Eurobarometer results on attitudes on data protection and electronic identity in the European Union. According to a survey conducted by the European commission, most Europeans trust Health/Medical institutions, national public authorities, banks/financial institutions and European Institutions to protect their information, but do not trust commercial companies such as shops/department stores, telecommunication and Internet companies.

The low results reported for ISP and internet companies are due to influence of the nature of institutions analysed and their exposure to respondents. All other categories of institutions are equally acknowledged by all demographic categories, while their structure is more balanced when it comes to usage. Internet related activities are directly related to their incidence rate within the general population (users of Internet) highly dependent on their usage experience and leverage. As a supplementary note, a cross analysis of trust in institutions based on the index of Internet use, reveals that the lowest trust value (11 percent) is assigned to very low Internet users and their trust in Internet companies.

Figure 1 indicates another area of concern, which is the further use of personal data by institutions other than the ones whom originally collected it, as 70 percent of the Europeans expressed their worries regarding their information use. Respondents from the United Kingdom (80 percent), Ireland (80 percent), France (79 percent), Portugal (78 percent) and the Czech Republic (77 percent) are the most concerned Europeans, while Swedish nationals close the country-based analysis with 37 percent (European Commission, 2011).

Figure 1. Europeans' trust in institutions to protect personal data (European Commission, 2011).

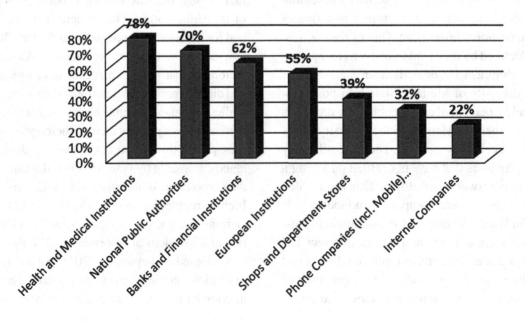

Table 2. Overview of current situation in Europe

Outdated regulations, comprising contradictory and confusing rules.
National enforcement current level, which led to the creation of national traditions that will be hard to be transferred at European level.
Lagging regulative process that affects the expansion of cloud computing and its full exploitation.
Conflicting parties that have different interests and expectations, not only at the European level, but also at global level.
The current position of the European Commission that is committed to propose and work on a regulation that meets Member States and industry representatives at half way, when interests differ.

Considering the fundamental principles defined by the Directive 95/46/EC, the much needed revision of the outdated provisions should take into account not only the current and future issues that affect the data protection rules (Millard, 2012) but also the public perception of this protection. Along with the increased globalisation of data flows, the global exposure of personal information exchanges, and the technological advancements, the arrival of cloud computing in the digital world is considered one of the main reasons for revising the above-mentioned Directive, given the international perspective of cloud computing that ensures instant data movements from one jurisdiction to another, including those outside EU jurisdictions (European Commission, 2012). Table 2 provides a summary of the current situation.

Directive 95/46/EC does not consider cloud computing along with other aspects such as globalisation and other technological advancements. Neelie Kroes, the Vice-President of the European Commission in charge of the Digital Agenda, identifies two areas of concern with Directive 95/46/EC, providers trust in European regulations and the workable characteristic of the rules. Kroes acknowledges that data protection rules are overdue, given that they were implemented in 1995 which is considered a pre-Internet era. A public consultation process on European cloud computing and the revision to Directive 95/46/EC took place between the 16th of May 2011 and 31st of August 2011 that gathered the opinions of 538 respondents. 42.75 percent of respondents declared that they represent a company. As a general guidance, 56.6

percent of the 152 individuals are optimistic that the new regulation will facilitate cloud computing, while preserving privacy and applying data protection rules rather than negatively affecting it. Within the companies' segment, a similar share of the population is confident that the GDPR will foster cloud computing (56.2 percent). The answers provided to open-ended questions show a high concern for data protection topics, one of the respondents stated that: "the DPD revision provides an important opportunity to reduce the complexity and costs associated with the current rules governing the international transfer of personal data inside and outside the European Union" (European Commission, 2011).

FUTURE DATA PROTECTION IN EUROPE

On the 25th January 2012 the European Commission released plans in the form of the General Data Protection Regulation (GDPR) to be a single law to unify data protection within the EU. The EU's European council has decided to aim for adoption of the GDPR in 2015 with a planned transition of the years before it takes effect. The implementation of the General Data Protection Regulation would lead to the following:

- The emergence of a unique set of regulations for the European cloud providers. The elimination of regulations' diversity calls for a sole enforcement authority for each company ("a one stop shop") – the one present on the market where the provider settled its main base. The same rule applies at individuals' level.

- The elimination of unnecessary administrative and reporting costs burden, which is expected to save businesses around € 2.43 billion each year. (European Commission, 2012) This measure implies that companies will require only one authorisation that will be valid across all EU Member States.

- The support provided to SMEs across Europe to grow, by exempting the large majority of them from the appointment of a data protection officer, while their data protection impact assessments will refer only to the data processing activities that bear high risks. They will also be exempted from the duty to document their data processing activities. According to the European approach, SMEs are considered the companies with less than 250 employees. Vivian Reding, the Vice-President of the European Commission in charge of Justice, Fundamental Rights and Citizenship, considers that the regulative process should start by "thinking small first" (Reding, 2012).

- The creation of clear regulations for international data transfer defined by streamlined approval processes that offer an automatic recognition of approval for all national authorities once one of them has given prior approval to the binding corporate rules.

- Companies and institutions will be obliged to notify data breaches to the national supervisory authority and the concerned individuals as soon as possible, ideally in 24 hours.

- The individuals' right to be forgotten is protected through the proposal – individuals will be able to request the deletion of the personal data from the provider's premises if there is no legitimate reason for continuing to keep the information. According to the Special Eurobarometer 359, the access to personal information stored by institutions should be a free service, although still around 28 percent of the Europeans are ready to pay for access, if needed. Europeans agree more when it comes to claiming their right to be forgotten, as 75 percent of them want to be able to delete their personal data whenever they decide, and not only when they choose to terminate the contract with the service/website or Internet provider (European Commission, 2011).

- The right to portability recognised to the individuals, change that is expected to increase the competition level among cloud computing providers. The right to portability is one of the main requirements coming from the European citizens, as they consider in a proportion of 71 percent that it is important to be able to transfer data (European Commission, 2011).

- The proposal drafted by the European Commission provides the area of international data transfers with more details and clarity, establishing its coverage, as well as the contractual terms that can replace the existence of an adequacy approval at the level of the third country (European Commission, 2012).A comparative view regarding the main principle of data protection within the international environment – the adequacy principle – is presented in Table 3.

The European Commission's Regulation will fill a legislative void that exists in the current technological environment, which has significantly evolved since 1995, when the current Directive was put in place. Each Member State has individually adapted its data protection procedures with the

Table 3. Comparative view of adequacy principle for directive 95/46/EC and the general data protection regulation

Topic	Directive 95/46/EC	General Data Protection Regulation
General principle	The current Directive established the principle of protection adequacy for the third country to which personal data is transferred for undergoing processing or after transfer processing.	The GDPR sets the conditions to be fulfilled by the controller and the processor, specifying also that compliance must include onward transfers from the initial third country or international organisation to a subsequent one.
Coverage	The Directive strictly refers to third country transfers.	The GDPR extends the scope of the regulations to third countries, territories or processing sectors within that third country, or international organisations.
Establishing protection adequacy	1. Considering all circumstances surrounding a data transfer operation or set of data transfer operations. 2. Particular consideration shall be given to the nature of the data, the purpose and duration of the proposed processing operation or operations, the country of origin and country of final destination, the rules of law, both general and sectoral, in force in the third country in question and the professional rules and security measures which are complied with in that country.	1. Considering the rule of law, relevant legislation in force, both general and sectoral, including public security, defense, national security and criminal law, the professional rules and security measures which are complied with in that country or by that international organisation, as well as effective and enforceable rights including effective administrative and judicial redress for data subjects. 2. Assessing the existence and effective functioning of one or more independent supervisory authorities in the third country or international organisation with established responsibilities in data protection. 3. The existence of international commitments the third country or international organisation in question has entered into.
Transfers by way of appropriate safeguards	Subsequent to the implementation of the current Directive, several safeguards regulations have been negotiated with third countries.	1. A controller or processor may transfer personal data to a third country or an international organisation only if it has provided appropriate data protection safeguards in a legally binding instrument. 2. The appropriate safeguards shall be provided by: e. Binding corporate rules; f. Standard data protection clauses adopted by the Commission; g. Standard data protection clauses adopted by a supervisory authority; h. Contractual clauses between the controller or processor and the recipient of the data authorised by a supervisory authority. 3. In the absence of a legally binding instrument, the controller or processor shall obtain prior authorisation for the transfer, or a set of transfers, or for provisions to be inserted into administrative arrangements providing the basis for such transfer.

current situation defined by an increased diversity that is blocking cloud computing from tapping its enormous potential. More and more public institutions, companies and individuals raise their voice to show that the Directive is outdated, insufficient and restrictive. Recently, researchers from CERN (European Organisation for Nuclear Research) declared that the delay in the creation of a proper European legislative framework for data protection is restricting them in scaling their activities through cloud computing (Curtis, 2012). However 90 percent of the Europeans are in favour of harmonised data protection regulations. Regarding the administrative level for the enforcement rules, two opposite poles forces emerge, with 44 percent of Europeans considering that enforcement should be conducted at the European level, while 40 percent would like to keep national level enforcement. Latvia, Luxembourg, Germany, France and Belgium are the main sustainers for European level enforcement, while Sweden, the United Kingdom, Denmark, Slovenia and Finland would cast their vote for national enforcement (European Commission, 2011).

Analyzing the proposed Regulation of the European Commission, criticism has emerged in two ways: (Reding, 2012)

- Part of the experts consider that the proposal goes too far and that only a minimum set of regulations should have been proposed, still offering Member States the possibility to explore more on their current traditions.
- Other experts consider that some of the rights are not fully protected through the proposed regulations, giving as example the right to be forgotten, which might be only partially protected through the data deletion from the initial cloud computing provider, given the indexing processes of companies, such as Google.

Potentially the most important concern of the current situation is that current discussions have a basis proposal that still has to pass through the European Parliament and EU Member States before being adopted and implemented. Given the different corners the Member States are in, there is a high probability that the GDPR may have to further wait before it comes into effect, however recent progress on the reform has now made it irreversible following a European Parliament vote (European Commission, 2014).

Table 4 provides an overview of potential issues between Directive 95/46/EC and the GDPR in regards to cloud computing.

DATA PROTECTION OUTSIDE EUROPE AND IMPACT ON CLOUD COMPUTING

Although at a first look the global world is defined by a clear majority of countries that were not able to tap on the cloud opportunities yet by establishing proper data protection policies. Figure 2 indicates regional distribution for cloud services and highlights how the cloud computing segment is concentrated in the hands of some major cloud computing powers: North America, Western Europe and Japan that hold an estimated 92.6 percent of the total cloud traffic in 2012. (Gartner, 2011)

Only recently, the European Union managed to raise interest for the United Sates to participate to discussions regarding data protection law adap-

Table 4. Cloud computing issues with directive 95/46/EC and the general data protection regulation

Current Issues	Future Issues
Outdated Directive	The inability of new regulations to capture the entire prevalence of cloud computing upon data protection
Diversity of regulations, which generates confusion and misinterpretation	The resistance of Member States to renounce at their traditional approaches in order to embrace a unitary perspective
Contradictory regulations	Member States will have to collaborate closely and act at the request of other national data protection authorities, given that each data holder will address the request to the national authority that will further need to follow the request and foster to its resolution
Data exposure to outside-EU countries	The need to balance and integrate EU's regulation with already established regulations of other countries

Figure 2. Cloud services regional distribution (Gartner, 2011).

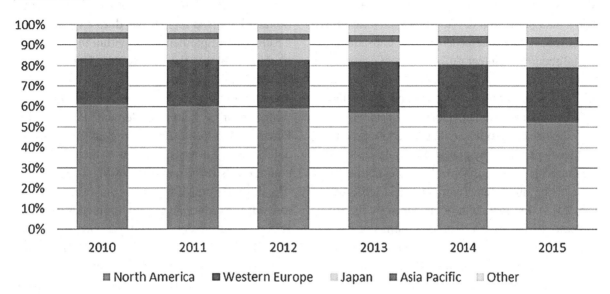

tion. The U.S. current out-dated and restrictive regulations are viewed as contradictory in parts by EU's representatives, however, there is a long journey from discussion panels to actual legislative reform. On a positive note, Japan, which is the third prominent segment in cloud computing, already benefits from a data protection law that is partially inspired by the European Union's perspective. A summary of the current situation is listed below.

- Vast environment that offers no easy path towards unification from data protection perspectives.
- Over 90 percent of the cloud computing world is concentrated in North America, part of the European Union and Japan.
- Timid steps made for aligning regulations among big drivers, with less interest shown in the North American segment.
- Increased interest deployed by Asian markets that own proper infrastructure and scalability, but are lacking proper regulations.

- Bilateral discussions held between U.S. and the European Union offer valuable insights required during EU's law reform.

DIFFERENCES IN DATA PROTECTION LAWS BETWEEN THE EU AND NON-EU COUNTRIES

When data is transferred from Europe to outside Europe using cloud computing services, data protection is perceived as one of the major obstacles. Where obstacles exist, opportunities also arise. The countries that are willing and have the capability to offer proper data protected environments will be the ones that see their cloud computing thriving.

After clearly stating in the beginning of 2011, the lack of interest of the United States officials to negotiate on data protection themes, European Commission Vice-President Viviane Reding acknowledged that discussions held in 2011 and 2012 revealed a firm commitment for personal data protection for both parties (Reding, Bryson,

2012). Both the European Union and the United States show interest when it comes to the other side's data protection developments, as indicated by the recent joint statement that "The transatlantic digital economy is integral to our economic growth, trade and innovation. Cross border data flows are critical to our economic vitality, and to our law enforcement and counterterrorism efforts. We affirm the need to promote data protection, privacy and free speech in the digital era while ensuring the security of our citizens. This is essential for trust in the online environment." (EU-US Summit, 2014). In practice the steps taken by the EU to approve Microsoft's cloud commitments was a good indication of this (EU Commission, 2014), however in practice it appears to be more difficult as only a few weeks later a judge in the US ordered Microsoft to hand over a customer's email, which were held on a server in Europe (BBC, 2014).

The recent regulation drafts presented in the beginning of 2012 were essential in bringing the EU's and US's regulatory systems closer, at least regarding guiding principles (Reding, Bryson, 2012).

The United States is probably one of the few countries empowered with the luxury of refusing or showing reduced interest when it comes to negotiating regulations with the European Union, Smaller countries however that are on the lookout for increasing their cloud computing reach, view the start of negotiations as an opportunity, rather than an imposed act. For example, Japan initiated its first private-sector data protection law in 2003 after publicly declaring that it targets to comply with Europe's data-export protection rules. (Adams, Murata, Orito, 2010) The US's self-regulatory system significantly differs from the soon to be one-stop-shop approach proposed by the European Union.

Differences in domestic data privacy systems are not a 21th century novelty. Going back to 1980 with the adoption of the OECD Guidelines and subsequent APEC forum, international efforts have been initiated for the development

of a common framework for data protection. (Reisman, 2012) Being a signatory of international, globalised regulations does not guarantee a follow-up implementation within the domestic market. This was the case for the United States that did not implement the OECD Guidelines after signing the document. As a consequence, a "safe harbor" system is implemented in line with Directive 95/46/EC for the organisations to be able to engage in transactions with their European counterparts (Privireal.org, 2005).

Although consistent steps have been made towards the reduction of the differences between Europe's data protection legal system and the countries that dominate outside the Europe framework, new collisions in ideas are expected to emerge once discussions start to take the form of adopted rules. Issues with the new EU proposal may arise if approved and implemented in the current format, as the regulation indicates about prohibited "transfers of personal data to countries which do not ensure an adequate level of protection." Currently 80 percent share of the global ICT market is still unable to meet this request coming (BSA, 2012), as the compromise of closing a contract between the data controller and the recipient that can ensure protection is "very difficult to implement, particularly in cloud computing that entails that continuous transfer of personal data" (European Parliament, 2012).

Rated with a lower impact on cloud activities is its positive effect on the competition level, the so-called "jurisdiction shopping" may come into play where users embark on a lookout for jurisdictions that can offer the protection level they require or that could bring competitive advantages. On the contrary, the 90 percent of individuals and organisations that feels overwhelmed by the general confusion when dealing with cross-border data transfers that should be a primary concern for the state institutions (European Parliament, 2012).

The European Union has set a very ambitious Digital Agenda that spans up to 2020, one major strategy of this is to "Accelerate cloud computing through public sector buying power" which will help build a single EU market for cloud computing (European Parliament, 2012). While analysing this opportunity of crossing European borders while enhancing cloud services, does lead the European Union to be criticised for the harsh regulations that would further isolate it from any other country or region that is not considered sufficiently developed from data protection perspectives, while the European Union has every right to fear crossing its borders through international data transfers, especially to countries that do not have a modern cloud regulative system in place.

Table 5 provides a simple impact matrix between different data protection laws between the EU and non-EU countries.

BINDING CORPORATE RULES

The outdated characteristic of Directive 95/46/EC currently in place and the undefined area of third countries adequacy assessment leave a gap in the data protection area that cannot be covered easily through legislative efforts. Indeed, the European Commission is actively engaged in reformation

processes that target to clarify the missing pieces, while modernising the legal framework, but this is viewed as a long-term result.

Besides the extended duration of legislative reforms, analysed proposals could be implemented in a very distinct format than the one when they were initially proposed. Taking all these aspects into consideration, it is imperative that at least a partial clarification and solution be introduced while the more advanced legislative process unfolds. "Binding corporate rules (BCR)" is a term that is increasingly used when it comes to international data transfers that imply third countries. The approval of the binding corporate rules given by one national authority is also enriched with expansion coverage power over all national authorities in the light of the Directive proposal.

After a successful application of binding corporate rules at the level of controllers, the Article 29 Data Protection Working Party advanced to another level by adopting in June 2012 a working document on binding corporate rules for processors, both companies and data protection authorities. BCR are viewed as "internal rules applicable to entities of a multinational company and contain key principles legally covering the transfers of personal data coming from the European Union".

Table 5. Impact of different data protection laws between the EU and non EU countries

Critical Impact	• Discussions held between world's economic powers are still conducted in the light of restricted domains, and not on a general, comprehensive level. • Regulations practiced by major players are contradictory and difficult to be tracked from EU's perspective. • Even if less differentiated regulations are defined, from development to actual implementation there is a hard and long road to be covered. • Increased diversity around cloud computing world, which leads to barriers in risks assessment for European institutions when crossing Europe's borders. • Very high confusion sensed among individuals and organisations regarding liability issues.
Medium Impact	• Different scales of interest across cloud computing world for submitting to a global set of regulations • Possible closure of EU's borders to unsecure countries, rated as medium given the fact that this regulation is not yet final; once and if implemented this situation will entail a critical impact to the industry.
Low Impact	• The influence deployed by smaller self-regulated countries – low impact at national, regional or global level, but could make the difference between profitability and bankruptcy for certain companies that operate in those designated environments • Jurisdiction shopping, that increases the competition among countries for assuring they get as much as possible from the global cloud market.

They are regarded as an alternative to the Safe Harbor Principles and the European Commission's Standard Contractual Clauses. When transcended at the level of processors, binding corporate rules should be able to provide clients with the security and privacy of their data under European Union data protection regulations. The Article 29 Working Party's working document provides processors with a conditions checklist that must be fulfilled for being granted their adequacy (Data Protection Working Party, 2012).

The A29 DPWP working paper also came as a response to the industry's numerous requests to move the usage of binding corporate rules at the level of processors as well. There are also voices that demand BCRs to be included for community cloud, considering that there might be cases when community members that belong to different corporate groups might own similar interests. Even though improvements at the level of binding corporate rules are definitely a step forward, their approval process remains a long and expensive procedure under the current regulations. While Member States grant approval based on diverse conditions, there is still a range of Member States that tends to remain on the safe side requesting an individual approval for each transfer under an already approved BCR (Hon & Millard, 2012).

If applied on a large scale, binding corporate rules may solve one of the main issues implied by both adequacy findings and Safe Harbor compliance, with their restrictive geographical reach. In a July 2012 paper on cloud computing adopted by the Article 29 Data Protection Working Party, the organisation states that companies that export data should act with increased diligence and question the statement of the data importer that it owns a Safe Harbor certification. Also, cloud clients should verify that standard contractual terms comply with national requirements regarding contractual data processing (Data Protection Working Party, 2012).

GLOBAL TECHNOLOGY ADOPTION AND TECTONIC PLATES

This chapter has highlighted the global nature of cloud computing and how it resulted in rapid adoption in many applications around the world. The chapter argues that with such global technology adoption, there are likely to be areas for clashes between nations and regions, much like the fault lines between tectonic plates. The example used is to focus on data protection regulation and explore the significant challenges and emergent issues from a legislative perspective. This provides interesting perspectives to inform policy makers covering data protection and cloud computing services and provision, as well as on a more generic level the global technology adoption processes and phenomena.

There may be many other areas for fault lines to emerge such as cultural differences. For example, due to historical reasons, many countries within Europe have as a culture of secrecy that would be almost unimaginable in the United States. One of the biggest social divides between the US and EU is highlighted in how European law protects confidentiality verses the US ethic of free speech and sharing feelings and information (Huie, et al, 2002). A specific example of the differences is how revelations that the US National Security Agency conducted surveillance on world leaders, such as German Chancellor Angela Merkel which is now causing series harm to transatlantic relations, simply because Europeans take it for liberty and that the individual has a right to information self determination to be a protected basic right (Porsher, et al, 2013).

For the adoption of a global technology modal it is recommended that the aspect of checking the legal data requirements for legislative feasibility before a technology is deployed to ensure legal compliance within a specific country or region which is taken from the framework for assessing and implementing HPC opportunities (Eldred, et al, 2014).

Figure 3 provides a framework related to the data protection laws and issues and consolidates the key findings from the research conducted in this chapter. Step one is to assess the data protection impact on the reach of jurisdictions as indicated in Table 1, if the impact is low then the potential solution could be implemented within the cloud, while if the impact is medium or critical the solution would need to be assessed against the current legal barriers within Directive 95/46/EC and against potential future issues with the General Data Protection Regulation as indicated in Table 4 and 5. The next step is to try and remove barriers either through adding safeguards (such as by using corporate binding rules), change the solution scope or ultimately by considering not using cloud.

This framework offers a practical approach for assessing the EU legal impact of going to a cloud computing solution and can easily be combined with other frameworks that look at measuring the risk of cloud computing. One specific modal is the practical framework for managing cloud computing risk (Foley 2013). This framework

Figure 3. Framework for assessing EU legal impact of going for a cloud computing solution

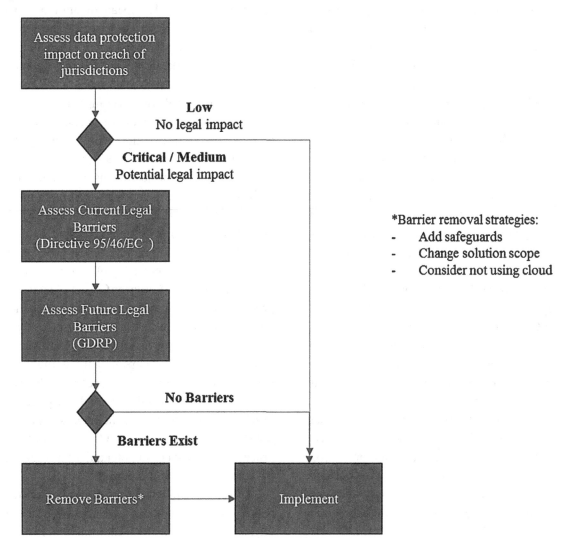

evaluates the risk of an organisation in an easy to follow low, medium high rating by assessing two variables: the criticality of the business process being supported and by the sensitivity of the data stored in the cloud, however this framework does not look at the reach of jurisdiction and the legal impact of the data and when combined with the framework for assessing EU legal impact of going for a cloud computing solution can offer a practical solution for organisations wanting to manage the risk of cloud computing.

Along with being relevant for other risk framework or modals it can also be relevant to other areas of cloud provision, for instance it could be applied to the financial services industry particularly in capturing the underlying fault lines of which data protection is a key issue. Approaches to financial risk modelling have not improved since after the global financial crisis of 2008 (Chang, 2014). The business intelligence as a service in the cloud modal offers a solutions to this via its dual approach to compute risk and pricing for financial analysis. However the BIaaS modal is not easy to fully implement due to privacy and data ownership issues (Change, 2014), such as how personal data which is operated by multinationals operating on different continents and using cloud services again operating across different continents may inadvertently be breaking EU law. Another example of use within the financial services is how the framework can be combined with the conceptual financial cloud platform that is based on the Operational Risk Exchange that includes 53 banks from 18 countries that use the platform to share operational risk data and provide useful feedback for participating banks about their calculations (Chang, 2014).

The framework for assessing EU legal impact of going for a cloud computing solution can ease the complexity by assessing the data protection impact of reach, the potential legal impact and then by implementing the necessary removal safeguards for legal compliance for both the BIaas and conceptual financial cloud platform.

CONCLUSION

With organisations benefitting from performance, innovation and technological evolution from cloud computing in recent years, a consequence has been that the already disparate application of EU's regulations has further deepened the confusion surrounding the current legal framework with the diversity and complexity that cloud brings. In such circumstances, organisations have often renounced their plans to enhance the usage of cloud computing or were forced to spend considerable resources in order to become legally compliant.

The solution of a unitary approach within the borders of the EU regarding data protection is desirable, however European institutions must proceed cautiously, while providing the proper conditions for following unitary implementation. If the latter fails, the new proposals may still generate confusion with only minimal improvements visible at the level of users. A comprehensive unity backed up by a sole regulatory perspective will be rather difficult to achieve, for this reason it is recommended that the critical first advancement should be that data protection institutions proceed with the recognition of approvals coming from one Member State to all the others. This measure would at least absolve cloud-computing providers of the multi-level approval granting process. For international data transfers that involve non-European Union countries, the European Commission should provide the proper conditions for data protection without raising unnecessary barriers. A closed environment will only hamper the implementation of technological advancements that have the ability to hike performance along with scale. Higher risk open environments could additionally be protected by more fiercely guarding data, such as by enforcing the use of dynamic encryption and encoding procedures which could potentially representing the missing piece of the puzzle.

It is recommended that contractual provisions be viewed as an indispensable ingredient for an efficiently protected cloud environment. In order for the cloud-computing industry to move to a more stable and consistent environment, countries and organisations must obey to the much-needed requirements of collaboration, communication and the ability to find common grounds. These directions should lead the objectives setting for cloud-computing major players, as after all "a healthy national market for cloud computing does not necessarily translate into a market that is attuned to the laws of other countries in a way that lets data flow smoothly across borders". "Countries that wall themselves off are doing real harm" (BSA, 2012).

This chapter has made contribution in the following areas. Firstly it provides a robust case study of clashes (or fault lines) on a global scale between the evolving data protection legislation in the EU and non-EU countries. It also provides some guidance on how to address these clashes. Secondly the chapter has made contribution in providing a snap shot of the current state, the thinking and processes around cloud-computing data protection issues before an expected major change in EU data protection legislation. As such it provides a base for future research to compare and explore the result of changes and future interventions. Thirdly, the chapter makes contribution by providing an example of the global technology adoption phenomena which are highlighting clashes between national, cultural and legal norms – the analogy we use are 'fault lines' between the global societal tectonic plates. The case example of data protection legislation also adds insight on how these fault lines can be addressed from a practical level. Consequently the chapter hopes to make contribution to practitioners (particularly cloud service providers and potential cloud service users), to technology adoption researchers and to policy makers.

This research has limitations in that it does not look further into the impact of the differences between EU and non-EU countries from a regional perspective and in terms of what proposal may come from third party countries.

The research also does not take into account other laws, which are closely linked with data protection such as privacy and human rights laws. Other aspects such as the technical advancements of moving data between different types of technology could also be covered. Additional work could build upon the framework for assessing EU legal impact of going for a cloud computing solution and could look at the fault-lines for the multi-dimensions for the business and technology environment bringing out a generic version for a wider set of issues such as social, ethical norms, politics, business practices, corporate rules, culture and technology, and infrastructure culture.

REFERENCES

Article 29 Data Protection Working Party, July 2012, Opinion 05/2012 on Cloud Computing. (2012). Retrieved February 4, 2014, http://ec.europa.eu/justice/data-protection/article-29/documentation/opinion-recommendation/files/2012/wp196_en.pdf

Article 29 Data Protection Working Party, June 2012, Press Release on Binding Corporate Rules for Processors. (2012). Retrieved February 4, 2014 http://ec.europa.eu/justice/data-protection/article-29/press-material/press-release/art29_press_material/20120619_pr_bcrwp_en.pdf

Berry, R., & Reisman, M. (2012). *Policy challenges of cross-border cloud computing.* Retrieved February 4, 2014 http://www.usitc.gov/journals/policy_challenges_of_cross-border_cloud_computing.pdf, p. 13-14

BSA. (2012). *Country reports.* Retrieved February 12, 2014, http://portal.bsa.org/cloudscorecard2012/countries.html

BSA. (n.d.). Retrieved from http://portal.bsa.org/cloudscorecard2012/countries.html

Chang, V. (2014). The business intelligence as a service in the cloud. *Future Generation Computer Systems, 37,* 512–534. doi:10.1016/j. future.2013.12.028

Chang, V., Li, C., & De Roure, D.W., Walters, R., & Chee, C. (2011). The financial clouds review. *International Journal of Cloud Applications and Computing, 1*(2), 41–63.

Chang, V., Walters, R. J., & Wills, G. (2013). The development that leads to the cloud computing business framework. *International Journal of Information Management, 33*(3), 524-538.

Chang, V., Walters, R., & Wills, G. (2014). Monte Carlo risk assessment as a service in the cloud. *International Journal of Business Integration and Management.*

CNIL. (2012). *Synthèse des réponses à la consultation publique sur le cloud computing lancée par la CNIL d'Octobre à Décembre 2011 et analyse de la CNIL.* Retrieved February 7, 2014, http://www.cnil.fr/fileadmin/images/la_cnil/actualite/Synthese_des_reponses_a_la_consultation_publique_sur_le_Cloud_et_analyse_de_la_CNIL.pdf, p. 10

Creese, S., Hopkins, P., Pearson, S., & Shen, Y. (2009). Data protection-aware design for cloud computing. Retrieved from http://www.hpl.hp.com/techreports/2009/HPL-2009-192.pdf

Curtis, S. (2012). *CERN says EU data protection laws are hindering cloud adoption.* Retrieved February 24, 2014, http://www.computerworlduk.com/news/cloud computing/3364456/cern-says-eu-data-protection-laws-are-hindering-cloud-adoption/

Directive 95/46/EC of the European Parliament and of the Council of 24 October 1995 on the Protection of Individuals with Regard to the Processing of Personal Data and on the Free Movement of Such Data. (1995). Retrieved January 7, 2014, http://eur-lex.europa.eu/LexUriServ/LexUriServ.do?uri=CELEX:31995L0046:en:HTML

Eldred, M. E., Orangi, A., Al-Emadi, A. A., Ahmad, A. A., O'Reilly, T. J., & Barghouti, N. (2014). *Reservoir simulations in a high performance cloud computing environment.* Society of Petroleum Engineers. doi:10.2118/167877-MS

ENISA. (2009). *Cloud computing, benefits, risks and recommendations for information security.* Retrieved January 21, 2014, http://www.enisa.europa.eu/act/rm/files/deliverables/cloud-computing-risk-assessment/at_download/fullReport

Europa. (n.d.). Retrieved from http://ec.europa.eu/avservices/video/player.cfm?ref=82655&sitelang=en

Europa.eu. (2012). *EU – US joint statement on data protection by European Commission Vice-President Viviane Reding and US Secretary of Commerce John Bryson.* Retrieved February 1, 2014, http://europa.eu/rapid/pressReleasesAction.do?reference=MEMO/12/192

European Commission. (2011a). *Special Eurobarometer 359: Attitudes on data protection and electronic identity in the European Union.* Retrieved January 7, 2014, http://ec.europa.eu/public_opinion/archives/ebs/ebs_359_en.pdf

European Commission. (2012a). *How will the EU's reform adapt data protection rules to new technological developments.* Retrieved January 9, 2014, http://ec.europa.eu/justice/data-protection/document/review2012/factsheets/8_en.pdf, p. 1

European Commission. (2012b). *Press release: Commission proposes a comprehensive reform of data protection rules to increase users' control of their data and to cut costs for businesses.* Retrieved February 3, 2014, http://europa.eu/rapid/pressReleasesAction.do?reference=IP/12/46&format=HTML&aged=0&language=EN&guiLanguage=en

European Commission. (2012c). *Proposal for a regulation of the european parliament and of the council on the protection of individuals with regard to the processing on personal data and on the free movement of such data.* Retrieved January 9, 2014, http://ec.europa.eu/justice/data-protection/document/review2012/com_2012_11_en.pdf

European Commission. (2014a). *Progress on EU data protection reform now irreversible following European Parliament vote.* Retrieved January 7, 2014, http://europa.eu/rapid/press-release_MEMO-14-186_en.htm

European Commission. (2011b). *Information society and media directorate-general, Cloud computing: Public consultation report.* Retrieved January 7, 2014, http://ec.europa.eu/information_society/activities/cloudcomputing/docs/ccconsultationfinalreport.pdf, p. 3-5

European Commission. (2014b). *Digital agenda: New strategy to drive European business and government productivity via cloud computing.* Retrieved January 21, 2014, http://europa.eu/rapid/press-release_IP-12-1025_en.htm

European Commission. (2011c). *Justice, commission decisions on the adequacy of the protection of personal data in third countries.* Retrieved January 9, 2014, http://ec.europa.eu/justice/policies/privacy/thridcountries/index_en.htm

European Parliament. (2012). *Directorate-general for internal policies, cloud computing.* Retrieved January 9, 2014, http://ec.europa.eu/information_society/activities/cloudcomputing/docs/cc_study_parliament.pdf, p. 21

February, B. S. A. (2012). *Global patchwork of conflicting laws and regulations threatens fast growing cloud computing market.* Retrieved February 12, 2014, http://ww2.bsa.org/country/News%20and%20Events/News%20Archives/global/02222012-cloudscorecard.aspx

Foley & Lardner LLP. (2013). *Cloud computing: A practical framework for managing cloud computing risk.* Retrieved February 5, 2014, http://www.foley.com/files/Publication/493fc6cc-aa03-4974-a874-022e36d12184/Presentation/PublicationAttachment/c9bd65f3-a6fd-4acb-96de-d1c0434f1eb7/CloudComputingPracticalFrameworkforManagingCloudComputingRisk.pdf

Gartner. (2011a). *Gartner reveals top predictions for IT organisations and users for 2012 and beyond.* Retrieved January 20, 2014, http://www.gartner.com/it/page.jsp?id=1862714

Gartner. (2011b). *Forecast: Public cloud services, worldwide and regions, industry sectors, 2010 – 2015.* Retrieved January 20, 2014, http://www.vertical.ch/fileadmin/News/Forecast_Public_Cloud_Services__Worldwide_and_Regions__Industry_Sectors__2010-2015__2011_Update.pdf

Huie, M. C., Laribee, S. F., & Hogan, S. D. (2002). The right to privacy in personal data: The EU prods the US and controversy continues. *9 TULSA J. COMP. &. INT'L L, 391*, 441.

IDC. (n.d.). Retrieved from http://www.idc.com/prodserv/idc_cloud.jsp

International Journal of Business Integration and Management Cloud Industry Forum. (2012). *USA cloud adoption & trends 2012*. Retrieved February 15, 2014, http://docs.media.bitpipe.com/io_10x/io_103375/item_496686/CIF%20white%20paper%20US%20Cloud_FINAL.pdf, p.12, 14

June, I. D. C. (2011). *European enterprises will spend $8.2 billion on cloud professional services in 2015*. Retrieved January 21, 2014, http://www.idc.com/getdoc.jsp?containerId=prUK22881811

June, I. D. C. (2012). *Third of western European retailers expect to increase spending on cloud computing by up to 25%*. Retrieved January 21, 2014, http://www.idc-ri.com/getdoc.jsp?containerId=prUK23533512&pageType=PRINTFRIENDLY

Ko, C. (2012). *Chinese government official: Is cloud HK's next advantage?* Retrieved January 9, 2014, http://www.asiacloudforum.com/content/chinese-government-official-cloud-hks-next-advantage

Kroes, N. (2012). *EU data protection reform and cloud computing*. Retrieved February 6, 2014, http://europa.eu/rapid/pressReleasesAction.do?reference=SPEECH/12/40&format=HTML&aged=0&language=EN&guiLanguage=en

Kuan Hon, W., & Millard, C. (2012). *Data export in cloud computing – How can personal data be transferred outside the EEA*. Retrieved February 5, 2014, http://www.cloudlegal.ccls.qmul.ac.uk/Research/researchpapers/55649.html

Lambo, T. (2012). Why you need a cloud rating score. *CloudSecurityAlliance*. Retrieved January 23, 2014, https://cloudsecurityalliance.org/wp-content/uploads/2012/02/Taiye_Lambo_Cloud-Score.pdf

Liebenau, J., Karrberg, P., Grous, A., & Castro, D. (2012). *Modeling the cloud: Employment effects in two exemplary sectors in the United States, the United Kingdom, Germany and Italy*. Retrieved February 9, 2014, http://www2.lse.ac.uk/management/documents/LSE-Cloud-report.pdf, p. 24

Lim, A. (2012). *Cloud computing data protection – Two considerations*. Retrieved January 22, 2014, http://event.idsirtii.or.id/wp-content/uploads/2011/10/Cloud-Data-Security-Two-Considerations-Anthony-Lim-Secure-Age-email.pdf

Microsoft. (2011). *Protecting consumers and promoting innovation and growth in cloud computing*. Retrieved January 9, 2014, http://www.microsoft.eu/Portals/0/Document/Technology%20Policy/MicrosoftGrowthinCloudWP_LV.pdf, p. 3

Microsoft. (n.d.a). *Cloud computing: A catalyst for European competitiveness*. Retrieved January 9, 2014, http://www.microsoft.eu/Portals/0/Document/Technology%20Policy/Cloud%20computing%20-%20a%20catalyst%20for%20European%20competitiveness.pdf

Microsoft. (n.d.b). *What is cloud computing*. Retrieved January 20, 2014, http://www.microsoft.eu/cloud computing/factsheets/whatiscloudcomputing.aspx

Onestopclick. (2012). *Over 70% CIOs confirm cloud computing benefits for UK business*. Retrieved January 21, 2014, http://hosting.onestopclick.com/technology_news/over-70-cios-confirm-cloud computing-benefits-for-uk-business_133.htm

Poscher, R., & Miller, R. (2013). *Surveillance and data protection in the conflict between European American legal cultures, security and defense*. John Hopkins University.

Reding, V. (2012). *Webpage.* Retrieved January 3, 2014, http://ec.europa.eu/avservices/video/player.cfm?ref=82655&sitelang=en

Summit, E. U.-U. S. Joint Statement. (2014). Retrieved March 14, 2014, http://eeas.europa.eu/statements/docs/2014/140326_02_en.pdf

ITU-T Technology Watch Report. (2012). *Privacy in cloud computing.* ITU-T.

The Department of Commerce Internet Task Force. (2010). *Commercial data privacy and innovation in the internet economy: A dynamic policy framework.* Retrieved January 20, 2014, http://www.commerce.gov/sites/default/files/documents/2010/december/iptf-privacy-green-paper.pdf

U.K. Information Commissioner's Office. (2010). *Data protection regulatory action policy.* Retrieved January 28, 2014, http://www.ico.org.uk/what_we_cover/taking_action/~/media/documents/library/Data_Protection/Detailed_specialist_guides/DATA_PROTECTION_REGULATORY_ACTION_POLICY.ashx

Vogel, T. (2012). *Storms threaten storage in the clouds.* Retrieved January 3, 2014, http://www.europeanvoice.com/page/3323.aspx?LG=1&ArtID=74223&SecName=Special%20reports&SectionID=5

Wessing, T. (2010). Cloud computing. Retrieved from http://www.taylorwessing.com/fileadmin/files/docs/Cloud_computing.pdf

World Economic Forum. (2010). *Exploring the future of cloud computing: Riding the next wave of technology-driven transformation.* Author.

ADDITIONAL READING

Adams, A., Murata, K., & Orito, Y. (2010). The Development of Japanese Data Protection (p. 95)., http://www.psocommons.org/policyandinternet/vol2/iss2/art5/, Retrieved January 5, 2014.

Asia Cloud Computing Association, March 2012, Asia Cloud Conference – Journey to the Cloud, p. 16

Banisar, D., & Davies, S. G. (1999, Fall). 1999, Global Trends in Privacy Protection: An International Survey of Privacy, Data Protection, and Surveillance Laws and Developments. *The John Marshall Journal of Computer & Information Law, XVIII*(1), 11. http://papers.ssrn.com/sol3/papers.cfm?abstract_id=2138799 Retrieved January 23, 2014

Bechtolsheim, A. (2008). Cloud Computing (p. 5)., http://netseminar.stanford.edu/seminars/Cloud.pdf, Retrieved January 1, 2014.

BSA. 2012, BSA Global Cloud Computing Scorecard. Retrieved February 12, 2014, http://portal.bsa.org/cloudscorecard2012/assets/PDFs/BSA_GlobalCloudScorecard.pdf, p. 1, 8-9

Eustace, D. 2011, Cloud Computing – Legal Considerations for Data Controllers. Retrieved February 17, 2014, http://www.dilloneustace.ie/download/1/Cloud%20Computing%20Legal%20Considerations%20for%20Data%20Controllers.pdf, p. 1

Gantz, J., & Toncheva, A. (2012). Cloud Computing's Role in Job Creation (p. 1)., http://www.microsoft.com/en-us/news/download/features/2012/IDC_Cloud_jobs_White_Paper.pdf, Retrieved January 20, 2014.

Greenleaf, G., October 2011, The Influence of European Data Privacy Standards Outside Europe: Implications for Globalization of Convention 108 (initial draft), p.1

Jaeger, P. T., Lin, J., Grimes, J. M., & Simmons, S. N. (2009, May). Where Is the Cloud? Geography, Economics, Environment, and Jurisdiction in Cloud Computing. *First Monday, 14*(5), http://firstmonday.org/htbin/cgiwrap/bin/ojs/index.php/fm/article/view/2456.Mell/2171. RetrievedJanuary62014. doi:10.5210/fm.v14i5.2456

Lim, A. 2012, Cloud Computing Data Protection – Two Considerations. Retrieved January 16, 2014, http://event.idsirtii.or.id/wp-content/uploads/2011/10/Cloud-Data-Security-Two-Considerations-Anthony-Lim-Secure-Age-email.pdf

Moos, F. 2012, Germany – DPA Guidance on Cloud Computing. Retrieved February 6, 2014, https://www.privacyassociation.org/publications/2012_01_01_germany_dpa_guidance_on_cloud_computing/

Newsletter, I. A. 2010, Cloud Computing: Silver Lining or Storm Ahead. Retrieved January 6, 2014, http://iac.dtic.mil/iatac/download/Vol13_No2.pdf, p. 23

Practical Law Company. April 2011, Data Protection: Canada. Retrieved February 7, 2014, http://ipandit.practicallaw.com/6-502-0556?source=relatedcontent

Practical Law Company. March 2012, Data Protection: United States. Retrieved February 7, 2014, http://ipandit.practicallaw.com/6-502-0467?source=relatedcontent

Privireal.org. United States: Data Protection – History of Data Protection in the United States, 2005. Retrieved February 6, 2014, http://www.privireal.org/content/dp/usa.php

Russell, J. March 2012, Japan Warns Google that its New Privacy Policy May Violate Data Protection Laws. Retrieved February 11, 2014, http://thenextweb.com/google/2012/03/01/japan-warns-google-that-its-new-privacy-policy-may-violate-data-protection-laws/

Tan, J. May 2012, Briefing: Data Protection Law in Singapore. Retrieved January 5, 2014, http://www.computerworld.com.sg/tech/it-governance/briefing-data-protection-law-in-singapore/

Technologies, C. A. May 2012, U.S. Companies View Cloud Computing as Key to Improved Data Protection. Retrieved January 23, 2014, http://www.ca.com/us/news/Press-Releases/na/2012/US-Companies-View-Cloud computing-as-Key-to-Improved-Data-Protection.aspx

KEY TERMS AND DEFINITIONS

Binding Corporate Rules: European Union rules to allow international organizations and groups of companies to be in compliance with EU Data Protection law when make intra-organisational transfers of personal data across borders.

Cloud Computing: A style of computing that provides scalable and elastic IT-enabled capabilities that are delivered as a service using Internet technologies.

Data Protection: The legal control over access to and use of data stored in computing systems.

Directive 95/46/EC: The European Union Director that regulates and protects individuals with regards to the processing of personal data.

General Data Protection Regulation: A planned European Commission regulation that will unify data protection within the European Union, as Directive 95/46/EC does not consider globalization and technological developments such as cloud computing and social networks.

Global Technology Fault Lines: Clashes between legal systems, cultural differences and business practice norms when applying technology.

Non-EU Data Protection Systems: Non-European Union legal systems that regulates and protects individuals with regards to the processing of personal data.

Section 2
Cloud Adoption Issues and Cases

Chapter 4

Analyzing French and Italian iPhone 4S Mobile Cloud Customer Satisfaction Presented by Organizational Sustainability Modeling

Victor Chang
Computing, Creative Technologies and Engineering, Leeds Beckett University, UK

ABSTRACT

This chapter explains the use of Organizational Sustainability Modeling (OSM), a model to evaluate the status of risk and return for Cloud Computing including Mobile Cloud, where the customer satisfaction rate is an important indicator. The authors describe how to use OSM to collect and analyze French and Italian 2011 data, in which the iPhone 4S Cloud service is used as the representation for Mobile Cloud industry. OSM data analysis shows that French and Italian data have declined customer satisfaction, being affected by the economic downturn. There are medium-high uncontrolled risks and good data consistencies in both countries. The use of 3D Visualization helps further data analysis and interpretation. Comparisons between French and Italian data are presented, and rationale for their similarities and differences are explained in detail. Additionally, OSM and other similar methods are compared. Due to the capabilities to support both quantitative and qualitative approaches with support from real case studies, OSM is a better method to analyze customer satisfaction in Mobile Cloud.

1. INTRODUCTION

Since the development of Cloud Computing in the industry, more organizations have adopted Cloud Computing for a variety of projects and services, including backup, experiments, web hosting, word processing, email, mobile services and highly specialized applications (Dinh et al., 2011; Marston et al., 2011; Chang et al., 2013 a). There are different types of reasons for adopting Cloud Computing. Some foresee business opportunities; some regard Cloud Computing as a

DOI: 10.4018/978-1-4666-8210-8.ch004

Copyright © 2015, IGI Global. Copying or distributing in print or electronic forms without written permission of IGI Global is prohibited.

platform to integrate their IT infrastructure; some use Cloud as a resource to develop applications which can be shared and reused. All the reasons mentioned above are the drivers for organizations to adopt Cloud Computing (Rochwerger et al., 2009; Marston et al., 2011). In all different types of Cloud adoption, there are industries that have more competition due to fast-growing areas in the global market and the user community. One such an area is Mobile Cloud, which is a fast-growing area due to the rise of smart phones, better infrastructures (such as 4G), better services and better applications (apps) available to a large number of users (Dinh et al., 2011; Qiang et al, 2012). Similarly, price wars between different smart phones, between different mobile service carriers and between different mobile apps have become more intense. For example, an iPhone 4S phone 8GB could be purchased with £20 per month for a two-year contract in 2014. In 2011, this would have cost £45 per month plus the additional fees to own the smart phones. Some researchers argue that the drop in price may not be accompanied by maintenance of quality of service. However, the 4G network has been more established and more mature than in 2011 and most users do not feel there is a huge difference between their service quality in 2011 and 2014. The Mobile phone and service industry is a competitive area. However, there is insufficient quantitative research investigating the Mobile Cloud service industry such as customer satisfaction, profitability or the business models. Although there are qualitative research projects in this area, they do not fully address the requirements and challenges in Mobile Cloud industry. We argue that concrete quantitative data and evidence must be fully demonstrated in support of any existing hypotheses. Additionally, innovative techniques for analyzing the user data is important to understand the consumer behavior, since users may change their habits and behaviours over shorter periods of time than other industries (Idongesit and Skouby, 2014). For example, some apps which were popular a few years ago could

face a challenge to survive if they did not update and evolve their services. One example is the Chinese version of Farmville, which had millions of users in 2009. They did not change their games and services for four years. They experienced a large decline in users due to other apps available, which could be free and could work on all different mobile operating systems. In 2013, the company filed a statement of bankruptcy.

Customer satisfaction is an important indicator for the service industry, since it offers evaluations to the services on offer and it provides valuable information for investors to decide the scale and amount of investment. If a company does not perform well in their customer satisfaction, there are consequences. First, customers may leave and join other service providers. Second, if there is a decline, depending on the scale of decline in maintaining existing number of customers, the company may experience financial difficulties due to reduced revenues and fewer investors willing to put in more funds. There are studies about direct relationship between maintaining customer satisfaction and profitability. Both Heskett and Schlesinger (1994) and Hallowell (1994) demonstrate the direct positive relationship between the improved customer satisfaction and profitability. Statistical data and empirical evidence presented by both groups of researchers assert that the loyal customers contribute to the profitability of the service industry. Although the short-term relationship cannot be easily identified, maintaining high customer satisfaction and profitability are related in the long-term. If a company struggles to maintain an acceptable level of customer satisfaction, they may experience a decline of existing customers with reduced revenue and poor corporate reputation. This will not help the company to be profitable in the long term, since they may lose out to competitors with similar services.

Cloud computing promises to revolutionize the provision of major computing services, bringing with it benefits for all types of users. These benefits vary from simplified administration for systems programmers to ready access to massive processing power on demand for desktop users. However, to gain the full benefits, a full commitment to Cloud computing is necessary and this brings with it a requirement for users to revise business processes and attitudes to computing services in addition to the immediately obvious systems changes (Barry, 2012). Therefore evaluation of a Cloud computing project must consider the balance of benefits and risks to the organization in the context of its environment in addition to technical considerations.

A number of methods that can analyze the customer satisfaction in the fast-growing Mobile Cloud service have been investigated. We realize that there is no quantitative method addressing this issue. Methods such as Weinhart et al (2009) and Klem et al (2009) are qualitative – they do not even present papers specific to Mobile Cloud industry. One of the recognized methods available to analyze investments is Capital Asset Price Modeling (CAPM) which is able classify risks into uncontrolled or managed types (Sharpe, 1990). CAPM takes proper account the risks associated with an investment and the context in which it is made. However Cloud computing projects present some particular challenges which are not well addressed by CAPM which has been developed as a generic technique for evaluating investments and business projects.

2. MODELS FOR ANALYZING RISK AND RETURN STATUS FOR MOBILE SERVICE

This section describes the method of analyzing risk and return. Return may mean profitability, customer satisfaction, or any goals that have to be accomplished. Risk may mean the uncontrolled and controlled risk. This classification is important as confirmed by Sharpe in this Nobel-winning model, Capital Asset Pricing Model (CAPM) (Sharpe, 1990). The supporting rationale is as fol-

lows. Each Cloud service needs to identify risks, classify whether they can be managed. Each Cloud service will expect some forms of uncontrollable risk, which include impact due to financial crisis, natural disaster and accidents (car, fire, flood and so). These events cannot be managed with the human intervention, although actions we provide can reduce the damage caused by those events. Hence, all Cloud Computing services including Mobile services should contain the status of return and risk (controlled and uncontrolled).

2.1 An Overview of Choosing Suitable Models

This section describes some of the suitable models for calculating risk and return. Monte Carlo simulations (MCS) have been widely used in financial analysis and computation. Longstaff et al demonstrate the use of Least Squared Method (LSM) to enable large-scaled computations to be completed in a short period of time (seconds). Chang et al (2011 a) follow their steps to make improved prototype and demonstrate the use of MCS for undertaking large-scaled simulations on private and public clouds, and they have contributions for developing financial analysis. However, Monte Carlo simulations require specific business cases of investment. Input key values should be determined and verified. With Cloud Computing, the use of public cloud does not require a high capital input, since it can cost as little as one dollar to buy a virtual machine as a service for computation. Monte Carlo simulation should be used for predicting the put and call prices of an investment. Additionally, MCS regards risk as a single entity (Teunis and Havelaar, 2000; Jampani et al., 2008) and does not have a definition to calculate the uncontrolled risk.

Black Scholes Models (BSM) have been used in financial derivatives and computation (Eberlein and Keller, 1995; Carr and Madan, 1999). This includes the use of Cloud Computing to calculate financial derivatives in both numerical forms and visualization (Chang et al., 2011 a; Chang 2014 a; 2014 b). Sharma et al (2002) demonstrate the use of their improved BSM for Cloud Computing and they focus on the service providers' points of view. However, Cloud Computing is not limited to service providers but includes a variety of organizations and users, including those in public clouds and community clouds, which may not even follow their recommendation. Additionally, BSM does not classify risks into uncontrolled and uncontrolled types.

Binomial Trees can be used to investigate the dependency of different factors contributing to the success of managing Cloud Computing projects. However, the model assumes that all the factors are dependent on each other, since the value of the probability can indicate the dependency relationship. For example, suppose the model determines two major factors, one contributing to 30% and the other 70% and the second main factor is divided into four other factors. The last factor (in the second main factor) then contributes to 10%, and the probability is thus 0.1. However, some risks are independent of each other. For example, if one Mobile service is managing all controlled risks under 2% (all stocks are available; all services are up-and-running; disruptions of services can be resumed within 2 hours), when the country experiences flood and the town was in a flood situation. Then there is no way to prevent a flood from happening to cause the damage. Similarly, the probability of having a flood is not dependent on the way that the business is managed. Thus, risks are not necessarily dependent; they can be independent. The better approach is to classify risks as uncontrolled or controlled before using Binomial Tree or dividing them into different percentages of probabilities.

2.2 Capital Asset Pricing Model

A key feature of Capital Asset Pricing Model (CAPM) is that it divides risks associated with an investment into two categories: those which

can be controlled and managed, and those which cannot. For example, when considering risk in a stock market portfolio, risks associated with the relative fortunes of individual companies arising from the foresight and proficiency of their management may be managed and ameliorated by spreading an investment across a variety of different companies. However, a general trading downturn is an inherent characteristic of this type of investment which cannot be avoided. There are researchers demonstrating that CAPM is suitable for Cloud Computing (Gentzoglanis, 2011). CAPM can be used for Cloud Computing except the improvement in the handling of big data and the requirements for adaptation for Cloud Computing (Chang, 2013).

CAPM can analyze uncontrolled and managed risk associated with the status of return. Comparing with models described in Section 2 and 2.1, CAPM appears to be more suitable. Although CAPM is a generic model suitable for any disciplines, it has two limitations; it struggles to handle large datasets and its focus on econometrics. At the time that CAPM was being developed, the extremely large digital datasets which are common today did not exist so there was no need for CAPM in its original from to be able to handle thousands of datasets at once. Thus, CAPM does not address how to handle large datasets. With the volume of data being generated by organizations adopting new technologies growing, the capacity to handle thousands of datasets is important for data-based research (Hey et al., 2009). This inability of basic CAPM models to handle data-intensive cases leads to longer computational times. This explains why it is necessary to handle big datasets due to the rapid data growth experienced by many organizations. To tackle this problem, researchers have developed revised models such as "International CAPM" which can compute a large number of financial datasets at once (Hamelink, 2000).

CAPM is focused on econometrics and calculation of investment portfolio risk and return analysis (Sharpe, 1990; Hull, 2009). It can be used as a generic solution but a more tailored approach is desirable for computing in which key input values correspond to technical rather than financial terms such as return on the market and risk-free rate in the market. For use in IT system adoption scenarios, CAPM needs to be redesigned. The required attributes and key performance indicators should be revised to focus on measuring expected and actual returns while keeping risk-control rate low. By doing this, the revised model will become a better fit to the task of risk analyses for organizations adopting large systems such as Cloud Computing.

3. OVERVIEW OF A PROPOSED MODEL: ORGANIZATIONAL SUSTAINABILITY MODELING (OSM)

As discussed in Section 2 and 2.1, the development of a new or improved model is necessary. While reviewing suitability of the models described earlier, CAPM is the one for further development. The main reasons are first, it is a generic model for analyzing risk and return. Second, it has the classification of uncontrolled and controlled risks. The areas for improvement include:

- Making the revised model suitable for evaluating Cloud Computing adoption.
- Modifying the model so that it can process the thousands of datasets or millions of datapoints at once without extra work.

The proposed model is called Organizational Sustainability Modeling (OSM), which help organizations analyze their risk and return status. It has several case studies to support its validity. These include:

- **Vodafone and Apple:** Analyze the profitability and risk. There was an actual 21-26% gain in the profitability after adopting Mobile /Cloud services.

- **SAP:** The use of SAP helps small and medium enterprises (SMEs) to manage their risks within 1% and helps SMEs to withstand the impact of the financial crisis.
- **University of Southampton:** The use of OSM helps analyzing the cost-saving of up to 22% due to the use of green Cloud Computing.

OSM revises and improves CAPM to assess risk and return analysis for organizations adopting large computer systems, such as the adoption of Cloud. The objective of OSM is to provide a systematic approach to help managers understand the status of risk and return of Cloud Computing projects and services.

3.1 Details about Organizational Sustainability Modeling (OSM)

Based on the original CAPM formula, OSM formula is

$$e = r_c + \beta \left(a - r_c \right) \tag{1}$$

where:

- a is the actual return (or performance) of a large computing systems project.
- e is the expected return (or performance) of a large computing systems project.
- r_c is the risk-control rate, the rate of manageable risk.
- β is the beta value which represents a measure of uncontrolled risk.

The challenge is to calculate beta which determines the uncontrolled risk value, because it is an implicit value making it difficult to quantify. Beta values can be calculated for each dataset from the expected return, the actual return and risk-control rate. One approach would be to collect many beta values and calculate a mean value. Another approach for calculating beta is to perform linear regression, where the gradient of the slope is the value for beta (Chang, 2013; Sharpe, 1990). Beta can be calculated by rearranging Equation (1), giving

$$\beta = \frac{e - r_c}{a - r_c} \qquad (2)$$

where a is the actual return of a large computing systems project, r_c is the risk-control rate, e is the expected return, and β is the beta value representing a measure of uncontrolled risk as before.

Given a number of datasets, the value for beta (β) is given by the gradient of a line through the datapoints. As with CAPM, OSM uses linear regression to compute a line of best fit. Ordinary Least Squares (OLS), as part of the OSM, is used to minimize the sum of squared vertical distances between the observed responses in the dataset and the line is the method used.

3.2 OSM Datasets Processing

This section describes how to proceed with OSM dataset processing. Chang (2014) explains how to use OSM to measure popularity of German iPhone 4S users in their evaluations of mobile services. In other words, OSM can be used to analyze similar cases for customer satisfaction measurement in using Mobile Cloud services.

Metrics collection can be undertaken by system automation on a regular basis, by surveys which need to be completed by a large sample size. Hundreds and thousands of datasets can be collected in this way while running experiments or conducting surveys over a period of time. This will ensure a large sample size for modeling but a numerous datasets makes analysis more complex and time-consuming (Huson et al., 2007).

The size of the data that OSM can handle is as follows. Each dataset contains up to 2,000 rows and 255 fields of records, which is then equiva-

lent to 510,000 datapoints. There are then 500 datasets involved, which becomes 500 x 510,000 = 255,000,000 datapoints for analysis, which is considered a big data analysis that data processing is completed within seconds to calculate key outputs for businesses. Chang et al (2011 b; 2011 c) explain details about how to process data and the algorithms involved with data processing.

3.3 OSM Outputs

As explained by Chang et al (2011 b, 2011 c) and Chang (2014 c, 2014 d), the OSM outputs are as follows.

- **Beta (β):** A measure of uncontrolled risk that may affect the project.
- **Standard Error of the Mean:** The range of the mean of the experimental results. Smaller standard errors imply more accurate and representative results.
- **Durbin-Watson [18, 19]:** A test to detect autocorrelation (a relationship between values separated from each other by a given time lag) in the residuals of a regression analysis. The value should be greater than 1. The value for Pr > DW corresponds to the negative autocorrelation test (residuals eventually wither off) and is in favored by OSM. The value of Pr > DW should ideally get as close as to 1 to reflect the accuracy of the OSM regression. The difference between 1 and Pr > DW can work out the p-value for the OSM analysis.
- **Mean Square Error (MSE):** An estimator to quantify the difference between estimated and actual values. A low MSE value means there is a high correlation between actual and expected return values.
- **R-Squared Value:** It is a value to test the regression fit. However, it is equivalent to the term "R-squared value for firm" used in econometrics to describe the percentage of risks in proportion to the external or inter-

nal organizations or factors (Teoh et al., 2006; Damodaran, 2008; Lee et al., 2009). For example, if an organization has an R-squared value (99.99% C.I) of 0.6 this means 60% of risks are from external bodies or the market, and 40% of risks come from the organization such as poor adoption decision, overspending, poor selection of equipment (resulting in accidents) and so on. Adoption of a large computer system also introduces risks and the R-squared value provides a good indication for the percentage and sources of beta risks.

3.4 Supporting Case Studies

There are several models proposed by Cloud Computing researchers. First, Weinhardt et al (2009) propose a framework for Cloud Computing and address the relationship between different levels of services. Their proposal can be used as a generic model for Cloud adoption. Klem et al (2009) propose their framework for Cloud Computing and explain that their approach can be adopted. Third, Sultan (2010) addresses the effectiveness of Cloud Computing for education and consolidates his conceptual ideas. However, none of these papers has real-life case studies to support their point of view, except Sultan (2014). However, this case study does not use his recommendation fully.

The original concepts proposed by Weinhardt et al (2009), Klem et al (2009) and Sultan (2010) proposals lack support from real-life case studies and demonstrations. We assert that any proposed models or frameworks should have support from real-life case studies and demonstrations, if they are not to be in a weak position for organizational adoption. Our OSM model has case studies used in different domains and applications of the user adoption. In this paper, we demonstrate that the use of OSM to analyze French and Italian data of user satisfaction of using iPhone 4S Mobile Cloud services. We interpret the outputs from OSM analysis which can offer useful information for the stakeholders and decision-makers.

4. FRENCH AND ITALIAN CASE STUDIES: ANALYZING THE RATE OF CUSTOMER SATISFACTION OF IPHONE 4S MOBILE SERVICE IN FRANCE AND ITALY

This section describes the case study in detail, which presents how OSM is used to help analyze the rate of customer satisfaction of using iPhone 4S Mobile Service in France. Current literature has concentrated on system design, development and deployment examples (Ganti et al., 2011 a; Rimal et al., 2011). There is little literature about surveys focusing on the customers and their ratings of satisfaction towards using Mobile Cloud services. It is crucial for businesses to understand consumer behaviours and preferences for mobile products and services. In order to define what to measure, propose how to measure and analyze data, a systematic method is required. OSM is the method to systematically compute all these data and explain the interpretations of these data, in the form of statistical modeling. Reporting the status of risk and return of such Cloud adoption is important, since it can provide stakeholders an overview about their service rating, risk monitoring and analysis about whether their strategies of offering Cloud services have met their expected targets. In this way, the businesses can be more adaptable to the fast-paced requirement changes for Cloud Computing, particularly Mobile Cloud, which is a fast-growing area.

4.1 Motivation for Using iPhone 4S: A Representation of Mobile Cloud and a Hypothesis

Chang et al (2011 c) presented their Vodafone/ Apple case study on Mobile Cloud which had an overall coverage of iPhone and iPad models. The generalization provides useful recommendations for potential and current investors (Chang et al., 2013 b). Based on our knowledge of investors' requirements, they feel analysis will be more useful if it can be focused on each specific model. This may include iPhone 4S model alone and its computational analysis about its business performance that focuses on status of return and risk. We assert that the integrated approach has the following advantages:

- It is cost-effective and can provide data and results in the minimum amount of spending.
- The quality of analysis is of a high standard, since it goes through a series of quality assurance (QA) processes.

French Telecom is one of the big European telecommunication service providers and is a major provider of iPhone 4S together with Orange, Vodafone and T-Mobile. France is well-known for its creativity and there are groups of active users for using mobile applications and services. However, the economic downturn has caused more job losses in France and towns with farming and leisure focus have been affected by downturn considerably (Cavailhes et al., 1994), and the same situation applies for 2011. This makes a huge decrease in the number of iPhone users, since customers have changed to cheaper mobile models with cheaper service fees, or are in the progress of doing so.

Telecommunication services in Italy are active and have major service providers offering iPhone 4S services. However, Italy is one of the worse economic performers in EU and has been hit in particular by Euro zone crisis in 2011. This puts Italy in a vulnerable position and is near to a recession level, which can lose several percentages of iPhone users due to its high prices.

In regard to the discussion in introduction about the relationship between the Mobile Cloud Service and user satisfaction, results in our previous papers (Chang et al., 2011 b; 2013 a; Chang, 2014 c, 2014 d) also demonstrate the direct relationship between the user satisfaction and the economic downturn or the business performance of the

invested company. In our previous work (Chang, 2014 c; 2014 d), results support the case that the customer satisfaction is related to the economic downturn. In other words, the customer satisfaction is influenced by a country's economy. Our rationale from that data analysis is that if the country is in economic crisis and customers either receive less pay or risk losing their jobs, they feel that Mobile service may cost them more than the necessities in life such food and accommodation. Based on the observations in our previous studies and the analysis of German and Spanish data, we propose the first hypothesis:

H1: The rate of customer satisfaction in Mobile Cloud Services can reflect the state of the economy.

The results in this section will justify whether our hypothesis can be validated. Both Heskett and Schlesinger (1994) and Hallowell (1994) demonstrate the direct positive relationship between the improved customer satisfaction and profitability. This concept is applicable to information and communication technologies including mobile phone industry and its new services (Dinh et al., 2011; Qiang et al, 2012). In other words, if there is high customer satisfaction, profitability is expected for businesses. Additionally, Mobile Cloud is a fast-growing area that needs more attention and better strategies (Marston et al., 2011; Idongesit and Skouby, 2014). The ability to purchase mobile phones and new services such as Mobile Cloud can provide good indications of the recovery of the economy due to the direct impact on consumer spending and billions of Euros of revenues generated in this sector (Worldpanel ComTech, 2011; USwitch survey, 2011). This means that if many people in Country A are willing to pay for new mobile phones with their monthly bills and new services, consumer spending tends to provide positive outcomes to the quarterly consumer spending data and quarterly GDP in its retail sales. In other words, all these contribute to positive results in the quarterly macroeconomic measurement of Country A. Thus, the rate of customer satisfaction in Mobile Cloud can reflect the recovery of the economy.

The OSM approach provides high quality of analysis at low cost. This can ensure a higher return for investors. In addition, market contests between smart phones, mobile clouds, service providers and mobile applications for Clouds have become more competitive than before and it is useful to keep track of market demands and consumer requirements so that our Cloud strategies and recommendation can be kept up-to-date.

4.2 Data Processing and Analysis Overview

This section describes the computational analysis of the collected datasets and explains the interpretations from the data. The source of data is from Kantar Worldpanel ComTech (2011), a market research company, as well as Anastaya (2011), a consulting firm specializing in data analysis. The author worked in Anastaya for a period of time as a part-time consultant. A thorough data analysis approach has been adopted to ensure data analysis can be unbiased and reflect the actual risk and return status of the mobile cloud adoption. The objective of this research is to analyze the rate of satisfaction and the rate of adoption in the EU zone such as France and Italy.

Although Kantar Worldpanel ComTech has published a report on the iPhone 4S business performance in EU, it does not provide detailed statistical and computational analysis. It only offers an estimated percentage of performance downgrade and does not provide any detailed analysis. Hence, we aim to offer a more comprehensive analysis with the following objectives:

- Compute the exact extent of performance downgrade (or improvement) in EU countries. In this paper, we focus on the French data because France is a country behind

EU policy with Germany. Italy is a country that has been particularly hit by economic downturn, although it still remains a G7 nation as one of the leading developed countries in the world.

- Our previous work already analyzed the German and Spanish data (Chang, 2014 c, 2014 d). Analyzing French and Italian data is a good reflection on how top-tier EU country performed in the economic crisis.
- To provide a rationale and analysis about their performance (downgrade) based on our results.

Datasets follow the requirements of the OSM Equation (2). Each row of data contains the numerical values for the actual value, expected value and risk-control rate of the French Mobile customer satisfaction. Similar steps are undertaken for the Italian data. Each row of datasets contains the actual and expected values of measurement, and risk-control rate associated with each pair of actual and expected values. The data processing takes each row of datasets – reading all data values; putting data values into the formulas; and then perform statistical regression while using OSM.

4.3 OSM Metrics

The use of OSM metrics is as follows.

1. The expected values included the 2010 to 2011 data taken a year before the study began. The actual values included the 2011 data, to investigate the usage of mobile cloud adoption in 2012.

2. The risk data between 2011 and 2012 was collected by Kantar Worldpanel ComTech. It was measured based on the percentage of dissatisfied users (although they were dissatisfied, they still used iPhone 4S services. This was a risk-control rate – if Apple could offer better and cheaper deals,

Table 1. OSM key statistics for French data in mobile cloud analysis

Beta	0.7723	Durbin-Watson (4th Order)	1.0439
96.12% of Risks: External and 3.88% of Risks: Internal		Pr>DW (Negative Autocorrelation: Maximum of 1) Positive Autocorrelation (p-Value)	0.9958 0.0042
Standard Error	0.0266	Regress R-Square (99.99 C.I)	0.9612
Mean Square Error (MSE)	0.00769	Regress R-Square (95 C.I)	0.9723

users would be happy to stay, based on their feedback) measured in major French cities: Paris, Lyon, Marseille, Toulouse, Lille and Nice.

3. In terms of the Italian data, the data collection process was identical to the point 1 and 2 above, except six Italian cities were chosen for customer satisfaction survey: Rome, Milan, Venice, Naples, Turin and Bologna.

After collecting the metrics, OSM data processing took place as described in Section 3.2. Results and analysis for French and Italian data will be presented as follows.

4.4 OSM Data Analysis for French Data

This section presents results of the French data analysis and explains the interpretations of all these key statistical values. All the data is based on between January 2011 and December 2011, which provides a twelve month period of customer satisfaction measurement for iPhone 4S. OSM can be modeled by statistical languages, in which SAS is more suitable than other languages since it can compute more in-depth analysis (Chang et al., 2011 b; 2011 c). The data is carefully calculated, examined and analyzed. Twelve months of data for this case study is sufficient to analyze its business performance, since this is a model specific approach and often Apple product performance can be determined within the first few months in the market release (Kantar Worldpanel

ComTech, 2011). SAS program for OSM is coded for computation and Table 1 shows the summary of OSM key statistics.

Further explanations are presented as follows:

- Beta is equal to 0.7723. The medium-high value suggests the project risk is maintained at an acceptable control rate.

- Standard error is 0.0266. The low value suggests most metrics are close to each other and the data has few extremes. There is an extremely high consistency between all metrics.

- The fourth order Durbin-Watson: It means Durbin-Watson has been regressed four times to get the most accurate values for analysis. Durbin-Watson value is 1.0439. Pr > DW is equal to 0.9958 and is very close to 1, showing that there is a high negative auto-correlation. Similarly, the positive p-value is 0.0042, which indicates that the possibility of extreme cases is very small and below 0.42%.

- The extremely low Mean Square Error (MSE) value suggests excellent consistency between actual and expected return values.

- Main regression R-square is 0.9612. This means 96.12% of the risks are from the externals such as the impacts of financial crisis that prevented users from spending more and 3.88% of the risks are from the internals such as the operations and strategies set by French telecommunication companies.

Table 2. OSM key statistics for Italian data in mobile cloud analysis

Beta	0.8070	Durbin-Watson (4th Order)	1.3801
58.05% risks external 41.95% risks internal		Pr>DW (negative autocorrelation: maximum of 1) Positive autocorrelation (p-value)	0.9792 0.0208
Standard Error	0.1117	Regress R-Square (99.99 C.I)	0.5805
Mean Square Error (MSE)	0.15311	Regress R-Square (95 C.I)	0.6637

4.5 OSM Data Analysis for Italian Data

All the steps are similar to sections above, except this is the analysis for Italian data. All the data is based on between January 2011 till December 2011, which provides a twelve month period of customer satisfaction measurement for iPhone 4S. Careful data analysis and examination has been applied and Table 2 shows the results.

Further explanations are presented as follows:

- Beta is equal to 0.8070. The medium-high value suggests the project risk is maintained at an acceptably controlled rate. The mobile service provider should be aware of the risk imposed by the price, service and customer satisfaction.
- Standard error is 0.1117. The low value suggests most metrics are close to each other and the data has few extremes. There is high consistency between all metrics.
- The first order Durbin-Watson: Durbin-Watson value is 1.3801. Pr > DW is equal to 0.9792 and is very close to 1, showing that there is a high negative auto-correlation. Similarly, the positive p-value is 0.0208, which indicates that the possibility outside the 95% confidence limit (0.05) is very low and unlikely.
- The low Mean Square Error (MSE) value suggests excellent consistency between actual and expected return values.

- Main regression R-square is 0.5805. It means 58.05% of the risks are from the externals such as the impacts of financial crisis that prevented users from spending more. 41.95% of the risks are from the internals such as the prices, the quality of service, operations and strategies set by telecommunication companies, which should consider lowering prices or offering incentives for existing customers.

5. 3D VISUALIZATION: FURTHER ANALYSIS TO SUPPORT FRENCH AND ITALIAN CASE STUDIES

OSM supports the development of 3D Visualization. The benefit is to consolidate interpretations from data analysis. Statistical analysis can only explain what each key OSM output means. 3D Visualization can provide an overview about the project by presenting the three key metrics: actual return value, expected return value and risk-controlled rate head-to-head. This also provides stakeholders a platform to double check with existing analysis, so that no other data analysis and interpretations can be missed. The shape presented by the 3D Visualization can consolidate interpretation of data analysis as demonstrated in our previous work (Chang et al., 2011 b, 2011 c; Chang, 2014 c; 2014 d). If there are spikes or bumps, it means that the project may experience a volatile period that can prevent the progress of the project, or delivery of the service to the users/customers. The most ideal situations can be:

- **An Overall Trend of Upward Movement:** This means that the project is on the way up, with increasing the expected return values and actual return values over the period of the project/service.

- **There Are Few Spikes and Bumps:** It means that the project is not having any volatile period or factors that contribute to the development of uncontrolled risk.

The focus of this chapter is to demonstrate that 3D Visualization can help interpret further data analysis, rather than the computational

5.1 OSM Data Analysis for French Data

Figure 1 shows visualization for customer satisfaction using iPhone 4S Mobile Cloud services in France between January and December 2011. The x-axis shows the actual rate of customer satisfaction is between -7.5 to -9.5%, and the y-axis shows the expected rate of customer satisfaction is between -6.0 to -7.5% and z-axis presents risk-control rate is between 1.2 and 1.8%. Although the decline was expected before the survey process and data collection, the actual rate of decline in customer satisfaction is higher than expected values. Possible reasons may include that the customers felt the prices were high, or the services were not improving, and issues in their previous iPhone and Mobile services left unresolved in their new contracts. The French data has only minor spikes and bumps, which means that the overall service between January and December 2011 was still considered a manageable experience for Mobile service providers. Similar to German data analysis (Chang, 2014 c; 2014 d), actual iPhone usage is lower than the expected rate. This may imply a large number of users did not continue with iPhone services and switch to cheaper models and services due to its higher prices and impact of downturn. 3D Visualization helps businesses interpret the likely causes for their downgrade in their business targets.

Figure 1. Visualization for customer satisfaction in using iPhone 4S mobile cloud services in France between January and December 2011

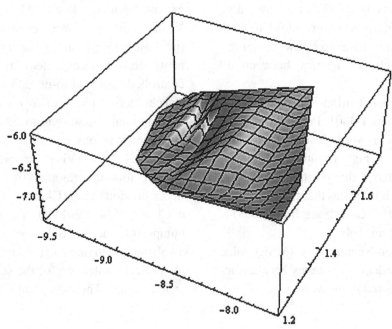

5.2 OSM Data Analysis for Italian Data

Figure 2 shows visualization for customer satisfaction in using iPhone 4S Mobile Cloud services in Italy between January and December 2011. The x-axis shows the actual rate of customer satisfaction is between -4.0 to -6.0%, and the y-axis shows the expected rate of customer satisfaction is between -3.0 to -5.0% and z-axis presents risk-control rate is between 1.0 and 1.8%. Although the decline was expected before the survey process and data collection, the actual rate of declined customer satisfaction is higher than expected values. However, the difference between French and Italian data is that R-squared in Italian data is much lower, with 58.05% for the external risk and 41.95% for the internal risk. Interestingly, numerous Italian feedback comments suggested that customers criticized the former prime minister's policy for telecommunication industry (that he was the tycoon) and regarded this risk as internal rather external. This may also

explain why there are more bumps and one major spike seen in Visualization suggesting the Mobile Cloud service might experience a turbulent period. Additionally, other possible reasons are similar to the French data: high prices, unimproved services and no value for money. 3D Visualization again can consolidate interpretation of data analysis in the Italian data.

5.3 Summary of 3D Visualization

The OSM metrics include actual return values, expected return values and risk-controlled rate, which can be computed as 3D Visualization. The aim is to help interpret the complex analysis into a format that the stakeholders and reviewers without statistical or computing backgrounds can understand. The use of visualization is crucial to the development of the organizational business intelligence strategy that can blend their business processes with the use of Cloud Computing services (Loshin, 2012).

Figure 2. Visualization for customer satisfaction in using iPhone 4S mobile cloud services in Italy between January and December 2011

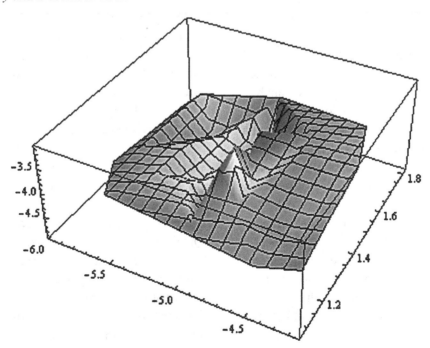

5.4 Testing of Our Hypothesis

Results of French and Italian data fully support our hypothesis. Since both countries had economic crises and this influenced the way they perceived spending more money on their Mobile Cloud services. The OSM outputs and interpretations show that the decline of the customer satisfaction is due to the higher expenses, services not improved and poor value for money. Thus, some customers left for cheaper services. However, more data analysis on more smart phone models and countries will help to fully validate our first hypothesis.

6. DISCUSSION

This section presents three topics for discussion. The first topic is general discussions about the OSM. The second topic is general discussion about Mobile Cloud services and competition with other vendors, as well as future direction that can influence Mobile Cloud services. The third topic is a comparison with other similar models.

6.1 General Discussions about OSM

This section presents the overall discussions with OSM and the comparison with the original model, CAPM. While CAPM is not designed to handle huge datasets and is not designed for analysis of system adoption such as Cloud Computing, OSM has an improved methodology and formula. OSM can compute thousands of datasets at once and is designed for Computing (including Cloud Computing) rather than being a generic model for risk and return. While identifying and collecting metrics for actual return values, expected return values, risk-control rates, OSM can calculate key values including beta, standard error and Durbin-Watson (with negative autocorrelation) to interpret the collected datasets. A project with good Cloud adoption including Mobile Cloud should have the following properties:

- **Low Beta:** The project has lower uncontrolled risk.
- **Low Standard Error:** Results of collected datasets have high consistency between one another.
- **Durbin-Watson:** The value is above 1, and negative autocorrelation test is as close as to 1 as possible. The positive autocorrelation is equivalent to the p-value, which should be 0.05 and below, to correspond that all datapoints are within the 95% confidence interval.
- R-squared values can identify the proportions and sources of beta risks. It should be above 0.5 and below 1.
- Mean Squared values and positive p-values should have low values to support accuracy of OSM analysis.

6.2 OSM for Mobile Cloud Survey Research and Future Direction in Mobile Cloud

OSM is the only model developed in academia that has numerous case studies that can analyze the risk and return status for projects with Cloud adoption, including Mobile Cloud Service. Our previous work has presented the case studies for Vodafone/Apple Mobile Cloud strategies in 2009 and iPhone 4S customer satisfaction in Germany between January and December 2011. This paper presents two case studies of analyzing French and Italian customer satisfaction data between January and December 2011.

Mobile Cloud is such a highly competitive area that services need to be constantly improved and prices should be reasonably adjusted (Marston et al., 2011; Dinh et al., 2011; Worldpanel ComTech, 2011; USwitch survey, 2011; Dinh et al., 2011; Qiang et al, 2012; Idongesit and Skouby, 2014). There are other mobile service providers offering Samsung, HTC, Sony and Nokia/Windows services that require further analysis. Future direction will focus on measuring and analyzing customer satisfaction for the following areas:

- Analysis of iPhone 4S for United Kingdom in 2011.
- Analysis of iPhone 5 and iPhone for United Kingdom in 2012 and 2013 respectively.
- Analysis of iPhone 5 and iPhone for Germany, France and Italy in 2012 and 2013.
- Analysis of Samsung high-end phones for United Kingdom, Germany, France and Italy in 2012 and 2013 respectively.
- Analysis of HTC, Sony and Nokia/ Windows Mobile Cloud services for United Kingdom, Germany, France, and Italy in 2012 and 2013 respectively.

We will work closely with consultancy firms that analyze the rate of customer satisfaction for Mobile Cloud services. Hypotheses will be set based on the observation of results and analysis. We will have more data and their interpretations to validate our first hypothesis: "H1. The rate of customer satisfaction in Mobile Cloud Services can reflect the recovery on economy" and we will use more varieties of phones and their services to validate. Currently, results in our analysis and interpretations in Section 4 and 5 support this hypothesis.

6.3 Comparisons with Similar Models

This section is focused on a comparison between OSM, CAPM and similar models, particularly the three models mentioned in Section 3.4. The reason to include them is because they proposed similar method years ago. We assert in Section 3.4 that all proposed frameworks or models should have the support from real-life case studies or demonstrations or both to make them justifiable for organizations for adoption. The criteria for comparison are explained as follows:

1. **Support Form Real Case Studies and Demonstrations:** Has been described earlier.
2. **Detail and Clarity of Using the Model/ Framework:** The proposed method should describe details about how to adopt and how to use. These should include what types of metrics, details in the data processing, what are the inputs and outputs and interpretation of results.
3. **Continuous Contributions to the Research Community:** This is different from point one. After the publication of their first or first few papers establishing their model/framework, the proposers should have continuous publication and regularly contribute new findings and improvements to their proposed method. Improvements should include any other areas such as the performance in data processing, improved technique, update from the first or first few papers and so forth.

Comparing OSM with the original models proposed by Weinhardt et al (2009), Klem et al (2009) and Sultant (2010), OSM is the model that has continuous contributions to the research community by publishing the improved technical performance, data processing, analysis of results. More importantly, there is strong support from case studies by Vodafone/ Apple, SAP, Universities of Southampton, Greenwich and Oxford, Leeds Metropolitan University, King's College London, and Guy's and St Thomas' NHS Trusts (GSTT), who have used Cloud Computing adoption and key metrics developed and recommended by OSM. This explains why Cloud Computing adoption should have strong support from real-life case studies and demonstrations. Other than OSM, Buyya et al (2009) have continuous contribution to the development of Cloud Computing projects and services. Table 3 shows similarities and differences between OSM and other methods.

Table 3. Comparisons between OSM and similar methods

Models and Criteria	Support from Real-Life Case Studies and Demonstrations	Detail and Clarity of Using the Model or Framework	Continuous Contributions to the Research Community
Weinhardt et al (2009)	The proposed method is a conceptual idea. It offers a generic recommendation. There is no any case study or demonstration based on this.	The proposed method is a conceptual idea and there is no detail about how to use and replicate their work.	They published three papers with similar content in 2009 and 2010. There is no any update since 2010.
Klem et al (2009)	The proposed method is a conceptual idea. It offers a generic recommendation. There is no any case study or demonstration based on this.	The proposed method is a conceptual idea and there is no detail about how to use and replicate their work.	They published three papers with similar content in 2009 and 2009. There is no any update since 2009.
Sultant (2010; 2014)	A case study was published in 2013 since his paper in 2010 (Sultan, 2014). Even so, that paper is about the investigation about how a NHS hospital uses Cloud Computing. It is not how the NHS hospital uses his model and makes positive impact.	The proposed method is a conceptual idea and discussions based on other people work before establishing his recommendation. There is no detail about how to use his model since they are all qualitative descriptions.	He published papers since 2010. Later on, there is an update in the case study in April 2014.
OSM (Chang et al. 2011 b; 2011 c; 2012 a; Chang 2013 a)	OSM has case studies for Vodafone/ Apple, SAP, Universities of Southampton, Greenwich and Oxford, Leeds Metropolitan University, King's College London, and Guy's and St Thomas' NHS Trusts.	Details have been presented. These include demonstrations in healthcare, finance, education and emerging areas.	Papers have been published to discuss the results, data processing, interpretation of analysis for continuous update and improvement.

7. CONCLUSION AND FUTURE WORK

Cloud computing is an emerging technology which promises to change the way organizations view their computing systems, as well as how consumers use and rate Cloud services. This includes Mobile Cloud industry, which is a competitive area. This paper presents the French and Italian data about the user satisfaction rate of using iPhone 4S Mobile Cloud services. French and Italian data have good consistency between all the values in the datasets and have medium-high uncontrolled risk. Figures in 3D Visualization can show whether there are spikes and bumps that need more investigation. This information is useful to the stakeholders to understand the status of risk and return. We also explain the use

of OSM in the data collection and analysis, and results computed by OSM. Results presented in this paper and our previous paper support the hypothesis that the rate of customer satisfaction in Mobile Cloud Services can reflect the recovery of the economy. We also compare OSM with other similar approaches. OSM and approaches proposed by Buyya et al (2009) can demonstrate continuous contributions to the research community. We also explain how to use OSM to analyze results and the results of good projects. Our future work includes the data analysis of other smart phone and their Cloud services in the United Kingdom, Germany, France, Italy and Spain, so that they can consolidate our hypotheses about the rate of customer satisfaction in Mobile Cloud Services in regard to the economic recovery in European countries.

REFERENCES

Anastaya. (2011). *Data analysis for mobile industry, white paper*. Author.

Barry, D. K. (2012). *Web services, service-oriented architectures, and cloud computing: The savvy manager's guide*. Newnes.

Buyya, R., Yeo, C. S., Venugopal, S., Broberg, J., & Brandic, I. (2009). Cloud computing and emerging IT platforms: Vision, hype, and reality for delivering computing as the 5th utility. *Future Generation Computer Systems*, *25*(6), 599–616. doi:10.1016/j.future.2008.12.001

Carr, P., & Madan, D. (1999). Option valuation using the fast Fourier transform. *Journal of Computational Finance, 2*(4), 61-73.

Cavailhes, J., Dessendre, C., Goffette-Nagot, F., Schmitt, B., & INRA-Dijon, . (1994). Change in the French countryside: Some analytical propositions. *European Review of Agriculture Economics*, *21*(3-4), 429–449. doi:10.1093/erae/21.3-4.429

Chang, V. (2013). *A proposed model to analyse risk and return for a large computing system adoption*. (PhD Thesis). University of Southampton.

Chang, V. (2014a). *Introduction to the risk visualization as a service*. Paper presented at the First International Workshop on Emerging Software as a Service and Analytics, Barcelona, Spain.

Chang, V. (2014b). An introductory approach to risk visualization as a service. *Open Journal of Cloud Computing*, *1*(1), 1–9.

Chang, V. (2014c). *The big data analysis for measuring popularity in the mobile cloud*. Paper presented at the First International Workshop on Emerging Software as a Service and Analytics, Barcelona, Spain.

Chang, V. (2014d). Measuring and analyzing German and Spanish customer satisfaction of using the iPhone 4S mobile cloud service. *Open Journal of Cloud Computing*, *1*(1), 19–26.

Chang, V., De Roure, D., Walters, R. J., Wills, G., & Barry, T. (2011b). Organisational sustainability modelling for return on investment: Case studies presented by a national health service (NHS) trust UK. *Journal of Computing and Information Technology*, *19*(3). doi:10.2498/cit.1001951

Chang, V., De Roure, D., Wills, G., & Walters, R. (2011c). Case studies and organisational sustainability modelling presented by cloud computing business framework. *International Journal of Web Services Research*, *8*(3), 26–53. doi:10.4018/JWSR.2011070102

Chang, V., Li, C. S., De Roure, D., Wills, G., Walters, R., & Chee, C. (2011a). The financial clouds review. *International Journal of Cloud Applications and Computing*, *1*(2), 41–63. doi:10.4018/ijcac.2011040104

Chang, V., Walters, R. J. & Wills, G. (2013a). Cloud storage and bioinformatics in a private cloud deployment: Lessons for data intensive research. In *Proceedings of Cloud Computing and Service Science* (LNCS). Berlin: Springer.

Chang, V., Walters, R. J. & Wills, G. (2013b). The development that leads to the cloud computing business framework. *International Journal of Information Management, 33*(3), 524-538.

Dinh, H. T., Lee, C., Niyato, D., & Wang, P. (2011). A survey of mobile cloud computing: architecture, applications, and approaches. *Wireless Communications and Mobile Computing*.

Durbin, J., & Watson, G. S. (1950). Testing for serial correlation in least squares regression: I. *Biometrika, 37*, 409–428. PMID:14801065

Eberlein, E., & Keller, U. (1995). Hyperbolic distributions in finance. *Bernoulli*, *1*(3), 281–299. doi:10.2307/3318481

Ganti, R. K., Ye, F., & Lei, H. (2011). Mobile crowdsensing: Current state and future challenges. *Communications Magazine, IEEE*, *49*(11), 32–39. doi:10.1109/MCOM.2011.6069707

Gentzoglanis, A. (2011). EVA and the cloud: An integrated approach to modelling of cloud computing. *International Journal of Modellling and Optimization*, *1*, 322–327.

Hallowell, R. (1996). The relationships of customer satisfaction, customer loyalty, and profitability: An empirical study. *International Journal of Service Industry Management*, *7*(4), 27–42. doi:10.1108/09564239610129931

Heskett, J. L., & Schlesinger, L. A. (1994). Putting the service-profit chain to work. *Harvard Business Review*, *72*(2), 164–174.

Hull, J. C. (2009). Options, futures, and other derivatives (7th ed.). Pearson, Prentice Hall.

Idongesit, W., & Skouby, K. E. (Eds.). (2014). *The African mobile story*. River Publishers.

Jampani, R., Xu, F., Wu, M., Perez, L. L., Jermaine, C., & Haas, P. J. (2008, June). MCDB: A Monte Carlo approach to managing uncertain data. In *Proceedings of the 2008 ACM SIGMOD International Conference on Management of Data* (pp. 687-700). ACM. doi:10.1145/1376616.1376686

Kantar Worldpanel ComTech. (2011). *Kantar worldpanel ComTech global consumer, white paper and VIP report*. Author.

Klems, M., Nimis, J., & Tai, S. (2009). Do clouds compute? A framework for estimating the value of cloud computing. In Designing e-business systems: Markets, services, and networks (pp. 110-123). Springer.

Lee, C. F., Lee, A. C., & Lee, J. (2010). *Handbook of quantitative finance and risk management*. Springer. doi:10.1007/978-0-387-77117-5

Longstaff, F. A., & Schwartz, E. S. (2001). Valuing American options by simulation: A simple least-squares approach. *Review of Financial Studies*, *14*(1), 113–147. doi:10.1093/rfs/14.1.113

Loshin, D. (2012). *Business intelligence: The savvy manager's guide*. Newnes.

Marston, S., Li, Z., Bandyopadhyay, S., Zhang, J., & Ghalsasi, A. (2011). Cloud computing—The business perspective. *Decision Support Systems*, *51*(1), 176–189. doi:10.1016/j.dss.2010.12.006

Qiang, C. Z., Yamamichi, M., Hausman, V., Altman, D., & Unit, I. S. (2011). *Mobile applications for the health sector*. Washington, DC: World Bank.

Rimal, B. P., Jukan, A., Katsaros, D., & Goeleven, Y. (2011). Architectural requirements for cloud computing systems: An enterprise cloud approach. *Journal of Grid Computing*, *9*(1), 3–26. doi:10.1007/s10723-010-9171-y

Rochwerger, B., Breitgand, D., Levy, E., Galis, A., Nagin, K., Llorente, I. M., & Galan, F. (2009). The reservoir model and architecture for open federated cloud computing. *IBM Journal of Research and Development*, *53*(4), 4–1. doi:10.1147/JRD.2009.5429058

Sharma, B., Thulasiram, R. K., Thulasiraman, P., Garg, S. K., & Buyya, R. (2012). Pricing cloud compute commodities: A novel financial economic model. In *Proceedings of the 2012 12th IEEE/ACM International Symposium on Cluster, Cloud and Grid Computing* (ccgrid 2012) (pp. 451-457). IEEE Computer Society. doi:10.1109/CCGrid.2012.126

Sharpe, W. F. (1990). *Capital asset prices with and without negative holdings*. Nobel-Prize Economics Lecture.

Sultan, N. (2010). Cloud computing for education: A new dawn? *International Journal of Information Management*, *30*(2), 109–116. doi:10.1016/j.ijinfomgt.2009.09.004

Sultan, N. (2014). Making use of cloud computing for healthcare provision: Opportunities and challenges. *International Journal of Information Management*, *34*(2), 177–184. doi:10.1016/j.ijinfomgt.2013.12.011

Teunis, P. F. M., & Havelaar, A. H. (2000). The beta poisson dose-response model is not a single-hit model. *Risk Analysis*, *20*(4), 513–520. doi:10.1111/0272-4332.204048 PMID:11051074

USwitch Survey. (2011). *USwitch's guide to mobile phones*. Author.

Weinhardt, C., Anandasivam, D. I. W. A., Blau, B., Borissov, D. I. N., Meinl, D. M. T., Michalk, D. I. W. W., & Stößer, J. (2009). Cloud computing–A classification, business models, and research directions. *Business & Information Systems Engineering*, *1*(5), 391–399. doi:10.1007/s12599-009-0071-2

KEY TERMS AND DEFINITIONS

3D Visualization: It is another service that can compute complex analysis in a way that the stakeholders can understand. The use of visualization can present the status of risk and return in a way that people without prior knowledge can understand.

Beta: It refers to the uncontrolled risk in Cloud adoption. The stakeholders must be able to know their values and devise the appropriate actions to lower and reduce beta. It can be computed through OSM analysis.

Cloud Computing Adoption for Organizations: This is an area to investigate why organizations adopt Cloud Computing and use it daily for their work. As closely related to the benefits of Cloud Computing adoption, some businesses use it to reduce the operational costs like CA technologies. Some organizations use it to allow the businesses to be more competitive since they can create virtual hardware much quicker, they can offer more types of services to customers, and they can integrate different types of services together. This area can also provide an in-depth study, since adoption depends on various factors apart from technical reasons. Organisational and financial reasons can motivate organizations for adoption. However, there are technical, financial and organizational risks which pose challenges for Cloud Computing adoption.

Cloud Computing: It consists of three major services: Infrastructure as a Service, Platform as a Service and Software as a Service and four main types of Clouds: Public Cloud, Private Cloud, Hybrid Cloud and Community Cloud. Cloud Computing is a technology-based (normally internet based) service that allows organizations to offer service delivery that supports the organizational IT strategy, design, transition, operation and continuous service improvement.

Customer Satisfaction Rate: It provides important results to the Mobile Cloud service providers. The higher the customer satisfaction rate, the more it can contribute to the success and profits of Cloud services on offer and their relative performance over their competitors.

Mobile Cloud: It is an emerging area that is one of the most profitable Cloud Computing services.

Organizational Sustainability Modeling (OSM): OSM is a method to analyze risk and return for Cloud Computing adoption. It helps organizations and stakeholders to understand the status and significance of their Cloud adoption with a comprehensive quantitative analysis.

R-Squared Values: They are used to determine whether the risks come from the external or internal sources.

Chapter 5
A Conceptual Model for Cloud Computing Adoption by SMEs in Australia

Ishan Senarathna
Deakin University, Australia

William Yeoh
Deakin University, Australia

Matthew Warren
Deakin University, Australia

Scott Salzman
Deakin University, Australia

ABSTRACT

Cloud Computing is an increasingly important worldwide development in business service provision. The business benefits of Cloud Computing usage include reduced IT overhead costs, greater flexibility of services, reduced TCO (Total Cost of Ownership), on-demand services, and improved productivity. As a result, Small and Medium-Sized Enterprises (SMEs) are increasingly adopting Cloud Computing technology because of these perceived benefits. The most economical deployment model in Cloud Computing is called the Public Cloud, which is especially suitable for SMEs because it provides almost immediate access to hardware resources and reduces their need to purchase an array of advanced hardware and software applications. The changes experienced in Cloud Computing adoption over the past decade are unprecedented and have raised important issues with regard to privacy, security, trust, and reliability. This chapter presents a conceptual model for Cloud Computing adoption by SMEs in Australia.

INTRODUCTION

Cloud Computing is an increasingly important area in the development of business services. Gartner Consulting defines Cloud Computing as "a style of computing in which scalable and elastic IT-enabled capabilities are delivered as a service using Internet technologies" (Plummer et al., 2009). Cloud Computing provides differ-ent types of services delivered under different deployment models on demand, and uses a pay-as-you-go method. Many developed countries are moving quickly to ensure the rapid adoption of Cloud Computing (Mudge, 2010).

In general, companies obtain Cloud Computing services (e.g. Software as a Service (SaaS)) from a Cloud Computing environment; they then have the opportunity to take advantage of new devel-

DOI: 10.4018/978-1-4666-8210-8.ch005

Copyright © 2015, IGI Global. Copying or distributing in print or electronic forms without written permission of IGI Global is prohibited.

opments in IT technologies at an affordable cost. Therefore, Cloud Computing is a cost effective IT solution which can benefit small, medium and larger organisations as well as governments and public services. For example, economies of scale for data centers (facilities used to house computer systems and associated components) can deliver cost savings of 5 to 7 times compared to typical total costs of computing (Armbrust *et al.*, 2010). Cloud Computing provides shared computing resources, software, storage and information on demand to Cloud Computing users.

"Cloud Computing" could potentially revolutionize the entire Information Communication Technology (ICT) industry (Tuncay, 2010). The actual size of the Cloud Computing market is unknown. WinterGreen Research (2010) estimated the global Cloud Computing markets at US$36 billion in 2008, and anticipated it would reach US$160.2 billion by 2015. Herhalt and Cochrane (2012) reported that the adoption of Cloud Computing in Australian organisations lagged behind the US levels by a year or more. A survey by Frost and Sullivan (2011) suggests that, in 2011, 43 per cent of businesses in Australia were using some form of cloud computing services, which was up from 35 per cent in 2010. In fact, the Australian Cloud Computing market is forecasted to reach US$3.33 billion in 2016 (Philsandberg, 2012).

SMEs play a critical role in any nation's economy as it is the fastest growing sector of most economies around the world and represents a high portion of all businesses and GDP (Paik, 2011). Similarly, SMEs in Australia account for 95 per cent of all businesses (MacGregor & Kartiwi, 2010). With considerably lower start-up costs, Cloud Computing benefits SMEs and reduces their need to purchase an expensive array of advanced hardware technology and software applications (Sultan, 2010; Chang 2013). Cloud Computing is a novel business model in terms of economy and flexibility, which is particularly valuable for SMEs, as Cloud Computing can be adopted with limited investment in infrastructure

(Mudge, 2010). Cloud Computing is commercially viable for many SMEs due to its flexibility and pay-as-you-go cost structure (Sultan, 2011), however, within the SME sector and despite potential benefits, the adoption rate of Cloud Computing is still relatively low in Australia compared to other countries in the Asian region (ACCA, 2012). This chapter presents a conceptual model for Cloud Computing adoption by SMEs in Australia. The issues of Cloud Computing adoption are explored within the chapter with the aim of identifying likely key factors that motivate or inhibit its use by SMEs. A further overarching research objective is to design and propose a model suitable for the adoption of Cloud Computing by SMEs in Australia by looking at the motivators and inhibitors of Cloud Computing adoption.

BACKGROUND

Cloud Computing Overview

Cloud Computing extends the current use of Information Technology as a service over the network, especially through the Internet (for instance, Software as a Service (SaaS), Platform as a Service (PaaS), and Infrastructure as a Service (IaaS). Its major goal is reducing the cost of IT services while increasing efficiency, flexibility, reliability, availability and processing. Cloud Computing has been defined differently by industry experts and researchers. So, the definition of Cloud Computing is also "Cloudy".

The National Institute of Standards and Technology (NIST) proposed a definition for Cloud Computing, "a model for enabling convenient, on demand network access to a shared pool of configurable computing resources (e.g., network, servers, storage, applications and services) that can be rapidly provisioned and released with minimal management effort or service provider interaction. This Cloud Computing model promotes availability and is composed of five essential characteristics and three service models and four deployment models" (Mell and Grance, 2011). In 1997, Cloud Computing was defined by Ramnath Chellapa as "a computing paradigm where the boundaries of computing will be determined by rationale rather than technical" (Chellappa, 1997). This was the first academic definition of Cloud Computing. According to Catteddu and Hogben (2009), Cloud Computing was defined by the European Network and Information Security Agency (ENISA) as an "on-demand service model for IT provision, often based on virtualisation and distributed computing technologies".

Another common academic definition of Cloud Computing was proposed by Buyya *et al.* (2009) as "a type of parallel and distributed system consisting of a collection of interconnected and virtualized computers that are dynamically provisioned and present as one or more unified computing resources based on service-level agreements established through negotiation between service provider and customer". Wang and Laszewski (2008) defined Cloud Computing as "a set of network enabled services, providing scalable, Quality of Service (QoS) guaranteed, normally personalized, inexpensive computing platforms on demand, which could be accessed in a simple and pervasive way". Luis *et al.* (2009) proposes the Cloud Computing definition as "a large pool of easily usable and accessible virtualized resources (such as hardware, development platforms and/or services). These resources can be dynamically reconfigured to adjust a variable load (scale), allowing also for an optimum resource utilization. This pool of resources is typically exploited by a pay-per-use model in which guarantees are offered by the infrastructure provider by means of customized SLAs". Founder of Oracle, Larry Ellison, says, "we've redefined Cloud Computing to include everything that we already do..." (Farber, 2008). Richard Stallman, founder of the Free Software Foundation and creator of the operating system GNU, says, "Cloud Computing was simply a trap aimed at forcing more people to buy into locked,

proprietary systems that would cost them more and more over time... it's stupidity. It's worse than stupidity: it's a marketing hype campaign" (Johnson, 2008). These different definitions showed that the different stakeholders, such as academicians, architects, consumers, developers, engineers and managers, consider Cloud Computing very differently (CSA, 2009).

Cloud Computing is being heavily promoted for mainstream adoption due to results of the latest advances in virtualisation technologies, combined with the acute realization of the increasing economic burden of maintaining proprietary IT infrastructures (Erdogmus, 2009). Cloud Computing is being perceived as a huge Internet data center in which hardware and software resources are virtualized, offering a variety of services to the customers. They use Cloud Computing from a service provider's pool of capacity and Cloud Computing infrastructure on a pay-as-you-go basis as an alternative to managing their own IT infrastructure (Lim *et al.*, 2009; Sultan, 2010). Cloud Computing offers benefits such as reduced IT overheads for the customers, greater flexibility, reduced TCO, on-demand services, and improved productivity (Wei *et al.*, 2009). According to Erdogmus (2009), economic benefits, simplification and convenience of the way computing services are delivered seem to be the key drivers to speed up the adoption of Cloud Computing. Farah (2010) highlights the Cloud Computing adoption as fast tracking cost reductions, increasing efficiency and, ultimately, creating a competitive advantage in any market.

There are many business areas where Cloud Computing has been adopted, including in higher education (Sultan, 2010; Wheeler and Waggener, 2009; Suess and Morooney, 2009), to provide solutions for human resources (Farah, 2010), software testing (Babcock, 2009), data back-up or archive services (Treese, 2008), Web 2.0 based collaborative applications (Orr, 2008), for storage capacity on demand (Kraska *et al.*, 2009), and for content distribution services (Fortino *et al.*, 2009). New IT approaches and services have taken advantage of Cloud Computing, for example, market-oriented allocation of resources (Buyya *et al.*, 2009), hard discrete optimization problems (Li *et al.*, 2009), corporate fraud detection using intelligence (Lodi *et al.*, 2009), collaborative business intelligence (Chow *et al.*, 2009), data mining algorithms and predictive analytics (Zeller *et al.*, 2009; Guazzelli *et al.*, 2009), software testing as a service (Ciortea *et al.*, 2009), e-government solutions (Cellary and Strykowski, 2009), and architecture and implementation courses at graduate level in Cloud Computing (Holden *et al.*, 2009).

Cloud Computing Services

Three service models are extensively used by the Cloud Computing community to categorize Cloud Computing services (Ahuja and Rolli, 2011; Dillon *et al.*, 2010; George and Shyam, 2010). Cloud Computing provides software (SaaS), platforms (PaaS), and infrastructure (IaaS) services on demand and pay-as-you-go. Software as a Service in Cloud Computing eliminates the need to install and run an application on the client's computer (Marston *et al.*, 2011). In addition, it is not necessary to worry about software licensing nor upgrading to latest versions. According to Sullivan (2010), there are various types of services that come under Software as a Service (SaaS), namely, Customer Relationship Management (CRM), Video Conferencing, IT Service Management, Accounting, Web Analytics, and Web Content Management etc. Similarly, Application Design, Development, Testing, Deployment, Hosting are services provided by Platform as a Service (PaaS). The development and deployment of applications without the cost and complexity of buying and managing the underlying hardware and software layers are facilitated by PaaS (Marston *et al.*, 2011). Further, Sullivan (2010) explains that Infrastructure as a Service (IaaS) provides services such as Server Space, Net Working (N/W) equipment, Memory, Storage Space and Computing Capabilities. Table 1 summarizes service models used in the Cloud Computing environment. The table describes

Table 1. Cloud computing service models

Services	Description
Software as a Service (SaaS)	Cloud Computing consumers release their applications in a hosting environment, which can be accessed through networks from various clients (e.g., Web browser, PDA, etc.) by application users. Cloud Computing consumers do not have control over the Cloud Computing infrastructure that often employs multi-tenancy system architecture to achieve economies of scale and optimization. Example applications of SaaS include SalesForce.com, Google Mail, Google Docs, and so forth.
Platform as a Service (PaaS)	PaaS is a development platform supporting the full "Software Lifecycle" which allows Cloud Computing consumers to develop Cloud Computing services and applications (e.g., SaaS) directly on the PaaS cloud. Hence, the difference between SaaS and PaaS is that SaaS only hosts completed Cloud Computing applications whereas PaaS offers a development platform that hosts both completed and in-progress Cloud Computing applications. An example application of PaaS is Google App Engine.
Infrastructure as a Service (IaaS)	Cloud Computing consumers directly use IT infrastructures (processing, storage, networks, and other fundamental computing resources) provided in the IaaS cloud. Virtualisation is extensively used in IaaS cloud in order to integrate/decompose physical resources in an ad hoc manner to meet growing or shrinking resource demand from Cloud Computing consumers. An example of IaaS is Amazon's EC2.
Data storage as a Service (DaaS)	The delivery of virtualized storage on demand becomes a separate Cloud Computing service – a data storage service. Note that DaaS could be seen as a special type of IaaS. The motivation is that on-site enterprise database systems are often tied to prohibitive upfront costs in dedicated servers, software licenses, post-delivery services, and in-house IT maintenance. DaaS allows consumers to pay for what they are actually using rather than the site license for the entire database. Examples of this kind of DaaS include Amazon S3, Google BigTable, and Apache HBase, etc.

(Adapted from Dillon *et al.*, 2010).

Table 2. Cloud computing deployment models

Deployments	Description
Public Cloud	The public cloud is used by the general public cloud consumers and the cloud service provider has the full ownership of the public cloud with its own policy, value, and profit, costing, and charging model. Many popular cloud services are public clouds including Amazon EC2, S3, Google AppEngine, and Force.com.
Private Cloud	The cloud infrastructure is operated solely within a single organisation, and managed by the organisation or a third party regardless whether it is located premise or off premise.
Hybrid Cloud	The cloud infrastructure is a combination of two or more clouds (private, community, or public) that remain unique entities but are bound together by standardized or proprietary technology that enables data and application portability.
Community Cloud	Several organisations jointly construct and share the same cloud infrastructure as well as policies, requirements, values, and concerns. The cloud community forms into a degree of economic scalability and democratic equilibrium. The cloud infrastructure could be hosted by a third-party vendor or within one of the organisations in the community.

(Adapted from Dillon *et al.*, 2010).

three main service models such as Software as a Service, Platform as a Service and Infrastructure as a Service. Some authors explain Database as a Service as a different service model, but it can be seen as a special type of service model under Infrastructure as a Service.

Cloud Computing Deployment Models

In reviewing the literature, services provided by Cloud Computing can be categorized according to the level of service and the way it is provided. Deployment models are recorded based on these characteristics. More recently, four Cloud Computing deployment models have been defined in the Cloud Computing community and are summarized in Table 2 (Dillon, *et al.*, 2010; Sasikala, 2011).

A public Cloud Computing service is available from a third-party service provider via the Internet. It is a cost-effective way to deploy IT solutions and provides many benefits such as being elastic and service-based. This is the commonly used model and is suitable especially for SMEs because it provides almost immediate access to hardware resources, with no upfront capital investments for users, leading to a faster time to market in many businesses. This treats IT as an operational expense

rather than a capital expense ('Opex' as opposed to a 'Capex' model) (Marston *et al.*, 2011). Private Cloud Computing provides greater control over the Cloud Computing infrastructure and can be managed within the organisation. Therefore, it is often suitable for large organisations as they are using larger installations (Marston *et al.*, 2011). Hybrid Cloud Computing is a combination of public and private Cloud Computing models which try to address the limitations of each (Zhang *et al.*, 2010). The community Cloud Computing infrastructure is controlled and shared by a group of organisations and supports a specific community that has shared concerns (e.g., mission, security requirements, policy, and compliance considerations) (Sasikala, 2011). According to Lawrence *et al.* (2010) the different business models are used in each deployment model differently.

Characteristics of Cloud Computing

Cloud Computing characteristics are more important to identify how Cloud Computing differs from information technology. These characteristics can be categorized into two - essential characteristics and common characteristics. According to Plummer *et al.* (2009), five essential characteristics of Cloud Computing were identified by NIST

Table 3. Cloud computing essential characteristics

Characteristics	Description
On-demand self-service	A consumer with an immediate need at a particular time slot can access computing resources (such as CPU time, network storage, software use, and so forth) in an automatic (i.e., convenient, self-serve) fashion without resorting to human interactions with providers of these resources.
Broad network access	These computing resources are delivered over the network (e.g., Internet) and used by various client applications with heterogeneous platforms (such as mobile phones, laptops, and PDAs) situated at a consumer's site.
Resource pooling	A Cloud Computing service provider's computing resources are 'pooled' together in an effort to serve multiple consumers using either the multi-tenancy or the virtualisation model, "with different physical and virtual resources dynamically assigned and reassigned according to consumer demand". The motivation for setting up such a pool-based computing paradigm lies in two important factors: economies of scale and specialization.
Rapid elasticity	For consumers, computing resources become immediate rather than persistent: there are no up-front commitments and contracts as they can use them to scale up whenever they want, and release them once they finish scaling down.
Measured service	Although computing resources are pooled and shared by multiple consumers (i.e., multi-tenancy), the Cloud Computing infrastructure is able to use appropriate mechanisms to measure the usage of these resources for each individual consumer through its metering capabilities.

(Adapted from Grance, 2010; Dillon *et al.*, 2010).

(National Institute of Standards and Technology) (Grance, 2010; Dillon *et al.*, 2010). The Cloud Computing essential characteristics are shown in Table 3. These five characteristics are crucial in a Cloud Computing environment.

Advantages of Cloud Computing

Cloud Computing offers a number of benefits to businesses based on its different deployment and delivery models (Voona and Venkantaratna, 2009; Buyya *et al.*, 2009; Miller, 2008; Catteddu and Hogben, 2009; Andrei and Jain, 2009; Sasikala 2011). The advantages of Cloud Computing are described in Table 4. These advantages vary based on the different deployment and delivery models.

Some Technical and Business Issues of Cloud Computing

As Cloud Computing is still in its infancy, current adoption is associated with numerous technical and business challenges. Table 5 describes some

of the issues such as the availability of a service, data confidentiality, data transfer bottlenecks, and legal jurisdiction.

Cloud Computing Adoption

Youseff *et al.* (2008) explored methods to foster rapid adoption of Cloud Computing by the scientific community. The adoption of Cloud Computing has been perceived differently by various prominent members of the computing community. For example, Microsoft did not originally foresee the trend toward Cloud Computing, which is being led by Amazon and Google (Cusumano, 2009). Even though many firms showed little early interest in Cloud Computing, with the maturation of virtualisation technology and the current almost explosive increase in interest in Cloud Computing, many firms are joining the Cloud Computing wave.

The Open Cloud Manifesto was signed by a group of 38 companies and academic organisations, calling for open standards in Cloud Computing (Merritt, 2009). This manifesto is an effort to promote common standards for Cloud Comput-

Table 4. Advantages of cloud computing

Advantages	Description
Cost-effectiveness	According to the literature, it is obvious that using Cloud Computing to run applications, systems, and IT infrastructure saves staff and financial resources.
Flexibility	Cloud Computing allows organisations to start a project quickly without worrying about upfront costs. Computing resources such as disk storage, CPU, and RAM can be added when needed. Therefore, a company could started on a small scale by purchasing necessary resources and added additional resources later.
Data safety	Organisations are able to purchase storage in data centres located thousands of miles away, increasing data safety in case of natural disasters or other factors. This strategy is very difficult to achieve with traditional off-site backup.
High availability	Cloud Computing providers such as Microsoft, Google, and Amazon have better resources to provide more up-time than almost any other organisations and companies do.
Ability to handle large amounts of data	Cloud Computing has a pay-for-use business model that allows academic institutions to analyze terabytes of data using distributed computing over hundreds of computers for a short-time cost.
Reduced costs	Cloud Computing technology is paid incrementally, saving organisations money.
Increased storage	Organisations can store more data than on private computer systems.
Highly automated	IT personnel need not to worry about keeping software up to date.
More mobility	Employees can access information wherever they are, rather than having to remain at their desks.
Allows IT to shift focus	No longer need to worry about constant server updates and other computing issues, and government organisations will be free to concentrate on innovation.

(Adapted from Yan, 2010).

ing in areas such as security, portability, interoperability, management, and monitoring. The National Institute of Standards and Technology is also working on Cloud Computing standards (NIST, 2009). If such standards are adopted by the majority of Cloud Computing vendors, it would make it easier to move applications from one Cloud Computing provider to another, which is currently not possible with some vendors, because of proprietary Cloud Computing applications. Although many major corporations, such as Advanced Micro Devices, Juniper, and IBM, along with the Open Cloud Consortium, are backing this manifesto, some major Cloud Computing partici-

Table 5. Technical and business issues of cloud computing

Issues	Description
Data confidentiality	Most academic libraries have open-access data. This issue can be solved by encrypting data before moving to the clouds. In addition, licensing terms can be negotiated with providers regarding data safety and confidentiality.
Data transfer bottlenecks	Accessing digital collections requires considerable network bandwidth, and digital collections are usually optimized for customer access. Moving huge amounts of data (e.g., preserving digital images, audios, videos, and data sets) to data centres can be scheduled during off hours (e.g., 1–5 a.m.), or data can be shipped on hard disks to the data centre.
Legal jurisdiction	Converting to Cloud Computing involves legal restraints. For example, there are legal restrictions prohibiting on the provider transmitting data outside of Australia without the prior approval of the agency (DFD, 2011b)(DFD, 2011b)(DFD, 2011b)(DFD, 2011b)(DFD, 2011b)(DFD, 2011b)(DFD, 2011b)(DFD, 2011b). Since Cloud Computing providers can be multi-national, it is imperative that such providers are aware of and abide by national regulations where they do business.

(Adapted from Yan, 2010).

pants, namely, Amazon, Microsoft, and Google, are conspicuously absent (Merritt, 2009). The Open Cloud Consortium, which includes Cisco Systems, Yahoo, and several academic partners, runs a Cloud Computing test bed and has developed Cloud Computing services benchmarks (Merritt, 2009). This movement toward Cloud Computing standards and the conspicuous absence of some major Cloud Computing providers appears to be a battle between some early major Cloud Computing participants to attempt to protect their initial market and the others that want to make Cloud Computing a more open, standardized technology. Such common standards could also make it easier and more affordable for potential Cloud Computing customers to participate in Cloud Computing. Cloud Computing providers, both existing and planned, have a vested interest in the future of Cloud Computing (Weiss, 2007).

There is currently widespread interest in Cloud Computing and the growth in the available options for using Cloud Computing. Low *et al.* (2011) found that Cloud Computing in the high-tech industry depends on the firm's technological, organisational and environmental contexts. There are many advantages, such as economy of scale and the availability of large computing resources (Greenberg *et al.*, 2008), ability to test their business plan quickly and increase business agility (Wang *et al.*, 2011). In addition, Cloud Computing providers can keep a very high level of availability, often with considerably less downtime than individual organisations (Greenberg *et al.*, 2008). Parthasarathy and Bhattacherjee (1998) and also Rogers (1962) found that when clients were displeased with a technology they had adopted, they tended to discontinue its use. Because of this issue, it is important for a Cloud Computing provider to maintain customer satisfaction to retain its clients. Maintaining customer satisfaction involves continuing to satisfy client needs, staying cost-competitive, maintaining system reliability and availability, and ensuring information security and confidentiality. One illustration of a process for

running a successful Cloud Computing organisation is given by Kaliski (2008). In describing how to promote a well-run Cloud Computing entity, Kaliski says that the Cloud Computing entity should run like a container ship or cruise liner, with standardized products, set costs, and non-interference with other customers' products. This model could appeal to cost-conscious, organized people. Various organisations are beginning to adopt Cloud Computing, ranging from individuals and small to larger organisations.

Although there is extensive current interest in Cloud Computing, there can be a gap between the promise of Cloud Computing and market adoption. Greenberg *et al.* (2008) anticipated that, while individuals are already adopting Cloud Computing for applications readily available, and small organisations will adopt Cloud Computing in the near term, it may take from fifteen to twenty years for larger corporations to convert to Cloud Computing. Aligning a company's technology and corporate strategy by addressing the needs of management, resource issues, and external factors improve organisational functioning (Chen *et al.*, 2008). Adopting Cloud Computing can meet the technology and corporate needs of smaller, resource poor organisations and individuals, while large organisations can afford to purchase and maintain their own large computing resources. As a result, larger organisations have less of an incentive to go to outside providers than do smaller organisations (SMEs) or individuals. An example of the gap between the potential and the actual are the recent survey results presented by Delahunty (2009), where the participant responses showed that eleven per cent of their firms currently use Cloud Computing for data and information storage, with another nineteen per cent considering using Cloud Computing. This leaves seventy per cent of the respondents showing little interest in Cloud Computing.

Even with the movement toward transitioning computing and storage applications to Cloud Computing, there are some applications that organisations are choosing not to. These applications are typically mission critical applications, which are expected to be retained by their owners rather than being transitioned to Cloud Computing (Greenberg *et al.*, 2008). These applications are retained in-house for reasons such as the criticality of response times or concerns about the inadvertent release of very sensitive information.

User training can further an organisation's adoption of Cloud Computing by making users more comfortable with using the technology (Marshall, 2008). The younger and more technology savvy workers may adopt Cloud Computing more easily than those who are technology averse. Even though some potential users adopt new technologies more rapidly than others, any user when faced with the ability to perform a job more easily, more completely, at lower cost, and faster, can find Cloud Computing attractive (Aljabre, 2012).

SMALL AND MEDIUM-SIZED ENTERPRISES (SMEs)

A number of definitions for SMEs exist, many coming from various governmental and official sources such as SME agencies, ministries, governmental institutions and national statistical institutions or bureaus around the world. The Australian Bureau of Statistics (ABS) defines a small business as having fewer than 19 employees, whereas micro businesses have fewer than 4 employees. Medium-sized enterprises are defined as businesses with from 20 to 199 employees (DIISR, 2011). For this study the following criteria (see Table 6) are considered to define the SMEs in Australia.

Some researchers have criticized these definitions for only using a simple quantitative criterion such as the number of employees (Brytting, 1999; Curran *et al.*, 1991). Van Hoorn (1979) proposed the five additional characteristics below to differentiate SMEs from larger firms, rather than considering only the number of employees:

1. A comparatively limited number of products, technologies and know-how;
2. Comparatively limited resources and capabilities;
3. Less-developed management systems, administrative procedures and techniques,
4. An unsystematic and informal management style;
5. Senior management positions held by either the founders of the firm and/or their relatives.

SMEs in Australia

SMEs account for 95 per cent of active businesses and employ 70 per cent of the nation's workforce (MacGregor and Kartiwi, 2010), thus, they are the major component of the Australian economy. Globally, SMEs make a substantial contribution to national economies and are estimated to account for 80 per cent of global economic growth. In Australia they contribute over 33 per cent of Australia's GDP (ASMEA, 2012). In other words, SMEs performs a critical role in the Australian economy, in particular, as suppliers to large firms, as customers of large firms, and as suppliers to end-user customers in their own right. Australia's SME sector plays a vital role in the new job venture creation, emerging export markets, sustainable

Table 6. SME definition

Micro Enterprises	Micro enterprises are enterprises with 0 to 4 employees.
Small Enterprises	Small enterprises are enterprises with 5 to 19 employees.
Medium-Sized Enterprises	Medium sized enterprises have greater than 20 and fewer than 199 employees.

(DIISR, 2011).

economic growth and business resilience (Wei, 2010). SMEs are also a significant customer segment for financial service providers (MacGregor and Kartiwi, 2010).

Australian SMEs use a wide range of ICT in their business operations with their use of Internet technologies. The Australian Communication and Media Authority reported that 94 per cent of SMEs in Australia were estimated to be connected to some form of Internet service (ACMA, 2010).

Cloud Computing Adoption in SMEs

Marks & Lozano (2010) proposed a Cloud Computing Reference Model that supports major business drivers. It consists of four supporting models such as Cloud Enablement Model, Cloud Deployment Model, Cloud Governance Model and Cloud Ecosystem Model. The Cloud Enablement Model describes different tiers of cloud services from them Cloud business tier that can be selected according to the user's business necessity. This Cloud Computing Reference Model corroborates the ideas of Surendro & Fardani (2012), who identifies the needs of SMEs. According to their survey carried out in Indonesia on IT needs and readiness to adopt Cloud Computing technologies, SaaS is the paramount business necessity of SMEs which is covered under Cloud Enablement Model. Further, this survey reveals that, type of cloud computing deployment that best fits the characteristics and needs of SMEs is the Public Cloud. However, such explanations tend to awkward with the Cloud Adoption Reference Model (CARM) introduced by Keung & Kwok (2012) as it completely based on confidential data.

Carr (2005) suggests that, in many instances, using Cloud Computing might provide the first opportunity for SMEs to try new software approaches in a cost effective manner. Often SMEs are unable to afford their own dedicated IT but have a sufficient IT budget to buy the

bandwidth and pay according to their need and usage (Monika *et al.*, 2010). In a Cloud Computing environment, SMEs can reduce their capital expenditure for IT infrastructure and, instead, utilize and pay for the resources and services provided by Cloud Computing (Rittinghouse and Ransome, 2009).

As previously explained, there are various types of business models related to Cloud Computing adoption, and their application depends on the nature and size of an enterprise (Handler *et al.*, 2012; Rahimli, 2013). Chang *et al.* in 2013 mentioned that a number of SMEs have followed the classification of the appropriate business models and even adopted a combination of different business models to improve performance of their businesses. According to Lawrence *et al.*, (2010), all direct and indirect go-to-market models in Cloud Computing are able to cater for SMEs needs, however, they are not necessarily suitable for large enterprises because of their scale and complexity. It has been found that the current charging pattern and other aspects of Cloud Computing make it more suitable for SMEs than for larger organisations (Misra and Mondal, 2010). Further, the public Cloud service provides a more valuable service to Micro-Small Businesses (non-employer business and with 1-4 employees) as they require many of the same business services provided to large organizations even though they may have only a PC and an Internet connection (Handler *et al*, 2012).

In addition, the findings of Sultan (2011) and Bharadwaj & Lal (2012) suggest that Cloud Computing is likely to be a more attractive option for most SMEs because of flexible cost structures and scalability. Traditional in-house Enterprise Resource Planning (ERP) implementation incurs high costs for SMEs, whereas, by using the Cloud they can buy ERP components relevant to their business and pay per component instead of buying a whole ERP suite (Sharif, 2010). Findings also show that SMEs can expand their usage and services easily using Cloud Computing. The Cloud services are more acceptable by SMEs because of relative advantage, flexibility and scalability features (Salleh *et al.*, 2012). In 2009, Gorniak demonstrated the first three reasons behind the possible use of cloud computing by SMEs is: 1) avoiding capital expenditure in hardware, software and IT support, information security by outsourcing infrastructure / platforms / services; 2) flexibility and scalability of IT resources; and 3) business continuity and disaster recovery capabilities. The prior Cloud Computing constructs previously identified were analyzed against the requirements of the different SMEs types (Table 7). The factors affecting Cloud Computing adoption is investigated separately for micro, small, and medium enterprises filling the research gap identified from the literature with micro organizations.

CONCEPTUAL MODEL

Cloud Computing provides different services which are delivered under various deployment models on demand, and uses a pay-as-you-go method. Several leading researchers in Cloud Computing domain attempt to develop Cloud Computing Business models (Papazoglou and Georgakopoulos, 2003; IBM, 2008; Hanna *et al.*, 2009; Chen *et al.*, 2010; Li, 2010; Chang *et al.*, 2013). In the design of a Cloud Computing adoption model, it is necessary to understand the differences between technology adoption and Cloud Computing adoption. Rather than directly applying the Technological, Organisation and Environment (TOE) framework in Cloud Computing adoption, Cloud Computing provides a complete service-based environment for SMEs.

Table 7. Analysis of cloud computing constructs in the SME context

Construct	Size of SME	References
Cloud Security	Micro	
	Small	(Sahandi *et al.*, 2012; Kelly, 2011; Monika *et al.*, 2010)
	Medium	(Sahandi *et al.*, 2012; Kelly, 2011; Monika *et al.*, 2010)
Cloud Privacy	Micro	
	Small	(Sahandi *et al.*, 2012)
	Medium	(Sahandi *et al.*, 2012)
Cloud Flexibility	Micro	
	Small	(Brian *et al.*, 2008; Sahandi *et al.*, 2012; Monika *et al.*, 2010; Salleh *et al.*, 2012)
	Medium	(Brian *et al.*, 2008; Sahandi *et al.*, 2012; Monika *et al.*, 2010; Salleh *et al.*, 2012)
Relative Advantage	Micro	(Handler *et al.*, 2012)
	Small	(Salleh *et al.*, 2012; Monika *et al.*, 2010)
	Medium	(Salleh *et al.*, 2012; Monika *et al.*, 2010)
Awareness of Cloud	Micro	(Handler *et al.*, 2012; Rath *et al.*, 2012)
	Small	(Rath *et al.*, 2012; Salleh *et al.*, 2012; Surendro & Fardani, 2012)
	Medium	(Rath *et al.*, 2012; Surendro & Fardani, 2012)
Quality of Service	Micro	
	Small	(Brian *et al.*, 2008; Keung & Kwok, 2012; Monika *et al.*, 2010; Salleh *et al.*, 2012)
	Medium	(Brian *et al.*, 2008; Keung & Kwok, 2012; Monika *et al.*, 2010; Salleh *et al.*, 2012; Chang *et al.*, 2013)

Various researchers indicate that adopting Cloud Computing includes expectations of the quality of service provided by Cloud service providers, such as availability, reliability and ongoing updating services (ITIIC, 2011). Therefore, the process is more important for SMEs than just the environmental factors considered in most of the technology/Cloud adoption models under the TOE framework. Thus, the proposed model is a variation of the TOE framework in regard to SME Cloud Computing adoption. This framework is considered to be a Technology, Organisation and Process (TOP) framework. The TOP multiple-perspectives approach can be used to best describe the factors influencing Cloud Computing adoption. A multiple perspectives method can be applied to any phenomenon, sub-system or system to analyze a problem in different ways (ASMEA, 2012). Linstone (2005) and Mitroff and Linstone

(2012) have used it to demonstrate the different ways of looking at a TOP model. Figure 1 presents the conceptual model.

The proposed conceptual model constitutes adoption factors under the technology, organisation and process contexts. Cloud security, Cloud privacy and Cloud flexibility are considered under the technology context. The organisational context includes relative advantages and awareness of Cloud Computing. The quality of service (QoS) of the Cloud is considered under the process context.

The biggest challenge with the security of Cloud Computing is the delegation of the confidentiality, availability and integrity of data to a third party. The security of Cloud Computing is complicated because of the multi-tenancy of the virtualized resources (Opala, 2012), and is one of the concerns about Cloud Computing that is delaying its adoption (Jamwal *et al.*, 2011).

Figure 1. Conceptual model for adoption of cloud computing for Australian SMEs

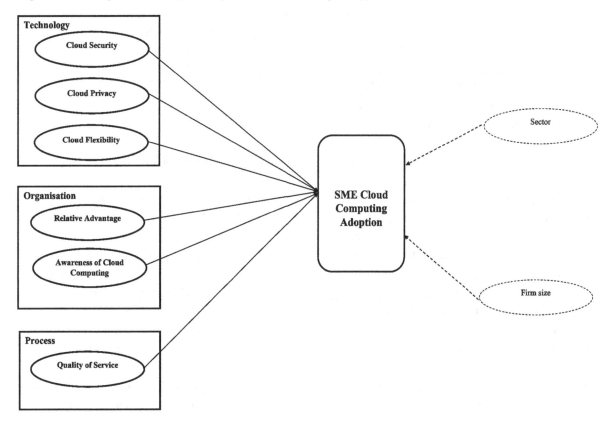

Further, privacy is also a leading reason for not adopting cloud solutions Pearson (2009). According to Pearson (2009), poor user control, loss of trustworthiness and lack of transparency create most of the privacy issues. In addition, lack of transparency creates legal issues that are caused by the Cloud's physical location which creates difficulties in determining its jurisdiction. Because of this key issue, the Australian government is extremely concerned about the location of outsourced personal data storage and there is a strong desire for Cloud services to be only located within Australia's borders (Hutley, 2012). Frequently, SMEs are not able to invest large amounts in IT infrastructure (Foster, Zhao, Raicu, & Lu, 2008) compared to larger organisations. However, a KPMG report (2009) on Australian lessons and experiences, shows that using Cloud Computing allows them to adopt innovative IT technologies quickly without paying upfront for capital investment (McCabe & Hancook, 2009). Further, Cloud Computing provides greater flexibility to encompass the innovations of the Australian government and industry (Mudge, 2010).

Dong *et al.* (2009) highlight the Cloud's ability to reduce costs, provide more flexibility, reduce development time, and allow for scalability and centralized data storage as some of the more significant gains in Cloud adoption. The Australian government traces the key drivers as, value for money for organisations adopting Cloud Computing, such as reductions in duplication and costs, leveraging economies of scale, increased savings through virtualisation, pay-as-you-use and, reduced energy use (DFD, 2011a). Further, with the characteristics of scalability and elasticity of services in the Cloud, relative advantages are more easily achieved. The Information Technology Industry Innovation Council (ITIIC) in Australia has published information on the importance of educating Australian business and consumers on how best to harness the benefits and manage the potential risks of adopting Cloud Computing solutions (ITIIC, 2011). They indicate that knowledge about Cloud Computing and its benefits for SMEs could be increased among the Australian business community; and similar statistics are indicated in the readiness index published by the Asia Cloud Computing Association (ACCA, 2012).

Previous studies have found that Cloud Computing is a service process where availability and reliability are coupled with ongoing service updates (ITIIC, 2011; Lippert & Govindarajulu, 2006)). Armbrust *et al.* (2010) have identified that business continuity and service availability are significant factors in considering Cloud adoption. Reliability is another thought-provoking feature of Cloud adoption. One of the most welcome characteristics of Cloud Computing compared with traditional IT provision, are the ongoing service updates. The debate continues on the QoS as an important characteristic in Cloud adoption with its combination of availability, reliability and ongoing service updates.

The constructs used to examine Cloud Computing adoption in this study are explored in Table 8. Based on the literature, six major adoption factors are identified for this study, namely: Cloud security, Cloud privacy, Cloud flexibility, relative advantages of Cloud, awareness of Cloud, and quality of service. These constructs are analyzed using theoretical, practitioner and government underpinnings.

RESEARCH APPROACH

Accurate methodological assumptions lead to the identification of research methods and techniques that are considered to be appropriate for the gathering of valid empirical evidence. Therefore, the cornerstone for undertaking successful research study depends on making the correct methodological assumptions (Myers & Avison, 2002). Correct assumptions shape "how we conduct research and how we use the results...the science that seeks to understand the underlying assumptions associated with different approaches is called the philosophy of science" (Polonsky & Waller, 2011, p. 4).

Table 8. Constructs used to examine cloud computing adoption (developed for this study)

Constructs	Academic	Government	Practitioner
Cloud Security	(Anthes, 2010; Behl, 2011; Bhayal, 2011; Jamwal et al., 2011; Krautheim, 2010; Lippert & Govindarajulu, 2006; Mahmood, 2011; Nir, 2010; Opala, 2012; Rittinghouse & Ransome, 2009; Ross, 2010; Sahandi et al., 2012; Sarwar & Khan, 2013; Subashini & Kavitha, 2011; Sultan, 2011; Wei et al., 2009; Yoon, 2009; Zhang et al., 2010)	(Anthony, 2012; DFD, 2011b, 2011c; ITIIC, 2011; Mudge, 2010; Sullivan, 2010)	(Carlin & Curran, 2011; Chakraborty, Ramireddy, Raghu, & Rao, 2010; Dave, 2012; Friedman & West, 2010; Herhalt & Cochrane, 2012; Hutley, 2012; Joanna & Chiemi, 2010; Kelly, 2011; Martin, 2010; McCabe & Hancook, 2009; Mudge, 2010)
Cloud Privacy	(Abadi, 2009; Grobauer et al., 2011; Jamwal et al., 2011; Katzan, 2010; Mark, 2011; Pearson, 2013; Sahandi et al., 2012; Sarwar & Khan, 2013; Sultan, 2010; Svantesson & Clarke, 2010; Tancock et al., 2013)	(Anthony, 2012; DFD, 2011b, 2011c; IMO, 2013)	(Friedman & West, 2010; Pearson, 2012);(Hutley, 2012; Wijesiri, 2010)
Cloud Flexibility	(MacGregor & Kartiwi, 2010; Marian & Hamburg, 2012; Marston et al., 2011; Mvelase et al., 2011; Opala, 2012; Son & Lee, 2011; Sultan, 2010; Wu, 2011)	(DFD, 2011a, 2011b; ITIIC, 2011; Sullivan, 2010)	(Herhalt & Cochrane, 2012; Joanna & Chiemi, 2010; McCabe & Hancook, 2009; Mudge, 2010; Ning, 2013)
Relative Advantage	(Cragg & King, 1993; Dong et al., 2009; George & Shyam, 2010; Kerr & Bryant, 2009; Lee, 2004; Li et al., 2011; Low, Chen, & Wu, 2011; Marston et al., 2011; Moghavvemi et al., 2012; Molla et al., 2006; Oliveira & Martins, 2011; Rogers, 2003; Shareef et al., 2011; Son & Lee, 2011; Thong, 1999; Tweel, 2012; Yang & Yoo, 2004; Yoon, 2009)	(DFD, 2011a; ITIIC, 2011)	(Herhalt & Cochrane, 2012; Hutley, 2012; McCabe & Hancook, 2009)
Awareness of Cloud	(Moghavvemi et al., 2012; Opala, 2012; Alshamaila et al., 2009; Shareef et al., 2011; Singh et al., 2013 ; Zhang et al., 2010)	(Anthony, 2012; ITIIC, 2011; Sullivan, 2010)	(ACCA, 2012; Hutley, 2012; Kelly, 2011; Martin, 2010; Ning, 2013; Pearson, 2012)
Quality of Service (QoS)	(Armbrust et al., 2010; Habib et al., 2012; Hailu, 2012; Lippert & Govindarajulu, 2006; Ross, 2010; Sarwar & Khan, 2013; Uusitalo et al., 2010; Wang et al. 2011)	(DFD, 2011a; ITIIC, 2011)	(Herhalt & Cochrane, 2012; Hutley, 2012; McCabe & Hancook, 2009; Scott, 1987; Wu & Chen, 2005)

Swanson and Holton (2005) suggest that "Quantitative research can be exploratory; it is used to discover relationships, interpretations, and characteristics of subjects, which suggest new theory and define new problems" (Swanson and Holton, 2005, p. 33). A considerable amount of literature has shown that the quantitative survey method can be used effectively to evaluate the acceptance of new technologies (Flick, 2009; Jahangir and Begum, 2007; Lease, 2005). A quantitative research method will therefore be applied in this research. The survey method is chosen as an efficient way to reach larger numbers of SMEs quickly, while protecting their anonymity. A longitudinal design would not have been appropriate to answer the research questions in a timely manner since such research requires years to complete. Interviews and direct observations would have been costly, difficult to schedule and time-consuming. An in-depth examination of previous research found that quantitative survey methodology had been successfully applied within each research study.

There are three phases in the research design. In phase one, academic and practitioner literature on technology adoption, Cloud Computing and SMEs will be studied to identify the key factors for successful Cloud Computing adoption by SMEs. In phase two, a structured questionnaire will be used to collect the quantitative data from Australian SMEs. A questionnaire is the major instrument to be designed for a survey to collect data from SMEs. Data analysis, model verification and modifications will be conducted in phase three.

DATA COLLECTION AND ANALYSIS

Quantitative research is most often used in studies with clearly-stated hypotheses that can be tested. It focuses on well-defined studies. A quantitative method discusses the problem from a broader perspective, often by providing a survey with specific answer alternatives (Merriam, 1998). Further the most of the cloud business models and frameworks proposed by leading researchers are quantitative (Armbrust *et al.*, 2010, Brandic *et al.*, 2009 and Buyya *et al.*, 2009). Therefore, it was decided that the best method to adopt for this investigation is surveys and this research will be performed using a survey data collection method and data will be collected by IT managers or decision-makers in the IT sections of selected SMEs.

Online surveys have numerous strengths compared to other survey methods (Evans & Mathur, 2005). The method is quite flexible as surveys can be conducted in several formats such as by e-mail with a link to a survey URL, or by e-mail with an embedded survey etc. Online surveys can be administered in a timely manner, minimizing the time taken in the field and for data collection (Kannan *et al.*, 1998). As a result of self-administered surveys, costs can also be kept down as postage or interviews are not required (Evans & Mathur, 2005). Further, the online surveys can use larger samples. The Australian Communications and Media Authority reported that 94 per cent of SMEs are estimated to be connected to some form of internet service (ACMA, 2010). With this high level of Internet usage by SMEs, an online survey tool is considered to be the best choice to collect data for this study, especially in Australia.

The most frequently-used ordered scale in survey instruments is a ranked one-to-five Likert type scale. However, this scale suffers some limitations. With only five points, two at the extreme ends and one midpoint, the scale suffers its own bounded parameters. Many respondents are reluctant to select extreme values, which leads to a restricted set of scores and making it difficult to measure differences. The seven-point Likert type scale avoids the limitations of the five-point scale and provides more flexibility such as a larger array of options (Carey, 2010). Therefore, an online survey questionnaire with a seven-point scale will be administered in Australia, to collect data for the study. The population for this study will be SMEs in Australia. The questionnaire has been pilot tested with 30 samples in an effort to assist in validating the questionnaire design. This pilot survey was developed by framing relevant questions under each of the six core variables identified from the literature survey. The questionnaire was divided into two parts. The first part of the survey captured the demographic details of the responding organisations and the second part of the survey captured perception of the security, privacy, relative advantage, quality of service of the Cloud Computing and the awareness of Cloud Computing. For each construct, three to six questions were formulated capturing the perception and adoption of Cloud Computing by SMEs. All of the reflective indicators of a construct were measured on a 7-point Likert scale using scales from "strongly disagree" to "strongly agree". Table

Table 9. Demographic characteristics of responding organisations

Survey (*n*=30)	Participants	Organisations
No. of Employees		
0 to 4 (micro)	18	60%
5 to 19 (small)	7	23%
20 to 199 (medium)	5	17%
State/Territory		
VIC	8	27%
NSW	7	23%
QLD	8	27%
WA	1	3%
SA	4	13%
TAS	2	7%
Use of Cloud Computing		
Yes	10	33%
No	20	67%

9 summarizes the demographic characteristics of responded organisations. The results show that 60% of organisations that responded were micro, 23% small, and 17% medium. Not surprisingly, states with larger populations provided higher response rates. Of the 30 organisations that responded, only 33% indicated that they were using some form of Cloud Computing.

Descriptive statistics are used to summarize the basic features of data. These summary measures include measurements expressing location, and dispersion. Relevant visualizations techniques will also be presented. With descriptive analysis, the raw data is transformed into a form that will make it easy to understand and interpret (Zikmund, 1994).

The reliability of the measurements have been verified using the Cronbach's alpha coefficient. The constructs are considered adequate when the Cronbach's alpha values are above the recommended value of 0.7 (Hair *et al.*, 2010; Malhotra, 2010). As shown in Table 10, Cronbach's alpha values exceed 0.7 for all constructs. Therefore, the questionnaire was taken as an acceptable instrument to be administered.

Factor analysis is commonly used in education (Hogarty *et al.*, 2005) and is considered an appropriate method for interpreting self-reporting questionnaires (Byrant *et al.*, 1999). Factor analysis is a multivariate statistical analysis method that has been used for many purposes, such as: reducing a larger number of variables into a smaller set of variables or factors; establishing dimensions between variables and latent constructs allowing formation and refinement of the theory; providing construct validity for self-reporting scales or instrument; addressing multicollinearity; developing theoretical constructs; and providing or disproving proposed theories (Tabachnick & Fidell, 2007). Exploratory factor analysis allows researchers to explore the main dimensions to generate a model from a relatively large set of latent constructs represented by a set of items (Swisher *et al.*, 2004). The aim of this study is to explore the large set of items and to generate a model for the adoption of Cloud Computing by SMEs. Exploratory factor analysis, therefore, will be performed as a multivariate analysis technique.

Regression Analysis is used to predict the value of a variable (dependent) based on the value of two or more other variables (independent). It is necessary to identify the influencing factors for Cloud adoption before developing an adoption model. Therefore, the results of the factor analysis will be used for regression analysis and variance tests. Further, most of previous Cloud adoption studies have based their analysis method on multiple regression

Table 10. Reliability validation

Overview	Cronbach's Alpha
Security	0.771
Privacy	0.733
Flexibility	0.722
Relative Advantage	0.754
Awareness	0.729
Quality of Service	0.819
Adoption	0.866

(Rahimli, 2013; Gupta *et al.*, 2013). It is therefore proposed that multiple regression be used to gain insight into the nature of the relationship between the independent variables and a dependent variable. The independent variables (factors) of this study are Cloud security, Cloud privacy, Cloud flexibility, relative advantage, awareness of Cloud Computing and quality of service of Cloud Computing. Cloud Computing adoption is the dependent variable of this study and is measured based on level of usage of Cloud Computing by SMEs.

SOLUTIONS AND RECOMMENDATIONS

This preliminary pilot-study set out with the aim of discovering the importance of enablers and inhibitors of Cloud Computing adoption in SMEs in Australia and develop a model for Cloud Computing adoption. The results indicate that the majority of SMEs are micro organisations and that they are situated in Victoria, Queensland and New South Wales. Results reveal that the Cloud Computing usage by the SME sector is comparatively less than other sectors, and that this observations needs to be investigated further. Considerably more work will need to be done to determine the enabling and inhibiting factors affecting Cloud Computing adoption in SMEs. Statistics reveal that there is a growing level of interest in Cloud adoption in Australia (Anthony, 2012). Hence, designing a more attractive adoption model is necessary for addressing the difficulties faced by SMEs in Australia.

FUTURE RESEARCH DIRECTIONS

The scope of this research will be limited to Australian SMEs. This can be expanded to other countries in the future. The research will be undertaken targeting a specific Cloud Computing deployment method known as Public Cloud Computing.

Studies could be done using other deployment methods as well. Many variables are available that can influence adoption decisions on Cloud Computing, but some of them are more important than others. This study, therefore, evaluates a few of the important factors but future studies could develop this study framework with other variables as well. Cloud Computing is a dynamic operational model, so influencing factors considered in this study may vary in future situations.

CONCLUSION

The literature indicates that the main inhibiting factor for Cloud Computing adoption is the fear of dispatching organisational data to a third party. It also indicates that Public Cloud Computing is more economical when compared to private Cloud Computing, and that all business models can be used in Public Clouds. In general therefore, it appears to be more beneficial for SMEs compared to larger organisations to adopt a Public Cloud Computing model, as it can provide them with a relatively better economic solution. Further, previous findings suggest that Cloud Computing adoption is more than just technology adoption. It includes a number of important changes such as cross-border data transfer, keeping data with a third party, remotely accessing resources and applications through the Internet and so on, which will need to be made when considering Cloud Computing adoption, but they do not necessarily apply to IT adoption. Furthermore, it is interesting to note that IT adoption mainly refers to in-house IT infrastructure, however, Cloud Computing adoption includes accessing resources outside the organisation through the Internet as a service. The research will be targeting a specific Cloud Computing deployment method known as Public Cloud Computing. The proposed model will be useful in a variety of countries exhibiting a range of economic settings as this is intended to be a generic Cloud adoption model for SMEs.

This research makes a number of contributions to research and practice. This study extends the current understanding of Cloud Computing adoption by SMEs (micro, small and medium enterprises) using a technology-based service adoption framework. The conceptual framework has been developed through the synthesis of a critical literature review for investigating Cloud Computing adoption by SMEs. Therefore, it bridges the research gap and contributes to the Cloud Computing adoption literature, especially in the context of SMEs. The study offers a view from the perspective of the process factors, in addition to the organisational and technical factors, to assess Cloud Computing adoption. On a practical front, these research findings offer insights for SMEs that are planning or are in the process of implementing a review of their Cloud Computing initiatives. Service providers can also use the model to understand the requirements of SMEs in their provision of the service. Further, it will be beneficial for consulting companies that are assisting SMEs with Cloud Computing implementation. In addition, the government could use the Cloud Computing model to assist with developing awareness, support programs and policies for SMEs.

REFERENCES

ACCA. (2012). *Cloud readiness index 2012*. Asia Cloud Computing Association.

ACMA. (2010). Australia in the digital economy: The shift to the online environment. *Communication Reports*, 2009–2010.

Ahuja, S. P., & Rolli, A. C. (2011). Survey of the state-of-the-art of cloud computing. *International Journal of Cloud Applications and Computing*, *1*(4), 34–43. doi:10.4018/ijcac.2011100103

Aljabre, A. (2012). Cloud computing for increased business value. *International Journal of Business and Social Science*, *3*(1), 234–240.

Andrei, T., & Jain, R. (2009). *Cloud computing challenges and related security issues: A survey paper*. Retrieved from http://www.cse.wustl.edu/~jain/cse571-09/ftp/cloud.pdf

Anthes, G. (2010). Security in the cloud. *Communications of the ACM*, *53*(11), 16–18. doi:10.1145/1839676.1839683

Anthony, B. (2012). *Forecast: Cloudy but fine: Privacy risks and potential benefits in the cloud*. Privacy Victoria - Office of the Victorian Privacy Commissioner.

Armbrust, M., Fox, A., Griffith, R., Joseph, A. D., Katz, R., Konwinski, A., & Zaharia, M. (2010). A view of cloud computing. *Communications of the ACM*, *53*(4), 50–58. doi:10.1145/1721654.1721672

ASMEA. (2012). *SME facts*. Retrieved from http://www.asmea.org.au/SMEFacts

Babcock, C. (2009). Ready for this? *Information Week*, *1250*, 22–30.

Behl, A. (2011). *Emerging security challenges in cloud computing*. WICT.

Bharadwaj, S. S., & Lal, P. (2012). *Exploring the impact of cloud computing adoption on organizational flexibility: A client perspective*. Paper presented at the International Conference on Cloud Computing Technologies, Applications and Management (ICCCTAM 2012). doi:10.1109/ICCCTAM.2012.6488085

Bhayal, S. (2011). *A study of security in cloud computing*. (PhD. Dissertation). Retrieved from ProQuest Dissertations and Theses. (UMI No: 1504430).

Brandic, I., Music, D., Leitner, P., & Dustdar, S. (2009). *VieSLAF framework: Enabling adaptive and versatile SLA-management*. Paper presented at the 6th International Workshop on Grid Economics and Business Models, Delft, The Netherlands.

Brian, H., Brunschwiler, T., Dill, H., Christ, H., Falsafi, B., Fischer, M., & Gutmann, R. (2008). Cloud computing. *Communications of the ACM*, *51*(7), 9–11. doi:10.1145/1364782.1364786

Brytting, T. (1999). *Organizing in the small growing firm: A grounded theory approach*. Stockholm School of Economics.

Buyya, R., Yeo, C. S., & Venugopal, S. (2009). *Market-oriented cloud computing: Vision, hype, and reality of delivering IT services as computing utilities*. Paper presented at the 10th IEEE International Conference on High Performance Computing and Communications.

Buyya, R., Yeo, C. S., Venugopal, S., Broberg, J., & Brandic, I. (2009). Cloud computing and emerging IT platforms: Vision, hype, and reality for delivering computing as the 5th utility. *Future Generation Computer Systems*, *25*(6), 599–616. doi:10.1016/j.future.2008.12.001

Byrant, F. B., Yarnold, P. R., & Michelson, E. (1999). Statistical methodology: Using confirmatory factor analysis (CFA) in emergency medicine research. *Academic Emergency Medicine*, *6*(1), 54–66. doi:10.1111/j.1553-2712.1999.tb00096.x PMID:9928978

Carey, V.A. (2010). *Questionnaire design for business research*. Academic Press.

Carlin, S., & Curran, K. (2011). Cloud computing security. *International Journal of Ambient Computing and Intelligence*, *3*(1), 14–19. doi:10.4018/jaci.2011010102

Carr, N. G. (2005). The end of corporate computing. *MIT Sloan Management Review*, *46*(3), 67–73.

Catteddu, D., & Hogben, G. (2009). *Cloud computing - Benefits, risks and recommendations for information security*. ENISA.

Cellary, W., & Strykowski, S. (2009). *E-government based on cloud computing and serviceoriented architecture*. Paper presented at the 3rd International Conference on Theory and Practice of Electronic Governance (ICEGOV '09), Bogota, Colombia. doi:10.1145/1693042.1693045

Chakraborty, R., Ramireddy, S., Raghu, T. S., & Rao, H. R. (2010). The information assurance practices of cloud computing vendors. *IT Professional*, *12*(4), 29–37. doi:10.1109/MITP.2010.44

Chang, V. (2013). Business integration as a service: Computational risk analysis for small and medium enterprises adopting SAP. *International Journal of Next-Generation Computing*, *4*(3).

Chang, V., Walters, R. J., & Wills, G. (2013). The development that leads to the cloud computing business framework. *International Journal of Information Management*, *33*(3), 524–538. doi:10.1016/j.ijinfomgt.2013.01.005

Chellappa, R. K. (1997). Intermediaries in cloud-computing: A new computing paradigm. INFORMS. Cluster: Electronic Commerce.

Chen, J., He, Y. B., & Jin, X. (2008). A study on the factors that influence the fitness between technology strategy and corporate strategy. *International Journal of Innovation and Technology Management*, *5*(1), 81–103. doi:10.1142/S0219877008001308

Chen, X., Wills, G. B., Gilbert, L., & Bacigalupo, D. (2010). Using cloud for research: A technical review. *TesciRes Report for JISC*.

Chow, R., Golle, P., Jakobsson, M., Shi, E., Staddon, J., Masuoka, R., & Molina, J. (2009). *Controlling data in the cloud: Outsourcing computation without outsourcing control.* Paper presented at the ACM workshop on Cloud Computing Security (CCSW '09), Chicago, IL. doi:10.1145/1655008.1655020

Ciortea, L., Zamfir, C., Bucur, S., Chipounov, V., & Candea, G. (2009). Cloud9: A software testing service. *SIGOPS Oper.Syst.Rev., 43*(4), 5–10. doi:10.1145/1713254.1713257

CSA. (2009). *Security guidance for critical areas of focus in cloud computing V2.1.* Cloud Security Alliance.

Curran, J., Blackburn, R. A., & Woods, A. (1991). *Exploring enterprise cultures: Small service sector enterprise owners and their views.* Kingston University.

Cusumano, M. (2009). Technology strategy and management: The legacy of Bill Gates. *Communications of the ACM, 52*(1), 25–26. doi:10.1145/1435417.1435429

Dave, A. (2012). The state of cloud computing security in Asia. *Trend Micro,* 1-5.

Delahunty, S. (2009, January). *State of enterprise storage.* Paper presented by Byte & Switch. InformationWeek Analytics.com, Manhassett, NY.

DFD. (2011a). *Opportunities and applicability for use by the Australian Government.* Cloud Computing strategic direction paper. DFD.

DFD. (2011b). *Better practice guide: Negotiating the cloud – Legal issues in cloud computing agreements.* DFD.

DFD. (2011c). *Better practice checklist: Privacy and cloud computing for Australian government agencies.* DFD.

DIISR. (2011). *Key statistics: Australian small business, Commonwealth of Australia 2011.* DIISR.

Dillon, T., Wu, C., & Chang, E. (2010). *Cloud computing: Issues and challenges.* Academic Press.

Dong, L., Neufeld, D., & Higgins, C. (2009). Top management support of enterprise systems implementations. *Journal of Information Technology, 24*(1), 55–80. doi:10.1057/jit.2008.21

Erdogmus, H. (2009). Cloud computing: Does Nirvana hide behind the Nebula. *IEEE Software, 26*(11), 4–6.

Evans, J. R., & Mathur, A. (2005). The value of online surveys. *Internet Research, 15*(2), 195–219. doi:10.1108/10662240510590360

Farah, S. (2010). Cloud computing or software as a service-which makes the most sense for HR? Employment relations today. *ABI/INFORM Global, 36*(4), 31.

Farber, D. (2008). Oracle's Ellison nails cloud computing. *CNET News.* Received from http://news.cnet.com/8301-13953_10052188-80.html

Flick, U. (2009). *An introduction to qualitative research* (4th ed.). Los Angeles, CA: SAGE Publications.

Fortino, G., Mastroianni, C., Pathan, M., & Vakali, A. (2009). *Next generation content networks: Trends and challenges.* Paper presented at the 4th Edition of the UPGRADE-CN Workshop on use of P2P, GRID and Agents for the Development of Content Networks (UPGRADE-CN '09), Garching, Germany. doi:10.1145/1552486.1552516

Foster, I., Zhao, Y., Raicu, I., & Lu, S. (2008). *Cloud computing and grid computing 360-degree compared.* Paper presented at the Grid Computing Environments Workshop. doi:10.1109/GCE.2008.4738445

Friedman, A. A., & West, D. M. (2010). Privacy and security in cloud computing issues in technology innovation. Center for Technology Innovation at Brookings (3).

George, F., & Shyam, G. (2010). Impact of cloud computing: Beyond a technology trend. *Systems Integration*, 262–269.

Gorniak, S. (2009). *Cloud computing European network and information security agency (ENISA)*. Retrieved from http://www.enisa.europa.eu/act/res/technologies/tech/dnssec/dnssec

Grance, T. (2010). The NIST cloud definition framework. National Institute of Standards and Technology.

Greenberg, A., Hamilton, J., Maltz, D. A., & Patel, P. (2008). The cost of a cloud: Research problems in data center networks. *Computer Communication Review*, *39*(1), 68–73. doi:10.1145/1496091.1496103

Grobauer, B., Walloschek, T., & Stocker, E. (2011). Understanding cloud computing vulnerabilities. *Security & Privacy, IEEE, 9*(2), 50–57. doi:10.1109/MSP.2010.115

Guazzelli, A., Zeller, M., Lin, W. C., & Williams, G. (2009). PMML: An open standard for sharing models. *The R Journal, 1*(1), 60–65.

Gupta, P., Seetharaman, A., & Raj, J. R. (2013). The usage and adoption of cloud computing by small and medium businesses. *International Journal of Information Management*, *33*(5), 861–874. doi:10.1016/j.ijinfomgt.2013.07.001

Habib, S. M., Hauke, S., Ries, S., Mühlhäuser, M., Antonopoulos, N., Anjum, A., & Rong, C. (2012). Trust as a facilitator in cloud computing: a survey. *Journal of Cloud Computing: Advances, Systems, and Applications, 1*(1), 19.

Hailu, A. (2012). *Factors influencing cloud-computing technology adoption in developing countries*. (PhD. Thesis), Retrieved from ProQuest Dissertations and Theses. (UMI No: 3549131).

Handler, D.P., Barbier, J., & Schottmiller. (2012). *SMB public cloud adoption: Opening a hidden market*. Cisco Internet Business Solutions Group.

Herhalt, J., & Cochrane, K. (2012). Exploring the cloud. *KPMG*, 1–46.

Hogarty, K., Hines, C., Kromrey, J., Ferron, J., & Mumford, K. (2005). The quality of factor solutions in exploratory factor analysis: The influence of sample size, communality, and overdetermination. *Educational and Psychological Measurement*, *65*(2), 202–226. doi:10.1177/0013164404267287

Holden, E. P., Kang, J. W., Bills, D. P., & Ilyassov, M. (2009). *Databases in the cloud: A work in progress*. Paper presented at the 10th ACM Conference on SIG-Information Technology Education (SIGITE '09), Fairfax, VA. doi:10.1145/1631728.1631765

Hutley, N. (2012). Modelling the economic impact of cloud computing. *KPMG*, 1–52.

IBM. (2008). *IT service management to enable the fulfilment of your SOA strategy*. White paper. IBM Global Services.

IMO. (2013). Better practice guide: Privacy and cloud computing for Australian government agencies. Australian Government.

ITIIC. (2011). Cloud computing: Opportunities and challenges. Information Technology Industry Innovation Council.

Jahangir, N., & Begum, N. (2007). Effect of perceived usefulness, ease of use, security and privacy on customer attitude and adaptation in the context of e-banking. *Journal of Management Research, 7*(3), 147–157.

Jamwal, D., Sambyal, A., & Sambyal, G. S. (2011). Cloud computing: Its security & privacy aspects. *International Journal of Latest Trends in Computing*, 2(1), 25–28.

Joanna, G., & Chiemi, H. (2010). *Exploring the future of cloud computing: Riding the next wave of technology driven transformation.* Paper presented at the World Economic Forum 2010.

Johnson, B. (2008). *Cloud computing is a trap, warns GNU founder Richard Stallman.* Retrieved from http://www.guardian.co.uk/technology/2008/sep/29/cloud.computing.richard.stallman

Kaliski, B. (2008). Multi-tenant cloud computing: From cruise liners to container ships. In *Proceedings of Third Asia-Pacific Trusted Infrastructure Technologies Conference.* Academic Press. doi:10.1109/APTC.2008.16

Kannan, P. K., Chang, A. M., & Whinston, A. B. (1998). Marketing information on the i-way: Data junkyard or information gold mine? *Communications of the ACM*, 41(3), 35–43. doi:10.1145/272287.272295

Katzan, H. (2010). On the privacy of cloud computing. *International Journal of Management & Information Systems*, 14(2), 1–12.

Kelly, L. (2011). The security threats facing SMEs. *Computer Weekly*, 11-12.

Keung, J., & Kwok, F. (2012). Cloud deployment model selection assessment for SMEs: Renting or buying a cloud. In *Proceedings of the 5th International Conference on Utility and Cloud Computing.* IEEE/ACM. doi:10.1109/UCC.2012.29

Kraska, T., Hentschel, M., Alonso, G., & Kossmann, D. (2009). Consistency rationing in the cloud: Pay only when it matters. *Proc. VLDB Endow*, 2(1), 253–264. doi:10.14778/1687627.1687657

Krautheim, F. J. (2010). *Building trust into utility cloud computing.* (PhD. Dissertation). Retrieved from ProQuest Dissertations and Theses. (UMI No: 3422891)

Lawrence, M.W.L., Brad, D.C.C., Chris, C., & Denna, M. (2010). Cloud computing business models for the channel. *A CompTI A Cloud/SaaS Community Resource*, 1–12.

Lease, D. R. (2005). *Factors influencing the adoption of biometric security technologies by decision making information technology and security managers.* Retrieved from ProQuest Digital Dissertations. (AAT 3185680).

Lee, J. (2004). Discriminant analysis of technology adoption behavior: A case of internet technologies in small businesses. *Journal of Computer Information Systems*, 44(4), 57–66.

Lee, M. K. O., & Cheung, C. M. K. (2004). Internet retailing adoption by small-to-medium sized enterprises (SMEs): A multiple-case study. *Information Systems Frontiers*, 6(4), 385–397. doi:10.1023/B:ISFI.0000046379.58029.54

Li, C. S. (2010). Cloud computing in an outcome centric world. Paper presented at IEEE Cloud 2010. Miami, FL.

Li, X., Troutt, M. D., Brandyberry, A., & Wang, T. (2011). Decision factors for the adoption and continued use of online direct sales channels among SMEs. *Journal of the Association for Information Systems*, 12(1), 1–31.

Li, Z., Wang, Y., Olivier, K. K. S., Chen, J., & Li, K. (2009). *The cloud-based framework for ant colony optimization.* Paper presented at the First ACM/SIGEVO Summit on Genetic and Evolutionary Computation (GEC '09), Shanghai, China. doi:10.1145/1543834.1543872

Lim, H., Babu, S., Chase, J., & Parekh, S. (2009). *Automated control in cloud computing: challenges and opportunities.* Paper presented at the 1st workshop on Automated control for datacenters and clouds (ACDC '09). Barcelona, Spain. doi:10.1145/1555271.1555275

Lodi, G., Querzoni, L., Baldoni, R., Marchetti, M., Colajanni, M., Bortnikov, V., & Roytman, A. (2009). *Defending financial infrastructures through early warning systems: The intelligence cloud approach.* Paper presented at the 5th Annual Workshop on Cyber Security and Information Intelligence Research (CSIIRW '09), Oak Ridge, Tennessee. doi:10.1145/1558607.1558628

Low, C., Chen, Y., & Wu, M. (2011). Understanding the determinants of cloud computing adoption. *Industrial Management & Data Systems, 111*(7), 1006–1023. doi:10.1108/02635571111161262

Luis, M. V., Luis, R. M., Juan, C., & Maik, L. (2009). A break in the clouds: Towards a cloud definition. *SIGCOMM Comput. Commun. Rev, 39*(1), 50–55.

MacGregor, R., & Kartiwi, M. (2010). Perception of barriers to e-commerce adoption in SMEs in developing and developed country: A comparison between Australia and Indonesia. *Journal of Electronic Commerce in Organizations, 8*(1), 61–82. doi:10.4018/jeco.2010103004

Mahmood, Z. (2011). Data location and security issues in cloud computing. In *Proceedings of IEEE International Conference on Emerging intelligent Data and Web Technologies.* IEEE. doi:10.1109/EIDWT.2011.16

Malhotra, N. (2010). *Marketing research: An applied orientation.* Pearson Education.

Marian, M., & Hamburg, I. (2012). *Guidelines for increasing the adoption of cloud computing within SMEs.* Paper presented at the 3rd International Conference on Cloud Computing, GRIDs, and Virtualization.

Mark, D. R. (2011). Cloud computing privacy concerns on our doorstep. *Communications of the ACM, 54*(1).

Marks, E. A., & Lozano, B. (2010). *Executive's guide to cloud computing.* Wiley.

Marshall, P. (2008). City in the cloud. *Government Computer News, 27*(28), 29–29.

Marston, S., Li, Z., Bandyopadhyay, S., Zhang, J., & Ghalsasi, A. (2011). Cloud computing — The business perspective. *Decision Support Systems, 51*(1), 176–189. doi:10.1016/j.dss.2010.12.006

Martin, L. (2010). *Awareness, trust and security to shape government cloud adoption.* Academic Press.

McCabe, B., & Hancook, I. (2009). Cloud computing: Australian lessons and experiences. *KPMG*, 1–20.

Mell, P., & Grance, T. (2011). The NIST definition of cloud computing (draft). *NIST Special Publication, 800*, 145.

Merriam, S. B. (1998). *Case study research in education: A qualitative approach.* San Francisco, CA: Jossey-Bass Publications.

Merritt, R. (2009). Vendors call for cloud computing standards. *EE Times.* Retrieved from http://www.eetimes.com/electronics-news/4081939/Vendors-call-for-cloud-computing-standards

Miller, M. (2008). *Cloud computing: Web-based applications that change the way you work and collaborate online.* Indianapolis, IN: Que Publishers.

Misra, S. C., & Mondal, A. (2010). Identification of a company's suitability for the adoption of cloud computing and modelling its corresponding return on investment. *Mathematical and Computer Modelling, 53*(3), 504–521.

Mitroff, I. I., & Linstone, H. A. (2012). *The unbounded mind: Breaking the chains of traditional business thinking*. New York: OxFord University Press.

Moghavvemi, S., Hakimian, F., & Feissal, T. M. F. T. (2012). Competitive advantages through it innovation adoption by SMEs. *Social Technologies, 2*.

Monika, S., Ashwani, M., Haresh, J., Anand, K., Madhvendra, M., & Vijayshri, T. (2010). Scope of cloud computing for SMEs in India. *Journal of Computing, 2*(5), 144–149.

Mudge, J. C. (2010). *Cloud computing opportunities and challenges for Australia*. Melbourne, Australia: ATSE.

Mvelase, P., Dlodlo, N., Williams, Q., & Adigun, M. O. (2011). Custom-made cloud enterprise architecture for small medium and micro enterprises. *International Journal of Cloud Applications and Computing, 1*(3), 52–63.

Myers, M. D., & Avison, D. (2002). *An introduction to qualitative research in information systems, a reader*. London: Sage.

Ning, X. (2013). *Personal health management system in cloud and adoption by older Australians: A conceptual research model*. Paper presented at the 21st Century Science Health, Agency, and Well-Being, Sydney, Australia.

Nir, K. (2010). Cloud computing in developing economies: Drivers, effects and policy measures. In *Proceedings of PTC'10*. PTC.

NIST. (2009). *Cloud computing*. Information Technology Laboratory. Retrieved from http://csrc.nist.gov/groups/SNS/cloud-computing/index.html

Opala, O. J. (2012). *An analysis of security, cost-effectiveness, and IT compliance factors influencing cloud adoption by IT managers*. (PhD. Dissertation). Retrieved from ProQuest Dissertations and Theses. (UMI No: 3527699)

Orr, B. (2008). Will IT of the future have its feet firmly planted in the "cloud"? *ABI/INFORM Global, 100*(9), 50.

Papazoglou, M. P., & Georgakopoulos, D. (2003). Service oriented computing. *Communications of the ACM, 46*, 25–28.

Parthasarathy, M., & Bhattacherjee, A. (1998). Understanding post-adoption behavior in the context of online services. *Information Systems Research, 9*(4), 362–379. doi:10.1287/isre.9.4.362

Pearson, S. (2009). *Taking account of privacy when designing cloud computing services*. Paper presented at the ICSE Workshop on Software Engineering Challenges of Cloud Computing (CLOUD'09). doi:10.1109/CLOUD.2009.5071532

Pearson, S. (2012). *Privacy, security and trust in cloud computing*. Springer.

Plummer, D.C., Smith, D.M., Bittman, T.J., Cearley, D.W., Cappuccio, D.J., Scott, D., Robertson, B. (2009). *Five refining attributes of public and private cloud computing*. Gartner.

Polonsky, M. J., & Waller, D. S. (2011). *Designing and managing a research project: A business student's guide*. Thousand Oaks, CA: Sage Publications.

Rahimli, A. (2013). Factors influencing organization adoption decision on cloud computing. *International Journal of Cloud Computing and Services Science, 2*(2), 141–147.

Rath, A., Mohapatra, S., Kumar, S., & Thakurta, R. (2012). *Decision point for adopting cloud computing for SMEs*. Paper presented at the The 7th International Conference for Internet Technology and Secured Transactions.

Rittinghouse, J. W., & Ransome, J. F. (2009). *Cloud computing: Implementation, management, and security*. New York: CRC Press.

Rogers, E. M. (1962). *Diffusion of innovations*. New York: The Free Press of Glencoe.

Ross, V. W. (2010). *Factors influencing the adoption of cloud computing by decision making managers*. (PhD. Dissertation). Retrieved from ProQuest Dissertations and Theses. (UMI No: 3391308)

Sahandi, R., Alkhalil, A., & Opara-Martins, J. (2012). SMEs' perception of cloud computing: Potential and security. In Collaborative networks in the internet of services. Springer.

Salleh, S. M., Teoh, S. Y., & Chan, C. (2012). *Cloud enterprise systems: A review of literature and its adoption*. Paper presented at the PASIS 2012.

Sarwar, A., & Khan, M.N. (2013). A review of trust aspects in cloud computing security. *International Journal of Cloud Computing and Services Science, 2*(2), 116–122.

Sasikala, P. (2011). Cloud computing in higher education. *International Journal of Cloud Applications and Computing, 1*(2), 1–13. doi:10.4018/ijcac.2011040101

Shareef, M. A., Kumar, V., Kumar, U., & Dwivedi, Y. K. (2011). e-Government adoption model (GAM): Differing service maturity levels. *Government Information Quarterly, 28*(1), 17–35. doi:10.1016/j.giq.2010.05.006

Sharif, A. M. (2010). It's written in the cloud: The hype and promise of cloud computing. *Journal of Enterprise Information Management, 23*(2), 131–134. doi:10.1108/17410391011019732

Singh, H. P., Bhisikar, A., & Singh, J. (2013). Innovative ICT through cloud computing. *IUP Journal of Computer Sciences, 7*(1), 37–52.

Son, I., & Lee, D. (2011). *Assessing a new IT service model, cloud computing*. Paper presented at the PACIS 2011, Queensland, Australia.

Subashini, S., & Kavitha, V. (2011). A survey on security issues in service delivery models of cloud computing. *Journal of Network and Computer Applications, 34*(1), 1–11. doi:10.1016/j.jnca.2010.07.006

Suess, J., & Morooney, K. (2009). Identity management & trust services: Foundations for cloud computing. *ABI/INFORM Global, 44*(5), 24.

Sullivan, D. (2010). The definitive guide to cloud computing. Realtime Publishers.

Sultan, N. (2010). Cloud computing for education: A new dawn? *International Journal of Information Management, 30*(2), 109–116. doi:10.1016/j.ijinfomgt.2009.09.004

Sultan, N. A. (2011). Reaching for the "cloud": How SMEs can manage. *International Journal of Information Management, 31*(3), 272–278. doi:10.1016/j.ijinfomgt.2010.08.001

Surendro, K., & Fardani, A. (2012). *Identification of SME readiness to implement cloud computing*. Paper presented at the International Conference on Cloud Computing and Social Networking (ICCCSN, 2012). doi:10.1109/ICCCSN.2012.6215757

Svantesson, D., & Clarke, R. (2010). Privacy and consumer risks in cloud computing. *Computer Law & Security Report, 26*(4), 391–397. doi:10.1016/j.clsr.2010.05.005

Swanson, R. A., & Holton, E. F. (2005). *Research in organizations: Foundations and methods of inquiry* (3rd ed.). San Francisco, CA: Berrett-Koehler Publishers.

Swisher, L. L., Beckstead, J. W., & Bebeau, M. J. (2004). Factor analysis as a tool for survey analysis. *Physical Therapy, 84*(9), 784–799. PMID:15330692

Tabachnick, B. G., & Fidell, L. S. (2007). *Using multivariate statistics*. Boston: Pearson Education Inc.

Tancock, D., Pearson, S., & Charlesworth, A. (2013). A privacy impact assessment tool for cloud computing. In Privacy and security for cloud computing. Springer.

Treese, W. (2008). Movin' to the cloud. *NetWorker, 12*(4), 13–15. doi:10.1145/1461981.1461985

Tuncay, E. (2010). Effective use of cloud computing in educational institutions. *Procedia: Social and Behavioral Sciences, 2*(2), 938–942. doi:10.1016/j.sbspro.2010.03.130

Tweel, A. (2012). *Examining the relationship between technological, organizational, and environment factors and cloud computing adoption*. (Doctoral Dissertation). Retrieved from ProQuest Dissertations and Theses. (UMI No: 3529668)

Uusitalo, I., Karppinen, K., Juhola, A., & Savola, R. (2010). *Trust and cloud services-an interview study*. Paper presented at the 2nd International Conference on Cloud Computing Technology and Science (CloudCom). doi:10.1109/CloudCom.2010.41

Van Hoorn, T. P. (1979). Strategic planning in small and medium-sized companies. *Long Range Planning, 12*(2), 84–91. doi:10.1016/0024-6301(79)90076-1

Voona, S., & Venkantaratna, R. (2009). *Cloud computing for banks*. Infosys Technologies Ltd.

Wang, L., & Laszewski, G. V. (2008). *Scientific cloud computing: early definition and experience*. Paper presented at the IEEE International Conference on High Performance Computing and Communications, Dalian, China. doi:10.1109/HPCC.2008.38

Wang, W. Y. C., Rashi, A., & Chuang, H. (2011). Toward the trend of cloud computing. *Journal of Electronic Commerce Research, 12*(4), 238–242.

Wei, D. (2010). The impact of emerging technologies on small and medium enterprises (SMEs). *Journal of Business Systems, Governance, & Ethics, 4*(4), 53–60.

Wei, J., Zhang, X., Ammons, G., Bala, V., & Ning, P. (2009). *Managing security of virtual machine images in a cloud environment*. Paper presented at the 2009 ACM Workshop on Cloud Computing Security, CCSW '09. New York, NY. doi:10.1145/1655008.1655021

Weiss, A. (2007). Computing in the clouds. *netWorker, 11*(4), 16–25. doi:10.1145/1327512.1327513

Wheeler, B., & Waggener, S. (2009). Above campus services: Shaping the promise of cloud computing for higher education. *ABI/INFORM Global, 44*(6), 52.

Wijesiri, S. (2010). *Cloud computing - A new wave in IT*. Retrieved from http://www.dailynews.lk/2010/07/22/fea15.asp

WinterGreen Research. (2010). *Worldwide cloud computing market opportunities and segment forecasts 2009 to 2015*. WinterGreen Research Inc. Retrieved from http://www.wintergreen-research.com/reports/CloudOpportunities.htm

Wu, W. (2011). Developing an explorative model for SaaS adoption. *Expert Systems with Applications, 38*(12), 15057–15064. doi:10.1016/j.eswa.2011.05.039

Yan, H. (2010). On the clouds: A new way of computing. *Information Technology & Libraries, 29*(2), 87–92.

Youseff, L., Butrico, M., & Da Silva, D. (2008). Toward a unified ontology of cloud computing. In *Proceedings of the Grid Computing Environments Workshop*. Academic Press. doi:10.1109/GCE.2008.4738443

Zeller, M., Grossman, R., Lingenfelder, C., Berthold, M. R., Marcade, E., Pechter, R., & Holada, R. (2009). *Open standards and cloud computing: KDD-2009 panel report.* Paper presented at the KDD '09: Proceedings of the 15th ACM SIGKDD International Conference on Knowledge Discovery and Data Mining, Paris, France. doi:10.1145/1557019.1557027

Zhang, Q., Cheng, L., & Boutaba, R. (2010). Cloud computing: State-of-the-art and research challenges. *Journal of Internet Services and Applications, 1*(1), 7–18. doi:10.1007/s13174-010-0007-6

Zikmund, W. G. (1994). *Exploring market research.* Dryden Press.

ADDITIONAL READING

Amini, M., Bakri, A., Sadat, S. N., Javadinia, A., Amir, S., & Tolooie, A. (2014). The Role of Top Manager Behaviours on Adoption of Cloud Computing for Small and Medium Enterprises. *Australian Journal of Basic & Applied Sciences, 8*(1).

Brimbela, F. (2013). *Adoption of cloud computing by SME's in emerging markets.* Brazil: Dublin Business School.

Bunce, B. (2013). Can Cloud Computing benefit SME's? *IS Practices for SME Success Series, 5.*

Carcary, M., Doherty, E., & Conway, G. (2013). The Adoption of Cloud Computing by Irish SMEs – an Exploratory Study. *The Electronic Journal of Information Systems Evaluation, 16*(4), 258–269.

Chang, V., Bacigalupo, D., Wills, G., & De Roure, D. (2010). A categorisation of cloud computing business models. *Paper presented at the Proceedings of the 2010 10th IEEE/ACM International Conference on Cluster, Cloud and Grid Computing.* doi:10.1109/CCGRID.2010.132

Chang, V., Wills, G., & De Roure, D. (2010). A review of cloud business models and sustainability. *Paper presented at the 2010 IEEE 3rd International Conference on Cloud Computing.* Retrieved from http://ieeexplore.ieee.org/stamp/stamp.jsp?tp=&arnumber=5558011

Collins, D.J., & Lam, K.P. (2014). *Selling the Cloud to Smaller Business Organisations.*

Dahiru, A. A., Bass, J., & Allison, I. (2014). *Cloud Computing: Adoption Issues for Sub-Saharan Africa SMEs.* The Electronic Journal of Information Systems in Developing Countries.

Dietmar, N., & Mark, S. (2014). Exploring the economic value of a cloud computing solution and its contribution to green IT. *International Journal of Business Process Integration and Management, 7*(1), 62–72. doi:10.1504/IJBPIM.2014.060605

Dillon, S., & Vossen, G. (2014). SaaS cloud computing in small and medium enterprises: A comparison between Germany and New Zealand: Working Papers, *ERCIS-European Research Center for Information Systems.*

Kelmendi, R. (2013). Cloud computing latency effect on small and medium enterprises. *Science, Innovation New Technology, 59.*

Korongo, J. N., Samoei, D. K., & Gichoya, D. M. (2013). Cloud computing: An emerging trend for small and medium enterprises. *Paper presented at the IST-Africa Conference and Exhibition (IST-Africa, 2013).*

Mohlameane, M., & Ruxwána, N. (2014). The Awareness of Cloud Computing: A Case Study of South African SMEs. *International Journal of Trade, Economics & Finance, 5*(1).

Prasad, A., Green, P., & Heales, J. (2014). Cloud computing service considerations for the small and medium enterprises. *Paper presented at the Americas Conference on Information Systems.*

Sabwa, B. A. (2013). Cloud Computing Adoption By Small And Medium Enterprises (SMEs). In *Nairobi County*. University of Nairobi.

Saedi, A., & Iahad, N. A. (2013). Developing an instrument for Cloud Computing adoption by Small and Medium-sized Enterprises. *Paper presented at the International Conference on Research and Innovation in Information Systems (ICRIIS 2013)*. doi:10.1109/ICRIIS.2013.6716757

Stieninger, M., & Nedbal, D. (2014). Diffusion and Acceptance of Cloud Computing in SMEs: Towards a Valence Model of Relevant Factors. *Paper presented at the 47th Hawaii International Conference on System Sciences (HICSS 2014)*. doi:10.1109/HICSS.2014.410

Welsh, G. (2013). Cloud Computing–An SME Perspective. *IS Practices for SME Success Series*, 135.

Whorrod, A. (2013). Public Cloud Security: A Question of Trust. *IS Practices for SME Success Series*, 143. Upra, R., & Chaisricharoen, R. (2014). Workgroup Distribution File System (WDFS) for personal cloud system. *Paper presented at the 4th Joint International Conference on Information and Communication Technology, Electronic and Electrical Engineering (JICTEE 2014)*.

Yu, J., & Ni, J. (2013). Development Strategies for SME E-Commerce Based on Cloud Computing. *Paper presented at the 7th International Conference on Internet Computing for Engineering and Science (ICICSE 2013)*. doi:10.1109/ICICSE.2013.9

KEY TERMS AND DEFINITIONS

Cloud Computing: Cloud computing is a model for enabling ubiquitous, convenient, on-demand network access to a shared pool of configurable computing resources (e.g., networks, servers, storage, applications, and services) that can be rapidly provisioned and released with minimal management effort or service provider interaction.

Community Cloud: A community cloud is a multi-tenant infrastructure that is shared among several organizations from a specific group with common computing concerns.

Database-as-a-Service (DBaaS): DbaaS is a service that is managed by a cloud operator (public or private) that supports applications, without the application team assuming responsibility for traditional database administration functions.

Hybrid Cloud: A hybrid cloud is a cloud computing environment in which an organization provides and manages some resources in-house and has others provided externally.

Infrastructure as a Service (IaaS): IaaS is a provision model in which an organization outsources the equipment used to support operations, including storage, hardware, servers and networking components. The service provider owns the equipment and is responsible for housing, running and maintaining it. The client typically pays on a per-use basis.

Platform as a Service (PaaS): PaaS is a way to rent hardware, operating systems, storage and network capacity over the Internet. The service delivery model allows the customer to rent virtualized servers and associated services for running existing applications or developing and testing new ones.

127

Private Cloud: A private cloud is a particular model of cloud computing that involves a distinct and secure cloud based environment in which only the specified client can operate.

Public Cloud: A public cloud is one based on the standard cloud computing model, in which a service provider makes resources, such as applications and storage, available to the general public over the Internet. Public cloud services may be free or offered on a pay-per-usage model.

Software as a Service (SaaS): SaaS is a software distribution model in which applications are hosted by a vendor or service provider and made available to customers over a network, typically the Internet.

Chapter 6

Analysis of Cloud Services on Business Processes in the Digitalization of the Consumer Product Industry

Ute Riemann

Business Principal Consultant, Business Transformation Services, SAP Deutschland AG & Co. KG, Walldorf, Germany

ABSTRACT

Nowadays, cloud computing is becoming popular within the business environment. Cloud services is not new, but the evolution of mobility, connectivity, and computing hardware has made it interesting for the business. Cloud services provides a way to increase the capacity or add capabilities dynamically without investing in new IT infrastructure, training new personnel, or licensing new software. Focusing on the consumer product goods (CPG) market with its mainly small and medium-sized companies, we see dramatic changes from the market demands, logistic challenges and price competition. The purpose of this chapter is therefore to present the positioning of cloud services in the CPG industry and to outline an approach that enables a typical company in the CPG industry to link the current capabilities of cloud services this to a business-process-driven evaluation approach to provide a transparency for the decision towards cloud services. The result of the business process investigation underlies assumptions and inductive conclusions.

INTRODUCTION

Cloud Computing in Consumer Product Industries

For CPG industry companies, the ability to quickly and accurately meet consumer demand is an increasingly complex challenge. Rapidly evolv-

ing consumer tastes are pressuring companies to continually introduce new products. Therefore it is essential to ensure that relevant products are in the right place at the right time. Doing this requires the ability to understand and anticipate changing consumer needs. To achieve and sustain competitive advantage and high performance in the future, consumer industry companies around

DOI: 10.4018/978-1-4666-8210-8.ch006

Copyright © 2015, IGI Global. Copying or distributing in print or electronic forms without written permission of IGI Global is prohibited.

the globe will need to meet a daunting set of new imperatives. At the same time cloud services introduces a new era in consumer products industries and changes the game. Cloud services is not new, but the evolution of mobility, connectivity, and computing hardware made it interesting for the information technology (IT) infrastructure of both small and large consumer product industries. Specifically, companies must:

- Serve the new digital consumers who are interacting with the companies, brands, and offerings in radically new ways to gain product information and share their opinions, demanding for more customized marketing and offers. Serving this consumer calls for excellence in customer-facing processes.

- Win the challenge where the traditional customer segmentation does no longer exit but turn out into a 1:1 marketing and selling. Thus it is necessary to help retailers – as it is the case at Villeroy & Boch - to grow their store sales and margins through consistent delivery of the right products, prices, and promotions, in return for more valuable shelf space and ideal product placement – even thinking of virtual product placements. This requires strong performance from data-analytics processes, innovative store concepts and a strong approach in an omni-channel management.

- Drive growth in emerging markets to stay competitive in the face of stagnation in developed markets, whether it's through acquiring new companies, setting up new operations overseas, or attracting consumers in emerging markets.

- Extract high performance from business processes, to scale up or down to meet the changing market needs that have come with globalization. This feat requires agile operating and supply chain models to serve consumers in developed and emerg-

ing markets alike. Meeting these requirements escalates the need for superior management of core and non-core business processes.

- Companies can profit from cloud as a new technology innovations and license models: they do not need to buy their own hardware infrastructure, but pay a monthly subscription for the use of resources on demand. They benefit from, for example, the achieving of better economies of scale, improving organizational flexibility, increasing speed to market, and spending improvements. They do not need to spend time on complex IT challenges and can concentrate on the issues of their core business. But there simultaneously are problems. Customers also could put their data at significant risk, due to the localization of this data in data centers and reduced levels of control. (Deloitte, 2013)

For CPG companies, the potential to deepen customer relationships at a lower cost with cloud services provides an interesting opportunity. Cloud services could play a prominent role in helping these companies to meet industry challenges like declining brand loyalty, enduring consumer frugality, growing prevalence of online and mobile commerce and the growing importance of dollar and discount retail channels. Furthermore, cloud services have the potential to help companies grow in a dynamic environment where new geographies are increasingly important, regulatory requirements are more demanding, and commodity costs are volatile. The potentially transformative benefits can outweigh the risks traditionally associated with cloud computing, and the risk of inaction. Cloud services constitute a transformative opportunity that could help consumer product companies lessen the constraints of existing business models in terms of customer relationships, growth and innovation.

Objective and Structure of the Chapter

The first step is to evaluate in detail the positioning of cloud services in the consumer products industry - and here especially for midsize companies such as Villeroy & Boch. Afterwards the evaluation of cloud services based on categorized End-to-End processes within the consumer products industry starts. The first part identifies End-to-End business processes for consumer products industries – exemplarily for Villeroy & Boch. Afterwards, those business processes, potential use cases and fraud indicators must be categorized. A measurement model will analyze the End-to-End business processes regarding their suitability to the cloud environment. The evaluation is based on evaluation criteria to identify the inherent benefit / risk factor of cloud services towards a business process in the light of a company within the CPG industry. For this reason, it is necessary to determine selection, scoring and weighting of useful criteria, which decision makers would consider. The result represents the attractiveness of End-to-End process regarding the implementation as a cloud solution and reflects potential use cases.

CLOUD SERVICES

Characteristics and Overview of Cloud Services

There are many definitions of cloud computing. Following three definitions that show the broadness of cloud services and that shall be the underlying definition within this chapter. One very comprehensive definition is by Brendl (2010) who defined cloud services as "collections of IT resources (servers, databases, and applications) which are available on an on-demand basis, provided by a service company, available through the internet, and provide resource pooling among multiple users." (Bisong, A., Rahman,

S.M., 2011) Another definition has been set by Mett, P., Timothy, G. (2009): "Cloud computing is a model for enabling ubiquitous, convenient, on-demand network access to a shared pool of configurable computing resources (e.g. networks, servers, storage, applications, and services) that can be rapidly provisioned and released with minimal management effort or service provider interaction. This cloud model is composed of five essential characteristics, three service models, and four deployment models." (Mett, P., Timothy, G. 2011) The National Institute of Standards and Technology defines cloud services as a model for enabling convenient, on-demand network access to a shared pool of configurable computing resources (eg networks, servers, storage, applications, and services) that can be rapidly provisioned and released with minimal management effort or service provider interaction. (Mell, P., Grance, T., 2009)

Leimeister et al. (2010) defines cloud services as "an IT deployment model, based on virtualization, where resources, in terms of infrastructure, applications and data are deployed via the internet as a distributed service by one or several service providers. The services are scalable on demand and can be priced on a pay-per-use basis". Marston et al. (2011) provide a definition from a business perspective that encompasses key benefits for business as well as its technological features, i.e. IT services "are delivered on-demand to customers over a network in a self-service fashion, independent of device and location....users pay for the service as an operating expense without incurring any significant initial capital expenditure, with the cloud services employing a metering system.

To summarize these facets: from a business perspective, the cloud service model is a model for providing and sourcing information technology services on a pay-per-use basis through web-based tools and applications. Cloud services are elastic, allowing them to be highly configurable, adaptable, and scalable, and requiring less up-front investment and ongoing operating expenditure than traditional IT models.

Cloud services represent a paradigm shift in the way systems will be deployed. They can serve as a vital improvement to the business by acting as a potential disruptive innovation for its employees. However, these business should be mindful in using cloud services, as well as which services deployed with which cloud deployment model (e.g. public or private clouds). Cloud service is intended to enable companies of all size to quickly procure and use a wide range of enterprise services on a pay-per-use basis. It will also help companies to scale up or down their IT infrastructure. Cloud services offers Financial, Technological & operational benefits to the user. It takes the technology, services, and applications that are similar to those on internet and turns them into a self-service utility. With the advent of cloud computing, the software service model would change from being an on premise model to an on-demand model. Cloud services uses two essential concepts

1. **Abstraction:** Cloud services abstracts the details of the system implementation from the users and developers. Applications run on physical systems that aren't specified, data is stored in locations that are unknown, administration of systems is outsourced to others, and access by users is ubiquitous.
2. **Virtualization:** Cloud services virtualizes systems by pooling and sharing resources. Systems and storage can be provisioned as needed from a centralized infrastructure, costs are assessed on a metered basis, multi-tenancy is enabled, and resources are scalable with agility.

Cloud services for some people is considered as an art technique that provides a flexible IT infrastructure that integrates high scalability and multi-tenancy as its supporting features. (Bhadauria, R. et al, 2008) Cloud services can be used in a private, public, community/managed or hybrid setting. (Cloud Security Alliance, 2009)

- **Public Clouds:** Public cloud services are provided off-premise by third-party providers to the general public and the computing resources are shared with the provider's other customers. The public cloud describes cloud services in the traditional mainstream sense, whereby resources are dynamically provisioned on a fine-grained, self-service basis over the Internet, via web applications/web services, from an off-site third-party provider who shares resources and bills on a fine-grained utility computing basis. It is typically based on a pay-per-use model, similar to a prepaid electricity metering system which is flexible enough to cater for spikes in demand for cloud optimization. (Enterprise Cloud Computing: Transforming IT, 2010) Public clouds are less secure than the other cloud models because it places an additional burden of ensuring all applications and data accessed on the public cloud are not subjected to malicious attacks.
- **Private Clouds:** Private cloud describes offerings that emulate cloud services on private networks. It is set up within an organization's internal enterprise datacenter. In the private cloud, scalable resources and virtual applications provided by the cloud vendor are pooled together and available for cloud users to share and use. It differs from the public cloud in that all the cloud resources and applications are managed by the organization itself, similar to intranet functionality. Utilization on the private cloud can be much more secure than that of the public cloud because of its specified internal exposure. Only the organization and designated stakeholders may have access to operate on a specific private cloud. (Arnold, S., 2009) Due to government regulations many organization are mandated to keep their servers, software and data within their own data centers; and

private clouds enable them to achieve this. By implementing cloud computing technologies behind their firewall, enterprises can enable pooling and sharing of computing resources across different applications, departments or business units. It requires significant up-front development costs, data center costs, ongoing maintenance, hardware, software and internal expertise when compared with public cloud.

- **Community Clouds:** They are similar to public clouds. However the communities are benefitted since they know who their neighbors are and hence fear less about the security and data protection.
- **Hybrid Clouds:** The hybrid cloud is considered when the enterprises seek to use a mix of public and private cloud capabilities. Public clouds would be used for general computing while customer data is kept within a private cloud, community cloud or a more traditional IT infrastructure. This option would be viable for businesses that have invested in their own IT infrastructure or have data protection responsibilities, but would like to take advantage of the scalability and flexibility that cloud computing affords. Public and private clouds would be integrated through web services. In other words: the hybrid cloud is a private cloud linked to one or more external cloud services, centrally managed, provisioned as a single unit, and circumscribed by a secure network. Global Netoptex Incorporated, 2009) It provides virtual IT solutions through a mix of both public and private clouds. (Kuyoro S. O. & Ibikunle F. & Awodele O., 2011)

Cloud Service Business Models

To classify the cloud service business models, eight types have been identified (Chang, V., et al, 2010): Service Provider and Service Orienta-tion, Support and Services Contracts, In-House Private Clouds, All- In-One Enterprise Cloud, One-Stop Resources and Services, Government funding, Venture capitals and Entertainment and Social Networking.

All of these eight models do fit into the cloud cube model (CCM) helping to explain the cloud service model with their basic characteristics, helping to identify the most appropriate cloud service model according to the business needs. (Chang, V., et al, 2010) Since this chapter focuses on the use of cloud service we will focus on those cloud service models that represent the provisioning of a cloud service. (Chang, V., et al, 2010) Three important models or developments will be explained to give a better understanding about what cloud computing is. One development is called software-as-a-service (SaaS), this model allows users to pay for the software per one use. Another development called platform-as-a-service (PaaS), which means that computing processing capacity is purchased on the web. Lastly, another development is infrastructure-as a-service (IaaS), which allows cloud computing users to pay for the technology on a pay per use basis. The following is a list of the three main types of services that can be offered by the cloud: (Sultan, N., 2009 and Ernst & Young, 2013)

- **Infrastructure as a Service (IaaS):** Computing, storage, and network communication services.
- **Platform as a Service (PaaS):** Database, development tools, and other components necessary to support the development and deployment of applications in the cloud.
- **Software as a Service (SaaS):** General applications, such as word processing, email, spreadsheet, and specialized application management.

The types of deployment models for cloud computing are:

Figure 1. Cloud services models based on NIST
Liu et al. NIST Cloud Computing, 2011.

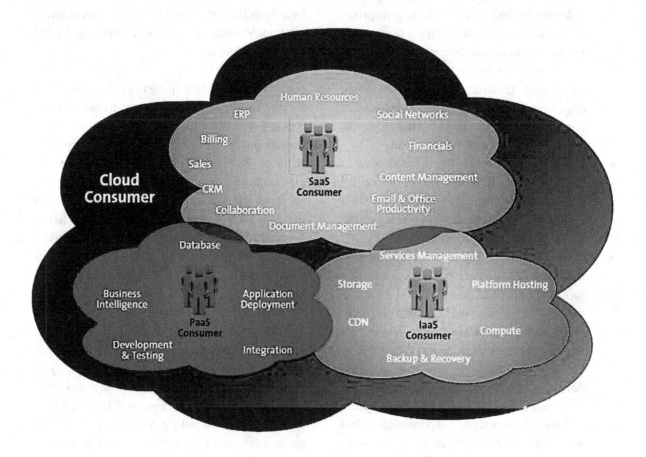

- **Private Cloud:** The cloud infrastructure is operated solely for an organization. It may be managed by the organization or a third party, or a combination of both, and may exist on or off the premises of the organization.
- **Public Cloud:** The cloud infrastructure is made available to the general public and is owned by an organization selling cloud services.
- **Community Cloud:** The cloud infrastructure is shared by several organizations and supports a specific community that has shared concerns (e.g., mission, security requirements, and compliance considerations). It may be managed by one of the organizations or a third party.

- **Hybrid Cloud:** The cloud infrastructure is a combination of two or more clouds (private, community, or public).

Since the demand for efficient and scalable business solutions emerges, many software providers lead the evolution in information technology (Gartner, 2013) in providing various cloud services to support their current customer base and generate new potential customers. (SAP AG, 2013) According to Gartner the IT industry is in a transition. By 2016 the growth of cloud computing will increase and "become the bulk of new IT spend". (Gartner, 2013) The international data collaboration (IDC) predicted in 2012 that "70% of CIOs will embrace a 'cloud first' strategy in

2016". (IDC, 2012) Furthermore, they reported that by 2016, LOB executives will be directly involved in 80% of new IT investments, in 2013 already 58%. (IDC, 2013) A major objective for the software companies in the cloud market is to deliver the right mix of cloud solutions in order to respond to new developments and changing market conditions. The current situation is that most customers have high investments in on-premises. Therefore it is necessary identify those services of value for the customers and to support a transition path for the customers "into the cloud". There is a long list of possible cloud use cases, which can be further extended. However there are several questions which need to be answered.

- Where and why does a cloud service make sense?
- Which use cases are interesting?
- What are risks and benefits that can be garnered from moving to the cloud?
- How do cloud solutions interoperate with existing on-premises landscapes?

Customers consider several aspects, before investing in cloud services (e.g. lifetime requirements, complexity of computation, size of the data set, organizational value, confidentiality, variability or volatility of data, and the need for scalability). Customers "ask for different things: faster innovation, faster time to value, more control, and all mobile and with a much better ease-of-use". (Schulze, 2014) They want systems, which can run their company. They need efficient and easy to use solutions, which improve productivity and reduce the total costs of ownership (TCO). Furthermore, those systems have to be adopted quickly and must be open for the integration with other applications. The cloud solution needs the right mix and must be flexible.

The Cloud Services Portfolio and Outlook Based on the Example of SAP

According to Gartner (Gartner, 2013) the use of cloud services is growing, and by 2016 this growth will increase to become the bulk of new IT spend, according to Gartner, Inc. 2016 will be a defining year for cloud as private cloud begins to give way to hybrid cloud, and nearly half of large enterprises will have hybrid cloud deployments by the end of 2017. According to Ed Anderson, research director at Gartner, segments such as software as a service (SaaS) and infrastructure as a service (IaaS) have even higher projected CAGR growth rates of 34.4 percent and 39.8 percent. Cloud services has a number of different providers that a business could choose from. Each one of these providers offers different functions within their cloud computing service. For instance, Google and IBM have already built different data centers that students can tap into over the Internet to program and research remotely. To describe the basic concepts into more detail the SAP cloud service portfolio is outlined into a little more detail. According to a CMI Report (Competitive & Market Intelligence, Global State Of The Market, March 2013) the various providers show different strengths and positions on the market. SAP leads in three of our 5 market categories; Salesforce leads in Cloud and Oracle leads in database & technology IBM's expansion into enterprise software and its presence in virtually all accounts make it a significant threat SAP must compete aggressively on any and all CRM deals, regardless of deployment model Supply chain analytics, where SAP has the capability to dominate, is the largest analytics the lines of business in all markets except NA GRC represents significant revenue potential in all markets Powerful partnering opportunities exist with telcos and IT outsourcers due to explosive growth of mobile managed services Now is the time to target existing BI and SAP Business Suite customers

Figure 2. Exemplarily visualization of the SAP SaaS solution portfolio
Based on SAP Cloud Applications Portfolio, by J. P. Wunderlich, 2013, Walldorf: SAP AG.

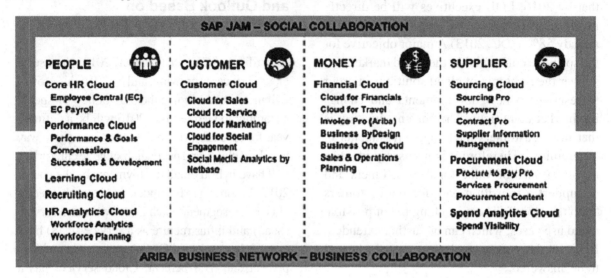

running Oracle and position SAP HANA banking, public sector, professional services, retail, telecom, consumer products, high tech, and insurance will each exceed $10 billion in market size by 2015. The providers do offer their individual service portfolio – as an example this is outlined in figure 2 by the SAP SaaS solution portfolio.

However, since this chapter will not investigate the benefits and risks of the various cloud service models in detail and for the sake of simplification the chapter will simplify the following sections in such a way that the specifics of a cloud service model is not considered in-depth and where we benefit from an idea to assume the "X as a service (XaaS)"; where the values of X we have been outlined above including Infrastructure, Hardware, and Platform. (Armbrust, A. et al., 2009)

For a software provider it is essential to understand the companies, the typical factor of the industry and the potential for cloud services to focus on the development of the specific services. For simplicity reasons let's take a deeper look at the consumer oriented service "Order-to-Cash" which is according to the understanding of the needs of the CPG industry a key processes to increase the customer loyalty. Here are five key challenges CPG companies have to address:

- Brand loyalty and cross channel management;
- Cross-channel management;
- Economic growth, particularly in emerging markets;
- Accelerated merger and acquisition (M&A) activity;
- Sales effectiveness and cost pressure ;
- Refine go-to-market strategies and align with emerging retail channels.

Having these benefits together with the overall value of an industry such as the CPG industry in mind the cloud service provider decided to invent dedicated key cloud services.

- Cloud services for integrated business planning which enables supply chain teams to build on a sales & operations planning to enable forecast demand consistently across plan dimensions, optimize the supply chain, minimize inventory costs, avoid capacity and material shortages, and react quickly to volatile demand with sales and operations planning.

- Cloud service for retail execution to increase consumer products sales teams' effectiveness by providing tools to help enable salespeople to optimize routes for store visits, facilitate visit planning with checklists and other planning aids, help ensure pricing and merchandising compliance, complete store audits, and manage reorders, returns and claims.
- Cloud services sales in general, including potential applications for consumer products companies as well as integration the ERP application.
- Cloud services for omni-channel management to support consumer products companies understanding how to move beyond traditional physical channels via an omni-channel strategy to reach, engage and serve the new always on consumer directly.

Summary: In a Nutshell, CPG Need to Build Better Customer Relationship for Less

The savvy use of cloud services has the potential to help CPG companies to achieve and sustain competitive advantage and high performance in the future. The companies need to confront a daunting set of new imperatives. These imperatives include serving the new digital consumer and driving growth in emerging markets. As CPG companies strive to achieve success, cloud services will play a major role. The cloud's potent combination of agility, scalability and efficiency supports the qualities that industry players will need to compete and win in the future. CPG companies have to face a number of stubborn challenges: declining brand loyalty, consumer frugality, the growing popularity of online and mobile commerce, and the expanding presence of dollar and discount retail channels. Combined, these factors are lowering CPG profit margins and degrading brand power. CPG companies advances in cloud computing seem to be dissipating the traditional

competitive advantages that come from economies of scale in developing a direct-to-consumer channel. Marketers are benefitting from cloud-based scalable technology infrastructure—platforms they use to develop direct-to-consumer online and mobile capabilities, and services they use to deploy e-commerce sites.

CPG companies have used cloud-based solutions to rapidly launch direct-to-consumer storefronts. Additionally it is necessary to build capabilities to narrowly target consumers based on predictive analysis of contextual information, including demographics, behaviors, and attitudes. The ROI for digital marketing has the potential to significantly exceed that of traditional marketing, thanks largely to the combined powers of cloud computing, social media, mobile devices, and analytics. Marketers now have the ability to narrowly and precisely target consumers with predictive models based on attributes like past purchases, prior responses to promotions, demographics, and location. As a result, they are better able to personalize interactions with consumers, including delivering target communications, which may increase awareness, build brands, cost-effectively promote products, increase revenue, and reduce unintended margin loss. Personalized marketing techniques are made possible by faster and cheaper computer processing, data storage, and network connectivity. Combined with mobile devices and social networks, improved targeting capabilities may create more impact for a CPG company's marketing buck. Increasingly, marketers can use targeted advertisements and promotions to grow incremental revenue and margin dollars at a lower marketing cost. Cloud services can potentially drive down the costs for manufacturing operations, packaging, and logistics and distribution. It becomes possible to deploy similar cloud-based inventory and supply chain management applications to eliminate inefficiency and drive down costs throughout the supply chain.

CLOUD SERVICES FOR THE CONSUMER PRODUCTS INDUSTRY

CPG companies have to balance a dilemma: With the advent of Web 2.0 and Industry 4.0, CPG companies are moving into the digital world and use social media to reach out to the customers. Social networking sites are used to increase the awareness of the service offerings of the CPG companies. Social media can be used to help the customer to get attracted to the new products, provide a "Sale of Living attitude" rather than a pure selling of products. Additionally customers are shifting to paperless billing, check bills in the mobile applications, and make payment over the web or mobile phone. Like other industries, CPG companies have to manage the impact of an ageing workforce though technology. CPG companies have to consider the field force automation with the aging workforce. Operations will have to be streamlined through technology to scale down headcount. At the same time CPG will need to adapt and automate their field workforces to increase their flexibility and meet customers' rising expectation in terms of service and reliability. Here again the digital trend will support these companies while using e.g. trends such as new workforce organization forms, global partner networks and virtual teams.

On the other hand-side, CPG companies are known for being very conservative in their IT spending, adoption of new IT technologies. Given the market structure, the size of companies and considering the sensitivity of customer data, many CPG companies are wary of the costs, security and privacy issues that emerge due to cloud computing. For this reason it is necessary to identify the potential industry business processes categories and the existing SAP cloud services portfolio to develop an adequate and attractive cloud service portfolio specified for this industry. The question to be answered is: "Why would cloud services be used in consumer products industry?"

Considering the costs, flexibility and operational benefits cloud services would seem to be a viable option for CPD companies. (Deloitte, 2012)

- First, cloud services have the potential to deepen consumer and customer relationships at a lower cost. For CPG companies, customer relationship economics are a natural starting point to leverage the cloud. Cloud services could improve the business impact of direct-to-consumer storefronts — perhaps even commoditizing them. Furthermore, this confluence of technologies has the ability to significantly improve marketing ROI as marketers more narrowly target consumers with personalized marketing. Also, cloud-based interfaces with retailers – which can help synchronize demand and supply – have the potential to reduce transaction friction of interacting with smaller retailers and small-footprint stores.

- Second, cloud services have the potential to increase agility related to new market growth with less upfront investment in IT. Cloud services could help efficiently deploy and scale IT infrastructure and sales capabilities in new markets, channels, and geographies. Additionally, cloud services could improve the economics of working with smaller suppliers with exchange platforms for visibility to demand and supply with smaller suppliers. For CPG companies, the ability to reconfigure their supply chains to embrace a broader array of small, local suppliers is increasingly important.

- Third, cloud services have the potential to drive faster, shorter innovation cycles by increasing accessibility of computing power during product design, formulation, and testing. Also, cloud computing could reduce cycle time for IT application development by bypassing in-house infrastructure setup times.

Cloud services are still in a nascent stage. Since CPG companies have to worry about the cost of the servers, software licenses, and maintenance fees and other IT infrastructure, large up-front capital expense need to be replaced with a low, pay-for-use operating expense, and the financial appeal of cloud computing is obvious. Therefore companies within the consumer product industry currently mainly focus on SaaS public cloud. Within this service model it is possible to assign the cloud suitability of the investigated industry business processes to the existing public cloud SaaS solution categories. The suitability reflects the industry attractiveness of a cloud product for the CPG industry. For this reason, the less important industry business processes of business functions are, the more cloud computing makes sense. Every application or tool offered by the cloud in this service model is abstracted and hence the staff would not have to learn the intricacies of the tools used. Developers can develop application and re-use or deploy the application across the organization. Developers are can rapidly procure the necessary IT infrastructure required for the business and thereby reducing the lead time.

Assignment of SAP Cloud Service Categories

The cloud offerings can be structured into five categories money, people, customer, supplier, and collaboration (Table 1).

The category money represents industry business processes of the business process category manage financial resources. The category people reflects the generic industry business process category develop and manage human capital. Customer stands for the business process category market and sells products and services. The area supplier focuses on the deliver products and services business process category. Collaboration is an overall category, which serves all industry business process categories, but mainly develops and vision strategy, manages environmental health and safety, manage external relationships, and manage knowledge, improvement, and change.

How May Cloud Services Be Used in CPG Industry?

A suitable cloud service business model should have the capability of translating new technologies into a service value proposition. Sustainability is the key. (Kinetic, 2009) Therefore – and first of all – it is necessary; to understand the specifics of the industry and the company where the cloud services should be applies to. The CPG environment together with the vital trend of digitalization may allow using cloud services to create agile production and logistic networks to other – even very small – partners. While creating this kind of dynamic supply chain networks all partners of these networks benefit from each other e.g. while using the cloud services on their behalf and therefore reducing their operational cost.

Within the CPG environment we are dealing with mainly companies that have are small to medium size companies. As we have seen in the previous paragraph, cloud services become financially interesting for these types of companies. According to a US study at least 70% of SMBs have reinvested money saved as a result of moving to the cloud in areas such as product development and innovation, marketing, and expanding into new markets and 36% have improved their customer service (36 percent) was cited as the main savings reinvestment for SMBs that have adopted the cloud. (Saunder, R., Praw, J., 2013).

In the following paragraphs, this finding is stated for the time being focusing especially the customer-facing cloud service as well as the supplier-facing cloud services may gain severe benefit for CPG companies. Let us consider an example of cloud services offered by SAP used in a CPG midsize company such as Villeroy & Boch. The following chapter is about to understand how CPG companies can benefit from the cloud's potent combination of agility, scalability and efficiency supports the qualities that industry players will need to compete and win in the future. Villeroy & Boch has two business areas serving

Table 1. Cloud service categories (example)

		Money	People	Customer	Supplier	Collaboration	Others
U1/D1	Develop Vision and Strategy					X	
U2	Acquire, Explore and Appraise Assets						X
U3	Develop and Deplete Assets						X
U4	Develop and Manage Upstream Technologies						X
U5/D6	Develop and Manage Human Capital		X				
U6/D7	Manage Information Technology						X
U7/D8	Manage Financial Resources	X					
U8	Acquire, Construct and Manage Support Facilities and Non-Productive Assets						X
U9/D10	Manage Environmental Health and Safety					X	
U10/D11	Manage External Relationships					X	
U11/D12	Manage Knowledge, Improvement and Change					X	
D2	Develop and Manage Products and Services						X
D3	Market and Sell Products and Services		X				
D4	Deliver Products and Services			X			
D5	Manage Customer Service		X				
D9	Acquire, Construct and Manage Property						X

Illustration, by Ute Riemann, 2014, Walldorf: SAP AG.

different market segments and market structures: the tableware with a retail-oriented market structure and the bathroom & wellness segment with a 3-tier market model. Cloud services serve the new digital consumer by excelling at customer-facing processes and extend the flexibility in dealing with the number of sometimes small and local suppliers. The end consumer can direct interact with the company, their brands, products and services in radically new ways. Today, consumers are using cloud based social media platforms such as Facebook and Twitter to get product information and share viewpoints about companies and their offerings The increasing use of mobile apps across multiple devices defines many consumers' online life, blurring the lines between their online and bricks-and-mortar worlds. Let's take a digital consumer of Villeroy & Boch who wants to buy a new bathroom. The consumer may visit a store to pick up information and examine the products. The consumer may also use a PC, smartphone, or tablet to search for information (including pricing) about the items of interest and to learn about the companies' quality and background. In addition, the consumer might use social media to see what their friends are saying about the company their products. And the consumer may email or phone a call center to ask questions about an article or peruse an online or printed catalog. How can cloud service help? The combination of cloud technologies and mobility are blurring the online and physical realms, creating new, unfamiliar terrain. Of course, Villeroy & Boch has known for a while now how to track consumers' online activities and generate customized insights from the data that activity creates. But savvy use of the cloud can help to achieve greater agility, scale, and efficiency in customer-facing processes. When combined with the consumerization of IT, mobility, and analytics, cloud services enables Villeroy & Boch to collect the huge volumes of data generated by consumers' 24/7 online activity. This potent blend of technology also puts Villeroy & Boch in a position to slice and dice data in more ways than ever, generating even better informed insights about how to serve the digital consumer based on the resulting analytics. Armed with insights extracted from the data, the businesses can generate smarter ideas for better serving end consumers.

As previously mentioned Villeroy & Boch serve two different market models: one retail market with their tableware articles and one wholesale market with the bathroom & wellness products. Moreover, cloud computing enables a one-to-one relationship between Villeroy & Boch and the end consumer that was previously not possible, as retailers traditionally had sole access to this type

of data. CPG companies may use cloud services to deploy new types of analytics; for example, by posing questions to consumers on a product's Facebook page and gathering responses. This process helps to gauge market size and interest and then rapidly generate multiple products. They can also quickly and inexpensively add innovative features to their websites.

In addition, cloud services allow context-based services. The services are location-based services that alert customers to the nearest own retail shop of Villeroy & Boch may know where the customer is, but they don't know the customer and what he or she is trying to do right now. Context-based services – combining real-time signals from the physical world with location data, online activities, social media, and other contextual inputs – can help deepen companies' understanding of customers' in-the-moment needs. These services comprise a kaleidoscope of context that can add up to rich user experiences and help companies turn insights into action. Cloud services can help by enabling Villeroy & Boch to gather and analyze more context-related data than ever. Cloud services enable Villeroy & Boch a closer collaboration with their own retail shops or retailers to win the war in the store by mastering data-analytics processes. One important element to win the war in the store do so by working with retailers to confirm that the right products are consistently on shelves and are made visible and alluring to shoppers through the right promotion, placement, and pricing strategies. Villeroy & Boch had realized a close collaboration with their own retail shops but still have external retailers of – as it is within the division bathroom & wellness – a 3-tier logistic chain. In today's market speed is essential. Traditionally, companies rolled out a new offering in stores, tested the launch's effectiveness, and made changes as needed based on the results of the testing. Now, with competition stiffer than ever, companies cannot afford to take a leisurely approach to bringing new products to market; they must get it right the first time, in real time. Doing so, they must gather immense volumes of data on shopper activity and promotion performance, and use it to develop future in-store strategies. That means navigating the shifts in relationships among manufacturers and their retail partners and suppliers. These players have begun sharing more information about consumer behavior with an eye to improving their business performance. But as this trend gathers momentum, companies such as Villeroy & Boch have started putting greater emphasis on priorities such as:

- Product traceability and recall;
- Managing product lifecycles;
- Monitoring promotion execution as well as optimizing retail execution.

At the same time, the new consumer interaction models are helping Villeroy & Boch to directly cultivate intimate, personal connections with end consumers. While companies connecting more directly with consumers will close, the information loops for Villeroy & Boch and benefit the retailer and their own shops by bringing more consumers to a retailer's stores. These evolving models are also presenting new opportunities to engage consumers in product development, making focus groups a thing of the past. In addition, as this trend deepens, consumer products companies can invest more resources in:

- Using social media for marketing and related analytics;
- Optimizing product assortment and retail space;
- Creating augmented reality merchandising.

For instance, a company can use cloud services to create a virtual image of what a display of products in table culture and/or bathroom & wellness would look like in a retailer's store and – even further – in the consumers own premise. The retailer can interact with the image, moving products around to see how a different configura-

tion might affect the appeal of the display and to consider how the display will look in the context of other displays in the store. This kind of service helps to establish planograms for merchandise displays in aisles and on shelves in their stores.

To succeed in today's shifting industry landscape; consumer product companies must use these technologies and other means to differentiate themselves from rivals. They can boost their chances of doing so by connecting directly with consumers through digital means; collaborating with their retail customers and suppliers to develop new value opportunities; and delivering information for decision making anytime, anywhere.

Winning the customer calls for agility, scale, and efficiency in companies' data-analytics processes. With cloud services, Villeroy & Boch can easily collect and analyze data about the effectiveness of their in-store strategies in addition to their own retail stores.

Cloud services support the positioning to drive growth in emerging markets by strengthening their infrastructure related processes. As spending stagnates among cash strapped consumers in developed markets, many companies are seeking to drive fresh growth in emerging markets. Those markets have a growing number of consumers who are entering the middle class and who have increasing purchasing power. As a result, companies are targeting them to drive new growth. To accomplish this growth the companies may need to swiftly execute activities such as getting employees from a newly acquired company integrated with existing systems, and deploying applications that will help them analyze consumer and market data. Capitalizing on this trend requires agility, scale, and efficiency in companies' infrastructure processes. Cloud services will enable companies to manage this feat swiftly and at a lower cost, and to shift from capital to operational expenditure. To fully serve the customer base in new markets or set up new operations overseas, companies do not have to build a new data center; instead, they can run their new operations remotely using cloud technologies. Cloud services may as well help to better manage key data and processes that cross all the regions where they do business – in emerging and mature markets alike. Take the End-to-End process "Market-to-Demand", covering the entire supply chain. As Villeroy & Boch goes even further global, the reach, number of links, and number of transactions generated in their supply chains all increase dramatically, creating ever more complexity. The variance and complexity makes it challenging to conduct critical activities such as tracing products or raw materials. Cloud computing promises to help surmount this challenge: instead of relying on one another's supply chain management technology and willingness to share data to perform such activities, all players along the supply chain could tie into one cloud-based system. That system would have the power and capacity to handle the huge volumes of transactional data generated along the global supply chain. It could also be scaled up or down quickly and easily. Moreover, the data managed by the system would be accessible by every player along the chain, anywhere and anytime, giving everyone real-time visibility into the entire supply chain and generating one unified picture of what is happening within the chain. This, in turn, would position companies to effectively and efficiently carry out processes critical to supply chain management.

Summary: Identification of the CPG Industry and Company Specifics

Identifying the key drivers of an industry or the company should not be considered as a one-time or annual event. To evaluate the cloud services use by measurement of their characteristics by key drivers it is required to stay attuned to the changes of the industry and company drivers that are affected by cloud services. If these drivers change (e.g. due to the digitalization of the entire market) the measurement must shift accordingly. In building a cloud specific scorecard for a CPG company it is therefore recommended to add the information how up to date the drivers are.

For consumer product companies the cloud adoption has the potential to transform the economics of the enterprises. Cloud services constitute a transformative opportunity that could help CPG lessen the constraints of existing business models in terms of customer relationships, growth, and innovation. For CPG companies, the potential to deepen customer relationships at a lower cost with cloud services presents an interesting opportunity. Cloud services combined with social computing, mobile technologies, and data analytics could play a prominent role in helping companies meet industry challenges like declining brand loyalty, enduring consumer frugality, growing prevalence of online and mobile commerce and the growing importance of dollar and discount retail channels. Furthermore, cloud services have the potential to help companies grow in a dynamic environment where new geographies are increasingly important, regulatory requirements are more demanding, and commodity costs are volatile. The potentially transformative benefits can outweigh the risks traditionally associated with cloud computing, and the risk of inaction.

BUSINESS PROCESSES IN A CLOUD ENVIRONMENT

In the previous chapter, it has been outlined that core processes such as consumer-facing, product-innovation-related and supply chain management oriented processes may have a great potential being applied to a cloud environment.

In general, it is fair to argue that cloud services are empowering consumer products companies to meet globalization challenges by extracting increased performance from their core and non-core business processes. As we saw earlier, in today's era of globalization, consumer products companies need agile and highly effective operating and supply chain models to serve consumers. They must also be able to scale their operations up or down quickly and easily based on changing market needs.

To accommodate this, companies must sharpen their focus on core business processes (designing products and services, interacting with customers) and optimize their use of non-core business processes (finance, procurement, controlling and human resources). To meet this imperative, companies need agility, scale, and efficiency in their business processes. Cloud services can help by enabling companies to optimize their core and non-core business processes.

On the other hand-side cloud services do have another level of risk due to that fact that processes and data are not managed solely by the company any more. Following the current discussion of "cloudification" of business processes all processes are considered similar in regards to their usability within the cloud. The truth is, that neither all processes have the same usability for cloud services not do they have the same importance for a specific company. Therefore it is essential to balance the previously benefits of cloud services with a company-specific value-creation for the "cloud-affinity" and the "cloud-usability" of a business process considering on one hand side the strategic importance, the benefit as well as the operational use of a process. For this it is a pre-requisite to formalize the description of the functional and non-functional interdependencies within the company-specific value chain within the various deployment- and governance alternatives (e.g. security, compliance, quality, adaptability) using a process framework that covers the entire process landscape of a company. With the use of this proposed methodology it becomes relatively easy to identify cloud-suitable processes and thus optimize the companies value generation tightly focused with the use of this new technology.

Process Framework for CPG Industries

The End-to-End process framework is used to classify the business process and to structure the processes according to their importance.

The analysis is important for companies involved in dynamic markets with rapidly changing technology to focus on the continuous improvement of those processes that are of key importance and to manage the risk of handling their core data in a new environment such as cloud. Risk can be defined as circumstances, which certainly change and with consequences for an enterprise. (Hillson, D. & Murray-Webster, R., 2007) Due to this uncertainty of future market conditions it is even more important to focus on the most important processes and this in the light of the uncertainty of the cloud technology in some cases. "It is more important to do the right things (improve effectiveness), than to do the things right (improve efficiency)". (Hofer, C. W., Schendel, D., 1978) After the identification of the business processes that are most important for the business sustainability, the company is able to manage a structured decision towards moving with their business processes into the cloud and ensure the company's sustainability in the future.

A Consumer Product Specific End-to-End Process Classification Framework

There are several frameworks available for defining and structuring the processes. Based on the renowned Process Classification Framework (PCF), a generic taxonomy of cross-functional business processes intended to outline and define End-to-End processes-specific to the consumer products industry. In the analysis of the generic value chain in the consumer products industry it becomes obvious that those processes are the key value driving processes that are essential to deliver the required services to the customer and that strengthen the customer relationship – in other words: those processes are key, that have a visible interface to the outside. The case is that those processes are of special relevance that to deliver a significant portion of the companies value, that are focused on the fulfilment of the customers' needs and consequently create a perceivable customer benefit. The specification of a company's value chain is different for each industry, business model, organization and strategic goals.

Process-Orientation

A process is a chain of activities tailored to the provisioning of dedicated services. A process is characterized by a services input, service output, a cycle time, handling time and the use of resources.

The starting point to identify the End-to-End processes should be the value chain of each company. To assess continuous business process improvement from a process point of view it is necessary to identify the company-specific value-chain. Michael Porter described the ways in which a company could organize its activities in order to achieve competitive advantage by making it hard for others to copy. The example of a typical value chain given by Porter included all external-facing processes, and in addition their supporting ones. Based on the corporate strategy, the market development as well as the evolving customer preferences we need to give those business processes prominence that are essential for the delivery of goods and services to the customers and/or stakeholders.

The additional step towards the building of a value chain that goes beyond the classical concept of Porter is to segment the value chain in regards to a value-based value chain driven by process value that will be added to the core business of each company and thus strongly linked to the P&L positions. The cost positions and their proportions within selected companies / segments will help to set the right focus and do give an indicator of the importance and value of the area for the business and thus for the significance of the process and its KPIs. Why bother on this value-based segmentation? As said above, it provides the focused context for all work on an efficient and focused value chain management. But most importantly the highest value add is to provide

clear definitions, boundaries and dependencies on the most important processes of a company. In a one-step approach the scope is tailored to a manageable but as well most important scope at the same time to let every discussion and activity relate to the core values of a company.

Especially those processes that do cover more than one business area are important as they are a typical candidate for optimization and thus to simplify integration with the use of cloud services. To allow a comprehensive company-wide process-analysis we need to consider the supporting processes ("Enablers") to a certain extend – however we will not consider them in detail in our paper. Exemplarily we will use the purchasing processes to describe our approach in a practical example.

End-to-End Processes of the CPG Industry

The most crucial process in the CPG industry includes mainly, customer-oriented processes and purchasing. For the CPG industry it is the same as for all other industries: Inputs are the triggers for a process; they may be tangible (e.g. a letter from a customer) or intangible (e.g. a need to develop a new service). The output in public sector is mainly taken by the service a person provides it. In other words: the outputs are mainly intangible and closely related to the process performance as well as to the limitations given e.g. by legal constraints. The constraints as well as the perceived level of service needs are the boundaries to be considered when it comes to process optimization as theses constraints need to be considered within the continuous improvement and consistently monitored to be included in the process models.

The – sometimes expensive – services provided by the companies in the consumer products industry are provided with the help of and operational framework consisting of processes and systems in the light of the legal constraints. While taking advantage of the cloud services we may be able to get support from the generic cloud effects. However, we have to consider issues of the cloud services and its changes to manage issues and requirements. These issues are not confined to the CPG industry: the IT systems are necessary to control, administer and enhance the business processes, constrained by regulation – independent from their technical realization. Thus, process compliance is a major topic for business processes in this environment. Failure to comply is no option at all – this is an even higher restriction as within other businesses. Therefore, we need to have a stable framework to dynamically capture all requirements while allowing the improvement of processes.

The End-to-End process identification answers the question which business processes of a company unit are essential to fulfil the customers' needs based on the business model, the market and the corporate strategy of a company. The expected optimization with the shift of business processes into the cloud will only bring a positive impact once the profit-relation of the respective ("What is the operational effect of the process?") the cost intensity and the fraud indication ("What may happen when the process is shifted to the cloud") is evaluated. End-to end processes for multi-industry value chains such as the CPG industry needs to combine horizontal and industry specific solutions:

- Collaborate better to enhance interagency information and resource sharing;
- Adapt better for increased transparency and shifting resource needs;
- Decide better by monitoring performance for informed actions for mission success;
- Operate better to improve fiscal conditions through a holistic government view.

Prior to the use of cloud services and the correlation to the corporate value chain – defined by the companies End-to-End processes – it is important to define meaningful and measurable indicators to allow a careful examination. These indicators need to be as industry-independent as

possible to allow on one hand side an application to mostly any industry, market- and competitive situation but on the other hand side need to be as specific as necessary to allow a process appraisal in regards to their cloud service usability. Following we will consider the following dimensions of indicators:

- **Result Relevance:** The importance of a process within the value chain of a company and its value for the operating results in its current status.
- **Cost Relevance:** It is necessary to check how cost intensive the current process is and which implications will change due to a "cloudification".
- **Security Relevance:** The dimension covers he assumption of possible frauds due to the use of the process. The indicator can be expressed e.g. in "number of interfaces to 3rd party systems" or "indication in regards to sensitive data". This will give an indication in regards to the potential use of cloud services

Overall, it is necessary to consider End-to-End processes that do cover the whole company (e.g. from customer order to the delivery of goods and/or services). The analysis of sub-processes does not allow identifying fundamental process optimization potentials and process risks. Especially in functional-structured organizations, this might lead to misleading assumptions and results, because one single process covers only one single organizational unit with no indication how the overall process works. To get a profound analysis and a sustainable business case it is essential to have an end-to-end focus to analyze the change of the overall process landscape and the corporate risk of a company from a process perspective. The in Figure 3 presented End-to-End process landscape is characterized by the separation of value-driven and supportive processes. The processes have been defined as part of an overall transformation program to have a cross-company guideline for future process enhancements and tool support. The herewith outlines End-to-End processes serve as an architectural principle to slice and dice the process and system topics for the designated key user.

This End-to-End process classification framework becomes most relevant to the specific process improvement needs and to enable a beneficial benchmarking. This generic framework has allowed Villeroy & Boch to define their End-to-End process framework most relevant to the specific process improvement needs. To assess the potential use cloud services from a process point of view it is necessary to identify the company-specific End-to-End processes.

Overall, it is necessary to consider End-to-End processes that do covert he whole company (e.g. from customer order to the delivery of goods and/or services). The analysis of sub-processes does not allow identifying fundamental process optimization potentials and process risks. Espe-cially in functional-structured organizations this might lead to misleading assumptions and results, because one single process covers only one single organizational unit with no indication how the overall process works. To get a profound analysis and a sustainable business case it is essential to have an end-to-end focus to analyze the change of the overall process landscape and the corporate risk of a company from a process perspective.

A process is a chain of activities tailored to the provisioning of dedicated services. A process is characterized by a services input, service output, a cycle time, handling time and the use of resources. (Mayer, R., 1998) The process is an element of a process landscape to gain transparency of the cost driver and the interfaces to other processes. The herewith proposed enhancement regarding the usability of cloud services relating to the continuity, the consistency and the governance of business processes while using cloud services. The answering of these questions is an important lever for the

Figure 3. Villeroy & Boch end-to-end process landscape
Own Illustration, by Ute Riemann, 2014.

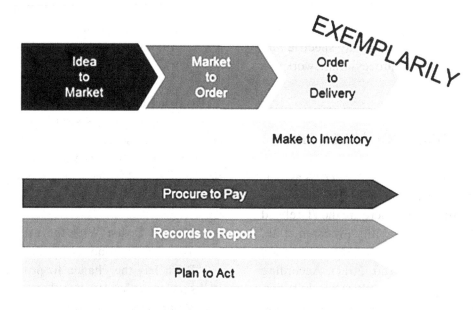

identification of the inherent costs, potentials and risks and serves as an element to support the decision whether and how to use cloud services for dedicated processes, for the identification of the most appropriate processes and the required establishment of process governance.

Summary: Developing End-to-End Process Framework for a Company of the CPG Industry

Developing an End-to-End process framework hinges on a clear understanding of the overall CPG industry, the company structure and the market approach. Moreover the process perspective is a prerequisite for cultivating the measurement of the cloud services on the processes and thus on the overall company for generating a true evaluation result that gains actionable results. The measurement system for the End-to-End processes or for the company as a whole can create value only when the processes are carefully identified and designed covering the industry and company uniqueness. Thus it is essential to take quality time to define and setup the own End-to-End process framework rather than to copy benchmarks or best practices as the processes may not be portable across companies since in the company specific and the company individual process framework lies their competitive value.

CLOUD SERVICES CHALLENGES

The current adoption of cloud services is associated with numerous challenges. Cloud services offer many advantages. There are the IT-related topics such as easy scalability (Marston et al., 2011), access to new software (Marston et al., 2011), and reliability (Yoo, 2011). According to Chang (Chang, V., 2011) there are three major challenges in the business context of cloud services.

- **Frameworks:**
  ○ Cloud business models and frameworks proposed are either qualitative or quantitative.
  ○ Each framework is self-contained, and not related to others' work. There are few frameworks or models which demonstrate linking both quantitative and qualitative aspects, and when they do, the work is still at an early stage.
- **Methodology:**
  ○ There is no accurate method for analyzing cloud business performance other than the stock market. The current available business model classifications and justifications can be successful but need more cases to support them and more data modelling to validate them for sustainability.
- **Communication between Cloud Types:**
  ○ Clouds from different vendors are often difficult to implement. This brings the question of portability, as portability of some applications from desktop to cloud is challenging referring to moving enterprise applications and services, and not just files or VM over clouds.

The benefits and risks can be structured into following main categories: security, costing model, charging model, service level agreements. (Kuyoro, S. O., et al 2011) The benefits – especially for a midsize and global acting accompany such as Villeroy & Boch are obvious:

- **Capital Costs:** With the use of a 'pay-as-you-go' economic model Villeroy & Boch has the chance to provide unique services using large-scale resources from cloud service providers and 'add or remove capacity from their IT infrastructure to meet peak or fluctuating service demands while paying only for the actual capacity used'. (Sotomayor, B. & Montero, R.S. & Llorente I. M. & Foster I., 2009)

- **Running Costs:** It can also be significantly cheaper to rent added server space for a few hours at a time rather than maintain proprietary servers.

Even though the business context is hard to predict the advantages of using cloud services are also beyond cost savings as cloud computing allows e.g. to avoid the expense and time-consuming task of installing and maintaining hardware infrastructure and software applications; and allow for the rapid provisioning and use of services to clients by optimizing their IT infrastructure. On the other hand there are the cloud service risks that are can directly applicable from the ITO literature such as business continuity, interoperability, auditability of data, not to forget the unsolved legal topics – just to name a few. (Lacity, M. C. & Willcocks, L. P., 1998)

So even though the risks are inherent and far away from being solved the significant (business) benefits that might not be affordable to the businesses, especially small and medium size companies led us to the requirement to invest in an in-depth analysis of how to get the best use and benefits of cloud services and how to best avoid fraud or mitigate the risks.

Therefore we need to find an approach that helps identifying especially the risks for one company, make the (business) risks transparent to allow the best decision towards cloud services. One core assumption in this chapter is, that the company's business opportunities and chances has to be set in focus rather than focusing on technology and IT management. As the End-to-End business processes reflect the core processes and thus the DNA of a company the outline approach considers this model as the fundamental layer to drive the evaluation.

IDENTIFICATION OF INDUSTRY BUSINESS PROCESSES FOR CLOUD SERVICES

Categorization of End-to-End Processes

As previously mentioned, cloud computing has both benefits and drawbacks, however it is vital to examine if these benefits and drawbacks are beneficial or detrimental to businesses when deciding whether or not to implement cloud computing. Although cloud computing has been recognized as a way to improve business, not all businesses are the same.

One of the questions is which of these industry business processes are suitable for cloud computing. Before an evaluation can be performed, it is necessary to categorize the business processes. A business function is an element of a company. Each industry business process is structured into procedures of activities. The elements of a company are described in Business Function Ontologies (BFO), to provide a hierarchy of different functions and an abstraction of available industry business processes of an organization as an independent classification. BFOs are a common vocabulary for business functions within enterprises. (Filipowska, A. & Hepp, M. & Kaczmarek, M. & Markovic, I., 2014). A company consists of several functional areas such as marketing, finance, human resources (HR), management, research and development, procurement, etc. (Abramowicz, W. & Filipowska, A., Kaczmarek, M. & Pedrinaci, C. & Starzecka, M. & Walczak, A., 2014). Business functions can be structured into support and core business functions. Core business functions "are activities of an enterprise yielding income" (European Comission, 2013). It is usually the primary activity of an enterprise such as logistics and production. Secondary activities can also be part of the core business, if they are important. Support business functions reflect all other secondary activities. (European Comission, 2013) Consumer Products

Industries require the typical support business functions finance, inventory, human resources, customer service, marketing and sales, procurement, and management and administration. Besides this general business functions, we have a specialty within Villeroy & Boch in the sense that this company serves different markets due both product lines tableware and bath & wellness. Tableware is a typical retail business with own points of sales whereas bath & wellness is managed within a 3-step business model as an indirect business-to-business model. Therefore, driven by the different markets and the variances in the products the processes do vary on level 2 and level 3 due to the variance within the product and business. However, in general and on End-to-End process level 1 the core business functions represent the typical industry process within the consumer products industry.

Selection, Scoring, and Weighting of Evaluation Criteria

Since the support of business processes by IT tools may become an expensive resource for organizations, cloud services seems to be a perfect alternative to overcome this costly "exercise". (Miller, M., 2009) To "over-simplify it: "The only requirements are a computer and an Internet connection. If these requirements are available for the user, documents can be easily accessed from anywhere". (Miller, M., 2009)

But is it that simple?

Unfortunately, it is not as the concept of cloud computing in business may sound ideal and easy to implement, but like all new technology being introduced into a business that already has a system and method in place it has both positive and negative aspects. (Abdulaziz, A., 2012)

To find the right answers if and where and how to get the benefits of cloud services it is essential to de-couple IT-driven arguments (e.g. scalability) from the business-driven arguments simply to find the most comprehensive and neutral set of pros and cons driven by the business and not by IT. Therefore,

the following scoring model is focused on the business perspective on cloud services – not saying that after having completed this "business exercise" the IT points of view needs to be added to get the full picture for one company. The process identification and selection answers the question that business processes of a corporate unit are essential to fulfill the customers and/or other stakeholders' needs based on the business model, the market and the corporate strategy of one company.

The expected optimization with the shift of business processes into the cloud will only bring a positive impact once the profit-relation of the respective ("What is the operational effect of the process?") the cost intensity and the fraud indication ("What may happen when the process is shifted to the cloud") is evaluated. Therefore, the business functions have to be evaluated based on useful evaluation criteria in regards to their risk and benefit business value level. Prior to the use of cloud services, it is important to define meaningful and measurable indicators to allow a careful evaluation. The criteria used play a key role in determining cloud services place in a company. For this reason, it is important to ground the indicators in some essential principles.

A sound set of indicators does two things: First, it improves the decision-making towards cloud services by helping to focus on those aspects of the business and business environment that create value. In the process it provides feedback to be used to evaluate the impact of cloud services towards the company strategy and though of future decisions. A well-thought out set of indicators thus act as both a guide and a benchmark for evaluating cloud service contribution to the company's strategy implementation. In addition, it provides a valid and systematic justification for process and IT tool support decisions. Cloud services cannot legitimately claim its benefit for a company unless it can show how it contributes to the company's success. An appropriately set of indicators allows explicating the links and thus lay the groundwork for investments in cloud services.

The measurement of cloud services shall be strategically meaning that it is essential to understand whether the considered indicators will provide the kind of information that will help to decide towards cloud services strategically. In addition, the set of indicators need to support "top down" thinking rather than a "bottom up" to guide the decisions underlying the measurement system. Understanding the impact of cloud services and developing construct-valid measures do form this top down approach.

In general the indicators are a sophisticated form of benchmarking, because they need to be as industry-independent as possible to allow on one hand side an application to mostly any industry, market- and competitive situation but on the other hand side need to be as specific as necessary to allow a process appraisal in regards to their cloud service usability.

This can be done by using a scoring model. "A scoring model is a formula that assigns points based on known information to predict an unknown future outcome". (Perrine, D., 2007) When implementing software solutions, the decision maker needs to consider business value, implementation and operational impact (Accenture, n.d.).

When we speak of indicators what is really meant? Good indicators require an understanding of and expertise in measurement of the industry, the processes and the cloud services. Therefore, the first step to identify "indicators with a meaning" is the following analysis is the selection and scoring of useful evaluation criteria with the adding of context to the indicators. This is the appeal of a benchmark – herein for the CPG industry. For doing this we will again come back to the dimensions of business value, cost and security relevance:

- **Business Value Relevance:** The importance of a process of a company and its value for the operating results in its current status.

- **Cost Relevance:** Defendant on the As-is processes wit is related systems it is necessary to check how cost intensive the current process is and which implications will change due to a "cloudification".

- **Security Relevance:** The dimension covers he assumption of possible frauds due to the use of the process. The indicator can be expressed e.g. in number of interfaces to 3rd party systems» or "indication in regards to sensitive data". This will give an indication in regards to the potential use of cloud services

Taking the outlined three main areas of business value, cost relevance and security relevance as a theoretical basis, I will commence defining the appropriate set of indicators. The selected set of indicators is taken by coincidence and needs to be detailed within a specific consulting context with the related specifics and optimization targets. Therefore, the following example serves as a demonstration that this systematic approach fits a gap in the overall analysis of business-driven security aspects – independent from a technical driven implementation approach. In a nutshell: the proposed process-optimization approach proposed herewith will allow an implementation independent analysis of the chances and risks of the selected implementation strategy in the context of cloud services.

The aspect 'business value' contains the criteria regular operational expenditures (OPEX), return on investment, internal policy and compliance regulations, government regulations, business impact, data privacy, and number of users and economy of scale. Regular operational expenditures are ongoing costs for running a system. The criterion is structured into the dimensions low, medium, and high. The higher the importance of this criterion gets, the lower the software solution types are scored. Regular costs are important for business functions and the belonging software solutions with a relatively low level of business impact. The return on investment (ROI) measures the financial return of capital expenditures (CAPEX). In addition, "the flexibility and agility of cloud computing allows a company to focus on its core competencies". (Sosonsky, B., 2011) The criterion is structured into dimensions low, medium and high. The higher the importance of a business function is, the lower the scoring is.

The cost relevance is the most common and obvious one since it analyses and measures the cost of the entire process.

The security relevance is the new dimension that shall be added to the discussion of business processes in the cloud. The security relevance expressed by fraud indicators is a new element in the overall process analysis to allow the estimation of the usability of cloud services for certain processes. Internal policy and compliance regulations affect processes as well. The criterion is divided into the following sub-criteria:

- **Number of Interfaces:** Interfaces to other processes or users are the "gateway» to interchange data. This can lead to a lack of trustworthiness as well to an issue regarding the compliance regulations.
- **Relevance of the Process for the Business:** Especially in regards to the business continuity management relevant.
- **Number of Compliance Rules:** (Sub-) processes need – dependent on the industry- fulfill legal requirements. Depending on the implementation this might lead to significant frauds.
- **Number of Roles:** The more people are involved the higher is the chance, that any of these persons might affect the process negatively and use the information for not-allowed purposes.
- **Value of the Assets Triggered by the Process:** If the assets of a company are affected by a process the initial value of each affected asset is of importance for the estimation of the risk within a dedicated environment.

Another important aspect is that each process can be (slightly) differently implemented according to the business model and/or business needs of each company (e.g. the detailed process covering the push or pull principle will be different in a detailed process or transaction level). This difference needs to be considered as well when applying and weighting the indicators. This simple example is intended to give a high level idea of the complexity and the variance of the factors that affect a process such as the Procure-to-Pay process and how complex as well important it is to establish a standardized fraud-analysis framework. The weighting of evaluation criteria is limited objective. Each decision maker or company must make this limited objective decision on its own. This may have a big influence on the result. The weighting of the criteria in the present study is based on expert interviews as well.

Prioritization of Industry Business Process Categories

As already mentioned the business processes guide the cloud service contribution towards the CPG Company. At the end this contribution shall, has to and need to be expressed quantitatively. Considering the approach to define a sustainable ROI for cloud service (Chang, V., 2012) the following business process-driven approach shall give an added value to the idea of building a business-driven ROI covering the various dimensions of cloud services.

Having the business process categories in the center of the analysis the proposed approach provides a scorecard that validates the cloud service contribution in terms of benefits and risks for a CPG company. Therefore, it is essential after having selected and scored the evaluation criteria to rate the industry business processes must be rated according to the dimension of each criterion.

Scaling, Weighting, and Measuring

Throughout the chapter, it has been emphasized that we have to consider the cloud specifics, the business industry specifics and the processes as the main three dimensions for measuring. Now the measuring system itself will be outlined to manage the cloud specifics and to evaluate its contribution to a CPG company. In choosing measures to evaluate the impact of cloud services on business processes one has to consider the scaling, weighting and measuring. Depending on the scale and weighting of the measurement criteria, the company gives importance to the various aspects measured. Measuring gives meaning to the indicators and to potential changes due to the use of cloud services. However, those measures are very likely to be company-specific. Therefore, the magnitude of those indicators is unique to each company and consequently the less useful it is for being used as a benchmark. For the purpose of this chapter, the definition of measurement is the company's process and system architecture and the company strategy. The properties that are most interesting are the value creating processes – in other words, the deliverables of a process and the value drivers that the deliverables influence, thinking of them as observable measures. The measurement process itself is not an end in itself. It has only value if the results contribute to a meaningful decision in regards to the use of cloud services. Measurement is defined as the process of assigning values to the identified indicators by following certain rules. The set of criteria needs to answer the question if the use of cloud services will produce a change in the company's performance and if so how significant. In short: the criteria need to be actionable. Therefor the following set of indicators has been defined assuming that criteria have a significant impact. Additionally indicators such as sensitivity of processed data and the data availability should be taken into consideration. Especially the data availability is important in this context as the most processes run through various instances, users and IT systems meaning that the data might have different system sources. For this reason the importance of each criterion must be analyzed in a preference matrix that is industry and company-specific. This matrix relates each criterion to another criterion. As an example we will apply fraud indicators to the processes and process steps of the End-to-End process of Procure-to-Pay. The values are standardizes with 1 (= low) to 5 (= high). With this rather simplified model is becomes clear, that the process steps do have diverse fraud profiles. Depending on the transformation and implementation – that will be integrated into the risk assessment – we will derive specific risk estimation.

Each criterion may have a positive or negative influence on the decision score of the cloud computing solution types. Therefore the cloud impact can be marked as a benefit or risk in the evaluation matrix. On the basis of the evaluation, it is possible to get a decision score, which indicates a prioritization of industry business

Table 2. Simplified charter for fraud indicator grid

Driver Indicator	Order Specification	Delivery	Pricing	Order	Fulfillment	Payment
Interfaces						
Relevance						
Compliance						
Roles						
Assets						

Own Illustration, by Ute Riemann, 2014.

process categories. The result of the evaluation is a scoring matrix and a decision score for each industry business process category and software solution type private cloud, public managed cloud and on-premises.

The measures explored are based on simple principles of measurement. Their advantage lies not so much in their degree of sophistication towards cloud-service specifics and business process details, but in their ability to help the company to focus on the activity of measurement in general. All of the criteria prompt to think about the processes and about their importance for the company. Most important, these simple measures allow to draw the attention with the core matter on "if and how to get use of cloud services".

Due to this decision score, it is possible to rank and prioritize business functions as industry business process categories. It is necessary to compare the decision score of different solution types of each business function, to prioritize them and decide either to implement industry business processes as a public cloud, private managed cloud, or on-premises solution. This priority based on the decision score is described as ranking per business function. Secondly, it is possible to order for example all private managed cloud decision scores, to get to know, which business function fits best to the corresponding solution type. It is striking that the scores of each software solution type of one business function are very close to each other, but very different compared to other business functions. This indicates the different requirements, challenges, and demands of various industry business processes. The higher the score is, the more challenges need to be overcome, to implement a business process as a solution of the belonging software solution type.

To illustrate the approach mentioned above, let's consider the End-to-End process Order-to-Cash within a CPG company. Although this is not the specific process for Villeroy & Boch, it is possible to be used since the process is applicable widely even though variances due to industry

and company specifics need to be considered. Therefore, the process and the typical criteria of a CPG company itself will illustrate the methodology. Above all the main three deliverables of the process is to allow a

- More customer segmentation even down to a 1:1 market with less control of the customer behavior.
- Organizational productivity for simple and fast processing with reasonable costs.
- Flexible collaboration to meet the flexible customer requirements and demands.

To apply this to the methodology, they are translated into the drivers of the processes that make up the End-to-End flow. Then the key cloud service indicators are named that may have influence on the overall processing to achieve the deliverables of the process. Based on the main three process deliverables it is possible to identify and weight those drivers and indicators that are most important for the company to allow a seamless process.

For this example the combination interfaces and selection is of high importance due to the fact, that various suppliers need to join an online platform, sharing their confidential price information based on the company's confidential offering. Let's now imaging that the company identified this factor combination as the most important fact considering a cloud service implementation and let's as well assume the company rates the fact of handling confidential data as a critical fact for using cloud services the scoring gives the hint to select the right path forward.

Again, for simplicity's sake, this example is limited to a few elements. Assuming the End-to-End process landscape of a company together with the most important indicators of cloud services the analysis becomes significantly complex. However this simple example shows that this analysis gives actionable results. For one thing, it gives an intuitive summary of how the cloud services impact the business process. It does alert to any issues

Table 3. Simplified charter for fraud indicator grid for the order-to-cash process at a typical CPG company

Driver Indicator	Order Specification	Delivery	Pricing	Order	Fulfillment	Payment
Interfaces	4	4	4	5	5	5
Relevance	4	3	1	4	5	3
Compliance	5	2	2	1	3	2
Roles	5	1	2	3	2	2
Assets	1	2	2	2	4	5

Own Illustration, by Ute Riemann, 2014.

that may be related to the use of cloud services and provides some guidance on if this process is suitable for the use of cloud services and what risks need to be addressed if this processes will be migrated to a cloud service solution. Note, though that guidance for if this processes is suitable for your company in regards to cloud services this is only a perceptual map. It does not tell of the process is in fact not suitable for the application of cloud services; it just shows the current perception. Therefore once this result is in place it is recommended to determine in detail this result.

Business Process Risk Management in a Cloud Environment

Risk analysis is useful to help organizations to understand the extent of business and operational risks, which can vary from time to time (Chang, V. 2014) For the business process owner it is important to know immediately which effects issues in the process (no matter if occurred in the cloud or not) has and to have the ability to assess the impact. Vice versa: if we do not want to be reactive we have to establish a federated framework that does allow an anticipation of the effects to evaluate the risk potential of a process. To achieve this we have to change the way in which processes are evaluated in the "the light of cloud" to ensure that all risk relevant indicators are maintained. The challenges an organization faces is when it adjusts the processes to meet the new potential of cloud services. The organization must ensure

that the processes are federated in such a way that they still meet the compliance requirements whilst at the same time prioritize the flexibility as a major benefit of using cloud services to be a competitive leader in the longer term. With the introduction of cloud services we have consider, that we cannot directly evaluate the processing system directly to achieve compliance even though the processing environment becomes an increasing integral part of the business process analysis. The business processes are the active part of the business. They describe the functions of the business, and involve resources that are used, transformed, or produced. A common definition of business process is (Davenport, T., 1992):

A process is simply a structured set of activities designed to produce a specified output for a particular customer or market. It implies a strong emphasis on how work is done within an organization, in contrast to a product's focus on what. A process is thus a specific ordering of work activities across time and place, with a beginning, an end, and clearly identified inputs and outputs: a structure for action.

It is not a new understanding that all businesses make some use of information technology, and it is important that their systems are really built to support the businesses of which they are an integrated part. The business is what ultimately defines the requirements on the information systems. Thus use of cloud services without a proper understanding of the context in which the process is to operate is a dangerous adventure. A business is a complex system, consisting of a hierarchical organization of departments and their functions. In order to get such an understanding, it is essential to make a comprehensive model of the business. Even though such a model is a simplified view of a complex reality it is important to cover all relevant dimensions to focus on the important aspects at a time. In the context of federated processes in the cloud environment we need to develop a model to make the core topics of process compliance in the cloud transparent to make them manageable. The traditional method for analyzing business processes is to draw business flow chart which divides the business process into a number of sections. This documentation method is limited to how the business process is built, organized and supported with any kind of IT. Important information such as rules that govern the execution of the business, the goals, and compliance rules cannot be captured in the traditional organizational view. A good business model contains all of this information on one side but reduces the complexity in such a way that the main information is kept and the overall model is manageable. With the increasing complexity using cloud services the capturing and documenting of this information in itself is be the basis for making better decisions that result in a business that runs more smoothly, and better protected against fraud for specifying the requirements of the cloud services. Since the technology is readily available to meet the technical changes and the regulatory requirements remain independent from the technology applied to a process we have to overcome the new threats arising with the use of cloud services enabling a simpler and flexible deployment of processes and process changes with a low cost of ownership and a manageable risk with the adoption of all factors that come along with the cloud services. Thus we need to know how to become compliant when defining the processes, stay compliant once we implement

the process / applying them to cloud services and remain compliant once we run and maintain each process using service in the cloud.

To better manage business process compliance in the cloud we propose to set up a comprehensive business model that covers these dimensions. By contrast to other existing frameworks we propose in analogy to the model of Eriksson-Penker (Eriksson, H.-E. Penker, M., 1999) and (Eriksson, H.-E. Penker, M., 1998) to develop a model that strictly separates the different views towards a process and that allows to create a framework to understand the dynamics and complexity of federated processes with the use of cloud services. Thus the framework addresses the issue that the business and IT "picture" is too complex such that they cannot be fully described by one single perspective but multiple point of views of different stakeholders are required. On the one hand, the model need to apply to the fundamentals of UML process modeling by selecting relevant aspects of the UML concept. On the other hand, our model adapts elements of the existing approaches for the process modularization and existing GRC frameworks. Each view needs to express a dedicated view towards the process dependent on the specific target the view shall depict. In our context the views need to capture the business view of the process, the cloud service and the GRC dimension. The overall view on a process is dynamically derived from the interactions with each other. In enforcing a strict separation of these views we separate business flows from cloud service logic from GRC KPIs.

Business Perspective

The central perspective is the business (process) perspective, which describes activities within the business and how they relate to and interact with the resources in the business to achieve a goal for the process. The business perspective is the center of business modeling. One of the primary motives for developing a business view on the processes is to increase the understanding of the business and facilitate communication about the business. The processes show the activities to achieve an explicit goal and their relationships with the resources participating in the process. As noted earlier, the business model cannot and should not contain all the details of the business. Thus, the model should focus on the core business processes from the company's value chain identified in a previous analysis as a pre-requisite. There are relationships between the process modules, between different processes that interact and there is a coupling of process (modules) to business goals. The model is a current snapshot and with the change of the process modules it will change and evolve according to the business changes. The model gives a fairly stable, because they give a clear picture of the roles and tasks in the overall organization.

Service Perspective

The business perspective and the process module descriptions are used to identify necessary information for the required cloud services that shall support the business. Ideally, large sections of the business perspective can be mapped directly onto cloud services. The strict separation allows the decision which cloud services are required to support which process module. Cloud services now allow for a whole new dimension of process module shifting. That dimension is defined by even more flexibility regarding outsourcing of process modules. Next to various technical questions it is important to stay aware of the business consequences of engaging processes inside the cloud. Ideally, the business process (modules) can be translated or mapped to one cloud service. Since this is not always the case the translation cannot always be translated into one cloud service, since there are cloud services that are not present at all in the business model, and vice versa. This makes a direct mapping between the "business world" as described by the business model and the cloud services impossible. Nevertheless, even

if a one-to-one mapping between the business perspective and the cloud service perspective is not possible, the way the business operates and the cloud services used to support it are more tightly integrated using our proposed framework. Each service has a standard interface communicating with each other. The benefits of technical modularization face rising complexity regarding process monitoring getting necessary as processes are autonomously executed in foreign organizations -- even in a trusted federation, since each organization has flexible integration capabilities of the received and processed information, using analytical tools, for example.

GRC/Compliance Perspective

Besides the business perspective and cloud service perspective the compliance framework – expressed in KPIs have to be described. This rising communication and monitoring effort is to be specified and must be addressed by adequate control mechanisms. This perspective determines the compliance requirements for the process and data managed in each process module. The use of cloud services is determined by the compliance perspective as the cloud services cannot precede the GRC / compliance perspective. Consequently, the GRC / compliance perspective has to be completed before the cloud service perspective can be specified. This problem is to be addressed by defined standards, regulations and GRC requirements to reach process goals and assure process information security.

Due to the multilayered nature of this problem, an information security management system has to be supported methodologically. Effective risk and compliance management always requires an implemented governance framework and addresses the main information security criteria of confidentiality, availability and integrity of the processed information as well as various regulatory obligations. To create value out of the separation of these views we have to link these views in a common framework. The framework needs to link the processes their compliance requirements and metrics for measurement and cloud services into a metrics structure to span all possible dimensions. With the focus of the most important processes alongside a company-specific value chain we are able to focus on those processes that are of key value for the company and thus having the highest fraud potential. As we begin to create the business processes, cloud services and compliance requirements we need to understand the business requirements first followed by the compliance requirements. Thereafter we have to answer the question if and if yes: which cloud service we deploy should do to help the business? For analysis, we turn to describe the fraud level of a business process (module) to capture the intended fraud-level of the business process (model) independent of any IT system. The business perspective is purely designed to describe the dynamics of the process (models) and their interdependencies. The cloud service view is the technical representation of the business perspective. It may be derived from the cloud service description. The process models from the business perspective need to be mapped to one or more cloud services.

Having designed this framework all three dimensions capture the intend and expected behaviors of the system covering the implication of the fraud level while creating various scenarios with the shift of process (models) into the cloud. When design is driven from analysis, we can be more confident that select the most appropriate processes for being applied into cloud services with a full transparency on the fraud level we are willing to accept and to manage.

Summary: The Business Process Prioritization Sets the Focus of the Cloud Service Use

The words criteria, scorecard and measuring seems to be on everyone's lips while trying to evaluate an impact of an emerging concept on the own compa-

nies situation. The chapter tries to demonstrate why the identification of the right dimensions, criteria and weighting is so important to measure the impact of cloud service on the company's processes. The chapter as well emphasized the importance of measurement as a foundational capability. The need for better measures becomes particularly acute in evaluating the complex situation such as the process landscape in relation to cloud services. The chapter introduces an approach to measure this complex set up. First the measures itself as a diagnostic tool are outlined. The emphasis here was on transparency as an indicator of the benefit and risks a cloud service may have capturing the fit to one's process.

With the help of fraud indicators from the GRC/compliance view we can use these metrics to identify the fraud level on each process module covering the whole business dimension with a link to the cloud services.

DETERMINATION ON BENEFITS AND RISKS FOR PROCESSES USING CLOUD SERVICES

The consummation of IT will continue to drive the customer in the future. The way of thinking will evolve. More and more customers will decide to implement cloud-based applications instead of on-premises solutions. Innovation will remain a top priority of them. Cloud services need to be accepted as an additional challenge of process governance covering the process quality. While using the processes within the cloud we need to consider the nature of cloud per se, e.g. cloud interfaces from and to the cloud as well as the type of cloud (public, private, and hybrid). It is therefore necessary to provide an adapted and continuous process quality management. To establish such an appropriate process quality management covering especially the topic of process compliance we need to derive and enhance the main pillars from the corporate governance, IT governance and process governance that are already established in any company. These enhancements will then cover mainly the process specifics in correlation with the cloud typology. One key element is the coverage of the policies while using cloud services. These policies are basically the rules and regulations that are essential for the valuation of a processes appliance to the cloud and especially those policies that consider the use of cloud services while running the processes and process data needs to be re-shaped for the appliance to the cloud. The target is therefore to establish a governance model that secures the governance topic within the cloud. (Guo et.al, 2010) Especially the coverage of the process compliance needs to be considered within the enhanced policies to allow a smooth and secure handling the fraud risks while running processes in the cloud. Compliance is the ensuring that business operations, processes, and practices are in accordance with a given prescriptive (often legal) document. (Governatori, G., Indulska, M., zu Muehlen, M., 2009) In a broader perspective, compliance is about unambiguously ensuring conformance to a set of prescribed and/or agreed upon norms. (Turetken, O., Elgammal, A.& van den Heuvel, W.-J., Papazoglou, M., 2004). Compliance is a multidimensional concern that applies to the entire business processes (BP) and its lifecycle phases impacting not only the BP control and data flow, but also management and governance aspects. (Turetken, O., Elgammal, A.& van den Heuvel & W.-J., Papazoglou, M., 2004) This, in combination with the cloud-specifics points towards a generic framework for analyzing the compliance-affinity throughout the entire process value chain of a company.

The compliance certification of business processes is therefore a key element targeting a sustainable process implementation in the cloud. Even though cloud is new to the process environment the policies need to follow the same regulations and requirements of those without taking advantage of the cloud services.

Even though processes are processed with the use of cloud services all rules, regulations and policies remain still valid and unchanged – by contrast additional regulations need to be considered, e.g. the control of processes in the cloud needs to be secured but becomes with the appliance of cloud more complex and vague as the level of control is more indirect compared to the control of a normal system landscape that handles the processes.

CONCLUSION

The consummation of cloud services will continue to drive the business process design and implementation in the future. More and more customers will decide to implement cloud-based applications instead of on-premises solutions. Innovation will remain a top priority of them and cloud services now allow for a whole new dimension defined by even more flexibility regarding outsourcing of process modules. All currently existing cloud service models are conceivable for the CPG industries. Especially part of the investigation were SaaS solutions. Customers in the CPG industry can profit from the advantages of cloud computing, such as the fast adoption and scalability of applications. Furthermore, cloud computing offers a fast and easy time to value. Consequently, customers can concentrate on their core business and speed up their business velocity. On the other hand, security remains one of the major topics in cloud computing. The cloud providers have to ensure data privacy and must win the customers confidence. Especially customer-oriented areas must prepare themselves for challenges of a new technology.

However, the decision towards cloud services is not an easy and simple one and deserves a structured approach. The presented framework specifically captures the dynamics of the business while, keeping the dynamics of cloud service and increases the quality of transparency in regards to process risk and compliance at the same time. Moreover the framework analysis provides a tendency of beneficial cloud product categories and industry business processes and addresses the issue that the business and IT "picture" is too complex so that they cannot be fully described by one single perspective but multiple points of view of different stakeholders are required.

To establish such an appropriate structure and framework covering especially the topic of process compliance we need to enhance and operationalize the main pillars from the corporate governance, IT governance and process governance that are already established in any company. These enhancements will then cover mainly the process specifics in correlation with the cloud typology. One key element is the coverage of the policies while using cloud services. These policies are basically the rules and regulations that are essential for the valuation of a processes appliance to the cloud and especially those policies that consider the use of cloud services while running the processes and process data needs to be re-shaped for the appliance to the cloud.

Even though cloud is new to the process environment the policies need to follow the same regulations and requirements of those without taking advantage of the cloud services – by contrast additional regulations need to be considered, e.g. the control of processes in the cloud needs to be secured but becomes with the appliance of cloud more complex and vague as the level of control is more indirect compared to the control of a normal system landscape that handles the processes. In general three main questions need to be answered as an outlook:

- What are the risks of each process that needs to be considered while shifting a certain process to the cloud?
- What are the stakeholders (e.g. auditors) and their requirements that need to be considered in terms of performing the requested controls?

- What are the needs of the process owner in regards to an estimation of the data processing of their processes using cloud services?

In the context of the CPG industry, cloud computing is particularly efficient in collection and analyses of huge volumes of sales data and in real time inventory management. (Ernst & Young and IE foundation, 2013) The challenges of cloud computing adoption are:

- **Information Security and Data Integrity:** Processing data with a cloud services provider followed by communication over the internet, as opposed to keeping it within the company network, increases data and information vulnerability. Key information security risks when processing data in the cloud are unauthorized modification to the network's logical or physical areas, unauthorized modification of systems or data and unauthorized deletion of data. A common concern for companies is the loss of control over their business information by trusting cloud providers with secure authentication, user credentials, and data management.
- **Compliance and Privacy:** Regarding privacy, a single data breach could cause considerable damage to the name of an organization, hurt its reputation and limit its growth potential, not to mention the direct costs caused by the leak. Organizations are obliged by law or industry regulations to store, trace and even not transfer certain information. Moving data to the cloud does not relieve the organization from its compliance obligations, but rather the contrary. Irrespective of where the data resides, the organization still has its obligations. Accordingly, the organization will need to have a firm grasp of the legal and regulatory requirements of each jurisdiction in which the organization and the cloud provider operate.

- **Standards and Interoperability:** Cloud service provides generally develop personalized services that meet the needs of their target public. However, for efficient interaction with the provider's applications, the companies' and the cloud providers' systems need to be able to talk to one another.
- Otherwise, the continuity of the process, the performance of the application, the inability to tailor applications and the overall efficiency of the desired services are jeopardized. Standards are under development, but this is a lengthy process.
- **Supplier Management and Governance:** Service level agreements or contracts often stipulate a user's ability to audit a supplier, the legal recourse available in the event of incidents and the owner of the data stored in the cloud. Often they contain essential details regarding key elements of the service; e.g. the level or percentage of availability and the storage space assigned. These terms are often not negotiable, especially for users of basic service packages.

To draw a conclusion: cloud service is well-arrived in the business perspective. To support a structured view and a sustainable success of cloud services in its various occurrences it is essentially to

- Support the use of cloud with a structured approach to identify and proactively manage the process risks with the use of appropriate fraud indicators.
- Provide an adequate level of security applied in enhanced policies to allow and up-to-date process governance with the coverage of all regulations that are in place while using cloud services.
- Establish a stable framework as a layer for a corporate framework covering the needs of a business perspective with the use of cloud services.

ACKNOWLEDGMENT

I would particularly like to give thanks to Thomas Ochs, CIO of Villeroy & Boch who supported me in giving insights of a mid-size company in the consumer products industry. I really appreciate to get his support to apply a theoretical approach to a real life business.

REFERENCES

Abdulaziz, A. E. (2012). Cloud Computing for Increased Business Value. *International Journal of Business and Social Science*, *3*(1), 235–238.

Abramowicz, W., Filipowska, A., Kaczmarek, M., Pedrinaci, C., Starzecka, M., & Walczak, A. (2014). *Organization Structure Description for the Needs of Semantic Business Process Management*. Retrieved from http://ceur-ws.org/Vol-472/paper3.pdf

Accenture. (2014). Our cloud strategy approach. Retrieved from http://www.accenture.com/Microsites/cloudstrategy/documents/cloud_diagram/index.html

Anderson, J. E., Wiles, F. A., & Young, K. P. (2008). The Impact of Cloud Computing on IS/IT Academics. *Issues in Information Systems*, *9*(1), 203–206.

Ariba. (2012). *Ariba Invoice Professional*. Retrieved from http://www.ariba.com/assets/uploads/documents/Datasheets/Ariba-Invoice-Professional.pdf

Armbrust, M., Fox, F., Griffith, R., Joseph, A. D., Katz, R., Konwinski, A., . . . Zaharia, M. (2009). Above the Clouds: A Berkeley View of Cloud Computing. Berketley, CA: UC Berkeley Reliable Adaptive Distributed Systems Laboratory.

Arnold, S. (2009). *Cloud computing and the issue of privacy* (pp. 14–22). KM World.

Bhadauria, R., Chaki, R., Chaki, N., & Sanyal, S. (2012). *A Survey on Security Issues in Cloud Computing.* School of Electronics and Communications Engineering, Vellore Institute of Technology, Vellore, India.

Bisong, A., & Rahman, S. (2011). An overview of the security concerns in enterprises. *International Journal of Network Security & Its Applications (IJNSA), 3*(1).

Brodkin, J. (2007). *IBM unveils cloud computing technologies for internet-scale computing on the way in spring. Network World.*

Buyya, R., Broberg, J., & Goscinski, A. (2011). Cloud computing principles and paradigms. Hoboken, New Jersey: John Wiley & Sons, Inc. doi:10.1002/9780470940105

Chang, D., Bacigalupo, G. W., & De Roure, D. (2010). *A categorization of cloud computing business models.* IEEE Xplore Digital Library.

Chang, V., Li, C., De Roure, D., Wills, G., Walters, R. J., & Chee, C. (2012). The Financial Clouds Review. In Grid and Cloud Computing: Concepts, Methodologies, Tools and Applications (pp. 1062-1083). Hershey, PA: Information Science Reference. doi:10.4018/978-1-4666-0879-5.ch503

Chang, V., Wills, G., Walters, R., & Currie, W. (2012). (in press). Towards a structured cloud ROI. *Sustainable Green Computing: Practices Methodologies and Technologies.*

Chang, V. (2014). An introductory approach to risk visualization as a service. *Open Journal of Cloud Computing, 1*(1).

Cloud Security Alliance. (2010). Top threats to cloud computing V1.0. Retrieved from http://www.cloud-securityalliance.org/topthreats/csathreats.v1.0.pdf

Davenport, T. (1992). *Process innovation: Reengineering work through information technology.* Harvard Business Review Press.

Deloitte. (2012). *Rethinking the role of IT for CPG companies using cloud computing to help escape the constraints of existing business economics.* Retrieved from https://www.deloitte.com/assets/Dcom-UnitedStates/Local%20Content/Articles/Consumer%20Business/Consumer%20Products/us_cp_rethinkingtheroleofIT_042512.pdf

Deloitte (2013). Moving to the Cloud? Engage internal audit upfront to manage risks. *Wall Street Journal.* Retrieved from http://deloitte.wsj.com/riskandcompliance/2013/12/11/moving-to-the-cloud-engage-internal-audit-upfront-to-manage-risks-2/?KEYWORDS=cloud

Eriksson, H.-E., & Penker, M. (1999). *Business Modeling with UML: Business patterns at work.* Wiley & Sons.

Eriksson, H.-E. & Penker, M. (1998). UML Toolkit. Wiley & Sons.

Ernst & Young and IE Foundation. (2013). Security solutions in consumer goods & retail. In Consumer Goods & Retail. Advanced series Foundation.

European Comission. (2013). Glossary: Business functions - statistics explained. Retrieved from http://epp.eurostat.ec.europa.eu/statistics_explained/index.php/Glossary:Core_business_function

Filipowska, A., Hepp, M., Kaczmarek, M., & Markovic, I. (2014.). Organisational ontology framework for semantic business prcoess management. Retrieved from http://www.heppnetz.de/files/OrganizationalOntologyFrameworkSBPM.pdf

Gartner. (2013). Gartner says cloud computing will become the bulk of new it spend by 2016. Retrieved from http://www.gartner.com/newsroom/id/2613015

Global Netoptex Incorporated. (2009). Demystifying the cloud: Important opportunities, crucial choices (pp. 4-14). Retrieved from http://www. gni.com

Goldberg, R. P. (1974). Survey of Virtual Machine Research. *IEEE Computer*, *7*(6), 34–45. doi:10.1109/MC.1974.6323581

Governatori, G., Indulska, M., & zu Muehlen, M. (2009). *Formal models of business process compliance*. JURIX.

Guo, Z., Song, M., & Song, J. (2010). *A governance model for cloud computing*. Paper presented at the Management and Service Science (MASS).

Haag, S., & Cummings, M. (2010). *Management information systems for the information age (8*[th] *ed.)*. New York: McGraw-Hill/Irwin.

Hillson, D., & Murray-Webster, R. (2007). *Understanding and managing risk attitude*. Aldershot: Gower Publishing Co Ltd.

Hofer, C. W., & Schendel, D. (1978). *Strategy formulation: analytical concepts*. West Pub. Company.

Huebscher, M. C., & McCann, J. A. (2008). A survey of autonomic computing degrees, models, and applications. *ACM Computing Surveys*, *40*(3), 1–28. doi:10.1145/1380584.1380585

IDC. (2012). *IDC releases market predictions for 2013: CIO agenda*. Retrieved from http://www. idc.com/getdoc.jsp?containerId=prUS24482213

IDC. (2013). *IDC predictions 2013: Competing on the 3rd platform*. Retrieved from http:// www.idc.com/research/Predictions13/downloadable/238044.pdf

International Business Machines Corp. (2006). *An architectural blueprint for autonomic computing*. White Paper Fourth Edition.

Lacity, M. C., & Willcocks, L. P. (1998). An empirical investigation of information technology sourcing practices: Lessons from experience. *Management Information Systems Quarterly*, *22*(3), 363–408. doi:10.2307/249670

Lewin, K. (2009). *Federal cloud computing initiative overview*. Retrieved from http://www. usaservices.gov/intergovt/ documents/StateWeb-Pres6-18.ppt

Linthicum, D. S. (2009). Cloud Computing and SOA convergence in your enterprise: A step-by-step guide (1st edition). Addison-Wesley Professional.

Liu, F. et al. (2011). NIST cloud computing reference architecture. *NIST Special Publication 500-292*.

Lohr, S. (2007). Google and IBM join in "cloud computing" research. *New York Times*. Retrieved from http://www.nytimes.com/2007/10/08/ technology/08cloud.html

Marston, S., Li, Z., Bandyopadhyay, S., Zhang, J., & Ghalsasi, A. (2011). Cloud computing: The business perspective. *Decision Support Systems*, *51*(1), 176–189. doi:10.1016/j.dss.2010.12.006

Mayer, R. (1998). Prozesskostenmanagement – State of the Ar (pp. 3-28). Horváth & Partners (Hrsg.).

Mell, P., & Grance, T. (2009). *The NIST definition of cloud computing*. Retrieved from http:// csrc.nist.gov/groups/ SNS/cloud-computing/ cloud-def-v15.doc

Mett, P., & Tomothy, G. (2011). *The NIST definition of cloud computing*. Retrieved from http://www.csrc.nist.gov/publications/nistpubs/800-145/SP800-145.pdf

Miller, M. (2008). *Cloud computing: Web-based applications that change the way you work and collaborate online*. Indianapolis: Que Publishing.

Nabil, S. (2009). Cloud computing for education: A new dawn? *International Journal of Information Management.*

Papazoglou, M. P., & Van den Heuvel, W. J. (2007). Service oriented architecture: Approaches, technologies and research issues. *The VLDB Journal, 16*(3), 389–415. doi:10.1007/s00778-007-0044-3

Parkhill, D. (1966). The challenge of the computer utility. Boston, MA: Addison-Wesley Educational Publishers Inc.

Perrine, D. (2007). *What is a scoring model?* Retrieved from http://www.scoringmodels.com/scoring%20models/what-is-a-scoring-model/

Platform Computing. (2010). Enterprise cloud computing: transforming IT. *A Platform Computing Whitepaper* (p. 6).

SAP AG. (2013). *SAP - The world's leading business software company*. Investor Presentation.

Saunders, R. & Praw, J. (2013). *Small and midsize businesses cloud trust study: U.S. study results.* Mircosoft Study.

Schulze, B. (2014). *SAP cloud strategy* [Interview]. Walldorf: SAP AG.

Schulze, B., Wemme, D., Schmidt, N., & Nelz, J. (2013). *Cloud 101 - Demystifying Cloud*. Cloud Week SAP.

Smith, R. (2009). Computing in the cloud. *Research Technology Management, 52*(5), 65–68.

Sosonsky, B. (2011). *Cloud computing bible.* Indianapolis: Wiley Publishing.

Sotomayor, B., Montero, R. S., Llorente, I. M., & Foster, I. (2009). Virtual infrastructure management in private and hybrid clouds. *IEEE Internet Computing, 13*(5), 14–22. doi:10.1109/MIC.2009.119

SuccessFactors. (2013). *Employee central*. Retrieved December 8, 2013, from http://www.successfactors.com/content/dam/successfactors/en_us/resources/brochures-product/employee-central.pdf

Turetken, O., Elgammal, A., van den Heuvel W.-J., & Papazoglou, M. (2004). *Enforcing compliance on business processes*. Tilburg: European Research Institute in Service Science (ERISS).

Wang, L., von Laszewski, G., Kunze, M., & Tao, J. (2008). *Cloud computing: A perspective study*. Eggenstein-Leopoldshafen, Germany: *Steinbuch Centre for Computing, Karlsruhe Institute of Technology.*

Wunderlich, J. P. (2013). *SAP cloud applications portfolio*. SAP AG.

Yoo, C. S. (2011). Cloud computing: Architectural and policy implications. *Review of Industrial Organization, 38*(4), 405–421. doi:10.1007/s11151-011-9295-7

KEY TERMS AND DEFINITIONS

Business Processes: A business process is a series of logically related activities or tasks (such as planning, production, or sales) performed together to produce a defined set of results.

Cloud Services: A cloud service is any resource that is provided over the Internet. The most common cloud service resources are Software as a Service (SaaS), Platform as a Service (PaaS) and Infrastructure as a Service (IaaS).

Consumer Product Industry: Consumer Product Goods – CPG industry is a type of good that is consumed every day by the average consumer. The goods that comprise this category are ones that need to be replaced frequently, compared to those that are usable for extended periods of time. While CPGs represent a market that will always have consumers, it is highly competitive due to high market saturation and low consumer switching costs.

End-to-End Processes: An end-to-end process refers to the beginning and end points of an overall process covering different business areas within a company. End-to-end embraces the philosophy that eliminating as many middle layers or steps as possible will optimize performance and efficiency in any process. An end-to-end process is always customer oriented.

Fraud Indicator: In IT systems fraud as a tort generally are the intentional misrepresentation or concealment of an important fact upon which the victim is meant to rely, and in fact does rely, to the harm of the victim. The concept of fraud is analyzed with the use of so called fraud indicators that give an indication in regards to the occurrence of a fraud.

Omni Channel Management: Omni channel management mean the seamless melding of the advantages of in-store (brick and mortar) shopping with the information-rich experience of online shopping.

Order-to-Cash: "Order to cash" (O2C or OTC) normally refers to the business process for receiving and processing customer sales. It follows "Opportunity to Order" and covers business-to-business (B2B) and business-to-consumer (B2C) sales.

Chapter 7
Cloud Computing for Rural ICT Implementations:
Methods, Models, and Architectures

Mohamed Fazil Mohamed Firdhous
University of Moratuwa, Sri Lanka

ABSTRACT

Half of the world's population live in rural areas and majority of them are in developing countries. The rural population face many challenges in their life compared to their urban counterparts. Some of these challenges include high unemployment rate, limited employment opportunities in their areas, high brain drain to more developed cities, lack of access to education and healthcare facilities. Information and communication technology has been identified as the enabling technology that can be used to overcome the present day problems. There are several ICT projects implemented across the world with the objective of helping these rural masses. But many of these projects face sustainability challenges due to lack of resources. In this chapter, the author takes an in depth look at how cloud computing can be leveraged successfully to address the sustainability problem of current rural ICT implementation.

INTRODUCTION

Cloud computing is one of the newest computing paradigms helping the people use computers and allied technologies more effectively (Shawish & Salama, 2014). Cloud computing has transformed the way how people access, use and pay for computing resources (Buyya, Yeo, Venugopal, Broberg, & Brandic, 2009; Chang, Walters, & Wills, 2013a). Prior to the arrival of cloud computing, the computing resources including especially hardware was either purchased outright or leased on fixed charges. It has been observed that the utilization or productivity of these resources was very low as most of these resources were just idling most of the time. On the contrary, cloud computing improves the resource utilization by making them available only when needed and releasing them to other users and applications when not in use (Kiruthika & Khaddaj, 2013). Also the cloud systems can be accessed using a variety of client hardware including desktop computers, laptop (portable) computers, tablet PCs, personal digital assistants, iPads and smart phones (Dihal, Bou-

DOI: 10.4018/978-1-4666-8210-8.ch007

Copyright © 2015, IGI Global. Copying or distributing in print or electronic forms without written permission of IGI Global is prohibited.

wman, de Reuver, Warnier, & Carlsson, 2013). Due to the advantages of cloud computing over traditional computing schemes, it can be successfully employed where traditional computing paradigms struggle or sometimes totally fail to deliver their services.

Traditionally, rural population living in far away from urban centers face several challenges in their life compared to their urban counterparts (Mtega & Malekani, 2009). Also majority of the rural population live in developing countries aggravating the issues further (Usman, Dutta, Habeeb, & Jean, 2013). The rural population suffer from poverty, high unemployment, lack of access to proper infrastructure and social services etc., (Mechanic & Tanner, 2007). In some areas, the poverty is so widespread that the majority of the population live on less than USD 1 a day below the absolute poverty level set by the World Bank (Ahmed, Hill, Smith, Wiesmann, & Frankenberger, 2007). Hence the rural population living in developing countries is considered the most vulnerable out of all the world population. In order to help these people overcome the current deficiencies, they need to be sufficiently empowered with new opportunities, skills and technologies (Sianipar, Yudoko, Adhiutama, & Dowaki, 2013).

The effective empowerment of rural youth is only possible by introducing them to the effective use of Information and Communication Technologies (ICT) (Alibaygi, Karamidehkordi, & Pouya, 2012). This is due to the fact that the ICT has been considered to be the enabling technology that could effectively bridge the gap between the rural and urban population (Songan, Hamid, Yeo, Gnaniah, & Zen, 2008). ICT empowers the rural population by providing them with new skills and opening up new opportunities that were hitherto confined to the people living in urban areas. The main advantage of ICT is the effective elimination of physical distance between people living across a wide geographic separation (Bargh & McK-

enna, 2004). Now people living in rural areas can participate in many activities and benefit from them without leaving their places of birth. This would effectively reduce one of the main problems challenging the sustainability of the rural communities. That is youth migration to urban areas looking for better employment and other opportunities. Youth migration affect the sustainability of rural communities by depriving the community of one of the most vital segment of the population (Ango, Ibrahim, Yakubu, & Alhaji, 2014; Ajaero & Onokala, 2013). When the youth migrate to the urban areas, the rural areas are left with an aging and underage population to look after their traditional livelihood, farming and other family endeavors. This would adversely affect the output of the farming activities and the family income unless the loss income is sufficiently compensated by the inward remittances of the migrants.

Governments and nongovernmental social activists have already identified the crucial role to be played by ICT in empowering the rural masses (Nag, 2011). Hence they have implemented several rural ICT projects with the objective of improving the quality of life of rural people. These projects have met with various successes and failures (Best & Kumar, 2008; Musiyandaka, Ranga, & Kiwa, 2013). One of the main issues identified for the failure of many rural ICT implementation is lack of financing and trained human resources for continuous maintenance of the projects.

In this chapter, the author takes a critical look at how cloud computing can be leveraged to mitigate the problems faced by traditional rural ICT implementations. The main focus of the chapter will be on the shortcomings of traditional ICT implementations and how the cloud based projects could successfully overcome these shortcomings. Finally the chapter presents the cloud computing based rural ICT architectures that could harness the maximum advantage from the implementations.

NEEDS AND CHALLENGES OF RURAL COMMUNITIES

According to a survey carried out by the United Nations, nearly half of the world population lives in rural areas (UN, 2011). The same survey found that the percentage of rural population in developing countries are much higher reaching as much as 75 percent of their national population in some countries. Many of these countries are concentrated in specific parts of the world such as Sub Saharan Africa, Latin American, South Asia and South Eastern Asia. Hence, it could be safely concluded that majority of the rural population live in developing countries. Developing countries in general suffer from various problems including large populations, lack of infrastructure facilities, large international and national debts, lack of employment opportunities resulting in high unemployment ratios, dependence of outdated technologies and high levels of corruption (Sloman, 2006; Faye, McArthur, Sachs, & Snow, 2004; Ragan & Lipsey, 2011). Hence the rural population living in the developing countries suffer a lot compared to others.

The rural population is generally characterized by certain disadvantages in social, cultural, economic and political arenas compared to the ones living in the urban centers (Scott, Gilbert, & Gelan, 2007). The challenges faced by the rural population include lack of opportunity for securing good and gainful employment, limited access to technical and professional education, problems in obtaining good healthcare at affordable prices and difficulty in benefiting from services provided by the governments (Hargraves, 2002). Traditionally, employment opportunities in rural areas are limited to agriculture or farming related jobs, and unemployment among the rural youth is also reported to be high (van der Geest, 2010). The farming activities carried out by the rural areas may not provide gainful employment to all the residents in the area as the extent of area cultivated and the number of workers needed are far less than the people available (Sundar & Srinivasan, 2009). Also, the farming activities carried out in rural areas generally employ casual workers only during certain seasons such as land preparation, planting and harvesting (Ovwigho, 2014; Chaudhry, Malik, & Ashraf, 2006). This forces many people to look for other employment opportunities outside farming during other times. Though it is possible to see large scale commercial farming activities using modern technologies in developed countries, generally the farmers in developing countries engage in subsistence agriculture (Khalif & Nur, 2013). The earnings from subsistence agriculture is very low compared to that of the economic activities carried out by the urban population (Thorlakson & Neufeldt, 2012). All the above make the rural farmers in developing countries very poor (Martin, Lorenzen, & Bunnefeld, 2013). Therefore, all these make the rural population the most vulnerable group and keep them trapped in this vicious cycle, unless there is an external intervention.

The rural areas in developing countries have very little manufacturing or industrial activities (Dave & Dave, 2012). The reasons for the zero or very less industrial activity in rural areas are manifold. Saxena (2012) has carried out an investigation into the problems associated with rural entrepreneurship with the objective of finding solutions to these problems. In his study, he has found that the rural enterprises are labor intensive rather than capital intensive automated industries providing the much needed employment opportunities to the rural youth. He opines that such industries are needed in more numbers in order to help overcome the rural unemployment problem. His study has found that the rural industries could be categorized into the following major categories. They are namely agro-based industry, textile industry, polymer and chemical based industry and engineering industry. In the study, he has identified the following problems to be the main barriers to the development of rural industries.

They are namely, inadequacy of capital due to the absence of tangible security and credit for this market segment, lack of markets for rural industrial products and heavy competition from large established industries, lack of aptitude and competency for rural entrepreneurs, lack of knowledge on modern facilities and techniques on the part of the rural industrialists and poor rural infrastructure facilities such as roads, reliable supply of energy, communication facilities etc. Saxena (2012) further states that all these problems could be easily overcome with the help and intervention of governments and nongovernmental agencies.

Establishing rural industries will also help reduce the labor migration from rural areas to urban centers. Labor migration creates social problems for both rural as well as urban areas (Abbass, 2012). The inward labor migration into the cities creates slums and other over populated areas creating many social and environmental problems (Davis, 2004). On the hand the outward migration of rural youth looking for employment opportunities in cities leave the elderly and minors in rural areas to look after themselves (Hendry & Kloep, 2004). The shortage of active youth participating in rural economic activities such as farming hampers development and productivity of this sector very badly (Obiora, 2014). Also the absence of youth affects small time trading activities such as restaurants, shops and other businesses in rural areas.

Compared to the urban population, rural counterpart face many problems in education as well. The educational opportunities and facilities in rural areas are also limited in terms of number and types of schools, facilities, opportunities etc. In many cases, even if schools are available in certain areas, they have many shortages including physical, academic and human resources (Fu, 2005; Tayyaba, 2012). Furthermore in many cases, there are other obstacles such as poverty and other social barriers prevent many children from attending school (Taneri & Engin-Demir,

2011). In some rural areas in developing countries, the schools are located far apart from population centers and students have to travel long distance to reach these schools (Roy, 2012). Due to inadequate transport facilities available in these areas, mostly students travel to the school and back on foot. This also discourages students to attend the schools regularly. Roy (2012), further states that in many areas the available education facilities are limited to primary schools. Due to this reason, the students who seek education beyond this level are forced to migrate to the nearest cities.

The main problems associated with rural schools is inadequate facilities for providing a proper teaching and learning environment (Roy, 2012). The types of resources required for providing a satisfactory learning environment can be categorized into physical resources, academic resources and human resources (Tayyaba, 2012). The physical resources include buildings, furniture, classrooms, assembly halls, other halls, administrative blocks, science rooms, libraries and workshop (Adeyemi, 2009). On the hand the academic resources required for proper delivery of education are teaching kit, teachers' guides, audio-visual aids, text books, laboratories and school library (Tayyaba, 2012). The human resources required to run a school effectively are the head of institution namely the principal or head teacher as in many schools, administrative and clerical staff, minor staff and most importantly the qualified and trained teaching staff (Owojori & Asaolu, 2010). Rural schools suffer from the shortages in all three kinds of resources.

Though the physical and academic resources could be obtained with the help of government, nongovernmental agencies or other philanthropists, rural schools find it difficult to recruit qualified teachers (Lowe, 2006; Hudson & Hudson, 2008). Many a times, even when teachers are recruited, it is difficult to retain them as they try to join urban schools the very first opportunity they get (Hammond & Post, 2000; Lowe, 2006; Hudson & Hudson, 2008). Also the teachers in rural schools are burdened with teaching multiple subjects in different grades. Many of the times, the teachers covering many subjects do not have proper training in all the subjects taught by them (Tayyaba, 2012).

The conditions at home outside school related factors also affect the educational performance of rural children. These conditions include less education of parents, fewer study aids at home, and low parental help and involvement in the achievements of children (Tayyaba, 2012). All in all, it can be said that the rural children have to face much more challenges and hurdles in obtaining a good education similar to that of their urban counter parts. Only a few students manage to overcome all these challenges and successfully reach their goals, while all the other are forced to join the labor market at an early age.

People living in rural areas have inequitable access to healthcare services compared to that of the urban population (Sibley & Weiner, 2011). This is mainly due to the fact that rural areas are mainly served by the public healthcare providers whereas the urban areas are served by both public and private providers who are better equipped with modern facilities but more expensive compared to public providers (Harris, et al., 2011). The types of hospitals or medical facilities available in rural areas is also far inferior to that are found in the urban centers (Lokhande & Kale, 2014). Rural areas are mainly served by rural hospitals and dispensaries that are equipped to handle only basic health issues (Lutfiyya, Bhat, Gandhi, Nguyen, Weidenbacher-Hoper, & Lipsky, 2007). On the other hand the urban hospitals are equipped with modern facilities capable of handling any kind of healthcare issues (Jones, Carr, & Dalal, 2011). Jones et al (2011), further stated that in addition to the access to fully equipped hospitals, the urban and suburban population have the advantage of attending specialized healthcare facilities in their own areas within few minutes of travelling. On the other hand, the rural population need

to travel long distance to the nearest urban or suburban centers to attend to such facilities. The main reason for the absence of specialized and/ or private healthcare institutions in rural areas is the financial non-viability of such projects. Compared to the urban and suburban areas, the rural population density is very low. Except for few cases, rural population on the whole is living in poverty with less or no means of affording such expensive treatment. Also, due to high rates of unemployment, under employment and low wages in rural areas, majority of the rural population is not covered by health insurance (Myhre & Hohman, 2012; Younis, 2003). Thus the rural areas lack the critical mass of patients to support the establishment, operation and maintenance of private or specialized healthcare facilities in those areas.

Due to the economic status of the rural population, they are compelled to attend to public or government sponsored (supported) healthcare facilities (Aitken, Backliwal, Chang, & Udeshi, 2013). Generally public healthcare facilities are overloaded compared to private hospitals and clinics (Saeed & Ibrahim, 2005). On the hand, the urban masses can attend private hospitals and avail better personalized care due to their better economic statuses coupled with employer sponsored insurance coverage (Harris, et al., 2011). Thus, it could be seen that the urban population are better placed in terms of access to improved and modern healthcare facilities.

Similar to any other profession, the rural areas find it difficult to attract the healthcare professionals as well. The healthcare professionals including specialists, general physicians, dentists, dental surgeons, nurses and other paramedics, and medical technicians find it lucrative to stay in urban and suburban areas compared to rural areas (Jones, Carr, & Dalal, 2011; Huttlinger, Ayers, Lawson, & Ayers, 2003). Jones et al., (2011) have found that though 20 percent of the American population live in rural areas, only 9 percent of physicians practice there. They further noted that the situation becomes worse as only 3 percent of the recent medical graduates prefer to live and work in rural areas. If the situation in developed world is like that the situation in developing countries is even worse (Araújo & Maeda, 2013). Many positions including that of the directors, chief medical officers etc., in government hospitals and clinics in rural areas remain unfilled due to unwillingness of professionals to move to rural areas (Al-Qudah, 2011). Hence it can be seen that the recruitment and retaining healthcare professionals in rural areas is a problem for both developed and developing countries. The only difference between these two parts of the world is that it is more acute as the problem is aggravated due to other factors such as non-availability of other resources such as good transport and communication facilities, high poverty levels and long distance between the nearest city and the rural areas.

Due to the disparity in access to healthcare facilities in urban and rural areas, the rural masses suffer from many adverse consequences. The main outcome of the above discussed shortcomings in rural areas include shorter life expectancy, higher death rates among young people, higher infant, child and maternal mortality rates, more deaths and disabilities resulting from injuries, and higher rates of suicide due to non-treatment of mental issues and depression (Jones et al., 2011).

The other major area of disparity between the urban and rural areas is public infrastructure such as roads, street lights, access to clean supplies, sanitation, waste management services, uninterrupted energy supplies and communication facilities (Amirullah, 2014). Development of infrastructure in rural areas is very important as economic development is possible only with efficient and sound infrastructure (Srinivasu & Rao, 2013). Hence the development of rural infrastructure will infuse new blood to the life of rural masses through economic enhancement and improved quality of life.

EFFECT OF ICT IN RURAL DEVELOPMENT

Information and Communication Technology (ICT) represents a complex, and heterogeneous but related group of goods, services and applications that are used to generate, process, transform, distribute, present and consume information through the modern computer and communication technologies (Dalal, 2006; Okiy & Ogbomo, 2011). They further state that though the traditional technologies would continue to play an important role for many people living across the globe, the new technologies need to be adopted and exploited for the empowerment of everyone including underprivileged.

Digital Divide

Digital divide has been defined as the disparity or social exclusion experienced between the group of people who are beneficiaries of the new and advanced services made available by the development of ICT and others who are not (van Dijk, 2008). Keniston (2004) have identified four major disparities that make the digital divide. These disparities are namely the gap between rich and poor, the gap between English speaking and non English speaking, the gap between rich and poor countries and the gap between the professionals employed in sunrise industries and others. The four digital gaps in detail are described below.

The first identified gap, the gap between the people who are rich, educated and powerful and others namely the poor and powerless can be found in any country irrespective of whether they are developed or developing, eastern or western, industrialized or non-industrialized etc. The rich and educated tend to be more computer literate and IT savvy compared to the poor creating the digital gap. Similar difference between the rich and poor exist in the ownership of computers at home and access to the Internet from home. All these things put together make the rich, educated and powerful to be part of the information age reaping maximum benefits from it.

The people who are fluent in English are in a better position to reap the benefits of ICT compared to others. This is mainly due to the fact that even if a person owns a computer and have access to the Internet, he or she will not be able to benefit from it, if he/she doesn't possess sufficient knowledge in English. This is mainly due to the fact that the English language dominates the Internet (Wolk, 2004; Atwell, et al., 2007). Majority of the websites on the Internet are authored and available in English (Crystal, 2006). Though the use of other languages like Chinese have seen an increase on the web in recent years, English would continue to dominate the information dissemination on the Internet and the World Wide Web (Danet & Herring, 2007). The dominance of English as the language of the Internet has created the second gap between the people, who benefit from the internet technologies and those who do not.

The gap between the rich and poor nations has been identified as another major hurdle from benefitting from the development of ICT. The main reason behind this disparity is that the people from rich counties are better positioned economically to afford computers, telephone connections and connectivity to the Internet at home (Gulati, 2008). Owning computers and access to the Internet is a prerequisite to gain competitive advantage from the development of ICT. In developing countries, many people use public Internet access points such as cyber cafes, telecenters and libraries to gain access to the Internet (Furuholt & Kristiansen, 2007). This provides a cost effective means for benefiting from the ICT as the cost of the computer and the Internet connection are shared by many (Cilesiz, 2004; Becker, Crandall, Fisher, Kinney, Landry, & Rocha, 2010). But there is a shortcoming associated with this kind of access as the telecenters open only during specific periods of a day and users need to wait for their turn, if the place is overcrowded. On the other hand having home access to the Internet provides users any time access giving them the maximum benefit and

flexibility (Asik, 2014). Hence living in a developed country provides an advantage over others in benefiting from the developments of ICT.

The final disparity is the one that exists between the professionals who are engaged in employments in the field of ICT commonly known as a "Sunrise Industry" and others (Kamaludeen & Thamodaran, 2014). The professionals engaged in jobs related to ICT are by nature required to follow the developments and advancements of the field against others who are required to take their own initiative to benefit from it (Ilavarasan & Parthasarathy, 2012). The employment opportunities in the ICT sector are considered to be more lucrative yielding higher pay and other benefits compared to other professional fields (Bhatnagar, 2006). Hence the professionals employed in the ICT industry have a better quality of life resulting from their improved economic conditions compared to others.

Empowering the Rural Population with ICT

In order to bridge the gap between the haves and have nots, it is necessary to bring the marginalized group into the mainstream (Sharma, 2005; Wong, Fung, Law, Lam, & Lee, 2009). The marginalized group requires empowerment for them to come out of the situation they are in currently (Rao, 2009). The empowerment must be carried out by teaching them with knowledge, skills and opportunities of the new generation that is capable of bringing a paradigm shift similar to the agriculture and industrial revolutions of the past. In recent times, the ICT has brought a similar paradigm change by converting many traditional industries and services and introducing many new products, services and employment opportunities. The penetration of ICT into human life has been so widespread, that it has effected total transformation of social, technological, political and economic life of people (Ogbomo & Ogbomo, 2008). ICT is capable of exerting direct impact on five specific areas of human life. They are namely technological, economic, occupational, spatial and cultural (Talvitie, 2004). The impacts effected by ICT can be summarized as follow. By introducing new tools, techniques and applications, ICT transforms the way technology has been used in human life. The development of ICT brings new products, services and opportunities helping the users gain competitive advantages over others by improving their economic status and quality of life. ICT has created new jobs, work ethics, workplaces, work relationships and structures. By removing the physical distance between people, ICT has changed the way, how people manage time and space in their day to day life. The impact on cultural aspect of human life is reflected through the generation, distribution and consumption of information among the different social units and how they interact with each other.

The governments and citizens' groups interested in the development and empowerment of the rural population have identified the power and capacity of ICT to effect the transformation expected. The ICT is expected to act as the equalizer by bridging the gap between the urban and rural population by removing the barriers and creating new opportunities (Kuriyan & Kitner, 2009). Thus, in the last two decades several rural ICT projects have been implemented throughout the world targeting various regions and social groups (Patil, Dhere, & Pawar, 2009). Several researchers have investigated the rural ICT development projects carried out all over the world for identifying the factors affecting success or failures of these projects (Pade, Mallinson, & Sewry, 2011; Best & Kumar, 2008; Ogbomo & Ogbomo, 2008; Gamage & Halpin, 2007; Narula & Arora, 2010).

Sustainability is one of the main factors that determines the effectiveness of a rural ICT project (Pade, Mallinson, & Sewry, 2011). They further state that a number of issues challenge the sustainability of rural ICT development projects. These challenges include limited access to infrastructure, limited formal education for users, insufficient training and capacity building, financial and political constraints, and social or cultural challenges. According to Best and Kumar (2008), the telecenters implemented by nongovernmental organizations (NGO) operated longer than the privately operated ones. The NGO operated ones had the financial backing from donors while the privately owned ones charged the customers for the services. Due to this, the privately owned ones suffered from financial constraints due to inadequate income from customers. Also these telecenters had certain technical issues including lack of voice communication facilities, inadequate customer support from service provider, lack of prior computer training of users and unreliable internet connectivity. The shortcomings for sustainability of rural ICT projects found by Ogbomo and Ogbomo (2008) include high cost of facilities, unavailability or lack of infrastructure, lack of skills and awareness, lack of information policy and its implementation, language barriers, little or no government support and political instability.

The other factor that affects the motivation of rural masses in participating and benefitting from these projects is their lack of English knowledge (Gamage & Halpin, 2007). This is one of the main contributing factors to the digital divide identified by Keniston (2004). This situation is further aggravated by the lack of experts available for developing contents and applications in the local languages (Narula & Arora, 2010). Teaching English to all the rural masses and bringing their knowledge to certain functional level would take a long time and incur high costs. Also, this would deviate the project from the main course to teaching English. Hence the most appropriate action to be taken to circumvent the adverse effects language barrier is to develop contents and applications in local languages. Training experts in local language application development for each and every project would result in enormous cost. Also these experts will not have sufficient work once the project has been implemented. Hence it is advisable to share these experts among multiple projects. There must be some central coordination among various rural ICT development projects, if resources are to be shared and pooled among them all.

Almost all the rural ICT projects implemented using internet kiosks for delivering the information and services to the intended users (Rao, 2004; Best & Kumar, 2008; Molawa, 2009; Narula & Arora, 2010). Prospective users are required to travel up to these kiosks and pay for the services they access. Also depending on the number of computers available in these kiosks, users may have to wait for some time for their turns during peak times. This would discourage even the enthusiastic users in the long run. Today, advanced handheld devices such as mobile phones, smart phones, personal digital assistants (PDA) and tablet PCs can also be used to access internet (Pocatilu, Alecu, & Vetrici, 2009). The penetration of mobile phone users across the world is increasing at a phenomenal rate, and in some countries, it has already exceeded their actual population figures (Hosman & Fife, 2012). On the other hand, the cost of mobile devices is also coming down on a daily basis, so everyone irrespective of their social status can afford these devices and services (Boulos, Wheeler, Tavares, & Jones, 2011). Hence it is advisable to move towards mobile devices for client access rather than centralized kiosk solutions. Also, if the applications are web based, then there is no much difference whether it has been accessed using a mobile device or a standalone computer.

According to Sewchurran and Brown (2011), three types of factors can be identified to affect the successful service delivery from a service providers' perspective. They have named these types of factors as enablers, inhibitors and hygiene factors. The enablers are a must for delivering a satisfactory service. On the other hand inhibitors if present, would impact the successful service delivery negatively. The third factors, the hygiene factors do not necessarily enhance the service delivery if present, but will negatively impact the service

delivery if absent. Hence they are also a necessary set of factors for successful delivery of ICT services. Service uptime and availability along with the presence of a Service Level Agreement (SLA) and compliance with it are major hygiene factors in successful service delivery. From a technical point of view, in order to provide a satisfactory service with predictable uptime and availability, it is necessary to have sufficient computing and other resources to meet the customer demands. If disaster management and mitigation is also taken into account, it is necessary to duplicate the entire system in another location. All these would add to the cost of service delivery. The best way to meet all these requirements is to collaborate with other service providers and have a common shared data center where the applications of multiple service providers can be hosted.

The primary objective of e-government projects is to improve the reach, enhance the base, minimize the processing costs, increase transparency, and reduce the cycle times (Rao, 2004). In order to achieve these objectives, the rural e-government applications have been developed with the aim of offering easy access to citizen services and improved processing of government-to-citizen transactions. The important points to note here is that from the technical point of view, it is important thereby to reduce processing cost and cycle time to provide easy access to the services. In addition to the above, the author has also identified the selection of appropriate technologies in terms of dependability, maintainability and cost effectiveness for rural connectivity and information processing solutions. The speed of implementations also plays a vital role in the success of these projects. The implementation model identified by the author includes several servers hosted by respective departments for offering the identified services. These servers are connected through Intranet/LAN to the delivery server where the e-government portal is hosted. This model has several shortcomings in terms of implementation and maintenance. When each department maintains its own server, the total (cumulative) cost of hardware and other resources become very high. Each department needs to have its own expertise for managing the systems and also the recurrent cost involved in maintaining and managing the systems including power consumption and consumables would also be considerably high. In addition to the cost, the implementation time for each system needs to go through the complete cycle starting from specification identification, purchase, installation to testing. Also, it is important to note that the utilization of these servers would be very low and most of the time they would become idle wasting precious resources and investments. It has been identified that even in large commercial data centers, the average server utilization lies between 4 and 18 percents (Malkowski, et al., 2012). The probable solution to reduce the cost and time of implementing and maintaining the systems while increasing the utilization is to consolidate and co-locate all the servers in a single data center such that they can share many of the resources and costs.

The above discussion clearly shows that sustainability of the facilities and operations is the main issue of the rural ICT projects. There are several factors affecting the sustainability of projects. These factors are given below:

- High implementation cost.
- Inadequate trained personnel for managing facilities.
- Lack of human resources for innovative application development.
- Few computers at telecenters.
- High maintenance cost.
- Poor performance of systems.
- Lack of English knowledge of users.
- Lack of computer skills for users.
- Lack of service agreements.
- Lack of network capacity.
- Lack of income.

The above factors can be grouped into three main categories as lack of finances for implementation and maintenance, lack of trained staff for sustainable operations, inadequate knowledge and skills of users.

CLOUD COMPUTING

Since its proposal few years back, cloud computing has become popular not only among the large businesses, but also among small and medium enterprises (Wang, 2013; Yeboah-Boateng & Essandoh, 2013). The growth of popularity of cloud computing is mainly attributed to the advantages it offers to businesses by eliminating unnecessary expenses on nonperforming investment on computers and allied resources. Cloud computing has brought a paradigm change in computing by converting the resources that hitherto required up front investments to services that can be paid on a pay-as-you-go model (Wang, 2013). Cloud computing delivers computing resources such as hardware, application development environment and hosting platform, software and others as services over the Internet (Buyya et al., 2009). Cloud resources are hosted on innovative virtualized systems that can be brought up and removed on demand (Bento & Bento, 2011). A single physical computer can host multiple virtual computers simultaneously without interfering with each other. Thus the same physical hardware resource can be allocated to multiple users as only active virtual machines require resources. Sharing the same resource among multiple users without affecting the performance improves the return on investments reducing the per user cost. It has been observed that through proper management of virtual systems, the utilization of hardware resources can be increased to more than 80 percent from mere 4-18 percent without virtualization (Malkowski, et al., 2012; Blagodu-

Figure 1. Capacity-utilization curve (AWS, 2012).

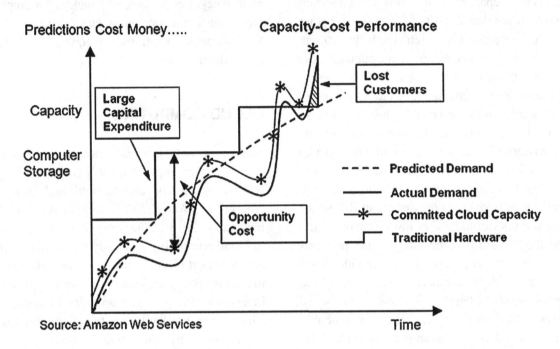

rov, Gmach, Arlitt, Chen, Hyser, & Fedorova, 2013). Increased utilization helps the service provider to get their return on investment much faster improving their profitability. Thus, cloud computing helps both service providers and clients simultaneously meeting their objectives. Figure 1 shows the demand-allocation pattern of computing resources under traditional and cloud computing scenarios.

Figure 1 clearly shows the advantage of cloud computing over traditional computing model. Under traditional computing model, resources have been procured in steps based on the projections of demand. This kind of acquisition of resources results in both over and under provisioning at various momentary demands resulting in losses during both periods. On the other hand cloud based resource provisioning closely follows the demand pattern in both short run as well as long run. Hence cloud computing gives 100 percent return on investment.

Advantages and Disadvantages of Cloud Computing

Though cloud computing provides several advantages to the user community, it has certain disadvantages as well. The advantages and disadvantages of cloud computing identified by Mirashe and Kalyankar (2010) and Badger, Grance, Patt-Corner, and Voas (2012) is summarized in Table 1.

The disadvantages identified above can be mitigated through the advanced technologies available today. The network connectivity can be made stronger by having multiple connections as the cost is now shared by multiple users. The users are free to define their own security by installing additional security features of their choice as cloud services can be treated very similar to any other raw computing services. In addition to this, now the service provider is in a better position to provide enhanced disaster mitigation schemes by duplicating the services at different locations.

Table 1. Advantages and disadvantages of cloud computing

Advantages	Disadvantages
Lower costs	Requires high speed reliable Internet connectivity
Improved performance	Storage of sensitive information in an outside location
Better resilience	Security issues
Improved power and capacity	
Co-location of human and other resources	
Better utilization of resources (hardware, software and liveware)	
Centralized decision making and management	
Centralized administration of resources (hardware and data)	
Universal access through the Internet	
Reduced Lead Time for Implementation	

Cloud Computing Delivery Models

Cloud computing delivery models are divided into four main categories, private, public, hybrid and community clouds (Bamiah & Brohi, 2011; Chang et al., 2013a). Each model has its own advantages and disadvantages with a significant impact on administration and decision making.

Private Cloud

The entire cloud infrastructure is installed in-house, owned and used by the employees and stake holders of a single organization. The main advantage of private cloud is that it can pool all the resources within an organization in one place and distribute them across multiple divisions based on real demands. The organization may also adopt a cost apportioning scheme based on the real usage between the divisions. The main disadvantage of this model is that the organization

needs to invest upfront on the system and manage on its own. Also, the organization requires qualified and skilled human resource to implement and maintain the system in house.

Public Cloud

The public cloud is implemented by a commercial organization and the services are sold to prospective customers for a fee. In choosing a public cloud service provider, the customers need to consider several factors including cost, reliability, customer support, etc. The customers are also free to select different component of the system from different providers and combine themselves based on the requirements. The main disadvantage of this model is that the vendor lock-in may occur, if the service provider's system is not standardized.

Hybrid Cloud

A hybrid cloud is formed, when an organization uses both the private and public clouds to meet its computing demands. An organization may set up a private cloud to meet its base demand and use the public cloud to handle the requests beyond that or it may use the private cloud to host its sensitive information while the rest is hosted in the public cloud. This model provides a cost effective solution while maintaining security and privacy of sensitive data.

Community Cloud

Community cloud is similar to public cloud, but the use of cloud infrastructure is limited only to a few selected organizations. The organizations that have similar interests and concerns may get together and form a cloud system to meet their requirements. The benefits realized from pooling the requirements and resources together this way will be realized by all the organizations involved. For meeting the requirements of rural ICT development, community cloud is the best model as all the organizations involved in these projects are bound together by a common objective "better quality of life for rural population".

Cloud Computing vs. Rural ICT Requirements

It is necessary to understand how cloud computing can meet the demands of rural ICT implementations. Table 2 lists the demands of the rural ICT projects against the advantages of cloud computing in a summary form.

From Table 2, it can be seen that cloud computing can meet the demands of rural ICT implementations successfully. Cloud computing is able to provide satisfactory solutions in terms of reducing the financial requirements, eliminating much of the human resource requirements from client side and concentrating more expensive and powerful hardware at the service provider. The resources at the service provider including hardware and expertise is shared among all the clients (projects) thus reducing the per project cost drastically.

IMPLEMENTATION ARCHITECTURES

In this section, the probable implantation architectures for server side (cloud provider) and client side are proposed. At the outset it is necessary to identify the right delivery model of cloud computing that would meet the requirements of rural ICT projects. By looking at the characteristics, benefits and detriments of private cloud, it can be seen that it is financially and technically not feasible to implement individual cloud system for each and every rural project. Also, there is no special advantage that can be gained by implementing a private cloud over traditional server room. Hence private cloud must be ruled out as a suitable model. Purchasing resources from a public cloud provider may give financial and technical benefits, but it will reduce the flexibility of the implementation. Thus public cloud is also not suitable for rural ICT implementations. Since the hybrid model is a combination of both public and private cloud, it will also be ruled out as an unsuitable model. The only option now remains is the community cloud model. The stakeholders of a community cloud system is

Table 2. Rural ICT demands vs. cloud computing

Rural ICT Demands	Cloud Computing
High cost of facilities	Pooled resources, reduced per user cost
In adequate infrastructure at client side	Can be accessed using variety of devices including smart phones, low cost computers, PDA etc.
High maintenance cost	Shared by many users (projects)
High operational cost	Shared by many users (projects)
Inadequate performance	Improved performance due to better, high quality devices at service provider
Long implementation lead time	Only incremental implementation as service provider has already installed the base system
Centralized delivery (telecenters)	Can be accessed using variety of devices including smart phones, low cost computers, PDA etc.
Unreliable Internet connectivity	Can have better access due to falling cost of broadband services
Lack of service provider support	Can have strong service level agreements
Absence of service level agreement	Possible to have service level agreements
Lack of skilled staff for operation and maintenance	Much of the operation and maintenance is moved to service provider
Lack of qualified staff for new application/content development	Pooled staff at the service/content provider
Lack of user skills and awareness	Better training facilities and minimum training on how to use

bound by common goals such as serving a community and common characteristics including the type of usage and resources required. Hence all the resources requirements of multiple projects serving a region can be pooled in a single cloud data center.

Design of Cloud Data Center

Since the cloud data center is to support many project and applications, it needs to be designed with future expansion including new projects in mind. Ghazali, Osman, Ahmad, Abas, Rahmat, and Firdhous (2013) have proposed a cloud data center design that can be remotely accessed by multiple telecenters. This proposal is very basic and no implementation details are given, in this chapter the author extends this proposal further into a more strong and rugged architecture. Figure 2 shows the proposed cloud data center architecture.

Proposed cloud data center shows two independent data centers created for the purpose of load sharing and disaster management. It is not necessary to setup both data centers at the beginning itself. The second data center can be established when the requirement comes up and the financing is available. The proposed data center is a modular one that can be established small with few servers and can be expanded easily with the rise in demand without modifying the underlying architecture. All the requests are first handled by the front end web servers and then forwarded to the back end servers depending on the resources required and performance expectations. The data center is protected by the external firewall from outside intruders and the internal firewall acts as barrier between data center network and the administrative network.

Figure 2. Proposed cloud data center

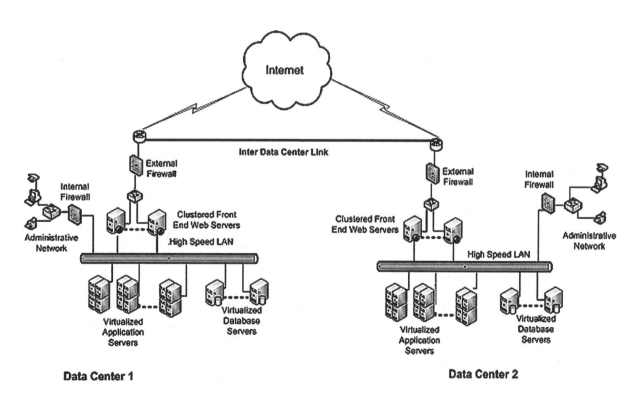

The administrative network is where all the application developers and system administrators will be housed. The internal firewall protects the data center from the administrative network zone as any user working in the administrative area need not have access to the entire data center. Also the internal firewall protects the administrative network from external intruders as they need to cross two firewalls before reaching the systems hosted there.

The cloud data center servers connected through a high speed data network. High speed data network removes any latency introduced by the network affecting the performance of the application, as a single application may need multiple resources hosted in multiple servers. Finally the entire data center is connected to the Internet via a high speed internet connectivity. If the connectivity needs protection from links or service provider failures, the links can be duplicated and connected to different service providers enabling multihoming.

Since the data center is connected to the Internet via a high speed connectivity, it is not necessary to have dedicated connectivity between client sites and the data center. The clients can access the data center servers through the Internet just by having a connection to the nearest Internet Service Provider (ISP). This allows even individual users with smart phones, home computers both laptop and desktop with internet connectivity to access the systems directly. If additional security is required between the users and the systems or for the data transmitted over the Internet, it is possible to create Virtual Private Networks (VPN) between the data center and the clients. Independent connectivity to the Internet increases the reach of the data center from the confines of a single region. This aids in improving the capability of enhancing the reachability of the project to a larger user base, sometimes even outside the political boundary of a single country.

Overall this a versatile design as the design is future safe and grow slowly with the increase in demand. Also the design provides sufficient security as the data center is protected by two firewalls, namely internal and external firewalls. In the event both data centers are established it provides additional safety against disasters as all the applications and data can be backed up in the other data center.

The human resource required to setup and maintain the data center must be skilled professionals with right qualifications. The type of personnel required are also varying as application developers, system administrators, network administrators and database administrators. But the number of personnel required is small as they are now employed at a single data center rather than at user access centers that are many. Also the per client cost of the professionals are also less as the data center is now accessed by many user access centers belonging to several projects.

Design of User Access Centers

The collective user access centers will be telecenters operating at various places in the region of interest. These telecenters will be accessing the cloud applications hosted as Software as a Service (SaaS) in data centers. Since the SaaS applications are developed as Web 2 applications, they can be accessed with any reasonable modern web browser. These web browsers are now available in many platforms including low and high end computers, smart phones, PDA etc., Hence the client access centers need to house high end computers. Reasonable low end, low cost commodity hardware based computers with modest resources and good web browser is sufficient to access the applications. Also, these low end computers do not need much storage space also as all the user data will be stored in the data center servers. Figure 3 shows the proposed user access center design.

The architecture shown in Figure 3 is a simple design that requires to interconnect all the computing and other devices in the center and to have an Internet connectivity. Many devices shown in the figure are optional. The firewall can be removed unless it is required to protect the center computers that are

Figure 3. Proposed user access center design

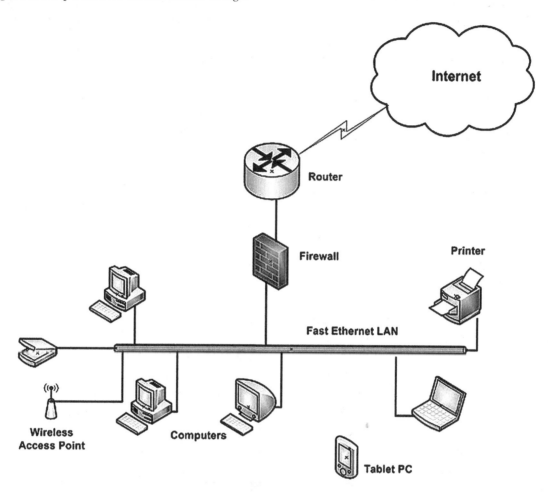

being used as zombie hosts by outsiders to attack other computers in the Internet. This problem can be easily handled by enabling personal firewalls in computers and enabling dynamic IP address allocation with minimal cost. The router can be replaced by a network modem, if 24*7 up persistent connectivity is not required. The network modem will create a dial up connection on demand. The downside of the dial up connection is its limited bandwidth. It is also possible to have reasonably high speed connectivity with ADSL (Asymmetric Digital Subscriber Line) or wireless broadband connections, if available. The wireless access point is included for the sake of completion only. This is also an optional component, if the provision of wireless access is not necessary.

Overall the design shown in Figure 3 is a low cost arrangement that can be duplicated with minimum cost and effort where needed. The cloud data centers can be accessed individually independent of the user access centers with right hardware (smart phones, home computers with internet connectivity) and user credentials.

The human resource required to manage the above user access center is minimal as the devices hosted are commodity hardware with a very simple network. This kind of technical personnel can be easily trained by selecting suitable school leavers with minimum aptitude. Cost of employing such technical personnel is also low compared to that of highly qualified computer professionals.

PORTING APPLICATIONS TO THE CLOUD

Once the data center has been setup, it is necessary to migrate the existing applications that have already been in use and develop new applications based on user requirements. Migrating the existing application to the new cloud environment is not a straight forward process, but requires the consideration of multiple factors along with careful planning (Chang, Walters & Wills, 2013b). The migration process must go through a specified workflow with clearly identified tasks and outcomes. Failure to follow a clearly identified steps along with measurable milestones may result in the failure of the entire migration process ultimately ending up with a system that is worse than the original system running on the traditional IT platform. Several frameworks, models and methods for the migration of traditional applications to the cloud platform have been proposed in literature (Andrikopoulos, Binz, Leymann & Strauch, 2013; Chang, 2013; Chang et al, 2013b). In this work, the author proposes the following seven step process for successful migration of traditional applications to the cloud environment.

Step 1: Define the applications and their associated workloads.

A workload is defined as the complete set of components and processes that are required for the proper functioning of an application. An application may have components from many off the self applications along with custom built units and scripts interacting with one another across multiple platforms. Then identify the components that can be ported directly to the cloud systems and components that require modifications or total redevelopment.

Step 2: Identify the requirement of cloud resources and have them provisioned.

Once the applications and their workloads have been identified, it is necessary to identify the resources required to run them. It is vital to identify the types of servers, storage and network along with their capacities, operating systems, other software and tools etc. Once the details are worked out, discuss with the prospective cloud service provider and have them provisioned.

Step 3: Establish a connectivity.

The next step is to create a secure and transparent bi-directional connectivity between the data center and the cloud system. When establishing this connectivity, leased lines are preferred over Internet VPNs as the performance of the VPNs may fluctuate affecting the performance of the applications.

Step 4: Deploy the applications.

Once everything is place including the hardware, tools and other things such as the secure connectivity, transfer the applications and other identified components to cloud.

Step 5: Maintain seamless connectivity between the cloud and traditional data center.

Until all systems have been successfully migrated, it is necessary to maintain a seamless connectivity between the migrated applications and other non migrated systems. This is similar to maintaining a hybrid system comprising a on premise system and cloud migrated system(s). The connectivity between the systems must be smooth, resilient and secure to maintain such a hybrid system successfully.

Step 6: Test and validate.

It is utmost important to make sure that all the applications function as they should be. Hence all the migrated applications must be tested for their functionality, reliability scalability, security and performance. These testing must be done in a controlled environment before the final launch.

Step 7: Disconnect the old systems.

Once every application has been migrated, tested and validate, it is time to disconnect the old systems.

When the above seven steps are followed properly, prospective cloud users will be able to enjoy the benefits of cloud computing without sacrificing the flexibility and security of the locally installed applications.

The following subsection discusses the implementation of Education as a Service (EaaS) as a rural ICT project. The section takes an in depth look at the advantages and sustainability challenges to the implementation of such projects along with how cloud computing could overcome these challenges. The subsection also proposes a cloud based e-learning system architecture along with an implementation model known as amalgamated e-learning platform. Finally the expected advantages of this model compared to traditional e-learning system has been enumerated.

Cloud-Based Rural Education

Once the cloud data center has been setup and the applications have been migrated, the next step is to get the users to actively participate and benefit from the investments. Cloud based education would be one of the most useful application to be run on a rural ICT implementation (Choubisa, 2012). This is mainly due to the reason that education has the power to empower the rural masses helping them to get out of the vicious cycle they are trapped in today. One of the main hurdles for taking education to the rural areas is the cost of the infrastructure and attracting the required human resources (Gulati, 2008). Cloud based ICT infrastructure provides an alternative to the traditional e-learning or e-education methods. Education as

a Service or EaaS in short refers to the delivery of educational services using cloud computing technology (Chang & Wills, 2013). EaaS defined broadly includes the cloud infrastructure, applications, services and contents delivered using the cloud computing technology to remote students. The delivery of education may take one or more of the forms of lectures, tutorials, assignments, quizzes, examinations and student support.

The advantages of EaaS compared to traditional teaching and learning methods include (Chang & Wills, 2013):

- Reduced environmental and financial cost.
- Shared infrastructure and load.
- Flexible payment schemes.
- Ability to pool resources from a geographically distributed locations.
- Making experiments more repeatable.

In addition to the above advantages, the following can also be considered as major pluses of cloud based EaaS.

- Wider reach crossing geographical and political boundaries.
- Improved return on investments.
- Ability to get the participation of experts from wider geographical area.
- Ability to enroll large number of students from various parts of the world.
- Ability to provide customized programs based on user requirements.
- Ability to incorporate wide range of resources including text, video, audio, speech and images.
- Flexibility for students to follow the programs on their leisure based on their requirements and resources.

Due to the advantages of cloud computing, many higher educational institutions including well established universities world over are adopting cloud based EaaS (Chang, 2012). The main reasons identified for this trend includes; flexibility, loss of students due to increased cost of education, reduced financing from governments towards higher education and the eagerness for adopting a transformational technology.

Odunaike, Olugbara and Ojo (2012) have identified 10 sustainability challenges facing the successful e-learning implementation s in rural areas. The sustainability challenges thus identified include financial support sustainability, stakeholders sustainability, social and political sustainability, technological sustainability, security sustainability, energy sustainability, internet connection sustainability, content development and management sustainability, training sustainability and best practice sustainability. If these challenges are not handled properly, they will totally undermine the success of the e-learning implementations. The authors have finally concluded that cloud computing would be able to overcome these sustainability challenges more than the tradi-

tional e-learning implementations due to its scalability, flexibility, availability, agility and cost effectiveness.

Masud and Huang (2012) have proposed a cloud based e-learning architecture that can be successfully adopted in a rural setting. The model has been a result of an in depth analysis between traditional e-learning systems and advantages and capabilities of cloud computing. In this model the roles of the educational institutions offering the services and vendors providing the necessary infrastructure has been clearly identified and defined. According to the authors, the institutions will be responsible for the education process including content management and delivery while the vendor must take care of system construction, maintenance, development and management. The separation of roles and responsibilities are advantages of this model as it clearly identifies the ownership along with the tasks and responsibilities assigned to them. Figure 4 shows the e-learning systems architecture proposed by authors.

Figure 4. E-learning system architecture (Masud & Huang, 2012).

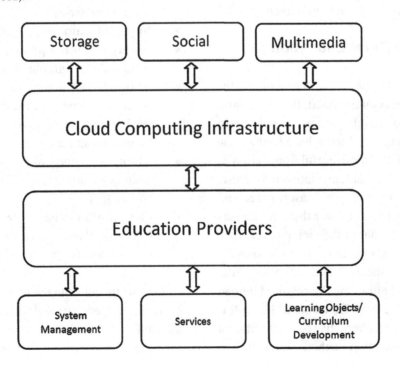

A blended learning model, combining tutors with the modern technology would result in a more productive output than using a single one. The delivery of the content can be made more effective with storage of contents that can be accessed offline at the leisure of the students with interactive contents, virtual collaborations between teachers and students and between students along with advising sessions.

In order to support the proposed objectives, it is necessary to have a strong infrastructure comprising hardware, software and administrative policies, rules and mechanisms. The necessary hardware will be provided by the cloud computing system along with the networking infrastructure used to access the cloud system. The software required for implementing a successful e-learning system comprises the operating system, learning management system and other management and administrative tools. The operating system provides the platform for hosting the learning management system and other applications and tools. The learning management system is the most important component of any e-learning system comprising the administration, documentation, tracking, reporting and delivery of e-learning education courses or training programs. There are many learning management systems available in the market that can be readily ported to the cloud computing systems. The administrative policies, rules and mechanism provide the framework for properly engaging all the resources including hardware, software and liveware (human resources) for the successful delivery of educational and training programmes using the cloud infrastructure. Figure 5 shows an overall view of the resources amalgamated together for the delivery of cloud based e-learning programmes.

Figure 5. Amalgamated e-learning platform
(Masud & Huang, 2012).

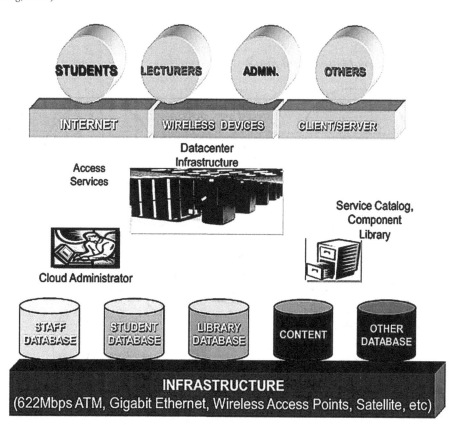

When a cloud based rural e-learning system has been designed, implemented and launched, it is expected to have the following technical benefits over the traditional systems in addition to reaching a large mass of enthusiastic learners spread across wide geographical region at a reduced cost. The expected technical benefits are as follows:

- Increased computing and storage capacities.
- High availability and security.
- Improved productivity due to virtualization.

MEASURING THE EFFECTIVENESS AND BENEFITS OF EaaS

After launching a cloud based rural e-learning system in a specific region, it is necessary to carry out an impact analysis for understanding the effectiveness and shortcomings of the projects. The lessons learnt from these impact studies would help future implementations of the same project or expansion and duplications of the project into some other regions. The benefits can be measured in four specific dimensions. These dimensions include economic benefits, functional benefits, operational benefits and social benefits as shown in Figure 6.

Economic Benefit Analysis

Economic benefits of a cloud based rural EaaS implementation can be carried out using the general economic and financial terms used for measuring the benefits of similar projects (Marengo & Marengo, 2005). The economic benefit analysis can be carried out using generic economic ratios such as return on investment (RoI), RoI ratio, total cost of ownership (TCO), TCO ratio, productivity, savings, cost ratio etc.

The RoI is calculated using the following simple formula as for any other project (Jones, 2012).

Figure 6. Dimensions of cloud based rural EaaS

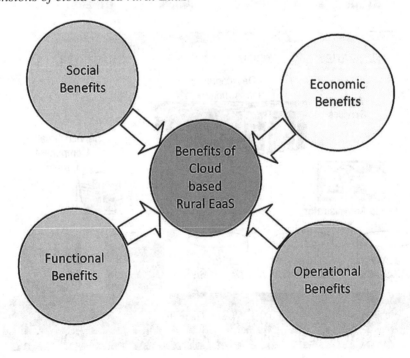

$$Return\ on\ Investment\left(RoI\right) = \frac{Net\ Income}{Total\ Investment}$$

Net income is calculated by subtracting the cost from the total income.

The RoI Ratio computed using the RoI of cloud based system and that of traditional system gives an insight into the advantage (or disadvantage) of cloud based implementation with respect to the traditional implementation. The formula for computing the RoI ratio is as follows:

$$RoI\ ratio = \frac{RoI_{cloud}}{RoI_{traditional}}$$

The TCO is calculated by computing the cumulative costs including the investments and operating costs throughout the life of the project (Ferrin & Plank, 2002). The TCO can be computed using the following formula:

$$Total\ Cost\ of\ Ownership\left(TCO\right)$$
$$= Initial\ Investment + Operational\ Cost + Upgrades$$

Similar to RoI ratio, a more meaningful TCO ratio could be computed by factoring the TCO of cloud based system with that of the traditional learning system computed using projected costs. The formula for computing TCO ratio is as follows:

$$TCO\ ratio = \frac{TCO_{cloud}}{TCO_{traditional}}$$

Productivity of the project can be computed using the total man power required to setup cloud based EaaS. The following is the formula for computing productivity (Syverson, 2011).

$$Productivity\left(P\right) = \frac{Value\ of\ EaaS\ System}{Total\ Man\ Hours}$$

Similarly, the Productivity ratio also can be calculated as given below.

$$P\ ratio = \frac{Productivity\ of\ Cloud\ based\ System}{Productivity\ of\ Traditional\ System}$$

Savings is the total amount of savings that can be achieved by adopting a cloud based solution compared to traditional solution. The savings can be calculated for the investment as well as for the entire project including all the operational and management costs throughout the life of the projects. The following are the formulas that can be used to compute savings.

$$Savings_{investment} = Investment_{traditional}\ \ \ Investment_{cloud}$$

$$Savings_{total} = TCO_{traditional} - TCO_{cloud}$$

where *TCO* is the total cost of ownership.

From the customers' point of view, the economic benefit can be computed using the cost metric or cost ratio (CR). The cost ratio is the fraction of the cost that a user will incur to access the cloud based system compared to a traditional system. The cost ratio can be computed as follows:

$$Cost\ ratio\left(CR\right)$$
$$= \frac{Unit\ Cost\ of\ Accessing\ Cloud\ based\ System}{Unit\ Cost\ of\ Accessing\ Traditional\ System}$$

where the unit cost is defined as the cost of accessing the resources for unit time (one hour).

Functional Benefits Analysis

Functional benefits of cloud based rural EaaS are the advantages that can be gained over traditional e-learning and face to face learning methods due to the additional features included within the system. The functional benefit analysis can be carried out either qualitatively or quantitatively or both by identifying inputs and indices to be computed for both types of analysis. Some of the indices that can be computed under functional benefits analysis include, ease of use factor, number of new features factor. Qualitative functional benefits can include emotional benefits that deals with some special emotional or psychological state due to certain feature of an offering (Sweeney & Webb, 2007).

The quantifiable functional benefits include the number of special features included in the cloud based EaaS compared to that of traditional e-learning systems, the number of hours a system is available and accessible to users compared to the other one, types of devices that can be used to access the system etc.

Operational Benefits Analysis

Operational benefits can be computed quantitatively by comparing the operational costs of cloud based EaaS with that of traditional e-learning implementations. Operational expenditure (OpEx) is the total money spent on operating and managing the IT infrastructure on a day to day basis (recurrent expenditure) including the salaries and wages of IT staff (Shimamoto, 2012) The metrics like OpEx ratio, Operational Productivity ratio (OPR) etc can be used to compute the operational benefits quantitatively.

The OpEx ratio is the ratio between the total expenditure incurred in one year for running a cloud based system to that of the traditional system.

$$OpEx\ ratio = \frac{Operational\ Expenditure_{cloud}}{Operational\ Expenditure_{traditional}}$$

The OPR is similar to that of the project, but takes only the man power required to operate the system. Similarly OPR ratio can also be computed as a comparative measure to evaluate the benefits of cloud based system. The following formulas can be used for computing these metrics.

$$OPR = \frac{Value\ of\ Operations\ per\ Year}{Total\ Man\ Hours}$$

$$OPR\ ratio = \frac{OPR_{cloud}}{OPR_{traditional}}$$

Social Benefits Analysis

The social benefit analysis is carried out to understand how a project that has been implemented in a rural area has improved the quality of life of the target group. The social benefits can be computed quantitatively be calculating various ratios similar to the ones shown above under economic, operational and functional benefit analysis. When computing the social benefits of EaaS, the metrics that can successfully be employed include; reachability index (RI), enrollment index (EI), graduation index (GI), outcome index (OI) etc. The meaning and the formulas that can be used to compute these metrics are discussed below.

Reachability index is the ratio of the number of prospective learners reached by a cloud based system to that of a traditional system. Larger this index better it is. The index can be computed as follows:

$$Reachability\ index\left(RI\right)$$
$$=\frac{No.\ of\ Prospective\ Learners_{cloud}}{No.\ of\ Prospective\ Learners_{traditional}}$$

Since the cloud based systems are hosted on the Internet, it has a larger reachability crossing political and geographic boundaries. Hence naturally cloud based EaaS would have a larger RI compared to traditional e-learning systems. The reachability of cloud based systems can be confined to practical values through policies restricting the access only to the people living in certain areas, age groups or other demographic factors.

The enrollment index computes the number learners enrolled in the programs in a cloud based system to that of traditional systems. Since the cloud based systems have a larger reachability and lower costs, it is generally expected to have a larger value larger than unity (one). The mathematical formula for computing EI is as follows.

$$Enrollment\ index\left(EI\right)$$
$$=\frac{No.\ of\ Enrolled\ Learners_{cloud}}{No.\ of\ Enrolled\ Learners_{traditional}}$$

Similarly the graduation index (GI) can be computed using the formula given below:

$$Graduation\ index\left(EI\right)$$
$$=\frac{No.\ of\ Graduates\ per\ Given\ Period_{cloud}}{No.\ of\ Graduates\ during\ the\ Same\ Period_{traditional}}$$

The outcome index (OI) could be used to compute how the standard of living of the rural masses has been improved due to the provision of EaaS compared to traditional e-learning systems. Different input values can be used to compute this index depending on the requirements. The possible inputs for computing this index include the number of graduates gainfully employed, total income of the graduates, reduction in the number of people living under poverty line etc. A sample index computation formula is used below.

$$Outcome\ index\left(OI\right)$$
$$=\frac{No.\ of\ Graduates\ Gained\ Employment\ in\ a\ Given\ Period_{cloud}}{No.\ of\ Graduates\ Gained\ Employment\ during\ the\ Same\ Period_{trad}}.$$

From the above discussion, it can be seen that the benefits of cloud based EaaS can be analyzed using a multi-pronged approach. The analysis can be carried out either qualitatively or quantitatively depending on the factors involved and the index computed. The data for analysis can be obtained from the system attributes, performance data, usage data and from users through survey. The final results obtained from the above analysis could be used to identify the virtues and shortcomings of the solution along with tangible benefits compared to traditional techniques and schemes.

The above indices can be computed by comparing two ICT implementations in similar settings, for example two villages having similar resources, facilities and needs. One village must be implemented with a cloud based ICT facility while the other one must have a traditional ICT implementation. On the contrary, it is possible to use the same village that has moved from traditional ICT implementation to cloud based ICT implementation. In this case, it is necessary to use the historical information with a specific time period such as one year.

CONCLUSION

This chapter took an in depth look at the problems involving rural population especially those living in the developing countries. Many researches have been carried out on how ICT can be used to empower the rural population. Also many projects have already been implemented at various places with the objective of providing the rural masses with new skills and opportunities for them to overcome the current situation they are in. These projects have met with various successes and failures due to different reasons. The main issue facing these projects is sustainability due to lack of funding and skilled human resources to operate them. In this work, the author proposes a cloud based solution for rural ICT development taking an in depth look at the advantages of cloud computing and how they can be leveraged to address the rural ICT issues. Then cloud data center and user access center architectures are proposed along with a methodology for porting traditional applications to the cloud infrastructure. The proposed architectures are modular, robust and secure meeting the basic requirement of low per project (user) cost. Education as a Service (EaaS) has been selected in this Chapter as a sample application to explain how cloud based rural ICT projects can be implemented in a real world setting. Finally a scheme for evaluating the effectiveness and benefits of implemented cloud based systems using EaaS as an example along with some metrics that can be used for this purpose were covered.

REFERENCES

Abbass, I. M. (2012). Trends of rural-urban migration in Nigeria. *European Scientific Journal*, 8(3), 97–125.

Adeyemi, T. O. (2009). The effective management of primary schools in Ekiti State, Nigeria: An Analytical Assessment. *Educational Research Review*, 4(2), 48–56.

Ahmed, A. U., Hill, R. V., Smith, L. C., Wiesmann, D. M., & Frankenberger, T. (2007). *The world's most deprived: characteristics and causes of extreme poverty and hunger*. Washington, DC: International Food Policy Research Institute.

Aitken, M., Backliwal, A., Chang, M., & Udeshi, A. (2013). *Understanding healthcare access in India: What is the current state?* Parsippany, NJ: IMS Institute for Healthcare Informatics.

Ajaero, C. K., & Onokala, P. C. (2013). The effects of rural-urban migration on rural communities of Southeastern Nigeria. *International Journal of Population Research*, 2013, 1–10. doi:10.1155/2013/610193

Al-Qudah, H. S. (2011). Impacts of new recruited doctors refrain from working in rural remote areas at Jordan Southern Badia Region. *International Journal of Business and Social Science*, 2(3), 186–194.

Alibaygi, A., Karamidehkordi, M., & Pouya, M. (2012). Using the Delphi technique to assess cost-effectiveness of rural information and communications technologies (ICT) centers in Iran. *Journal of Agricultural Extension and Rural Development*, 4(20), 552–555.

Amirullah. (2014). Public private partnership in infrastructure development of rural areas: Opportunities and challenges in India. *The International Journal of Humanities & Social Studies*, 2(2), 1-6.

Ango, A. K., Ibrahim, S. A., Yakubu, A. A., & Alhaji, A. S. (2014). Impact of youth rural-urban migration on household economy and crop production: A case study of Sokoto metropolitan areas, Sokoto State, North-Western Nigeria. *Journal of Agricultural Extension and Rural Development*, 6(4), 122–131. doi:10.5897/JAERD2013.0547

Araújo, E. C., & Maeda, A. (2013). *How to recruit and retain health workers in rural and remote areas in developing countries: A guidance note*. Health, Nutrition and Population (HNP) Discussion Paper. Washington, DC: World Bank.

Asik, O. (2014). *Location optimization to determine telecenter network in rural Turkey*. MS Thesis, Cornell University, Ithaka, NY.

Atwell, E., Arshad, J., Lai, C.-m., Nim, L., Asheghi, N. R., Wang, J., & Washtell, J. (2007). Which English dominates the World Wide Web, British or American? In *Proceedings of the Corpus Linguistics Conference* (pp. 1-13). Birmingham, UK.

AWS. (2012). *Capacity vs Utilization Curve.* Retrieved May 15, 2013, from http://www.amazon.com/economics

Badger, L., Grance, T., Patt-Corner, R., & Voas, J. (2012). *Cloud computing synopsis and recommendations. Special Publication.* Gaithersburg, MD: U.S. Department of Commerce, National Institute of Standards and Technology.

Bamiah, M. A., & Brohi, S. N. (2011). Exploring the cloud deployment and service delivery models. *International Journal of Research and Reviews in Information Sciences, 1*(3), 77–80.

Bargh, J. A., & McKenna, K. Y. (2004). The internet and social life. *Annual Review of Psychology, 55*(1), 573–590. doi:10.1146/annurev.psych.55.090902.141922 PMID:14744227

Becker, S., Crandall, M. D., Fisher, K. E., Kinney, B., Landry, C., & Rocha, A. (2010). *Opportunity for all: How the American public benefits from internet access at U.S. libraries.* Washington, DC: Institute of Museum and Library Services.

Bento, A., & Bento, R. (2011). Cloud computing: A new phase in information technology management. *Journal of Information Technology Management, 22*(1), 39–46.

Best, M. L., & Kumar, R. (2008). Sustainability failures of rural telecenters: Challenges from the Sustainable Access in Rural India (SARI) project. *Information Technologies & International Development, 4*(4), 31–45. doi:10.1162/itid.2008.00025

Bhatnagar, S. (2006). India's software industry. In V. Chandra (Ed.), *Technology, adaptation, and exports: How some developing countries got it right?* (pp. 95–124). Washington, DC: World Bank.

Blagodurov, S., Gmach, D., Arlitt, M., Chen, Y., Hyser, C., & Fedorova, A. (2013). Maximizing server utilization while meeting critical SLAs via weight-based collocation management. In *Proceedings of the IFIP/IEEE International Symposium on Integrated Network Management* (pp. 277-285). Ghent, Belgium.

Boulos, M. N., Wheeler, S., Tavares, C., & Jones, R. (2011). How smartphones are changing the face of mobile and participatory healthcare: An overview, with example from {eCAALYX}. *Biomedical Engineering Online, 10*(24), 1–14. http://www.ncbi.nlm.nih.gov/entrez/query.fcgi?cmd=Retrieve&db=PubMed&list_uids=21466669&dopt=Abstract PMID:21466669

Buyya, R., Yeo, C. S., Venugopal, S., Broberg, J., & Brandic, I. (2009). Cloud computing and emerging IT platforms: Vision, hype, and reality for delivering computing as the 5th utility. *Journal of Future Generation Computer Systems, 25*(6), 599–616. doi:10.1016/j.future.2008.12.001

Chang, V. (2012). Three Greenwich Case Studies in Private Cloud Migration and Adoption. Retrieved from http://eprints.soton.ac.uk/357189/1/VC_Greenwich_tech_paper.pdf

Chang, V. (2014). Cloud Bioinformatics in a Private Cloud Deployment. In J. Rodrigues (Ed.), *Advancing Medical Practice through Technology* (pp. 205–220). Hershey, PA: IGI Global.

Chang, V., Walters, R. J., & Wills, G. (2013a). The Development that Leads to the Cloud Computing Business Framework. *International Journal of Information Management, 33*(3), 524–538.

Chang, V., Walters, R. J., & Wills, G. (2013b). Cloud Storage and Bioinformatics in a Private Cloud Deployment: Lessons for Data Intensive Research. In I. I. Ivanov, M. van Sinderen, F. Leymann, & T. Shan (Eds.), *Cloud Computing and Services Science* (pp. 245–264). Berlin, Heidelberg: Springer.

Chang, V., & Wills, G. (2013). A University of Greenwich Case Study of Cloud Computing: Education as a Service. In D. Graham, I. Manikas, & D. Folinas (Eds.), *E-Logistics and E-Supply Chain Management: Applications for Evolving Business* (pp. 232–253).

Chaudhry, I. S., Malik, S., & Ashraf, M. (2006). Rural poverty in Pakistan: Some related concepts, issues and empirical analysis. *Pakistan Economic and Social Review, 44*(2), 259–276.

Choubisa, K. (2012). Cloud Computing & Rural Development. *International Journal of Information Technology and Knowledge Management, 6*(1), 98–100.

Cilesiz, S. (2004). Internet cafés: Bridges of the digital divide. *International Conference on Society for Information Technology & Teacher Education*, Atlanta, GA.

Crystal, D. (2006). Language and the internet (2nd ed.). Cambridge: Cambridge University Press. doi:10.1017/CBO9780511487002

Dalal, P. (2006). *Use of ICT for women empowerment in India*. New York: United Nations.

Danet, B., & Herring, S. C. (Eds.). (2007). *The multilingual internet: Language, culture, and communication online*. Oxford: Oxford University Press. doi:10.1093/acprof:oso/9780195304794.001.0001

Dave, D., & Dave, R. (2012). Role of non-farm sector in rural development. *National Monthly Refereed Journal of Research in Arts & Education, 1*(7), 7–16.

Davis, M. (2004). Planet of slum. *New Left Review, 26*, 5–34.

Dihal, S., Bouwman, H., de Reuver, M., Warnier, M., & Carlsson, C. (2013). Mobile cloud computing: State of the art and outlook. *Info, 15*(1), 4–16. doi:10.1108/14636691311296174

Faye, M. L., McArthur, J. W., Sachs, J. D., & Snow, T. (2004). The challenges facing landlocked developing countries. *Journal of Human Development, 5*(1), 31–68. doi:10.1080/14649880310001660201

Fu, T. M. (2005). Unequal primary education opportunities in rural and urban China. *China Perspectives, 60*, 2–8.

Furuholt, B., & Kristiansen, S. (2007). Internet cafés in Asia and Africa – Venues for education and learning? *The Journal of Community Informatics, 3*(2).

Gamage, P., & Halpin, E. F. (2007). E-Sri Lanka: Bridging the digital divide. *The Electronic Library, 25*(6), 693–710. doi:10.1108/02640470710837128

Ghazali, O., Osman, B., Ahmad, A., Abas, A., Rahmat, A. R., & Firdhous, M. (2013). Cloud powered rural telecenters – A model for sustainable telecenters. In *Proceedings of the 4th International Conference on Rural ICT Development* (pp. 136–142). Malacca, Malaysia.

Gulati, S. (2008). Technology-enhanced learning in developing nations: A review. *International Review of Research in Open and Distance Learning, 9*(1), 1–16.

Hammond, L. D., & Post, L. (2000). Inequality in teaching and schooling: Supporting high-quality teaching and leadership in low-income schools. In R. D. Kahlenberg (Ed.), *A Notion at Risk: Preserving Public Education as an Engine for Social Mobility* (pp. 127–167). New York: The Century Foundation.

Hargraves, M. (2002). Elevating the voices of rural minority women. *American Journal of Public Health, 92*(4), 514–515. doi:10.2105/AJPH.92.4.514 PMID:11919041

Harris, B., Goudge, J., Ataguba, J. E., McIntyre, D., Nxumalo, N., Jikwana, S., & Chersich, M. (2011). Inequities in access to health care in South Africa. *Journal of Public Health Policy, 32*, 102–123. doi:10.1057/jphp.2011.35 PMID:21730985

Hendry, L. B., & Kloep, M. (2004). To stay or not to stay? – that is the question: Rural youths' views on living in Scandinavia. *Barn, 22*(4), 33–52.

Hosman, L., & Fife, E. (2012). The use of mobile phones for development in {Africa}: Top-down-meets-bottom-up partnering. *The Journal of Community Informatics, 8*(3).

Hudson, P., & Hudson, S. (2008). Changing pre-service teachers' attitudes for teaching in rural schools. *Australian Journal of Teacher Education, 33*(4), 67–77. doi:10.14221/ajte.2008v33n4.6

Huttlinger, K., Ayers, J. S., Lawson, T., & Ayers, J. (2003). Suffering it out: Meeting the needs of health care delivery in a rural area. *Online Journal of Rural Nursing and Health Care, 3*(2), 17–28.

Ilavarasan, V. P., & Parthasarathy, B. (2012). Limited growth opportunities amidst opportunities for growth: An empirical study of the inter-firm linkages of small software firms in India. *Journal of Innovation and Entrepreneurship, 1*(4), 1–12.

Jones, L. R. (2012). Return on Investment Analysis: Applying a Private Sector Approach to the Public Sector. *Prime Journal of Business Administration and Management, 2*(1), 426–435.

Jones, I., Carr, D. L., & Dalal, P. (2011). Responding to rural health disparities in the United States: The geography of emergency care and telemedical technology. *Networks and Communication Studies, 25*(3-4), 273–290.

Kamaludeen, P., & Thamodaran, V. (2014). Role of information technology in unit linked insurance plans marketing. *Tactful Management Research Journal, 2*(4), 1–3.

Keniston, K. (2004). Introduction: The four digital divides. In K. Keniston & D. Kumar (Eds.), *IT Experience in India: Bridging the Digital Divide* (pp. 11–36). Delhi: Sage Publishers.

Khalif, A., & Nur, A. (2013). The African farmer and the challenge of food security in Africa. *Development, 56*(2), 257–265. doi:10.1057/dev.2013.25

Kiruthika, J., & Khaddaj, S. (2013). System performance in cloud services: Stability and resource allocation. In *Proceedings of the 12th International Symposium on Distributed Computing and Applications to Business, Engineering & Science* (pp. 127-131). Los Alamitos, CA. doi:10.1109/DCABES.2013.30

Kuriyan, R., & Kitner, K. R. (2009). Constructing class boundaries: Gender, aspirations, and shared computing. *Information Technologies and International Development, 5*(1), 17–29.

Lokhande, T. N., & Kale, V. P. (2014). Spatial distribution of health care facilities in Nanded District (Maharashtra) India. *Online International Interdisciplinary Research Journal, 4*(I), 316–325.

Lowe, J. M. (2006). Rural education: Attracting and retaining teachers in small schools. *Rural Educator, 27*, 28–32.

Lutfiyya, M. N., Bhat, D. K., Gandhi, S. R., Nguyen, C., Weidenbacher-Hoper, V. L., & Lipsky, M. S. (2007). A comparison of quality of care indicators in urban acute care hospitals and rural critical access hospitals in the United States. *International Journal for Quality in Health Care, 19*(3), 141–149. doi:10.1093/intqhc/mzm010 PMID:17442745

Malkowski, S., Kanemasa, Y., Chen, H., Yamamoto, M., Wang, Q., Jayasinghe, D., . . . Kawaba, M. (2012). Challenges and opportunities in consolidation at high resource utilization: non-monotonic response time variations in n-tier applications. In *Proceedings of the Fifth IEEE International Conference on Cloud Computing* (pp. 162-169). Honolulu, HI. doi:10.1109/CLOUD.2012.99

Marengo, A., & Marengo, V. (2005). Measuring the Economic Benefits of E-Learning: A Proposal for a New Index for Academic Environments. *Journal of Information Technology Education*, *4*, 329–346.

Martin, S. M., Lorenzen, K., & Bunnefeld, N. (2013). Fishing farmers: Fishing, livelihood diversification and poverty in rural Laos. *Human Ecology*, *41*(5), 737–747. doi:10.1007/s10745-013-9567-y

Masud, M. A. H., & Huang, X. (2012). An E-learning System Architecture based on Cloud Computing. *World Academy of Science. Engineering and Technology*, *6*, 738–742.

Mechanic, D., & Tanner, J. (2007). Vulnerable people, groups, and populations: Societal view. *Health Affairs*, *26*(5), 1220–1230. doi:10.1377/hlthaff.26.5.1220 PMID:17848429

Mirashe, S. P., & Kalyankar, N. V. (2010). Cloud computing. *Journal of Computing*, *2*(3), 78–82.

Molawa, S. (2009). The "first" and "third world" in Africa: Knowledge access, challenges and current technological innovations in Africa. In *Proceedings of the First International Conference on African Digital Libraries and Archives*, (pp. 1-14). Addis Ababa, Ethiopia.

Mtega, W. P., & Malekani, A. W. (2009). Analyzing the usage patterns and challenges of telecenters among rural communities: Experience from four selected telecenters in Tanzania. *International Journal of Education and Development Using Information and Communication Technology*, *5*(2), 68-87.

Musiyandaka, D., Ranga, G., & Kiwa, J. F. (2013). An analysis of factors influencing success of ICT4D projects: A case study of the schools computerisation programme in Mashonaland West Province, Zimbabwe. *The Journal of Community Informatics*, *9*(4).

Myhre, D. L., & Hohman, S. (2012). Going the distance: Early results of a distributed medical education initiative for royal college residencies in Canada. *Rural and Remote Health*, *25*(12), 1–7. PMID:23110637

Nag, B. (2011). Mass media and ICT in development communication: Comparison & convergence. *Global Media Journal*, *2*(2), 1–29.

Narula, S. A., & Arora, S. (2010). Identifying stakeholders' needs and constraints in adoption of ICT services in rural areas: The case of india. *Social Responsibility Journal*, *6*(2), 222–236. doi:10.1108/17471111011051739

Obiora, C. J. (2014). Agriculture and rural development versus youth rural-urban migration: The menace. *Journal of Agriculture Economics and Rural Development*, *2*(2), 58–61. doi:10.12966/jaerd.05.05.2014

Odunaike, S. A., Olugbara, O. O., & Ojo, S. O. (2012). Using Cloud Computing to Mitigate Rural E-Learning Sustainability and Challenges. *World Congress on Engineering and Computer Science*, (pp. 1-6) San Francisco, CA, USA.

Ogbomo, M. O., & Ogbomo, E. F. (2008). *Importance of information and communication technologies (ICTs) in making a heathy information society: A case study of Ethiope East Local Government Area of Delta State* (pp. 1–8). Nigeria: Library Philosophy and Practice.

Okiy, R. B., & Ogbomo, E. F. (2011). Supporting rural women's use of information and communication technologies for sustainable economic development in Ethiope-East Local Government Area of Delta State, Nigeria. *Journal of Information Technology Impact*, *11*(1), 71–84.

Ovwigho, B. O. (2014). Factors influencing involvement in nonfarm income generating activities among local farmers: The case of Ughelli South Local Government Area of Delta State, Nigeria. *Sustainable Agriculture Research*, *3*(1), 76–84. doi:10.5539/sar.v3n1p76

Owojori, A. A., & Asaolu, T. O. (2010). Critical evaluation of personnel management problems in the Nigerian school system. *International Journal of Educational Sciences*, *2*(1), 1–11.

Pade, C., Mallinson, B., & Sewry, D. (2011). Sustainable rural ICT project management practice for developing countries: Investigating the Dwesa and RUMEP projects. *Information Technology for Development*, *17*(3), 187–212. doi:10.1080/02681102.2011.568222

Patil, D. A., Dhere, A. M., & Pawar, C. B. (2009). ICT and empowerment of rural and deprived women in Asia. *Asia-Pacific Journal of Rural Development*, *19*(1), 1–22.

Pocatilu, P., Alecu, F., & Vetrici, M. (2009). Using cloud computing for e-learning systems. In *Proceedings of the 8th WSEAS International Conference on Data Networks, Communications and Computers* (pp. 54-59). Baltimore, MD.

Ragan, C. T., & Lipsey, R. G. (2011). Challenges facing the developing countries. In C. T. Ragan, & R. G. Lipsey (Eds.), Macroeconomics (13th ed.). Don Mills, ON: Pearson.

Rao, S. S. (2009). Role of ICTS in India rural communities. *The Journal of Community Informatics*, *5*(1).

Rao, T. P. (2004). ICT and e-governance for rural development. In *Proceedings of the Symposium on Governance in Development: Issues, Challenges and Strategies* (pp. 1-13). Anand, Gujarat, India.

Roy, N. K. (2012). ICT–enabled rural education in India. *International Journal of Information and Education Technology*, *2*(5), 525–529. doi:10.7763/IJIET.2012.V2.196

Saeed, A., & Ibrahim, H. (2005). Reasons for the problems faced by patients in government hospitals: Results of a survey in a government hospital in Karachi, Pakistan. *JPMA. The Journal of the Pakistan Medical Association*, *55*(1), 1–3. PMID:15816698

Saxena, S. (2012). Problems faced by rural entrepreneurs and remedies to solve it. *IOSR Journal of Business and Management*, *3*(1), 23–29. doi:10.9790/487X-0312329

Scott, A., Gilbert, A., & Gelan, A. (2007). The urban rural divide: Myth or reality? SERG Policy Brief 2. London, UK: The Macaulay Institute, Socio Economic Research Group.

Sewchurran, E., & Brown, I. (2011). Successful ICT service delivery: Enablers, inhibitors and hygiene factors - A service provider perspective. In *Proceedings of the Institute of Computer Scientists and Information Technologists Conference* (pp. 195-204). Cape Town, South Africa.

Sharma, M. (2005). Information and communication technology for poverty reduction. *Turkish Online Journal of Distance Education*, *6*(2).

Shawish, A., & Salama, M. (2014). Cloud computing: Paradigms and technologies. In F. Xhafa & N. Bessis (Eds.), *Inter-cooperative collective intelligence: Techniques and applications* (pp. 39–67). Heidelberg: Springer. doi:10.1007/978-3-642-35016-0_2

Shimamoto, D. (2012). A Strategic Approach to IT Budgeting: How Organizations can Align Technology Spending with their Overall Mission and Goals. *Journal of Accountancy*.

Sianipar, C. P., Yudoko, G., Adhiutama, A., & Dowaki, K. (2013). Community empowerment through appropriate technology: Sustaining the sustainable development. *Procedia Environmental Sciences*, *17*, 1007–1016. doi:10.1016/j.proenv.2013.02.120

Sibley, L. M., & Weiner, J. P. (2011). An evaluation of access to health care services along the rural-urban continuum in Canada. *BMC Health Services Research*, *11*(20), 1–11. PMID:21281470

Sloman, J. (2006). Economics (6th ed.). Upper Saddle River, NJ: Prentice Hall.

Songan, P., Hamid, K. A., Yeo, A., Gnaniah, J., & Zen, H. (2008). Challenges to community informatics to bridging the digital divide. In F. B. Tan (Ed.), *Global information technologies: Concepts, methodologies, tools, and applications* (pp. 2121–2133). Hershey, PA: Information Science Reference. doi:10.4018/978-1-59904-939-7.ch152

Srinivasu, B., & Rao, P. S. (2013). Infrastructure development and economic growth: Prospects and perspective. *Journal of Business Management & Social Sciences Research*, *2*(1), 81–91.

Sundar, K., & Srinivasan, T. (2009). Rural industrialisation: Challenges and proposition. *Journal of Social Science*, *20*(1), 23–29.

Sweeney, J. C., & Webb, D. A. (2007). How Functional, Psychological and Social Relationship Benefits Influence Individual and Firm Commitment to the Relationship. *Journal of Business and Industrial Marketing*, *22*(7), 474–488.

Syverson, C. (2011). What Determines Productivity? *Journal of Economic Literature*, *49*(2), 326–365.

Talvitie, J. (2004). Incorporating the impact of ICT into urban and regional planning. *European Journal of Spatial Development*, 1-32.

Taneri, P. O., & Engin-Demir, C. (2011). Quality of education in rural schools: A needs assessment study. *International Online Journal of Educational Sciences*, *3*(1), 91–112.

Tayyaba, S. (2012). Rural-urban gaps in achievement, schooling conditions, student, and teachers' characteristics in Pakistan. *International Journal of Educational Management*, *26*(1), 6–26. doi:10.1108/09513541211194356

Thorlakson, T., & Neufeldt, H. (2012). Reducing subsistence farmers' vulnerability to climate change: Evaluating the potential contributions of agroforestry in western Kenya. *Agriculture & Food Security*, *1*(15), 1–13.

UN. (2011). *World urbanization prospects: The 2011 revision*. New York, NY: United Nations, Department of Economic and Social Affairs, Population Division.

Usman, A., Dutta, D., Habeeb, O., & Jean, A. (2013). Sustainable energy in rural communities of Bongouanou: Utilizing solar energy as a source for electricity. In *Proceedings of the IEEE Global Humanitarian Technology Conference: South Asia Satellite* (pp. 15-20). Trivandrum, India. doi:10.1109/GHTC-SAS.2013.6629881

van der Geest, K. (2010). *Rural youth employment in developing countries: A global view*. Rome, Italy: United Nations Food and Agriculture Organization.

van Dijk, J. (2008). One Europe, digitally divided. In A. Chadwick & P. N. Howard (Eds.), *The Routledge handbook of internet politics* (pp. 288–304). London: Routledge.

Wang, D. (2013). Influences of cloud computing on e-commerce businesses and industry. *Journal of Software Engineering and Applications*, *6*(06), 313–318. doi:10.4236/jsea.2013.66039

Wolk, R. M. (2004). The effects of English language dominance of the internet and the digital divide. In *Proceedings of the International Symposium on Technology and Society* (pp. 174-178). Worcester, MA, USA. doi:10.1109/ISTAS.2004.1314348

Wong, Y. C., Fung, J. Y., Law, C. K., Lam, J. C., & Lee, V. W. (2009). Tackling the digital divide. *British Journal of Social Work*, *39*(4), 754–767. doi:10.1093/bjsw/bcp026

Yeboah-Boateng, E. O., & Essandoh, K. A. (2013). Cloud computing: The level of awareness amongst small & medium-sized enterprises (SMEs) in developing economies. *Journal of Emerging Trends in Computing and Information Sciences*, *4*(11), 832–839.

Younis, M. Z. (2003). A comparison study of urban and small rural hospitals financial and economic performance. *Online Journal of Rural Nursing and Health Care*, *3*(1), 38–48.

KEY TERMS AND DEFINITIONS

Cloud Computing: Refers to the Internet based computing where computing resources have been hosted remotely and clients access them and pay for only usage.

Data Centers: A place where all the server grade computing systems and workforce of an organization's are located and the processing and data storage are taking place.

Digital Divide: The disparity in life between the people who avail the benefit of computers and the Internet and who do not.

EaaS: The delivery of educational service using the cloud technology.

Rural IT Implementation: The Information and communication Technology projects implemented with the objective of enhancing the quality of life of the rural masses.

SaaS: The software delivery model where remotely hosted software is delivered over the internet and charged on usage basis.

Telecenter: A place equipped with computing equipment and the Internet where casual users can access them and pay for.

Utility Computing: The computing paradigm where users are allowed to access computing resources over the internet and pay for it based on usage.

Section 3
Current Cloud Advances

Chapter 8
A Resource Allocation Model for Desktop Clouds

Abdulelah Alwabel
University of Southampton, UK

Robert John Walters
University of Southampton, UK

Gary B. Wills
University of Southampton, UK

ABSTRACT

Cloud computing is a new paradigm that promises to move IT a step further towards utility computing, in which computing services are delivered as a utility service. Traditionally, Cloud employs dedicated resources located in one or more data centres in order to provide services to clients. Desktop Cloud computing is a new type of Cloud computing that aims at providing Cloud capabilities at low or no cost. Desktop Clouds harness non dedicated and idle resources in order to provide Cloud services. However, the nature of such resources can be problematic because they are prone to failure at any time without prior notice. This research focuses on the resource allocation mechanism in Desktop Clouds.The contributions of this chapter are threefold. Firstly, it defines and explains Desktop Clouds by comparing them with both Traditional Clouds and Desktop Grids. Secondly, the paper discusses various research issues in Desktop Clouds. Thirdly, it proposes a resource allocation model that is able to handle node failures.

INTRODUCTION

Cloud computing is a new model that promises to move IT services a step further towards utility computing, which means providing computing services as a utility service. Traditionally, a Cloud service provider (CSP), such as Amazon, employs computing resources located in data centres in

order to provide Cloud services to clients. The computing resources are dedicated to providing these services (i.e., they are made for this purpose). This type of Cloud computing is called Traditional Clouds throughout this paper. Desktop Cloud computing is a new type of Cloud computing that aims to provide Cloud capabilities by harnessing computing resources that would otherwise remain

DOI: 10.4018/978-1-4666-8210-8.ch008

Copyright © 2015, IGI Global. Copying or distributing in print or electronic forms without written permission of IGI Global is prohibited.

idle. This ambition can be achieved by combining both Cloud computing and Volunteer computing in order to form Desktop Clouds. This new type of Cloud computing is motivated by the success of Desktop Grid projects, such as SETI@home (Anderson & Fedak, 2006), in harnessing idle computing resources instead of relying on specific-made resources to form a Grid. Desktop Clouds harness non-dedicated and idle resources in order to provide Cloud services. For example, a university may wish to use its IT resources when they become idle to form a Cloud. The resources can be any type of computing nodes, normal PCs for example. The main motivation for Desktop Clouds is to reduce the expense of acquiring Cloud services.

This chapter focuses on the resource allocation mechanism in Desktop Clouds. The resource allocation mechanism in Cloud computing is concerned with the following question: how to allocate resources in a way that can maximise the profits for the service providers without affecting the performance of these servers. Maximisation of profit can be achieved by saving power consumption in the physical nodes that are employed by CSPs. The Desktop Cloud is a new Cloud type that employs idle and non-dedicated resources to provide Cloud services. However, the nodes in Desktop Clouds are prone to failure at any time without prior knowledge. A failure event in a physical node can be caused as a result of connectivity problems, crashes and so on. A failure event, in this context, includes if an owner of physical machine that is serving in a Desktop Cloud, decides to disconnect his/her machine without prior notice. Therefore, Desktop Clouds have brought a new dimension, the high failure rate of nodes, to the problem of resource allocation in Clouds. The contributions of this chapter are threefold:

- The chapter explains Desktop Clouds as being a new Cloud computing model. A comparison is given between Desktop Clouds against Traditional Clouds and Desktop Grids.

- Several research issues in Desktop Clouds are discussed. Attention is given to failures in physical nodes within Desktop Clouds.
- The chapter proposes a resource allocation model that is able to handle node failures.

The rest of the paper is organised as follows: a background section gives an overview of Desktop Clouds as a new Cloud computing model. Several advantages of Desktop Clouds are compared with Traditional Clouds and discussed. The section compares and contrasts Desktop Clouds with related large-scale systems (Traditional Clouds and Desktop Grids). The subsequent section discusses several research issues that need further attention from researchers of Desktop Clouds. An analysis of the failures in Desktop Cloud physical nodes is conducted to show the importance of having a resource allocation mechanism that can handle such failures. After that, the taxonomy of resource allocation mechanisms in the literature is described. Furthermore, a failure-aware resource allocation model is proposed, along with a discussion about its effectiveness.

Background

The success of Desktop Grids motivated the idea of applying the same concept to the Cloud. Desktop Clouds exploit computing resources of any form to build Clouds. Hence, the term Desktop comes from Desktop Grids because both Desktop Clouds and Desktop Grids are based on harnessing Desktop PCs and laptops. Similarly, the term Cloud comes from Cloud paradigm because Desktop Cloud aims to provide services based on the Cloud business model.

Several synonyms for Desktop Cloud have been used in the literature, such as Ad-hoc Cloud, Volunteer Clouds and Non-Dedicated Clouds. The literature shows that very little work has been undertaken in this direction. Ad-hoc Cloud is the idea of harvesting distributed resources within an organisation to form a Cloud (Kirby,

Dearle, Macdonald, & Fernandes, 2010). Nebula (Chandra & Weissman, 2009; Weissman et al., 2011) is a project aiming to exploit distributed resources in order to create a Volunteer Cloud which offers services free of charge. Cloud@ home (V. D. Cunsolo, Distefano, Puliafito, & Scarpa, 2009; V. Cunsolo & Distefano, 2010) is a project representing the @home philosophy in Cloud computing. The goal of Cloud@home is to form a new model of Cloud computing that is contributed to by individual users over the Internet. In addition, Cern has announced an initiative to move their Desktop Grid project, called LHC@ home, towards the Cloud (Harutyunyan et al., 2012). In addition, Andrzejak et al. (2010) suggest that non-dedicated resources can be exploited by Cloud providers in case their local infrastructure cannot meet consumer requests at peak times.

Desktop Cloud is a new Infrastructure-as-a-Service Cloud model that exploits computing resources such as computer desktops when these resources to serve as nodes within the Cloud system. Each Cloud node can work, virtually, as a server in a datacentre to end users in Cloud computing. Virtualisation allows each Cloud node to host multiple VMs. Desktop Cloud can be defined as:

It is an IT paradigm that enables online access to idle computing resources based on virtualisation technology to allow users to provision services rapidly and scale up and down according to demand of users.

The overview architecture of Desktop Clouds is shown in Figure 1. The architecture shows that a Desktop Cloud consists of several layers. The resource layer is responsible for aggregating the physical nodes that form the Desktop Cloud infrastructure. Physical machines can be connected by way of LAN or WLAN. Clients contact the service layer in order to submit their demands. The virtual layer plays an important role in isolating clients from physical nodes by way of virtualisation; a

method similar to that used in Traditional Clouds. The isolation improves security and prevents unauthorised access between two parties. Users are assigned virtual machines that are allocated to physical machines by a resource allocator. The physical layer manages the Cloud nodes in terms of allocating VMs requested by clients. The layer implements a resource allocation mechanism that is tolerant of the failures that can happen in physical nodes.

There are several scenarios to show how a Desktop Cloud can be built. For example, suppose a group of universities decides to benefit from its computing resources to form a Desktop Cloud. The resources can range from PCs and laptops to servers, each of which is called a Cloud node. The idea is that when a node becomes idle, it joins the Cloud. This scenario has been previously implemented to execute Grid tasks on computers when they are idle. This scenario can be seen as a private Desktop Cloud. Another scenario that can be considered is that of a universal Desktop Cloud. In this scenario, people are asked to contribute

Figure 1. Overview architecture of desktop clouds

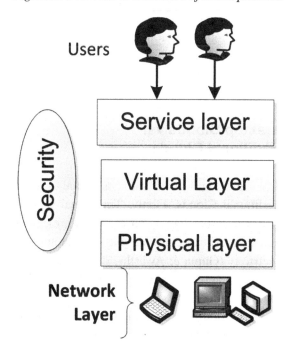

their own computing resources via the Internet to be used sometime by Cloud clients (V. Cunsolo, Distefano, Puliafito, & Scarp, 2009). This scenario can be considered as a public Desktop Cloud. A question can be raised in this context in respect of why people would be willing to donate their machines. People can be encouraged to participate in Desktop Cloud to serve science within research communities. For example, the SETI@home Desktop Grid project had more than 300,000 contributors willing to serve the research community (Anderson & Fedak, 2006).

Figure 2 fits in terms of reliability of resources and service delivery. The figure shows that both Desktop Clouds and Traditional Clouds are service oriented, which means that computing is provided as a service, while Grids and Desktop Grids are more application oriented. Application oriented means that users submit small batches of jobs to Grids or Desktop Grids (Zhang, Chen, & Huo, 2010). Furthermore, the graph depicts that the infrastructure used for both Desktop Clouds and Desktop Grids is quite similar because they both employ the same types of physical machine; which can be highly volatile. Therefore, Desktop Clouds and Desktop Grids have low reliability. In order to elaborate further on the meaning of Desktop Clouds, the following two sections describe the similarities and differences of Desktop Clouds when compared to Traditional Clouds and Desktop Grids.

Desktop Clouds vs. Traditional Clouds

Desktop Clouds have some advantages over Traditional Clouds. Firstly, Traditional Clouds have a negative impact on the environment as their data centres consume massive amounts of electricity (Gupta & Awasthi, 2009). Each data centre contains a massive number of computing nodes running at the same time, which require extra electricity for cooling. Rasmussen (2007) estimates that cooling accounts for about 40%

Figure 2. Desktop clouds Position2

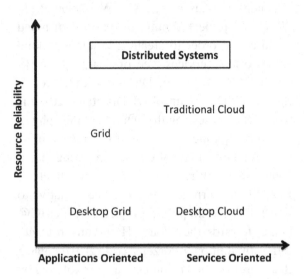

of the electricity consumed in data centres. In contradiction, computing nodes used in Desktop Clouds are already in use before joining the Cloud, so no extra electricity for cooling and maintenance is required. However, a Desktop Cloud still consumes extra electricity, as a Desktop Cloud's node would remain idle if it did not join the Cloud. This extra electricity consumption penalty can be small because it has been shown that an idle machine consumes about 70% of the total electricity power consumed when the machine is fully utilised (Kusic, Kephart, Hanson, Kandasamy, & Jiang, 2008). Therefore, about 30% more power consumption is needed if an idle machine runs at full utilisation when joining a Desktop Cloud.

The second advantage is the cost effectiveness of Desktop Clouds in terms of running, maintenance and service usage. For service providers, there is no need to build new data centres to meet the increasing demands of the future. Consumers will get their services at lower prices, if not free, compared to Traditional Clouds. Thirdly, Desktop Clouds have a positive impact towards environment; helping to reduce energy consumption, as it utilises already-running resources which would otherwise remain idle. Some studies show that the average percentage of local resources that are idle within an organisation totals about 80% (Arpaci et al., 1995). Furthermore, Traditional Clouds are built on top of a limited number of data centres located around the globe. Therefore, they are inefficient in terms of data mobility between clients and CSPs and pay little attention to the location of clients (Weissman et al., 2011). Finally, Traditional Clouds are centralised, which raises the issue that there could be a single point of failure issue if a Cloud service provider goes out of business. In contrast, Desktop Clouds manage and offer services in a decentralised manner.

There are some similarities and differences between Desktop Clouds and Traditional Clouds. Both Desktop Clouds and Traditional Clouds have the same essential characteristics of Cloud computing (Vaquero, Rodero-Merino, Caceres, & Lindner, 2009), as Table 1 shows. The characteristics are elasticity, on-demand self-service, virtualisation, service delivery model and ease of use. Both Desktop Clouds and Traditional Clouds share the elasticity feature. Elasticity means that a Cloud's user can acquire computing services and scale up or down according to their needs in a short time. The services are online self-service which means that Cloud services can be acquired and released in an automatic way. Both Traditional Clouds and Desktop Clouds employ virtualisation to separate VMs from physical machines. The model of services delivered by Cloud systems should implement the 'pay per use' base. The model means that Cloud services are delivered on a time-based contract between a CSP and customers. Users in Desktop Clouds are not expected to pay for their usage, but they can gain services on the same principle. For example, a Desktop Cloud's user can gain a couple of VMs, for example for three hours, similar to what happens in Traditional Clouds. The 'ease of use' principle means that clients can use a specific service without the need to make lots of changes to their work. Both Traditional Clouds and Desktop Clouds let their users harness services without making significant changes to their code.

Table 1. Essential characteristics of cloud systems

Feature	Traditional Cloud	Desktop Cloud
Elasticity	√	√
On-demand Self-service	√	√
Virtualisation	√	√
Service Delivery Model	√	√
Ease of Use	√	√

However, there are several differences between Desktop and Traditional Clouds, as depicted in Table 2. The first is in the resource layer; Desktop Cloud is made of resources that are non-dedicated, i.e., not they are not made to be part of the Cloud infrastructure. The physical nodes in Desktop Clouds are expected to be highly volatile due to the fact that they can fail unexpectedly without prior notice. The failure of nodes can be as a result of machines crashing, connectivity problems or even because the owner of a physical machine decides to leave the Cloud. Resource high volatility can have a negative impact on availability and performance (Marosi, Kovács, & Kacsuk, 2012). To the contrary, the infrastructure of Traditional Clouds consists of a large number of computing resources located in data centres made to serve clients in the Cloud. Secondly, resources in Desktop Clouds can be distributed across the globe, provided that anyone can contribute from anywhere. However, resources in Traditional Clouds are limited to the locations of the data centres hosting them.

Table 2. Traditional clouds vs. desktop clouds

Feature	Traditional Clouds	Desktop Clouds
Resources	Dedicated	Non-dedicated and Volatile
Cost	Relatively High	Cheap
Location	Limited	Distributed
Services	Reliable and Available	Low Availability and Unreliable
Heterogeneity	Heterogeneous	Very Heterogeneous

Although resources in both Desktop Clouds and Traditional Clouds are heterogeneous, they are more heterogeneous and varied in Desktop Clouds.

Desktop Clouds vs. Desktop Grids

Desktop Grids are distributed systems which utilise idle resources to perform large computation tasks in scientific projects at low costs (Kondo, Taufer, & Brooks, 2004). The Desktop Grid is derived from Grid computing. Grid computing is a geographically distributed computational platform integrating large-scale, distributed, complex and heterogeneous resources working together to form a virtual super computer. Grid was motivated by the research community with the aim of solving a specific problem by sharing computing resources (I. Foster, Kesselman, & Tuecke, 2001). Grid computing emerged in the late nineties with a vision to progress to a utility age whereby computing is provided as a utility service just like electricity. The vision of providing computing services as utility services is shared by Grids and Clouds. In addition, many researchers think that Cloud computing has evolved from Grid computing (Ian Foster, Zhao, Raicu, & Lu, 2008). These reasons have caused some sort of confusion between Grids and Clouds. Therefore, several papers have been published in order to compare and contrast Grids with Clouds, such as Ian Foster et al. (2008), Bégin et al. (2008), Vaquero et al. (2008) and Zhang et al. (2010).

The comparison between Grids and Traditional Clouds can help us to understand the difference between Desktop Grids and Desktop Clouds. Table 3 summarises the similarities and differences between Grid computing and Traditional Clouds. First of all, they both rely on dedicated resources that are very reliable. In fact, some of the Grid infrastructure can be used as parts for Cloud infrastructure. Cloud implements virtualisation to abstract physical machines. Virtualisation enables resource multiplexing; meaning more than a VM can be assigned to the same physical node. Cloud

Table 3. Grids vs. traditional clouds

Feature	Grids	Traditional Clouds
Resources	Dedicated and Reliable	Dedicated and Reliable
Resource Multiplexing	Not Employed	Employed
Business Model	Project Oriented	Pay Per Use
Application Domain	Research Projects	Various Purposes
Quality of service	Guaranteed (at application level)	Guaranteed by CSPs

offers services on a 'utility base', which means that users gain services and pay for their actual usage only, whereas the business model in Grids is based on a 'project oriented' model which means that every client is assigned a certain time to use a particular service. It does not matter if the client actually uses this service or not (Ian Foster et al., 2008). As mentioned before, Grid computing was motivated by research communities to serve and solve some research problems. Therefore, it is quite normal to have a single purpose Grid project. For example, neuGrid is a Grid project that enables neuroscientists to carry out research regarding degenerative brain diseases (Redolfi et al., 2009). Cloud computing, on the other hand, offers services to a wide range of customers with various purposes. In addition, both Grids and Clouds can achieve QoS guarantees, but at different levels. For the former, it is at the application level that users can implement some sort of mechanisms to ensure QoS, while it is granted by CSPs for the later.

Desktop Clouds can be confused with Desktop Grids in a similar way to the confusion between Clouds and Grids. Table 4 shows a comparison of Desktop Clouds and Desktop Grids. The Table can be seen as a summary of the comparison of Desktop Clouds; with Traditional Clouds from one side and Grids against Traditional Clouds on the other side. Resources have the same features, such as being undedicated and unreliable in both

Desktop Grids and Desktop Clouds. In fact, a Desktop Cloud can be built on top of a Desktop Grid infrastructure. However, Desktop Clouds employ virtualisation that enables resource sharing between users via resource multiplexing. Finally, Desktop Clouds follow the business model offered by Traditional Clouds in terms of scalability and elasticity. Users in Desktop Clouds can acquire VMs as they desire, and scale them up or down according to their needs. Desktop Grids employ the 'project oriented' concept that is used by Grids. The Desktop Grids' main application domain is research projects because researchers use idle resources to help them solve complex research problems. This goal is shared with Desktop Clouds, but can be more generic. For example, Desktop Clouds can be used by CSPs in Traditional Clouds when a CSP owned data centre(s) cannot meet user demand. Thus, Desktop Clouds can have more generic purposes than Desktop Grids, thanks to the business model that enables them to deal with several clients.

RESEARCH CHALLENGES

This section describes several research issues that need further attention in Desktop Clouds. Some of these challenges are inherited from Cloud computing, while others are driven by the employed highly volatile resources.

Security and Data Protection

Security is considered to be one of the major concerns that prevents organisations from migrating to the Cloud (Dillon, Wu, & Chang, 2010; Chang and Ramachandran, 2014). A study shows that an attacker can gain critical information about a particular VM using a cross-VM side channel attack; by placing a malicious VM on the same physical machine that hosts the target VM (Ristenpart, Tromer, Savage, & Shacham, 2009). More concerns arise in Desktop Clouds, especially when both consumers and contributors are from the

Table 4. Desktop grids vs. desktop clouds

Feature	Desktop Grids	Desktop Clouds
Resources	Non-dedicated	Non-dedicated
Infrastructure	Unreliable	Unreliable
Resource Sharing	Not Supported	Supported
Business Model	Project Oriented	Cloud Model
Application Domain	Research Projects	Generic Purposes

public. In Desktop Clouds, there are three parties that need to be protected against security threats: consumers, contributors and the CSP. In addition to threats brought by in Traditional Clouds, all parties take on risk themselves when they participate in a Desktop Cloud. Contributors can put their private data at risk by allowing VMs to be hosted on their machines. Likewise, consumers are vulnerable to malicious contributors. Nodes in Desktop Clouds are more likely to be vulnerable to security attacks due to weaknesses in firewalls and local antivirus software, compared to Traditional Clouds.

Therefore, the Desktop Cloud service provider should implement some mechanisms to prevent several attacks. Virtualisation can play an important role in isolating the host completely from guest operating systems and thus, preventing any unwanted access from either party. Trust mechanisms can be applied in this way. For example, a Desktop Cloud can maintain a table that contains some history information about both consumers and contributors. The table can help in deciding which parties are trustworthy enough to join a Desktop Cloud, as either a contributor of consumer. Furthermore, Desktop Clouds should rely on autonomous mechanisms, such as security certification to prevent various attacks from hackers (Cao, Li, & Xia, 2009). In addition, encryption mechanisms can help to protect the consumers' data from hosted machines. Desktop Cloud service providers should implement detector mechanism to detect malicious VMs and shut them down.

Adoption of Cloud

Adoption of Cloud is considered a research challenge in Traditional Clouds. The question is what drives small and medium enterprises to move to Cloud computing. Chang et. al., (2014) discuss several advantages of adopting Cloud computing for such organisations. The advantages can be classified into non-functional (such as elasticity and QoS), economical (such as low running costs) and technological (such as multi-tenancy) attributes. However, data portability can be a challenge from the perspective of organisations against migration to the Cloud. Data portability means that users of Cloud computing can migrate their data from a service provider to another provider. Data portability requires standard protocol between Cloud service providers. Desktop Cloud is no exception in this context. However, this issue requires further attention because there are no available standard protocols that can be used. To illustrate that adoption of Cloud can be delivered smoothly, Chang (2014) design and implement Business Intelligence as a Service in the Cloud to allow clients and host organisation about the risk with regard to the investment. This is a successful example for Cloud adoption for all the stakeholders, company users and their clients.

Node Failure

Nodes usually in Desktop Clouds are expected to fail at any time without prior knowledge. Desktop Grid is no exception in this context since the underlying infrastructure is quite similar. A Desktop Cloud can be built on top of the Desktop Grid's infrastructure. Therefore, studying the failure events that happen in the physical nodes in a Desktop Grid can help in designing a fault tolerance mechanism to reduce the negative impact of failures. Failure Trace Archive (FTA) is a public repository containing traces of several distributed and parallel systems ranging from Supercomputing and Grids to Desktop Grids (Javadi, Kondo,

Iosup, & Epema, 2013). Traces of two Desktop Grids have been gathered from the archive: Notre Dame and SETI@home Desktop Grids. Although the archive provides traces of the node behaviour, it needs some analysis to calculate the failure rate. The failure rate means the number of nodes that fail in a given hour of a day (h) in an FTA as following:

$$failure\ rate(h)$$
$$= \frac{number\ of\ failed\ nodes\ at\ h}{total\ number\ of\ nodes} * 100$$

Table 5 estimates of the literature; resource unavailability can reach up to 50% in such infrastructure (Kondo et al., 2004). Figure 3 shows the average hourly failure rate for Notre Dame and SETI@home Desktop Clouds. The hourly average failure rate is an average failure rate per hour in 30 days; this means calculating the average failure rate when $h=1$ at day 1,2 to 30. Each failure rate at an hour is independent from the others. The average spans between 7% and 20% for SETI@home, while it is between 9% and 16% for Notre Dame Desktop Cloud.

Resource Management

The resource manager in Desktop Clouds is responsible for ensuring that the quality of services provided is within user acceptance level. This role

Table 5. Failure rate summary table

	Notre Dame	SETI@home
Number of nodes	503	961
Running hours	720	720
Minimum failure rate	5.37%	5.41%
Maximum failure rate	23.26	54.42%
Mean (Average)	9.60%	10.26%
Median	8.95%	9.37%
Standard deviation	3.10	3.79

Figure 3. Average hourly failure rate

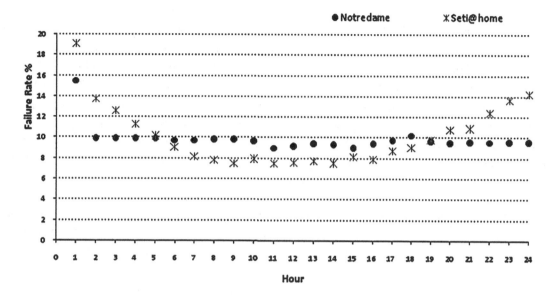

also includes aggregating and selecting resources amongst a large pool of very heterogeneous resources. The resource aggregation mechanism, implemented at the resource management level, is concerned with choosing the best match of resources to each request in order to improve the overall performance. In addition, monitoring these resources is quite important to observe resource behaviour to detect failures. Furthermore, the study of the nodes' behaviour in Desktop Grids, as described in the previous section, shows that the rate of failure events in nodes is quite high. The failures in the nodes have a direct impact on the quality of service provided to clients. Therefore, fault recovery mechanisms are crucial in order to improve reliability and QoS in this environment. The resource allocation mechanism relies on replication to ensure that the services are not interrupted. However, replication techniques can affect the availability of nodes that are ready to serve new requests. Therefore, virtualisation can be employed to improve resource availability by assigning replicas to resources that are already busy hosting VMs. The next section discusses resource allocation mechanisms in the literature from the perspective of node failures.

Taxonomy of Resource Allocation Mechanisms

Cloud management is responsible for coordinating and monitoring the virtual machines allocated to physical resources. The Cloud resource management, according to Sotomayor et al. (2009), should provide Cloud users with a uniform view of the virtualised resources. The full VM life cycle should also be managed and monitored by the management component. It is responsible for maintaining the level of performance required in the SLA contract. The resource allocation in Cloud computing is the process which involves placing VMs into PMs with the purpose of satisfying the SLA requirements. It also involves the migration of VMs from one PM to another for various reasons, for example to maintain the performance of VMs or to improve utilisation. Several works in this context show that there is a possibility to achieve this goal by implementing the right resource allocation policy. The policy should take into consideration:

1. Placing a new VM,
2. Migrating a VM to another PM, and

3. Monitoring the running VM in case any performance degradation occurs (Mills, Filliben, & Dabrowski, 2011).

In Traditional Clouds, the literature shows that the focus of researchers is on how to minimise the power consumption of physical nodes in order to maximise the revenue for Cloud service providers. The researchers are motivated to tackle this issue because the cost of power consumption in data centres accounts for a large amount of the total cost of data centre maintenance (Barroso & Hölzle, 2009). The idea behind it is that better utilisation leads to more idle servers. Subsequently, idle servers can be switched to a safe mode (e.g., sleep, hibernation) in order to reduce the cost of energy consumption in servers. Meisner et al. (2009) show that an idle machine may consume at least 60% of the total power consumed when it is fully utilised. This chapter discusses several works that have been carried out on how to improve the resource allocation mechanism from performance, costs and utilisation perspectives. The works are limited to resource allocation, which deals with managing virtual machines only.

Resource Allocation Techniques in Traditional Clouds

In Cloud computing the problem of allocation of resources can be formulated as follows: there are a set of VMs and a set of PMs. Several works in this context show that there is a possibility to achieve this goal via implementing the right resource allocation policy. The policy should take into consideration:

1. Placing a new VM,
2. Migrating a VM to another PM, and
3. Monitoring the running VM in case any performance degradation occurs (Mills et al., 2011).

The challenge is how to tradeoff between lowering energy consumption and maintaining an acceptable level of performance. It has been shown that assigning various VMs to PMs can be classified as a type of Bin Packing problem (A Beloglazov & Buyya, 2010). The Bin Packing problem in its classic form, means packing as many objects of different volumes into the least possible number of bins (Garey & Johnson, 1985). However, the problem needs further attention because it involves another vector. The number of VMs placed in each PM can cause performance degradation of the VMs if the number exceeds a certain level (Srikantaiah, Kansal, & Zhao, 2008), therefore causing more SLA violations. It can also lead to PMs consuming more energy than normal due to the state of overutilization (A Beloglazov & Buyya, 2010). Therefore, the Bin Packing problem has to be extended to involve allocating as many VMs as possible to the same PM under two restrictions: violation of SLA and excessive power consumption due to overutilization.

Several Bin Packing heuristic solutions for VM placement have been evaluated by Mills et al. (2011). The authors have investigated First Fit (FF), Least Fit First (LF) and Next Fit (NF) algorithms for node-selection decisions in Traditional Clouds. Their experiments showed that the LF algorithm is slightly better in terms of utilisation. Similar works have been undertaken in Jiang et al. (2012) to evaluate FF, NF and Best Fit (BF) algorithms with regard to performance. The study concluded that the BF algorithm has the best performance. However, the heuristic algorithms cannot guarantee better results, as the aforementioned studies have shown. Therefore, the resource allocation policies should define several steps to establish better results.

Load balancing, Static-Greedy and Round-Robin resource allocation policies are implemented in open-source resource management for Traditional Clouds, such as Eucalyptus, OpenNebula and Nimbus (Sotomayor et al., 2009). The load balancing policy chooses a PM with the least used resources (CPU and RAM) to host the new VM. The Static-Greedy mechanism allocates a VM to the PM with the least number of running VMs. If the chosen PM cannot accommodate the new VM, then the next least VM running PM will be allocated. Round Robin is an allocation policy, which allocates a set of VMs to each available physical host in a circular order without any priority. For example, suppose three VMs are assigned to two PMs. The RR policy will allocate VM1 to PM1, then VM2 to PM2 and then allocate VM3 to PM1 again. Although these policies are simple and easy to implement, they have been criticised for being under-utilisation mechanisms which waste energy.

Power-Aware Resource Allocation

Srikantaiah et al. (2008) have studied the relationship between energy consumption, resource utilisation and performance in resource consolidation in Traditional Clouds. The researchers have investigated the impact of resource high utilisation on performance degradation when various VMs are consolidated to the same physical node. A notion of optimal point was introduced into their work. They argued that there is an optimal utilisation point, which allows placing several VMs at the same physical node without affecting the performance level. Once the utilisation point is reached in a PM, no new VMs are placed. The proposed policy relies on calculating the optimal point for utilisation. After calculation of the utilisation optimal point, the policy can employ a heuristic algorithm for VM placement, as they defined the consolidation problem as a multi-dimensional Bin Packing problem. They have shown that the consumption of power per transaction results in a 'U' curve shape. Their experiment found that CPU utilisation at 70% is the optimal point. However, this point can vary according to the specification of the physical machines and workloads used in the experiment. Their approach is criticised for the fact

that the technique used depends on the type of the workload and the nature of the targeted machines (Graubner, Schmidt, & Freisleben, 2011).

Verma et al. (2008) have presented 'pMapper', a power and performance aware framework for VM placement and migration in virtualised systems. In pMapper, the monitoring engine collects current performance and power status for VMs and PMs in case any migration is required. The allocation policy in pMapper employs *mPP*, which is an algorithm that places VMs on servers with the aim of reducing the power consumed by these servers. The algorithm has two phases. The first is to determine a target utilisation point for each available server based on the power model for each of them. The second phase employs a First Fit Decreasing (FFD) algorithm to place VMs on servers with regard to the utilisation point for each server. The optimisation in the framework considers reducing the cost of VM migration from one server to another. The migration cost is calculated by a migration manager for each candidate PM in order to determine which node is to be chosen. The work is criticised for the fact that it does not handle strict SLA requirements (Anton Beloglazov, Abawajy, & Buyya, 2012). The proposed allocation policy deals with static VM allocation where the specification of VMs remains unchanged. This is not the case in Cloud computing, where clients can scale up or down in a dynamic manner. In addition, it requires prior knowledge of each PM in order to compute the power model.

Liao et al. (2012) have proposed a prototype of 'GreenMap', a VM-based management framework under the constraint of multi-dimensional resource consumption in clusters. GreenMap dynamically allocates and reallocates VMs to a set of PMs within a cluster at runtime. There are four modules in the framework: clearing, locking, trade-off and placement modules. The clearing module is responsible for excluding VMs that are not appropriate for dynamic placement. A VM can be inappropriate if the resource demand is unpredictable or has a short timescale of demand variation. The locking module monitors the SLA violation caused by the workloads. In the case of SLA violation occurring, the module will switch to a redundant VM to execute the workload. The trade-off module evaluates the potential of a new placement generated by the placement module with respect to performance and cost trade-off. The placement module performs a strategy for reallocating live VMs into another physical resource to save power based on a configuration algorithm. The algorithm starts by randomly generating a new placement configuration. The placement module then delivers the configuration to the trade-off module. Their experiments have shown that it can save up to 69% in a cluster with some performance degradation. However, the study does not consider the overhead of the placement module.

A Beloglazov & Buyya (2010) and Anton Beloglazov et al. (2012) have proposed an algorithm to allocate virtual machines to physical resources within data centres with a target to reduce power consumption. They aimed to develop an algorithm that can reduce power consumption in physical machines, without violating the SLA agreement between a Cloud provider and users. The researchers argued that assigning a group of VMs to as small a number of physical nodes as possible, will result in saving power (Buyya, Beloglazov, & Abawajy, 2010). The energy-aware resource algorithm (Anton Beloglazov et al., 2012) has two stages: VM placement and VM optimisation. The VM placement technique aims at allocating VMs to PMs using a Modified Best Fit Decreasing (MBFD) algorithm. The MBFD algorithm is based on the Best Fit Decreasing (BFD) algorithm, which uses no more than 11/9 * OPT + 1 bins (OPT is the optimal number of bins) (Vazirani, 2003). The MBFD algorithm sorts VMs in descending order according to their CPU utilisation in order to choose power-efficient nodes first.

The second stage is the 'optimisation step' that is responsible for migrating VMs from PMs that are either over-utilised or under-utilised. However, VM migration may cause unwanted overheads that should be avoided unless it affects either power consumption or performance. Therefore, the authors have set two thresholds for utilisation: the lower and upper utilisation thresholds. If the total utilisation of the CPU of a physical node falls below the lower threshold, it indicates that this host might consume more energy than it needs. Similarly, if the utilisation exceeds the upper threshold then the performance of the hosted VMs can degrade. Then, some VMs should migrate to another node in order to lower the level of utilisation. They concluded that the Minimisation of Migrations (MM) policy could save up to 66% of energy with performance degradation of up to 5%. It has shown that the MM policy minimises the number of VMs required to migrate from a host, with utilisation remaining above the upper threshold.

Failure-Aware Resource Allocation

The aforementioned works have studied the resource allocation mechanisms with the aim of minimising costs without affecting performance. However, they have paid little attention to the reliability of resources. Therefore, there is no explanation of how the allocation policy should behave in the event of failure. The authors in Javadi et al. (2012) have addressed the issue of node failure in hybrid Clouds, i.e., private and public Clouds. The problem is formulated as following: a private Cloud with limited resources have a certain number of nodes with a high failure-rate. The question is how to minimise the dependency of the public Clouds in order to achieve better QoS, given the fact that sending workload to a public Cloud means costing more money. They have proposed a failure-aware resource provisioning for hybrid Clouds. The 'time-based brokering strategy' is proposed to handle failure nodes in private Clouds, by directing tasks that are required long term into a public Cloud. The decision of forwarding a task to a public Cloud is based on its request duration. If it is more than the mean request duration, then the task will be forwarded to a public Cloud. Although the proposed strategy considers a public Cloud to solve the issue of failure in nodes, the decision mechanism based on request time can be used to assign tasks to more reliable nodes within a faulty private Cloud.

Resource Management Model

This section presents a model that represents the resource management function in Desktop Clouds. The goal of the model is to propose a resource allocation mechanism that can deal with resource failure in an efficient way. The mechanisms implemented in Traditional Clouds focus mainly on cost-effective trade-offs only. In Desktop Clouds, the resource management function should consider the faulty physical machines (PMs). The proposed model replicates virtual machines (VMs) in order to reduce the impact of node failures on the performance of VMs. In addition, the model tries to keep the effect of replication at a minimum by using VM consolidation steps to improve the resource utilisation and thus, resource availability.

Resource Allocation Model

Figure 4 depicts an abstract for managing resources. The abstracts represents the full lifecycle of IaaS Desktop Cloud where users request sets of VMs. The created VMs are used to process a set of tasks submitted by users. The purpose of the abstract is to help to study the resource allocation mechanism used in Desktop Clouds. The allocation mechanism is implemented within the resource management abstract. The allocation mechanism receives requests to create VMs to serve various tasks. It then maps VMs to physical nodes.

The model starts by receiving workload and VM requests sent by the 'Service Analyser' component. The component works as an entry point for the model. The 'Scheduler' component is responsible for scheduling each task in the workload to be processed in the 'Execution' component. The 'Scheduler' component helps to test the scalability of the model. The 'Execution' component executes each task with its associated VM instance. The VM instance is allocated and managed by the 'Allocator' component. The 'Monitor' component monitors the behaviour of the running VMs by getting updates from the 'Execution' component. The allocator is responsible for allocating VMs

Figure 4. Resource management abstract

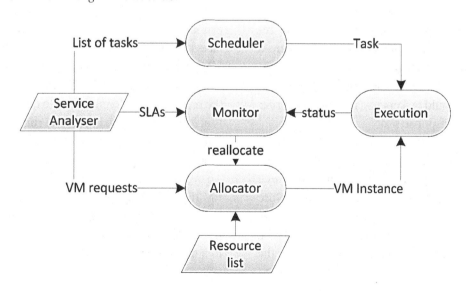

Figure 5. Resource allocation model

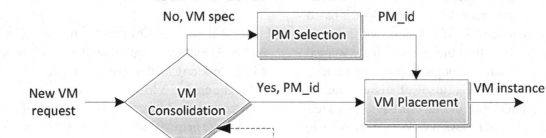

to PMs. The next section presents the resource allocation model that is implemented in both components: 'Allocator' and 'Monitor'.

The resource allocation mechanism in Cloud computing is the process of allocating VM instances to physical nodes. The allocation of resources is not a trivial step in Desktop Clouds as it has several limitations. Firstly, the mechanism has to be able to handle the failure of physical nodes. Secondly, it must allocate VMs to PMs with the aims of improving the resource utilisation and saving power consumption. In addition, it is vital that the resource allocation mechanism maintains the accepted level of performance offered to the customers. The mechanism should allocate resources in a dynamic manner to ensure that there is no intermittent service during the execution time. Finally, the overhead of the resource allocation mechanism should be kept to a minimum in order to reduce the response time.

The model presents a failure tolerant technique that depends on replicating the requested VMs. The aim of this model is to design a resource allocation mechanism that can handle failure events in PMs without affecting performance. Performance means that a VM continues to be running even with the presence of failures in the

node which hosts it. The 'PM Pool' in the model is a list containing all PMs that are ready to serve in the Desktop Clouds. The 'Allocated PMs' are a list of all Allocated PMs (meaning the physical nodes that host at least one VM). The model contains the following entities:

VM Replication

The 'VM Replication' is responsible for replicating the requested VM in order to improve the resilience of the model against failure. When a new request arrives, the 'VM replication' will replicate the request, so that two copies are created, namely, primary and replica VMs. The replication process is based on the idea that more than one version of the VM will be run simultaneously. The VM replica is assigned to another PM. The reason for deploying the replica to a different PM is to ensure that there is at least one version of the VM running in case a failure occurs. The disadvantage of the replication process is that it affects the availability of PMs. To avoid this situation, the replica is allocated to a PM that is already hosting a VM if at all possible.

This method will improve the resource utilisation and will keep the effect on the available nodes to a minimum level. When the 'VM Replication' receives a VM request, it sends it to the 'PM Selection' to choose a PM to host the new VM. Another copy is sent to the 'VM Consolidation' to allocate it to a PM that is already hosting a VM. The 'VM Replication' ensures that the VM and its replica will not be assigned to the same PM. This is achieved by assigning those VMs the same VM ID, in order to let the 'VM Consolidation' recognise them, so as to avoid assigning a replica VM to the primary VM.

VM Consolidation

The 'VM Consolidation' unit is responsible for allocating a replica to a PM. It is better from the point of utilisation to consolidate the replica with other VMs. The aim of this step is to improve utilisation and minimise the number of running PMs. The desired PM is the one with the least utilisation. However, it is not always possible to find a host that can host the replica.

The 'VM Consolidation' component gets a list of all PMs that host VMs from the 'Allocated PMs' unit. According to these details, the component will decide whether to allocate the replica to one of the listed PMs. The PM that can meet the requirements of the new VM with the least utilisation will be chosen. The 'VM Placement' will be notified by the ID of the chosen machine to allocate the replica. If no PM can host, then a new request will be sent to the 'PM Selection' in order to choose a new PM.

PM Selection

The 'PM Selection' unit is responsible for choosing a new PM among a pool of available PMs to host a new VM. The physical nodes in the Desktop Clouds are highly dispersed. Therefore, there is a need for a method to choose the most suitable PM for each requested VM. The selection process should pick the PM with the best capability to host more than one VM for future requests. Once the PM is picked up, its ID will be sent to the 'VM Placement'. If there is no PM that can host the new VM, then the 'PM Selection' should reply with a rejection, as no available PM can host the new VM. Then, the requested VM should be moved to a waiting list until resources become available.

VM Placement

This component simply receives the ID of a PM from either 'VM Consolidation' or 'VM Selection'. It then allocates the new requested VM to this PM. The 'VM Placement' sends an update to the 'Allocated PMs' pool to add the new PM to the list of PMs that are hosting VMs. The new VM instance is created and is ready to process the tasks coming from the 'Scheduler' in the resource management model.

Monitor

The 'Monitor' component is responsible for monitoring the running VMs during the execution time. The component periodically checks the status of each running PM. If a PM is down, it means that all VMs that are associated with this PM have stopped running. Each VM that is hosted in the PM has a replicated version. The monitor will inform the 'VM consolidation' to create a new replication for each VM that is hosted in the failed PM. This step is important to avoid reaching the 'complete failure' status. The 'complete failure' status means the failing of a primary VM and its replications. Therefore, the monitor should create a new VM replica for each VM that is found to be down.

DISCUSSION

The proposed model aims to provide an acceptable level of tolerance to failures in physical nodes within a Desktop Cloud. The model employs a replication technique to copy a VM; if one is lost due to a failure in its hosted machine, another copy remains alive in another host. However, the replication technique affects the availability of resources to serve new requests. The VM consolidation technique is used to assign a VM replica to the machine with the best utilisation level from a pool of PMs, in order to improve utilisation. Better utilisation, in this context, increases the availability of resources. Instead of allocating each primary VM and its replica to the same physical host, the primary VM is assigned in PM selection to the node with the least utilisation to improve reliability. The replica will be assigned to the host with the best utilisation to reduce the effect of replication on availability.

The model can improve the reliability of VMs by ensuring that another copy of it exists. However, this technique has some drawbacks. Firstly, there is still a chance that a VM can be lost if a failure were to occur simultaneously in both the PM that runs the primary copy of the VM and its replica. This situation can be set as a complete failure state and the model cannot handle such failures. In addition, the cost of creating a VM replica and keeping it matched to the primary VM can be quite high in Desktop Clouds; data transfer can be costly due to limited bandwidth and low connectivity. However, this cost can be less expensive than using VM checkpointing techniques (Oliner, Rudolph, & Sahoo, 2006) which can cause performance degradation in VMs in Desktop Clouds. Checkpointing techniques require a one-to-one relationship between VMs and the physical nodes in the faulty environment to improve performance. If a node fails while hosting many VMs, the performance will be affected in each of these VMs. Therefore, the proposed resource allocation model remains a better solution to handle node failures in Desktop Clouds.

CONCLUSION AND FUTURE DIRECTIONS

Desktop Clouds represent a new direction in the Cloud Computing paradigm. Traditional Clouds provide computing services based on resources that are dedicated for this purpose. In contrast, the aim of the Desktop Cloud is to provide Cloud services on top of non-dedicated resources. Cloud computing is seen as a legitimate successor to Grid computing. Desktop Grids emerged to provide the same vision as the Grid, on resources scattered across the Internet. Likewise, Desktop Clouds bring this vision to the Cloud era. Security and data protection can be considered a research concern that needs some attention. Add to that, the infrastructure of Desktop Clouds consists of resources that are prone to failure for a variety of reasons without prior knowledge. It is been shown that the average rate of failure in one hour can reach up to 10% within a Desktop Cloud's physical nodes. Thus, the resource management component should implement a resource allocation mechanism that can handle such failures.

The resource allocation mechanism in Cloud computing provides the ability to allocate virtual machines to physical machines with the aim of satisfying the performance requested by users. In addition, the mechanism involves various steps to improve resource utilisation and reduce running costs. Several resource allocation mechanisms in Traditional Clouds have been discussed in this chapter. The reviewed mechanisms focus on reducing the costs of running physical nodes without affecting the performance of Cloud services. However, the mechanisms cannot be effective in Desktop Clouds because they do not give the requisite attention to the failure events that can occur in physical machines during running time. Therefore, this chapter presented a model for designing a resource allocation mechanism that takes failure events into consideration. The model depends on the replication of virtual machines. The downside of the replication techniques is that it can reduce the availability of the physical nodes. Therefore, the model employs a consolidation step in order to reduce the negative impact on availability.

One future research direction is to find the optimal number of replications for a VM to keep the effect on performance caused by failures to the minimum under availability constrain. This means that finding a number of replication that improves systems tolerance to failures while keeping utilisation at acceptable level. However, optimal replication number can be influenced by the failure rate which can be varied depending on the nature of physical nodes. For example, an optimal replication number when failure rate at 10% is less than when the failure rate is at 40% and so on. Therefore, another possible idea for research is to develop an online adaption technique to keep monitoring the failure rate during run time to adjust the number of replication according the current recorded failure rate. The monitor component can employ live migration techniques to improve utilisation and reduce power consumption while maintaining the required performance level.

REFERENCES

Anderson, D. P., & Fedak, G. (2006). The computational and storage potential of volunteer computing. In *Proceedings of the Sixth IEEE International Symposium on Cluster Computing and the Grid (CCGRID'06)* (pp. 73–80). doi:10.1109/CCGRID.2006.101

Andrzejak, A., Kondo, D., & Anderson, D. P. (2010). Exploiting non-dedicated resources for cloud computing. In *Proceedings of the 2010 IEEE Network Operations and Management Symposium - NOMS 2010* (341–348). doi:10.1109/NOMS.2010.5488488

Arpaci, R. H., Dusseau, A. C., Vahdat, A. M., Liu, L. T., Anderson, T. E., & Patterson, D. A. (1995). The interaction of parallel and sequential workloads on a network of workstations. *Science* (Vol. 23). ACM. Retrieved from http://portal.acm.org/citation.cfm?id=223618

Barroso, L. A., & Hölzle, U. (2009). *The Datacenter as a computer: An introduction to the design of warehouse-scale machines* (Vol. 4, pp. 1–108). Synthesis Lectures on Computer Architecture. doi:10.2200/S00193ED1V01Y-200905CAC006

Bégin, M. E., Jones, B., Casey, J., Laure, E., Grey, F., Loomis, C., & Kubli, R. (2008). An EGEE comparative study grids and clouds - Evolution or revolution? *EGEE III Project Report, 30,* 1–33. Retrieved from http://wr.informatik.uni-hamburg.de/_media/teaching/sommersemester_2009/egee-grid-cloud.pdf

Beloglazov, A., Abawajy, J., & Buyya, R. (2012). Energy-aware resource allocation heuristics for efficient management of data centers for Cloud computing. *Future Generation Computer Systems, 28*(5), 755–768. doi:10.1016/j.future.2011.04.017

Beloglazov, A., & Buyya, R. (2010). Energy efficient resource management in virtualized cloud data centers. In Proceedings of the 10th IEEE/ACM International Conference on Cluster, Cloud and Grid Computing (pp. 826–831). Washington, DC: IEEE Computer Society. Retrieved from http://dl.acm.org/citation.cfm?id=1845139

Buyya, R., Beloglazov, A., & Abawajy, J. (2010). Energy-efficient management of data center resources for cloud computing: A vision, architectural elements, and open challenges. *arXiv preprint arXiv:1006.0308,* (Vm), 1–12. Retrieved from http://arxiv.org/abs/1006.0308

Cao, B. Q., Li, B., & Xia, Q. M. (2009). A service-oriented qos-assured and multi-agent cloud computing architecture. *Cloud Computing*, 644–649. Retrieved from http://www.springerlink.com/index/97H153M34UK4L000.pdf

Chandra, A., & Weissman, J. (2009). Nebulas: Using distributed voluntary resources to build clouds. In Proceedings of the 2009 conference on hot topics in cloud computing (pp. 2–2). USENIX Association. Retrieved from http://citeseerx.ist.psu.edu/viewdoc/summary?doi=10.1.1.148.7267

Chang, V. (2014). The business intelligence as a service in the cloud. *Future Generation Computer Systems*, *37*, 512–534. doi:10.1016/j.future.2013.12.028

Chang, V., & Ramachandran, M. (2014). *A proposed case for the cloud software engineering in security*. Paper presented at the first international workshop on Emerging Software as a Service ESaaSA 2014, Spain, 3-5 April.

Chang, V., Walters, R., & Wills, G. (2014). Review of cloud computing and existing frameworks for cloud adoption. In M. Ramachandran (Ed.), *Advances in cloud computing research*. Nova Publishers. Retrieved from http://eprints.soton.ac.uk/358094/

Cunsolo, V., & Distefano, S. (2010). From volunteer to cloud computing: Cloud@ home. In *Proceedings of the conference on computing frontiers* (pp. 103–104). Retrieved from http://dl.acm.org/citation.cfm?id=1787304

Cunsolo, V., Distefano, S., Puliafito, A., & Scarp, M. (2009). Cloud@ home: Bridging the gap between volunteer and cloud computing. In *Proceedings of the 5th international conference on Emerging intelligent computing technology and applications (ICIC'09)*. doi:10.1007/978-3-642-04070-2_48

Cunsolo, V. D., Distefano, S., Puliafito, A., & Scarpa, M. (2009). Volunteer computing and desktop cloud: The cloud@ home paradigm. In *Proceedings of the Eighth IEEE International Symposium on Network Computing and Applications, 2009 (NCA 2009)* (pp. 134–139). IEEE. doi:10.1109/NCA.2009.41

Dillon, T., Wu, C., & Chang, E. (2010). Cloud computing: Issues and challenges. In *Proceedings of the 24th IEEE International Conference on Advanced Information Networking and Applications* (pp. 27–33). IEEE. doi:10.1109/AINA.2010.187

Foster, I., Zhao, Y., Raicu, I., & Lu, S. (2008). Cloud computing and grid computing 360-degree compared. In *Proceedings of the Grid Computing Environments Workshop, 2008 (GCE'08)* (pp. 1–10). IEEE. doi:10.1109/GCE.2008.4738445

Foster, I., Kesselman, C., & Tuecke, S. (2001). The anatomy of the grid: Enabling scalable virtual organizations. *International Journal of High Performance Computing Applications*, *15*(3), 200–222. doi:10.1177/109434200101500302

Garey, M., & Johnson, D. (1985). A 71/60 theorem for bin packing. *Journal of Complexity*, *106*, 65–106. doi:10.1016/0885-064X(85)90022-6

Graubner, P., Schmidt, M., & Freisleben, B. (2011). Energy-efficient management of virtual machines in Eucalyptus. In Proceedings of the 2011 IEEE 4th International Conference on Cloud Computing (pp. 243–250). IEEE Computer Society. Retrieved from http://ieeexplore.ieee.org/xpls/abs_all.jsp?arnumber=6008716

Gupta, A., & Awasthi, L. K. L. (2009). Peer enterprises: A viable alternative to Cloud computing? In Proceedings of the 2009 IEEE International Conference on Internet Multimedia Services Architecture and Applications (IMSAA) (Vol. 2, pp. 1–6). IEEE. Retrieved from http://ieeexplore.ieee.org/xpls/abs_all.jsp?arnumber=5439456

Harutyunyan, A., Blomer, J., Buncic, P., Charalampidis, I., Grey, F., Karneyeu, A., & Skands, P. et al. (2012). CernVM co-pilot: An extensible framework for building scalable computing infrastructures on the cloud. *Journal of Physics: Conference Series*, *396*(3), 032054. doi:10.1088/1742-6596/396/3/032054

Javadi, B., Abawajy, J., & Buyya, R. (2012). Failure-aware resource provisioning for hybrid Cloud infrastructure. *Journal of Parallel and Distributed Computing*, *72*(10), 1318–1331. doi:10.1016/j.jpdc.2012.06.012

Javadi, B., Kondo, D., Iosup, A., & Epema, D. (2013). The Failure trace archive: Enabling the comparison of failure measurements and models of distributed systems. *Journal of Parallel and Distributed Computing*, *73*(8), 1208–1223. doi:10.1016/j.jpdc.2013.04.002

Jiang, D., Huang, P., Lin, P., & Jiang, J. (2012). Energy efficient VM placement heuristic algorithms comparison for cloud with multidimensional resources. *Information Computing and Applications*, 413–420. Retrieved from http://www.springerlink.com/index/K08740211M1W7834.pdf

Kirby, G., Dearle, A., Macdonald, A., & Fernandes, A. (2010). An approach to ad hoc cloud computing. *Arxiv preprint arXiv:1002.4738*. Retrieved from http://arxiv.org/abs/1002.4738v1

Kondo, D., Taufer, M., & Brooks, C. (2004). Characterizing and evaluating desktop grids: An empirical study. *International Parallel and Distributed Processing Symposium 2004, 00*(C). Retrieved from http://ieeexplore.ieee.org/xpls/abs_all.jsp?arnumber=1302936

Kusic, D., Kephart, J. O., Hanson, J. E., Kandasamy, N., & Jiang, G. (2008). Power and performance management of virtualized computing environments via lookahead control. *Cluster Computing*, *12*(1), 1–15. doi:10.1007/s10586-008-0070-y

Liao, X., Jin, H., & Liu, H. (2012). Towards a green cluster through dynamic remapping of virtual machines. *Future Generation Computer Systems*, *28*(2), 469–477. doi:10.1016/j.future.2011.04.013

Marosi, A., Kovács, J., & Kacsuk, P. (2012). Towards a volunteer cloud system. *Future Generation Computer Systems*. doi:10.1016/j.future.2012.03.013

Mills, K., Filliben, J., & Dabrowski, C. (2011). Comparing VM-placement algorithms for on-demand clouds. In *Proceedings of the 2011 IEEE Third International Conference on Cloud Computing Technology and Science* (pp. 91–98). doi:10.1109/CloudCom.2011.22

Oliner, A., Rudolph, L., & Sahoo, R. (2006). Cooperative checkpointing: A robust approach to large-scale systems reliability. In *Proceedings of the 20th annual international conference on Supercomputing (ICS '06)* (pp. 14–23). Retrieved from http://dl.acm.org/citation.cfm?id=1183406

Rasmussen, N. (2007). Calculating total cooling requirements for data centers. *American Power Conversion, White Paper #25*. Retrieved from http://68.170.159.58/Portals/0/CalculatingTotalCoolingRequirements.pdf

Redolfi, A., McClatchey, R., Anjum, A., Zijdenbos, A., Manset, D., Barkhof, F., & Frisoni, G. B. et al. (2009). Grid infrastructures for computational neuroscience: The neuGRID example. *Future Neurology*, *4*(6), 703–722. doi:10.2217/fnl.09.53

Ristenpart, T., Tromer, E., Savage, S., & Shacham, H. (2009). Hey, you, get off of my cloud: Exploring information leakage in third-party compute clouds. In Proceedings of the 16th ACM conference on computer and communications security (pp. 199–212). ACM; Retrieved from http://portal.acm.org/citation.cfm?id=1653687 doi:10.1145/1653662.1653687

Sotomayor, B., Montero, R. R. S., Llorente, I. M., & Foster, I. (2009). Virtual infrastructure management in private and hybrid clouds. *IEEE Internet Computing*, *13*(5), 14–22. doi:10.1109/MIC.2009.119

Srikantaiah, S., Kansal, A., & Zhao, F. (2008). Energy aware consolidation for cloud computing. In HotPower'08: Proceedings of the 2008 conference on Power aware computing and systems. Berkeley, CA: USENIX Association. Retrieved from http://www.usenix.org/event/hotpower08/tech/full_papers/srikantaiah/srikantaiah_html/

Vaquero, L. M., Rodero-Merino, L., Caceres, J., & Lindner, M. (2009). A break in the clouds: Towards a cloud definition. *Computer Communication Review*, *39*(1), 50–55. http://portal.acm.org/citation.cfm?id=1496100 doi:10.1145/1496091.1496100

Vazirani, V. (2003). Approximation algorithms (2nd ed., p. 380). New York: Springer.

Verma, A., Ahuja, P., & Neogi, A. (2008). pMapper: Power and migration cost aware application placement in virtualized systems. In *Proceedings of the 9th ACM/IFIP/USENIX International Conference on Middleware* (*Middleware '08)* (pp. 243–264). New York: Springer-Verlag. Retrieved from http://dl.acm.org/citation.cfm?id=1496966

Weissman, J. B., Sundarrajan, P., Gupta, A., Ryden, M., Nair, R., & Chandra, A. (2011). Early experience with the distributed nebula cloud. In Proceedings of the fourth international workshop on Data-intensive distributed computing (pp. 17–26). ACM. Retrieved from http://portal.acm.org/citation.cfm?id=1996019

Zhang, S., Chen, X., & Huo, X. (2010). The comparison between cloud computing and grid computing. In Proceedings of the 2010 International Conference on Computer Application and System Modeling (ICCASM) (Vol. 11, pp. V11–V72). IEEE. Retrieved from http://ieeexplore.ieee.org/xpls/abs_all.jsp?arnumber=5623257

KEY TERMS AND DEFINITIONS

Cloud Business Model: A model to charge end users according to their actual usage.

Cloud Computing: A new computing paradigm that offers computing services based on pay-per-use business model.

Cloud Node: A physical node that is located in the infrastructure level in Cloud computing.

Desktop Cloud: A new approach of providing Cloud computing services by employing normal PCs, laptops, etc.

Elasticity: Means that users can acquire services and scale up or down according to their needs in a short time.

Fault Tolerant mechanism: A mechanism that tries to reduce the effect of failure events.

Resource Allocation Mechanism: The mechanism of allocating a virtual machine to a physical machine.

Traditional Cloud: The traditional way of providing Cloud services by employing computing infrastructure designed for this purposes such as data centres.

Chapter 9
Performance Evaluation of Multi-Core Multi-Cluster Architecture (MCMCA)

Norhazlina Hamid
University of Southampton, UK

Robert John Walters
University of Southampton, UK

Gary B. Wills
University of Southampton, UK

ABSTRACT

A multi-core cluster is a cluster composed of numbers of nodes where each node has a number of processors, each with more than one core within each single chip. Cluster nodes are connected via an interconnection network. Multi-cored processors are able to achieve higher performance without driving up power consumption and heat, which is the main concern in a single-core processor. A general problem in the network arises from the fact that multiple messages can be in transit at the same time on the same network links. This chapter considers the communication latencies of a multi core multi cluster architecture, investigated using simulation experiments and measurements under various working conditions.

INTRODUCTION

Chen, Wills, Gilbert, & Bacigalupo (2010) define cloud computing as an emerging business model that delivers computing services over the internet in elastic self-serviced, self-managed and cost-effective manner. Cloud computing doesn't yet have a standard definition, but a good working description of it is to say that clouds, or clusters of distributed computers, provide on-demand resources and services over a network, usually the Internet, with the scale and reliability of a data centre. Cloud computing provides a pool of computing resources which includes network, server, storage, application, service and so on that is required without huge investment on its purchase, implementation and maintenance that can be accessed through the Internet. The basic

DOI: 10.4018/978-1-4666-8210-8.ch009

Copyright © 2015, IGI Global. Copying or distributing in print or electronic forms without written permission of IGI Global is prohibited.

principle of cloud computing is to shift the computing tasks from the local computer into the network (Sadashiv & Kumar, 2011). Resources are requested on-demand without any prior reservation and hence eliminate overprovisioning and improve resource utilization.

Cloud computing has changed the way both software and hardware are purchased and used. An increasing number of applications are becoming web-based since these are available from anywhere and from any device. Such applications are using the infrastructures of large-scale data centres and can be provisioned efficiently. Hardware, on the other side, representing basic computing resources, can also be delivered to match the specific demands without the user/consumer having to actually own them. As more organisations adopt cloud, the need for high availability platform and infrastructures, the cluster, to facilitate and distribute the load across multiple processors is evolving (Chang, Walters, & Wills, 2014). The deployment of clustered applications in Cloud infrastructures supports the capabilities of resource configuration and ensures communication between shared resources (Kosinska, Kosinski, & Zielinski, 2010).

The emergence of High Performance computing (HPC) that includes Cloud computing and Cluster computing has improved the availability of powerful computers and high speed network technologies. It can be concluded that the main target of HPC is better performance in computing. HPC aims to leverage cluster computing to solve advanced computation problems. While cluster computing has been widely used for scientific tasks, cloud computing was set out for serving business applications. Dillon et al. (2010) have pointed out that the current cloud is not geared for HPC for several reasons. Firstly, it has not yet matured enough for HPC; secondly, unlike cluster computing, cloud infrastructure only focuses on enhancing the overall system performance; and thirdly, HPC aims to enhance the performance of a specific scientific application using resources across multiple organisations. The key difference is in elasticity, where for cluster computing the capacity is often fixed, therefore running an HPC application can often require considerable human interaction, such as tuning based on a particular cluster with a fixed number of homogenous computing nodes (Schubert, Jeffery, & Neidecker-Lutz, 2010). This is contrasted with the self-service nature of cloud computing, in which it is hard to know how many physical processors are needed. In order to achieve higher availability and scalability of an application executed within cloud resources, it is important to supplement the capabilities of management services with high performance cluster computing to enable full control over communication resources.

Motivation of the Studies

In the past, there has been a trend to increase a processor's speed to get better performance. Moore's Law, which states that the number of transistors on a processor will double approximately every two years has been proven to be consistent due to the transistors getting smaller in successive processor technologies (Intel, 1997). However, reducing the transistor size and increasing clock speeds causes transistors to consume more power and generate more heat (D. Geer, 2007). These concerns limit cost-effective increases in performance which can be achieved by raising the processor speed alone. These issues gave computer engineers the idea of designing the multi-core processor, a single processor with two or more cores (Burger, 2005).

Multi-core processors are used extensively in parallel and cluster computing. As far back as 2009, more than 95% of the systems listed in the Top 500 supercomputer list used dual-core or quad-core processors (Admin, 2009). The motivation in this realm is the advances in multi-core processor technology that makes them an excellent choice to use in cluster architecture (Soryani, Analoui, & Zarrinchian, 2013). From the combination of cluster computing and multi-core processor, the multi-core cluster architecture has emerged. The multi-core cluster architecture becomes more powerful due to the combination of faster processors and faster interconnection (Bethel & Howison, 2012). The implementation of multi-core cluster supports high availability and enables scalability for cloud computing architecture (Kosinska et al., 2010).

Overall performance of multi-core clusters is always determined by the efficiency of its communication and interconnection networks (Dally & Towles, 2004). Hence, performance analysis of the interconnection networks is vital. A general problem in the network may arise from multiple messages being in transmission at once on the same network links and this will cause delays. Such delays increase the communication latency of the interconnection network and it is therefore important to minimise this. A high communication latency of interconnection network can dramatically reduce the efficiency of the cluster system (Shainer et al., 2013).

Many studies (Ichikawa & Takagi, 2009; Lei, Hartono, & Panda, 2006; Ranadive, Kesavan, Gavrilovska, & Schwan, 2008) have been carried out to improve the performance of multi-core cluster but few clearly distinguish the key issue of the performance of interconnection networks. Although the cluster interconnection network is critical for delivering efficient performance, as it needs to handle the networking requirements of each processor core (Shainer et al., 2013), existing models do not address the potential performance issues of the interconnection networks within multi-core clusters.

Scalability is a very important aspect to examine when evaluating clusters. Abdelgadir, Pathan, & Ahmed (2011) find that having good network bandwidth and faster network will produce better scalability of clusters. Scaling up by adding more processors to each node to increase the processing power creates too much heat (Burger, 2005). The conventional approach to improving cluster throughput is to add more processors, but there is a limit to the scalability of this approach; the

infrastructure cannot provide effective memory access to unlimited numbers of processors and the interconnection network(s) become saturated (Shahhoseini, Naderi, & Buyya, 2000). Technological advances have made it viable to overcome these problems by combining multiple clusters of heterogeneous networked resources into what is known as a multi-cluster architecture (Abawajy & Dandamudi, 2003). Apart from scalability and multi-core systems, private cloud solution offers another approach. Chang (2014) explains a private cloud design and implementation to demonstrate the business intelligence as a service. The benefit allows the stakeholders to understand the relationship between risk and return in financial investment (Chang, 2014).

This chapter will describe a scalable approach to building heterogeneous multi-cluster architecture and is the first investigation into network latency within such architecture. The rest of the chapter is organized as follows: introduction of cluster computing. Next section gives an overview of the multi-core cluster, interconnection networks and multi-cluster architecture. Subsequent section introduces the new architecture of the cluster followed by the communication network involved in the new architecture followed by a section describing the research methodology which includes simulation models and simulation results. The last section concludes the chapter and describes future work.

CLUSTER COMPUTING

A computer cluster can be defined as "a collection of individual computers" (Baldassari, Kopec, Leshay, Truszkowski, & Finkel, 2005), "connected to each other by fast local area networks" (Baker & Buyya, 1999) which "work together to form a single computer" (Baker, Apon, Buyya, & Jin, 2000). In their 2002 paper, Buyya, Hai and Cortes described cluster computing as a fusion of the fields of parallel, high-performance, distributed, and high-availability computing.

A cluster is deployed to increase performance and availability, and clusters are more cost-effective than a single computer of comparable speed. There are many kinds of computer cluster, ranging from some of the world's largest computers to collections of throwaway personal computers. Clustering was among the first computer system architecture techniques for achieving significant improvements in overall performance, user access bandwidth and reliability (T. L. Sterling, 2002). The emergence of cluster platforms was driven by a number of academic projects such as Beowulf, Berkeley NOW and HPVM (Sadashiv & Kumar, 2011).

A computer cluster can provide fast and reliable services to computationally intensive applications. In 1999, Baker and Buyya described cluster computing as being capable of providing similar or better performance and reliability to traditional mainframes or supercomputers, and the network will be one with a high bandwidth and low latency. If designed correctly, better fault tolerance at a much lower hardware cost can be achieved. Their work found that many applications have successfully used clusters, including computationally intensive ones such as quantum chemistry and computational fluid dynamics.

The key components of a cluster include multiple standalone computers (PCs or Workstations), operating system, interconnection networks, middleware, parallel programming environments and applications (Yeo et al., 2006). This chapter will focus on cluster interconnection networks. Interconnection networks enable data packets to be transferred between logical elements distributed among a set of separate processor nodes within a cluster through a combination of hardware and software support (T. Sterling, Apon, & Baker, 2000). The nodes in a cluster communicate over high-speed networks using a standard networking protocol such as TCP/IP or a low-level protocol. There are a number of high performance network technologies such as Ethernet, Asynchronous Transfer Mode (ATM), Scalable Coherent Interface (SCI), Infiniband and Myrinet (Petrini, Frachtenberg, Hoisie, & Coll, 2003).

Advantages of Cluster Computing

Clusters offer several advantages over traditional supercomputers. The use of clusters as a computing platform is not just limited to scientific and engineering applications, and there are many business applications that can benefit from the use of clusters (Buyya, Hai, & Cortes, 2002). Cluster computing also reduces costs, improves network technology and increases processing power (Admin, 2010). A clustered system brings fault-tolerance and support for rolling upgrades. The following list highlights some of the reasons why workstation clusters are preferred (Haddad, 2006):

- High Availability;
- Scalability;
- Performance;
- Rapid Response to Technology Improvements;
- Manageability;
- Cost Efficient Solutions;
- Expandability and Upgradeability;
- Transparency;
- Flexibility of Configuration.

A common use for clusters is website hosting where a cluster will spread visitors over all the computers in the cluster in order to spread the load between them (Admin, 2010). This will prevent an overload, causing a crash that could bring the system down. This ensures that the system is always available, which is not possible with a single computer system. Other benefits to cluster computing include sharing a common directory, having access to the same programs as everyone else, reducing the need to authenticate a document from another computer, which can reduce the number of flagged security alerts, and sharing a network (Hope & Lam, n.d.). Clusters can also be used in data mining applications to provide the storage and data management services for the data set being mined and computational services required by the data filtering, preparation and mining tasks.

Challenges in Cluster Computing

Apart from all the benefits, there are research challenges in cluster computing, as follows (Sadashiv & Kumar, 2011):

- **Middleware:** To produce a software environment that provides an illusion of a single system image, rather than a collection of independent computers.
- **Program:** The applications that run on the clusters must be explicitly written and incorporate the division of tasks between nodes.
- **Elasticity:** The capability to adapt to changing potential requirements, for example the variance in real-time response time when the number of service requests changes dramatically.
- **Scalability:** Ability to scale to meet the additional requirements of a resource. This can affect the performance of the system.

Processor

The processor is the logic circuitry that responds to and processes the basic instructions that drive a computer; in the simplest terms, it is the computer's brain (Rouse, 2006). It is the part that interprets instructions and executes calculations. The processor tells the computer what to do and when to do it, decides which tasks are more important and prioritises them to fulfil the computer's needs. Stevens (1986) mentioned that the term 'processor' has generally replaced the term 'central processing unit' (CPU), and the processor in a personal computer, or one embedded in small devices, is often called a microprocessor. A microprocessor is a computer that has been made on a single chip of silicon about 4 to 6 millimetres square and ½ millimetre thick, and contains a minimum of a few thousand transistors (Stevens, 1986). Stevens also states that most of the chips called microprocessors are not in fact complete computers, but

rather the central processing units of computers. Personal computer systems are usually built from CPU-only chips and the term 'microprocessor' is therefore applied to any chip that contains the whole of a CPU. Each generation of processors has grown smaller, faster, dissipating more heat and consuming more power (Schauer, 2008).

Multi-Core Processor

In 1965, Gordon Moore made his famous observation, the so-called "Moore's Law", which predicted that the number of transistors per integrated circuit would double every year and the speed would double every two years (Intel, 1997). Over more than four decades, this has driven the impressive growth in computer speed and accessibility. Decreasing transistor switching times by reducing transistor size and shortening the distances between the transistors has increased speed further (Schauer, 2008). These have contributed to a faster processor clock frequencies by having more transistors to work with and it has allowed more complex computation or implementations that can be clocked more rapidly. However, Lei, Qi and Panda (2007) identified that it becomes more difficult to speed up processors nowadays by increasing frequency. As processor frequencies increase, the amount of heat produced by the processor increases with it (Pase & Eckl, 2005). These concerns make it less cost-to-performance effective to increase the processor clock rate. The solution is to reduce the transistor size because smaller transistors can operate at lower voltages, and this allows the processor to produce less heat. Unfortunately, David Geer (2005) demonstrated that as a transistor gets smaller, it will be less able to block the flow of electrons. Also, increasing clock speeds causes transistors to switch faster and thus generate heat and consume more power (D. Geer, 2007). These issues gave computer engineers the idea of designing a single processor with multiple processing cores which means to place two or more processing cores on the same chip (Burger, 2005).

Multi-core processors are the answer for the deficiencies of single-core processors by increasing bandwidth while decreasing power consumption (Burger, 2005). Multi-core processors are developed to adhere to reasonable power consumption and heat dissipation. By dividing the workload into different cores, multi-core processors can speed up application performance by running at lower frequencies while minimising the use of power and heat generation (Lei et al., 2007). Multi-core processors don't necessarily run as fast as the highest performing single-core models, but they improve overall performance by handling more work in parallel (David Geer, 2005).

According to an Intel report, in 2015 a typical processor will likely consist of up to hundreds of cores where part of the core will be dedicated to specific purposes, providing a huge performance potential (Rauber & Runger, 2010). Despite the huge performance potential, many issues remain unsolved and need further attention, such as high communication latency in interconnection networks.

Multi-Core Processor vs. Single-Core Processor

Processors were originally developed with only one core. A core is a complete computational engine or a processing element in a processor (Burger, 2005).

A single-core means only one processing element within a single processor and a multi-core processor combines two or more processing elements in a single processor, on a single chip or multiple chips (Roy, 2008). A single-core can perform one task at a time while a multi-core can divide the work between two or more execution cores, allowing more work to be done within a given clock cycle (Burger, 2005). Clock cycle is the time that sets the speed of the computer processor. A dual-core processor contains two cores (e.g., Intel Core Duo); a quad-core processor contains four cores (e.g., AMD Phenom II X4) and a hexa-core processor contain six cores (e.g., Intel Core i7 Extreme Edition 980X).

Multi-Core Processor Basic Design

Schauer (2008) identified the basic overview of multi-core architecture. Although manufacturer designs differ from one another, multi-core architectures need to adhere to certain aspects. The basic multi-core architecture, as in Figure 1 includes:

- Processor;
- Core;
- L1 and L2 Cache;
- Main memory.

Figure 1. Multi-core processor

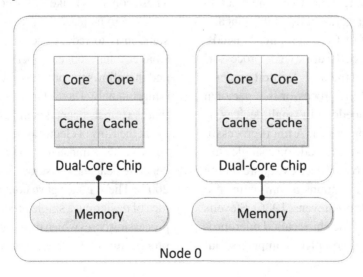

In the processor, there is a core and cache. Cache is a very fast memory used to store data frequently used by the processor. The main memory is very large, but slower than a cache and is used to store files. For example, most systems have between 1GB to 4GB of main memory compared to the 32KB to 2MB of the cache. If the data is not located in the cache or main memory, the system must retrieve it from the hard disk, which takes more reading time than the memory system. When two cores are set side-by-side, communications between the cores and with the main memory are accomplished by using either a single communication bus or an interconnection network.

Advantages and Challenges of Multi-Core Processor

Besides the main advantage of having a multi-core processor, which is better performance, there are many more advantages such as (Burger, 2005; Karmakar, 2011):

- **Scalability:** Instead of having to replace a computer to increase the number of processors, the user can simply replace the single multi-core processor with one containing more CPU cores using only a single socket.
- **Compatibility:** Various single and multiple thread programs can be mixed on a multi-core computer.
- **Minimise Power and Lessen Heat:** Multi-core processors have been designed to be able to minimize power consumption and decrease the temperature.
- **Evolution Toward Multi-Core Software:** Most application vendors have developed software that could take advantage of multithreading capabilities to utilise the benefits of a multi-core processor based system fully.
- **Pricing and Licensing:** Intel states that a multi-core processor will cost less than an equivalent fast single-core processor, both

in terms of the initial price and overhead use. In terms of licensing, Microsoft, the world's largest software vendor, has announced that they will consider a multi-core processor as a single processor for licensing purposes (Burger, 2005).

Multiple cores on a single processor give rise to some problems and challenges (Karmakar, 2011; Lei et al., 2007; Schauer, 2008) such as interconnection networks performance, cache coherence, multithreading, parallel programming and starvation. Performance evaluation of cluster in this chapter will focus on interconnection networks performance. A faster network means a lower latency of communication in interconnection network and memory transactions. In order to get optimal performance, it is crucial to have an in-depth understanding of application behaviours and trends in multi-core clusters.

Multi-Core Cluster

In the past, several parallel machines with different architectures have been built as viable platforms for High-Performance Computing (HPC) (Qian, 2010), such as distributed shared memory and clusters of multiprocessors. However, with the emergence of high-speed networks, the HPC community has adopted network based computing clusters as cost-effective platforms (Hope & Lam, n.d.) to achieve high performance. High performance is a computational activity requiring more than a single computer to execute a task (Qian, 2010). The trend has been shifting towards cluster systems with multi-core (Wu & Taylor, 2013), which will be the focus of this research. The Top500 supercomputer list published in November (Admin, 2013) showed that multi-core processors have been widely deployed in clusters of parallel computing, and more than 95% of the systems are using dual-core to quad-core processors. Another trend in this realm is the advances in multi-core processor technology that make them an excellent choice to use in clustered nodes (Soryani et al., 2013). Due to their greater computing power and cost-to-performance effectiveness, cluster computing uses multi-core processors extensively (Chai, 2009).

The architecture of multi-core cluster is a combination of cluster computing and multi-core processors. Multi core clusters typically have a hierarchical memory structure, where cores from the same processor share L2 caches (Fengguang, Moore, & Dongarra, 2009). On the other hand, cores belonging to distinct processors built from the same node share the main memory (RAM or DRAM) and cores belonging to different nodes do not share any memory resource. High performance can be achieved when executing parallel applications with tasks being allocated to the cores according to the application communication pattern and environment characteristics (Silva, Drummond, & Boeres, 2010). Tasks that communicate more frequently should be allocated to the same node avoiding remote communication. However, depending on the amount of task computation and data to be processed, the allocation of multiple tasks to the same processor can be a bottleneck due to the resources being shared by the processor cores (Soryani et al., 2013).

A multi-core cluster has a lot of advantages, and nowadays more software is being designed to run with multiple threads. Burger (2005) also states multi-core technology allows systems to run tasks in parallel that previously would have required multiple processors, and multi-core clusters are more easily scalable and can put more processing power in a smaller package that uses less power and generates less heat for the computational power derived. As it gains in popularity, the multi-core cluster will provide greater advantages in speed, scalability and flexibility (Creel & Goffe, 2007; David Geer, 2005).

A multi-core cluster can be used to run two programs side by side and when an intensive program is running, such as an audio visual scan, video conversion or CD ripping, another core can be utilised to run the browser to check emails, scanning for viruses or using another application (Burger, 2005). A multi-core cluster really shows its capabilities when using a program that can utilise more than one core, called parallelisation, to improve the program's efficiency (Karmakar, 2011). Programs such as graphic software and games can run multiple instructions at the same time and deliver faster, smoother results (Creel & Goffe, 2007).

Another motivation for using a multi-core cluster is the reduction of the execution time of computation-intensive application programs. Although minimising the communication between nodes may reduce the execution time, it does not solely guarantee the optimal execution time (Ichikawa & Takagi, 2009). B. Javadi, Akbari, Abawajy & Nahavandi (2006) states it always depends on the effectiveness of its interconnection network to determine the overall performance of a cluster system.

Interconnection Networks

An interconnection network is a physical connection between the different components of a parallel system, and it can be used in a classification of multi-core cluster systems. A network is characterised by the media it uses to carry messages, the way the network links devices and the expansiveness of the network (Sullivan, Lewis, & Cook, 1988). In multi-core cluster systems, the interconnection network is used to connect the nodes with each other (Peh, 2001) and is used to connect the processors with the memory modules. In a network, a node is a connection point, either a redistribution point or an end point for data transmissions (Rouse, August 2006).

The main task of the interconnection network is to transfer messages from a specific processor to a specific destination which can be another processor or a memory module (Gramsamer, 2003). The objective of the interconnection network is to perform the message transfer correctly as quickly as possible, even if several messages have to be transferred at the same time (Rauber & Runger, 2010). Interconnection networks are an attractive alternative to dedicated wiring because they allow limited wiring resources to be shared by several low-duty-factor signals (Dally & Towles, 2004). Some interconnect technologies used in high-performance computers include Gigabit Ethernet (Koibuchi et al., 2011), Myrinet and QsNet (Qian, 2010). Each interconnect provides a different level of programmability, raw performance and integration with the operating system.

Interconnection networks are critical in achieving high performance in clusters (Shainer et al., 2013). While ideal networks support both high bandwidth and low latency, there often exists a trade-off between these two parameters (Dally & Towles, 2004). For example, a network that supports high bandwidth tends to keep the network resources busy, often causing contention for the resources which will increase the latency of the messages. Contention occurs when two or more messages want to use the same shared resource in the network. With a good combination of network topology, routing technique and flow control mechanism, this problem can be minimised (Dally & Towles, 2004).

Network Topology

The topology describes the interconnection structure used to connect different processors or processors and memory modules. The most common topologies that are used for interconnection networks are shared bus and crossbar switches. However, shared bus and crossbar switches do not scale well with the growth of the processor numbers (Khosravi, Khorsandi, & Akbari, 2011). Many network topologies have been proposed for clusters in which fat-tree topology are among the most popular. Fat-tree topology derives from a popular class multistage interconnection network, Butterfly-Fat-tree (Furhad, Haque, Kim, & Kim, 2013). In Fat-tree topology, Figure 2, each node in the tree is represented by a set of coordinates (level, position), where 'level' denotes the level in the tree and 'position' denotes the location using right to left ordering. The vertical levels are numbered from zero, starting at the leaves. The leaves in the trees correspond to nodes and the upper levels represent routers. Fat-tree topology can be scalable with more processing nodes, and the regularity of the processing node connection can also be exploited to develop more efficient parallel algorithms (Lin, 2003).

Figure 2. An 8-port 2-tree constructed by proposed algorithm

Fat-Tree Topology

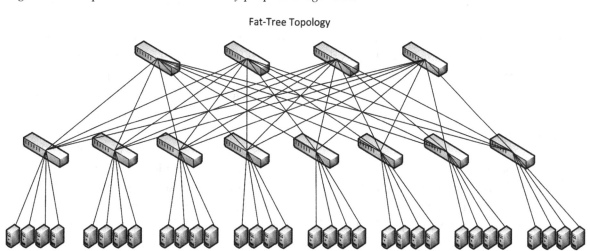

Routing Technique

Routing techniques determine the paths messages follow in the network from a sender to a receiver (Dally & Towles, 2004). A path is a series of nodes along which the message is transferred. Two important aspects of the routing technique are the routing algorithm and the switching strategy. The routing algorithm determines the path to be used for the transmission, and a good routing algorithm balances the load uniformly regardless of the offered traffic pattern, while the switching strategy determines how a message is transmitted along a path that has been selected by the routing algorithm (Rauber & Runger, 2010). Two basic switching strategies are circuit switching and packet switching. In circuit switching, the entire path from the source node to the destination node is established and reserved until the end of the transmission of the message. For packet switching, the message to be transmitted is partitioned into a sequence of packets that are transferred independently of each other through the network from the sender to the receiver.

There are three main routing techniques: deterministic, oblivious and adaptive. The deterministic technique always sends the packet in the shortest direction; the oblivious technique randomly picks a direction for each packet, while the adaptive technique sends the packet in the direction for which the local channel has the lowest load. While adaptive routing changes the path of packets dynamically, deterministic routing, which will be used in this work, determines a path statically and it has the following advantages (Koibuchi, Watanabe, Kono, Akiya, & Amano, 2003):

- It guarantees the FIFO packet delivery, which is required with several message passing libraries.
- It makes the detection and tracing of misrouted packets much easier than adaptive routing, since there is a pre-determined path between each pair of hosts.

Routing is carefully designed to avoid deadlocks. A deadlock occurs in an interconnection network when a group of packets is unable making progress because they are waiting on one another to release a resource; usually this is a buffer or channel (Dally & Towles, 2004). Deadlocks can be avoided by eliminating cycles in the resource dependence graph by imposing a partial order on the resources and then insisting that an agent allocate resources in ascending order. The simplest deadlock-free deterministic routing used in such networks is Up*/Down* routing (Sancho, Robles, & Duato, 2004; Schroeder et al., 1991).

Up*/Down* routing is based on an assignment of direction (up and down) to network channels where a spanning tree whose node (also called vertex) corresponds to a switch in the network, based on building a breadth-first search spanning tree (BFS) used in Autonet (Schroeder et al., 1991). Based on this spanning tree, the "up" end of each link is defined as:

- The end whose switch is closer to the root in the spanning tree.
- The end whose switch has the lower identifier, if both ends are at switches at the same tree level.

To avoid deadlocks while still allowing all links to be used, this routing scheme uses the following Up*/Down* rule: a legal route must traverse zero or more links in the up direction followed by zero or more links in the down direction (Sancho et al., 2004). Thus the Up*/Down* rule prohibits any packet transfer from the down direction to the up direction. The Up*/Down* rule can never deadlock because of the ordering imposed by the spanning tree, and no deadlock-producing loops are possible (Schroeder et al., 1991). It also guarantees deadlock-free routing since no cycles are formed among paths with the above rule while still allowing all hosts to be reached (Koibuchi, Akiya, Watanabe, & Amano, 2003). Although Up*/Down* routing was originally an adaptive routing, it can be implemented as a deterministic routing by choosing a single path from several alternative paths (Koibuchi, Jouraku, & Amano, 2002).

Flow Control Mechanism

Once a topology has been chosen and the path has been determined, the resources such as channel and buffer will be managed by the flow control mechanism. Flow control determines how a network's resources, such as channel bandwidth, buffer capacity and control state, are allocated to messages as they progress along their route in the network (Gramsamer, 2003). Channel bandwidth transports messages between nodes; buffers are storage implemented within the nodes, such as registers and memories that allow messages to be held temporarily at the nodes. The control state tracks the resources allocated to the packet within the node and the state of the packet's traversal across the node (Dally & Towles, 2004). The fact that multiple messages can be in transmission and attempt to use the same network link at the same time will cause a problem in the network. If this problem happens, some of the message transmission must be blocked while other messages are allowed to proceed (Kumar, Grama, Gupta, & Karypis, 1994).

A good flow control forwards packets with minimum delay and avoids deadlock (Dally & Towles, 2004). Flow control can be divided into two methods: bufferless and buffered (Rauber & Runger, 2010). Bufferless flow control uses no buffering and simply allocates channel and bandwidth to competing packets, while buffered flow control can store a packet in a buffer, preventing the waste of the channel bandwidth caused by dropping or misrouting packets. This work will focus on buffered flow control and one of widely used buffered flow control is store-and-forward flow control.

Store-and-forward flow control is a packet switching mechanism where the message to be transmitted is partitioned into a sequence of packets (Rauber & Runger, 2010). Each packet is sent separately to the destination according to routing information. Store-and-forward flow control allocates channel bandwidth and buffer resources to packets, and the resources are used by one packet at a time. With store-and-forward flow control, each node along a route waits until a packet has been completely received or stored and then forwards the packet to the next node.

Store-and-forward flow control has risen in popularity in cluster systems due to its ability to achieve optimal performance in terms of throughput (Bahman Javadi, Abawajy, & Akbari, 2006). Store-and-forward allows the utilisation of the full bandwidth for every connection and it can quickly release the connection as soon as the packet has passed the connection which reduces the risk of deadlocks (Rauber & Runger, 2010). This work will take the challenge to apply store-and-forward flow control to evaluate the performance of interconnection networks in a multi-core cluster.

Messages, Packet, and Flits

A message is a logically contiguous group of bits that are delivered from a source terminal to a destination terminal (Dally & Towles, 2004). Because messages may be arbitrarily long, resources are not directly allocated to messages, and messages are divided into one or more packets. A packet is the basic unit of routing, and sequencing and control state is allocated to packet. Flits, or flow control digits, are the basic unit of bandwidth and storage allocation used by most flow control mechanisms (Bahman Javadi, Abawajy, & Akbari, 2008a). Figure 3 illustrates the partitioning of a message, packet and flit (Rauber & Runger, 2010). Since a packet is a part of a message, in this work, message and packet will be used interchangeably.

Figure 3. The partitioning of a message into packets and of packets into flits (Rauber & Runger, 2010).

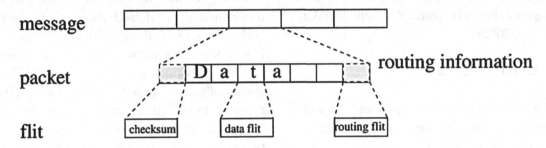

Multi-Cluster Architecture

Multi-cluster architecture is a multiple cluster system that is connected via the cluster interconnection networks where each cluster system/node has multiple processors. Multi-clusters were introduced to address the main concern of a basic cluster system which has limited service capacity of its common resources, something that causes an increase in the waiting time of the processor as the number of processors increases (Shahhoseini et al., 2000). Using more powerful common resources is the conventional method for decreasing waiting time, but the capacity of servicing of the resources such as effective memory access time and the interconnection network bandwidth is saturated by the technology and their structures. To overcome the problems, advances in computational and communication technologies have made it economically possible to combine multiple clusters of heterogeneous networked resources to develop a large-scale system known as a multi-cluster system (Abawajy & Dandamudi, 2003).

Multi-Core Multi-Cluster Architecture (MCMCA)

A multi-core cluster is a cluster where all the nodes in the cluster have multi-core processors. In addition, each node may have multiple processors (each of which contains multiple cores). With such cluster nodes, the processors in the node share both

memory and their connections to the outside. A new architecture known as the Multi-Core Multi-Cluster Architecture (MCMCA) is introduced in Figure 4. The structure of MCMCA is derived from a Multi-Stage Clustering System (MSCS) (Shahhoseini et al., 2000) which is based on a basic cluster using single-core nodes. The MCMCA is built up of numbers of clusters where each cluster is composed of numbers of nodes. The numbers of nodes are determined at run time. Each node of a multi-core cluster has more than one processor. Cores on the same chip share local memory, but have their own cache. The interconnection network connects the cluster nodes.

Communication Network

The performance of a cluster system depends on its communication latency of the interconnection network. The research conjecture is that low communication latency is essential to achieving a faster network and increasing the efficiency of a cluster. In order to understand the communication network of the Multi-Core Multi-Cluster Architecture (MCMCA), this section first explains in detail the different types of communication networks.

There are five communication networks in MCMCA. Three of them are commonly found in any multi-core cluster architecture, these are: the intra-chip communication network (AC); the inter-chip communication network (EC) and the intra-cluster network (ACN). The new communi-

Figure 4. Overview of the proposed Multi-Core Multi-Cluster Architecture (MCMCA)

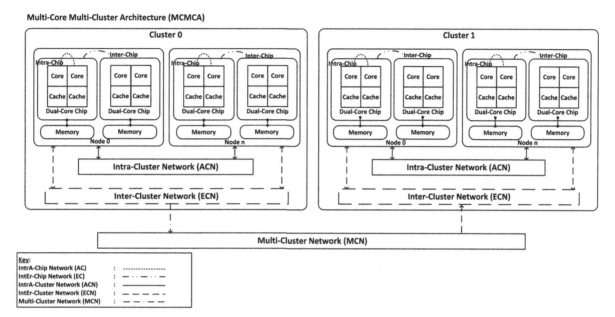

cation networks introduced in this chapter are the inter-cluster network (ECN) and the multi-cluster network (MCN).

The communication between two processor cores on the same chip is the intra-chip communication network (AC), as shown in Figure 5. Messages from source A to destination B travel via the AC communication network, which acts as a connector between two processor cores on the same chip.

Figure 6 shows an inter-chip communication network (EC) for communicating across processors in different chips but within a node. Messages travelling to different chips from source A in the same node first have to communicate within the chip via the intra chip communication network (AC), and then travel between the chips via the EC network to reach their destination B. Each node has two communication connections which are intra cluster network (ACN) for transmission within a cluster and inter cluster network (ECN) for transmission between clusters.

An intra-cluster network (ACN) is used for messages within a cluster. In order for messages to cross the nodes, messages have to communicate with the intra-chip communication network (AC) and the inter-chip communication network (EC) to pass between chips. Then messages travel via the ACN to enter different nodes to reach their destination, as shown in Figure 7.

Messages travelling from source A to destination B between clusters communicate via two communication networks to reach other clusters, as shown in Figure 8. An inter cluster network (ECN) is used to transmit messages between clusters. The clusters are connected to each other via the multi cluster network (MCN). When the messages reach the other cluster, they have to communicate with the ECN of the target cluster before arriving at their destination.

All levels of communication are critical in order to optimise the overall performance of the Multi-Core Multi-Cluster Architecture (MCMCA). The overall communication latency gathered from all communication networks will be calculated. The derived simulation results will be analysed for comparison between the existing architecture and the MCMCA architecture.

Figure 5. Communication network flow A for message passing between two processor cores on the same chip

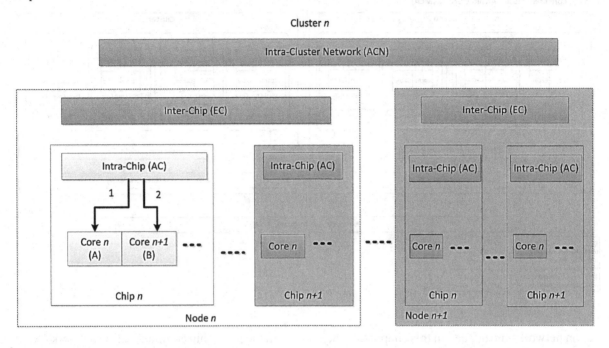

Figure 6. Communication network flow B for message passing across processors in different chips, but within a node

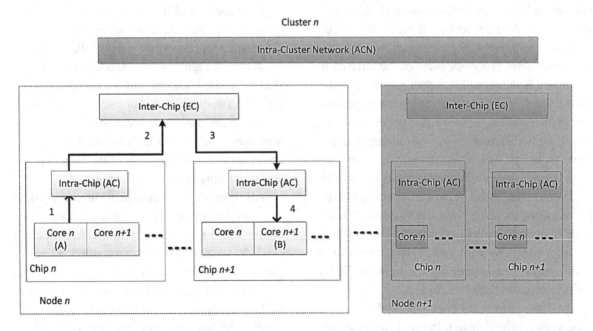

Figure 7. Communication network flow C for message passing between processors on different nodes but within the same cluster

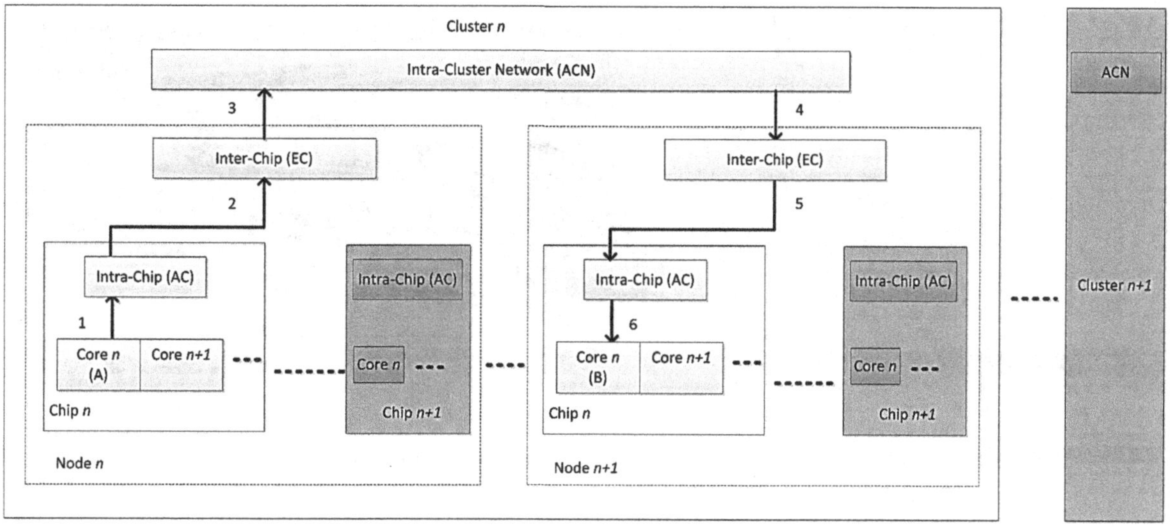

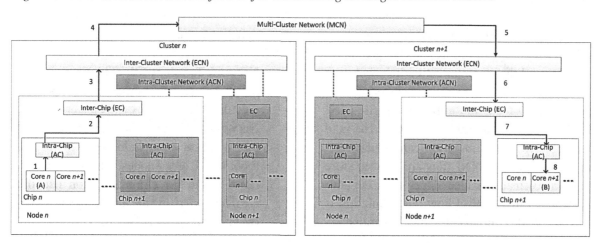

Simulation Development

Simulation models of Multi-core Multi-cluster Architecture have been developed using OMNeT++ network simulation software. OMNeT++ is an open source discrete event simulation tool that can be used in the design and analysis of systems in which state changes are discrete (Jingjing, Ponomarev, & Abu-Ghazaleh, 2012). Figure 9 shows the overview of the OMNeT++ simulation interface.

The structure of the model including its modules and their interconnection is defined in OMNET++'s topology description language, NED. NED consists of simple module declarations, compound module definitions and network definitions (Varga & Hornig, 2008). Simple module declarations describe the interface of the module: gates and parameters. Compound module definitions consist of the declaration of the module's external interface such as gates and

Figure 8. Communication network flow D for transmitting messages between clusters

Figure 9. Overview of OMNeT++ simulation interface

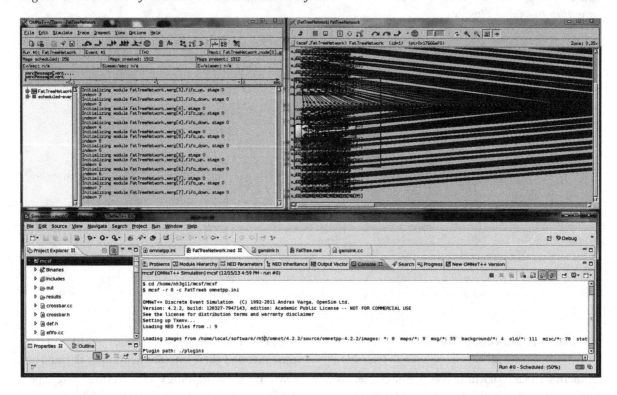

parameters and the definition of submodules and their interconnection. Network definitions are compound modules that qualify as self-contained simulation models. The OMNeT++ package includes an Integrated Development Environment which contains a graphical editor using NED as its native file format. The editor can be used to edit the network topology either graphically or in NED source view.

Unlike many formats of deterministic discrete event simulation, the model is built at run time to form a topology that represents the geometric structure and the communication links between the modules. At the start of each execution, the simulator reads the initialisation file (.INI file) that tells the tool which network file is to be simulated. The simulation can behave with different inputs and INI files are used to store these values, usually called omnetpp.ini, containing settings that control how the simulation is executed. In this initialisation file the parameters

of the model, such as number of cores per node, number of clusters, number of messages to be generated, message length (M), flit length (F) and inter-arrival time, are specified. INI files provide a great way to specify how these parameters change and enable simulation to run with any parameter combination.

The topology and the communication links between the modules are represented by the NED file. Six module files have been built to describe the simulation model.

- **Network Topology File:** This file describes the building blocks of the fat-tree topology, including cores, nodes and clusters.
- **Network Interface File:** This file contains the interface of module types in fat-tree topology. Cores, nodes, clusters, switch, channel and the communication network are declared in this file and connections between them are established.

- **Communication Switch:** This file acts as the connection for each switch and router in the model and it will determine how a message is transmitted along a path that has been selected by the routing algorithm.
- **Routing File:** This file determines the path and schedules the routing algorithms for the packets in all communication networks based on FIFO (First-In-First-Out), and it represents a single server queue that has the same service rate for each packet.
- **Message Generator File:** Packets are generated by this file following the assumption that the message destinations are uniformly distributed.
- **Message Delete File:** This file will destroy the packets after each generation is completed and will gather event information for statistics.

When the simulation is started, it will show how the messages hop from module to module following the routing algorithm. The Message Generator file will generate the messages which will be divided into a sequence of packets at each tree node, following the assumptions that the message destinations are uniformly distributed by using a uniform random number generator. In order to get the message to its destination, a packet will access the processor through a chip, and a chip can contain one or more processors. The processor will then divide the packets into the number of cores. If the first processor is busy, it will pass the packets to another processor in the same chip within the same cluster, before passing the packets via the communication network to other idle processors in other chips between the clusters. Packets will access the chips, processors and cores in its cluster first before accessing other clusters via communication network.

The routing file will determine the path the packets will follow in the network from the source to the destination. If there is a situation where more than one packet needs to use the same route, the communication switch will determine which packet can go through first or if the packet needs to queue (buffer) until the route is available. Each packet is time stamped after its generation and the message completion time is defined in the Message Delete file on each tree node to compute message latency. The Message Delete file receives a message, tests the packet type, prints a message and then deletes the packet before gathering the statistics for every event in the simulation for analysis of the results. Several print-out messages about the events and the type of messages generated and received are displayed in another window.

To illustrate the architecture, a model of the architecture is developed by the simulation program. The simulation model applies fat-tree topology that describes the geometric structure used for the arrangement of switches and communication links to connect the processors. Two levels of communication switch represent the intra-chip (AC) and inter-chip (EC), while each node in the tree represents the processor. The dotted line represents the route taken by a packet from source to destination. Figure 10 illustrates the packet travelling path in the OMNeT++ simulation model.

A packet travelling from source node to destination node will go up through internal switches of the tree until it finds the Nearest Common Ancestor (NCA) and then is transmitted down to the destination node. In this algorithm, each packet experiences two phases, an ascending phase to get a NCA, followed by a descending phase. For example, a packet is to be sent from node 0:A to node 4:E and the switch connected to the source node is SW010. The packet will travel up in ascending phase to the NCA through switch SW001 and then go down in descending phase through switch SW012 until it reaches the destination node 4:E. More examples are discussed in Table 1.

Figure 10. Illustration of packet travelling path in OMNeT++ simulation model

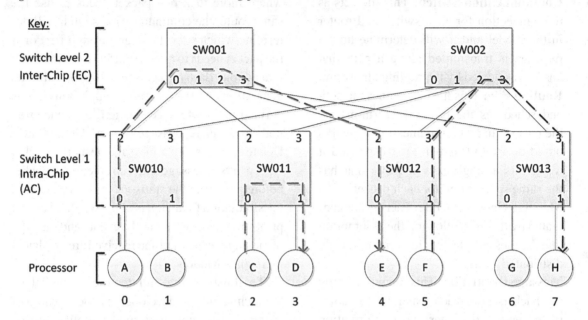

Simulation Model

Early stages of simulation experiments under various configurations and design parameters have been completed. The performance evaluation focused on communication latency in the MCMCA architecture. As a preliminary study, the communication network performance and experiment are based on a single-core multi-cluster architecture. A simulation model has been developed to measure the performance of single-core multi-cluster architecture. The evaluation was then compared to the model of multi-cluster architecture presented by Javadi, Akbari, & Abawajy (2006) with the given configuration and parameters to match the work in their papers. The configuration of the simulation was based on the list of interconnection network parameters in Table 2.

This work focuses on measuring steady-state performance of a network; the performance of a network with a stationary traffic source after it has reached steadiness. A network has reached steadiness when its average queue lengths have reached their steady-state values. To measure

Table 1. Examples of routing algorithms

Source	Destination	Switch	In_Port	Out_Port	Communication Network
0:A	4:E	010	0	2	Intra-chip (AC)
		001	0	2	Inter-chip (EC)
		012	2	0	Intra-chip (AC)
2:C	3:D	011	0	1	Intra-chip (AC)
5:F	7:H	012	1	3	Intra-chip (AC)
		002	2	3	Inter-chip (EC)
		013	3	1	Intra-chip (AC)

Table 2. Interconnection network parameter

Parameter	Intra-Cluster (ACN)	Inter-Cluster (ECN)
Network Latency	0.01s	0.02s
Switch Latency	0.01s	0.01s
Network Bandwidth	1000b/s	500b/s

(Bahman Javadi, Mohammad K. Akbari, et al., 2006).

steady-state performance, the simulation experiments were conducted in three phases: warm-up, measurement and drain (Dally & Towles, 2004). The network has necessarily reached a steady state once the network is warmed up (Bahman Javadi et al., 2008a). This means that the statistics of the network are stationary and no longer changing with time, which will determine an accurate estimation. Statistics were gathered in each simulation experiment.

The simulation model is built on the basis of the following assumptions which are used in similar studies (Bahman Javadi, Abawajy, & Akbari, 2008b; Bahman Javadi, Mohammad K. Akbari, et al., 2006; Yulei, Geyong, Keqiu, & Javadi, 2012):

1. The underlying system is a large-scale cluster with two types of communication networks: intra-cluster network and inter-cluster networks.
2. Each processor generates packets independently, following a Poisson distribution and inter-arrival times are exponentially distributed.
3. The destination of each message is any node in the system with uniform distribution.
4. The numbers of processors and cores in all clusters are the same and the cluster nodes are homogeneous.
5. The communication switches are input buffered and each channel is associated with a single packet buffer.
6. Message length is fixed.

SIMULATION RESULTS AND DISCUSSION

The simulation of the single-core multi-cluster simulation model has been examined with a number of cases. When the simulation is started, a message will travel in the network following the routing algorithm which will determine the path from the source to the destination. A long message will be divided into one or more packets and each packet will be partitioned into a sequence of flits, a flow control digit, to make sure the resources can be allocated directly to the messages.

The performance under various workload conditions has been evaluated. The first case was for an 8 single core cluster system with message length (M) = 32 flits, flit lengths (F) of 256 bytes and 512 bytes. The second case was performed by the same 8 single core cluster system and the same flit lengths (F) of 256 bytes and 512 bytes, but with a longer message length (M) = 64 flits.

Results in Figure 11 are derived from computer simulation based on the first case with message length (M) = 32 flits while Figure 12 depicts the results of the second case with message length (M) = 64 flits. The X axis of the graph represents the traffic generation rate, while the Y axis denotes the communication latency.

Simulation experiments have revealed that the results obtained from the single-core multi-cluster architecture closely match the results from the model of multi-cluster architecture presented by Javadi et al. (2006), when compared. The results have shown that as the traffic rate increases, the average communication latency increases following the assumptions that the messages have to wait for resources before traversing into a network. At low traffic rates, latency will approach zero-load latency. The zero-load latency assumption is that a packet has never contended for network resources with other packets. The results confirm that the simulation model is a good basis to measure the communication latency for a large-scale cluster, and can be extended to multi-core multi-cluster architecture.

Figure 11. Average latency of 8-cluster system with M=32 flits, F=256 bytes and 512 bytes

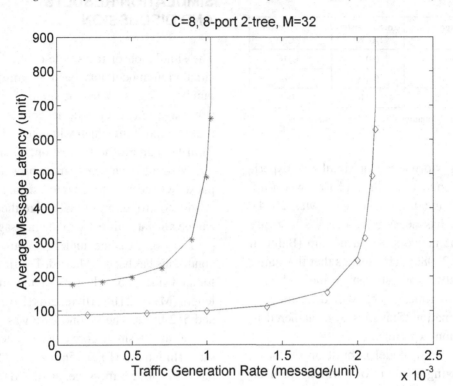

Figure 12. Average latency of 8-cluster system with M=64 flits, F=256 bytes and 512 bytes

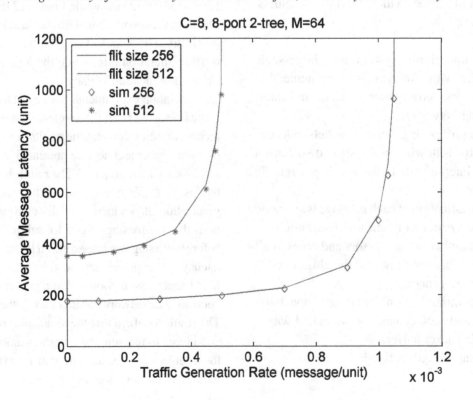

CONTRIBUTION

Multi-core cluster architecture is clusters composed of multi-core nodes that are connected via an interconnection network, or networks. This architecture typically imposes high communication latency, especially for communication between processors located on different nodes (Lei et al., 2007). The possibility of bottlenecks and contention which contribute to high communication latency may prevent this architecture from achieving better performance (Silva et al., 2010). A high communication latency interconnect can dramatically reduce the efficiency of a cluster (Shainer et al., 2013).

The objective of this work is to produce a new architecture to investigate the performance of a multi-core multi-cluster architecture. The validity of the architecture will be demonstrated by computer simulation and experimental measurements within the simulation.

The new architecture will involve five communication networks compared to three in the existing multi-core cluster architecture. The performance measurements will focus on overall communication latency within the simulation model and the simulation results will be analysed for comparison with published results of existing cluster architectures. This research will apply multi-cluster architecture for a more scalable approach and this is the first investigation into employing multi cluster architecture within multi-core cluster architecture.

CONCLUSION AND FUTURE DIRECTIONS

This chapter has presented an architecture for measuring the performance of communication networks in Multi-Core Multi-Cluster Architecture (MCMCA). Preliminary stages of the research involved the development of the single-core multi-cluster simulation model. Simulation experiments have been conducted to evaluate the single core multi-cluster and baseline results were produced. Simulation results demonstrated that the simulation model is a good basis to measure the communication latency for a large scale cluster, and can be extended to MCMCA.

Our future work will be developing a simulation model for MCMCA. Experiments will be run in simulation to investigate the model's performance under various configurations. This will provide communication network performance results for comparisons to be made between the model of the MCMCA and models of existing cluster architectures (Bahman Javadi, Mohammad K. Akbari, et al., 2006; Lei et al., 2007). The simulation will measure communication latency of a cluster when applying multi-core processor technology, under a multi-cluster architecture environment. The approach taken and accuracy of the simulation outcome will make it a good reference for predicting the performance behaviour of MCMCA.

At the end, this research will benefit not only cluster architecture, but also high performance computing architecture including cloud computing. More research in high performance computing, especially cloud computing is now based on cluster architecture to solve its limitation especially in satisfying peak workload performance (Chang, Walters, & Wills, 2013; Kosinska et al., 2010; Moreno-Vozmediano, Montero, & Llorente, 2011). This research will also provide an alternative platform for high performance computing that will provide several benefits such as high availability, fault tolerance and infrastructure cost reduction.

REFERENCES

Abawajy, J. H., & Dandamudi, S. P. (2003). Parallel job scheduling on multicluster computing system. In *Proceedings of the 2003 IEEE International Conference on Cluster Computing*.

Abdelgadir, A. T., Pathan, A.-S. K., & Ahmed, M. (2011). *On the performance of MPI-OpenMP on a 12 nodes multi-core cluster. Algorithms and architectures for parallel processing* (pp. 225–234). Springer.

Admin. (2009). TOP500 Highlights - November 2009. Retrieved from http://www.top500.org/lists/2009/11/highlights

Admin. (2010). What is cluster computing. Retrieved from http://www.ccgrid.org/tag/cluster-computing

Admin. (2013). Top500 Supercomputer Sites.

Baker, M., Apon, A., Buyya, R., & Jin, H. (2000). Cluster computing and applications. Retrieved from http://www.buyya.com/papers/encyclopedia.pdf

Baker, M., & Buyya, R. (1999). Cluster computing: The commodity supercomputer. *Software–Practice and Experience, 29*(6), 551-576.

Baldassari, J. D., Kopec, C. L., Leshay, E. S., Truszkowski, W., & Finkel, D. (2005, April 4-7). *Autonomic cluster management system (ACMS): A demonstration of autonomic principles at work.* Paper presented at the 12th IEEE International Conference and Workshops on the Engineering of Computer-Based Systems, 2005. ECBS '05.

Bethel, E. W., & Howison, M. (2012). Multi-core and many-core shared-memory parallel raycasting volume rendering optimization and tuning. *International Journal of High Performance Computing Applications, 26*(4), 399–412. doi:10.1177/1094342012440466

Burger, T. W. (2005). Intel Multi-Core Processors: Quick Reference Guide.

Buyya, R., Hai, J., & Cortes, T. (2002)... *Cluster Computing, 18*, 5–8.

Chai, L. (2009). *High performance and scalable MPI intra-node communication middleware for multi-core clusters. PhD.* The Ohio State University.

Chang, V., Walters, R., & Wills, G. (2013). Cloud storage and bioinformatics in a private cloud deployment: Lessons for data intensive research. In I. Ivanov, M. van Sinderen, F. Leymann, & T. Shan (Eds.), *Cloud computing and services science* (Vol. 367, pp. 245–264). Springer International Publishing. doi:10.1007/978-3-319-04519-1_16

Chang, V., Walters, R. J., & Wills, G. (2014). Review of cloud computing and existing frameworks for cloud adoption. In *Advances in cloud computing research*. Nova Publishers.

Chen, X., Wills, G. B., Gilbert, L., & Bacigalupo, D. (2010). *Tecires report: Using cloud for research: A technical review*. University of Southampton.

Creel, M., & Goffe, W. L. (2007). Multi-core CPUs, clusters, and grid computing: A tutorial. *Computational Economics, 32*(4).

Dally, W. J., & Towles, B. P. (2004). *Principles and practices of interconnection network*. Morgan Kaufmann.

Dillon, T., Chen, W., & Chang, E. (2010). *Cloud computing: Issues and challenges.* Paper presented at the 2010 24th IEEE International Conference on Advanced Information Networking and Applications (AINA).

Fengguang, S., Moore, S., & Dongarra, J. (2009). *Analytical modeling and optimization for affinity based thread scheduling on multicore systems.* Paper presented at the IEEE International Conference on Cluster Computing and Workshops, 2009. CLUSTER '09.

Furhad, H., Haque, M., Kim, C.-H., & Kim, J.-M. (2013). An analysis of reducing communication delay in network-on-chip interconnect architecture. *Wireless Personal Communications*, 1–17. doi:10.1007/s11277-013-1257-y

Geer, D. (2005). Industry trends. *Chip Makers Turn to Multicore Processors*, *38*, 11–13.

Geer, D. (2007). For programmers, multicore chips mean multiple challenges. *Computer*, *40*(9), 17–19. doi:10.1109/MC.2007.311

Gramsamer, F. (2003). *Scalable flow control for interconnection networks. Doctor of Tecnical Sciences thesis*, Swiss Federal Institute of Technology Zurich.

Haddad, I. (2006). *The HAS architecture: A highly available and scalable cluster architecture for web servers*. PhD thesis, Concordia University, Library and Archives Canada.

Hope, L., & Lam, E. (n.d.). A review of applications of cluster computing. *World*, 1-10.

Ichikawa, S., & Takagi, S. (2009). *Estimating the optimal configuration of a multi-core cluster: a preliminary study*. Paper presented at the 2009 International Conference on Complex, Intelligent and Software Intensive Systems. CISIS '09.

Intel. (1997). Moore's law and Intel innovation. Retrieved from http://www.intel.com/about/companyinfo/museum/exhibits/moore.htm?wapkw=moore+laws

Javadi, B., Abawajy, J. H., & Akbari, M. K. (2006). *Modeling and analysis of heterogeneous loosely-coupled distributed systems Technical Report TR C06/1*. Australia: School of Information Technology, Deakin University.

Javadi, B., Abawajy, J. H., & Akbari, M. K. (2008a). A comprehensive analytical model of interconnection networks in large-scale cluster systems. *Concurrency and Computation*, *20*(1), 75–97. doi:10.1002/cpe.1222

Javadi, B., Abawajy, J. H., & Akbari, M. K. (2008b). Performance modeling and analysis of heterogeneous meta-computing systems interconnection networks. *Computers & Electrical Engineering*, *34*(6), 488–502. doi:10.1016/j.compeleceng.2007.09.007

Javadi, B., Akbari, M. K., & Abawajy, J. H. (2006). A performance model for analysis of heterogeneous multi-cluster systems. *Parallel Computing*, *32*(11–12), 831–851. doi:10.1016/j.parco.2006.09.006

Javadi, B., Akbari, M. K., Abawajy, J. H., & Nahavandi, S. (2006). *Multi-cluster computing interconnection network performance modeling and analysis*. Paper presented at the 2006 International Conference on Advanced Computing and Communications. ADCOM 2006.

Jingjing, W., Ponomarev, D., & Abu-Ghazaleh, N. (2012). *Performance analysis of a multithreaded PDES simulator on multicore clusters*. Paper presented at the 26th Workshop on Principles of Advanced and Distributed Simulation (PADS), 2012 ACM/IEEE/SCS.

Karmakar, N. (2011). *Multi-core architecture. The new trend in processor making* (p. 44). India: North Maharashrta University.

Khosravi, A., Khorsandi, S., & Akbari, M. K. (2011). *Hyper node torus: A new interconnection network for high speed packet processors*. Paper presented at the 2011 International Symposium on Computer Networks and Distributed Systems (CNDS).

Koibuchi, M., Akiya, J., Watanabe, K., & Amano, H. (2003). Descending layers routing: A deadlock-free deterministic routing using virtual channels in system area networks with irregular topologies. In *Proceedings of the 2003 International Conference on Parallel Processing*.

Koibuchi, M., Jouraku, A., & Amano, H. (2002). *The impact of path selection algorithm of adaptive routing for implementing deterministic routing* (pp. 1431–1437).

Koibuchi, M., Watanabe, K., Kono, K., Akiya, J., & Amano, H. (2003). Performance evaluation of routing algorithms in RHiNET-2 cluster. In *Proceedings of the 2003 IEEE International Conference on Cluster Computing*.

Koibuchi, M., Watanabe, T., Minamihata, A., Nakao, M., Hiroyasu, T., Matsutani, H., & Amano, H. (2011). *Performance evaluation of power-aware multi-tree ethernet for HPC interconnects*. Paper presented at the 2011 Second International Conference on Networking and Computing (ICNC).

Kosinska, J., Kosinski, J., & Zielinski, K. (2010). *The concept of application clustering in cloud computing environments: The need for extending the capabilities of virtual networks*. Paper presented at the Fifth International Multi-Conference on Computing in the Global Information Technology (ICCGI).

Kumar, V., Grama, A., Gupta, A., & Karypis, G. (1994). *Introduction to parallel computing*. Canada: The Benjamin/Cummings Publishing Company, Inc.

Lei, C., Hartono, A., & Panda, D. K. (2006). *Designing high performance and scalable MPI Intra-node communication support for clusters*. Paper presented at the 2006 IEEE International Conference on Cluster Computing.

Lei, C., Qi, G., & Panda, D. K. (2007). *Understanding the impact of multi-core architecture in cluster computing: A case study with intel dual-core system*. Paper presented at the Seventh IEEE International Symposium on Cluster Computing and the Grid. CCGRID 2007.

Lin, X. (2003). *An efficient communication scheme for fat-tree topology on infiniband networks*. M.Sc thesis, Feng Chia University Taiwan.

Moreno-Vozmediano, R., Montero, R. S., & Llorente, I. M. (2011). Multicloud deployment of computing clusters for loosely coupled MTC applications. *IEEE Transactions on Parallel and Distributed Systems*, 22(6), 924–930. doi:10.1109/TPDS.2010.186

Pase, D. M., & Eckl, M. A. (2005). A comparison of single-core and dual-core opteron processor performance for HPC I. IBM.

Peh, L. S. (2001). *Flow control and microarchitectural mechanism for extending the performance of interconnection networks*. PhD Thesis, Stanford University.

Petrini, F., Frachtenberg, E., Hoisie, A., & Coll, S. (2003). Performance evaluation of the quadrics interconnection network. *Cluster Computing*, 6(2), 125–142. doi:10.1023/A:1022852505633

Qian, Y. (2010). *Design and evaluation of effiecient collective communications on modern interconnects and multi-core clusters*. PhD thesis, Queen's University, Canada.

Ranadive, A., Kesavan, M., Gavrilovska, A., & Schwan, K. (2008). Performance implications of virtualizing multicore cluster machines. In *Proceedings of the 2nd workshop on System-level virtualization for high performance computing*. Glasgow, Scotland. doi:10.1145/1435452.1435453

Rauber, T., & Runger, G. (2010). *Parallel Programming for Multicore and Cluster Systems*. Springer.

Rouse, M. (2006). Node. Retrieved from http://searchnetworking.techtarget.com/definition/node

Rouse, M. (2006). Processor. Retrieved August 2, 2012, from http://whatis.techtarget.com/definition/processor

Roy, P. V. (2008). The challenges and opportunities of multiple processors: Why multi-core processors are easy and internet is hard. Retrieved from http://www.ist-selfman.org/wiki/images/5/54/Vanroy-mc-panel.pdf

Sadashiv, N., & Kumar, S. M. D. (2011). Cluster, grid and cloud computing: A detailed comparison. In *Proceedings of the 6th International Conference on Computer Science & Education (ICCSE)* (pp. 477-482). doi:10.1109/ICCSE.2011.6028683

Sancho, J. C., Robles, A., & Duato, J. (2004). An effective methodology to improve the performance of the up*/down* routing algorithm. *IEEE Transactions on Parallel and Distributed Systems*, *15*(8), 740–754. doi:10.1109/tpds.2004.28

Schauer, B. (2008). Multicore processors-A necessity. *ProQuest*. Retrieved from http://www.techrepublic.com/resource-library/whitepapers/multicore-processors-a-necessity/

Schroeder, M. D., Birrell, A. D., Burrows, M., Murray, H., Needham, R. M., Rodeheffer, T. L., & Thacker, C. P. et al. (1991). Autonet: A high-speed, self-configuring local area network using point-to-point links. *IEEE Journal on Selected Areas in Communications*, *9*(8), 1318–1335. doi:10.1109/49.105178

Schubert, L., Jeffery, K., & Neidecker-Lutz, B. (2010). The future of cloud computing: opportunities for european cloud computing beyond 2010 (p. 66). European Commission, Information Society and Media.

Shahhoseini, H. S., Naderi, M., & Buyya, R. (2000). Shared memory multistage clustering structure, an efficient structure for massively parallel processing systems. In *Proceedings of the Fourth International Conference/Exhibition on High Performance Computing in the Asia-Pacific Region, 2000.*

Shainer, G., Lui, P., Hilgeman, M., Layton, J., Stevens, C., Stemple, W., & Kresse, G. (2013). Maximizing application performance in a multi-core, NUMA-aware compute cluster by multi-level tuning. In J. Kunkel, T. Ludwig, & H. Meuer (Eds.), *Supercomputing* (Vol. 7905, pp. 226–238). Berlin Heidelberg: Springer. doi:10.1007/978-3-642-38750-0_17

Silva, J. M. N., Drummond, L., & Boeres, C. (2010). *On modelling multicore clusters.* Paper presented at the 22nd International Symposium on Computer Architecture and High Performance Computing Workshops (SBAC-PADW), 2010.

Soryani, M., Analoui, M., & Zarrinchian, G. (2013). Improving inter-node communications in multi-core clusters using a contention-free process mapping algorithm. *The Journal of Supercomputing*, 1–26. doi:10.1007/s11227-013-0918-7

Sterling, T., Apon, A., & Baker, M. (2000). Cluster computing white paper. Cluster Computing.

Sterling, T. L. (2002). *Beowulf cluster computing with Windows computers* (p. 445). MIT Press.

Stevens, R. (1986). *Understanding Computers.* Oxford: Oxford University Press.

Sullivan, D. R., Lewis, T. G., & Cook, C. R. (1988). *Computing today: Microcomputer concepts and application.* USA: Houghton Mifflin Company.

Varga, A., & Hornig, R. (2008). An overview of the OMNeT++ simulation environment. In *Proceedings of the 1st international conference on Simulation tools and techniques for communications, networks and systems & workshops*. Marseille, France.

Wu, X., & Taylor, V. (2013). Performance modeling of hybrid MPI/OpenMP scientific applications on large-scale multicore supercomputers. *Journal of Computer and System Sciences*, 79(8). doi:10.1016/j.jcss.2013.02.005

Yeo, C., Buyya, R., Pourreza, H., Eskicioglu, R., Graham, P., & Sommers, F. (2006). In A. Zomaya (Ed.), *Cluster computing: High-performance, high-availability, and high-throughput processing on a network of computers handbook of nature-inspired and innovative computing* (pp. 521–551). US: Springer.

Yulei, W., Geyong, M., Keqiu, L., & Javadi, B. (2012). Modeling and analysis of communication networks in multicluster systems under spatio-temporal bursty traffic. *IEEE Transactions on Parallel and Distributed Systems*, 23(5), 902–912. doi:10.1109/tpds.2011.198

KEY TERMS AND DEFINITIONS

Cluster Computing: A group of computers, which work together to form a single computer, connected to each other by fast local area networks.

High Performance Computing (HPC): Any computational activity requiring more than a single computer to execute a task.

Interconnection Network: A connection between two or more computer networks via network devices such as routers and switches, to exchange traffic back and forth and guide traffic across the complete network to their destination.

Multi-Cluster: A multiple cluster system that is connected via the cluster interconnection networks where each cluster node has multiple processors.

Multi-Core Cluster: A multi-core cluster is a computing cluster where all the nodes in the cluster have multi-core processors, each of which contains multiple cores.

Multi-Core Processor: A multi-core processor combines two or more processing elements in a single processor, on a single chip or multiple where a multi-core can divide the work between two or more execution cores, allowing more work to be done within a given clock cycle.

Network Simulation: The process of creating a model of an existing or proposed network, which provides an alternative designs to be evaluated without having to experiment on a real network, which may be costly, time-consuming or impractical to do.

Chapter 10
A Formal Framework for Cloud Systems

Zakaria Benzadri
University of Constantine 2, Algeria

Chafia Bouanaka
University of Constantine 2, Algeria

Faïza Belala
University of Constantine 2, Algeria

ABSTRACT

Cloud Computing is an emerging topic with high potentials in the IT industry. Its offered services need to be adapted to deal with variations caused by hostile environment, such as the Internet. Hence, a challenging issue in Cloud systems architecture is to model and analyze cloud-based services. However, few work has been dedicated to guarantee safe and secure adaptable services. The main objective of this chapter is to propose a formal framework for specifying cloud systems and offering analysis support to model-check their inherent properties. Based on Bigraphical Reactive Systems, the formalization process is achieved via the definition of the BiCloud-Arch model. Then, cloud architecture dynamics is formalized by a set of generic reaction rules to be applied on the obtained bigraphical model. This chapter also addresses a mapping from the proposed model (BiCloud-Arch) to a Maude-based formal executable specification (BiCloud-2M). On this basis, the proposed BiCloud Maude-based Model Checker (BMMC) is used to formally verify some Cloud system properties.

1. INTRODUCTION

Cloud computing is actually attracting more attention, as a promising model for delivering Information and Communication Technology (ICT) services via the generalization of service reuse to all computer resources. It involves dynamic and on demand provisioning of shared computing resources (Mell et al., 2011). The main principle behind this model is to offer computing, storage and software as a service attempting to reduce IT capital and operating expenditures. Hence, it promotes service availability, emphasizes resource reuse rationalization and provides opportuni-

DOI: 10.4018/978-1-4666-8210-8.ch010

Copyright © 2015, IGI Global. Copying or distributing in print or electronic forms without written permission of IGI Global is prohibited.

ties for reducing software development costs. Although cloud computing scope is enlarging, it is accompanied with a concentration of risks and brought issues. On the other hand, cloud systems are becoming more and more complex, since large organizations have to manage increasingly heterogeneous cloud systems: hundreds of services, thousands of servers, hundreds of thousands of transactions, more and more users spread over the world, whether customers or suppliers. Consequently, there are still many obstacles slowing down cloud computing model adoption and growth. Many obstacles have been identified by Armbrust et al. (2009), we list in what follows the most significant ones for our work:

- **Bugs in Large-Scale Distributed Systems:** It is difficult to anticipate and avoid bugs during system development, it is more difficult to find and fix them in a running system. Thus, proposing a model being sufficiently expressive while remaining reasonably analyzable is recognized as an ideal solution.
- **Service Availability and Quick Scalability:** Availability of service is the degree to which a service is available upon customer demand; it is measured regarding customer's perception of a service, i.e., customers' frustration whenever their services are no more available, whereas performance failure is being caused by an unexpected higher number of customers' demands. The opportunity is then to scale-up quickly as a response to customer's demand.

Identifying runtime service bugs while maintaining service availability is a complicated task regarding cloud systems architecture and complexity. Since, they allow formal verification of complex software systems giving rise to high quality, more correct software compared to conventional design methods, "formal methods are an effective approach to ensure cloud systems

reliability, by providing a high evaluation assurance level 'EAL7'"; according to (ISO 15408).

To obtain formal executable and analyzable cloud models, we define a new theoretical framework for cloud systems. The proposed framework extends our previous works (Benzadri et al., 2013) and (Benzadri et al., 2014) that are also part of our contribution in this chapter. The presented framework is composed of three main stages (see Figure 1):

Step 1: Designing cloud architecture and its shape shifting using Bigraphical Reactive Systems; BRS for short, BRS are an elegant solution to model cloud computing architecture and its dynamics.

Step 2: Obtaining Maude-based executable specifications, Maude language presents an excellent solution to implement the obtained cloud bigraphical model (proposed in Step 1).

Step 3: Verifying some cloud systems inherent properties using a Maude-based model checker. Via a judicious coupling of BRS and Maude, dynamic cloud architectures are analyzed and verified.

The framework will be detailed according to the identified main phases (see Figure 1) of cloud systems specification and verification. Each phase presentation begins by recalling necessary concepts, then presenting its resulting model. The chapter is organized as follows. Section 2 discusses related work. Section 3 presents an overview of cloud computing. Section 4 is dedicated to a brief description of Bigraphical Reactive Systems and their essential concepts. Then, our bigraphical cloud architecture formalization (BiCloud-Arch) is presented and illustrated through a well-known case study of the Cloud-Health system. Section 5 presents an overview of Maude's main concepts, and defines the proposed Maude-based executable specification for cloud architecture (BiCloud-2M). Section 6 exploits the proposed executable specification to verify cloud inherent

Figure 1. A formal framework for cloud systems

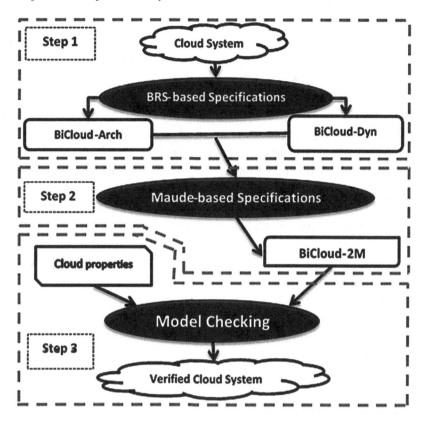

properties formally using the proposed BiCloud Maude-based Model Checker (BMMC). Section 7 is dedicated to an evaluation and discussion of the presented framework. Finally, conclusion and future work are addressed in section 8.

2. RELATED WORK

In the literature, several frameworks have been recently provided but do not deal with all fundamental concepts of cloud computing. They particularly focus on cloud computing financial and technological aspects; MobiCloud (Cloud Framework for Mobile Computing and Communication) proposed by Dijiang et al. (2010), is a new cloud framework for MANETs that focuses on interrelated system components including resource and information flow isolations. It enhances

communication by addressing trust management, secure routing, and risk management issues in the network. The need to establish a foundation for providing trust in the Cloud systems has been given in the work of Imad M. Abbadi (2013). The authors have identified challenges to be considered for trustworthy secure Cloud provenance, and proposed a framework for trustworthy Cloud's provenance. In the work of Chang et al. (2010), the research purpose is to test financial aspect of applications when running on the Clouds, and ensure enterprise level of portability, speed, accuracy and reliability. The authors propose the Financial Cloud Framework (FCF), which contains business models, forecasting, sustainability, modeling, simulation and benchmarking of financial assets. The improved version of such a framework has led to risk visualization as a service to present risk and simplify the level of difficulty to understand risk (Chang, 2014 a). While there are different types of risks and demands to handle, the further development of such a project has then established into the Business Intelligence as a Service, which includes risk visualization, risk tracking and risk calculation with regard to the prices, so that the stakeholders can monitor the status of their investment and make a better judgment of their decision-making process (Chang, 2014 b).

With regard to the recommendation for Cloud Computing adoption, the work in Chang et al (2013) aims to present technical and business challenges for organizational Cloud adoption, and describe four key areas to be addressed (Classification; Organizational Sustainability Modelling; Service Portability and Linkage). The Cloud Computing Business Framework (CCBF) has been proposed to help organizations achieving Cloud design, deployment, migration and services. The framework has been used in several organizations offering added values and positive impacts. Similarly, Tan C. et al. (2013) discuss the adoption and reliability of the SaaS model. They propose a framework that enables an organization to assess its current IT landscape and provides readiness assessment for SaaS adoption. The framework adapts Business Aligned IT Strategy as a foundation. Nattakarn P. et al. (2013) identify the necessary perspectives to capture benefits of cloud computing. Then, they propose a conceptual framework for cloud computing benefits. Their framework accounts for the different business areas and organizational levels where each of the benefits manifests. CBKMF for Ontology Cloud-Shadow Model-based Knowledge Service Framework in the work of Feng W. et al. (2012), is a framework that uses the definition and operation from an ontology cloud model that is able to reflect new-knowledge-view and knowledge's characters such as uncertainty, inconsistency, time-varying and sociality. The authors also discuss recent research on knowledge management and particular advantages that can arise and help to solve problems still existing in other frameworks.

Ricardo J. et al. (2013) propose an ontology-enriched framework for cloud-based Enterprise Interoperability. The proposed framework allows knowledge, decisions, and responsibilities to be exchanged about negotiations. It is supported by a reference ontology and uses cloud-computing as the paradigm to deploy services on the network. T. Chandrakumar and S. Parthasarathy (2014) explore the available literature on cloud ERP systems, suggest factors to be considered in cloud ERP, and propose a framework for evaluating cloud ERP systems. Their framework is grounded on software engineering parameters involved in the development of cloud ERP.

Additionally, there are other works that adopt formal methods for cloud computing. In the work of Y. Jarraya et al. (2012), a formal framework for specifying virtual machine migration and the associated security policies in the cloud is presented using a process algebra approach, it allows verifying the preservation of the global security policy within the new configuration after virtual machines migration. Dong, et al. (2010) and Grandison, et al. (2010), gave some discussion and exploration on establishing relationships between virtualization and cloud computing. Throughout their work, they attempt to give out a formal definition of cloud computing from a virtualization viewpoint using its theoretical basic concepts. Luo, et al. (2011) propose an access control model to achieve a fine-grained, data confidentiality and scalability via a formal definition of the HABAC model (Hierarcy Attribute-Based Access Control). Freitas & Paul (2012) present an abstract formalization of federated cloud workflows using the Z notation. They define various properties using rules restricting valid options in two categories: security and cost.

Whether adopting formal methods or not, the aforementioned previous works are limited and focus solely on enhancing the financial and technological aspects of cloud computing. Consequently, cloud computing lacks a theoretical framework that associates a clear semantics to its basic concepts: service delivery and deployment models. This framework might be able to support major cloud computing concepts specification and allows formal analysis of high level services provided over the cloud computing architecture. Within this perspective, we propose a semantic framework to specify cloud systems. Besides, it offers analysis support to model-check their inherent properties. Differences with the aforementioned frameworks include the adopted approach, the main focus, and the inclusiveness of the solution.

3. CLOUD COMPUTING

In this section, we briefly recall a largely adopted definition of cloud computing. Then, we recall the three service models and the four deployment models of cloud.

According to Mell et al. (2011), "Cloud computing is a model for enabling convenient, on-demand network access to a shared pool of configurable computing resources (e.g., networks, servers, storage, applications, and services) that can be rapidly provisioned and released with minimal management effort or service provider interaction. This cloud model promotes availability and is composed of five essential characteristics, three service models, and four deployment models".

Main characteristics of cloud computing are: On-demand self-service, broad network access, resource pooling, rapid elasticity and measured service.

Diverse dimensions can be adopted to classify cloud computing, two commonly used categories are: cloud deployment models and service models.

- From the cloud deployment models viewpoint, cloud computing can be classified as public cloud, community cloud, private cloud and hybrid cloud. The public cloud is provisioned for open use by everyone. However, the private cloud is provisioned for exclusive use by a single organization comprising multiple consum-

ers. Community cloud is provisioned for exclusive use by a specific community of consumers; organizations that have shared concerns. Finally, hybrid cloud is a composition of two or more distinct cloud computing services (private, community, or public) for the same entity.

- From a service model viewpoint, cloud computing can be classified into three service models: Infrastructure as a Service (IaaS), Platform as a Service (PaaS) and Software as a Service (SaaS). SaaS provides services to end users, while IaaS and PaaS provide services to Independent Software Vendor (ISV).

4. A BIGRAPH-BASED SPECIFICATION FOR CLOUD ARCHITECTURE

Albeit, various models were adopted for cloud architecture specification: Petri Nets in the work of Fitch et al. (2012) and Fang et al. (2013), Semantic Technology in the work of Hu et al. (2009), MDA in the work of Howard et al. (2010), Agent-based in the work of Sim et al. (2012), or Component Model in the work of Cosmo et al. (2012); they do not deal with the main concepts recurring in cloud computing; service locality and interaction. In this context, Bigraphical Reactive Systems (BRS) model is an elegant solution and formal approach to describe cloud architecture, particularly:

- The model emphasizes both locality and connectivity that can be used to specify location and interconnection of cloud system entities.
- BRS Reaction rules, that provide to bigraphs the ability to reconfigure themselves, are very useful to formalize cloud system dynamics, especially cloud system scalability.

In this section, BRS will be adopted to describe cloud architecture (step 1 of Figure 1). Before presenting our bigraphical formalization, a brief recall of Bigraphical Reactive Systems and their essential concepts is introduced. Then, bigraph-based specification of cloud architecture and its dynamics is presented. Finally, our cloud formalization approach is illustrated through a well-known case study of the Cloud-Health.

A. Bigraphical Reactive Systems

The notion of bigraph was proposed in the early 2000s by Milner (2009) to model important aspects of ubiquitous systems, focusing on mobile connectivity and mobile locality. It provides a general theory unifying existing ones, and providing necessary concepts to represent many existing calculi (CCS, π-calcul, X-calcul, etc.) for concurrency and mobility. A bigraph as an ordinary graph is composed of nodes and edges, although nodes in a bigraph can be nested giving rise to hierarchical and larger bigraphs. It is the resulting graph of composing a place and a link graphs. The place graph consists of a forest of trees; each one with its own root and serves to model locality or containment of the attached entities. The link graph models system connectivity or assembly and is composed of a set of nodes and a set of hyper-edges; meaning that each edge has multiple tentacles. Connection points between nodes and edges tentacles are called ports.

I. Bigraph Elements

A basic bigraph signature takes the form (S, ar) with S a set of controls specifying kinds of bigraph nodes, and a map ar: S $\rightarrow$ N assigning an arity, a natural number, to each control. The signature is denoted by S when the arity is understood. A bigraph over S assigns to each node a control, whose arity indexes ports of the underlying node, where links may be connected. In addition to arity, each control indicates which nodes are atomic (node

empty), and which of the non-atomic nodes are active (node permitting reaction inside) or passive (Milner, 2009).

A bigraph consists of a place graph; expressing the physical locations of nodes, and a link graph; representing interconnection between theses nodes, hence the prefix "BI" in bigraph. The formal definition of a bigraph is as follows:

Definition 1 (Bigraph): A bigraph is a 5-tuple (V, E, ctrl, prnt, link): (m, X) $\rightarrow$ (n, Y); also written <GP, GL>, consisting of a concrete place graph GP = (V, ctrl, prnt):m$\rightarrow$n and a concrete link graph GL = (V, E, ctrl, link): X $\rightarrow$Y.

Within a place graph, the hierarchy of nodes reflects a child/parent relationship to mean that the inner nodes are children of the outer (containing) node. The formal definition of a place graph is:

Definition 2 (Place Graph): A place graph is a 3-tuple (V, ctrl, prnt): m$\rightarrow$n having an inner interface m and an outer interface n, both are finite ordinals, used to index place graph sites and roots respectively. V is a finite set of nodes, ctrl:V$\rightarrow$S is a control map assigning controls to nodes drawn from a set that is called a signature. prnt: m$\uplus$ V $\rightarrow$V $\uplus$ n is a parent map indicating the parent of each node.

A link graph consists of a hyper-graph that describes the linkage of a bigraph. The formal definition of a link graph is as follows:

Definition 3 (Link Graph): A link graph is a quadruple (V, E, ctrl, link): X $\rightarrow$Y having an inner interface X and outer interface Y; called respectively the inner and outer names of the link graph. V and E are sets of nodes and edges respectively, ctrl: V $\rightarrow$S is a control map, and link: X $\uplus$ P $\rightarrow$E $\uplus$ Y is a link map; with P a set of ports. We shall call X $\uplus$ P the link graph points, and E $\uplus$ Y its links.

II. Reaction Rule

Once bigraph structure is presented, its dynamics will be formalized through a BRS (Bigraphical Reactive System) consisting of a category of bigraphs and a set of reaction rules that may be applied to transform these bigraphs.

Definition 4 (Reaction Rule): A reaction rule takes the form (R, R', O) where R: $m \rightarrow n$ is a bigraph called redex (the pattern to be changed), R': $m' \rightarrow n'$ is also a bigraph called reactum (the changed pattern), and O: $m' \rightarrow m$ is a map of ordinals establishing the correspondence between inner interfaces of R and R'.

III. Algebra of Bigraphs

Additionally to graph theory based definitions that are insufficient to model reasoning, bigraphs are dotted with an algebraic representation that defines the algebra of bigraphs with different forms of composition giving rise to larger bigraphs. The language of terms is summarized as follows:

- U.V: Nesting (U contains V),
- U|V: Prime product,
- U||V: Parallel product,
- U⊗V: Tensor product (Juxtaposition),
- U∘V: Composition.

While nesting a bigraph within another bigraph is realized via the composition operation "∘", placing them side-by-side is achieved using the juxtaposition operation "⊗" which is a useful way for combining bigraphs.

BRS basic concepts introduced here will be exploited to give a precise semantics to dynamic cloud architecture. Thus, a formal definition of Cloud architecture is defined via a specific bigraph, noted BiCloud-Arch.

B. Cloud Architecture Specification

Cloud architecture is generally composed of two essential parts: the front-end and the back-end; that are usually connected via internet. While Front-end encloses customer's computer and necessary interface to access the cloud, the back-end contains cloud services. In BRS modeling, this corresponds to the specification of two independent bigraphs: one for the front-end customers (Cloud Customers Bigraph) and the other one for the back-end services (Cloud Services Bigraph). Cloud architecture dynamics in terms of interactions between the two bigraphs will be established via reaction rules. We begin by presenting the specification of cloud architecture using bigraphs, which is called BiCloud-Arch.

I. Cloud Services

A cloud service is modeled by a node representing an abstraction of three different service delivery models that collaborate to ensure front-end requests: Infrastructure as a Service (IaaS), Platform as a Service (PaaS) and Software as a Service (SaaS). We propose a formal definition of Cloud Services Bigraph that captures essential concepts of cloud services. The control attached to each node allows us to distinguish among the three service delivery models; while nodes of control IaaS and PaaS are active, nodes of control SaaS are atomic. To offer several access modes to cloud services, we propose that each node (cloud service) will be dotted with three ports: Public, Private, and Community. Then, we spread the formal definition of bigraphs by the notion of port type, defining a new map (tp_{CSB}); the new map (tp_{CSB}) assigns a type $t \in PT_{CSB} = \{PbP, CmP, PrP\}$, to each node port $p \in P_{CSB}$, $tp_{CSB}: P_{CSB} \rightarrow PT_{CSB}$, where:

- $tp_{CSB}(p) = PbP$ if p is Public Port,
- $tp_{CSB}(p) = CmP$ if p is Community Port,
- $tp_{CSB}(p) = PrP$ if p is Private Port.

Definition 5 (Cloud Services Bigraph): A Cloud Services Bigraph takes the form:

$$CSB = (V_{CSB}, E_{CSB}, ctrl_{CSB}, GP_{CSB}, GL_{CSB}, tp_{CSB}):$$
$$<m_{CSB}, X_{CSB}> \rightarrow <n_{CSB}, Y_{CSB}>.$$

where V_{CSB} represents all cloud service nodes, E_{CSB} is a finite set of edges, $ctrl_{CSB}: V_{CSB} \rightarrow S_{CSB}$ is a control map that assigns a control to each cloud service. Controls range over the signature $S_{CSB} = \{IaaS, PaaS, SaaS\}$ with a map ar: $S_{CSB} \rightarrow N$ assigning an arity to each control.

Since each cloud service has three ports, $ar(IaaS)=ar(PaaS)=ar(SaaS)=3$. X_{CSB} is the inner face and Y_{CSB} is the outer face. GP_{CSB} represents its place graph and GL_{CSB} represents a link graph, such that, $link_{CSB}: X_{CSB} \uplus P_{CSB} \rightarrow E_{CSB} \uplus Y_{CSB}$, is a link map, with $P_{CSB} = \{(v,i) \mid i \in ar(ctrl_{CSB}(v))\}$ is the set of ports.

In this definition, we propose a suitable signature for CSB as follows: $S_{CSB} = \{IaaS: (3, active), PaaS: (3, active), SaaS: (3, atomic)\}$.

II. Cloud Customers

A Cloud customer represents any entity that requests a cloud service. Two types of cloud customers are identified: End users (EU) accessing only SaaS, and Independent Software Vendor (ISV) accessing IaaS and PaaS. Thus, we model Cloud customers as nodes equipped with specific controls to be able to distinguish between both types of Cloud customers. We now give a formal definition of the Cloud Customers Bigraph (CCB) which captures all of these concepts.

Definition 6 (Cloud Customers Bigraph): The Cloud Customers Bigraph formalizing customer's model takes the form:

$$CCB = (V_{CCB}, E_{CCB}, ctrl_{CCB}, GP_{CCB}, GL_{CCB}):$$
$$<m_{CCB}, X_{CCB}> \rightarrow <n_{CCB}, Y_{CCB}>.$$

where V_{CCB} represents all cloud customer nodes, E_{CCB} is a finite set of edges, $ctrl_{CCB}: V_{CCB} \rightarrow S_{CCB}$ is a control map that assigns a control to each cloud customer where the signature S_{CCB} is defined by $S_{CCB} = \{EU, ISV\}$. Also the map ar: $S_{CCB} \rightarrow N$ assigns an arity to each control, where $ar(EU)=ar(ISV)=x$ and $x>0$. X_{CCB} is the inner face and Y_{CCB} is the outer face. GP_{CCB} represents its place graph and GL_{CCB} represents the link graph. Therefore, the link map $link_{CCB}: X_{CCB} \uplus P_{CCB} \rightarrow E_{CCB} \uplus Y_{CCB}$, is defined such that the set of ports: $P_{CCB} = \{(v,i) \mid i \in ar(ctrl_{CCB}(v))\}$, i.e., a port is represented as pair consisting of a node (from V) and an index.

The signature of CCB is $S_{CCB} = \{EU: (x, atomic), ISV: (x, atomic)\}$.

III. Service-Customer Interaction

We have defined the structure of both cloud services and customers in separate bigraphs. Their juxtaposition forms the BiCloud-Arch model and represents the interaction between customers and services in terms of service request/response. Formally, the proposed BiCloud-Arch model is defined as follows:

Definition 7 (BiCloud-Arch): A BiCloud-Arch formalizing cloud architecture, takes the form $CSB \otimes CCB: I_{CSB} \otimes I_{CCB} \rightarrow J_{CSB} \otimes J_{CCB}$, where:

```
CSB⊗CCB =<GP_CSB⊗GP_CCB, GL_CSB⊗GL_CCB>,
with:
GP_CSB⊗GP_CCB: m_CSB+m_CCB →n_CSB+n_CCB is de-
fined by
GP_CSB⊗GP_CCB = (V_CSB⊎V_CCB, ctrl_CSB⊎ctrl_CCB,
prnt_CSB⊎ prnt_CCB).
GL_CSB⊗ GL_CCB: X_CSB⊎X_CCB →Y_CSB⊎Y_CCB is de-
fined by
GL_CSB⊗GL_CCB = (V_CSB⊎V_CCB, E_CSB⊎E_CCB,
ctrl_CSB⊎ctrl_CCB, link_CSB⊎ link_CCB).
```

Figure 2. Place/link graph of Bicloud-Arch

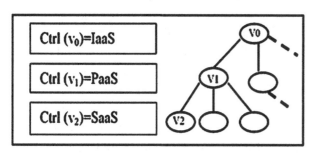 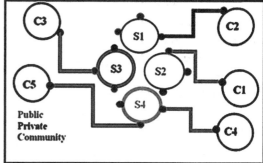

Interconnecting cloud architecture elements is modeled via two distinct relations: hierarchy of cloud services imbrication (IaaS, PaaS and SaaS), and interaction for service request/response. Formally, BiCloud-Arch model offers two types of independent graphs: BiCloud-Arch place graph (GP$_{CSB}$⊗GP$_{CCB}$) and BiCloud-Arch link graph (GL$_{CSB}$⊗GL$_{CCB}$) that will be exploited as follows:

BiCloud-Arch Place Graph

The place graph of BiCloud-Arch formally expresses cloud services and customers location. The hierarchy of cloud services within the place graph (as shown in Figure 2) is modeled with respect to the defined constraints (see definition 8), where a node of control IaaS (infrastructure) can only contain nodes of control PaaS (platform), also, a node of control PaaS can only contain nodes of control SaaS (software), finally, a node of control SaaS does not contain any nodes.

Definition 8 (Hierarchy Constraints for BiCloud-Arch nodes):

- $\forall$ U, N in V$_{CSB}$, (U.N ∧ ctrl$_{CSB}$(U)=IaaS) => ctrl$_{CSB}$(N)=PaaS.
- $\forall$ U, N in V$_{CSB}$, (U.N ∧ctrl$_{CSB}$(U)=PaaS) => ctrl$_{CSB}$(N)=SaaS.
- $\forall$ U in V$_{CSB}$, ctrl$_{CSB}$(U)=SaaS => {v in V$_{CSB}$ | U.N} = ∅.

BiCloud-Arch Link Graph

The Cloud deployment models expressed in terms of interconnections between cloud services and cloud customers are well defined via the link graph of BiCloud-Arch (GL$_{CSB}$ ⊗ GL$_{CCB}$). To identify service deployment model, we define a new function (see definition 9) depm: V$_{CSB}$ → DM, where V$_{CSB}$ represents all cloud services and DM= {Public, Private, Community, Hybrid}. The defined function takes as input a cloud service, and returns the type of the used port as a cloud deployment model. Whenever a cloud service is connected to cloud customers via various ports types, then the cloud service is deployed as a hybrid cloud. The identification of the cloud deployment model consists of exploring the links between customer and service, and according to the type of used port, the cloud deployment model is identified.

Definition 9 (Cloud Deployment Models):

Formally, $\forall$ s $\in$ V$_{CSB}$, Ps={(s,i) | i $\in$ ar(ctrl$_{CSB}$(s))} represents the set of ports of s and $\exists$ pb, pr, cm $\in$ Ps, such that: tp(pb)=PbP, tp(pr)=PrP, and tp(cm)=CmP. $\exists$ e $\in$ E$_{CSB}$, $\exists$ c $\in$ V$_{CCB}$ and Pc={(c,i) | i $\in$ ar(ctrl$_{CCB}$(c))} represents the set of ports of c and p $\in$ Pc. Such that:

- $link_{CSB}(s,\textbf{pb})=e$ and $link_{CSB}(c,p)=e$ → depm(s)= **Public.**
- $link_{CSB}(s,\textbf{pr})=e$ and $link_{CSB}(c,p)=e$ → depm(s)= **Private.**
- $link_{CSB}(s,\textbf{cm})=e$ and $link_{CSB}(c,p)=e$ → depm(s)= **Community.**
- (depm(s) = Public and (depm(s) = Private or depm(s) = Community)) OR
- (depm(s) = Private and (depm(s) = Public or depm(s) = Community)) OR
- (depm(s) = Community and (depm(s) = Private or depm(s) = Public)) → depm(s) = **Hybrid.**

Example

The link graph of Figure 2 represents the various cloud deployment models; it represents possible service interactions in terms of service demand/response relationship between cloud services and customers. It contains five customers: C1, C2, C3, C4, C5 and four cloud services: S1, S2, S3, S4 interconnected as follows:

- Cloud customer (C2) is relied to cloud service (S1) via its community port (CmP). Then (S1) is deployed as a community cloud (green color). So, depm(S1)= Community.
- Cloud customer (C1) is relied to cloud service (S2) via its public port (PbP). Then (S2) is deployed as a public cloud (blue color). So, depm(S2)= Public.
- Cloud customer (C3) is relied to cloud service (S3) via its private port (PrP). Then (S3) is deployed as a private cloud (red color). So, depm(S3)= Private.

- Cloud customers (C4) and (C5) are relied to the cloud service (S4), the first one with a public port (blue color) and the second one with a private port (red color). Then (S4) is deployed as a hybrid cloud (orange color). So, depm(S4)= Hybrid.

We have defined the (BiCloud-Arch) model in terms of its static structure. Two separate bigraphs are identified to represent both cloud services and customers. The juxtaposition of the two given bigraphs defines the cloud architecture model (BiCloud-Arch) focusing on the cloud deployment models.

C. Cloud Architecture Dynamics

Additionally to cloud structural aspects formalization, BRS is expressive enough to be adopted for representing cloud dynamics; in terms of reaction rules that give possible ways in which a cloud system might be reconfigured. Hence, we define two generic reconfiguration rules (BiCloud-Dyn): Service Allocation Reaction Rule (SARR), and Scalability Reaction Rule (SCRR).

I. Service Allocation Reaction Rule

Since service request and liberation are modeled as interconnection/disconnection between a customer port and a service one, reaction rule for service allocation and its dual one or deallocation affect bigraph linkage only. We define service allocation reaction rule (SARR) as follows: [R, R', n] (see Figures 3) where the redex (R) —the left-hand pattern—can match any cloud service (IaaS, PaaS or SaaS) and customer (EU or ISV) controls.

Figure 3. Cloud service allocation/deallocation

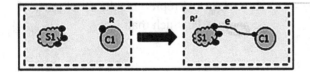

Figure 4. Scaling-up/down reaction rules

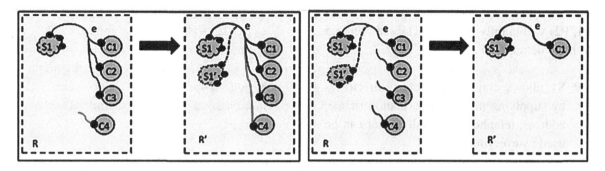

Figure 3 shows a cloud customer (C1) allocating a cloud service (S1), and a cloud customer (C2) liberating a cloud service (S2).

II. Scalability Reaction Rule

The need for cloud services scalability is justified by system surcharge with customer requests rendering system services unavailable. One solution for cloud services unavailability is a scaling-up of the cloud system, by creating new instances of the concerned cloud service (loaded in memory). This instance will be responsible for taking charge of new customer demands (by doubling cloud service initial bandwidth). A garbage collector can be automatically triggered when cloud customers

liberate a cloud service. It models a scaling-down of a cloud system. Thus, we define a meta-rule; representing cloud system scaling up and down respectively (see Figure 4).

To formalize service scalability, we assume here that each cloud service becomes unavailable when it is used by a fixed number (i=3) of cloud customers.

D. Cloud Health Specification

Cloud-Health is a cloud system allowing doctors to exchange information concerning their patients. We present this example in order to illustrate how the BiCloud-Arch model is able to capture and formally represent all cloud system elements.

Figure 5. Cloud-health bigraph

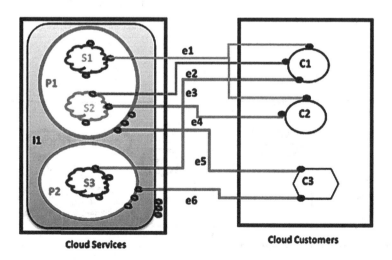

Let us suppose that we have the following cloud services: three SaaS (S1, S2, S3) in two PaaS (P1, P2) within only one IaaS (I1), see Figure 5 for more details.

- S1 allows consulting doctors directories by supplying multiple information (name, address, telephone, specialty), that can be used by everyone.
- S2 allows supplying administrative or medical information of every patient. It can be used by the community of the doctors. Only private access is allowed to patients in order to modify their administrative information.
- S3 allows every doctor to manage his medical office. This service is only used by the concerned doctor.

The cloud-health administrator ensures a smooth running of these three applications by supplying private access to PaaS (P1) and (P2).

According to our formalization approach, the BiCloud-Arch model associated to this example may have the following entities (see Figure 5):

- S1, S2, S3, P1, P2, I1∈V$_{CSB}$, where:
- ctrl$_{CSB}$(S1)= ctrl$_{CSB}$(S2)= ctrl$_{CSB}$(S3)= SaaS,
- ctrl$_{CSB}$(P1)= ctrl$_{CSB}$(P2)= PaaS, and
- ctrl$_{CSB}$(I1)= IaaS.
- C1, C2, C3 ∈V$_{CCB}$, where:
  - o ctrlCCB(C1)= ctrlCCB(C2)= EU

(represents respectively a doctor and a patient), and
  - o ctrlCCB(C3)= ISV (represents the administrator).
- e1, e2, e3, e4, e5, e6 ∈ E, with each edge representing a connection between cloud customers and cloud services.

The place graph, specifying the hierarchy of Cloud-Health entities, and the link graph, specifying its interconnection are represented in Figure 6.

Obviously, the proposed function depm(-) that specifies the deployment model of a given cloud service, returns for our case the following values:

- depm(S1)=Public (edge e1 in Figure 6),
- depm(S2)=Hybrid (edge e2 and e4 in Figure 6),
- depm(S3)=Private (edge e3 in Figure 6),
- depm(P1)=Private (edge e5 in Figure 6), and
- depm(P2)=Private (edge e6 in Figure 6).

5. EXECUTABLE SPECIFICATION FOR BICLOUD-ARCH MODELS

A set of tools is proposed for BRS edition, execution and verification. However, during their exploration, we have been confronted with several limitations;

Figure 6. Cloud-health place/link graph

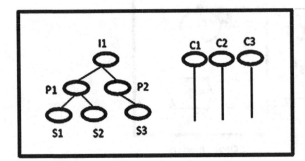
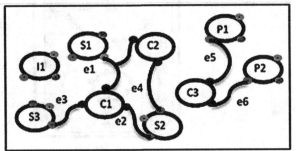

- BPL Tool in the work of Glenstrup et al. (2008), is the first implementation of bigraphical reactive systems with binding. It allows manipulation, simulation and visualization of bigraphs and bigraphical reactive systems. The proposed tool can be used either through the included web and command line user interfaces or as a programming library. However, it presents limits during its manipulation, because it does not allow expressing all bigraph concepts.
- Bigredit in the work of Faithfull et al. (2013), acronym for "bigraph editor". The tool uses the Eclipse Graphical Editing Framework, and permits creating bigraph diagrams and defining reaction rules. But, it remains restrictive and does not correspond to our expectations.
- BigMC in the work of Perrone, et al. (2012), is a model-checker designed to operate on Bigraphical Reactive Systems (BRS). Although it is the unique tool for model checking bigraphs, it remains very limited in the specification of properties to be verified.

Based on this observation, an appropriate specification language is needed to execute BiCloud-Arch specifications formally. We choose Maude, a language and system based on rewriting logic (Manuel, et al., 2007); that offers the possibility of executing and formally verifying specifications, as a foundation for implementing the Executable Specification of BiCloud-Arch.

In this section, we present a high-level overview of Maude's main concepts. Then, we define a mapping of BiCloud-Arch concepts into Maude language. The resulting executable model is called BiCloud-2M.

A. Maude Language

Maude is a high-performance reflective language based on rewriting logic that allows expression of concurrent and nondeterministic computation. Rewriting logic is a universal logic, in which we can consistently represent and simulate other theories. It represents the static aspect of systems by equational theories, and the dynamic by rewriting theories describing the possible transitions between states of concurrent systems (Manuel et al., 2007).

Maude is a declarative language, simultaneously emphasizing three dimensions:

- **Simplicity:** Programs in Maude are implemented as simply as possible and have clear meaning.
- **Expressiveness:** In Maude language not only applications, but entire formalisms, other languages, and other logics can be naturally expressed.
- **Performance:** Maude implementation yields system performance competitive with other efficient programming languages.

Maude system includes two main components Core-Maude and Full-Maude. Core-Maude component implements a rewriting engine and provides the basic constructs of Maude language. The Full-Maude component is itself a meta-level implementation written in Core-Maude to extend it with object-oriented concepts. In what follows, we describe the basic syntactic constructs (introduced in the work of Manuel, et al. (2007) and McCombs, (2003)) of Core-Maude that is used to define the BiCloud-2M specification.

I. Modules

A module is the basic unit of specification and programming in Maude. It provides a collection of sorts and a collection of operations on these sorts, as well as the necessary information to reduce and rewrite expressions that the user inputs into the Maude environment.

There are two types of modules in Core-Maude: the functional module (fmod) and the system module (mod).

```
fmod NAME is ... endfm
mod NAME is ... endm
```

II. Sorts and Variables

A sort is a category for values that describes any type of them, including lists and stacks of other values. It is declared within the module, with the key word sort and a period at the end. There are also sub-sorts, which are further specific groups all belonging to the same sort.

```
sort Fraction.
sorts Fraction Rational.
subsort Fraction < Rational.
```

A variable is constrained to range over a particular sort or kind. It is declared with the key words var or vars.

```
var x: number.
vars c1 c2 c3: color.
```

III. Operations

In a Maude module, an operator is declared with the keyword op followed by its name. An operation declaration specifies its domain and co-domain of values and optionally attributes declaration specifying its properties as associativity, commutatively.

```
op zero: -> Zero.
op s_: Nat -> NzNat.
op sd: Nat Nat -> Nat.
```

IV. Equations

Equations are used to define the semantics of operations. They are declared using the keyword eq.

$$eq\ 0 + N = N .$$

$$eq\ s(M) + N = s(M + N) .$$

V. Rewrite Laws

Rewriting logic consists of two key ideas: states and transitions. States are situations that, alone, are static, and transitions are the transformations that map one state to another. A rewrite law (rewrite rule) declares the relationship between states and transitions between them. We declare a rewrite law with the key word rl.

```
rl [raincloud]: sunnyday => rainyday.
```

B. BiCloud-2M Specification

Based on a judicious coupling between BRS theory as a semantic framework and Maude language as an executable specification language, we propose the BiCloud Executable Specification (BiCloud-2M) that combines logical reflection and hierarchical structuring of the underlying adopted theoretical framework. The following table summarizes the correspondence between Cloud computing; formalized with Bigraphical reactive systems, and their equivalent in Maude language.

BiCloud-2M is implemented in Maude as system modules. Figure 7 gives a basic overview of the defined modules and their sub-module dependencies;

Table 1. Correspondence table cloud/Bigraph/Maude concepts

Cloud Computing	Bigraphical Reactive Systems (BiCloud-Arch)	Maude Language (BiCloud-2M)
Service and Customer	Nodes	Operators
Service models and Customers types	Controls	Sorts
Structure (State)	Bigraph	Sort
Dynamics	Reaction rules (BiCloud-Dyn)	Rewrite rules

I. Bigraph Module

The *Bigraph* module includes sort and operator declarations for Bigraphs theory;

```
mod Bigraph is
protecting QID. protecting NAT.
sorts Bigraph Node Edge Port Control.
subsorts Node < Bigraph . subsorts
Edge < Port.
op null:-> Bigraph [ctor].
op _|_:-> Bigraph Bigraph [ctor comm
assoc id: null] ….
endm
```

Each basic concept of a bigraph is specified through the declaration of different sorts (node, edge, port, bigraph, control). Where a Node is sub-sort of Bigraph, and an Edge is sub-sort of Port. Thus, the Prime product operator (_|_) allows the juxtaposition of nodes or bigraphs, since it takes as arguments two bigraphs (nodes being a sub-sort of bigraph).

II. BiCloud-Arch Module

The syntax and semantics of cloud architecture elements are defined in the *BiCloud-Arch* module;

- The Service operator allows specifying a cloud service.

```
sort Vs.
subsorts Vs< Node,
op service<_;_;_>[_].{ _ }: Qid Ss S_
State Port Bigraph -> Vs [ctor].
```

- It takes as arguments:
  - A Quoted Identifier to specify its name;
  - A Control (Ss) specifying its service delivery model;
  - An Attribute specifying a service state (available, unavailable, and cloned);
  - A set of Edges connected to its three ports;

Figure 7. Overview of BMMC modules

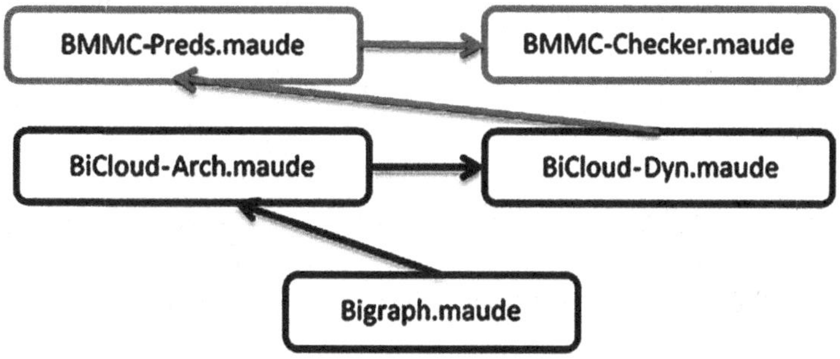

○ A set of nodes that may be included in it.
- The Customer operator allows specifying a cloud customer.

```
sort Vc.
subsorts Vc< Node.
op customer<_;_;_;_>[_]: Qid Sc Qid
Port Edge -> Vc [ctor].
```

- It takes as arguments:
  ○ A Quoted Identifier to specify its name;
  ○ A Control (Sc) specifying its customer type;
  ○ A Quoted Identifier to specify the requested service;
  ○ A Port specifying on which the requested service will be delivered;
  ○ An Edge connected to its port.
- Service models and Customer types are specified as a specific Sort in *BiCloud-Arch* module;

```
sorts Ss Sc.
subsorts Ss < Control. subsorts Sc<
Control.
op IaaS: -> Ss [ctor].
op PaaS: -> Ss [ctor].
op SaaS: -> Ss [ctor].
op EU: -> Sc [ctor].
op ISV: -> Sc [ctor].
```

Cloud services and customers signature is represented by the sorts Ss and Sc, both are sub-sorts of the sort Control (defined in *Bigraph* module).

III. BiCloud-Dyn Module

Cloud system dynamics has been formalized with *BiCloud-Dyn* module, containing a set of rewrite rules corresponding to *BiCloud-Dyn* reaction rules. Several rewrite rules are defined in terms of service delivery and deployment models; we present here only the meta-rules.

In the following, we assume that the term [Req] in customer operator characterizes a service requester, while the term [Lib] represents a customer who liberates a requested service.

- **Rewrite Rule for Service Allocation:**

```
rl [Service-allocation]:
service< i ; cs:Ss; available >[
e1, e2, e3 ].{ b2 } | customer< i1
; cc1:Sc ; i ; PbP >[ Req ] | b1 =>
service< i ; IaaS; available >[ e1,
e2, e3 ].{ b2 } | customer< i1 ;
cc1:Sc ; i ; PbP >[ e1 ] | b1 .
```

It shows a cloud customer (i1) requesting a cloud service (i) that is available. In this case the rewriting engine will directly allocate the cloud service to the customer; by affecting the term (e1) to customer edge space.

- **Rewrite Rule for Service Liberation:**

```
rl [Service-liberation]:
customer< i1 ; cc:Sc ; i ; p:Port
>[ edge na ] | b1 => customer< i1 ;
cc:Sc; i ; p:Port >[ Lib ] | b1 .
```

It expresses a cloud customer (i1) liberating a cloud service (i) by affecting the term (Lib) to its edge space.

- **Rewrite Rule for Scaling-Up:**

```
rl [Scaling-up]:
service< i ; cs:Ss; available >[ e1,
e2, e3 ].{ b2 } |
customer< i1 ; cc1:Sc ; i ; p1:Port
>[ edge n1 ] | customer< i2 ; cc2:Sc
; i ; p2:Port >[ edge n2 ] | cus-
```

```
tomer< i3 ; cc3:Sc ; i ; p3:Port >[
edge n3 ] | customer< i4 ; cc4:Sc ; i
; PbP >[ Req ] | b1 => service< i ;
cs:Ss; unavailable >[ e1, e2, e3 ].{
b2 } | service< i ; cs:Ss; cloned >[
e1, e2, e3 ].{ null } | customer< i1
; cc1:Sc ; i ; p1:Port >[ edge n1 ] |
customer< i2 ; cc2:Sc ; i ; p2:Port
>[ edge n2 ] | customer< i3 ; cc3:Sc
; i ; p3:Port >[ edge n3 ] | cus-
tomer< i4 ; cc4:Sc ; i ; PbP >[ e1 ]
| b1 .
```

The scaling up is achieved by creating a new instance of an unavailable cloud service. A cloud service becomes unavailable when it is used by a fixed number (i=3) of cloud customers.

- **Rewrite Rule for Scaling-Down:**

```
rl [Scaling-down]:
service< i ; cs:Ss; unavailable >[
e1, e2, e3 ].{ b2 } | service< i ;
cs:Ss; cloned >[ e1, e2, e3 ].{ null
} |
customer< i1 ; cc1:Sc ; i ; p1:Port
>[ Lib ] | customer< i2 ; cc2:Sc ; i
; p2:Port >[ Lib ] |
customer< i3 ; cc3:Sc ; i ; p3:Port
>[ Lib ] | b1 =>
 service< i ; cs:Ss ; available >[
e1, e2, e3 ].{ b2 } | b1 .
```

The scaling down is achieved when three cloud customers liberate a cloud service. In this case the rewrite engine changes service state to available and destroys its cloned instance.

C. Running Example

In order to illustrate the defined BiCloud-2M specification, let us go back to our health system example and consider the following scenario; a doctor must consult medical information of his patients at each appointment, to browse their state history and consult the performed treatments. In our case study, the SaaS (S2) allows doctors to consult medical information of every patient. Whenever this service (S2) becomes unavailable due to the high number of doctor's requests, a possible reconfiguration of the specified cloud system can be applied in order to take in new doctor's request using the Scaling up rewrite rule.

We consider the service (S2) of control SaaS being started in the cloud and four customers (doctor's) (C1, C2, C3 and C4) of control EU requesting it via its community port. The BiCloud-2M state defining this example is:

```
service< `S2 ; SaaS ; available>[
edge 1, edge 2, edge 3 ].{ null } |
customer< `c1 ; EU ; `S2 ; CmP >[ Req
] | customer< `c2 ; EU ; `S2 ; CmP >[
Req ] |
customer< `c3 ; EU ; `S2 ; CmP >[ Req
] | customer< `c4 ; EU ; `S2 ; CmP >[
Req ].
```

Initially, each customer is a service requester. So, it is given the term [Req] instead of the edge space. We specify the behavior of this specification via the execution of the following command:

rewrite in BiCloud-2M: service< `S2
; SaaS ; available>[edge 1, edge 2,
edge 3].{ null } |
customer< `c1 ; EU ; `S2 ; CmP >[Req
] | customer< `c2 ; EU ; `S2 ; CmP >[
Req] |
customer< `c3 ; EU ; `S2 ; CmP >[Req
] | customer< `c4 ; EU ; `S2 ; CmP >[
Req].

In this case, the system applies service allocation rule up to the fourth customer. Once, the service becomes unavailable due to its saturation (i=3), the system automatically (by running the scaling-up rule) adds an instance (cloned) of this service (S2) to respond to new customers demands (including that of customer C4). The result will be:

```
rewrites: 5 in 1628036047000ms cpu
(0ms real) (0 rewrites/second) result
Bigraph:
service< `S2 ; SaaS ; unavailable>[
edge 1, edge 2, edge 3 ].{ null } |
service< `S2 ; SaaS ; cloned>[ edge
1, edge 2, edge 3 ].{ null } |
customer< `c1 ; EU ; `S2 ; CmP >[
edge 2  ] | customer< `c2 ; EU ; `S2
; CmP >[ edge 2  ] |
customer< `c3 ; EU ; `S2 ; CmP >[
edge 2  ] | customer< `c4 ; EU ; `S2
; CmP >[ edge 2  ]
```

The fact that the proposed Maude-based specification (BiCloud-2M) is executable gives rise a flexible model of cloud system constituting a prototype for the verification phase.

6. MODEL CHECKING BICLOUD-2M SPECIFICATION

The term model checking was coined by Clarke and Emerson (1986) in the early eighties. Model checking is a verification technique that examines all possible system scenarios in a systematic manner. It explores the largest possible state spaces to show that a given system model truly satisfies a certain property. A technical definition of model checking is as follows:

Model checking is an automated technique that, given a finite-state model of a system and a formal property, systematically checks whether this property holds for (a given state in) that model (Baier, et al., 2008).

On this basis, two specification levels are identified:

- **System Specification Level:** We consider the proposed cloud system specification describing its dynamic aspects (see section 4). Then we map it to Maude; a system based on rewriting logic that offers the possibility of executing and formally verifying the proposed specification (see section 5).
- **Property Specification Level:** In terms of mathematical logic, properties should be described in a precise and unambiguous manner to state and prove our system specification. This is typically done using a property specification language. In particular, we use a linear temporal logic (LTL) as a property specification language to specify relevant properties of a cloud system.

Thus, in this section, we propose a BiCloud Maude-Based Model Checker (BMMC) in which the proposed BiCloud-2M specification can be easily verified (step 3 in Figure 1). We exploit it to check that our proposed model satisfies two important properties; one concerns service availability and the other concerns quick scalability.

A. BiCloud Maude-Based Model Checker Principal

The use of rewriting logic via its Maude language, offers an executable and analyzable specification that takes advantage of tools developed around Maude environment. We implement the BiCloud Maude-based Model checker using the model-checker for linear temporal properties of Eker et al. (2002).

We define two additional system modules (see Figure 7):

- **The BMMC-Preds Module:** Represents the system property specification expressed in linear temporal logic. We note that relevant state predicates are typically part of the property specification. So, we propose two state predicates to identify whether a service is cloned or a customer is a service requester. These predicates can be parameterized with service and customer operators; their semantics is defined as follows:

```
...
subsort Bigraph < State.
op requester: -> Prop . op cloned: ->
Prop.
eq customer< i1:Qid ; c:Sc ; i2:Qid
; p:Port >[ Req ] | b |= requester =
true.
eq service< i1:Qid ; c:Ss ; cloned
>[e1, e2, e3].{ b1 } | b |= cloned =
true.
...
```

- **The BMMC-Checker Module:** Checks LTL formula using a given initial state. For our example, an initial state may be specified by the following configuration system: a service (s2) of control SaaS allowing doctors to consult medical information of every patient and four doctor's (C1, C2, C3 and C4) of control EU requesting it via its community port.

```
...
op initial1: -> Bigraph.
eq initial1 = service< 'S2 ; SaaS ;
available>[ edge 1, edge 2, edge 3
].{ null } |
customer< 'c1 ; EU ; 'S2 ; CmP >[ Req
] | customer< 'c2 ; EU ; 'S2 ; CmP >[
Req ] |
customer< 'c3 ; EU ; 'S2 ; CmP >[ Req
] | customer< 'c4 ; EU ; 'S2 ; CmP >[
Req ].
...
```

B. Properties Specification

The BMMC Maude-based implementation can be used to check that our formal model satisfies some important properties, or obtain a useful counter-example showing that the property in question is violated. We deal here with significant properties such as service availability and quick scalability (which are very important compared to the presented case study).

I. Cloud Service Availability Property

Cloud service availability is fulfilled if system model (in its canonical final states) does not contain an unsatisfied customer request. It is formally specified with the following LTL formula:

```
...
O [] not (requester).
...
```

II. Quick Scalability Property

Quick scalability of cloud services is verified if all terminal states, in which no further rewrites are possible, contain at least one instance of a cloned cloud service. The corresponding LTL formula is defined:

```
...
O [] (cloned).
...
```

Figure 8 shows model checking results of service availability and quick scalability properties. We conclude that the proposed model verifies the desired properties.

We highlight here that this set of properties may be extended by other ones. Besides, we note that a practical tool implementing this analysis type of cloud systems has been developed.

Figure 8. Verification results

```
\IIIIIIIIIIIIIIIIIII/
--- Welcome to Maude ---
/IIIIIIIIIIIIIIIIIII\
Maude 2.6 built: Mar 31 2011 23:36:02
Copyright 1997-2010 SRI International
Sun Dec  8 15:05:38 2013

Maude>
Maude>
Maude>
Maude>

Maude> reduce in BMMC_CHECK : modelCheck(initial1, O [] ~requester) .
rewrites: 11 in 14099565028ms cpu (1ms real) (0 rewrites/second)
result Bool: true

Maude> reduce in BMMC_CHECK : modelCheck(initial1, O [] cloned) .
rewrites: 10 in 14099565028ms cpu (1ms real) (0 rewrites/second)
result Bool: true
```

7. DISCUSSION

Much as service-oriented architecture (SOA), cloud architecture must be defined, governed, and managed independently, (Marks et al., 2010).

As cloud computing has emerged from the industry, the hard work of formalization is still needed. Existing work falls into two main categories. The first category classifies studies according to their formalization interest. As already mentioned in the related work section, the aforementioned work is limited and focused solely on enhancing the financial and technological aspects of cloud computing;

- Financial (or business) aspects as in the work of Chang et al. (2010), Chang et al. (2014), Tan, C. et al. (2013) and Nattakarn P. et al. (2013),
- Technological aspects; for virtualization as in the work of Y. Jarraya et al. (2012), Dong, et al. (2010) and Grandison, et al. (2010), for security as in the work of Dijiang, H. et al. (2010), Imad M. Abbadi (2013) and Freitas & Paul (2012), or for

enterprise IT as in the work of Ricardo J. et al. (2013) and T. Chandrakumar and S. Parthasarathy (2014), etc.

Consequently, cloud computing lacks a theoretical framework that associates a clear semantics to its basic concepts: service delivery and deployment models.

The second category of studies concerns cloud computing formalization; Petri Nets in the work of Fitch et al. (2012) and Fang et al. (2013), Semantic Technology in the work of Hu et al. (2009), MDA in the work of Howard et al. (2010), Agent-based in the work of Sim, et al. (2012), or Component Model in the work of Cosmo, et al. (2012). They do not deal with all cloud architectural important concepts, such as services elasticity.

Within this perspective, we have proposed a semantic framework to specify and verify cloud systems. Differences with the aforementioned frameworks include the adopted approach, the main focus, and the inclusiveness of the solution;

- **Adopted Approach:** Bigraphical Reactive Systems are adopted as a semantic framework for their main characteristics of locality and connectivity (very useful when specifying cloud systems), which are absent in most formal models. To the best of our knowledge, our approach (Benzadri et al., 2013) was the first attempt to provide a formal definition of Cloud Computing using BRS theory.

- **Main Focus:** Cloud computing lacks a theoretical framework for its basic concepts: service delivery and deployment models. The proposed framework is able to support major cloud computing concepts specification and allow formal analysis of high level services provided over the cloud computing architecture.

- **Inclusiveness of the Solution:** The proposed framework and its integration in Maude are able to support the specification of major cloud architecture concepts and allow formal analysis of high level services provided over the cloud. Maude language is used to complete BRS formalism by implementing the obtained cloud bigraphical model. It allows us to execute and analyze the formal specification of cloud computing architecture and its dynamics.

8. CONCLUSION

In this chapter, we have proposed a formal framework where cloud computing architecture may be specified and analyzed. Therefore, we have adopted Bigraphical Reactive Systems (BRS) as a semantic model for dynamic cloud architecture specification. BRS seem adequate for two reasons. On the one hand, the model emphasizes both locality and connectivity that can be used to specify location and interconnection of cloud architecture entities. On the other hand, a set of reaction rules, providing to bigraphs the ability to reconfigure themselves, are very useful to formalize cloud architecture dynamics, especially cloud services elasticity. Two different bigraphs have been associated to both cloud services and customers by enriching them with new sorts of nodes and ports. Their juxtaposition (Cloud Services Bigraph and Cloud Customers Bigraph) gives rise to the suited BiCloud-Arch. We have particularly shown how the proposed BiCloud-Arch model provides a flexible theoretical framework where cloud service delivery and deployment models can be naturally defined. A nice consequence of this axiomatization is that the proposed Maude-based executable specifications (BiCloud-2M) have been exploited to formally verify some cloud systems inherent properties. This would not have been possible without the proposal of the BiCloud Maude-based Model Checker (BMMC).

In our ongoing work, we plan to exploit meta-modeling and model transformation tools to conceive a graphical interface and a BiCloud-2M specification generator in order to facilitate the exploitation of our proposed approach, thereby permitting graphical editing and automatic generation of the corresponding specifications.

REFERENCES

Abbadi, I. M. (2013). A framework for establishing trust in cloud provenance. *International Journal of Information Security*, *12*(2), 111–128. doi:10.1007/s10207-012-0179-0

Armbrust, M., Fox, A., Griffith, R., Joseph, A. D., Katz, R. H., Konwinski, A., . . . Zaharia, M. (2009). Above the clouds: A Berkeley view of cloud computing. Technical Report UCB/EECS-2009-28. EECS Department, University of California. Berkeley

Baier, C., & Katoen, J. P. (2008). *Principles of model checking* (p. 994). MIT Press.

Benzadri, Z., Belala, F., & Bouanaka, C. (2013). Towards a formal model for cloud computing. In *Proceedings of the International Conference on Service Oriented Computing Workshops* (p. 381-393).

Benzadri, Z., Bouanaka, C., & Belala, F. (2014). *Verifying cloud systems using a bigraphical maude-based model checker.* Paper presented at the 4th International Conference on Cloud Computing and Services Science (ESaaSA 2014).

Chandrakumar, T., & Parthasarathy, S. (2014). A framework for evaluating cloud enterprise resource planning (ERP). In Continued rise of the cloud: Advances and trends in cloud computing (pp. 161–175). doi:10.1007/978-1-4471-6452-4_7

Chang, V. (2014 a). An introductory approach to risk visualization as a service. *Open Journal of Cloud Computing, 1*(1), 1–9.

Chang, V. (2014 b). The business intelligence as a service in the cloud. *Future Generation Computer Systems, 37*, 512–534. doi:10.1016/j.future.2013.12.028

Chang, V., Walters, R. J. and Wills, G. (2014). The development that leads to the cloud computing business framework. *International Journal of Information Management, 33*(3), 524-538. ()10.1016/j.ijinfomgt.2013.01.005

Chang, V., Wills, G., & De Roure, D. (2010). *Towards financial cloud framework: Modelling and benchmarking of financial assets in public and private clouds.* Paper presented at IEEE Cloud 2010, the third International Conference on Cloud Computing, 5-10 July, Miami, Florida, USA.

Clarke, E. M., Emerson, E. A., & Sistla, A. P. (1986). Automatic verification of finite-state concurrent systems using temporal logic specifications. *ACM Transactions on Programming Languages and Systems, 8*(2), 244–263. doi:10.1145/5397.5399

Clavel, M., Durán, F., Eker, S., Lincoln, P., Martí-Oliet, N., Meseguer, J., & Talcott, C. (2007). All about Maude - a high-performance logical framework: How to specify. Berlin, Heidelberg: Springer.

Cosmo, R., Zacchiroli, S., & Zavattaro, G. (2012). Towards a formal component model for the cloud. In G. Eleftherakis, M. Hinchey, & M. Holcombe (Eds.), Software engineering and formal methods (p.156-171). Berlin Heidelberg: Springer.

Common Criteria, (2012). Common criteria for information technology security evaluation. CCMB-2012-09-003.

Dong, H., Hao, Q., Zhang, T., & Zhang, B. (2010). Formal discussion on relationship between virtualization and cloud computing. In *Proceedings of the 2010 International Conference on Parallel and Distributed Computing, Applications and Technologies (PDCAT)* (pp. 448–453). doi:10.1109/PDCAT.2010.41

Eker, S., Meseguer, J., & Sridharanarayanan, A. (2002). The Maude LTL model checker. In *Proceedings of the 4th International Workshop on Rewriting Logic and its Applications (WRLA 2002). (Vol. 71, pp. 115-142)*. Elsevier.

Faithfull, A. J., Perrone, G. D., & Hildebrandt, T. (2013). *Big red: A development environment for bigraphs.* EASST Electronic Communications.

Fang, X., Wang, M., & Wu, S. (2013). A method for security evaluation in cloud computing based on petri behavioral profiles. In Z. Yin, L. Pan, & X. Fang (Eds.), *Proceedings of The Eighth International Conference on Bio-Inspired Computing: Theories and Applications (BIC-TA) (pp. 587-593)*. Berlin Heidelberg: Springer.

Feng, W., Jiang, Z., Maoxiang, C., & Shoulin, S. (2012). An ontology cloud-shadow model based knowledge service framework. In *Proceedings of the 2012 International Conference on Communication, Electronics and Automation Engineering.*

Fitch, D. F., & Xu, H. (2012). A Petri net model for secure and fault-tolerant cloud-based information storage. In *SEKE* (pp. 333–339). Knowledge Systems Institute Graduate School.

Freitas, L., & Watson, P. (2012). Formalizing workflows partitioning over federated clouds: Multi-level security and costs. In *Proceedings of the IEEE Eighth World Congress on Services (SERVICES)* (pp. 219–226).

Foster, H., & Spanoudakis, G. (2010). Formal methods in model-driven development for ser-vice- oriented and cloud computing. Retrieved from http://citeseerx.ist.psu.edu/viewdoc/downl oad?doi=10.1.1.232.8422&rep=rep1&type=pdf

Glenstrup, A.J., Damgaard, T.C., Birkedal, L., and Højsgaard, E. (2008). An implementation of bigraph matching. Retrieved from http://cs.au.dk/~birke/papers/implmatch.pdf

Grandison, T., Maximilien, E., Thorpe, S., & Alba, A. (2010). Towards a formal definition of a comput-ing cloud. In *Proceedings of the 6th World Congress on Services (SERVICES-1), 2010* (pp. 191–192).

Hu, L., Ying, S., Jia, X., & Zhao, K. (2009). To-wards an approach of semantic access control for cloud computing. In M. Jaatun, G. Zhao, & C. Rong (Eds.), *Lecture notes in computer science* (Vol. 5931, pp. 145–156). Berlin Heidelberg: Springer.

Huang, D., Zhang, X., Kang, M., & Luo, J. (2010). MobiCloud: Building secure cloud framework for mobile computing and communication. In *Proceedings of the Fifth IEEE International Sym-posium on Service Oriented System Engineering (SOSE)*, *27*(34), 4-5. doi:10.1109/SOSE.2010.20

Jarraya, Y., Eghtesadi, A., Debbabi, M., Zhang, Y., & Pourzandi, M. (2012). Cloud calculus: Security verification in elastic cloud computing platform. In *Proceedings of the International Symposium on Security in Collaboration Technologies and Sys-tems (SECOTS 2012)* (pp. 447-454). IEEE Press.

Luo, S. X., Liu, F. M., & Ren, C. L. (2011). A hierarchy attribute-based access control model for cloud storage. In *Proceedings of the International Conference on Machine Learning and Cybernetics (ICMLC)* (Vol. 3, pp. 1146–1150). doi:10.1109/ICMLC.2011.6016897

Marks, E., & Lozano, B. (2010). *Executive's guide to cloud computing*. Wiley Publishing.

McCombs, T. (2003). Maude 2.0 Primer. Re-trieved from http://maude.cs.uiuc.edu/primer/maude-primer.pdf

Mell, P., & Grance, T. (2011). The NIST definition of cloud computing. Technical Report 800-145, National Institute of Standards and Technology (NIST), Gaithersburg, MD

Milner, R. (2009) *The space and motion of com municating agents*. Cambridge University Press. doi:10.1017/CBO9780511626661

Nattakarn, P., Xiaofeng, W., & Pekka, A. (2013). Towards a conceptual framework for assessing the benefits of cloud computing. In *Proceedings of the 4th International Conference, ICSOB 2013*. Potsdam, Germany.

Perrone, G., Debois, S., & Hildebrandt, T. T. (2012). A model checker for bigraphs. In S. Os-sowski & P. Lecca (Eds.), *SAC, ACM 1320–1325*. doi:10.1145/2245276.2231985

Ricardo J., Adina C., Carlos C, Moisés D., Parisa G. (2013) Ontology enriched framework for cloud-based enterprise interoperability. *Concurrent engineering approaches for sustainable product development in a multi-disciplinary environment*. Springer.

Sim, K. M. (2012). Agent-based cloud comput-ing. *IEEE Transactions on* Services Computing, *5*, 564–577.

Tan, C. et al.. (2013). An evaluation framework for migrating application to the cloud: Software as a service. In *Proceedings of 2nd International Conference on Logistics, Informatics and Service Science* (pp 967-972). doi:10.1007/978-3-642-32054-5_135

KEY TERMS AND DEFINITIONS

BiCloud Maude-Based Model Checker: (BMMC): A bigraphical maude-based model checker in which the proposed BiCloud-2M specification can be easily verified.

BiCloud-2M: An executable model, representing the mapping of "BiCloud-Arch" into Maude language.

BiCloud-Arch: A proposed bigraph-based model, formalizing cloud architecture via the juxtaposition of two specific bigraphs (CSB and CCB). It represents the interaction between customers and services in terms of service request/ response.

BiCloud-Dyn: A set of generic reaction rules that gives possible ways in which a cloud system might be reconfigured.

Cloud Customers Bigraph (CCB): A specific bigraph-based model that formalizes cloud customer types: End users (EU) accessing only SaaS, and Independent Software Vendor (ISV) accessing IaaS and PaaS.

Cloud Services Bigraph (CSB): A specific bigraph-based model that captures essential concepts of cloud services. It represents an abstraction of service delivery models: Infrastructure as a Service (IaaS), Platform as a Service (PaaS) and Software as a Service (SaaS).

Cloud-Health: A proposed case study of a cloud system, that allows doctors to exchange information concerning their patients. It is presented in order to illustrate how the BiCloud-Arch model is able to capture and formally represent all cloud system elements.

Scalability Reaction Rule (SCRR): A reaction rule for cloud system scaling up and down.

Service Allocation Reaction Rule (SARR): A reaction rule for service allocation and its dual one or deallocation. It affects bigraph linkage only.

Chapter 11

Building Clouds:
An Integrative Approach for an Automated Deployment of Elastic Cloud Services

Leonard Heilig
University of Hamburg, Germany

Stefan Voß
University of Hamburg, Germany

Lars Wulfken
Amazon Web Services, Germany

ABSTRACT

The highly automated and scalable nature of cloud computing encourages practitioners and scholars to reconsider software delivery processes. To efficiently leverage the benefits of elastic clouds, applications are typically provisioned and deployed several times a day in different environments and regions. Related procedures must support agile development and deployment of software components as well as the associated management of different versions and configurations. To efficiently utilize auto-scaling mechanisms, the latency produced by provisioning and deployment activities needs to be reduced while ensuring consistency, repeatability and reliability. In this chapter, an integrative process-oriented approach to improve the overall quality and performance of deployment processes is presented. Based on a comprehensive analysis of requirements, the proposed process considers the link between deployment and configuration management as well as tools and organizational aspects. Further, related research challenges and a case study focusing on the Adobe Shared Cloud are presented.

1. INTRODUCTION

Cloud computing fundamentally transforms the way software applications and hardware systems are designed, delivered and consumed (Marston et al., 2011). Several economic and technical potentials are associated with adopting cloud computing, but most important are a high degree of automation, the option to dynamically scale applications according to unexpected or anticipated demand, and usage-based pricing models without involving monetary investments. In this regard, Chang et al.

DOI: 10.4018/978-1-4666-8210-8.ch011

Copyright © 2015, IGI Global. Copying or distributing in print or electronic forms without written permission of IGI Global is prohibited.

(2014) describe characteristics of cloud computing and provide an extensive overview on cloud adoption frameworks. Especially software companies can benefit from the high flexibility and cost-effectiveness of cloud computing. Typically, software delivery involves several complex activities being carried out in several environments, before software components become finally available to customers. Within these deployment processes, the quality of software components needs to be extensively validated in order to comply with functional and non-functional quality of service (QoS) requirements as well as to avoid outages once software components are delivered to customers. In particular agile development teams require efficient deployment processes allowing an autonomous and continuous integration of components within short development cycles. During operations, the performance and quality of software components must be ensured under volatile demands and conditions. In contrast to traditional computing infrastructures, the high elasticity of cloud infrastructure allows cloud application providers to adapt their services according to certain conditions, for example, by automatically adding or removing underlying computing resources. Economically, the latter implies that unnecessary expenses for unused or underused infrastructure can be reduced (Rodero-Merino et al., 2010). Auto-scaling mechanisms, however, require that involved software components are deployed within a very short time span. As provisioning and deployment activities normally take, if automated, several minutes to complete, novel mechanisms are required to significantly reduce deployment time. Consequently, a high degree of deployment automation is essential for ensuring the performance and quality of software components throughout their entire lifecycle from development to phase out. More specifically, automated deployment is essential to realize continuous integration and a cost-efficient and QoS-compliant scaling behavior. To leverage the high degree of automation in cloud environments, however, cloud application

providers must establish standardized deployment processes by considering best practices, tools and organizational aspects.

In general, the overall complexity and heterogeneity of cloud infrastructure and deployed application services is growing (Breitenbücher et al., 2013). A prerequisite for efficiently managing complex software systems and enabling automated deployment is the adoption of configuration management practices. In this regard, it is important to analyze specific requirements of cloud-based software components in order to efficiently deliver and manage multiple versions of those components in different cloud environments (e.g., testing, staging, production) and multiple regions (e.g., EU, US, etc.) while ensuring consistency, a high service level and business continuity. For example, provisioning activities to build underlying infrastructure resources need to be adapted to the deployment of software components. These provisioning activities can be standardized and automated by using dedicated interfaces of the cloud infrastructure provider. A high degree of standardization facilitates that processes are repeatable, testable, auditable and accurate (Karunakaran, 2013). Furthermore, auto-scaling mechanisms must be integrated to trigger deployment processes for scaling software systems to changing conditions. To fully utilize cloud capabilities both in development stages and during operations, it becomes increasingly important to establish a standardized end-to-end process model connecting all these different activities by simultaneously considering cloud-specific requirements, tool support and organizational aspects.

Although configuration management is an inherent part of most development and deployment activities in most software organizations, a lack of integrative cloud-based end-to-end approaches can be identified both in practice and academia. An integrative approach is essential for improving the overall quality and performance of software delivery and operations of elastic software components in cloud-based environments. To fully understand the requirements of modern deployment processes, this chapter describes requirements on automated cloud-based deployment processes, which are identified in a practical context. This includes requirements for establishing a continuous delivery of software components, while ensuring repeatability, testability, reproducibility, and measurability of deployment processes. Requirements on supporting elastic cloud applications services by means of monitoring and auto-scaling are also identified and discussed. Given this catalog of requirements, a process model for establishing an automated deployment and efficient management of elastic cloud services in different environments and multiple regions is proposed. The process considers a pre-baking strategy to significantly reduce deployment time of components based on a configuration management system. In general, the proposed process model considers all activities being important to ensure a high quality and performance of components and applications in cloud environments including provisioning and cloud testing procedures. Besides that, the process model reflects the dependencies between automated deployment and configuration management activities. Organizational and cultural aspects as well as tool support are discussed in order to provide a basis for adoption. Based on the proposed automated deployment process and prior research, current research challenges, such as related to the area of decision analytics, are discussed. A case study focusing on the *Adobe Shared Cloud* demonstrates the potential benefits resulting from an application of the proposed deployment process for cloud application providers. As such, the chapter analyzes the state-of-the-art regarding configuration management in the context of automated deployment in the cloud and proposes, based on shortcomings of existing systems and a comprehensive requirements analysis, a novel approach for improving the delivery and management of elastic cloud application services, which is important both in research and practice. Further, research challenges are identified to guide future research activities.

The remainder of this chapter is organized as follows. Section 2 provides a background on virtualization techniques, configuration strategies and standards. Section 3 presents related work on configuration management and deployment in cloud environments. The requirements on deployment processes and configuration management are briefly discussed in Section 4. Based on the identified requirements, an integrative approach to automatically manage deployment of elastic application components during development and operations is presented in Section 5, considering testing strategies, organizational aspects, and tool support. Resulting research challenges and ideas to solve these challenges are discussed in Section 6. To evaluate results, a case study with a focus on the Adobe Shared Cloud is provided in Section 7. Finally, a conclusion and future research activities are presented in Section 8.

2. BACKGROUND

The most common form of cloud computing adoption is Infrastructure as a Service (IaaS). IaaS enables to access a broad range of virtualized, configurable, and on-demand computing resources (e.g., server systems, storage systems, etc.) without requiring interaction with the cloud infrastructure provider (Mell & Grance, 2011). Usage-based pricing schemes and automated scaling mechanisms foster the development of cost-effective, elastic and scalable cloud application services. Technically, distributed cloud applications are deployed on multiple virtual machines (VMs), which are configured based on user-defined requirements (e.g., processing power, memory, storage capacity, etc.). Typically, additional configurations and installations of middleware must be performed before a service component can be deployed and launched. Traditionally, these steps take a serious amount of time and are usually not fully documented and repeatable, which does not support the delivery of elastic cloud services and may lead to critical faults. Given the enhanced automation in cloud environments, cloud infrastructure providers support the creation of different VMs through a management console and usually proprietary interfaces. A VM image contains all elements and data necessary to be launched as VM. Most cloud infrastructure providers allow storing the current state of VMs as specific VM image containing, for example, a specific software stack or middleware. Although this reduces the burden of installing and configuring a basic server instance, manual or semi-automated provisioning and deployment processes are highly inefficient.

Configuration management is concerned with policies, processes and tools to build and maintain changing software components and underlying infrastructure systems. Related activities involve source/version management, change management as well as build and release management (Sommerville, 2011). A configuration management system refers to all tools and systems that support configuration management activities (e.g., version control, build automation, provisioning, etc.). In cloud environments, configuration management builds a foundation for an automated construction, configuration, and adaption of cloud environments containing VMs that host different, interwoven components of one or several cloud application services. As indicated, standardized and automated deployment processes are crucial to leverage the benefits of configuration management and enable fast and efficient scaling of cloud-based applications. Regarding the flexibility and performance of VM configurations, three basic strategies for incorporating configuration management can be identified in practice:

1. **Bootstrapping Strategy:** The aim is to minimize the number of VM images in order to better support the individual configuration of VMs and software components during runtime. VM images typically include only an installed operating system. Each time a software component is deployed, the VM can be provisioned with additional software (e.g., specific middleware, runtime environment) and configured based on specific settings, which are maintained in the configuration management system. As this strategy provides a high degree of flexibility in terms of individual configuration, it primarily supports development teams where demands on underlying software stacks and hardware often vary. The flexibility, therefore, implies a high degree of complexity in cloud environments.

2. **Baking Strategy:** In contrast to the bootstrapping strategy, the baking strategy aims to produce self-contained VM images that can be launched without further configuration. The configuration process for creating those VM images is referred to as *baking*. Changes are incorporated through the creation of new VM images. After selecting a baked VM image containing the required middleware, software stack and other configurations, a component can be deployed and launched immediately. The performance benefits of a baking strategy are essential for production environments. In particular, auto-scaling mechanisms are highly dependent on a fast deployment of cloud-based service components.

3. **Pre-Baking Strategy:** A pre-baking strategy aims to find a good compromise between a bootstrapping and a baking strategy. The main difference is that VM images are configured solely to a certain extent and can be further adapted during deployment. The extent to which a VM image is pre-configured impacts both the flexibility and performance of deployment and requires a decision to handle the corresponding trade-off.

In order to support elastic cloud services, the proposed automated deployment process (see Section 5) focuses on a pre-baking strategy. Thereby, a certain degree of flexibility is ensured, which is important to use region and/or environment-specific configurations without increasing the number of VM images. The creation of VM images is supported by different standards. A widely discussed standard is the Open Virtualization Format (OVF), which represents an XML-based open and extensible standard for the packaging of portable VM images. OVF builds a profound basis to describe VM images and allows the specification of platform-specific requirements. It further provides a foundation for managing the metadata of several VM images and versions of VM images in a version control system. Prior research provides extensions for OVF, for instance, to specify scaling rules (see Section 3). Thus, it can be used to create and manage VM images in an automated deployment process. Before an integrative approach for supporting deployment processes is presented, the following section discusses requirements that need to be taken into account for ensuring a high quality and performance of software delivery in cloud environments.

3. RELATED WORKS

Automated and on-demand deployment and provisioning of services has been investigated in several works. In the following, we will focus on publications that consider configuration management in particular with the focus on deployment processes in cloud environments. Mietzner and Leymann (2008) present a generic architecture to manage provisioning services of Software as a Service (SaaS) applications using the Web Service Business Process Execution Language (WS-BPEL). Based on a unified provisioning API, a generic process is defined to forward provisioning requests to specific (composite) provisioning services. However, a corresponding method to describe, translate and manage provisioning requests remains unspecified. Cerbelaud, Garg, and Huylebroeck (2009) investigate the varieties of image management and instance provision-

ing mechanisms for different open source cloud management platforms. The paper provides an extensive overview and evaluation of VM-based cloud platform characteristics, in particular with regard to provisioning options including cluster building, cloud bursting and control mechanisms. Although the authors describe means to create and manage VMs from a repository, the management of different image versions and configurations is not considered. Konstantinou et al. (2009) present a model-driven approach and a corresponding prototype to manage the configuration and provisioning of infrastructures and applications in the cloud. The basic idea of this paper is to use an abstract representation of virtual appliances (VAs) capturing configuration parameters that are transformed in multiple steps until a cloud platform-specific deployment and configuration plan is constructed. This description is used to build the cloud environment, generate VMs, and to configure the software stack. Although the idea to iteratively construct virtual resources is valuable in many ways, the process is highly dependent on individual experts and focuses on a clear separation of roles. This, however, is contrary to common approaches largely focusing on automation and the alignment of development and operations roles (see Section 5.4). Celesti et al. (2010) propose a concept to enable cross-cloud federation. The paper, however, focuses rather on the steps to discover and select heterogeneous cloud platforms than on the actual provisioning implementation. Rodero-Merino et al. (2010) propose an abstraction layer to enable cross-cloud federation, referred to as *Claudia*. The authors extend OVF to support automated scalability, deployment time customization and to specifically set network configurations. The extension enables the definition of diverse scalability options, such as service component scale up/down, scale in/out on a federated cloud and smart scaling by applying certain business rules. Chapman et al. (2011) also extend the OVF to express service requirements, elasticity rules and provisioning constraints. The authors propose to define Key Performance Indicators (KPIs) for measuring resource requirements on the application level to reduce overprovisioning. A service manifest expresses the resource needs of a component (e.g., CPU, memory requirements, etc.) that can be expanded or reduced during operations by applying elasticity rules and monitoring. A deployment descriptor is generated based on the service manifest in order to provision a respective VM. The complete provisioning of VMs, however, can take a large amount of time, which may result in temporary capacity restraints. Nevertheless, the paper provides the foundation for semantically describing component requirements used in automated deployment processes. Juve & Deelman (2011) propose a generic deployment process that accesses a deployment descriptor (specifying the cloud provider, a specific image and instance type, number of nodes, etc.) to start and configure a computing cluster in a specific cloud environment. The management of configurations is not discussed in their paper. Moreno-Vozmediano, Montero, & Llorente (2011) investigate the deployment of computing clusters on multiple cloud environments for solving loosely coupled Many-Task Computing (MTC) applications. Utilizing the OpenNebula platform for accessing different cloud environments (e.g., Amazon EC2, Elastic Hosts), the study demonstrates the existence of potential cost- and performance benefits of using multicloud computing clusters. On the cloud application level, however, interoperability and vendor lock-in is still a problem. Sampaio & Mendonça (2011) propose to utilize the Open Cloud Computing Interface (OCCI) to forward OVF-based provisioning descriptors to specific cloud environments using a respective cloud adapter. Although the approach may enable the provisioning of VMs in different cloud environments based on a standardized description of requirements, cloud-based applications may also rely on specific underlying services (e.g., in terms of storage, load balancing, etc.), which may not support a translation from an interoperable

specification to a vendor-specific implementation. Diaz et al. (2012) present a framework for creating and managing abstract images and uniform image registration for different cloud platforms (e.g., Nimbus, OpenNebula, Eucalyptus) and HPC Clusters (e.g., Bare Metal). Based on the requirements of users regarding the operating system, software and libraries to be installed, an abstract image template is generated containing all metadata needed to create cloud platform-specific images. These images can be customized and stored in a central repository accessible by other users through an image catalog. By registering the image for the targeted platform, the image is appropriately customized involving different network configurations, etc. By conducting some computational experiments, the authors demonstrate the potential time savings of using pre-defined base images compared to the provisioning of VMs from scratch. Breitenbücher et al. (2013) underline the importance of portability of components between different cloud platforms that may provide proprietary tools for supporting the creation of environments and the scalability of components (e.g., AWS CloudFormation, AWS Elastic Load Balancing). The authors propose to use conversion descriptors for adapting scripts to cloud platform-specific scripts based on TOSCA (Topology and Orchestration Specification for Cloud Applications)-compliant topology model components, but without specifying how the conversion of those scripts into platform-specific environments work.

4. REQUIREMENTS

In this section, requirements for establishing a highly reliable and efficient automated deployment process are identified and discussed. In general, the main objective is to support automated deployment processes for deploying and managing highly scalable, reliable and available cloud applications by simultaneously considering organizational and economic aspects.

4.1 Continuous Delivery

Distributed applications used in practice and research are typically developed iteratively and incrementally by several development teams. A frequent, or even continuous, delivery of components enables short development iterations and feedback cycles, reduces risks, and facilitates a faster time-to-market (Humble & Farley, 2011). The resource requirements of components may, however, fluctuate during operations. The option to dynamically provision cloud resources on-demand enables the adaption of the underlying infrastructure according to changing resource requirements, but also implies that a component may need to be rapidly deployed several times a day depending on the changing conditions. Setting up the resources and deploying the components involves several critical steps that must be repeated each time a component is deployed. A high degree of automation of these procedures is important to reduce costs and time needed to deliver the components to internal or external customers. As an automated deployment allows developers to manage the deployment processes mostly by themselves, the awareness of quality and responsiveness to errors during and after development would likely be increased. During operations, an automated deployment enables the adaption of applications to volatile requirements influenced by different external factors, such as by the number of users accessing the cloud-based application.

4.2 Repeatability

In order to reduce risks, increase accuracy and leverage the potentials of scalable cloud environments, automated deployment processes must be repeatable for new and existing components. The general steps being performed to dynamically deploy components usually differ only in applied configuration parameters. By managing those configurations in a distributed configuration management system, it is possible to fully standardize the deployment process. It also allows repeating certain deployment processes for reproducing a specific state of the environment, further discussed in Section 4.4.

4.3 Testability

The deployment process of components involves several types of tests being performed on different testing levels (e.g., unit testing, integration testing, etc.), further explained in Section 5.3. To extensively validate that the component runs as expected, tests are usually executed in different environments before the cutover to a production environment is made through which customers access and use the cloud application. To enable automated deployment processes, tests must also be executed and validated automatically (e.g., based on test results). As the complexity of tests and test results increases during the deployment process, it is important to detect errors in an early stage of deployment, or even better, before the deployment is launched. Consequently, an efficient testing strategy needs to be defined based on a standardized, automated deployment process. An individual and expressive feedback in form of test results must be provided to developers in order to ensure that errors can be addressed immediately. Automated measures to abort and/or rollback deployment processes must be performed if the developer is not able to fix problems in order to ensure a stable state in an environment shared by multiple developers. If the developer is not able to reconstruct a major problem in the local environment, it should be possible to run a cloned version of the exact environment.

4.4 Reproducibility

Released cloud applications are often operated in different versions and multiple regions. As the development, testing, staging and production environments continuously evolve, it becomes increasingly difficult to reconstruct an unexpected behavior or to test an update of components in the current environments as they may differ from the corresponding production environment. Consequently, it is important to store the version of components and environments in a configuration management system in order to allow the deployment of specific components in specific environments, which are built based on a separately launched cloud testing environment. A high reproducibility allows reconstructing states of a system at various points in time, which also improves a better auditability of cloud application environments, further discussed in Section 4.6.

4.5 Scalability

The most common way to scale applications services in cloud environments is the dynamic provisioning and deployment of component replicas that are connected to a load balancer splitting and distributing the load onto several VMs hosting identical components, also referred to as scaling up and down. Most of the cloud infrastructure providers allow to automatically scale applications based on predefined rules. In order to quickly respond to an increasing traffic or processing load, the time to provision VMs and deploy the affected component must be as small as possible, also requiring a high parallelization of automated deployment processes. Ideally, the process to scale up and down takes only a few seconds. The configuration and installation of the operating system and middleware, however, take a large portion of time to complete.

In a federated cloud, it is conceivable that components are deployed in cloud environments of different cloud providers, for instance, to reallocate components to an external cloud due to local resource limitations (e.g., in case of a hybrid cloud), to lower the risk of a complete failure or to dynamically select the cheapest cloud infrastructure provider taking economic factors into account (Rodero-Merino et al., 2010). The deployment of resources in a federated cloud environment, however, is still an enormous challenge due to a lack of interoperability between different clouds, which usually leads to a vendor lock-in.

Regarding the utilization of VMs, auto-scaling could also involve intelligent mechanisms that (re-)allocate components to VMs based on the available capacity in order to reduce operational expenses. For example, instead of deploying three components to three small VMs it could make more sense to bundle components on one bigger instance (see, e.g., Rodero-Merino et al., 2010). Running multiple components on one VM, however, might cause reliability and security issues. Instead, the reallocation of components could focus on reducing costs by minimizing overprovisioning.

4.6 Auditability

An automated deployment involves making changes to business-critical production environments. These environments may contain sensitive corporate data, such as customer records, and/or play a vital role in supporting crucial business processes and transactions. Consequently, it is important to track all changes being made to both components and environments. Due to the important role of production environments, the deployment of components into these environments is usually triggered manually by an operations team after the components are completely validated in the staging environment. The access to the staging and production environments must be restricted. Thus, auditability in the context of cloud deployment also means that each access to configuration management systems must be documented in order to comply with compliance regulations.

4.7 Monitoring

An efficient management of applications in complex environments further requires measures to monitor and control the overall system. A monitoring system is operated on top of a cloud environment to collect and process data of the contained components, middleware and infrastructure systems. In testing environments, this bird's eye perspective helps to identify and analyze problems, in particular with regard to the integration of components into an environment. In a wider sense, monitoring helps to analyze dependencies between software components and shared systems (e.g., databases, access management) valuable for improving the overall system architecture. During operations, monitoring is essential to analyze and better understand the behavior of the overall system and the external factors influencing this behavior. The gathered data, usually delivered as log records, build the basis for applying intelligent decision support for managing the overall system more efficiently. This includes not only the identification of recurring problems, but also enables the prediction of certain aspects (e.g., traffic load prediction) used to proactively manage the system according to QoS requirements as well as economic factors (see, e.g., Heilig & Voß, 2014a). A deployment process should be able to automatically react to those decisions during operations.

4.8 Measurability

Automated deployment processes are highly dependent on the use of metrics to quantify and measure performance and quality criteria. Metrics, such as the number of completed/failed builds and tests, or the mean duration time of deploy-

ment processes, can be used to identify recurring problems and for establishing a continuous improvement process as well as to adapt tool support and organizational aspects.

5. PROCESS-ORIENTED CLOUD DEPLOYMENT

Considering the requirements on automated deployment processes formulated in Section 4, an approach to standardize and automatize component-based deployment processes for building elastic cloud applications is presented.

5.1 Generic Component Lifecycle

The general lifecycle of components can be described with four generic phases: development, deployment, operations, and phase out. As depicted in Figure 1, the deployment phase is not only important for the rollout of application components from testing into different production environments, but plays a vital role for enabling continuous improvement and auto-scaling for elastic cloud applications. In the following, the generic phases and dependencies are briefly described.

- **Development:** Cloud applications are decomposed to service components that are developed and updated iteratively by several development teams.

Figure 1. Service component lifecycle

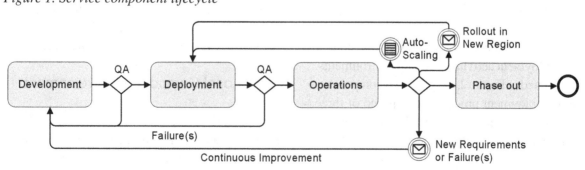

- **Quality Assurance (QA):** Involves procedures to prevent errors and defects in cloud applications in order to ensure that the application meets QoS requirements and service specifications before it is delivered to customers.
- **Deployment and Rollout:** Service components are built and deployed in different environments in multiple regions. After the quality of components is certified in a stepwise manner in testing and staging environments, the cutover to a production environment is made, which means that the component is delivered to the customer.
- **Operations:** Involves all activities for ensuring a high service level of deployed cloud applications in production environments. This includes an efficient management of the overall system, for instance, through monitoring and auto-scaling mechanisms. As customers extensively use the application in this phase, problems and/or new requirements may occur during operations, which need to be addressed by additional development activities triggering new deployment processes.
- **Phase Out:** The lifecycle of components ends by replacing or removing them from the production environment. As other components may depend on those components, it is important to plan and test phase out procedures in order to prevent business-critical outages.

5.2 Cloud Deployment Process Model

The proposed approach focuses on provisioning and deployment activities in cloud environments. As depicted in Figure 2, the proposed component-based deployment process is composed of three main phases covering the lifecycle of components from development to operations. The basic idea of this approach is to prepare not only components

to be deployed, but also VMs on which the components are executed. The pre-configured VM images are classified into Base Machine Images (BMIs) and Component Machine Images (CMIs). A BMI is a pre-configured VM containing at least an operating system, according to a bootstrapping strategy. Based on the specifications of a component, a BMI can be selected from a VM repository in order to individually provision the VM with a component-specific software stack and the component itself. Again, this package is stored as a pre-configured, reusable CMI that can be repeatedly deployed as VM in different environments. By this, the mean deployment time can be reduced while guaranteeing repeatability and reproducibility, further discussed in Section 5.2.4.

Configuration management plays a key role in the proposed deployment process. The distributed configuration management is accessible for all environments and is used to efficiently manage the overall application and environment landscape over time, including component versions and their dependencies, tests, and environment configurations on different layers. Consequently, a configuration management system contains information and tools to manage the evolution of large and complex software and infrastructure systems. In addition, a configuration management system promotes a better collaboration between development teams working on the same application and ensures that changes to the system are restricted and documented. The main reason is, though, that a configuration management system is essential for the automation of provisioning and deployment processes and provides a basis for the management of elastic cloud services. In the following, the phases of the proposed component-based automated deployment process are described in detail.

5.2.1 Local Component Development

Components are developed in the local environment of cloud software engineers. For each component, dependencies and configuration parameters,

Figure 2. Component-based automated deployment process

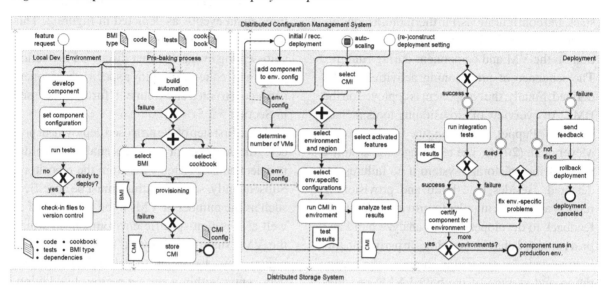

which are necessary to run the component in a specific runtime environment, are specified. Before the source code, corresponding unit tests and configuration items are committed to source control, each component must be built and intensively tested in the local environment in order to avoid failures in subsequent phases of the deployment process. Build processes are automated by using build automation tools, such as Apache Ant and Apache Maven (an overview on build tools is provided in Humble & Farley, 2011). To get a better test coverage in an early phase of development, parts or entire environments could be simulated through mocking objects using configuration parameters of specific environments, further discussed in Section 5.3. This testing process can be, for instance, complemented by collaborative code quality reviews. The individual developer should be able to trigger the automated deployment process by committing all files to source control, also referred to as version control. Tools for source control include Git, Mercurial, and Perforce (see, e.g., Humble & Farley, 2011). Typically, continuous integration tools, such as Jenkins (see, e.g., Hüttermann, 2012), are used to detect changes in the code repository in order to automatically trig-

ger corresponding build processes and unit tests. Build or test failures are reported and therefore satisfy testability requirements. If build processes and tests are successful, build artifacts (e.g., binary code, executable) are stored.

5.2.2 Pre-Baking

Given the build artifacts, a new CMI is created. This process, referred to as *pre-baking*, selects a BMI based on the requirements defined for the component (e.g., hardware requirements, such as number and type of processors, memory, etc.). A packaging tool, such as Packer (Packer, 2014), is used to build a VM image based on the BMI configuration file. The configuration file is also used to specify the cloud infrastructure provider, allowing the creation of BMIs for different cloud platforms. The packaging tool can also be used to install a provisioning agent so that the corresponding VM is able to provision itself autonomously through a connection to a provisioning tool. For each component, the provisioning tool maintains a provisioning configuration file (also referred to as cookbook or service manifest). This machine-readable configuration file is used to provision the BMI with the necessary middleware, software stack and configurations. Furthermore, a monitoring agent is installed in order to retrieve information on the VM and component during runtime. The sequence of provisioning activities can be defined. Finally, the component is deployed on the BMI. An overview of provisioning tools including Chef, Puppet, and CFEngine is presented in Meyer et al. (2013). The resulting CMI is stored in a distributed storage system if no failures are detected. Besides that, build and provisioning reports are stored in order to provide continuous feedback to developers and to analyze build and provisioning behavior over time. In particular, this is important for generating metrics. The preparation and storage of pre-baked VMs provides substantial advantages over traditional approaches. Depending on the degree of pre-configuration, a component can be started at best within seconds, which is especially important for building elastic cloud services, further discussed in Section 5.2.4.

5.2.3 Iterative Deployment

Once the pre-baked CMI is stored, it is used as an image for flexibly creating and deploying duplicates of the component in several environments. In general, it can be distinguished between testing, staging and production environments, whereas a staging environment is literally the final assembly line before the component is delivered to the customer accessing the production environment. The staging environment mirrors the production environment and is normally used to perform user acceptance, load and performance testing. Before a new component can be deployed into an environment, it must be added to the environment manifest. The environment manifest is a configuration file that specifies the overall system architecture including all dependencies between components and infrastructure elements. Thus, it is important to maintain versions of those settings in the configuration management system supporting reproducibility of certain environments.

The deployment process can be initiated through three main events, as depicted in Figure 2. This includes initial or recurring deployment events, auto-scaling events (further discussed in Section 5.2.4) and requests to deploy a specific component in a reconstructed environment (further discussed in Section 5.2.5).

In the first step of the proposed deployment process, the deployment request is analyzed in order to select an associated CMI from the repository. Subsequently, several settings must be specified, such as the number of VMs to be provisioned as well as a region-specific environment in which the VMs shall be deployed. The selection of a region may also imply to determine a specific data center within a certain region. In addition, the deployment process includes a mechanism to deactivate functionality of components, for instance, in case that some functionalities should only be available to certain regions or customer groups. Based on the environment configuration, specific configurations required for integrating the component into a specific environment are applied to the CMI (e.g., network settings). After the CMI is fully configured, it is used to launch one or several VMs in a respective environment. In testing environments, several QA procedures are performed to ensure that the component is integrated appropriately. This includes several testing activities, further described in Section 5.3. If those testing activities report that the component runs without any issues in the environment, the component is certified for this environment so that it can be deployed to another testing environment until it reaches the staging environment and, after being validated by the operations team, finally the production environment. Feedback mechanisms ensure that the developer of the component gets comprehensible test results so that errors or defects can be addressed immediately. In case that the developer is not able to handle errors or defects within a specific timeframe, a rollback mechanism transforms the environment into its original state by using corresponding configurations. Only if the component is certified in all environments, the cutover to the production environment can be made. The cloud application provider maintains an image catalog that lists all available BMIs and CMIs, which can be re-used for the deployment of different components.

5.2.4 Auto-Scaling

The proposed deployment process can be coupled with rule-based or dynamic auto-scaling mechanisms, provided by cloud infrastructure providers. The approach primarily supports scaling up / down mechanisms, but is not restricted to support scaling in / out mechanisms once the interoperability among different cloud infrastructure providers is established. Using a packaging tool, though, enables to create cloud platform specific CMIs, which can be deployed given that respective environment configurations exist and that components are independent from platform-specific functionality. To this extend, the reallocation of components to reduce overprovisioning is not considered extensively. An option to reduce overprovisioning would be to better determine the size of BMIs based on the average utilization of components and redeploy such components on a new BMI. Typically, a component is connected to a load balancer that monitors and allocates the traffic across multiple instances of the component as well as across multiple datacenters within one region. In addition, a message queue can be used to buffer and distribute requests to duplicated components. If the load exceeds the available capacity or defined thresholds, the load balancer automatically triggers corresponding deployment processes. The average time to deploy the corresponding components for reacting to certain loads can be significantly reduced through the use of pre-baked CMIs. Especially in production environments, an integrated auto-scaling mechanism plays an important role for satisfying QoS requirements of customers.

5.2.5 Environment Reconstruction

As the configuration management maintains versions of environments, components and their relationship, all system states can be reconstituted. This enables not only rollback mechanisms, but also that specific system states can be tested and analyzed in separately launched testing environments, for instance, to simulate and analyze phase out procedures. The proposed deployment process allows, based on cloud capabilities, to (re-)build complete environments according to blueprints given by system architecture and configuration settings.

5.3 Testing

The automated deployment process is, as discussed in the previous sections, highly dependent on automated testing procedures. In general, software testing has become more difficult, mainly because of the variety of programming languages, external libraries, operating systems and hardware platforms used in distributed application systems (Myers, Thomas, & Sandler, 2004). Software testing is considered as an essential activity in the component lifecycle ensuring that the overall application meets functional and non-functional QoS requirements of customers. In this section, a testing strategy is presented supporting the proposed automated deployment process by utilizing cloud computing capabilities. In this context, automated means to perform testing activities in a cloud environment are briefly discussed.

5.3.1 Testing Strategy

The testing strategy determines how functional and non-functional properties of components are tested during development and operations. Generally, the integration of a component into an environment is tested on several levels. For each level, different types of tests are executed in order to ensure a high test coverage. A high test coverage increases the chance of detecting faults and errors before the component is used by the customer. Thus, it reduces the risk of failure to comply with requirements, specified in Service Level Agreements (SLAs), which would have economic and/or legal impact. To combine testing activities with automated deployment processes, it is important that testing results are measurable and comparable with quantified and reasonable testing objectives (Zhu, Hall, & May, 1997).

As depicted in Figure 3, it becomes increasingly difficult to identify and analyze sources of faults and errors the more the deployment procedure is progressed, mainly due to the increasing complexity and level of abstraction. The costs of fixing those problems correlate with the increasing complexity; thus, it is preferable to detect and fix problems in an early stage of development. Furthermore, checked-in component errors may impact the work of other developers deploying components in shared development environments. To reduce costs, it is essential that each component is extensively tested in the local environment of developers in order to minimize or exclude potential errors on the component level. This includes all changes being applied to the component through refactoring activities. Therefore, a comprehensive set of unit tests has to be maintained for each component. As unit tests intend to validate isolated parts of the component often being dependent on data or methods of other components, subsystems (e.g., databases), and/or

external functionality provided by third parties, it is necessary to include mock objects into certain unit tests in order to simulate the behavior of external functionality. The component and environment configurations stored in the configuration management system can be used as a basis for generating mock objects for new components. By mimicking the interfaces specification of subsystems or other components, a mock object is used to simulate expected and unexpected behavior of subsystems (e.g., different return codes, erroneous data, etc.) in order to test whether the component is able to handle this behavior correctly. The deployment process automatically executes the unit tests once the developer has put all source and test files into version control.

Unit tests are executed in all development, staging and production environments in order to detect occurring faults and errors immediately. As a high system availability is very important for cloud-based applications, regression tests must be implemented to automatically re-test components whenever components are changed (e.g., to fix errors, improve feature, refactoring, etc.). Each change is deployed using the proposed standard deployment process, thus, allowing executing certain test procedures automatically. As complex tests may require large amounts of processing time, it is useful to maintain additional smoke and sanity tests, which verify basic functionalities of components to decide whether it is reasonable to further proceed with the test-

Figure 3. Testing strategy

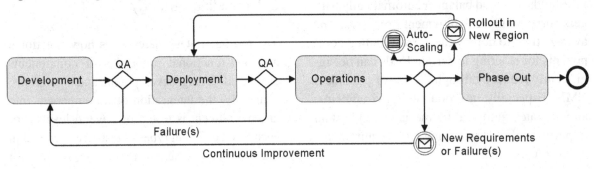

ing procedure. Test results should facilitate an efficient error treatment (for example, by means of error visualization, notifications). Moreover, test results must be standardized in a way that they can be used to automatically trigger certain procedures (e.g., deployment of new VMs in case of performance issues).

5.3.2 Cloud Testing

The on-demand and pay-per-use characteristics of cloud computing are increasingly used to enhance testing activities based on cloud-based environments. The primary objective of cloud testing is to better simulate observed and/or predicted user traffic in the staging environment. By providing different types of tests including load tests, stress tests and latency tests, cloud testing aims to evaluate the performance, scalability, security and measurement of cloud applications based on economic scales and pre-defined SLAs (Gao, Bai, & Tsai, 2011). The simulation of multiple usage scenarios, such as with millions of users accessing the system, allows to design and evaluate tests according to QoS requirements and SLAs, for instance, with regard to economic factors. In this context, it becomes increasingly important to have systematic approaches and standards for defining QoS requirements; the latter is still regarded as research challenge (Gao, Bai, & Tsai, 2011). Regarding the proposed deployment process, the developer initially defines QoS requirements for a component, e.g., by specifying service-oriented policies (see, e.g., Gao, Bai, & Tsai, 2011) that are managed and extended through a configuration management system. Cloud-based testing environments are invoked by the deployment process when needed. Consequently, cloud testing enables a scalable and cost-effective way of providing testing environments on-demand.

As cloud-based components are primarily managed by metadata describing, for instance, input and output data types or allowed input parameters, it is possible to automatically generate test cases based on interface specifications. As those tests run against a specific component or system interface from the outside, this kind of testing type is a good candidate to be provided as a cloud testing service (Bai et al., 2011). Test cases validating the enforcement of policies on QoS requirements could be created, executed and tested similarly.

Third-party providers offer some of the mentioned testing procedures as a service. After defining test parameters initially, these services can be frequently invoked by automated deployment processes. An overview of those testing tools (e.g., SOASTA, iTKO) is presented in Bai et al. (2011). Note that the use of third-party testing provider is not without any managerial, application-related or legal issues (see, e.g., Gao et al., 2011). For instance, the use of real testing data (e.g., customer records) might cause legal problems and would require that testing data must be generated synthetically. However, using third-party cloud testing services relieves the burden on designing, deploying, maintaining and managing certain test frameworks. Pay-per-use pricing models further increase the attractiveness of using cloud testing services to further increase flexibility and reduce expenditures for resource- and normally cost-intensive testing procedures. Consequently, cloud testing services enable a cost-effective and automated testing alternative, which can be used to further enhance automated deployment processes.

5.4 DevOps

To facilitate a successful adoption of the proposed deployment process in enterprises, it is essential that organizational and cultural aspects are taken into account. Often, development and operations teams act like silos and aim to improve, at most, their own processes to meet their respective objectives. While the main objective of operations is to ensure that the systems keep running smoothly according to defined service levels, development teams are increasingly organized in an agile fashion aiming to continuously create, test and integrate new components and features into operations within short development cycles. To avoid goal conflicts, the component delivery process must be improved as a whole. This implies that shared objectives for both development and operations are formulated meaning that everybody involved in the deployment process is accountable for meeting those goals. Based on a standardized deployment process, some of those goals can be measured based on metrics (e.g., average time to deploy a component into the production environment, mean time between failures – MTBF, etc.). Additionally, a decisive factor for streamlining the recurring cloud application delivery process from development to operations is that people from development (e.g., programmers, testers, QA personnel) and people from operations (e.g., database administrators, network experts) efficiently collaborate based on information, knowledge and tool sharing, policies and standards, automated processes, monitoring and measurement techniques (Hüttermann, 2012). These are core principles of the DevOps paradigm aiming to encourage greater collaboration between development and operations teams involved in software delivery processes in order to produce and deliver valuable software applications faster and more reliably (Humble & Farley, 2011). In addition, to utilize the potential of DevOps, a common culture of trust and sharing needs to be established in the organization. Although mostly interpersonal factors are important to establish this culture, appropriate tools, for instance a shared configuration management system, are necessary to support collaboration. The culture is also important to establish continuous improvement for configuration management activities and deployment processes. The proposed deployment process contains all aspects that are important to support DevOps for improving the overall delivery process of cloud applications.

6. RESEARCH CHALLENGES

Although the presented deployment process provides a blueprint for establishing highly automated, standardized, repeatable, scalable, testable, and auditable deployment processes, several research challenges can be identified before the potentials of the proposed model can be completely utilized. In this section, important research challenges are discussed as well as ideas to overcome those obstacles relevant for the adoption of the proposed automated deployment process in contemporary organizations.

6.1 Size of VM Images

For a high elasticity and scalability of cloud-based applications, the deployment of preconfigured VM images is proposed in the previous sections. While the instantiation of pre-configured and provisioned VM images is very fast, the size of VM images, usually in the order of gigabytes, may lead to a performance bottleneck when the demand for scaling increases. To read a CMI from the disk and transfer it over the network may consume precious time (Peng et al., 2012). In particular in multi-regional cloud environments, it is crucial to distribute and manage VM image duplicates in multiple regions or to find mechanisms to improve collaborative sharing in order to maximize the amount of available VM images in different environments for reducing network latency. Prior research concentrating on peer-to-peer network sharing (see, e.g., Peng et al., 2012), VM distribution networks (see, e.g., Chen et al., 2009), and low-latency VM cloning (see, e.g., Lagar-Cavilla et al., 2009) have already demonstrated the large potential for improvement. Those mechanisms must be incorporated in automated deployment processes and managed through a distributed configuration management system. In addition, CMIs might be frequently updated leading to multiple VM image versions, which may need to be distributed across several environments. Thus, VM image version control may help to reduce the huge network transmission overhead of transmitting VM images, further described in the next section.

6.2 VM Image Version Control

Although large collections of pre-configured VM images (e.g., BMIs and CMIs) provide new opportunities for scaling and to enforce the reuse of components for several purposes (Ammons et al., 2011), it is essential to enable version control for VM images. While several studies focus on VM checkpointing, migration, and image storage (see, e.g., Wood et al., 2011), only a few works can be found on version control of VM images. Tang, Wong, & Lee (2012) propose *CloudVS*, a version control system for managing different versions of VM images by using redundancy elimination. The applied redundancy elimination algorithm aims to minimize the network transfer bandwidth and storage overhead by storing only the initial VM image and deltas representing the new or changed content of the VM image (Tang et al., 2012), commonly referred to as deduplication. Given the amount of VM image data and transfer bandwidth, the storage and management of VM image versions can be optimized by using exact and approximate/heuristic approaches. In this regard, more research is required to further improve VM image management, especially in the context of multi-region cloud environments.

6.3 Cost Control and Cloud Service Pricing

In cloud environments it is crucial to understand the cost factors and drivers as a basis for running cost-effective applications. In this scope, it is comparably important to constantly monitor the accruing costs of all components in the different testing, staging and production environments in order to control budgets for development environments and cost model assumptions of the production system. This highly incorporates the elaboration of deployment and scaling policies, including the automated tear down of unused or abandoned VMs. Costs should be transparent at any time to the development and operations team. While an extensive monitoring system can track the use of cloud resources to measure resource utilization and calculate corresponding costs, it becomes increasingly important to provide mechanisms for reducing costs while satisfying QoS requirements. Cost control is a prerequisite for economic static and dynamic pricing models. An overview of decision analytics approaches to control costs (e.g., QoS-aware service selection and resource allocation) and support cost-effective pricing decisions, presented in Heilig & Voß (2014a), identify a lack of integrative approaches and a gap between scientific work and practical application of proposed approaches.

6.4 Cloud Interoperability and Vendor Lock-In

In recent years, cloud interoperability has been extensively discussed in the cloud computing community incorporating a challenge for both research and practice (see, e.g., Armbrust et al., 2010; Leavitt, 2009). The importance of cloud interoperability in cloud computing research is also shown in a comprehensive scientometric analysis of cloud computing literature presented in Heilig & Voß (2014b), which further provides important statistics to better understand the evolution, current state and trends of cloud computing research. Prior research, reviewed in the previous section, shows that federated clouds are supported by certain open cloud platforms, but also that the proprietary interfaces of specific cloud providers (e.g., Amazon Web Services, Rackspace) are still a problem resulting in vendor-specific processes, environments and applications (vendor lock-in). The clear differentiation between component-specific configuration and environment-specific configuration management could help to maintain provider-specific environments while being able to produce individual VMs based on a standardized VM image format and a multi-cloud supporting packaging tool, as suggested by the proposed deployment process model. This would not solve the cloud interoperability problem, but could be an option for improving the deployment and management of cloud services in multiple vendor-specific cloud environments. Further research is required to explore multi-cloud deployment and configuration management.

7. CASE STUDY: ADOBE SHARED CLOUD

This section gives insights into a Platform as a Service (PaaS) solution of Adobe, namely the Adobe Shared Cloud. The Shared Cloud implements a large amount of cloud-based software components to support major Adobe application services, such as Creative Cloud, Acrobat.com, and the Digital Publishing Suite. The platform is globally deployed in three regions – the US, Europe and Asia – and consists of multiple environments on the way to production. The underlying cloud infrastructure is operated by Amazon Web Services. The following case study reflects the benefits of an automated and standardized deployment process for cloud application providers. In general, current results show that automated deployment processes have a great impact on the performance and quality of development and operations activities as well as on the overall quality and cost-effectiveness of deployed components.

7.1 Team Setup

The Shared Cloud development team consists of multiple Scrum teams. These teams consist of 5-7 developers and a product owner, who is responsible for managing feature requests and changes. The teams are organized in a way that they are able to independently create software components from design to deployment. A tooling team supports those development teams by providing build and deployment tools. Those teams are co-located to enable an efficient communication and collaboration. Besides that, a globally distributed operations team supports the global deployment and operations of the cloud platform. Following the DevOps paradigm, some operations specialists are available on-site in order to enable an efficient communication and collaboration between development and operations teams.

7.2 Component Deployment

The development teams' performance is to a large extent dependent on an automated deployment process, which enables them to rapidly get feedback in certain environments and automatically promotes components to the next stage. In general, each development team frequently and autonomously triggers deployment procedures to a testing environment in order to carry out several QA activities. This includes provisioning tests, in which the configuration of the used VM image is tested, and integration sanity tests to validate the integration of the component into the environment. The latter procedure is extended by system tests, in which testing workflows are executed to test interdependencies between components. Acceptance tests include different performance tests and functional tests. Once these testing layers are passed, components are promoted to a stage environment, where they have to pass provisioning and sanity tests once again. Besides that, extensive load and performance tests with different usage patterns are performed to ensure that the component fully complies with certain QoS requirements (e.g., availability, response time) and scales well. SOASTA CloudTest (SOASTA, 2014) is currently used for those tests, which enables the simulation of global Internet traffic and real-time analytics. Finally, the staging environment's configuration is deployed to a non-live production environment and – once tests are passed – it is gradually activated for customers. To summarize, deployment procedures involve a lot of complex steps and activities in several environments to finally release a component. According to recent evaluations, the proposed automated deployment process greatly enhances the performance of agile development teams at Adobe, enabling an accurate, reliable, fast and repeatable deployment of software components supporting short development cycles.

7.3 Operations and Scaling Behavior

Once components are rolled out to production environments in different regions, the operations team is responsible for monitoring QoS parameters of components and for handling outages or performance degradations. First experiences with automated deployment processes based on a pre-baking strategy indicate that the components' startup time can be reduced significantly. In a wider sense, this provides the foundation for a cost-efficient and QoS-compliant scaling by utilizing the benefits of elastic cloud infrastructures.

8. CONCLUSION

The adoption of cloud computing for the delivery of elastic cloud applications is highly dependent on an automated and standardized deployment process and configuration management activities. These two aspects complement each other and provide a foundation to efficiently manage cost-effective and elastic cloud applications according to functional and non-functional QoS requirements. In this chapter, essential requirements of scalable cloud software applications are identified and discussed. On this basis, a novel process model to standardize and automate deployment processes is proposed. The process model reflects the interconnections between deployment processes and configuration management activities. The proposed process model composes all activities necessary for realizing a deployment of components in multiple environments and regions,

auto-scaling, and a reconstruction of certain cloud environments. The process model describes the entire lifecycle of cloud-based application components and considers organizational and cultural aspects as well as the use of tools to support process activities. A mechanism to significantly reduce latency of provisioning and deployment activities is also considered by the proposed deployment process. The potential benefits for enterprises that adopt cloud infrastructure services are demonstrated in an Adobe case study. Consequently, the approach considers many important aspects regarding configuration management in the cloud that are not yet covered in the current literature.

The chapter further describes the current state-of-the-art concerning cloud deployment as well as limitations and research challenges that need to be addressed to further enhance automated deployment processes. Thus, this chapter is intended as a starting point for implementing a highly efficient and qualitative deployment of elastic applications in cloud environments using a pre-baking strategy. An efficient deployment of cloud applications is relevant for both practice and academia. Several studies indicate the importance of automated deployment processes for scientific computing applications. The reproducibility of configurations may help to better compare different cloud environment and application settings. For further research, we intend to incorporate models and methods from the area of decision analytics into the prototype implementation of the proposed deployment process in order to measure and improve the performance of different degrees of pre-configuration and auto-scaling procedures. Based on dynamic monitoring data, methods to minimize costs of elastic cloud applications under QoS constraints shall be considered as well as related dynamic cloud pricing models. Moreover, it is essential to solve the identified research challenges in order to facilitate an effective adoption of cloud computing in global and national companies providing multitenant software applications in global cloud environments.

REFERENCES

Ammons, G., Bala, V., Mummert, T., Reimer, D., & Zhang, X. (2011). Virtual machine images as structured data: the Mirage image library. In *Proceedings of the 3rd USENIX conference on Hot topics in cloud computing. HotCloud 2011* (pp. 1–6).

Armbrust, M., Fox, A., Griffith, R., Joseph, A. D., Katz, R., Konwinski, A., & Stoica, I. et al. (2010). A view of cloud computing. *Communications of the ACM, 53*(4), 50–58. doi:10.1145/1721654.1721672

Bai, X., Li, M., Chen, B., Tsai, W.-T., & Gao, J. (2011). Cloud testing tools. In *Proceedings of the IEEE 6th International Symposium on Service Oriented System Engineering. SOSE 2011* (pp. 1–12). doi:10.1109/SOSE.2011.6139087

Breitenbücher, U., Binz, T., Kopp, O., Leymann, F., & Wettinger, J. (2013). Integrated cloud application provisioning: interconnecting service-centric and script-centric management technologies. In *Conferences on the move to meaningful internet systems* (pp. 130–148). OTM. doi:10.1007/978-3-642-41030-7_9

Celesti, A., Tusa, F., Villari, M., & Puliafito, A. (2010). How to enhance cloud architectures to enable cross-federation. In *Proceedings of the IEEE 3rd International Conference on Cloud Computing. CLOUD 2010* (pp. 337–345). doi:10.1109/CLOUD.2010.46

Cerbelaud, D., Garg, S., & Huylebroeck, J. (2009). Opening the clouds: qualitative overview of the state-of-the-art open source VM-based cloud management platforms. In *Proceedings of the 10th ACM/IFIP/USENIX International Conference on Middleware. Middleware 2009* (pp. 1–8).

Chang, V., Wills, G., & Walters, R. J. (2014). Review of cloud computing and existing frameworks for cloud adoption. In Advances in Cloud Computing Research.

Chapman, C., Emmerich, W., Márquez, F. G., Clayman, S., & Galis, A. (2011). Software architecture definition for on-demand cloud provisioning. *Cluster Computing, 15*(2), 79–100. doi:10.1007/s10586-011-0152-0

Chen, Z., Zhao, Y., Miao, X., Chen, Y., & Wang, Q. (2009). Rapid provisioning of cloud infrastructure leveraging peer-to-peer networks. In *Proceedings of the IEEE 26th Conference on Distributed Computing Systems. ICDCS 2009* (pp. 324–329). doi:10.1109/ICDCSW.2009.35

Diaz, J., von Laszewski, G., Wang, F., & Fox, G. (2012). Abstract image management and universal image registration for cloud and HPC infrastructures. In *Proceedings of the IEEE 5th International Conference on Cloud Computing. CLOUD 2012* (pp. 463–470). doi:10.1109/CLOUD.2012.94

Gao, J., Bai, X., & Tsai, W.-T. (2011). Cloud testing-issues, challenges, needs and practice. *Software Engineering, 1*(1), 9–23.

Heilig, L., & Voß, S. (2014a). (to appear). Decision analytics for cloud computing: A classification and literature review. *Tutorials in Operations Research.* doi:10.1287/educ.2014.0124

Heilig, L., & Voß, S. (2014b). A scientometric analysis of cloud computing literature. *IEEE Transactions on Cloud Computing. DOI: (preprint version).*10.1109/TCC.2014.2321168

Humble, J., & Farley, D. (2011). *Continuous delivery: Reliable software releases through build, test, and deployment automation.* Upper Saddle River, NJ: Addison-Wesley.

Hüttermann, M. (2012). *DevOps for developers.* New York: Apress.

Juve, G., & Deelman, E. (2011). Automating application deployment in infrastructure clouds. In *Proceedings of the IEEE 3rd International Conference on Cloud Computing Technology and Science. CloudCom 2011* (pp. 658–665). doi:10.1109/CloudCom.2011.102

Karunakaran, S. (2013). Impact of cloud adoption on agile software development. In Z. Mahmood & S. Saeed (Eds.), *Software Engineering Frameworks for the Cloud Computing Paradigm* (pp. 213–234). London: Springer. doi:10.1007/978-1-4471-5031-2_10

Konstantinou, A. V., Eilam, T., Kalantar, M., Totok, A. A., Arnold, W., & Snible, E. (2009). An architecture for virtual solution composition and deployment in infrastructure clouds. In *Proceedings of the 3rd International Workshop on Virtualization Technologies in Distributed Computing. VTDC 2009* (pp. 9–18). doi:10.1145/1555336.1555339

Lagar-Cavilla, H. A., Whitney, J. A., Scannell, A. M., Patchin, P., Rumble, S. M., De Lara, E., & Satyanarayanan, M. et al. (2009). SnowFlock: Rapid virtual machine cloning for cloud computing. In *Proceedings of the 4th ACM European Conference on Computer systems. EuroSys 2009* (pp. 1–12). doi:10.1145/1519065.1519067

Leavitt, N. (2009). Is cloud computing really ready for prime time? *Computer, 42*(1), 15–20. doi:10.1109/MC.2009.20

Marston, S., Li, Z., Bandyopadhyay, S., Zhang, J., & Ghalsasi, A. (2011). Cloud computing – The business perspective. *Decision Support Systems, 51*(1), 176–189. doi:10.1016/j.dss.2010.12.006

Mell, P., & Grance, T. (2011). The NIST definition of cloud computing. *NIST Special Publication, 800*(145), 7.

Meyer, S., Healy, P., Lynn, T., & Morrison, J. (2013). Quality assurance for open source software configuration management. In *Management of resources and services in cloud and sky computing* (pp. 1–8). MICAS. doi:10.1109/SYNASC.2013.66

Moreno-Vozmediano, R., Montero, R. S., & Llorente, I. M. (2011). Multicloud deployment of computing clusters for loosely coupled MTC applications. *IEEE Transactions on Parallel and Distributed Systems, 22*(6), 924–930. doi:10.1109/TPDS.2010.186

Myers, G. J. Badgett, T., & Sandler, C. (2004). The art of software testing. Hoboken, NJ: John Wiley & Sons.

Packer. (2014). Packer. [Online] Retrieved March 20, 2014, from: http://www.packer.io

Peng, C., Kim, M., Zhang, Z., & Lei, H. (2012). VDN: Virtual machine image distribution network for cloud data centers. In *Proceedings of the IEEE 31st International Conference on Computer Communications. INFOCOM 2012* (pp. 181–189). doi:10.1109/INFCOM.2012.6195556

Rodero-Merino, L., Vaquero, L. M., Gil, V., Galán, F., Fontán, J., Montero, R. S., & Llorente, I. M. (2010). From infrastructure delivery to service management in clouds. *Future Generation Computer Systems, 26*(8), 1226–1240. doi:10.1016/j.future.2010.02.013

Sampaio, A., & Mendonça, N. (2011). Uni-4Cloud: An approach based on open standards for deployment and management of multi-cloud applications. In *Proceedings of the 2nd International Workshop on Software Engineering for Cloud Computing. ICSE 2011* (pp. 15–21). doi:10.1145/1985500.1985504

SOASTA. (2014). CloudTest – cloud based load and performance testing. Retrieved July 21, 2014, from http://www.soasta.com/products/cloudtest

Sommerville, I. (2011). *Software engineering* (9th ed.). Boston, MA: Pearson.

Tang, C. P., Wong, T. Y., & Lee, P. P. (2012). CloudVS: Enabling version control for virtual machines in an open-source cloud under commodity settings. In *IEEE Network Operations and Management Symposium. NOMS 2012* (pp. 188–195). doi:10.1109/NOMS.2012.6211898

Wood, T., Ramakrishnan, K. K., Shenoy, P., & Van der Merwe, J. (2011). CloudNet: Dynamic pooling of cloud resources by live WAN migration of virtual machines. In ACM SIGPLAN Notices (vol. 46, pp. 121–132). doi:10.1145/1952682.1952699

Zhu, H., Hall, P. A., & May, J. H. (1997). Software unit test coverage and adequacy. *ACM Computing Surveys*, 29(4), 366–427. doi:10.1145/267580.267590

KEY TERMS AND DEFINITIONS

Auto-Scaling: A process to automatically adopt the underlying infrastructure according to current software application requirements in order to maintain performance during peak time and to reduce expenses at off-peak times.

Cloud Computing: A paradigm of providing virtualized computing resources and services through a network. While providers of these resources and services aim to achieve economies of scale and cost reductions by optimizing resource utilization and energy consumption under consideration of guaranteed quality levels, consumers are mostly attracted by on-demand use options, scalability, flexible pricing schemes and high degree of automation.

Cloud Deployment: All tasks, processes, actors and systems that are involved in making software applications available to the end user through a cloud.

Configuration Management: Configuration management is concerned with policies, processes and tools to build and maintain changing software components and underlying infrastructure systems. Related activities involve source/version management, change management as well as build and release management.

DevOps: A portmanteau describing principles that encourage a better collaboration between development and operations teams in order to increase the quality and performance of the overall software delivery process.

Pre-Baking Strategy: A least common denominator of software packages and configurations is pre-installed on a virtual machine image in order to reduce the overall deployment time of software applications using this type of virtual machine.

Virtualization: A key enabling technology for cloud computing that allows the sharing of computing resources among multiple users by creating virtual machines acting like real computing resources while being separated from the underlying physical hardware resources and isolated from other virtual machines running on the same hardware. This further enables a flexible resource allocation and scheduling.

Section 4
Proofs-of-Concept and Demonstrations

Chapter 12
Cloud Services for Healthcare:
Insights from a Multidisciplinary Integration Project

Konstantinos Koumaditis
University of Piraeus, Greece

George Vassilacopoulos
University of Piraeus, Greece

George Pittas
University of Piraeus, Greece

Andriana Prentza
University of Piraeus, Greece

Marinos Themistocleous
University of Piraeus, Greece

Dimosthenis Kyriazis
University of Piraeus, Greece

Flora Malamateniou
University of Piraeus, Greece

ABSTRACT

Healthcare organisations are forced to reconsider their current business practices and embark on a cloud adoption journey. Cloud-Computing offers important benefits that make it attractive for healthcare (e.g. cost effective model, big data management etc.). Large Information Technology (IT) companies are investing big sums in building infrastructure, services, tools and applications to facilitate Cloud-Computing for healthcare organisations, practitioners and patients. Yet, many challenges that such integration projects contain are still in the e-health research agenda like design and technology requirements to handle big volume of data, ensure scalability and user satisfaction to name a few. The purpose of this chapter is (a) to address the Cloud-Computing services for healthcare in the form of a Personal Healthcare record (PHR) and (b) demonstrate a multidisciplinary project. In doing so, the authors aim at increasing the awareness of this important endeavour and provide insights on Cloud-Computing e-health services for healthcare organisations.

INTRODUCTION

The introduction of Cloud-Computing and its business models have been some of the biggest changes impacting not only the IT sector but also several others including healthcare. The impact of Cloud-Computing on healthcare can be characterized as a positive change as it provides integration at a manageable cost and it introduces a new market of services. These two issues will be analyzed in the following paragraphs.

DOI: 10.4018/978-1-4666-8210-8.ch012

Copyright © 2015, IGI Global. Copying or distributing in print or electronic forms without written permission of IGI Global is prohibited.

Doctor's clinics, hospitals, and healthcare organisations (e.g., insurance bodies) require fast access to medical data, computing and large storage facilities which are not provided in the traditional settings (e.g., legacy systems). Additionally, in today's fast communication world medical data needs to be shared across various settings and geographical locations in a fast secure way without limitations (e.g., errors, cost) that might cause significant delay in treatment and loss of time. Recently, cloud technology has started replacing legacy healthcare systems and offers easier and faster access to medical data (e.g., exam results, patients history, etc.) as defined by the way it is stored (e.g., public, private or hybrid). Literature depicts that Cloud-Computing offers significant benefits to the healthcare sector with its business (e.g., pay-as-you-go) model and integration capability (Kuo, 2011). Renowned global IT players like Microsoft, Oracle, Amazon have already heavily invested in more powerful, reliable and cost-efficient cloud platforms, extending their new offerings for e-health services, such as Microsoft's HealthVault, Oracle's Exalogic Elastic Cloud, and Amazon Web Services (AWS) (Zhang, Cheng, & Boutaba, 2010).

The integration that can be achieved from such Cloud-Computing healthcare services is conceptualized under the term integrated patient centered care (Leventhal, Taliaferro, Wong, Hughes, & Mun, 2012). Integrated patient centered care reflects on integrated Healthcare Information Systems (HIS) (with elements as e-health cloud services) requiring coordination across professionals, facilities, support systems that is continuous over time and between patient visits (Singer et al., 2011). This approach is observed on national healthcare strategies that encourage patient involvement in their healthcare treatment. For example, the American Recovery and Reinvestment Act of 2009 (ARRA) laid down by the U.S. government is encouraging businesses in the healthcare industry to utilize certain applications of electronic records (Black et al., 2011). Follow-

ing similar legislative opportunities worldwide, patients increase their involvement with cloud healthcare services (Axelsson, Melin, & Söderström, 2011). This is a growing involvement, seen in parallel with mechanisms for the collection of information (obtained by mobile and other sources) in order to develop an enhanced, complete and integrated view of citizens health status.

This is an emerging area of e-health and a new market segment for contemporary organizations, given the term m-health (Chatterjee, Chakraborty, Sarker, Sarker, & Lau, 2009). According to a recent report m-health applications that are published on the two leading platforms, iOS and Android, has more than doubled in only 2.5 years to reach more than 100,000 apps (e.g., 1st quarter of 2014) with a market revenue of USD 2.4bn in 2013 and projections to grow to USD 26bn by the end of 2017 (Research2guidance, 2014). The major source of income for m-health application publishers will come from services (69%). These services typically involve backend structures of servers and/or teams of medical staff which monitor and consult with doctors, patients and general healthcare-interested individuals. Sarasohn-Kahn (2010), identified that a major mobile application vendor provides 5,805 health, medical and fitness applications with 73% of them used by patients and 27% by healthcare professionals (Sarasohn-Kahn, 2010). A big advantage to the growth of this market is the parallel advance of the smartphones. Evidently, the latest generation of smartphones is increasingly viewed as handheld computers rather than as phones, due to their powerful on-board computing capability, capacious memories, large screens and open operating systems that encourage application development (Boulos, Wheeler, Tavares, & Jones, 2011). Additionally, another promising area that allows people to be constantly monitored regarding their physical condition is the integration of sensing and consumer electronics. Market experts forecast that monitoring services will correspond to about US$ 15 billion market pool in 2017 (Chowdhury, Krishnan, & Vishwanath, 2012). These services either as m-health and/or via the internet in-home networks, can aid residents and their caregivers by providing continuous medical monitoring, memory enhancement, control of home appliances, medical data access, and emergency communication (Alemdar & Ersoy, 2010).

The aforementioned approaches empower the patients and allow them to take their own measurements, and provide verbal and written inputs (Clemensen, Rasmussen, Denning, & Craggs, 2011). In a technological respect the empowerment happens through information-sharing, offering the patients a visual overview of their course of treatment, letting the patients take their own measurements, and letting them provide verbal and written inputs (Clemensen et al., 2011). Many of these applications are based on Service Oriented Architecture (SOA) as e-health services can be easily delivered to both desktop and mobile computer devices using, for instance, JavaScript and HyperText Markup Language (HTML). Based on the SOA paradigm e-health services can be exposed and run over cloud (in the form of SaaS) (Poulymenopoulou, Malamateniou, & Vassilacopoulos, 2012).

Therefore, it is evident that Cloud-Computing can be used to provide efficient, scalable, portable, interoperable and integrated IT infrastructures that are cost effective and maintainable. Yet, despite the significant importance of these technologies, the healthcare sector has not paid much attention on these technologies. The healthcare industry is a laggard in the adoption of cloud services and this is mainly due to the challenges (e.g., financial, security, interoperability etc.) that such shift holds. As a result, many standalone applications exist in the area of healthcare providing services and supporting the activities of all actors involved such as patients, healthcare professionals, laboratories, hospitals.

At this point emphasis must be placed in past failures of IT systems in industry in general and healthcare in particular and have cost millions of Euros and even the death of patients (Avison & Young, 2007; Dwivedi et al., 2013). For that reason, it is of high importance to research the Cloud Services for Healthcare from a multidiscipline perspective (e.g., technological, medical, business and academic).

PERSONAL HEALTHCARE RECORDS (PHR)

Most developed countries are facing important overall problems regarding health care services, such as:

1. Aging population with increased demand on specialized health care services (e.g., chronic diseases),
2. Need for increased efficiency with limited financial resources (e.g., staff/bed reduction),
3. Requirements for increased accessibility of care outside hospitals (e.g., home care) to name a few.

To these problems, advances in information and communication technologies have provided considerable assistance in the form of Electronic Healthcare Records (EHRs). Yet, it seems that traditional EHRs, which are based on the 'fetch and show' model, provide limited functionality that does not cover the spectrum of the patients' needs. Therefore, new solutions as the PHRs appeared to narrow this gap. In more detail, PHRs' data can come from various sources like EHRs, health providers (e.g., e-Prescibing, e-Referal), and/or directly from the patient him/herself – including non-clinical information (e.g., exercise habits, food and dieting statistics, etc.) (Koufi, Malamateniou, & Vassilacopoulos, 2013). The PHR concept is a new multidiscipline area of research, with crucial aspects as it deals with the wellbeing of patients.

Three general PHR models have been proposed (Detmer, Bloomrosen, Raymond, & Tang, 2008):

1. The stand-alone model,
2. Electronic Health Record (EHR) system, and
3. The integrated one, which is an interoperable system providing linkage with a variety of patient information sources such as EHRs, home diagnostics, insurance claims etc.

The main types of health information supported by PHRs are problem lists, procedures, major illnesses, provider lists, allergy data, home-monitored data, family history, social history and lifestyle, immunizations, medications and laboratory tests (Halamka, Mandl, & Tang, 2008; Tang, Ash, Bates, Overhage, & Sands, 2006). Widely known PHR platforms in terms of centralized web-based portals include Dossia (www.dossia.org) and Microsoft Health Vault (www.healthvault.com) platforms. Many systems presented in literature offer integration with already established PHRs platforms (Reti, Feldman, & Safran, 2009; Zhou, Yang, Álamo, Wong, & Chang, 2010). Early experiences from the adoption of PHR-based systems have been found to be positive, showing that such systems can be feasible, secure, and well accepted by patients (Jennett & Watanabe, 2006). Nonetheless, today's EHRs and PHRs are far from being what the citizens consider as of value to their health, since for the public view, health means more than being disease-free.

Following this trend for patients' empowerment, academics, practitioners and patients advocate in favor of the patient centered healthcare systems. Still the aforementioned advocates have not yet reached a concise definition of Patient-Centered e-health (PCEH) that is shared across the research disciplines that focus on health and Information Technology (IT) (Wilson & Strong, 2014). The lack of consensus can be attributed, amongst other,

1. On the number of challenges that are involved in transitioning healthcare delivery to a more patient-centered system, and
2. The lack of proof-of-concept through well-documented and effective PCEH projects.

Thus, the challenge to integrate and redesign existing healthcare systems towards a more patient-centered exists (Leventhal et al., 2012).

To this end, the authors introduce in this chapter a list of PHR/EHR approaches and provide a brief introduction for each in the following section.

CURRENT PHR/EHR CLOUD-COMPUTING PROJECTS

Literature includes various examples of PHR and EHR approaches with different themes, addressing various aspects and produced in diverse settings (e.g., industry, academia etc.). This composes a mosaic of different examples that individual researchers of the field and/or developers need to consider before embarking in the Cloud-Computing e-health journey. Studying past endeavors one may learn from the successes and diverge from the mistakes of others. Therefore, our intentions for presenting such examples extend from providing a helpful list of recent PHR/EHR projects to illustrate unique techniques to implement Cloud services, describe ways to resolve the integration challenges faced, provide recent advances from academia and industry and highlight lessons learned and recommendations. The authors acknowledge that this is not an exhaustive list of examples but a suitable one for the theme and audience of this book.

To provide a better illustration and help the reader understand this important integration issue, the authors researched the literature and depict herein a twofold categorization of the findings, such as:

1. PHR/EHR solutions and/or
2. PHR/EHR components.

This provides a useful categorization in the current ongoing PHR issues discussion. Starting with the PHR/EHR below the identified projects are presented in an alphabetical list.

- **CareCloud:** Offers several approaches ranging from SaaS, to data analytics and IaaS. It offers healthcare practices a way to manage their practice with a plethora of tools. CareCloud allows the management of patient records, appointments, billing and reporting. Charts solution provides an easy to use EHR system. CareCloud also has solutions for doctor – patient virtual interaction (SUCRE, 2014).

- **ClearHealth Office:** A solution for small practices (fewer than ten physicians or 20,000 encounters per year) that can be distributed in two forms. The one is on premises and the second is cloud based. The first one (on premise), requires hardware and detailed setup processes. The second one is a cloud solution that removes the need for hardware and the problems with detailed setup. It is called HealthCloud and promises to deliver ready-to-go installations of ClearHealth Office on fully managed and secured datacenters owned by Amazon. This service is suitable for US practitioners, interested in self-serving their installations (ClearHealth, 2013).

- **EMC Electronic Health Record Infrastructure Solutions:** Consist of integrated, validated solutions with industry-leading healthcare ISV partners, clinical applications, and best-in-class hardware, software, and services to help caregivers to move forward with their EHR deployment. EMC provides the supporting IT infrastructure aligned with clinical services needs for the highest levels of performance, availability, security, virtualization, and integration (EMC, 2014).

- **Healthcare Trustworthy Platform:** A multilevel Personal Health Record (PHR) platform based on the Trustworthy Cloud Technology that allows people to share health data while guaranteeing security and privacy. It aims to integrate of third party applications and give them access to user's health data (e.g., view, add and update). It also provides a high security model which allows the patients to decide how and with whom to share data (Tclouds, 2014).

- **HealthVault:** The most popular solution in our list is the well-known HealthVault. It is being distributed through Windows Azure cloud server, which is already widely implemented in business environments and in some public administrations. Microsoft HealthVault provides one place to store and access of health information online. It supports interoperability with other healthcare providers. There is a growing list of devices such as pedometers, blood pressure monitors, blood glucose monitors, and even weight scales which work with HealthVault. In that way the users, don't have to enter anything by hand, just upload their data directly to HealthVault from compatible devices (Microsoft, 2014).

- **Medscribler:** A SaaS solution for recording patient data. It uses mobile technologies such as tablets and smartphones and handwriting recognition software to allow ease submission of patient data. It is an EMR solution that provides a quick and intuitive way to update medical records of patients. These records can be stored in a cloud. This solution provides an innovative approach to the problems of mobile practicing of medicine. The doctor is able to update patient records via a network connection and thus has no need for bulkier equipment than a tablet computer (Medscribbler, 2014).

- **OpenEMR:** A free and open source Electronic Health Records (EMR) and medical practice management application that can run on multiple platforms. OpenEMR is supported by a community of volunteers and professionals. This software can be implemented into a cloud as SaaS. It supports cloud structures, encryption, remote access and web browser access (OpenEMR, 2014).

- **SOFTCARE:** A multi-cloud-enabled platform which has developed a prototype of a monitoring system for seniors that allow caregivers (formal and informal) and senior users to get real-time alarms in dangerous or potentially dangerous situations and warnings on long-term trends that could indicate a future problem. It is based on Artificial Intelligence techniques that allow the recognition of daily activities based on the data obtained from an accelerometer (bracelet device) and location information (AAL-Europe, 2013).

- **X1.V1:** Another integration platform is X1.V1. It offers effective tools to generate reports about
  ○ The general healthcare status of the population,
  ○ The quality of healthcare performance, and
  ○ The financial costs. In that way, it facilitates the cooperation among the different caregivers in the provision of diagnosis and treatment. Another intuitive feature is that it enhances epidemic diseases and cancer detection rate (Deadalus, 2014).

- **Zappa:** An open source, extensible, scalable and customizable cloud platform for the development of e-Health/m-Health systems. It aims at delivering resources as services over Internet (Cloud-Computing). Moreover, the platform is intended to provide uninterrupted monitoring with the goal of obtaining some information that can be subsequently analyzed by physicians for diagnosing. It has also been developed two e-Health applications based on that platform:
  ○ Zappa App,
  ○ Cloud Rehab (Ruiz-Zafra, Benghazi, Noguera, & Garrido, 2013).

Having described the PHR/EHR solutions, the second part of list, the PHR/EHR components are depicted.

- **Cloud Rehab:** is a full m-Health system that is used to monitor the daily activities of patients with severe brain damage. It is a component to the Zappa cloud platform mentioned above. Cloud Rehab consists of two applications
  ○ Web application, and
  ○ Android application. Web application is being used by the medical staff to manage patients' medical information. Whereas, android application is being used by the patient. The mobile application monitors heart rate and sends the data to the cloud (Ruiz-Zafra et al., 2013).

- **DAPHNE:** A Data as a Service (DaaS) platform for collecting, managing and analyzing wellness data in order to provide healthy lifestyle and preventive medicine (Daphne, 2013). DAPHNE platform is open to hardware and software developers, providing data for different personalised health services, both for the citizen and the service provider.

- **EMC Collaborative Healthcare Solutions:** Provides a patient-centric infrastructure to "content-enable" Picture Archiving and Communication System, Hospital Information System, and Electronic Medical Record applications for accessing all relevant clinical, financial, and operational data. Based on open standards, the solution is in accordance with the Integrating the Healthcare Enterprise initiative that promotes the coordinated use of established standards. Their solution enhances operational agility through the abstraction of applications and infrastructure, improves financial performance by managing physical and virtual assets with highly automated tools, and secures access to and prevents loss of protected health information (SUCRE, 2014).

- **VIGOR++:** An international research project that aims to create a personalised gastrointestinal tract model, which facilitates accurate detection and grading of Crohn's disease. VIGOR++ processes multiscale information from patients, including laboratory, MRI, colonoscopy and microscopy (histopathology) data. Its techniques are integrated in the 3DNetMedical.com medical imaging cloud service, to make them immediately available in a clinically usable environment (Vodera, 2014).

- **Zappa App:** An m-Health system used to monitor the heart rate, temperature and blood pressure of the patient. It is a component to the Zappa cloud platform which is mentioned above. In addition, Zappa App is able to save the vital sign values, detect health problems and share information with a doctor or medical staff that are in the same place as the patient (Bluetooth) (Ruiz-Zafra et al., 2013).

The aforementioned categorized list is presented in Table 1. The first column is an arithmetic count of the projects, the second the name, the third the type based on our categorization, the fourth the description and the last column the reference for each.

The aforementioned PHR/EHR solutions utilize the Cloud-Computing advances to achieve common goals, therefore they hold similarities such as:

1. Integration,
2. Interoperability, and
3. Lower business expenses.

All of the aforementioned approaches try to integrate different systems to manage medical information based on a centralized system hosted on cloud. Furthermore, they try to provide users with the ability to access the systems through different type of operating systems (e.g., Windows, Linux, and MAC OS) and devices (e.g., desktop, laptop, tablet, smartphones, and medical sensors). The solutions presented in Table 1 leverage Cloud-Computing benefits to lower expenses both on Operating Expenditure (OPEX) and Capital Expenditure (CAPEX) at the health section. For example, solution number [7] can run in different systems, while [1,4,9] support integration of different type of systems resulting to lower business expenses.

Apart from the similarities, the above mentioned solutions also have differences between them, such as:

1. Different type of users,
2. Different target territories, and
3. Different type of devices.

For example, solution number [8] is designed for senior people, [2] for small practices and [11] for patients with severe brain damage, [2] targets USA practitioners and [11, 15] address mobile devices implementations.

The aforementioned Cloud-Computing solutions hold several merits and aim at the same goal, provide better e-health services. Yet, due to the critical nature of healthcare and the importance of successful implementation of such endeavors, there is still need for rigorous research that can carefully examine the development steps and provide "best-fit" technologies. To accommodate this need the authors' involvement in a multidiscipline e-health integration project that utilizes Cloud-Computing. This endeavor is analyzed in the following section.

Table 1. Requirements: proposed technologies

	Name	Type	Description	Reference
1.	CareCloud	EHR	An easy to use EHR system which provides solutions for doctor – patient virtual interaction.	(SUCRE, 2014)
2.	ClearHealth Office	EHR	Provides an open source solution for running a small practice.	(ClearHealth, 2013)
3.	EMC Electronic Health Record Infrastructure Solutions	PHR/ EHR	Provides clinical applications, hardware, software, and services.	(EMC, 2014)
4.	Healthcare Trustworthy Platform	PHR	PHR platform for sharing securely health data and providing integration with 3rd party applications.	(Tclouds, 2014)
5.	HealthVault	PHR	Provides one place to store and access all health information online.	(Microsoft, 2014)
6.	Medscribler	EHR	SaaS solution providing intuitive way to solve the mobile's practicing issues of medicine.	(Medscribbler, 2014)
7.	OpenEMR	EHR	Free and open source Electronic Health Records (EHR) and medical practice management application that can on multiple platforms.	(OpenEMR, 2014)
8.	SOFTCARE	PHR	Multi-cloud-enabled platform monitoring senior people.	(AAL, 2013)
9.	X1.V1	PHR/ EHR	Integrated platform with intuitive features statistical reports about patients, caregivers and financial costs)	(Deadalus, 2014)
10.	Zappa	PHR/ EHR	Extensible, scalable and customizable cloud platform for the development of e-Health/m-Health systems.	(Ruiz-Zafra et al., 2013)
11.	Cloud Rehab	COM/ NT	M-health system monitor daily activities of patients with severe brain damage	(Ruiz-Zafra et al., 2013)
12.	DAPHNE	COM/ NT	Data as a Service (DaaS) platform for collecting, managing and analyzing wellness data in order to provide healthy lifestyle and preventive medicine	(Daphne, 2013)
13.	EMC Collaborative Healthcare Solutions	PHR/ EHR	Provides a patient-centric infrastructure to "content-enable" Picture Archiving and Communication System, Hospital Information System, and Electronic Medical Record applications.	(SUCRE, 2014)
14.	VIGOR++	COM/ NT	Personalised gastrointestinal tract model, which facilitates accurate detection and grading of Crohn's disease.	(Vodera, 2014)
15.	Zappa App	COM/ NT	M-health system for monitoring the heart rate, temperature, blood pressure of patient	(Ruiz-Zafra et al., 2013)

PROVIDING INTEGRATED E-HEALTH SERVICES FOR PERSONALIZED MEDICINE UTILIZING CLOUD INFRASTRUCTURE (PINCLOUD)

The proposed project *Providing INtegrated e-health services for personalized medicine utilizing CLOUD* infrastructure (PINCLOUD), seeks to integrate different application components,

leading to the provision of an end-to-end personalized disease monitoring and medical data service "anytime, anywhere", which ensures an independent living regardless of age (Koumaditis et al., 2014). Additionally, from a managerial and research perspective it can be emphasized that the multidiscipline nature of this project provided a multidiscipline R&D team. The authors of this chapter are part of this team covering a wide

Figure 1. Providing integrated e-health services for personalized medicine utilizing cloud infrastructure

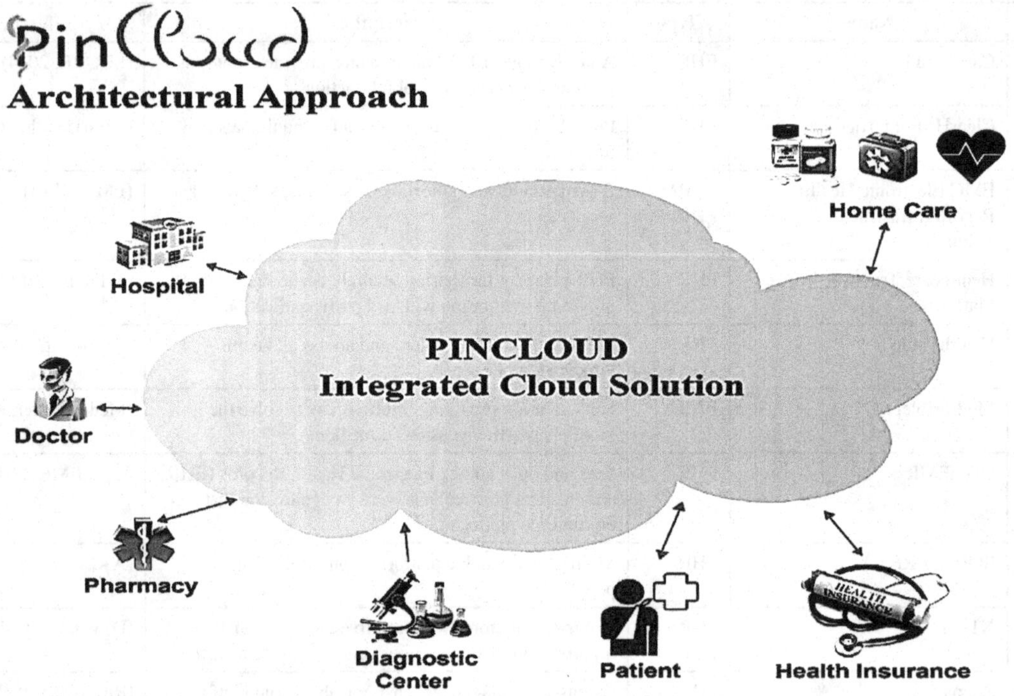

range of disciplines from healthcare professionals, IT experts, researchers from both academia and business.

Introduction

The scenario upon which PINCLOUD is developed, as seen in Figure 1, plays as such: a patient governs his\her PHR that can be remotely monitored by a doctor located either at a hospital or at an individual medical office. Complementary to the PHR's stored information the doctor monitors the patient using a home-care platform that receives and analyses patient's medical data. The proposed home-care platform will include among others the following services:

1. Asthma or COPD disease management;
2. Hyper-tension disease management;
3. Diabetes monitoring;
4. ECG monitoring;

5. Video/Audio Access to physicians for remote consultation;
6. Remote picture and text archiving and communication service (back-up/long term archiving complementary to infrastructure operated by hospitals); and
7. Fall Prevention and Detection Services.

The doctor can access the patient's PHR online through the PINCLOUD Integrated Cloud Solution. The latter can support the doctor in decision making and results in better quality of health service. In more detail, the doctor retrieves and updates the patient's medical data and can also use the proposed on-line system to:

1. Prescribe a new medicine;
2. Fill in an e-referral for specific exams (e.g., blood test);
3. Inform and advise his/her patient; or
4. Ask the patient to visit the hospital.

Following the doctor's advice, the patient visits a pharmacy, or a diagnostic center or a hospital. At the final stage, the healthcare service providers (doctors, hospitals, diagnostic centers) and pharmacies interact with the health insurance organisation to compensate all outstanding orders and medical actions.

MAIN IDEAS AND REQUIREMENTS

Service and data availability is crucial for healthcare providers who cannot effectively operate unless their applications are functioning properly and patients' data are available in a consistent manner. This is also the case for PINCLOUD. PINCLOUD's services (e.g., E-Prescription, E-Referral, Home-Care and PHR) ought to be available continuously with no interruptions or performance degradation since they will be used for decision making regarding the patients wellbeing.

New development projects, as PINCLOUD need to reinsure service availability to the participating healthcare providers and other organizations. In addition, hardware and software installations, upgrades, and reconfigurations have to be managed and maintained without any service interruptions that may cause problems. In order to achieve the availability in a cost efficient way the use of Cloud-Computing seemed to be the appropriate solution and thus the PINCLOUD was designed based on its features. Features such as cost-saving, agility, efficiency, resource consolidation, business opportunities and Green-IT are relevant and applicable to the healthcare sector (Chang et al, 2011; Chang, 2013b; Chang 2014).

Moreover, PINCLOUD potentially will be responsible for the governance of a big volume of medical and thus sensitive data. The protection of such data is paramount. At this stage of the project the protection of these data is achieved with a Private Cloud delivery model. A Private Cloud model is operated by a single organiza-

tion. In the private cloud, the technology resides within an organization's own data centre and the resources are deployed as needed to the different departments. In our project, a private IT company which is part of the consortium has provided the Private Cloud's infrastructure. In that way, the developers can overcome the challenges associated with other Cloud models (e.g., Public, Hybrid) since the ability to manage and control sensitive patient data remains within the organization.

As mentioned above, PINCLOUD is based on the well-known Cloud-Computing three service models' structure, namely:

1. Software as a Service (SaaS),
2. Platform as a Service (PaaS), and
3. Infrastructure as a Service (IaaS).

The way that PINCLOUD is decoded in the three models is depicted in Figure 2 and it is explained in the following paragraphs.

Respectively, PINCLOUD provides the user interaction through SaaS. In theory, SaaS is the capability provided to the consumer to use the provider's applications running on a cloud infrastructure (Mell & Grance, 2009). The applications are accessible from various client devices through either a thin client interface, such as a web browser (e.g., web-based email), or a program interface. PINCLOUD as depicted in Figure 2, offers four applications:

1. E-prescription,
2. E-referral,
3. Home-Care, and
4. PHR.

These applications provide the main functionality required and are being consumed by End-Users (e.g., Patients, Doctors, Hospitals/Labs and Insurance Bodies). All these users access the PINCLOUD through user-interface provided as a service. For example, a PINCLOUD registered user can have access to his/her medical record online.

Figure 2. PINCLOUD's services and actors

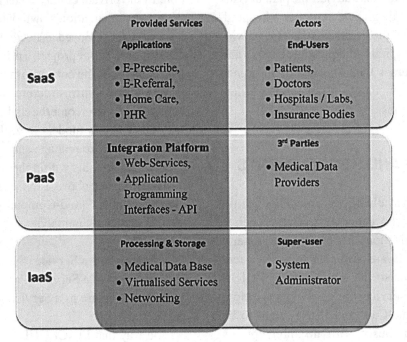

In addition, PINCLOUD takes advantage of PaaS service model. Literature presents PaaS as the capability provided to the consumer to use and or deploy into the cloud infrastructure consumer-created or acquired applications created using programming languages and tools supported by the provider (Mell & Grance, 2009). Accordingly, the R&D team takes advantage of the PaaS model and provides open source components as Web-Services and Application Programming Interfaces (APIs) that facilitate the integration with third parties (e.g., Medical Data Providers, Hospitals). For example, when a hospital decides to be integrated in the PINCLOUD system, it can allocate and consume the Web-services' API that the R&D team have created.

The processing and storage capability of PINCLOUD is based on IaaS model. IaaS is the capability provided to the consumer to provide processing, storage, networks, and other fundamental computing resources while the consumer can deploy and run arbitrary software, which can include operating systems and applications

(Mell & Grance, 2009). PINCLOUD takes advantage of the IaaS and provides data processing and storage of medical data. IaaS consists of multiple Virtual Machines (VM), Medical Data Base and Network Infrastructure. In the given case, multiple VMs are utilized with each one dedicated to a specific service (e.g., Database, Access Control, Backup). The Medical Data Base handles the data processing and storage while network infrastructure handles the connectivity between the different VMs. The only user who is responsible for the smooth operation of the VMs and the services running on them is the PINCLOUD's administrator.

What is more, the proposed architecture encompasses a mechanism that aims at dynamic deployment of application services in cloud infrastructures. The mechanism incorporates a monitoring framework that collects information, both on infrastructure and on application levels. With respect to the infrastructure metrics, CPU and memory are monitored on different time intervals, while number of users, response time, and location of requests are collected on the application level. Based on the aforementioned information, different deployment policies are put in place (e.g., deployment of additional VMs or deployment in different locations) so as to enable provision of quality of service guarantees for the presented cloud healthcare application.

To this end, one of the first responsibilities assigned to the R&D team was to list the requirements of the blueprint architecture. Counting several meetings and long brainstorming sessions with the cooperating partners and their project teams, various requirements were highlighted. In this section, the authors present the most relevant to the theme of this publication (e.g., relating to Cloud-Computing issues), such as:

- Virtualization,
- Healthcare Interoperability,
- Security,
- Big Volume of Data,
- Scalability,
- Responsive,
- Content Management,
- Dynamic and Scalable User Interface.

Based on the above aforementioned requirements the R&D team embarked on the design and implementation of the PINCLOUD application and technologies. The conceptualization, development steps and direction taken to accommodate the project requirements are depicted in the following section.

DESIGN AND IMPLEMENTATION

'Virtualization' is at the core of most cloud architectures. The concept of virtualization allows an abstract representation of logical and physical resources including servers, storage devices, networks and software. The basic idea behind it is to pool all physical resources and their management as a whole, meeting the individual

demands from these shared resources (Lupse, Vida, & Stoicu-Tivadar, 2012). In our case, we used multiple Virtual Machines (VM) each one running one service. For example, Data storage, Data processing, interconnectivity with 3rd parties' medical providers and user interface were placed in Individual VMs. Using Virtualization has many benefits including:

1. Easier replication and cloning a VM than physical server,
2. Lower down time in case of failure,
3. Lower power consumption and saving resources by running multiple Virtual Machines (VM) within the same physical server (Chang, 2013a).

Another requirement is the interoperability which is the ability of two or more systems or components (e.g., two or more HIS) to exchange data and use the information that has been exchanged (Lupse et al., 2012). Legislation surrounding e-Health communications promote a standardized communication process with standards and protocols. For example, the Integrating the Healthcare Enterprise (IHE) organization provides standards (e.g., HL7, DICOM, etc.) to enhance the interoperability and information sharing (IHE, 2012). An enabler of these standards is the SOA paradigm. An example of this is the recognised Healthcare Services Specification Program (HSSP) program, which is a collaborative effort between standards groups HL7 and OMG to address interoperability challenges within the healthcare sector, operating on SOA (HSSP, 2013). To ensure interoperability with 3rd parties, PINCLOUD adopts HL7 CDA (Clinical Document Architecture). The HL7 CDA standard is a document markup standard that specifies the structure and semantics of "clinical documents" for the purpose of data exchange (Lupse et al., 2012). In that way, PINCLOUD achieves integration with the providers' HIS and also data integrity.

Another important requirement that was taken under consideration is the security and protection of information against unauthorized access. As different users including:

1. Patients,
2. Doctors,
3. Hospitals,
4. Insurance companies, and
5. Pharmacies access the system, sensitive information may be provided only to authorized users (Narayanan & Giine, 2011).

In our case, Access Control is a critical part of PINCLOUD due to the large amount of sensitive medical data and the multiple users who interact with it. Access rights to resources must be granted at the right time to the right users in order to avoid unauthorized access to medical data. For example, a doctor should be given access to medical history of a patient only after patient's approval. In that way, we can reinsure protection against unauthorized access and distribution of medical data.

PINCLOUD is a multidiscipline e-health integration project. The need for this integrated approach to handle big volume of medical data is critical. Big data is high-volume, high-velocity and high-variety information assets that demand cost-effective, innovative forms of information processing for enhanced insight and decision making (Altman, Nagle, & Tushman, 2013). The systems need to handle and store these big amounts of medical data in a secure and consistent manner. A plateau of well-known database systems exists, most of them based on SQL, yet those cannot handle big data since they are not scalable (Cuzzocrea, Song, & Davis, 2011). Thus, one of the early motivation was to research and examine contemporary systems to handle large volume of data appropriate for the purpose of this project. Our research surfaced several interesting results like:

1. The current trend for big data is document based databases, and
2. Two of the most prominent database systems are Couchbase and MongoDB (COUCHBASE, 2014; MongoDB, 2013).

The latter are open source document based databases and from the on-going examination seem promising and fit for the purpose of this project.

Another important feature that was taken under consideration is the scalability. Due to the type (e.g., numerous different users and real time data streaming) of the application the developers needed to ensure its availability regardless of the number of concurrent connections. The only way to achieve this is through technologies which support scalability and take advantage of Cloud-Computing features. Due to the familiarization of the R&D team with SOA it was considered as the best practice available. Yet, the challenging part was to select the appropriate technologies to implement SOA. In a process to scan the spectrum of available "best-fit" solutions the R&D team examined various technologies, but dropped most of them since they are not compatible with the big data paradigm. From the examination process, the most prominent ones are nodejs and scala. These are highlighted since both

1. Support the aforementioned document based databases,
2. Provide high flexibility, and
3. Offer high availability (;).

As stated, it is important for the PINCLOUD integrated service users to access the web from their mobile devices. Thus, it was essential to provide the ability to the users to have access to the application through multiple devices such as:

1. Desktops,
2. Laptops,
3. Tablets, and
4. Smartphones.

One of the important tasks was to insure that the system will provide the best user experience on all the aforementioned devices. This may provide higher adoption rates of the applications. The responsiveness was insured by adopting responsive interface which is the optimal viewing experience (e.g., easy reading and navigation with a minimum of resizing, panning, and scrolling) across a wide range of devices (Marcotte, 2011). After analyzing various frameworks that support responsive design at the moment on top of our list is bootstrap (Bootstrap, 2014). Bootstrap is developed and distributed free by Twitter Company and allows easy and quick responsive design implementation.

Another consideration taken was the dynamic User Interface (UI). Many cases in healthcare emphasize the correlation of a good UI with the high adoption rates and vise-versa. Therefore the need to make sure that the best practices and state of the art technologies will be followed for this issue, was ever-present. HTML5 is the latest version of the well-known HyperText Markup Language (HTML) and provides features which facilitate not only the user interaction but also the developing phase (Pilgrim, 2010). PINCLOUD is set to adhere to a healthy adoption percentage and thus a user friendly web interface to the end-users was a requirement. Therefore, the HTML5 which provides portability across different mobile platforms was utilized (Preuveneers, Berbers, & Joosen, 2013).

Additionally an issue the R&D team had to tackle was how to consume the web-services (e.g., different options exist like server-side and client-side consumption). For consuming the web services various options of JavaScript frameworks had to be considered (e.g., AngularJS, Backbone.js, CanJS and Ember.js). Through an evaluation of these frameworks and promoting the client-side consumption two were selected:

1. AngularJS, and
2. ember.js.

The more promising one is AngularJS, developed by Google which is widely used lately as it provides dynamic and scalable User Interface (UI) (Google, 2014; Tilde, 2014).

In order to facilitate the administration of the web application's content, several Content Management Systems (CMS) that provide state of the art features such as

1. Extensibility,
2. Remote access,
3. Users management, were considered.

Currently, top of our list are Liferay and Drupal (Drupal, 2014; Liferay, 2014). Liferay is the most widely known java based CMS, while Drupal is based on PHP Hypertext Preprocessor. Both of them are open source solutions having very large communities which provide support and security updates. In that way, the R&D team can focus on the improvement of the core features of PINCLOUD and not at the updates (e.g., security updates). For our needs, Liferay approach was a favorite due to the familiarization of the R&D team with Java.

An illustrative view of the aforementioned requirements alongside the proposed solutions are depict in Table 2.

Table 2. Requirements: proposed technologies

Requirements	Proposed Solutions
Virtualization	Virtual Machines (VM)
Healthcare Interoperability	HL7 CDA Standard, DICOM
Security	Private Cloud, Role Based Access Control
Big volume of data	Document Based Databases (Mongodb, Couchdb)
Scalability	SOA, nodejs, Scala
Responsive User Interface	Twitter Bootstrap, Foundation, Skeleton
Dynamic and scalable User Interface	AngularJS, ember.js, HTML5
Content Management	Liferay CMS, Drupal

Figure 3. E-prescription process

Currently PINCLOUD is in its implementation phase, upon which the various components such as:

1. PHR platform,
2. E-prescribing and e-referral, and
3. Homecare applications, are being developed and tested (Lab of Medical Informatics, 2014).

The implementation is based on the technologies addressed in this section. In the next Section an example of the E-Prescribing Analysis is highlighted.

E-PRESCRIBING BUSINESS PROCESS

In this section the authors provide an analysis of the E-Prescription Service. This analysis is highlighted as to offer a suitable example of a complex business process addressed in our work. This close examination aids the reader to understand the configuration of E-Prescribing throughout the different Cloud-Computing models (SaaS, PaaS and IaaS). The analysis id presented with the aid of two Figures:

Figure 4. E-prescription analysis

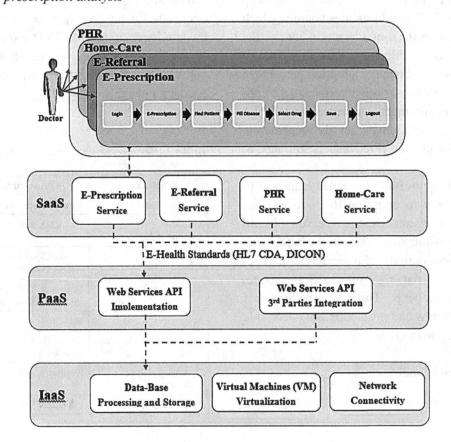

1. Figure 3 that depicts the business process, and
2. Figure 4 that illustrates the configuration of the E-Prescription through the different Cloud-Computing models.

Analysis

After a patient examination the doctor (e.g., general practitioner) prescribes medicines to a patient using the PINCLOUD application. Yet, before the doctor gain access to the E-Prescription service, he/she needs to be authenticated using his credentials through the web interface (Login) of the PINCLOUD. This step is the first step of the sequence depicted in Figure 3. After a successful user authentication, he/she is prompted four options to select, such as:

1. PHR,
2. Home-Care,
3. E-Referral, and
4. E-Prescription.

These four options are the main services provided through the PINCLOUD platform.

In the scenario presented in this sub-section the doctor selects E-Prescription. Subsequently, he/she locates the patient using the patient's Social Security Number (S.S.N.) which is unique for each patient. Before the doctor can prescribe the medicine, it is required by the system to register the diagnosed disease and any relevant treatment comments (e.g., free text) that he/she feels is applicable. The patient's disease is encoded based on the Worlds Healthcare Organization International Statistical Classification of Diseases and Related Health Problems that is now at its 10th Revision (e.g., ICD 10). ICD10 standard is considered as a best practice and therefore applicable in PINCLOUD. The next sequence in the business process, allows the doctor to select the drugs through a suggested drugs' list. The suggested

list corresponds to the diagnosed disease and the patient's medical history which is stored in PINCLOUD storage infrastructure. The doctor is not limited to the listed drugs but he/she can also choose other drugs beyond the listed ones based on his professional judgment. The doctor can also fill the dosage (e.g., number of pills) and other information of usage (e.g., frequency, oral etc.) for each selected drug. After filing all the information for the prescribed drugs, the system validates the selection of drugs based on their interaction on issues such as:

1. Other drugs,
2. Patient's allergies, and
3. Medication history.

Consequently, if the cross-checking produces no alerts, the prescription is stored waiting to be processed in Pharmacies.

As mentioned in the introduction, PINCLOUD is divided into three service models (e.g., SaaS, PaaS and IaaS). To be more specific, SaaS provides all the PINCLOUD's services such as:

1. PHR,
2. Home-Care,
3. E-referral, and
4. E-Prescribe.

The SaaS connects users to aforementioned services while providing basic functions such as

1. Web interface,
2. A secure communication, and
3. Authentication control.

In order to support the scalability, the application can be installed on multiple machines which are clustered. The use of HTTPS protocol guaranties a lightweight security and makes the application compliant with HIPAA security regulations.

Additionally, PINCLOUD takes advantage of PaaS by providing two kinds of APIs, the first one is for the interconnectivity between the different provided services and the storage, while the second one provides the ability to 3rd parties to connect with PINCLOUD.

The R&D team used Representational state transfer (REST) architectural style to develop the web services APIs. With REST it is feasible to design unique URLs dynamically to represent remote health records objects as needed. The frontend sends HTTP requests over Secure Sockets Layer (SSL) to obtain a JavaScript Object Notation (JSON) of the desired medical data. With REST, the identification of the resources (doctor, patient, lab results, drugs, medical exams) is straightforward. There is no need for the client to create complex requests to query the server. To be compliant with HIPAA security regulations, a POST method is used and the sensitive information (e.g., a query on a patient name) is passed in the body of the request as a JSON object over an SSL connection. All request and response headers have a content type "application/json" which means that complex queries and responses are in the form of JSON arrays or JSON objects. In addition to this, each time the user logs in, the server provides a security token which is mediatory each time the user is calling any API operation. This installment is placed for authentication reasons.

As the Figure 4 depicts, APIs run on PaaS and they handle the communication between the SaaS and IaaS. The exchanged information between those two services follows the E-health standards such as

1. Health Level 7 (HL7) for transferring clinical and administrative data,
2. Clinical Document Architecture (CDA) for encoding, structure and semantics of clinical documents, and
3. Digital Imaging and Communications in Medicine (DICOM) standard for handling, storing, printing, and transmitting information in medical imaging.

Table 3. Examples API operations

POST /users/login	Login of user
GET /users/{userId}/patient/{SSN}	Retrieve patient profile
POST /users/{userID}/patient/{SSN}/prescription/add	Create a new prescription
GET /users/{userID}/patient/{SSN}/prescription/{prescriptionId}	Return specific prescription

The First API includes operations for the aforementioned SaaS services. More specificly, it includes all the required operations as they are depicted in Table 3, like:

1. Login of user,
2. Retrieve patient's profile,
3. Creation of a new prescription, and
4. Specific prescription retrieval.

The API operations were designed to be versatile, secure and easy to use.

The second API is designed for 3rd parties (e.g., medical providers) which interact with PINCLOUD. Currently, it is under development. These providers already use their own solutions which have different architecture. This makes the integration difficult. The aim of the API is to facilitate the integration with 3rd parties' solutions. Additionally, the integration can be facilitated using e-health standards like HL7 CDA.

In Figure 4, the IaaS back-end functions are depicted, including amongst others:

1. The storage servers with their database system,
2. The virtual machines, and
3. Networking functions.

In more detail, the IaaS in our case, consists of three different kinds of servers:

- **Primary Servers:** Virtual Machines (VM) running the PINCLOUD applications. These servers are responsible for performing most of the computation.
- **Specific Servers:** Virtual Machines (VM) whose main task is to manage the communication with the database and with other servers.
- **Control Server:** Virtual Machine (VM) which monitors the overall PINCLOUD status. This server is responsible for creating and removing virtual machines dynamically based on dynamically changed requirements (e.g., too many concurrent users).

Moreover, IaaS provides a network which interconnects all the VMs by establishing a secure connection between them in order to complete all the requests between PINCLOUD application services.

User Interface

The aim of the R&D team is also to provide a user friendly web interface. Thus a balance between implementation of the required functionality required to complete a task and how the task is exposed through the user interface is needed. In other words, the user interface should not only be functional but also usable. To achieve this, the R&D team follows the user interface development process which is presented below in three phases, like:

1. Design,
2. Implementation, and
3. Testing.

At the current moment, the project is at the implementation phase.

- The Design Phase includes:
  - Determination of the initial requirements and goals for PINCLOUD,
  - Identification of use cases,
  - Conceptual design,
  - Logical design, and
  - Physical design.
- The Implementation Phase includes:
  - The prototyping of mockups that focus on the interface and user interaction, and
  - Building the user interface and preparation for upcoming design changes.
- The Testing Phase is set build test and evaluation scenarios and run those with various users.

To provide a clear view of the implementation phase, an example of the UI screens are presented below. The screens are divided in five main sections, like:

1. Patient's Information (seen in Figure 5),
2. Disease (seen in Figure 6),
3. Reasoning (seen in Figure 6),
4. Featured Prescription Drugs (seen in Figure 6), and
5. Suggested Medical Treatment (seen in Figure 7).

Starting with the 'Patient Information' screen, as seen in Figure 5, based on which the Doctor retrieves the patient's profile information prior to prescribing the drugs. In more detail, he/she needs to query using a unique identifier Social Security Number (SSN) and the PINCLOUD returns the patient's profile details.

Afterwards, as it is depicted in Figure 6 the doctor fills the diagnosed disease and any relevant comments (e.g., free text). The doctor chooses the "add drug" button in order to prescribe a new drug.

Figure 5. Screen: patients' information

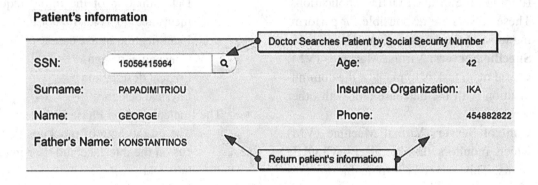

Figure 6. Screen: disease-reasoning-featured prescription drugs

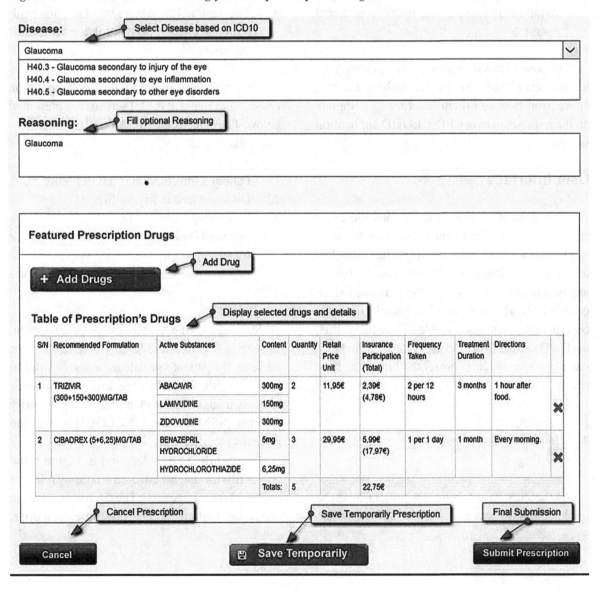

Figure 7. Screen: suggested medical treatment

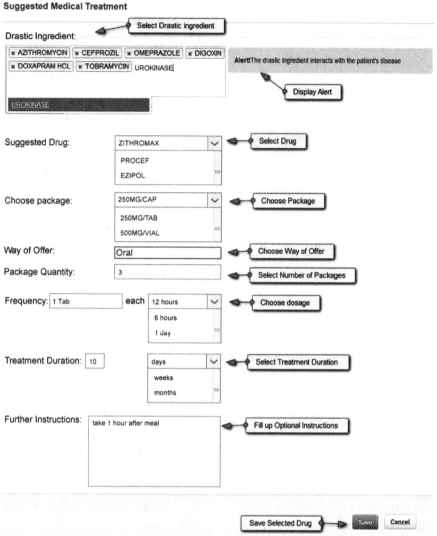

After the selection of the "add drug" selection, a modal window appears, as Figure 7 depicts. The doctor fills the drastic ingredients for the suggested treatment based on the diagnosed disease and PIN-CLOUD returns a list of suggested drugs to let the Doctor select the appropriate one. Afterwards, he/she chooses amongst several characteristics, such as:

1. Package of the selected drug,
2. Way of offer (e.g., oral),
3. Quantity,
4. Frequency (e.g., 1 pill every 6 hours), and
5. Treatment duration (e.g., 10 days).

Additionally, an option to include further instructions exists. In the event of a drastic ingredient interacting with patient's disease then PINCLOUD returns a message (alert) and prevents the doctor from adding the selected drug. Otherwise, the system displays the table of the selected drugs as it is depicted in Figure 6 (bottom half of figure). Finally the Doctor can:

1. Cancel the entered details in case of mistake,
2. Save temporary the prescription to be used later, and
3. Submit the final prescription.

EXPECTED BENEFITS

PINCLOUD project is set to build a reliable, secure and extensible platform warranting stakeholder collaboration and hopefully enjoying public trust. The expected benefits for all participant organizations include:

1. The development of integrated healthcare services that improve quality of service and reduce costs;
2. Business process reengineering, improvement, simplification and integration;
3. Enhanced decision making for health organizations and significant reductions to medical errors;
4. Standardization, automation, synchronization, better control and communication;
5. Improved coordination, management and scheduling of specific health supply chains and services;
6. Development of monitoring systems that improve quality of care of patients at home;
7. Establishment of an infrastructure that provides up-to-date information;
8. Development of an innovative organizational environment for the participating hospital using horizontal processes instead of the traditional hierarchical organization;
9. Implementation of an extensible and maintainable infrastructure that can be enriched with other medical services;
10. Development of an appropriate, sustainable technological framework that can be deployed and applied in other relevant situations and environments;
11. Investigation of state-of-the art technologies and novel research that extends the body of knowledge;
12. Significant research outcomes and publications of excellent quality;
13. Production of new platforms, infrastructures, and solution that can be further exploited;
14. Knowledge and expertise gained can lead to competitive advantage; and
15. Production and export of technical know-how for all the participants.

The results of the proposed project are of great importance for the businesses that deal with the e-health sector as they will gain the potential to achieve competitive advantages through the project. The area of healthcare is significant and the need for advanced and innovative IT solutions in this area is apparent too. Thus, the participant enterprises will have the opportunity to:

1. Develop an integrated platform that can be used by other organizations in the future;
2. Better understand and analyze the complexities of the Greek healthcare environment;
3. Experiment and implement innovative integrated solutions that can be turned into products;
4. Gain expertise and know-how on a complex area;
5. Sell these products and know-how at national and international level since PINCLOUD seeks to develop an innovative solution;
6. Obtain and reinforce experiences that can be used for the development of other network-oriented systems; and
7. Extend their business activities.

The benefits for both healthcare organizations include among others:

1. Specifications of processes for the management of healthcare processes;

2. Simplification and acceleration of business processes;
3. Better management of healthcare tasks;
4. Personalized disease monitoring and cost calculation;
5. More efficient operation; and
6. Economies of scale.

The benefits to the academic institutions participating in the project are equally important and include:

1. Knowledge exchange and transfer;
2. Engagement in innovative research;
3. Investigation of state of the art technologies;
4. Opportunity to publish research articles of high quality;
5. Prospect to conduct applied research and combine theory and practice.

FUTURE RESEARCH

Cloud-Computing has transformed the way many healthcare organizations work and offer healthcare services. In the previous section the benefits of such an endeavor alongside the steps taken so far to realize the implementation of a secure and reliable system, were analyzed. Yet, further research is required both in the testing and evaluation of our design and implementation.

To this end, the R&D team engineered several mechanisms to test and evaluate PINCLOUD and its components. For example, a proof-of-concept test will be implemented to check the communication of various sensors with the main PHR. The results of this test will be examined by healthcare professionals and provide initial evaluation of the technologies used. Additionally, testing mechanisms have been designed for the other components (e.g., e-prescribing and e-referral) as well. Besides, PINCLOUD will be implemented in two different cloud IaaS providers so as to study the interoperability in two different settings.

The results of this test will provide insights into the utilized technologies (e.g., Table 2) and if needed reconfigurations and adjustments will be implemented. The authors expect the results of this test to be the subject of our next publication.

CONCLUSION

The current trend of adopting Cloud-Computing in the medical field can tackle several HIS challenges from integration of legacy systems to well needed reduction of cost. Standardized Cloud Services for Healthcare can be beneficial to patients, practitioners, insurance companies, pharmacies, etc.

Yet, as discussed in this chapter, several approaches with similarities and differences are proposing the integration of the Cloud Services for Healthcare in the form of a PHR. This patient centered approach over the cloud is a relative new issue that requires thorough examination with a multidiscipline lens. To aid this discussion the authors presented their involvement in a multidiscipline project and highlighted the steps taken so far from design and implementation, to technology considerations and decisions on current trends. The reader through this presentation has the chance to understand how a complex idea addressed by PINCLOUD as the E-Prescribing correlated through the three Cloud-Computing service models (SaaS, PaaS amd IaaS). Therefore, the authors believe that the issues highlighted in this chapter will provide useful insights and guidance for e-health developers concerned with the integration of Cloud Services in healthcare.

REFERENCES

AAL-Europe. (2013). Ambient assisted living catalogue of projects 2013. Retrieved April 18, 2014, from http://www.aal-europe.eu/

Alemdar, H., & Ersoy, C. (2010). Wireless sensor networks for healthcare: A survey. *Computer Networks*, *54*(15), 2688–2710. doi:10.1016/j.comnet.2010.05.003

Altman, E. J., Nagle, F., & Tushman, M. L. (2013). Innovating without Information Constraints: Organizations, communities, and innovation when information costs approach zero. *Harvard Business School Organizational Behavior Unit Working Paper* (14-043).

Avison, D., & Young, T. (2007). Time to rethink health care and ICT? *Communications of the ACM*, *50*(6), 69–74. doi:10.1145/1247001.1247008

Axelsson, K., Melin, U., & Söderström, F. (2011). *Analyzing best practice and critical success factors in a healthcare information systems case-Are there any shortcuts to succesfull IT implementation?* Paper presented at the 19th European Conference on Information Systems – ICT and Sustainable Service Development, Helsinki, Finland.

Black, A. D., Car, J., Pagliari, C., Anandan, C., Cresswell, K., Bokun, T., & Sheikh, A. et al. (2011). The impact of eHealth on the quality and safety of health care: A Systematic overview. *PLoS Medicine*, *8*(1), e1000387. doi:10.1371/journal.pmed.1000387 PMID:21267058

Bootstrap. (2014). Bootstrap. Retrieved April 18 2014, from http://getbootstrap.com/

Boulos, M. N., Wheeler, S., Tavares, C., & Jones, R. (2011). How smartphones are changing the face of mobile and participatory healthcare: An overview, with example from eCAALYX. *Biomedical Engineering Online*, *10*(1), 24. doi:10.1186/1475-925X-10-24 PMID:21466669

Chang, V. (2013a). A case study for business integration as a service. Trends in e-business, e-services, and e-commerce: impact of technology on goods, services, and business transactions. Hershey, PA: IGI Global.

Chang, V. (2013b). *Cloud computing for brain segmentation technology*. Paper presented at the IEEE CloudCom 2013. http://eprints.soton.ac.uk/357188/

Chang, V. (2014). Cloud computing for brain segmentation–a perspective from the technology and evaluations. *International Journal of Big Data Intelligence*, *1*(3).

Chang, V., De Roure, D., Wills, G., John Walters, R., & Barry, T. (2011). Organisational sustainability modelling for return on investment (ROI): Case studies presented by a National Health Service (NHS) trust UK. CIT. *Journal of Computing and Information Technology*, *19*(3), 177–192. doi:10.2498/cit.1001951

Chatterjee, S., Chakraborty, S., Sarker, S., Sarker, S., & Lau, F. Y. (2009). Examining the success factors for mobile work in healthcare: A deductive study. *Decision Support Systems*, *46*(3), 620–633. doi:10.1016/j.dss.2008.11.003

Chowdhury, M., Krishnan, K., & Vishwanath, S. (2012). *Touching lives through mobile health: Assessment of the global market opportunity*. India: PricewaterhouseCoopers.

ClearHealth. (2013). ClearHealth smart. simple. sustainable. Retrieved April 15, 2014, from http://clear-health.com/

Clemensen, J., Rasmussen, J., Denning, A., & Craggs, M. (2011). *Patient empowerment and new citizen roles through telehealth technologies - The early stage*. Paper presented at the Third International Conference on eHealth, Telemedicine, and Social Medicine Gosier France.

COUCHBASE. (2014). COUCHBASE NoSQL Database. Retrieved April 15, 2014, from http://www.couchbase.com

Cuzzocrea, A., Song, I.-Y., & Davis, K. C. (2011). Analytics over large-scale multidimensional data: the big data revolution! In *Proceedings of the ACM 14th international workshop on Data Warehousing and OLAP*. Glasgow, Scotland, UK. doi:10.1145/2064676.2064695

Daphne. (2013). Daphne data-as-a-service platform for healthy lifestyle and preventive medicine. Retrieved April 15, 2014, from http://www.daphne-fp7.eu/node/21

Deadalus. (2014). Interoperability Platform X1.V1. Retrieved April 17, 2014, from http://dedaluschina.com.cn/products-solutions/interoperability-platform-x1-v1/

Detmer, D., Bloomrosen, M., Raymond, B., & Tang, P. (2008). Integrated personal health records: Transformative tools for consumer-centric care. *BMC Medical Informatics and Decision Making*, 8(1), 45. doi:10.1186/1472-6947-8-45 PMID:18837999

Drupal. (2014). Drupal open source content management platform. Retrieved April 18, 2014, from https://drupal.org/

Dwivedi, Y., Ravichandran, K., Williams, M., Miller, S., Lal, B., Antony, G., & Kartik, M. (2013). IS/IT project failures: A review of the extant literature for deriving a taxonomy of failure factors. In Y. Dwivedi, H. Henriksen, D. Wastell, & R. De' (Eds.), *Grand successes and failures in IT public and private sectors* (Vol. 402, pp. 73–88). Berlin Heidelberg: Springer. doi:10.1007/978-3-642-38862-0_5

EMC. (2014). Electronic health record infrastructure solutions. Retrieved April 17, 2014, from http://greece.emc.com/industry/public-sector/electronic-health-record-infrastructure.htm

Google. (2014). Angularjs. Retrieved April 15, 2014, from https://angularjs.org/

Halamka, J., Mandl, K., & Tang, P. (2008). Early experiences with personal health records. *Journal of the American Medical Informatics Association*, 15(1), 1–7. doi:10.1197/jamia.M2562 PMID:17947615

HSSP. (2013). Healthcare services specification program. Retrieved January 19, 2013, from http://hssp.wikispaces.com/

IHE. (2012). Integrating the healthcare enterprise. Retrieved March 1, 2011, from http://www.ihe.net/

Jennett, P., & Watanabe, M. (2006). Healthcare and telemedicine: Ongoing and evolving challenges. *Disease Management & Health Outcomes*, 14(1).

Koufi, V., Malamateniou, F., & Vassilacopoulos, G. (2013). An Android-enabled PHR-based system for the provision of homecare services. *International Journal of Measurement Technologies and Instrumentation Engineering*, 3(2), 1–18. doi:10.4018/ijmtie.2013040101

Koumaditis, K., Themistocleous, M., Vassilacopoulos, G., Prentza, A., Kyriazis, D., Malamateniou, F., Mourouzis, A. (2014). *Patient-centered e-health record over the cloud*. Paper presented at the International Conference on Informatics, Management and Technology in Healthcare, Attica, Greece.

Kuo, A. M.-H. (2011). Opportunities and challenges of cloud computing to improve health care services. *Journal of Medical Internet Research*, 13(3), e67. doi:10.2196/jmir.1867 PMID:21937354

Lab of Medical Informatics. (2014). Providing integrated eHealth services for personalized medicine utilizing cloud infrastructure. Retrieved April, 17, 2014, from http://pincloud.med.auth.gr/en

Lausanne, É. P. F. d. (2014). Scala. Retrieved April 18, 2014, from http://www.scala-lang.org/

Leventhal, T., Taliaferro, P., Wong, K., Hughes, C., & Mun, S. (2012). The patient-centered medical home and health information technology. *Telemedicine Journal and e-Health*, *18*(2), 145–149. doi:10.1089/tmj.2011.0130 PMID:22304440

Liferay. (2014). Liferay. Retrieved April 18, 2014, from http://www.liferay.com/

Lupse, O. S., Vida, M. M., & Stoicu-Tivadar, L. (2012). *Cloud computing and interoperability in healthcare information systems*. Paper presented at the The First International Conference on Intelligent Systems and Applications, INTELLI 2012.

Marcotte, E. (2011). *Responsive web design*. Editions Eyrolles.

Medscribbler. (2014). Medscribbler. Retrieved April 16, 2014, from http://www.medscribbler.com/

Mell, P., & Grance, T. (2009). The NIST definition of cloud computing. *National Institute of Standards and Technology*, *53*(6), 50.

Microsoft. (2014). HealthVault. Retrieved April 15, 2014, from https://www.healthvault.com

Mongo, D. B. I. (2013). MongoDB (from "humongous") is an open-source document database, and the leading NoSQL database. Retrieved April 15, 2014, from http://www.mongodb.org/

Narayanan, H. A. J., & Giine, M. (2011). *Ensuring access control in cloud provisioned healthcare systems*. Paper presented at the Consumer Communications and Networking Conference (CCNC), 2011. IEEE. doi:10.1109/CCNC.2011.5766466

Nodejs. (2014). Node.js platform. Retrieved April 15, 2014, from http://nodejs.org/

OpenEMR. (2014). OpenEMR a free and open source electronic health records. Retrieved April 15, 2014, from http://www.open-emr.org

Pilgrim, M. (2010). *HTML5: up and running*. O'Reilly Media, Inc.

Poulymenopoulou, M., Malamateniou, F., & Vassilacopoulos, G. (2012). Emergency healthcare process automation using mobile computing and cloud services. *Journal of Medical Systems*, *36*(5), 3233–3241. doi:10.1007/s10916-011-9814-y PMID:22205383

Preuveneers, D., Berbers, Y., & Joosen, W. (2013). The future of mobile e-health application development: exploring HTML5 for context-aware diabetes monitoring. *Procedia Computer Science*, *21*, 351–359. doi:10.1016/j.procs.2013.09.046

Research2guidance. (2014). *mHealth application developer economics 2014: The state of the art of m-health app publishing* (pp. 43). Retrieved from http://mhealtheconomics.com/mhealth-developer-economics-report/

Reti, S. R., Feldman, H. J., & Safran, C. (2009). Governance for personal health records. *Journal of the American Medical Informatics Association*, *16*(1), 14–17. doi:10.1197/jamia.M2854 PMID:18952939

Ruiz-Zafra, Á., Benghazi, K., Noguera, M., & Garrido, J. L. (2013). *Zappa: An open mobile platform to build cloud-based m-health systems. Ambient Intelligence-Software and Applications* (pp. 87–94). Springer.

Sarasohn-Kahn, J. (2010). *How smartphones are changing health care for consumers and providers* (1st ed., pp. 23). California HealthCare Foundation. Retrieved from http://www.chcf.org/

Singer, S., Burgers, J., Friedberg, M., Rosenthal, M., Leape, L., & Schneider, E. (2011). Defining and measuring integrated patient care: Promoting the next frontier in health care delivery. *Medical Care Research and Review*, *68*(1), 112–127. doi:10.1177/1077558710371485 PMID:20555018

SUCRE. (2014). Sucre state of the art report. Retrieved April 13, 2014, from http://www.sucreproject.eu

Tang, P., Ash, J., Bates, D., Overhage, J., & Sands, D. (2006). Personal health records: Definitions, benefits, and strategies for overcoming barriers to adoption. *Journal of the American Medical Informatics Association*, *13*(2), 121–126. doi:10.1197/jamia.M2025 PMID:16357345

Tclouds. (2014). TClouds - Trustworthy clouds healthcare scenario. Retrieved April 15, 2014, from http://www.tclouds-project.eu/downloads/factsheets/tclouds-factsheet-15-healthcare.pdf

Tilde. (2014). Emberjs. Retrieved April 15, 2014, from http://emberjs.com/

Vodera. (2014). VIGOR++ virtual gastrointestinal tract. Retrieved April 15, 2014, from http://www.vigorpp.eu/

Wilson, V., & Strong, D. (2014). Editors' introduction to the special section on patient-centered e-health: Research opportunities and challenges. *Communications of the Association for Information Systems*, *34*(15).

Zhang, Q., Cheng, L., & Boutaba, R. (2010). Cloud computing: State-of-the-art and research challenges. *Journal of Internet Services and Applications*, *1*(1), 7-18.

Zhou, F., Yang, H., Álamo, J., Wong, J., & Chang, C. (2010). Mobile Personal Health Care System for Patients with Diabetes. In Y. Lee, Z. Z. Bien, M. Mokhtari, J. Kim, M. Park, J. Kim, & I. Khalil et al. (Eds.), *Aging friendly technology for health and independence* (Vol. 6159, pp. 94–101). Berlin Heidelberg: Springer. doi:10.1007/978-3-642-13778-5_12

KEY TERMS AND DEFINITIONS

CAPEX: Capital Expenditure.

HIS Integration: The alignment of HIS in an interoperable environment.

HIS Interoperability: The ability of HIS to work together and exchange information.

HIS: Information systems designed to facilitate healthcare services.

IaaS: Infrastructure as a Service.

OPEX: Operational Expenditure.

PaaS: Platform as a Service.

PCEH: Patient Centered e-health.

SaaS: Software as a Service.

SOA: An architectural paradigm to build ecosystems of services.

Chapter 13
Genome Sequencing in the Cloud

Wei Chen
The University of Texas MD Anderson Cancer Center, USA

Bo Peng
The University of Texas MD Anderson Cancer Center, USA

Yun Wan
School of Arts & Science, University of Houston - Victoria, USA

Christopher I Amos
Geisel School of Medicine, Dartmouth College, USA

ABSTRACT

This chapter discussed the latest development of using cloud-computing technology for genome sequencing in bioinformatics field. It introduced the definition of genome sequencing and cloud computing, discussed the current status of NGS in cloud with the example of Nimbix. It also provided a rich source of cloud computing related service providers and technologies for references. Finally, it discussed the challenges of conducting NGS in a cloud environment.

INTRODUCTION

Bioinformatics is an inter-disciplinary field that has grown rapidly over the last two decades along with breakthroughs in both biotechnologies and information technologies. It relates to the study of methods about how to store, retrieve and analyze biological data, such as nucleic acid (DNA/RNA) and protein sequences, structures, functions, pathways and genetic interactions (http://en.wikipedia.org/wiki/Bioinformatics). The high-throughput data generated especially from next generation sequencing (NGS) is a challenge for its management, extraction and analysis. The Human Genome

Project began in 1990 and aimed at mapping and identifying the approximately 20,000-25,000 genes in human genome, and determining the sequences of the 3 billion base pairs that comprise human DNA. With the successful completion of the Human Genome Project in 2003, new needs emerged for rapidly and efficiently identifying single nucleotide polymorphisms (SNPs), copy number variations (CNVs), structural variations (SVs) and insertions and deletions (indels). Thus, the focus has shifted to understanding the roles or functions of genetic variations in the context of gene-gene and gene-environment interactions and cell signaling pathways, especially on genes

DOI: 10.4018/978-1-4666-8210-8.ch013

Copyright © 2015, IGI Global. Copying or distributing in print or electronic forms without written permission of IGI Global is prohibited.

for complex diseases and the development of personalized therapies. Only 1.1-1.4% of the genome is spanned by exons (coding sequence for amino acids) and the remaining sequence comprises introns (non-coding regions), intergenic regions or other sequences such as micro RNA that control expression of genes. Less than 1% of all SNPs lead to variation in proteins possibly causing damage, so the task of determining which SNPs have functional consequences remains an open challenge (Venter et al., 2001).

The increasingly data-intensive nature of life sciences, especially driven by the Human Genome Project and recently next generation sequencing data, demands high-speed data transfer, big data storage, optimized processing and efficient analyses in Petabyte and Exabyte scale. This leaves two options for most research organizations to enhance their computing infrastructure and support such initiatives: either build one's own cluster computing infrastructure, or use a cloud-based approach, that is a private cloud, or publically available cloud computing services like Amazon EC2.

The challenge for both options is there are few off-the-shelf tools to help integrate, analyze and visualize such massive amounts of data, which forces most bioinformatics researchers to search for solutions by themselves. In this chapter, we first introduce genome sequencing and cloud computing technology, then explain the current techniques of genome sequencing in the cloud with a list of available cloud computing service and software for genome sequencing. Then we discuss the challenges of this new trend.

GENOME SEQUENCING

Since the 1970s, the genome sequencing technology has experienced three stage of development. They were typically classified as zero generation sequencing used in the 1970s, first generation sequencing used in the 1980s to 1990s, and second generation sequencing adopted since the 2000s.

The first generation genome sequencing method is called Sanger sequencing and used cycle sequencing to generate a ladder of increased dye-labeled products, which are subjected to high-resolution electrophoretic separation. The four-channel spectrum is used to trace the sequence to fluorescently labeled fragments (Sanger & Coulson, 1978). Second generation genome sequencing is called clonally PCR amplified molecule sequencing (Shendure & Ji, 2008). The sequencing steps include fragmentation, library generation, amplification, sequencing and analysis. The raw sequence reads of whole genome sequencing may be produced in 5 days, followed by 3 weeks of mapping the reads to genome and generating raw genomic features (e.g. SNPs) and finally months of data analysis to uncover the biological meaning. The raw uncompressed sequencing data obtained by one Illumina HiSeq run can be 1.5 Terabyte, or 1400+ CDs of data over 1.7 m tall. Sequencing platforms in this category include Illumina Genome Analyzer/HiSeq (Illumina Inc.), ABI SOLiD (Life Technologies Corp.), and Roche 454 pyrosequencing. The third generation sequencing or next-next generation sequencing is called true single molecule sequencing (Harris et al., 2008). This category includes much more sensitive yet expensive sequencing by synthesis without amplification using true Single Molecule Sequencing (tSMS) or Heliscore technology HeliScopeSingle Molecule Sequencer (Helicos Biosciences Corp.), Ion Torrent technology uses a semiconductor (Life Technologies Corp.), SMRT technology (Pacific Biosciences Inc.), DNA nanoball technology (Complete Genomics Inc.), or Nanopore technology (Oxford Nanopore Technologies Inc.). The third generation sequencing produces longer reads but currently has higher error rates than earlier generations of sequencing approaches. The sequence assembly is easier because of the longer reads.

Table 1. Comparison of conventional and next generation DNA sequencing technologies

	Conventional	**Next Generation**
Step 1	DNA fragmentation	DNA fragmentation
Step 2	*In vivo* cloning and amplification	*In vitro* adaptor ligation
Step 3	Cycle sequencing	Generation of PCR colony array
Step 4	Electrophoresis and color spectrum	Cyclic array sequencing
Platform(s)	Sanger Sequencing	Illumina/Solexa, ABI SOLiD, Roche 454, Polonator, HeliScope
Length	up to 1000 bp	13 bp - 350 bp
Accuracy	99.999%	much lower (about 99-99.5%), needs intensive QC
Cost	$0.50 / kbp or $500 / mbp	<$1 - $60 /mbp

In a broader term, the next/second generation sequencing and the next-next/third generation sequencing are referred together as Next Generation Sequencing (NGS). Metzker (2010) gave a comprehensive review of sequencing technologies, NGS instruments, and the broad range of applications for such purpose. Table 1 lists the comparison of conventional sequencing to next generation(s) of sequencing in terms of general steps, length in base pairs produced, accuracy and cost.

The major difference between conventional and next generation sequencing technology is the trade-off between accuracy and computing cost. As noted in Table 1, the reading accuracy decreases and base calling error increases with the advance of newer sequencing technology, which increases the burden in sequencing data quality control (QC). For next generation sequencing, the read length is much shorter and raw accuracy is at least ten fold less accurate than for conventional sequencing. NGS increases the SNP calling accuracy by increasing coverage, i.e. how many times each fragment is covered.

The central dogma of molecular biology is that the genetic information is passed from DNA to RNA through transcription, then from RNA to functional protein through translation. DNA-seq involves the sequencing of DNA, which currently includes whole genome sequencing, whole genome sequencing to sequence all the exons of all the genes, and targeted gene sequencing to sequence only interested genes (either all exons or just hotspots in amplicon-based cancer panels). But 80% of the human genome is transcribed even though only 1% codes for proteins, so a current research trend also focuses on investigating the function of the majority non-coding RNA (Kellis et al., 2014). RNA-seq uses RNA extracted from cells directly to study the gene expression and transcriptional regulation. CHIP-seq provides a way to find where the transcription factors bind on the genomic DNA to understand gene regulation. Bisulfite sequencing (BS-seq) uses bisulfite treatment of DNA to determine its patterns of methylation. These sequencing technologies complement DNA-seq to provide rich information about genetic variants, transcriptome dynamics, transcription factor binding profile, epigenetic modifications, and other information of the human genome.

The real cost of accurate sequences produced by NGS is incurred via intensive downstream sequence QC steps and bioinformatics analysis on the huge amount of data obtained all in a sudden generated by the need to resequence the same bases many fold times to assure coverage of the genome. As a result, future NGS needs very efficient and scalable yet cheaper computing to suit this growing need. This trend is intensified because the cost of sequencing a base is dropping faster than the cost of storing a byte, therefore the computing power is not efficient enough to keep up with all the data that are being generated (Stein, 2010). Clearly we need very efficient and scalable yet cheaper computing to suit this growing need.

As noted in the previous discussion, the most important feature for NGS is the large amount of data generated. Next generation sequencing technology produces raw sequences much faster yet is fragmented over the entire genome into smaller pieces, each 25-500 nucleotides long, collected from random locations in the genome. Through sequencing many billions of reads, with 20-fold to 30-fold oversampling to ensure each nucleotide of the whole genome is covered, for one individual human's DNA, the final raw and intensity genome data set size is about 1 to 2 TB. This amount of data could be compressed into 100GB for transmission purpose (Ben Langmead, Schatz, Lin, Pop, & Salzberg, 2009). The coverage for highly degraded DNA, such as from FFPE samples to detect somatic mutations from cancer patients, is as high as 2000-fold. The subsequent computing intensive quality control steps include comparing every read to the others in different fold (usually drop read depth < 10, genotype quality <20), mapping or aligning the billions of reads to the reference human genome sequence obtained using conventional sequencing, finding the differences (genetic variations) and meaningful differences between the new sequence and reference genomes (de novo, non-synonymous, coding indels, and/ or causing damage to protein degradation). After mapping/ alignment of all fragments to human reference genome, the reduced data set size is around 200 GB. When we further compare data in this set with human reference genome, it may yield only 1 GB of summary variation data. The final analysis outcome data is around only 1MB. One can see here the significant data reduction

through each step from obtaining clean, accurate and really meaningful information out of the raw sequencing data, which means the requirement of powerful computing (Bock et al., 2005).

Currently, there are a few popular open-source tools such as BWA (Li & Durbin, 2009), TopHat (Trapnell, Pachter, & Salzberg, 2009), BOW-TIE (B. Langmead, Trapnell, Pop, & Salzberg, 2009), IGV (Thorvaldsdottir, Robinson, & Mesirov, 2013), SAMtools (Li et al., 2009), Picard (http://picard.sourceforge.net.), FastQC (http://www.bioinformatics.bbsrc.ac.uk/projects/fastqc), GATK (McKenna et al., 2010), MuTect (Cibulskis et al., 2013), Cufflink (Trapnell et al., 2010), Pindel (Ye, Schulz, Long, Apweiler, & Ning, 2009), Breakdancer (Chen et al., 2009), ANNOVAR (Wang, Li, & Hakonarson, 2010), VarScan2 (Koboldt et al., 2012), SNPEff (Cingolani et al., 2012), Variant Tools (San Lucas, Wang, Scheet, & Peng, 2012), RNA-eXpress (Forster, Finkel, Gould, & Hertzog, 2013), and Macs (Zhang et al., 2008) are used for alignment, QC, variant calling, functional analysis and quantification. Ivan Karabaliev of Eagle Genomics compiled a very cool "periodic table" summary of most of the bioinformatics tools available at http://elements.eaglegenomics.com/. However, almost all these NGS tools are under active development, being updated frequently, working in Linux environment only, and requiring intensive computing and advanced computational skills to run them.

Meanwhile, cloud computing offers scalable, on-demand, cost-effective, light weight yet high performance computing with different security levels of public accessibility, enabling easier big data sharing for team-based, national even internationally collaborative research, as well as more efficient big data processing using computationally expensive software. The combination of large data set and computing intensive nature of NGS is a natural fit for cloud computing. Next, we will briefly review the development of cloud computing.

CLOUD COMPUTING

Cloud computing refers to both applications software delivered as a Service via Internet and the hardware and system software in a data center that provide those services (Armbrust et al., 2010). The former is usually referred as Software as a Service (SaaS) and the latter as Platform as a Service (PaaS) or Infrastructure as a Service (IaaS). In PaaS model, cloud providers deliver a computing platform and solution stack typically including operating system, programming language execution environment, database, and web server. Application developers can develop and run their software solutions on a cloud platform without the cost and complexity of buying and managing the underlying hardware and software layers. The underlying computer and storage resources of some PaaS providers can scale automatically to match application demand so cloud user does not have to allocate resources manually.

The purpose of the cloud computing is to share computing (infrastructure, hardware, servers, system software, application software), storage, data, services, and/or network in a flexible, scalable, high performance common place ("cloud"), providing high availability, location independence, resource sharing, thus leading to improved efficiency, performance, reduced enterprise cost and greener IT. It may soon evolve from a mere competitive advantage to a necessity for most organizations.

Public cloud, including their applications, storage, and other resources, are made available to the general public by Cloud service providers. Community cloud shares infrastructure between several organizations from a specific community with common concerns (security, compliance, jurisdiction, etc.), whether managed internally or by a third-party and hosted internally or externally. Hybrid cloud is a composition of two or more clouds (private, community or public) in the same environment that remain unique entities but are bound together, offering the benefits of multiple deployment models. Private cloud is maintained by the organization. Sometimes, the private cloud could also be managed by a third party. This is mainly to maintain a high level of data security.

Cloud computing is a distributed computing technology that originated from cluster computing (Becker et al., 1995) and virtualization technology (Barham et al., 2003). Cluster computing originated from a divergent research stream from supercomputing in 1990s. It was initially motivated by the low cost computing needs and used Ethernet to connect a cluster of low-end x86-based PC or workstations to achieve the computing performance of a high-end supercomputer.

In 1994, two NASA scientists successfully launched the first Linux Cluster with 24 x486 PC equipped Linux OS networked together by Ethernet (Becker et al., 1995). Later, Linux Clusters became the hardware infrastructure of two Google founders in 1996, thus cementing its position as the standard cloud computing hardware infrastructure in 2000s. While Ethernet is the dominant cloud computing networking protocol for local area network, new technologies such as Infiniband are being promoted and implemented to further improve transmission speed, not just between computers but also between I/O devices within the computer, removing the inefficiency of traditional bus architecture. In the near future, we may observe competing full stack communication protocols in cloud computing architecture to replace Ethernet (Pfister, 2001).

IBM pioneered virtualization technology in 1970s on its System/370 mainframe computer. However, because of the popularity of distributed computing in later 1970s, virtualization technology was not further explored until the late 1990s when Mendel Rosenblum, a Stanford computer professor revitalized it on Intel x86 systems (Rosenblum, 2004). Later he, his wife and his student together launched a company called VMware in 1998. Their virtualization technology fulfilled an immediate need of increasing power hungry data centers by large companies because of under-utilization of workstation servers.

Virtualization technology became more popular with the introduction of Xen, an open source software created by Ian Pratt and his team in Cambridge University (Barham et al., 2003). Because of its open source nature and low usage cost, Xen was widely adopted by ecommerce companies like Amazon.com and became the infrastructure software for Amaon.com EC2. Amazon EC2 in turn became the most popular cloud computing platform for many companies that need a public cloud computing solution for their organization.

The infrastructure of cloud computing can be divided into two categories. The first is Google/Hadoop architecture. Google pioneered the combination of low-end Linux PC server cluster and highly redundant Google File System to compensate the high failure rate of PC servers. Google also invented MapReduce algorithm to allow easy implementation of parallel computing by applications. Starting from 2003, Google began to release its architecture design to public (Ghemawat, Gobioff, & Leung, 2003) and such design were being replicated by Yahoo as an open source system Hadoop (Borthakur, 2007). Yahoo, Microsoft, Facebook, Twitter and almost all major ecommerce companies subsequently adopted Hadoop/MapReduce architecture, making it the most popular cloud-computing platform for large ecommerce companies.

The popularity of Hadoop/MapReduce platform also made it a frequently used platform in NGS data processing. It is open source, scalable, provides load balancing, fault tolerance and transparent replication, and is especially suitable for jobs with single large input yet reduced output. It processes data in chunks mapped using name node and data nodes on chunkservers (nodes) managed by master server and gives out small output (reduce step), e.g. ElasticMapReduce by Amazon can shrink/enlarge based on the job needs. It also provides data locality, and eliminates the need to network transfer of very big data. Furthermore, it can be installed on regular cheaper commodity servers instead of expensive custom supercomputers, either locally or in the cloud, therefore is cost-effective.

NGS applications that can benefit from MapReduce/Hadoop include those involving large amounts of data processing, scaling up for large number of parallel jobs, or query type jobs. Dr. Ron Taylor of Pacific Northwest National Laboratory expected that in the near future, Hadoop running on regular commodity servers would take over traditional custom supercomputers in high performance parallel computing and become the dominant open source big data solution for NGS analysis (Afgan et al., 2010).

Hadoop uses a Map/Reduce execution engine to implement its fault-tolerant distributed computing system over the large data sets stored. MapReduce is like the 'ecosystem' of Hadoop and is an easy-to-use general-purpose parallel programming model tailored for large dataset analysis. Developers only need to write two functions: Map (converts an input key/value pair to a set of intermediate key/value pairs), and Reduce (merges together all intermediate values associated with a given intermediate key) to drive thousands or tens of thousands of computers processing and integrating the data. The framework automatically handles all low level details such as data partitioning, scheduling, load balancing, machine failure handling and inter-machine communication. Originated from Google File System, the Hadoop Distributed File System (HDFS) is a distributed file system designed to run on commodity hardware, with the differences from other distributed file systems being highly fault-tolerant and to be deployed on low-cost hardware. HDFS is suitable for applications for large data sets by providing high throughput access to application data. High-level language, pipe and streaming such as Pig / Biopig, Hive and Hbase built on top of Hadoop ease the use of Hadoop.

Pig is designed for batch processing of data. Biopig is an analytic toolkit for NGS data with tools such as BLAST. Hive is a data warehouse framework built on top of Hadoop. HBase adds a distributed, fault-tolerant scalable database, built on top of the HDFS file system, with random real-time read/write access to data. Hbase can store and analyze any sort of complex data, allowing researchers to combine diverse forms of data for a more complete view of gene activation and disease pathways. Mahout is an Apache project for building scalable machine learning libraries, with algorithms focus on clustering, classification, data mining (frequent itemset), and evolutionary programming, which are extremely useful for bioinformatics. Pydoop is a Python MapReduce and HDFS API for Hadoop that allows complete MapReduce applications to be written in Python.

There are more and more applications using Hadoop/MapReduce/Hbase in NGS like Cloud-Burst, Crossbow, Contrail and Myrna (Afgan et al., 2010). Hadoop provides the data locality (e.g. HDFS provides interfaces for applications to move themselves closer to where the data is located) and scalable parallel computing. So the huge raw sequencing data and workflows should be stored immediately in cloud and the preprocessing that has simple I/O (big data in and smaller data out) should be done in the Hadoop/MapReduce/Hbase based cloud computing infrastructure to distribute many similar tasks. Therefore the Hadoop/MapReduce/Hbase with well-maintained bioinformatics specific framework such as BioLinux, CloudMan and Galaxy bundle is the ideal infrastructure for sequencing preprocessing pipeline or workflow, and the raw sequencing data should reside close to such infrastructure if not reside right on the same cloud provider.

Though a powerful architecture as it is, Google/Hadoop is not as convenient as Amazon EC2 in terms of serving the needs of many traditional companies especially when they want to migrate a portion of their existing computing needs to a cloud platform. This is because Google/Hadoop does not provide virtualization technology for users. A parallel computing task such as genome sequencing has to utilize the function supported by MapReduce directly when being deployed on a Google/Hadoop platform to fully utilize its strength.

In contrast, the Amazon cloud platform, though using a similar Linux cluster, implements a virtualization platform on top of the cluster, and makes the underlying infrastructure transparent to users. Thus, users can create whatever server instance(s) they prefer and migrate their computing needs to such virtual instance on Amazon EC2 with ease. In addition, Amazon also provides related SQS, S3 service to complement messaging communication and storage needs for users. All these service could be pooled together to provide a complete virtual computing environment for any enterprise. In fact, many small ecommerce star-ups have been using Amazon Cloud to host their websites and currently Amazon maintains about 1% of all Web traffic due to its hosting services.

Proper adoption of cloud computing could bring significant benefit for organizations because it provides a cost-effective means to accommodate computing need fluctuation, allowing a company to smooth out demand peak without large infrastructure investment commitment. A recent Carbon Disclosure Project report estimated U.S. organizations that moving to the cloud could save $12.3 billion in energy costs and the equivalent of 200 million barrels of oil by 2020 (Reeve, 2011). In the domain of NGS, cloud computing provides on-demand and unlimited computing resources to users without the burden of maintaining expensive facility by user themselves.

Both Google/Hadoop and Amazon cloud architecture have their pros and cons in NGS. Users should first evaluate their own technical infrastructure and computing needs and then make the selection based on self-analysis.

In addition to public cloud computing solution, many research institutes of genome sequencing may adopt private or hybrid cloud computing solution due to practical needs, policy restrictions on data transfer, as well as challenges in moving large amount of data over networks.

A private cloud computing infrastructure could be implemented either with Google/Hadoop style or Amazon style. Both options need IT professionals to put together open source components, including Linux server and Xen-like virtualization tools. Because implementing open source solution needs IT professionals with more expertise in cloud computing domain and domain knowledge in NGS, sometimes, it makes more sense for an organization to use customized solutions from companies like IBM, which provide a flexible combination from private to hybrid cloud computing solutions as well as support.

IBM provides a Workload Deployer solution for private cloud computing. This solution includes blade servers, middleware and virtualization for organizations to build their own cloud infrastructure and providing virtual server for genome sequencing needs. IBM also provides tools like WebSphere Cast Iron to integrate private and public cloud computing services. In the bioinformatics field, IBM provides the customized cloud computing solution, PowerGene, to match users' needs. Recently IBM announced the launching of IBM PureGene v1.0 with IBM genomic pipeline (IGP) available in either cloud-based PaaS flavor or Gateway and Cluster flavors in January 2014, which is an open, scalable and end-end system framework based on the reference architecture for genomics platform.

In addition to the above infrastructures and solutions, other popular cloud computing service providers include Rackspace, CenturyLink/Savvis, Salesforce.com, Verizon/Terremark, Joyent, Citrix, Bluelock, Microsoft, and VMware. Meanwhile, new startup services kept propping up. For example, Bina Technologies, Inc. founded by several Stanford and UC Berkeley professors with expertise in HPC computer engineering, statistics and molecular biology also provides similar private, public or hybrid cloud computing through scalable NGS Bina Genomic Analysis Platform with Hadoop implementation (http://www.binatechnologies.com/technology). Bina claimed to be able to perform ultra-fast genomic data analysis with the ability to process a 40X whole human genome for several hours, comparing to >10 days

normally. Their Platform is said to be not only fast but also very accurate. They have been able to accelerate the popular BWA aligner with the Broad Institute's Genome Analysis Toolkit (GATK).

NGS IN CLOUD

Currently there have been hot debates in many biomedical research institutions or groups on whether they should go to cloud computing. Here we provide some general guidelines.

Generally it is recommended one would benefit a lot from going to cloud computing such as public cloud or bioinformatics specific cloud when there is no in-house computing infrastructure, such as high performance cluster or grid, that can do extensive parallel computing and no existing trained personnel that can do the complex bioinformatics tasks. Even for an organization that has both infrastructures in place cloud computing may still be a valuable approach for managing and processing data. Reasons that cloud computing would be employed include: the service frequently experience temporarily spikes in computing resource demands, one has massive data to share or work with from multiple sites that lack robust local computing resources, the computation is too expensive locally but does not require intensive I/O, or the data is already in cloud, such as from sequencing companies. We can predict that the bioinformatics community would benefit more and more from cloud computing, especially with the trend of lowered cloud service cost, faster internet bandwidth, improved security and privacy laws, more open-minded collaboration and data sharing, etc. Figure 1 is a brief summary of factors that favor cloud computing.

However, each institution has to do a thorough work system analysis based on their own situations before applying these guidelines.

We can obviously see strong evidence from federal and international policies and strategies favoring the adoption of cloud computing in NGS

Figure 1. Factors leading to cloud computing

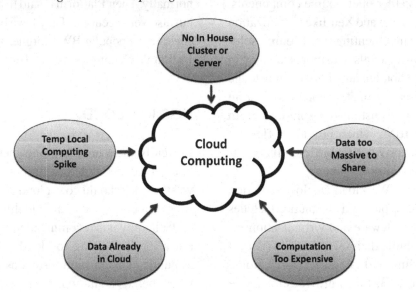

from the 1000 Genomes Project (Waltz, 2012). For example, NIH funded about $1.5 million for the development of Galaxy, an open source software suite for genomic data analysis capable to be uploaded to AWS cloud.

The 1000 Genomes Project is an international public-private consortium participated by about 20 countries, including multiple US National Institutes, leading research institutions and major sequencing companies. The central goal of the 1000 Genomes Project is to make the data of 2600 people from 26 populations as widely available as possible to accelerate medical discoveries, and to develop core technologies for data collection, management, analysis and extraction. The National Center of Biotechnology Information (NCBI) and the European Bioinformatics Institute (EBI) in the UK played a lead role in organizing the project, and the National Human Genome Research Institute (NHGRI) under NIH, Wellcome Trust of London and BGI-Shenzhen of China are major funders.

The 1000 Genomes Project data available on AWS cloud is the exemplar of new White House Big Data Initiative. The White House Office of Science and Technology Policy announced "The public-private collaboration demonstrates the

kind of solutions that may emerge from the Big Data Research and Development Initiative." The NIH Director Francis S. Collins, M.D., Ph.D. also stated that "The explosion of biomedical data has already significantly advanced our understanding of health and disease. Now we want to find new and better ways to make the most of these data to speed discovery, innovation and improvements in the nation's health and economy." At least six federal science agencies including the NIH, NSF, DOD and DOE were initially engaged in the Big Data Initiative, and over $200 million was put in "to a collaborative effort to develop core technologies and other resources needed by researchers to manage and analyze enormous data sets" (Waltz, 2012).

The data set reached 200 terabytes by March 2012, which sets "a prime example of big data that has become so massive that few researchers have the computing power to use them". NCBI and Amazon developed the systems in cloud that accommodate the unique types and sizes of files necessary for transferring, storing and accessing massive amounts of sequence data after their lengthy and fruitful collaboration. AWS posted the data for free as a public data set, providing a centralized repository on AWS (http://s3.amazonaws.com/1000genomes/), which can be seamlessly accessed through Amazon Elastic Compute Cloud and Amazon Elastic MapReduce with the highly scalable resources needed to power big data and high performance computing applications often needed in research. Researchers pay only for the additional AWS resources they need to further process or analyze the data. "The 1000 Genomes Project's sequence data set is the world's largest set of data on human genetic variation and is freely available for downloading from NCBI and EBI, but those without a robust local computing capacity may find it easier to use in the cloud. In the first week after cloud availability, 3,000 researchers accessed the data." (Waltz, 2012)

So cloud access expands the universe of researchers who have access to the data availability, enables other uses with constraints on computing power, such as for bioinformatics education, also enables users to analyze the data much more quickly without the time-consuming downloading of data and because users can run their analyses over many servers at once. "Putting the data in the cloud provides a tremendous opportunity for researchers around the world who want to study large-scale human genetic variation but lack the computer capability to do so." As said by AWS's principal product manager, "We're excited to help scientists gain access to this important data set by making it available to anyone with access to the Internet. This means researchers and labs of all sizes and budgets have access to the complete 1,000 Genomes Project data and can immediately start analyzing and crunching the data without the investment it would normally require in hardware, facilities and personnel. Researchers can focus on advancing science, not obtaining the resources required for their research." The systems also provide a framework for software providers and the latter could add different data processing tools for scientists to use.

AN EXAMPLE OF NGS IN CLOUD

The Current trend of cloud computing utilization in the bioinformatics field is Platform-as-a-Service with mainstream NGS analytical tools readily available, in which users can create a new instance of an application, then clone and modify existing applications via a user-friendly web interface or command line in Linux. There are a few existing research applications for conducting bioinformatics in private cloud environment (Chang, 2013). Here we give an example of using public cloud computing environment.

Figure 2 explains the basic procedures of NGS data analysis in cloud computing. To conduct NGS in the public cloud, we need to first create a storage account and computing account with the cloud provider. After that we need to move NGS data to the cloud storage account using the primary access key provided by service provider. We also need to have an instance in the cloud for bioinformatics tools used to process and analyze data. We will review the procedures in detail using Nimbix as example.

Nimbix

Nimbix is a Dallas-based cloud computing service provider. Their cloud solution, Nimbix Accelerated Compute Cloud (NACC), includes the Accelerated Genomics Cloud (TAGC) for bioinformatics and recently added JARVICE Nimbix's Platform as a Service offering. NACC is a large heterogeneous HPC cluster that includes a pool of Nimbix resources, ranging from high memory multi-core systems to specialized FPGA-based servers from Convey Computing. These resources can be reconfigured to provide the best performance across a range of applications and workflows. These may include reference mapping, de novo assembly, functional annotation, variant analysis and RNA expression profiling, provided by its Convey Bioinformatics Suite.

Figure 2. NGS in the Cloud

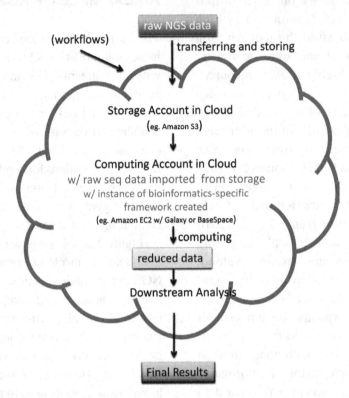

Launching Workloads in NACC

NACC has two easy ways to launch workloads, either through its web portal at https://nacc. nimbix.net/landing#tasks or via an Application Programming Interface (API) call from local server. The Nimbix web interface (https://nacc. nimbix.net) has three tabs: "Dashboard" for user profile, jobs and apps stat and monitoring, "Computing Tasks" for choosing the desired tools, and "Task Builder" for actually setting up tasks and submitting jobs. Fig 2illustrates an example of launching the workload through its web interface to choose human reference genome, upload two paired-end raw sequence files (.fastq) from the publically accessible 1000 genomes sequencing data from NCBI, and run BWA to align sequence reads to build hg19 of the human reference genome. The computation was performed in Nimbix bioinformatics cloud

on their Convey hybrid-core platforms in May 2013. Nimbix has since updated the portal and added two new tabs for JARVICE.

Raw data can be uploaded from Amazon S3 storage account, Dropbox, or SFTP from local storage server, by using NACC id and API key. The output files were saved to user's NACC repository. User would get email or SMS notifications for events such as job submission, starting, ending, and completion of file transfer. A video tutorial about how to run a simple BWA workload is available from YouTube: http://www.youtube. com/watch?v=eLrIbfbwRaE.

If one wants to submit jobs from a local Linux server we can use curl. In that case, we need to save the job description at API confirm step into a text file in JSON format. We can modify the file in JSON format with different input files and parameters, and submit a job using a curl command like:

```
curl -k - -header "Content-
Type:application/json" -X POST -d "@
nameofyourjsonfile" https://api.nim-
bix.net:4081/nimbix/nacc_upload
```

Data Movement Options

Nimbix provides a few ways to move data in and out of Nimbix or NACC storage. The data is not backed up and there is no service level agreement on data protection. Essentially, one can just use SFTP, or Globus, to pull files up or down including the intermediate .sai output files. The BAM file is available at sftp://drop.nimbix.net (using NACC id and API key for access). The transfer speed of data to NACC repository via Aspera transfers can reach as high as 1 Gbps. On SFTP and the portal, the password in the JSON format file is transmitted over an encrypted connection. For example, after creating a SFTP session using command

```
$sftp nacc_username@drop.nimbix.net:/
data
```

and API key from NACC as password, you could use command

```
sftp>put pathtofile/datafilename.
fastq.gz
```

to upload a file. Users who prefer a graphical user interface could connect with another ftp client or using Globus Online.

As to the questions on the security aspect, any data used in one's workload runs is loaded via encrypted transit and all processing is done behind a firewall. No end users have access to the servers in NACC except via the API. So that no one uses SSH to communicate with the servers. Each user has their own storage space that is accessible with their ID, password and security key.

Most of the applications mentioned above leverage one of their Convey Computer servers. While other applications might leverage Intel

Figure 3. Nimbix web interface
(© Copyright, Nimbix Inc.. Used with permission).

multicore servers, GPU enabled servers, or DSP Accelerators. The hourly rates ranged from $1.50 to $15.00 depending on the number and resource type being used, which allows users to analyze, for example, a dozen human genomes at significant coverage at a cost of around $1000. The cost per hour for standard BWA workflow has recently been lowered from $17.50 to $5.50 per hour.

Nimbix does not use virtualized servers in NACC. The platform consists of physical servers with specialized hardware accelerators (GPUs, DSPs, FPGAs, etc...). This enables them to provide a higher level of performance than other cloud solutions like Amazon EC2 but uploading a VM image with pre-configured tools is not an option. However, Nimbix allows the creation of workflow automation, and it is also straightforward to provide a "tools server" that would enable users to work on their datasets post alignment.

Nimbix's JARVICE is also a Platform-as-a-Service offering, which allows you to quickly create NAEs (Nimbix Application Environments) with different configurations based on one's needs. These NAEs are akin to Amazon's AMIs, but their NAEs run at bare-metal speeds and offers interconnect speeds all the way up to 56GB FDR Infiniband. There is no hypervisor, which means none of the stability or performance issues associated with virtual machines. There is no over subscription either because only one NAE runs on a server at one time. You get all of the resources of that machine. You are basically able to *create* new NAEs, *clone* existing NAEs, *delete* (unneeded NAEs) or *start* previously saved ones via the portal or a simple JSON API call. Which means additional NAEs can be spun up on demand programmatically by orchestrating NAEs via API. Another of the exciting things is they added 3D Linux Desktops. Users are now able to spin up powerful 3D desktops and as long as their application supports OpenGL and runs on Linux leverage them from multiple locations. They have had customers as far away as Moscow work with them and they were very happy with the performance. JARVICE will make it easier for customers to install and test their own custom code and then promote it into their NACC catalog and then take advantage of the simple pay-per-use pricing and scale-out capabilities of NACC on-demand for their processing needs. The applications can be setup as private or public.

Limitation of our research includes that we haven't compared the more time-consuming part of the downstream NGS workflow (only bwa was tested at Nimbix) and we haven't tried JARVICE, which is highly flexible for individual pipeline needs coming from different sequencing platforms, library preparations, software combinations, etc..

CLOUD TOOLS FOR NGS

Nimbix is only one example of NGS in Cloud service providers. We collected a list of similar service providers as well as NGS solution providers in Table 2. It lists names, URL's, reference and a brief introduction of most available cloud-based or cloud enabling bioinformatics applications. Even though we have made efforts to compose as complete a list as possible by searching all related literatures, this list is not exhaustive because new bioinformatics tools are being developed rapidly in this fast-growing field. Nevertheless, the list still could serve as a good reference for those who are seeking to use bioinformatics tools for cloud computing.

CHALLENGES

Lacking standards to handle data privacy, security, compliance and jurisdiction of cloud computing in bioinformatics area is the major challenge for current NGS. The big data trend in NGS not only place a high demand on storage, transfer, management and data mining, but also forces a paradigm change in making policies and strategies on using cloud computing for the research in biomedical sciences. Despite of the advantages cloud computing can offer, challenges remain as compared to traditional local computing. They include but not limited to: privacy, security, data transfer, human resource, and other hidden costs.

Table 2. Current cloud services available for bioinformatics

Application	URL and Brief Introduction
Atlas2 Cloud	http://sourceforge.net/projects/atlas2cloud/ a framework for personal genome analysis in the cloud
BaseSpace	http://basespace.illumina.com/home/index genomic cloud computing provided by Illumina
BG7	http://bg7.ohnosequences.com/ a new approach for bacterial genome annotation designed for next generation sequencing data
Biodoop	http://biodoop.sourceforge.net/core/ a suite of tools for computational biology with efficient, distributed implementation of computationally demanding and/or data-intensive tasks
BioNode	https://github.com/pjotrp/cloudbiolinux/tree/bionode a ready-made bioinformatics VM image for scalable computing for evolutionary genomics
BioVLAB-MMIA	http://microbial.informatics.indiana.edu/biovlab/ A Reconfigurable Cloud Computing Environment for microRNA and mRNA Integrated Analysis
Cloud BioLinux	http://cloudbiolinux.org/ pre-configured and on-demand bioinformatics computing for the genomics community
CloudAligner	http://cloudaligner.sourceforge.net/ a fast and full-featured MapReduce based tool for sequence mapping
CloudBlast	http://ammatsun.acis.ufl.edu/amwiki/index.php/CloudBLAST_Project combining MapReduce and virtualization on distributed resources for bioinformatics applications
CloudBrush	https://github.com/ice91/CloudBrush A de novo next generation genomic sequence assembler based on string graph and MapReduce cloud computing framework
CloudBurst	http://cloudburst-bio.sourceforge.net/ highly sensitive read mapping with MapReduce
CloudLCA	http://sourceforge.net/p/cloudlca/home/Home/ finding the lowest common ancestor in metagenome analysis using cloud computing
CloudMan	http://usecloudman.org delivering cloud compute clusters
CloudMap	http://usegalaxy.org/cloudmap a cloud-based pipeline for analysis of mutant genome sequences
CloVR	http://clovr.org/ a virtual machine for automated and portable sequence analysis from the desktop using cloud computing
CRdata.org	http://CRdata.org a cloud-based, free, open-source web server for running analyses and sharing data and R scripts with others
Crossbow	http://bowtie-bio.sourceforge.net/crossbow/ a scalable software pipeline for whole genome resequencing analysis
eCEO	http://www.comp.nus.edu.sg/~wangzk/eCEO.html an efficient Cloud Epistasis computing model in genome-wide association study
elasticHPC	http://www.elasticHPC.org a package for personalized cloud-based bioinformatics services
Eoulsan	http://transcriptome.ens.fr/eoulsan/ a cloud computing-based framework facilitating high throughput sequencing analyses
FX	http://fx.gmi.ac.kr an RNA-Seq analysis tool which runs in parallel on the cloud

continued on following page

Table 2. Continued

Application	URL and Brief Introduction
Galaxy	http://galaxyproject.org/ an open, scalable, web-based platform for data intensive biomedical research
GMS	http://gma-bio.sourceforge.net Genome Mappability Score for reliability of short read mapping, which leverages the parallelism of cloud computing to analyze large genomes
Hadoop-BAM	http://hadoop-bam.sourceforge.net/ a novel library for the scalable manipulation of aligned NGS data in the Hadoop distributed computing framework
Jamboree	http://code.google.com/p/tcgajamboree/ a space for TCGA organizations to share data, tools, web applications and visualizations in an environment with a variety of cloud and local services
Microbase2.0	http://www.microbase.org.uk/ a generic framework for computationally intensive bioinformatics workflows in the cloud
MR-MSPolygraph	http://compbio.eecs.wsu.edu/MR-MSPolygraph/ a MapReduce implementation of a hybrid spectral library-database search method for large-scale peptide identification
Myrna	http://bowtie-bio.sf.net/myrna a cloud-computing pipeline for calculating differential gene expression in large RNA-Seq datasets
PeakRanger	http://www.modencode.org/software/ranger/ a scalable peak caller software package that works equally well on punctate and broad sites
Roundup	http://roundup.hms.harvard.edu/about/ the comparative genomics tool using cloud computing
RUM	http://www.cbil.upenn.edu/RUM/ an alignment, junction calling, and feature quantification pipeline specifically designed for Illumina RNA-Seq data
SeqWare Query Engine	http://sourceforge.net/apps/mediawiki/seqware created using modern cloud computing technologies and designed to support database information from thousands of genomes
SIMPLEX	http://simplex.i-med.ac.at a cloud-enabled autonomous analysis pipeline, which comprises the complete exome analysis workflow
SOLiDzipper	http://szipper.dinfree.com a High Speed Encoding Method for the NGS data
SPRINT	http://r-sprint.org/ The Simple Parallel R Interface (SPRINT), a package for biostatisticians with easy access to HPCs and parallelized functions to R in cloud
Tavaxy	http://www.tavaxy.org integrating Taverna and Galaxy workflows with cloud computing support
Usm	http://usm.github.com Universal Sequence Maps, Javascript libraries and Apps for related iterated mapping techniques such as Chaos Game Representation (CGR)
VAT	http://vat.gersteinlab.org a computational framework to functionally annotate variants in personal genomes within a cloud-computing environment
Yabi	http://ccg.murdoch.edu.au/yabi an online research environment for Grid, High Performance and Cloud computing
YunBe	http://tinyurl.com/yunbedownload gene set analysis in the cloud

Firstly, although cloud computing is particular effective when a lot of computation is expected such as molecular dynamic simulations, in genomics, data processing usually coupled with large amount of data transfer. With the increasing amount of data generated in genome sequencing, transferring massive amount of data to the cloud becomes not only time consuming but also cost prohibitive for small laboratories with standard network bandwidth.

Moreover, by transferring the data to the cloud, one would create a data redundancy that is not efficient, unless the output from the sequencers is directly transferred to the cloud. Reference-based compression can ameliorate some of these issues. For example, a 10-fold reduction of a 300 GB BAM file will reduce the overall cost to approximately $4 for transferring the data to the cloud and storing them for 10 days, in addition to reducing the transfer time considerably (approximately 1 hour) (Sboner, Mu, Greenbaum, Auerbach, & Gerstein, 2011).

If the data set size is too large for online transfer or policy regulations prevent users from using public cloud computing services (for example, internal review board requirements), users may construct a private computing environment in Hadoop or Singleton mode, which is easier to use and debug when things go wrong though it needs more expertise from IT professionals and extra cost (Ben Langmead, Hansen, & Leek, 2010). If public cloud computing is necessary, one solution is using the cloud storage service and link it with computing service. For example, using Amazon's EC2 and S3 together could partially solve the problem though transference of initial data set may still be a challenge in such case.

There has been improvement in file transfer protocol and software that enables transferring of huge genomic data over Internet recently. One example of such improvement is the GeneTorrent software used by CGHUB (https://cghub.ucsc.edu/), which makes it possible to distribute huge BAM files from the TCGA project. Another one

is widely used Aspera (http://asperasoft.com/), which was used by BGI to reach nearly 10 gigabits per second between US and China (http://www.genomics.cn/en/news/show_news?nid=99118). There is also other work in progress such as improving the performance of SSH over its inefficient use of buffer.

Secondly, cloud computing has to ensure the data from human subjects remain private. However, users usually have to upload all the data to a cloud to have it processed and any privacy incident could cause disclosure of private information of human subjects (Ryan, 2011). Although some companies already provide tools to deal with these issues in the cloud, the legal aspects of handling genomic data are still in formation. In the United States, Health Insurance Portability and Accountability Act (HIPAA) compliance, especially rules regarding the storage of patient information still prevents the utility of cloud computing service for the processing of clinical data. For example, in November 2013, FDA ordered 23andme, a direct-to-consumer genomics service company, to stop selling its Personal Genome Service because it is not in compliance with HIPAA. One solution to the privacy issues could come from a government regulated federated online cloud computing environment where a researcher can conduct his/her genomics research in accordance with the legal framework (Chute et al., 2011). An alternative organization is Biomedical Informatics Research Network (BIRN). BIRN is created to address both technological and sociological challenges in biomedical data sharing for data to be share among researchers and made accessible and useful the end result to the larger scientific community eventually. The challenges with federated organization or voluntary sharing organization mainly come in two aspects. The first aspect is the high cost of moving data in clinical settings to the outside environment while maintaining the privacy requirements. Another aspect is researchers who have data are often unwilling to give the data to a central storage location not under their control (Helmer et al., 2011). In this scenario, it is important that there is definition of a shared common legal and ethical framework if data are shared nationally or internationally. We could use high-level summaries (VCF files) for data reduction which are considerably smaller than the whole set of mapped reads (only ~ 170 MB for ~ 3 million SNPs, ~ 8 MB for 300,000 indels, and ~ 0.2 MB for ~ 1,500 structural variations), and have the advantage of reducing the potential privacy issues related to NGS data (which reveals more of the individual and includes the potential for a full characterization that can be abused dangerously) (Ozdemir et al., 2011).

Finally, there is a lack of standards for cloud computing in NGS. Some computational frameworks, such as Galaxy, do provide users with several tools to perform data analysis. However, the tools provided in such systems are far from complete and the usage of such tools takes a lot of learning efforts. An unpredictable amount of time has to be spent on comparing and choosing suitable and reasonable software tools, learning how to install, configure and execute them, estimating the effects of tuning the parameters, interfacing input/output formats for serial modules in the pipeline, and debugging and streamlining. Sometimes, this latter phase is more time consuming than the actual processing time (Goddard, Wilson, Cryer, & Yamashita, 2011). In addition, whether the sequencing and initial data analyses are carried out externally or in house, researchers have to face the downstream analyses of NGS tailored to specific research projects. Hundreds of tools have been developed to unravel the complexity of biological mechanisms hidden in the sequence reads. Maintaining fast updating reference databases and bioinformatics tools in the cloud is also challenging. In contrast to the cost of hardware, the cost of projected human resources is difficult to predict at the current state with rapid technology development. No streamlined, standardized approach is yet available for the users, either an experienced or a casual one. Hence, users have

to commit considerable efforts to properly install, configure and using such services. In addition to standardization, there are also opportunities for startup companies to develop Health-as-a-Service solution to address NGS needs, that is provide a ready-to-use solution to facilitate user adoption (Chang, Wills, & Walters, 2011). Kuo (2011) provided a more comprehensive review of opportunities and challenges of NGS in cloud computing environment.

Recommendation for Future Project Development

PaaS cloud computing service is getting more mature and rapidly gaining market popularity, largely because it not only provides the computing platform but also the solution stack. It provides more than everything including team work and technical support needed for application development and deployment, but still gives the freedom to customers to create applications easily suiting their own special needs using the tools and environment provided.

In particular, Hadoop/HDFS based platform provides scalable, fault-tolerant, and cost-effective solution for parallel computing needed for big data coming from NGS. The potential market for big data from NGS has gained attention by many cloud computing providers. In addition to previously mentioned, the recent international ICGC-TCGA DREAM Somatic Mutation Calling Challenge is sponsored by Google Cloud (http://seqan-swers.com/forums/showthread.php?t=40294). A Google Cloud Storage bucket is provided to access challenge data and all computation and submissions can be performed on the Google Cloud Platform.

PaaS provider implementing Hadoop/MapReduce algorithm provides the scalable platform delivered as a server or desktop, with optimized NGS tools installed even template workflows available. Users can create new NGS applications or workflows via web interface as well as command-line in Linux. NGS data could reside locally without worry, instead of being uploaded to the public cloud, which also minimizes the network transfer of large data.

We think this would be the trend for cloud computing service to NGS data for life science companies and institutions. Ideally these cloud service providers could work seamlessly with customers together to gather requirements and design highly customized, user-friendly yet flexible applications for NGS workflows, therefore relieving the burden of the bioinformaticians and lab technicians from frequent hardware and software upgrades, maintenance, repair and optimization so they can concentrate on analyzing information obtained from the big NGS data more productively.

CONCLUSION

Cloud and big data are the two megatrends of this decade. Their proper hybridization will shape the way life science companies and research institutions build infrastructure and handle data. The "big data" complexity in bioinformatics can be simplified by cloud computing as already shown by dozens of successful cases, especially demonstrated in high-throughput sequence data analysis.

In this chapter, we provided a comprehensive introduction of next generation genome sequencing in cloud computing environment. We introduced the concept of *avant-garde* genome sequencing and cloud computing technologies, especially the Hadoop/MapReduce algorithm, described the big data problem NGS is facing and how it can benefit from scalable cloud computing. We also introduced the basic procedures of NGS in cloud computing using Nimbix cloud as example. Current bioinformatics tools or framework in the cloud were examined and list was provided. We introduced 1000 genomes data in AWS and Galaxy as examples of the current US government sponsored efforts.

It is predictable that more and more bioinformatics research will be moved to cloud computing in the near future for low cost and high flexibility, especially with the trend of improved technologies, dropping of service price and more security guarantee. The current non-technical changes of NGS in cloud computing includes privacy, security, compliance, and open standards. Future research direction should concentrate on how to solve above issues in cloud computing and solve the bottleneck of big data transfer as well as on methods for further data compression.

Our future plan is to conduct a thorough NGS workflow analysis in a flexible PaaS offering that adopts the Hadoop/MapReduce algorithm.

ACKNOWLEDGMENT

We would like to sincerely thank Steve Hebert, Paul Garrison and Rob Sherrard from Nimbix Inc. for their offering the free cloud computing testing, around-the-clock technical support, and constructive discussion and review of related content during the preparation of this book chapter.

REFERENCES

Afgan, E., Baker, D., Coraor, N., Chapman, B., Nekrutenko, A., & Taylor, J. (2010). Galaxy CloudMan: Delivering cloud compute clusters. *BMC Bioinformatics*, *11*(Suppl 12), S4. doi:10.1186/1471-2105-11-S12-S4 PMID:21210983

Armbrust, M., Fox, A., Griffith, R., Joseph, A. D., Katz, R., Konwinski, A., & Stoica, I. et al. (2010). A view of cloud computing. *Communications of the ACM*, *53*(4), 50–58. doi:10.1145/1721654.1721672

Barham, P., Dragovic, B., Fraser, K., Hand, S., Harris, T., Ho, A., & Warfield, A. et al. (2003). Xen and the art of virtualization. *Operating Systems Review*, *37*(5), 164–177. doi:10.1145/1165389.945462

Becker, D. J., Sterling, T., Savarese, D., Dorband, J. E., Ranawak, U. A., & Packer, C. V. (1995). BEOWULF: A parallel workstation for scientific computation. In *Proceedings of the International Conference on Parallel Processing*.

Bock, C., Reither, S., Mikeska, T., Paulsen, M., Walter, J., & Lengauer, T. (2005). BiQ Analyzer: Visualization and quality control for DNA methylation data from bisulfite sequencing. *Bioinformatics (Oxford, England)*, *21*(21), 4067–4068. doi:10.1093/bioinformatics/bti652 PMID:16141249

Borthakur, D. (2007). The Hadoop distributed file system: Architecture and design. *Hadoop Project Website*, *11*, 21.

Chang, V. (2013). Cloud bioinformatics in a private cloud deployment. Advancing medical practice through technology: Applications for healthcare delivery, management, and quality (p. 205). Hershey, PA: IGI Global.

Chang, V., Wills, G., & Walters, R. (2011). *The positive impacts offered by Healthcare Cloud and 3D Bioinformatics*. Paper presented at the 10th e-Science All Hands Meeting 2011, York.

Chen, K., Wallis, J. W., McLellan, M. D., Larson, D. E., Kalicki, J. M., Pohl, C. S., & Mardis, E. R. et al. (2009). BreakDancer: An algorithm for high-resolution mapping of genomic structural variation. *Nature Methods*, *6*(9), 677–681. doi:10.1038/nmeth.1363 PMID:19668202

Chute, C. G., Pathak, J., Savova, G. K., Bailey, K. R., Schor, M. I., Hart, L. A., . . . Huff, S. M. (2011). *The SHARPn project on secondary use of Electronic Medical Record data: Progress, plans, and possibilities*. Paper presented at the AMIA Annual Symposium Proceedings.

Cibulskis, K., Lawrence, M. S., Carter, S. L., Sivachenko, A., Jaffe, D., Sougnez, C., & Getz, G. et al. (2013). Sensitive detection of somatic point mutations in impure and heterogeneous cancer samples. *Nature Biotechnology*, *31*(3), 213–219. doi:10.1038/nbt.2514 PMID:23396013

Cingolani, P., Platts, A., Wang, L. L., Coon, M., Nguyen, T., Wang, L., & Ruden, D. M. et al. (2012). A program for annotating and predicting the effects of single nucleotide polymorphisms, SnpEff: SNPs in the genome of Drosophila melanogaster strain w1118; iso-2; iso-3. *Fly*, *6*(2), 80–92. doi:10.4161/fly.19695 PMID:22728672

Forster, S. C., Finkel, A. M., Gould, J. A., & Hertzog, P. J. (2013). RNA-eXpress annotates novel transcript features in RNA-seq data. *Bioinformatics (Oxford, England)*, *29*(6), 810–812. doi:10.1093/bioinformatics/btt034 PMID:23396121

Ghemawat, S., Gobioff, H., & Leung, S.-T. (2003). *The Google file system*. Paper presented at the ACM SIGOPS Operating Systems Review. doi:10.1145/945449.945450

Goddard, A., Wilson, N., Cryer, P., & Yamashita, G. (2011). Data hosting infrastructure for primary biodiversity data. *BMC Bioinformatics*, *12*(Suppl 15), S5. doi:10.1186/1471-2105-12-S15-S5 PMID:22373257

Harris, T. D., Buzby, P. R., Babcock, H., Beer, E., Bowers, J., Braslavsky, I., . . . Efcavitch, J. W. (2008). Single-molecule DNA sequencing of a viral genome. *Science, 320*(5872), 106-109.

Helmer, K. G., Ambite, J. L., Ames, J., Ananthakrishnan, R., Burns, G., Chervenak, A. L., & Macciardi, F. et al. (2011). Enabling collaborative research using the biomedical informatics research network (BIRN). *Journal of the American Medical Informatics Association*, *18*(4), 416–422. doi:10.1136/amiajnl-2010-000032 PMID:21515543

Kellis, M., Wold, B., Snyder, M. P., Bernstein, B. E., Kundaje, A., Marinov, G. K., & Hardison, R. C. et al. (2014). Defining functional DNA elements in the human genome. In *Proceedings of the National Academy of Sciences of the United States of America*, *111*(17), 6131–6138. doi:10.1073/pnas.1318948111 PMID:24753594

Koboldt, D. C., Zhang, Q., Larson, D. E., Shen, D., McLellan, M. D., Lin, L., & Wilson, R. K. et al. (2012). VarScan 2: Somatic mutation and copy number alteration discovery in cancer by exome sequencing. *Genome Research*, *22*(3), 568–576. doi:10.1101/gr.129684.111 PMID:22300766

Kuo, A. M.-H. (2011). Opportunities and challenges of cloud computing to improve health care services. *Journal of Medical Internet Research*, *13*(3), e67. doi:10.2196/jmir.1867 PMID:21937354

Langmead, B., Hansen, K. D., & Leek, J. T. (2010). Cloud-scale RNA-sequencing differential expression analysis with Myrna. *Genome Biology*, *11*(8), R83. doi:10.1186/gb-2010-11-8-r83 PMID:20701754

Langmead, B., Schatz, M. C., Lin, J., Pop, M., & Salzberg, S. L. (2009). Searching for SNPs with cloud computing. *Genome Biology*, *10*(11), R134. doi:10.1186/gb-2009-10-11-r134 PMID:19930550

Langmead, B., Trapnell, C., Pop, M., & Salzberg, S. L. (2009). Ultrafast and memory-efficient alignment of short DNA sequences to the human genome. *Genome Biology*, *10*(3), R25. doi:10.1186/gb-2009-10-3-r25 PMID:19261174

Li, H., & Durbin, R. (2009). Fast and accurate short read alignment with Burrows-Wheeler transform. *Bioinformatics (Oxford, England)*, *25*(14), 1754–1760. doi:10.1093/bioinformatics/btp324 PMID:19451168

Li, H., Handsaker, B., Wysoker, A., Fennell, T., Ruan, J., Homer, N., & Durbin, R. et al. (2009). The Sequence Alignment/Map format and SAMtools. *Bioinformatics (Oxford, England)*, *25*(16), 2078–2079. doi:10.1093/bioinformatics/btp352 PMID:19505943

McKenna, A., Hanna, M., Banks, E., Sivachenko, A., Cibulskis, K., Kernytsky, A., & DePristo, M. A. et al. (2010). The genome analysis toolkit: A MapReduce framework for analyzing next-generation DNA sequencing data. *Genome Research*, *20*(9), 1297–1303. doi:10.1101/gr.107524.110 PMID:20644199

Metzker, M. L. (2010). Sequencing technologies—the next generation. *Nature Reviews. Genetics*, *11*(1), 31–46. doi:10.1038/nrg2626 PMID:19997069

Ozdemir, V., Rosenblatt, D. S., Warnich, L., Srivastava, S., Tadmouri, G. O., Aziz, R. K., . . . Joly, Y. (2011). Towards an ecology of collective innovation: Human variome project (HVP), rare disease consortium for autosomal loci (RADical) and data-enabled life sciences alliance (DELSA). *Current pharmacogenomics and personalized medicine, 9*(4), 243.

Pfister, G. F. (2001). An introduction to the infiniband architecture. *High Performance Mass Storage and Parallel I/O, 42*, 617-632.

Reeve, R. (2011). Building a 21st century communications economy: Technical report, carbon disclosure project in support with AT&T.

Rosenblum, M. (2004). The reincarnation of virtual machines. *Queue*, *2*(5), 34. doi:10.1145/1016998.1017000

Ryan, M. (2011). Cloud computing privacy concerns on our doorstep. *Communications of the ACM*, *54*(1), 36. doi:10.1145/1866739.1866751

San Lucas, F. A., Wang, G., Scheet, P., & Peng, B. (2012). Integrated annotation and analysis of genetic variants from next-generation sequencing studies with variant tools. *Bioinformatics (Oxford, England)*, 28(3), 421–422. doi:10.1093/bioinformatics/btr667 PMID:22138362

Sanger, F., & Coulson, A. (1978). The use of thin acrylamide gels for DNA sequencing. *FEBS Letters*, 87(1), 107–110. doi:10.1016/0014-5793(78)80145-8 PMID:631324

Sboner, A., Mu, X. J., Greenbaum, D., Auerbach, R. K., & Gerstein, M. B. (2011). The real cost of sequencing: Higher than you think! *Genome Biology*, 12(8), 125. doi:10.1186/gb-2011-12-8-125 PMID:21867570

Shendure, J., & Ji, H. (2008). Next-generation DNA sequencing. *Nature Biotechnology*, 26(10), 1135–1145. doi:10.1038/nbt1486 PMID:18846087

Stein, L. D. (2010). The case for cloud computing in genome informatics. *Genome Biology*, 11(5), 207. doi:10.1186/gb-2010-11-5-207 PMID:20441614

Thorvaldsdottir, H., Robinson, J. T., & Mesirov, J. P. (2013). Integrative Genomics Viewer (IGV): High-performance genomics data visualization and exploration. *Briefings in Bioinformatics*, 14(2), 178–192. doi:10.1093/bib/bbs017 PMID:22517427

Trapnell, C., Pachter, L., & Salzberg, S. L. (2009). TopHat: Discovering splice junctions with RNA-Seq. *Bioinformatics (Oxford, England)*, 25(9), 1105–1111. doi:10.1093/bioinformatics/btp120 PMID:19289445

Trapnell, C., Williams, B. A., Pertea, G., Mortazavi, A., Kwan, G., van Baren, M. J., & Pachter, L. et al. (2010). Transcript assembly and quantification by RNA-Seq reveals unannotated transcripts and isoform switching during cell differentiation. *Nature Biotechnology*, 28(5), 511–515. doi:10.1038/nbt.1621 PMID:20436464

Venter, J. C., Adams, M. D., Myers, E. W., Li, P. W., Mural, R. J., Sutton, G. G., . . . Holt, R. A. (2001). The sequence of the human genome. *Science, 291*(5507), 1304-1351.

Waltz, E. (2012). 1000 genomes on Amazon's cloud. *Nature Biotechnology, 30*(5), 376–376. doi:10.1038/nbt0512-376

Wang, K., Li, M., & Hakonarson, H. (2010). ANNOVAR: Functional annotation of genetic variants from high-throughput sequencing data. *Nucleic Acids Research*, 38(16), e164. doi:10.1093/nar/gkq603 PMID:20601685

Ye, K., Schulz, M. H., Long, Q., Apweiler, R., & Ning, Z. (2009). Pindel: A pattern growth approach to detect break points of large deletions and medium sized insertions from paired-end short reads. *Bioinformatics (Oxford, England)*, 25(21), 2865–2871. doi:10.1093/bioinformatics/btp394 PMID:19561018

Zhang, Y., Liu, T., Meyer, C. A., Eeckhoute, J., Johnson, D. S., Bernstein, B. E., & Liu, X. S. et al. (2008). Model-based analysis of ChIP-Seq (MACS). *Genome Biology*, 9(9), R137. doi:10.1186/gb-2008-9-9-r137 PMID:18798982

KEY TERMS AND DEFINITIONS

AWS: Amazon Web Space.

Cloud Computing: Computing services by providers.

EC2: Amazon Elastic Computing Cloud.

Galaxy: A framework for integrating computational tools in bioinformatics (http://usegalaxy.org).

Hadoop/MapReduce: A scalable, load-balancing environment or platform frequently used to distribute and accelerate the computation in Linux clusters or in cloud computing.

IaaS: Infrastructure as a Service.

NGS: Next generation sequencing.

Nimbix: A cloud platform for pure High Performance Computing (http://www.nimbix.net/).

PaaS: Platform as a Service.

S3: Amazon's Simple Storage Service.

SaaS: Software as a Service.

Chapter 14
An SNMP Based Traffic Characterisation Paradigm for Green–Aware Networks

Kiran Voderhobli
Leeds Beckett University, UK

ABSTRACT

This chapter describes a novel approach to study network patterns in a data centre with the aim of reducing power consumed. Cloud infrastructures rely on numerous networked devices in data-centers to provide virtualization and sharing of resources. Network traffic is one of the key contributors to power consumption. Numerous techniques to develop power-aware data-centers have been proposed in the recent years. Virtualization management is based on many critical decisions including work-load, utilization, location of physical resources etc. This chapter takes a unique network management angle to greening a data center. It describes how Simple Network Management Protocol (SNMP) has a great potential to characterize traffic which can then feed into decisions for management of virtualized entities.

INTRODUCTION

Affordable Business Computing

The business model of subscription based computing has brought affordable IT services into the realms of everyone. Cloud computing has proved to be a very cost-effective means of sourcing IT, even for smaller firms and some third-world countries, where availability of powerful hardware and software resources are an expensive affair (Avram, 2014; Marston et al, 2011). Since cloud computing is considered as a business model, the cloud based resources are available in various profiles like private, public, community and hybrid clouds to address the requirements of various classes of users (Gupta, Seetharaman & Rudolph Raj, 2013). The cloud model allows for provisioning of Infrastructure as a Service (IaaS) which involves allocation of virtualised resources on demand. This could be software or specialist hardware like networking equipment, data store etc. Software as a Service (SaaS) gives users access to software via the Internet. This could be as simple as a word processor or as complex as any full-scale ERP software. Platform as a Service (PaaS) offers ser-

DOI: 10.4018/978-1-4666-8210-8.ch014

Copyright © 2015, IGI Global. Copying or distributing in print or electronic forms without written permission of IGI Global is prohibited.

vices related to backend platforms, middle-ware, SDKs and frameworks. More recently, there has also been focus on specific business related functionalities that could be delivered via the cloud. For example, Business Intelligence as a Service (BIaaS) delivers services like dataset analysis, financial analysis, stock analytics, business trends analysis etc. (Chang, 2014). Such services can help businesses off-load their "number crunching" tasks to the capabilities of cloud computing. The above features of the cloud are strong motivations for businesses to embrace cloud based business computing (Ramachandran & Chang, 2014). The business advantages combined with the inherently green property of the cloud, is another strong incentive to adopt cloud computing.

Cloud Network Operations and Energy

In the modern business computing landscape, cloud based IT infrastructure seems to be the norm. The low cost of computing and ease of access to powerful hardware and software resources is the rationale for adopting cloud based computing solutions. Cloud computing has revolutionised the way applications and services are delivered to businesses and end-users. The innovation of the cloud has helped mask the technicality of powerful computing resources from end-users. Subscribing to cloud based services alleviates the problem of having to build an IT infrastructure from scratch. In the last few years, the number of companies using cloud based infrastructures has constantly been on a rise due to Green policies widely adopted. Governments and corporate bodies have started to push for IT policies that have lower carbon footprints. Since cloud computing allows for sharing of resources, it reduces the need to deploy more hardware, thereby reducing power consumption. But traditional sustainability policies have only considered high level operations rather than looking at how data processing and data flow could contribute to efficiency in green

computing. Network operations arising from virtualisation contribute to power consumption. It is therefore important to consider network operations in a cloud infrastructure to optimise operations that will help reduce energy consumption. One key aspect that is often overlooked is the behaviour of packet transmission and network activity. Management operations of virtualisation should be based on continuous evaluation of network activity as this could be vital to saving power. There must be a body of knowledge that will help save power when there really is a scope to do so. In order to derive this body of knowledge, traffic patterns of virtualised instances (like a VM) must be studied.

Virtualisation

Virtualisation is a concept where instances of resources (be it hardware or software) are shared on the same platform base. It provides for abstraction of various services by emulating actual resources based on user needs and subscription requirements (Marston, Li, Bandyopadhyay, Zhang & Ghalsasi, 2011). For example, Network Service virtualisation allows for multiple instances of a network service like a router to be supported by the same hardware platform. Another example is applications being virtualised using VMs. Virtualisation is one of the fundamental principles that makes cloud infrastructure work. The "green benefits" can clearly be appreciated due to lesser number of electricity sources needed to support multiple applications. On the cloud, this benefit is compounded. Although instances of each of these applications and services are spawned on a "need-to" basis, it must be remembered that greater the number of virtualisation instances, the greater is the demand on supporting hardware. The end result is with each new instance of a virtualised service, the number of entities sharing the hardware resources increases. This then has a rippling effect on performance, network throughput, QoS etc. In a cloud infrastructure, it is not enough to just consider a piece of hardware for optimization, but grave thought needs to be given to the operations of these virtualised services. It is important to remember that each VM, could be a key contributor to network traffic. Hence optimisation must be done at the granularity of each VM and not each hardware entity.

Chapter Context

This chapter examines one of the means of gathering traffic patterns or characteristics from the live network which will enable a network manager to look for windows of opportunities for energy saving. Furthermore, the traffic related data gathered from the network could be used to automate the process of saving energy based on current network scenarios. The scheme discussed in this chapter will be especially useful for a data centre in a cloud based environment that processes high volumes of network traffic flowing from and to virtualised applications. In a computing intensive facility like a data centre, it becomes increasingly difficult to judge the values of various network attributes that could possibly contribute to energy saving. One of the reasons for this is that the scale of traffic and the distributed environment makes it difficult to assimilate traffic characteristics that could feed into energy saving decisions. For example, link utilisation, inter-flow and intra-flow delays between connections are difficult to gather on a large network. In this chapter, a scheme to apply Simple Network Management Protocol (SNMP) to characterise traffic in a data centre context will be considered. This will be used to model a paradigm for gathering vital network statistics that could potentially reveal areas of energy saving. There is a need for autonomic systems that require minimal interference from a Network Manager to evaluate changing network conditions to save energy. This chapter is a premise to the research being currently conducted at Leeds Beckett University which explores the using of SNMP to save energy. Although this chapter only explains the proposed system in context of Virtual Machines, it is expected that the research will be extended to virtualisation of network hardware in due course.

MOTIVATION

Need for Newer Systems for Cloud Infrastructure

With distributed computing, came the advent of cloud computing that supported Software as a Service (SaaS) and Platform as a Service (PaaS). Although cloud based services result in significant reduction in power consumption obtained by un-dedicated resources, there is still a lot of scope to reduce power consumption within data centres (Chang, Walters & Wills, 2012). Mouftah and Kantarci (2013) say that even with the rise in cloud infrastructure, concerns about green-house gases are getting serious because the reliance of ICT on cloud environments will add up to rising power consumption. Therefore, research into energy saving models and algorithms has gained importance in the recent years. It is believed that there is always a scope to save more energy through software/hardware optimisations and new algorithms geared towards green themes.

Network Traffic from Telecommunication Systems

Charaviglio and Mellia (2013) have said that power consumption can be attributed to three sources namely, telecommunication systems, data centres and end-user terminals. One of the motivations for this chapter is to address the first of the above sources in relation to network level power consumption. Telecommunication systems include network devices and the usage of these devices is based on applications running in the cloud infrastructure. The traffic being generated on the network is related to the number of applications interfacing with the network. Bilal et al (2014) highlight the fact that the current IT generation is dealing with Exascale computing where around 10^{18} floating point operations are done every second, most of which are on a Data Centre Network (DCN). They argue that DCNs are one of the top energy consumers in a cloud infrastructure due to power hungry network devices. As rightly pointed out in the above publication, energy could be saved by specialist techniques like traffic consolidation, link management etc. Given the scale of the problem it is evident that novel methods of identifying and characterising network traffic are needed to look for scope in power saving. Guelzim and Obaidat (2013) mention that one of the best practices in creating a green computing architecture is understanding power consumption and impact. This chapter has stemmed from the above best practice which tries to address the issue of identifying the contributors to power consumption. The chapter presents a scheme to gather intelligence about network activities generated by each Virtual Machine (VM) being hosted on servers in a cloud centre.

RELATIONSHIP BETWEEN POWER CONSUMPTION AND NETWORK TRAFFIC ON THE CLOUD

The Link between Packets and Power

Modern data centre infrastructure engineers are always conscious about energy consumption. There has been tremendous attention to energy efficiency of server farms and data centres and this will only continue to rise with the increasing dependency on cloud infrastructure. The typical means of making a data-centre energy efficient is refining the hardware of various network components and towards innovations in cooling, chip-level and processor level optimisations. However, the scope of "greening" a network is much more than hardware optimisations. It has to be acknowledged that network devices operate based on supply and demand of data (i.e., network traffic). In order to accommodate the massive volumes of network traffic, the network infrastructures are in surplus. Some of these devices need to be put into

energy saving mode when they are not participating in forwarding packets (which could happen many times during the day). Also, there are gaps in traffic flows where the inter-arrival rates of packets could be fluctuating and this could also be a consideration to save energy (Christensen, Gunaratne, Nordman & George 2004).

In a recent study on performance evaluation on green data centre, a multitude of factors that contribute to energy utilisation in a data centre were discussed (Peoples, Parr, McLean, Scotney & Morrow 2013). In this context, the authors list management of virtualised instances as one of the must-haves for efficient green management of data centres. Some VM related operations mentioned were VM migration, VM set-up/tear-down and the timing of these operations to ensure green-efficiency. In another research that adds weight to the importance of VM management for green networks, Yang et al. (2014) propose a novel method to evaluate the load on each physical machine that supports virtualisation. This is expressed as a ratio that is used as a threshold which when exceeded enough to compromise on quality, allows for VMs to be migrated to another physical machine. The researchers used a dedicated VM management platform to take decisions regarding various operations on the VMs (migrate, spawn, pause, start etc.) based on the level of activity on a physical machine. Corradi et al. (2012) stress the importance of having fewer physical servers to support maximum VMs whilst at the same time not compromising on performance. They say there are network related constraints that affect the location of a VM in terms of which physical machine it is actually running on. When it comes to VM consolidation, each VM is hungry for resources available on the physical machine. There is a competition for resources and this includes networking resources as well; for example, a large number of VMs relying on a limited number of network interfaces. The situation thereby imposes a restriction on the maximum utilisation of a network interface by a VM. Furthermore, idle VMs still continue to utilise some resources although they are not engaged at that moment in time. For example, some VMs could just be maintaining TCP connections while not actually transmitting or receiving packets.

Modern Approaches

It is only in the recent years that vendors have started considering energy savings mechanisms based on traffic patterns and depending on network devices to be responsible for taking suitable actions accordingly. Some of the approaches included

- Task forwarding to other routers where routers could off-load a set of tasks to a peer router if doing so saves energy. This depends on a number of factors including routing algorithm employed, the number of tasks depending on a particular router, topology, link utilisation, etc.
- Optimising port allocation where a port or a sub-set of ports could be shared by multiple applications to avoid having to dedicate ports (and thereby allowing certain devices to be dormant to save power).
- Activating or de-activating network operations on a "need-to" basis.
- Processors could be turned on or off based on gaps in traffic flow (Christensen et al, 2004). Similarly protocols could be given the intelligence to control transmitters (Safwat, Hassanein & Moufta 2002)
- Predicting idle times whereby a processor could be put into sleep mode (Christensen et al, 2004). The more the idle time the more is the power saved due to longer duration of CPU being in sleep mode. Therefore, it is advisable to schedule tasks (network related or otherwise) together to ensure that the shortest time slice is consumed to dispatch those tasks. The end result is potentially large gaps of inactivity that are windows for power saving.

There has been a lot of focus recently regarding developing specific algorithms to consider network traffic as a parameter to reduce power consumption. Once such example is by Xu et al. (2013), where the authors developed a strategy for power-aware routing specific for data centres. In the above literature, it is stressed that traffic characteristics are key contributors to power consumption. For example, there are various schemes that change routing mechanisms based on traffic, load, utilisation etc. Moving a packet from point A to point B consumes energy, albeit a little, it compounds to huge energy consumption for the overall network. In modern times, traffic densities have increased due to surge in demands from popular applications such as social media, e-commerce, gaming etc. If these are cloud based services, the actual cost of power consumption by a vendor/customer needs to be calculated (and perhaps be reflected in the pricing).

Although network traffic cannot be avoided, it would be beneficial to activate network devices on an on-demand basis to save energy. But these kinds of decisions are local based on statistics of local links and devices. Therefore getting a true picture for overall network traffic state needs more than just a local-view. This is especially true in cloud environments as energy saving should consider traffic present in the large cluster of servers rather than just intermediate devices like hubs and routers.

Despins et al. (2012) say that there are trade-offs between network performance and energy savings. Assuming it is possible to allocate multiple network applications on the fly to any server, consideration must be given to how those applications will complete for resources. For example, allocating a server with multi-core processor with numerous network applications (or VMs) rather than to distribute those applications evenly could save power, but there could be potential problems when it comes to available bandwidth, delays, etc. Therefore, any new paradigm must take into account the level of network activity being performed at each VM to save power, but not disrupt QoS as demanded by those applications. The paradigm proposed in this chapter takes into consideration these factors. It is not just about collecting SNMP data from various VMs, but it is also about using that data to form a well-balanced decision that does not compromise on QoS.

USING NETWORK MANAGEMENT PRINCIPLES FOR VIRTUALISED RESOURCES

SNMP in Context of Virtualisation

Simple Network Management Protocol (SNMP) has been widely accepted as a de-facto standard for network management. The SNMP standard as defined by RFC 1213 (IETF, 1991), allows a network manager to monitor and manage managed entities. Managed entities could be anything on a network, like PCs, routers, servers etc. The communication mechanism of network management is based on client server architecture. Each device on the network has a database known as Management Information Base (MIB), which could be queried by a network manager on a periodic basis. Most network management platforms allow for automation of this polling. The MIB on each device holds very up-to-date statistics of the device it is running on. Although some values in the MIB are static, most values change over time to reflect changes in traffic and device behaviour. Examples of such variables are rate of unicast packets, number of incoming octets at an interface, number of packets dropped due to errors, number of packets forwarded etc. When SNMP was standardised many years ago, it was only designed to manage physical network entities, not virtual ones. However recent evaluations suggest that SNMP is ideal in a virtualised cloud environment.

The reason green computing falls under the realms of Network Management is because virtualisation alone is not the answer to making a cloud infrastructure green. There are more critical decisions to be taken like

- What is the maximum number threshold of a server in hosting VMs before QoS drops? As the number of VMs increase, the competition for resources increases as well. Therefore, thrusting arbitrary number of VMs to a physical machine is not encouraged. There must be a systematic process that evaluates the ability of each physical machine.
- Under what circumstances could a VM be migrated to another server to reduce power consumption on the current server?
- How to determine the link states within a data-centre which could warrant migrating of VMs to another server where CPU clock cycles are not used to the fullest?
- How to share information among servers in a data centre to enable autonomic offloading of VMs to minimize power consumption?

In order to take above decisions based on traffic patterns, SNMP could be used to derive vital network related statistics from each of the VMs, to evaluate exactly how network active a VM is at any given point of time. This means that at autonomic mechanism of polling the VMs for MIB data and to share the information across the network must exist.

Kazandjieva et al. (2013) in a recent publication said that the level at which data required is to be collected to take decisions for green computing is not clear. They claim that data collected is either at a macro level or a micro level, both of which don't give the full picture. Therefore, a sensible approach to green computing should consider the aggregate of all contributors to power consumption. One of the key contributors in a cloud environment is the micro scale network activities that happen at the granularity of each VM. Now, the challenge is to aggregate this data over an entire cloud's server farm. The aggregate will act as a parameter to critical energy saving decisions. SNMP based data collection would be ideal to collect such data.

The traditional view of Network Management involved a network manager monitoring a network for various attributes including link performance, packet transmission, busy nodes, top talkers, network traffic forecasting etc. The typical set-up involved a management station and managed entities. Communication between management station and managed entities is using a mix of techniques like packet sniffing, exchange of CMIP/SNMP data and RMON probes. SNMP MIB-II as defined in RFC 1213 accounts for a very exhaustive list of objects that gather most up-to-date data of the device they are installed on. The concepts of network management could be used to automate the process of collecting network statistics which could then feed into an evaluation system. The evaluation system will analyse traffic data and look at windows of opportunity for saving energy. Although it might be difficult to imagine a cloud based data centre as a traditional network, the principles of distributed network communications are still the same. Therefore, Network Management paradigms could be modified to suit the purpose of making data centres green.

Related Work

Research that treats Green-IT as a network management problem have been gaining momentum. For many years optimising computing resources to be green was an afterthought. But these days, network infrastructures are being built with energy savings as one of the key requirements. In a recent work carried out by Blanquicet and Christensen (2008), they demonstrate a scheme using SNMP MIB (Management Information Base) where an energy aware network management system is used to gather vital statistics that enables network

devices take decisions like waking up or putting ports to sleep. The work they carried out created a custom MIB to extend the functionality of SNMP to green IT. The custom MIB objects were used record power states of devices on the network. Subsequently, the values of these MIB objects would be analysed to put interfaces to sleep mode.

Some recent research has shown that the idea of employing SNMP to virtualised environments is becoming important. For example Daitx et al (2011) used a SNMP based platform to manage virtual networks. The authors highlight the effectiveness of virtual networks as an ideal cost-effective alternative to deployment of real networks. They use SNMP as a means to gather vital network related data to manage virtualisation that happens at the core network. The virtualisation relates to network resources, like a virtual router that is representative of a real physical router. The choice of SNMP for a management interface was considered ideal due to the fact that virtual devices mirror the attributes of real devices. In other words, packet statistics, performance, port related data etc. can be collected for a virtual device in a similar fashion to data collection on a physical device. Therefore, traditional network management principles can be extended to virtual devices. The related paper, describes how the researchers developed a custom Management Information Base that was specifically created to extend SNMP based management to virtual devices. The reasoning behind this decision was that even virtualised entities become managed objects that could be queried by a network manager. The authors describe that there are two levels of management planes – the physical router and the instances of routers that are running on top of this physical router. Each of the virtual instances has virtual ports from which statistical data can be collected. In order to provision SNMP data collection from virtual devices, the authors created an "extended MIB". From the results published by the authors, it can be seen that an SNMP based approach has been very effective in gathering management data from virtualised routers. Similar work was carried out by Hillbrecht and de Bona (2012) where they created "Virtual Machine MIB" to manage Virtual Machines using SNMP where each time a VM is created, entries are made in the MIB that record the current attributes of the VM in terms of memory, CPU utilisation etc. Therefore, it is possible to keep track of the VMs performance on a real-time basis.

In other research by Benson et al. (2010), the researchers used SNMP to collect network related logs from a busy data centre. The publication describes how with SNMP polling, it was possible to gather data at a coarse granularity, which was then in turn used to derive finer statistics. Traffic characteristics were collected for various data centres for a mix of different traffic profiles. Different sets of network applications were used to create a realistic traffic profile. The coarse data collected via SNMP polling was used to gain knowledge about the traffic characteristics of the links in the data centre.

THE PROPOSED MODEL

Objectives of the Model

As said before, this chapter sets the premise for a novel approach to VM management, where decisions on VM management are taken to ensure that it promotes green networking theme on the cloud infrastructure. It explains the nature of the system that will be built as a part of this research in the near future. The idea is to extend SNMP based "request and response" model into virtualisation. The objectives of the proposed model are

- To be autonomic in information gathering from each VM that feeds into a knowledge base.
- SNMP polling to be done at local server level. This means that each server that is hosting one or more VM will send localised

SNMP queries to form a local knowledge base. Only specific information from this knowledge base is shared across the network to peer servers. This de-centralised approach avoids unnecessary polling traffic across the network.

- The knowledge base must be adequate enough to take decisions regarding VM operations like migrating a VM, suspending a VM etc.
- To support an "analytical engine" per physical machine that is responsible for gathering information from VMs and processing the data to form live statistics. This engine will also be responsible for starting, stopping and migrating VMs.
- The overall goal should be to distribute VMs in such a fashion that uses minimal physical machines to host all the VMs.
- All of the above objectives must be met without compromising Quality of Service.

All of the above objectives are based on the fact that every active VM uses resources like CPU, network interface etc. Keeping a VM active when it is not engaged in network based operations is only going to consume power. It might be beneficial to migrate it to another physical system that is already encountering a high amount of load. It is also important to note that by using SNMP, it allows the model to query error related MIB objects, like for example packets dropped. These kinds of MIB objects could be used to find a balance between "greening" and Quality of Service. There is no point in migrating a VM to a physical machine if that target machine is already encountering bottlenecks. There are many MIB objects that are indicators of such problems on the network.

Design of the Proposed Model

The presentation of the proposed model will start from a view of how virtualisation takes place at the level of an individual physical machine. This understanding is important before venturing into how data can be accessed from the VMs running on this machine. Although VMs are running on one physical machine, the machine itself is able to distinguish between the VMs based on unique IP addresses. Figure 1 gives a broad view of the components that exist in on a server that hosts many VMs. As can be seen from the figure, each VM has its own set of applications, operating system, virtual ports. These rely on the real resources of the physical machine.

Now, the important thing to remember is that each of these VMs can have their own IP address, if configured in a way that does not share the host's IP address. Each VM can therefore be addressed individually using their IP address, which is in fact a necessity for SNMP agent and manager interaction. Specific network applications in VMs can be addressed by their port numbers. Since the VMs can be treated as separate machines, it is possible to have SNMP

MIBs record live statistics. The physical machine can send snmp_get queries to the MIB agents on the virtual machines. Each physical machine will have an SNMP query generator that will be able to identify the VMs uniquely and send them periodic polls. From this point forward, the SNMP query generator will be referred to as VM Active Stats Poll Engine – VASPE in short.

The architecture that this research proposes seems like a localized approach, but in reality the complete system is distributed due to the requirement that some elements of locally collected information must be transmitted across the network in order to take decisions on VM migrations. Leinwand and Conroy (1996) describe a distributed NMS architecture as a setup of peer Network Managers responsible for sending management related queries to a sub-set of the network. For example one peer-NM could be responsible for collecting network management data for a specific subnet. Each of

Figure 1. A broad view of the components of a physical machine in a data centre

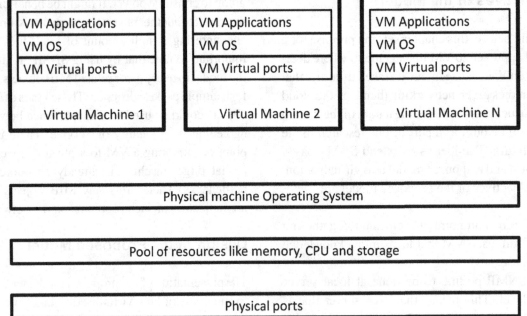

these peer network management platforms could maintain a local database that is relevant to that particular segment or group of the network. The reason for maintaining a local database is to store most up to date statistics that would help take decisions at a local level. Decisions that need to be taken based on overall state of the network are assisted by information stored in the global database. Periodically, some information collected at a local level is propagated to the global databases to keep the knowledge of overall status up to date. Recalling from previous sections, decisions regarding migrating of VMs to other physical systems require the knowledge of utilization levels and performance of other physical machines. Utilization is one of the indicators of whether a system can take more load or not.

Network Level View of the Model

The proposal presented in this chapter, extends the concept of a distributed NMS explained by Leinwand and Conroy (1996). An illustration of the overall model is given below, and shows how the schema works at the network level. Figure 2 is comparable to the view of a peer network manager querying VMs, where a set of VMs form the subset of the network. As can be seen, each physical machine will be equipped with a local database. The VASPE has the responsibility to update the local database and propagate relevant information to global databases. Also, the local database will interface with an "analytical" engine that is able to control VMs based on global and local network statistics (such as utilisation, load at peer nodes etc.).

Figure 2. A network level view of the proposed system

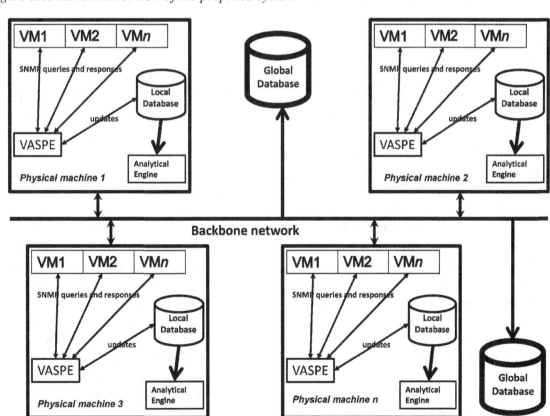

Each of the analytical engines is able to send signals across the network that allow it to set up connections with other peers in order to migrate VMs and awaken machines on the network, if need be.

The reasoning behind this setup is to separate the functionalities of "data mining" and "control" to two entities. The VASPE provides for data mining with its constant SNMP polling. The Analytical Engine, as the name suggests performs reasoning based on the SNMP data and provides control features. Analytical Engines will be designed in such a fashion that peer engines will be able to exchange and negotiate parameters prior to VM migration and/or task offloading. Some of these parameters may be related to maintaining the connection to end-user systems whilst VMs are migrated. Any decision taken by the Analytical Engine will be determined based on thresholds of various statistics.

To give an idea of how the proposed system is expected to work, a step-by-step example could be considered. It is to be noted that below, "utilisation" is considered as an example, but the principle could be extended to any statistic.

- In the Figure 2, each physical machine has the ability to spawn VMs based on demand. For each spawned VM, there exists a SNMP MIB that records scalar, counter and tabular values right from the moment they are created. Each of these VMs also respond to snmp queries like snmp_get addressed to a designated port (usually port 161 for SNMP standard)

- However, the behaviour of the VMs and network dependency can only be determined over a period of time, which in turn might have implications over the capacity of each physical machine.

- Therefore, the VASPE constantly queries the VMs using SNMP polling. VASPE is aware of newly spawned VMS and starts querying them for appropriate SNMP data.

Data is collected at different time intervals and differences/variations in value of SNMP variables feed into statistics (explained below).

- Based on the data gathered, it calculates statistics that otherwise are not readily available. For example, it can calculate the current utilisation at the physical network interface of the machine it is resident on. Furthermore, based on incoming and outgoing octets of packets it can even record what proportion of the total utilisation is contributed by any given VM. All these are recorded in the local database. The current utilisation of this physical machine is recorded in the global database, which can be accessed by other physical machines.

- The Analytical Engine, keeps on evaluating the status of the physical machine it is resident on. It observes how many Virtual Machines are currently active and how these contribute to the overall utilisation at the physical interface. At this juncture, numerous logical paths exist. One possibility is - the utilisation of a physical machine so low that it does not warrant keeping the machine in an active state to save energy. But if it is decided to put this machine into power saving mode, alternative physical machines must be found to relocate the existing VMs of the physical machine that needs to be put into power saving mode.

- The Analytical Engine now needs to find an alternative physical machine that is already active but whose utilisation has not exceeded the threshold. This decision is taken based on the values of utilisation recorded for each physical machine in the global database. To recall, the information in the global database is updated by the peer VASPEs situated across the network.

- Once a suitable machine is identified, peer Analytical Engines negotiate the parameters to migrate the VM(s). Once the

VM are migrated, the VASPE at the physical machine which is about to be put into power saving mode will update the global databases regarding its intent to go into a dormant state.

- The Analytical Engine, initiates a hardware interrupt that puts the host physical machine into power saving mode.

Like the case above, there could be many more possibilities to save energy as network conditions change. Another common possibility is a situation where the Analytical Engine has detected that the current utilisation of a physical machine is exceeding a threshold value thereby compromising on QoS of each co-existing VM. To alleviate this problem it might be wise to identify a VM that is heavily contributing to the overall utilisation and trying to migrate it to a different machine with a lot lesser utilisation at the network interface. Again, the local database is useful in identifying the overheads caused by VMs whilst the global database helps in identifying a potential candidate machine to port a VM. All this provided, migrating a VM does not overwhelm the target physical machine. If no suitable machine can be found to migrate a VM due to maximum utilisation, a dormant machine could be activated and delegated to host VMs. The dormant and active status of machines is available via the global database.

It can be seen from the above cases that at any given point of time, only the right amount of physical machines are in normal power consumption mode. Adopting a model as described helps bring some structure in the way VMs are allocated and managed, plus bringing in the benefits of power saving.

Addressing the "VM Ping-Pong" Problem

Initial dry runs revealed that VMs might be rapidly designated across multiple physical machines due to fluctuations in network scenarios. For example,

assuming that a VM has just been relocated to a different physical machine, a peculiar scenario arises whereby the target physical machine's analytical engine feels that the same VM could be re-assigned to a different physical machine to save energy. If this happens repeatedly, it can be described as "VM ping-pong problem". This is not just with the case of VMs. Any virtualised resource could encounter the same treatment. Since analytical engines base their decisions on local and global databases, any match in thresholds criteria and presence of a suitable candidate virtual resource will be considered for reallocation to different hardware. Therefore, design of the model must include an algorithm to prevent this from happening. One approach would be to implement a table of fair allocations. This table could hold the number of reallocations and time of last reallocation for each VM. Although VM migration can easily be masked from the end user, the rationale for preventing the "ping-pong" problem is to reduce unnecessary network traffic and overheads of performing frequent migrations.

Using SNMP Based Thresholds

It has been highlighted that SNMP MIB data will be extracted from local VMs, which will then be synthesised periodically for vital decision making. It would be beneficial to look at how SNMP data feeds into threshold settings. To reiterate, one of the ways of optimising VM allocation to physical machines is based on utilisation at the interfaces of each of these machines. Of course, other deciding factors could be memory usage, CPU usage/load, queue buffering capacity etc. But for now, interface utilisation alone will be considered as a factor for VM allocation. Future models in this research will incorporate other factors as well.

In order to calculate utilisation at an interface, the VASPE needs to query the MIB of the physical machine and not the VM. The interface would be shared by various VMs and therefore the overall utilisation will be due to total contribution of data flowing in and out of various virtual interfaces (of VMs). SNMP polling will take place continuously at different time intervals. The MIB objects *ifInOctets* and *ifOutOctets* give the values of number of incoming and outgoing bytes (in octets) respectively. Assuming polling is done at time *now* and *now+t*, the total bytes sent and received from the interface can be calculated as follows (Leinwand and Conroy, 1996)

```
Total Bytes per second = (ifInOctets
now+1 - ifInOctets now) + (ifOutOctets
now+1 - ifOutOctets now)
Time difference = (now+t) - (now)
Bytes per sec = total bytes per sec-
ond / time difference
Utilisation = (Bytes per sec * 8)/
ifSpeed
```

ifSpeed is the MIB object that has the value of the interface's speed, in this case the interface of the physical machine. It is certain that data centre machines will have multiple interfaces, and therefore the VASPE needs to calculate the overall interface utilisation based on traffic flowing through all the interfaces. The utilisation calculated above is refreshed in the global databases. The local databases at each physical machine will hold the values for "total packets sent" and "total packets received" of individual VMs. Therefore, the VASPE needs to send SNMP queries to the IP address of each VM to collect this information.

```
Packets received = ifInUcastPkts +
ifInBroadcasts + ifInMulticasts
Packets sent = ifOutUcastPkts + if-
OutBradcasts + ifOutMulticasts
```

Whilst overloading a machine which is already high in terms of utilisation is a sure way of compromising QoS, there are other indicators that can be signs of a poor interface that is subject to errors on a physical machine. For example, the values of the MIB objects *ifInDiscards* and *ifInErrors* might be signs of problems at the interface (though not always).

Statistics such as the ones shown above could form the basis for various thresholds. The model that will be developed as a part of this research will incorporate low and high thresholds. Low thresholds will be useful in determining situations of under-performance of a data centre machine. In other words, there could be a powerful piece of hardware consuming significant power to host a set of VMs that are mostly idle in terms of network traffic. A low threshold is therefore an indication that there is an opportunity to save energy. Also, when VMs are killed over time due to end-user actions, certain statistics are bound to fall below a threshold. Automatic clean-up processes could also then be triggered. A high threshold on the other hand often means that the machine is running at its optimum capacity, and delegating any further tasks would be detrimental to the performance of other virtualised entities. The thresholds should be set and customised by a data centre manager. The Analytical Engine will enforce these thresholds.

CONTRIBUTION TO KNOWLEDGE

The proposed system, once developed will alleviate the problem of characterising large volumes of network traffic that are typical to a cloud data centre. So far energy savings considered higher level factors, but the networking community has acknowledged that more needs to be done to minimise power consumption. The innovative part of this project is that it has the scope to go down to the finest level of packet characterisation. The idea presented considers network packets as one of the consumers of energy. The key contributions of the chapter are

- Presentation of a novel distributed system that self-regulates allocation and re-allocation of virtual machines with the objective of reducing power consumption. The system is innovative because it acts as an automatic network manager that performs tasks related to virtualisation based on energy optimisation.

- SNMP was traditionally used for corporate LAN and WAN management, but with the proposition described in this chapter the SNMP concepts have been extended and applied in context of green cloud computing. This is only possible because in this research green computing has been considered as a network management problem rather than as a new field.

- The novel approach to SNMP based traffic characterisation has built-in ubiquitous element to it. Every physical and virtual machine is aware of its responsibility to adhere to SNMP requests and control information to act in a manner that is consisted with the green theme of the overall network.

- The concepts presented in this chapter could also be extended to other network devices that could be virtualised. For example virtual and physical routers could be queried for SNMP data to derive a knowledge base. Virtual router allocation/migration can be performed on similar lines. Furthermore, statistics related to links can also be obtained in this fashion. Eventually, all this will also be addressed in the proposed system, thereby offering a single paradigm for traffic based energy saving.

- Although for the sake of an example, interface utilisation was considered as a deciding factor for VM migration, the model allows a network manager to base the decisions on a number of factors. These could be layered to offer multi-level decision making. Therefore, the schema will support custom decision making. This is ideal as VM control could be dependant on the type and scale of the data centre.

- The system allows for further fine tuning to gather data about inter-flow and intra-flow gaps in traffic. What this means is that it offers scope for saving energy between new connections and between packet flow gaps in existing connections. There are dedicated MIB objects related to IP flows, TCP connections, UDP data streams etc. As long as traffic patterns can be obtained and thresholds set, it is possible to refine the decision making at fine granularity.

- There is a lot of scope for a system such as the one described here to be implemented as a part of a Green Operating system. Green Operating systems are currently in development that embed green themes into processor management, kernel based controls, hardware scheduling etc. (Pachouri, Sharma, Tewari & Kaushik 2010). Since an OS also is responsible for providing networking facilities, a SNMP traffic characterisation system would be an ideal addition for future networks. Deploying the resultant OS, in any network would result in a green aware network from the ground-up rather than as an add-on.

FUTURE WORK

Simulations

The project is still in its preliminary stage. The next step is to create a simulated model that can be tested for various network scenarios. Network Simulator 2 (NS2) will be chosen as the simulator to build this model. NS2 has customisable modules for all the elements that build the network. NS2 does not have features to simulate virtualisation, but modifications to existing modules can help simulate virtual machines. After all, each virtual machine is a source of traffic that interfaces with live interfaces. The plan is to modify the traffic generation model in NS2 to implement a built-in SNMP agent and relevant parts of RFC 1213 MIB. Each NS2 node will also have routines for the functionality of VASPE and the Analytical Engine. Therefore each time a traffic generation module is instantiated it inherits the implementation of the MIBs and the functions to respond to SNMP requests. Similarly, when a node is instantiated it has the ability to send SNMP requests to the hardware node elements and also to virtual traffic generators. Further modifications are needed to emulate port sharing, internal routing etc. Description of detailed programmatic development and deployment is beyond the scope of this chapter and will be covered in subsequent publications as the model gets developed and refined.

Evaluating SNMP Overheads

Although the schema sounds beneficial at this preliminary stage, one of the top priorities of future work is to evaluate the overheads of SNMP polling. Going back to the point made earlier about all packet transmission consuming energy, it is quite obvious that constant SNMP polling itself is going to add to overheads. SNMP packets are still network traffic that could have implications on QoS. Each SNMP request and the resulting response are going to add to utilisation and power consumption. This should not end up like a scenario similar to that of spending 10 watts to save a watt! Indeed, frequent polling will result in very up-to-date and accurate statistics that will result in a more informed judgement on VM management. However, overhead costs of such queries might negate the benefits or not be significant enough to warrant deployment of the system. On the other hand, more widely spaced SNMP queries will cost little in terms of power consumption and network traffic overheads. But the data gathered might not be precise enough to form conclusive judgements. This is something that needs investigation and it might be possible to establish what the reasonable levels of polling might be, to find the right balance.

Measuring Hardware Overheads

It is not just network overheads that need to be considered. There is also the issue of hardware overheads. Such a complex distributed SNMP based system needs hardware support just like any other software. The processes related to VASPE and Analytical Engine will be dependent on the host system for computing resources. The system should be tested to ensure that it does not "leech" off resources that have to be made available for virtualisation.

Accommodation for Finer Statistics

In complex situations, VM management might need to be based on a chain of criteria, some of which could boil down to very specific network elements or traffic flows. For example, values related to flows between two end points or packet inter-arrival rate at a specific port. Further work will involve identifying all such values and their relationship to power saving possibilities. Also, this links back to the previous point about SNMP overheads. Overheads are increased when more SNMP MIB variables are queried. So one of the questions future research should tackle is "how much data analysis granularity can be achieved before the overheads offset any real benefits of having access to such data"? Again, these overheads are compounded the number of VMs being queried increases.

CONCLUSION

This chapter presented a novel concept to datamine network traffic related statistics that aids in management of virtual machines for energy saving. The concept involves using network management principles using SNMP to create a knowledge base that can be synthesised by a virtualisation management system. This is made possible by treating each virtual machine as an independent system that is able to respond to SNMP queries. As a part of the system, the functionalities of three entities were specified. These entities are VM Active Stats Poll Engine, the Analytical Engine and local/global databases (knowledge bases). These are required to extract data from the virtual plane and the physical plane, calculate statistics, analysis and decision making. Migrating of Virtual Machines from one physical machine to another with the aim of maximum usage of a physical machine, promotes a green architecture. The VM management system takes into account network statistics before finding a physical system to host a VM. It is believed that this concept can also be extended to manage other virtual network devices. The concept and related model development is still in its preliminary stages and further research is needed to establish practicality and efficiency of this concept. There is no doubt that a network management view of energy optimisations on the cloud is necessary. However, enforcing network management methods of gathering network data itself adds to overheads. Therefore, it is too early to say anything about the efficiency of this approach. Work on building a simulated system reflecting the principles given herein has already begun. Future publications will throw light on detailed system development, experimentation to test efficiency and determining overheads.

REFERENCES

Avram, M. (2014) Advantages and challenges of adopting cloud computing from an enterprise perspective. In *Proceedings of the 7th International Conference Interdisciplinary in Engineering (INTER-ENG 2013)*.

Benson, T., Anand, A., Akella, A., & Zhang, M. (2010). Understanding data centre traffic characteristics. *Computer Communication Review*, *40*(1), 92–99. doi:10.1145/1672308.1672325

Bilal, K., Saif Ur Rehman, M., Osman, K., Abdul, H., Enrique, A., Vidura, W., & Samee, K. et al. (2014). A taxonomy and survey on Green Data Centre Networks. *Future Generation Computer Systems*, *36*, 189–208. doi:10.1016/j. future.2013.07.006

Blanquicet, F., & Christensen, K. (2008) Managing energy use in a network with a new snmp power state MIB. In *Proceedings of 33rd IEEE conference on Local Computer Networks, LCN 2008* (pp 509-511). doi:10.1109/LCN.2008.4664214

Chang, V. (2014). The business intelligence as a service in the cloud. *Future Generation Computer Systems*, *37*, 512–534. doi:10.1016/j. future.2013.12.028

Chang, V., Wills, G., Walters, R., & Currie, W. (2012). Towards a structured cloud ROI: The University of Southampton cost-saving and user satisfaction case studies. Sustainable ICTs and management systems for green computing (pp. 179–200). Hershey, PA: IGI Global. doi:10.4018/978-1-4666-1839-8.ch008

Chiaravigli, L., & Mellia, M. (2013). *Energy-efficient management of campus pcs. In Green communications: Theoretical fundamentals, algorithms, and applications*. CRC Press.

Christensen, K., Gunaratne, C., Nordman, B., & George, A. (2004). The next frontier for communications networks: Power management. *Computer Communications*, *27*(18), 1758–1770. doi:10.1016/j.comcom.2004.06.012

Corradi, A., Fanelli, M., & Foschini, L. (2014). VM consolidation: A real case based on OpenStack Cloud. *Future Generation Computer Systems*, *32*, 118–127. doi:10.1016/j. future.2012.05.012

Daitx, F., Esteves, R. P., & Granville, L. Z. (2011) *On the use of SNMP as a management interface for virtual networks*. In the *Proceedings of the IFIP/IEEE International Symposium on Integrated Network Management* doi:10.1109/INM.2011.5990689

Despins, C., Labeau, F., Labelle, R., Cheriet, M., Leon-Garcia, A., & Cherkaoui, O. (2012). *Green communications for carbon emission reductions: Architectures and standards. Green communications: Theoretical fundamentals, algorithms, and applications*. CRC Press.

Guelzim, T., & Obaidat, M. (2013). *Green computing and communication architecture. Handbook of green information and communication systems* (pp. 209–227). Elsvier.

Gupta, P., Seetharaman, A., & Rudolph Raj, J. (2013). The usage and adoption of cloud computing by small and medium businesses. *International Journal of Information Management*, *33*(5), 861–874. doi:10.1016/j.ijinfomgt.2013.07.001

Hillbrecht, R., & de Bona, L. C. E. (2012) A SNMP-based virtual machines management interface. In *Proceedings of the IEEE fifth International conference on Utility and Cloud Computing UCC-2012* (pp 279-286).

IETF. (1991) RFC 1213 Management Information Base. Retrieved June 7, 2014, from http://www.ietf.org/rfc/rfc1213.txt

Kazandjieva, M., Heller, B., Gnawali, O., Levis, P. & Kozyrakis, C. (2013) Measuring and analyzing the energy use of enterprise computing systems. *Sustainable Computing: Informatics and Systems, 3*, 218-229.

Leinwand, A., & Conroy, F. K. (1996). *Network management – A practical perspective* (2nd ed.). Addison-Wesley.

Marston, S., Li, Z., Bandyopadhyay, S., Zhang, J., & Ghalsasi, A. (2011). Cloud computing — The business perspective. *Decision Support Systems, 51*(1), 176–189. doi:10.1016/j.dss.2010.12.006

Mouftah, H., & Kantarci, B. (2013). *Energy-efficient cloud computing: A green migration of traditional IT. Handbook of Green Information and Communication Systems* (pp. 295–329). Elsvier.

Pachouri, A., Sharma, M., Tewari, T., & Kaushik, P. (2010). Green operating system: Future low power operating system. *International Journal of Computers and Applications, 1*(21), 77–80. Foundation of Computer Science.

Peoples, C., Parr, G., McClean, S., Scotney, B. W., & Morrow, P. J. (2013). Performance evaluation of green data centre management supporting sustainable growth of the internet of things. *Simulation Modelling Practice and Theory, 34*, 221–242. doi:10.1016/j.simpat.2012.12.008

Ramachandran, M., & Chang, V. (2014). *Cloud security proposed and demonstrated by cloud computing adoption framework*. Paper presented at the first international workshop on Emerging Software as a Service and Analytics, Barcelona, Spain, 3-5 April.

Safawat, A., Hassanein, H., & Moufta, H. (2002) A MAC-based performance study of energy aware routing schemes in wireless ad-hoc networks. In *Proceedings of the Global Telecommunications Conference, 2002. GLOBECOM '02*. IEEE.

Xu, M., Shang, Y., Li, D., & Wang, X. (2013). Greening data centre networks with throughput guaranteed power aware routing. *Computer Networks, 57*(15), 2880–2899. doi:10.1016/j.comnet.2012.12.012

Yang, C., Liu, J., Huang, K., & Jiang, F. (2014). A method for managing green power of a virtual machine cluster in cloud. *Future Generation Computer Systems, 37*, 26–36. doi:10.1016/j.future.2014.03.001

KEY TERMS AND DEFINITIONS

Network Management: The set of techniques used to monitor a network for a range of problem scenarios based on live statistics and remote monitoring principles.

SNMP: Simple Network Management Protocol is the de-facto standard for managing networks that works on the basis of a network manager querying the MIB (Management Information Base) which is resident in devices of the network.

Traffic Characterization: The process of identifying network traffic patterns based on transmission rates, load, utilization, and network activities of end-devices.

VASPE (VM Active Stats Poll Engine): An entity that hosts a set of processes that use SNMP queries to gather statistics from virtualised entities, which in turn feed into critical VM management functions.

Virtualization Management: Covers the range of techniques employed in a cloud infrastructure to assign virtualized entities to physical entities and also encompasses resource management to support virtualisation based on real-time decisions.

Virtualization: The principle of creating various levels of abstraction of hardware and software resources to enable them to be shared by different users and applications.

Chapter 15
Cloud–Based Infiltration Detection System for Military Purposes

ChandraMani Sharma
Institute of Technology and Science, Ghaziabad, India

Deepika Sharma
Govindam Business School, India

Harish Kumar
Institute of Technology and Science, India

ABSTRACT

Massive military manpower is deployed on borders to keep a vigilant eye on possible infiltration from neighboring countries. This traditional approach is prone to errors because of human factors. To make border surveillance more effective, countries have installed CCTV cameras on borders but generally such systems are passive in nature and require human operators to keep an eye on the captured video footage. This chapter describes a cloud based approach for infiltration detection in border defense environments. The processing of video data, in cloud, and the real-time response are the factors that make system suitable for military purposes. As far as affordability is concerned, the governments can easily bear expense of establishing a private cloud for implementing visual surveillance. This chapter represents pertinent research of authors in the field of visual surveillance as well as other state-of-the-art breakthroughs in this area. The chapter is of multi-disciplinary significance in the field of cloud computing, video & image processing, behavioral sciences, and defense studies.

INTRODUCTION

With the increasing number of incidents of infiltration across borders, it is imperative for countries to enrich their troops with automated anti-infiltration systems. In recent few years, the defense funds of countries in the world are mammoth (see Table 1) and increasing over years. It is evident from the history of evolution of Information Technology that several I.T. tools and technologies emerged

DOI: 10.4018/978-1-4666-8210-8.ch015

Copyright © 2015, IGI Global. Copying or distributing in print or electronic forms without written permission of IGI Global is prohibited.

Table 1. Top 10 spending countries on defense for year 2013

S. No.	Name of Country	Total Defense Spending (Billion USD)	% of GDP	World Share (In %)
1	United States of America	682.0	4.4	39.0
2	People's Republic of China	166.0	2.0	9.5
3	Russia	90.7	4.4	5.2
4	United Kingdom	60.8	2.5	3.5
5	Japan	59.3	1.0	3.4
6	France	58.9	2.3	3.4
7	Saudi Arabia	56.7	8.9	3.2
8	India	46.1	2.5	2.6
9	Germany	45.8	1.4	2.6
10	Italy	34.0	1.7	1.9

(Source: Research Report of SIPRI).

from defense applications e.g., ARPANET paved the way of modern Internet which plays a very vital role in today's time. Likewise the assignment problem was first applied during World War-II by Britain as it has limited number of soldiers to protect its borders. By using assignment problem Britain's army effectively optimized the allocation of soldiers. Today, assignment problem has many other useful applications in Computer Science in solving various problems. Popularly, there are four types of clouds (public, private, hybrid & community), which offer three types of services-Infrastructure as a Service, Platform as a Service and Software as a Service (Chang et al.; 2013).

A lot of work has been done in the field of visual surveillance. Hu (2004) presents a survey of visual surveillance systems and he has presented the picture of visual surveillance. Shah et al. (2007) discuss the concept of visual surveillance in realistic scenarios. Kim et al. (2010) also present a survey on intelligent visual surveillance. The general approach of visual surveillance involves four basic steps namely— object segmentation, object classification, object tracking and object activity recognition (Hu et al. 2004). The various visual surveillance systems available mainly differ in terms of the underlying methods used to

achieve the objectives of visual surveillance. The concept of cloud based visual surveillance is rare and contains lots of research scope.

LITERATURE SURVEY ON RELATED RESEARCH

The aim is to develop robust methods for the successful implementation of a visual surveillance system. It is the broad range of applications of visual surveillance that draws the attention of research community to carry out more advanced research in this field. IEEE sponsored the IEEE International Workshop on Visual Surveillance on three occasions, in India (1998), the U.S. (1999), and Ireland (2000). Recent developments in human motion analysis are briefly introduced (Wang et al., 2003). It is noticeable that, after the 9/11 incident in US and 26/11 incident in India, visual surveillance has received more attention not only from the academic community, but also from industry and governments. Terrorist activities have become a major threat to the people at large. So the need for research, in visual surveillance and underlying methodologies, has become the need of the day. Visual surveillance has been investigated worldwide under several large research projects. For example, the Defense Advanced Research Projection Agency (DARPA) supported the Visual Surveillance and Monitoring (VSAM) project in 1997, whose purpose was to develop automatic video understanding technologies that enable a single human operator to monitor behaviors over complex areas such as battlefields and civilian scenes. Furthermore, to enhance protection from terrorist attacks, the Human Identification at a Distance (HID) program sponsored by DARPA in 2000 aims to develop a full range of multimodal surveillance technologies for successfully detecting, classifying, and identifying humans at great distances. The European Union's Framework V sponsored Advisor, a core project on visual surveillance in metro stations. There have been a number of famous visual surveillance systems. The real-time visual surveillance system W4 employs a combination of shape analysis and tracking, and constructs models of people's appearances in order to detect and track groups of people as well as monitor their behaviors even in the presence of occlusion and in outdoor environments. This system uses a single camera and grayscale sensor. The VIEWS system at the University of Reading is a three-dimensional (3-D) model based vehicle tracking system. The Pfinder system developed by Wren et al. (1997) is used to recover a 3-D description of a person in a large room. It tracks a single non occluded person in complex scenes, and has been used in many applications. As a single-person tracking system, TI, developed by Olsen et al. (1997) detects moving objects in indoor scenes using motion detection, tracks them using first-order prediction, and recognizes behaviors by applying predicates to a graph formed by linking corresponding objects in successive frames. This system cannot handle small motions of background objects. The system at CMU (Lipton et al., 1998) can monitor activities over a large area using multiple cameras that are connected into a network. It can detect and track multiple persons and vehicles within cluttered scenes and

monitor their activities over long periods of time. The first IEEE workshop on Visual Surveillance was organized at IIT Bombay in Jan, 1998 and it gave a bit momentum for the research and development in the area of visual surveillance. Still there has been no remarkable progress in India in the development of the video surveillance systems. The systems developed so far are equipped with simple functionality; they require human intervention and lack the features & characteristics needed for real-time applications. Viable hardware support suitable for developing robust surveillance systems is available on the open market. As far as hardware support is concerned, companies like Sony and Intel are marketing the equipments suitable for visual surveillance, e.g., active cameras, smart cameras, infrared cameras etc.

NECESSITY OF CLOUD-BASED INFILTRATION DETECTION SYSTEM

The following reasons explain the need for cloud-based infiltration detection systems:

- The borders of a country may be scattered over wide geographic range. Cloud-based surveillance provides effective command and control over scattered geographic regions.
- Analytical surveillance reports can be made readily available to the concerned authorities. So, they can take necessary measures to retaliate and check infiltration.
- Setting-up cloud based infrastructure is majorly one time investment and it can yield long term gains. Preferably, governments can set-up their private clouds. It cuts cost and optimizes the number of personnel required to keep the borders safe from possible infiltration.
- Even if the infiltration could not be stopped for some reason, then with such a system in place, it can be helpful in identifying and tracing the intruders.

But here a big question arises; can the cloud service providers can be relied upon for hosting highly sensitive military data? Further, if data is compromised or service providers maliciously misuse this sensitive data then it can be disastrous for countries. These risks can be easily mitigated or optimized at country level. Seeing the increasing budget of defense funds of the countries, it may not be a big deal for the governments to establish private clouds with dedicated infrastructure. The cloud based systems solve various problems of modern business in a cost effective and reliable manner. Also, they imbibe more intelligence to approaches and business processes. Chang (2014) discusses an architectural framework for business intelligence as a service in the cloud.

TYPES OF CLOUD STORAGE SYSTEMS

Kulkarni et al. (2012) discuss the following types of cloud storage structures. Each of these types has its own advantages and limitations. Selecting the correct underlying storage system can greatly impact the success or failure of implementing cloud storage.

1. **Object Storage Systems:** The motivation for object storage systems is simple - there is a need for having storage systems which can do more I/O computational work thereby relieving the hosts to do other processing work. Object storage mainly has two key characteristics: Individual objects and extended metadata. In such storage systems, data is stored and retrieved in the form of objects and these individual objects are accessed by a global handle. The handle may be a key, hash or a URL.
2. **Relational Database Storage Systems (RDS):** Relational Database storage systems aims to move much of the operational bur-

den of provisioning, configuration, scaling, performance tuning, backup, privacy, and access control from the database users to the service operator, offering lower overall costs to users. Due to this, the hardware costs and energy costs incurred by users are likely to be much lower because they are paying for a share of a service rather than running everything themselves.

3. **Distributed File Storage Systems:** This is a file system that allows access to files from multiple hosts sharing via a computer network and hence makes it possible for multiple users on multiple machines to share files and storage resources. The client nodes do not have direct access to the underlying block storage but interact over the network using a protocol. This makes it possible to restrict access to the file system depending on access lists or capabilities on both the servers and the clients, depending on how the protocol is designed.

THE PROPOSED FRAMEWORK

The proposed framework contains hardware as well as software components. The hardware component contains sensory devices, communication infrastructure and processing servers while the software component contains methods for object motion segmentation, object classification, and object activity recognition. The proposed cloud based framework is to be implemented in the government private cloud due to the sensitivity of defense context. A video is a coherent sequence of frames (images). The experiments, presented here in this chapter, are performed with the live video streams captured by CCTV Cameras. The calculations have been done on individual frame and group of frames (as per need).

Hardware Components

- **Sensory Devices:**
  - Optical CCTV Cameras.
  - Night Vision Cameras.
  - Thermal Sensors.
- **Communication Infrastructure:**
  - Transmission Media.
  - Transmission Technology.
- **Processing Servers:**
  - CCTV cameras are connected to local centers.
  - Local centers are connected to nodal centers.
  - Nodal centers are connected to regional centers.
  - Regional centers are connected to zonal centers.
  - Finally zonal centers are connected to country centers.

The administrators of the system can configure and customize how they want the system to work. The analytic processing can take place either locally or at a centralized point as needed. It is possible to share analytical reports seamlessly with other centers for effective command and control. The communication and information flow is bidirectional and can flow either top to bottom or from bottom to top. It means that a country center can share essential information to any of the local centers and vice versa. The other centers in hierarchy are connected in the same way and follow a customized way of information flow.

Figure 1 presents the schematic diagram of the proposed system. In this architectural diagram the video captured by sensory devices (such as IP cameras) is sent to the cloud servers for processing. To ensure secure delivery of data and credentials to cloud, 256-bit SSL secured network infrastructure should be used. Further, on remote client sites, the users of the system are provided authentication user IDs and passwords to log on to the system. To tackle the problem of intermit-

tent network bandwidth, dual Internet lines can be used. Further, to make this process more reliable, Edge Recording and Video Tickling features are used. Edge Recording lets the video be stored at local storage media (such as SD card) in case of network failure and transmits it to the cloud server once problem is rectified. Video Tickling smartly records the video when there is a change in the scene (such as owing to motion). To overcome the problem of data loss due to catastrophic problems, data can be replicated at various storage centers.

PROCESS OF VIDEO CONTENT ANALYSIS

The surveillance video captured by cameras is sent to the server for processing. There are three different tasks that take place at server namely analytical processing, report generation and storage of video data. The analytical processing at the server takes place once motion is detected in streamed video that considerably saves on the unnecessary processing overhead of analyzing every frame of live-streamed video. On detection of motion, the next step is to segment the objects and to classify them into three different categories including human, vehicle and animal. Finally, the activities of these objects is identified and at the same time, if any suspicion is found, then analytic reports/notifications are sent to the concerned authorities.

OBJECT SEGMENTATION

Object segmentation in a video aims at detecting regions corresponding to moving objects of interest. Detecting moving regions provides a focus of attention for later processes such as tracking and behavior analysis because only these regions need be considered for subsequent processing. The result of object segmentation is a set of segments covering the entire video frame, or a set of contours extracted from that.

Figure 1. Architectural diagram of the proposed cloud-based visual surveillance system

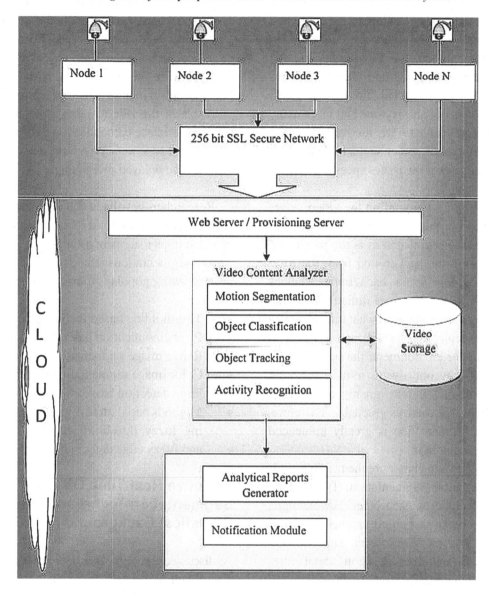

Figure 2. Process of object segmentation

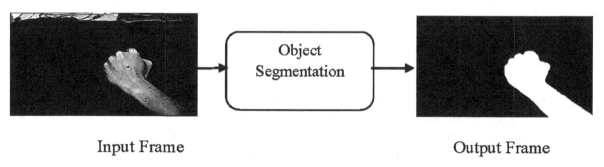

Each of the pixels in a region is similar with respect to others in characteristic or computed property, such as color, intensity, or texture. In motion segmentation, the foreground and the background are separated and objects of interest, in a video, are extracted. The task of object segmentation is not an easy one and faces many challenges. Researchers are motivated to find the new methods of object segmentation to get a winning edge over the issues specified below:

- Changing background, in the video, poses a serious problem before object segmentation. Since segmentation is the process of separating the background from the foreground. If in scene, background changes rapidly then it becomes difficult to decide what is background and what is foreground.
- When deploying surveillance systems in an outdoor environment, the lighting conditions may not always remain constant, for example, it may greatly affected by sunlight that changes gradually. Therefore, object segmentation is greatly influenced by changing light.
- Occlusion and clutter are the next big challenges before segmentation. Two objects may occlude on each other. For example, a person can be behind another person or a tree or some other object. This situation leads to incorrect decision about foreground and background.
- Automatic operation of the object segmentation is another challenge. Especially, with the surveillance applications today that require the process of object segmentation to be automatic. Therefore the object segmentation technique used in this case must have the attribute of automatic operation.
- In the context of the surveillance systems the real-time operation of the system is an indispensable requirement. Therefore the object segmentation should be as quick as possible and must be capable of process-

ing the video input in real-time. Another aspect here is of the memory storage. If the object segmentation strategy is not capable of processing the input video frames in the real-time then system will have to store the frames in memory and because of the huge size of the video signals generated by the surveillance camera(s) it will be quite inefficient to store such a huge amount of data for the delayed processing.

Researchers have been delving into the field of image segmentation for a long time but the area of video object segmentation is rather new. The various segmentation methods can be categorized into following popular groups (Zhang; 2006):

- Thresholding based methods;
- Pixel classification based methods;
- Range image segmentation methods;
- Color image segmentation methods;
- Edge detection based methods;
- Methods based on fuzzy set theory (including fuzzy thresholding, fuzzy clustering and fuzzy edge detection etc.).

Adaptive Real-Time Object Segmentation Technique Based on Statistical Background Modeling

As discussed earlier, the task of object segmentation is a difficult one and faces many challenges and there exists no single technique which can address all the challenges of object segmentation alone. Object segmentation techniques are designed, keeping in mind, the specific requirements of the application. For visual surveillance application object segmentation technique must perform well in contexts where the environment is outdoor, with varying lighting conditions, background in the video scene may change. Furthermore, the speed of the technique should be fast enough to process the video in real-time. So keeping in mind all these requirements, a technique for object segmentation is proposed in this section.

Figure 3. The proposed object segmentation method

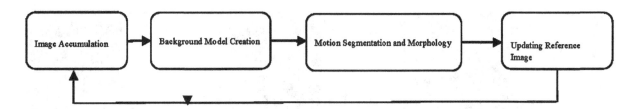

The proposed object segmentation technique will have many advantages like elimination of shadows and ghosts, high execution speed, adaptability to the background changes and lighting conditions. Use of hue and saturation, the difference between the actual object and its shadow is sought therefore we have used HSV color-space to mitigate the problem of shadows. The background is learned for some time and a statistical background model, involving variance and covariance values is constructed from this learning. The variance to estimate absolute variations in a pixel's value and covariance to estimate the variations relative to the other pixels' values. The averaged frame differencing reduces the processing cost of the technique. The background model gets updated to adapt the changes. Morphological operations and connected components are used to smooth the segmentation results.

The Proposed Object Segmentation Method

A block diagram of the proposed methodology is shown in Figure 3. Each of its components are explained in following subsections.

A detailed discussion and implementation details of this method can be found in our another work Kushwaha et al. (2014).

Experimental Results of Object Segmentation

See Figure 4.

OBJECT CLASSIFICATION

The outcome of the object segmentation task is the foreground separated from the background. The foreground generally consists of many moving objects of interest (e.g. human beings in case of surveillance applications). So here our goal is to give a name tag to the objects moving in the foreground and to classify them into different classes. The process of categorizing the objects into the different classes is called object classification. Different moving regions may correspond to different moving targets in natural scenes. For instance, the image sequences captured by surveillance cameras mounted in road traffic scenes probably include humans, vehicles and other moving objects such as flying birds and moving clouds, etc. To further track objects and analyze their behaviors, it is essential to correctly classify moving objects. Object classification can be considered as a standard pattern recognition issue. The task of object classification is very crucial in visual surveillance and this paves the path to object tracking and object activity recognition.

Haar-Like Features in Object Classification

Haar-like features are digital image features used in object recognition. They owe their name to their intuitive similarity with Haar wavelets and were used in the first real-time face detector. Historically, working with only

Figure 4. Object segmentation results

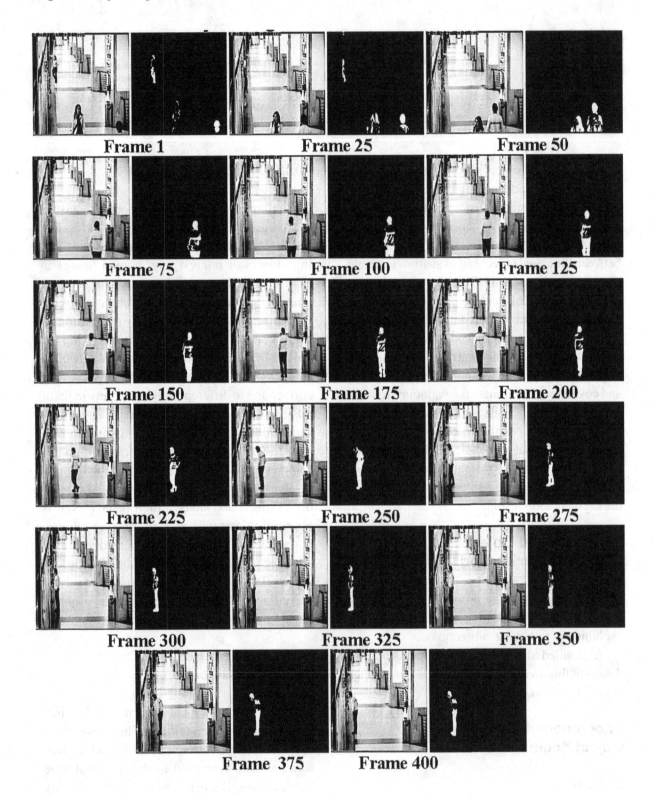

image intensities (i.e., the RGB pixel values at each and every pixel of image) made the task of feature calculation computationally expensive. Viola & Jones (2001) adapted the idea of using Haar wavelets and developed the so called Haar-like features. A Haar-like feature considers adjacent rectangular regions at a specific location in a detection window, sums up the pixel intensities in these regions and calculates the difference between them. This difference is then used to categorize subsections of an image. For example, let us say we have an image database with human faces. It is a common observation that among all faces the region of the eyes is darker than the region of the cheeks. Therefore a common haar feature for face detection is a set of two adjacent rectangles that lie above the eye and the cheek region. The position of these rectangles is defined relative to a detection window that acts like a bounding box to the target object (the face in this case). In the detection phase of the Viola-Jones object detection framework, a window of the target size is moved over the input image, and for each subsection of the image the Haar-like feature is calculated. This difference is then compared to a learned threshold that separates non-objects from objects. Because such a Haar-like feature is only a weak learner or classifier (its detection quality is slightly better than random guessing) a large number of Haar-like features is necessary to describe an object with sufficient accuracy. In the Viola-Jones object detection framework, the Haar-like features are therefore organized into something called a classifier cascade to form a strong learner or classifier. The key advantage of a Haar-like feature over most other features is its calculation speed. Due to the use of integral images, a Haar-like feature of any size can be calculated in constant time (approximately 60 microprocessor instructions for a 2-rectangle feature).

Object Classification for Visual Surveillance Based on Haar-like Features and State-Wise Additive Modeling Using a Multiclass Exponential Loss Function

Object classification puts objects, in a video, into different prescribed classes. Here, a real-time multiclass classifier based on Haar-like features and State-wise Additive Modeling using a Multiclass Exponential Loss Function (SAMME) is described. The proposed scheme can classify the objects, in video, into two classes: 'human' and 'car'.

The Proposed Object Classification Method

In the proposed technique, Integral Image representation is used for fast feature evaluation and boosting of cascaded classifiers is performed using SAMME. A more robust classifier is created by linearly combining the multiple weak classifiers. Based on this learning, the objects in the video are classified into classes Humans and Cars. The motion segmented video data is passed to the classifier system in order to obtain high computational speed. The basic steps of the proposed technique are as follows:

Sample Collection

The sample images for training the classifier are collected first. We have collected images for three classes; humans, cars and images which belong neither of these two from our own captured images and images from standard datasets like CalTek101, MIT-CMU datasets. We have created our own data set which consists of 4,000 images of humans, 3,500 images of cars and 5,000 images which are neither humans nor cars. These images were resized to dimension 60x60 and they consist of

Figure 5. Rectangle features

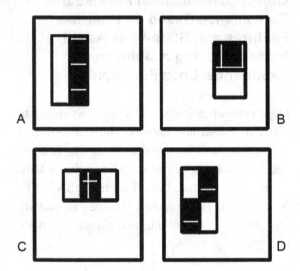

only one object per image. This was performed in order to make the classifier learn more domain information from a small number of images and this helps to improve the accuracy of the classifier.

Integral Image and Haar-Basis Functions

Simple Haar-like features, which are reminiscent of Haar-basis functions (Viola & Jones), are used. Use of features, instead of pixels, makes the classifier system work fast and helps in encoding the domain knowledge with finite quantity of data. Here we have used three types of features; two-rectangle features, three-rectangle features, and four-rectangle features. Differences between sums of pixels gives the value of two-rectangle feature. The regions are horizontally or vertically adjacent and have the same size and shape (shown in Figure 5). A three-rectangle feature is used to compute the sum within two outside rectangles subtracted from the sum in a center rectangle and a four-rectangle feature computes the difference between diagonal pairs of rectangles.

The number of features in a small detection window can be very high .For example a base detection window of size 25x25 contains more

than 200,000 such rectangle features, which are very difficult to compute. To speed up the computation process, we use the Integral Image representation proposed by Viola & Jones (2001) to compute the rectangle features. The Integral Image, $ii(\alpha, \beta)$ (shown in Figure 6) at location (α, β) contains the sum of all pixels above and left of (α, β) and can be computed in a single pass over image using the following pair of equations.

$$\omega(\alpha, \beta) = \omega(\alpha, \beta - 1) + i(\alpha, \beta) \qquad (1)$$

$$ii(\alpha, \beta) = ii(\alpha - 1, \beta) + \omega(\alpha, \beta) \qquad (2)$$

where, $\omega(\alpha, \beta)$ is the cumulative row sum and $i(\alpha, \beta)$ is the original image.

Multiclass Boosting with SAMME

We use Stage-wise Additive Modeling using a Multiclass Exponential loss function (SAMME) for boosting the cascade of multiclass classifiers. Viola & Jones (2001) used binary AdaBoost for their face detection system which fails in case of multiclass classification because of certain constraints over classifier's accuracy. The proposed

Figure 6. Integral image

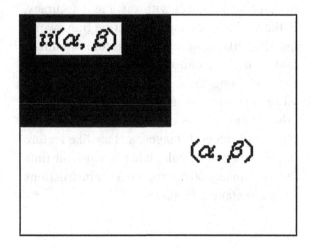

method has three classes of classification and a modified AdaBoost is used for this. SAMME is an extension of AdaBoost with a modification. The key for applying SAMME for multiclass problem is that the component classifiers are no longer required to achieve accuracy greater than 50%, but instead it need only be better than random guessing. Suppose we are given a set of training data $\{(\sigma_1, c_1), \ldots (\sigma_n, c_n)\}$, where the input vector $\sigma_i \in R^p$, and the c_i qualitatively assumes values in a finite set $\{1, 2, \ldots, K\}$ where K is the number of classes. The training data are independently and identically distributed samples from an unknown probability distribution. The goal is to find a classification rule $\phi(\sigma)$ from the given training data, so that for a given new σ, we can assign it to a class label c from $\{1, \ldots, K\}$.

Results of Object Classification

We have performed object classification experiments, with the proposed technique, on several videos, captured in real outdoor environment. The results, with two such representative videos, are given in Figure 7 and Figure 8 using the proposed approach. In these results, red windows are used for classifying the humans and blue windows are used to classify the cars. Figure 7 shows the object classification results with natural lighting conditions while Figure 8 shows the classification results in the low lighting condition.

One can observe from the results presented in Figure 7 that there are three human objects and one car in the video. The video was shot at a frame resolution of 640×480 and frame rate of 20 frames per second. The video consists of total 1600 frames and we have posted results at difference of 25 frames. At the start of the video the humans start moving towards camera and later on follow the random motion paths. The car shown in the video has been parked and does not move in video. The proposed technique is capable of handling partial inter-class and intra-class oc-

clusions. Video frames nos. 50, 225, 250 and 275 have the partial human to human occlusion and frames nos. 1025, 1050 and 1400 show the occlusion between car and human. The proposed method classifies the objects even in these frames accurately and in case of full occlusion proposed method has the capability of resuming quickly. As it is clear from the results given in Figure 7 and Figure 8 that the human objects have varying poses of their bodies while walking in the video. They acquire various views like frontal, side and back. Moreover the shape of their bodies also changes as being in motion. Unlike various existing classification methods, the proposed method classifies the various objects accurately irrespective of their views of appearance.

Many existing object classification schemes require the lighting conditions to be good in the video and can work only in presence of the statically good light. But from a practical point of view it is not desirable. In visual surveillance the videos are captured in the outdoor environment and fluctuations in the lighting are unavoidable. The classification results using proposed technique in poor lighting condition are given in Figure 8. The video for this experiment was shot in the evening at University of Allahabad campus. The resolution of video frames is 640×480 and was shot at frame rate of 20 frames per second. The video consists of a total 800 frames. The classification results with this video are given below starting from frame number 25 to frame number 800 at a difference of 25 frames. It can be observed that in the video three humans and one car appear. Humans are walking in random directions. The car has been parked and does not move. The humans while walking cause occlusion within themselves and with car. Frames 250 and 675 show the partial occlusion between humans where one human is partially occluded from another. Frames 625, 650, 725, 750, 775 and 800 show the occlusion between car and human. In frame number 625 and 650, one human object occludes the car while in frame number 725, 750, 775 and 800 two humans appear before car

Figure 7. Object classification with the proposed technique in normal lighting condition

Figure 8. Object classification with the proposed technique in poor lighting condition

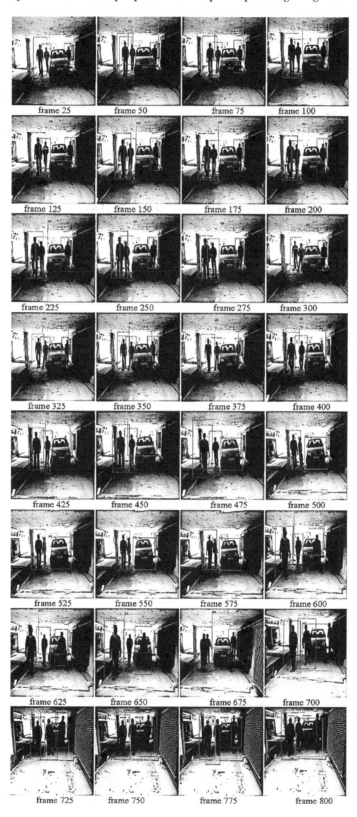

and occlude it. It is evident from the results that the proposed technique accurately classifies the objects in all the aforementioned frames.

We have tested the proposed method on several other realistic videos shot in outdoor environment. The average execution speed on these videos has been observed as 23 frames per second. The detection accuracy of the proposed classifier system has been estimated in our experiments between 79% and 98%. The tradeoff between the accuracy and the execution speed can be customized easily depending upon the user's requirement. The execution speed can be increased by slightly decreasing the detection accuracy and the detection accuracy can be increased by a slight decrement in execution speed.

OBJECT TRACKING

Object tracking is the process of locating a moving object(s), over time, in a video sequence. It has a variety of uses, some of which are: human-computer interaction, security and surveillance, video communication, augmented reality, traffic control, and video editing. Object tracking plays a vital role in visual surveillance and is a necessary step to be taken before analyzing the activities of an object of interest. Object tracking is a time consuming process due to the amount of data that is contained in video.

The objective of video tracking is to associate target objects in consecutive video frames. The association can be especially difficult when the objects are moving fast relative to the frame rate. Another situation that increases the complexity of the problem is when the tracked object changes orientation over time. For these situations video tracking systems usually employ a motion model which describes how the image of the target might change for different possible motions of the object.

Object Tracking Techniques

After detection of an object in a video sequence captured by a surveillance camera, the next step is to track these objects (human, vehicle etc.) in the subsequent frames of the video stream. Several object detection techniques have been proposed in literature. These techniques can be grouped on the basis of, single object trackers vs multi-object trackers, 2-D model based trackers vs 3-D model based trackers etc. For object tracking purpose different cues can be used e.g., color, shape, texture, motion pattern, velocity etc. The task of object tracking is a complex one and for a tracker to be practically useful, it has to be accurate. Detecting objects before tracking, is taking momentum for fulfilling such requirements. The concept of particle filtering can also be used for estimating the position distribution of an object in the subsequent frame.

Figure 9. Tracking an object across a video frame sequence

Particle Filter and Object Tracking

Particle filter based tracking techniques are very popular because of their ease of implementation and their ability to represent a non-linear object tracking system in presence of non-Gaussian nature of noise. Various object tracking techniques based on particle filtering are found in literature. Lanvin et al. (2003), proposed an object detection and tracking technique and solved the non-linear state equations using particle filtering. Algorithms which attempt to find the target of interest without using segmentation have been proposed for single target tracking based on cues such as color, edges and textures (Brasnett et al., 2005).

However single object trackers suffer from the problem of false positives when severe occlusions occur because of hidden first order Markov hypotheses. The problem of tracking multiple objects using particle filters can be solved in two ways. One is by creating multiple particle filters for each track and another one is by having a single particle filter for all tracks. The second approach works fine as long as the objects under tracking are not occluded but in case of occlusion when objects come close by, these techniques fail to track the objects.

Design of Particle Filter for Human Tracking

For tracking purpose, particle filter has been used. In our approach, uncertainty about human's state (position) is represented as a set of weighted particles, each particle representing one possible state. The filter propagates particles from frame i-1 to frame i using a motion model, computes a weight for each propagated particle using an appearance model, then re-samples the particles according to their weights. The initial distribution for the filter is centered on the location of the object, detected first time. The steps are as given below:

1. **Prediction:** The tracking of a human object is done from one video frame to another by predicting its position in the next frame when the position of the frame is known in the previous frame. If $\alpha_{j,i}$ and $\alpha_{j,i-1}$ represent the positions of an object j in i and i-1 frames then a distribution $\theta(\alpha_{j,i}\alpha_{j,i-1})$, over human object j's position in frame i, is predicted using the belief of its position in frame i-1. We define a motion model for predicting the position of a human object from frame to frame. We use a second-order auto-regressive dynamical motion model for object's position prediction in frames. Non-Gaussian noise is considered in our motion model by a random noise variable. In this autoregressive motion model we assume the next state λ_t of the system as a function of some previous states and a noise random variable Θ_t, as given below:

$$\lambda_t = f(\lambda_{t-1}, \lambda_{t-2}, \ldots\ldots\ldots, \lambda_{t-p}, \Theta_t) \qquad (3)$$

Here, a second-order linear autoregressive model for estimating the position of an object in current frame by using the information of its position in the last two frames is constructed as shown in equation (4).

$$\alpha_{j,i} = 2 * \alpha_{j,i-1} - \alpha_{j,i-2} + \Theta_i \qquad (4)$$

2. **Likelihood-Measurement for Particles:** We measure the likelihood $\theta(\psi^k \alpha_{j,i}^{(k)}, \psi_j)$, for each propagated particle k using a color histogram-based appearance model. Where ψ_j is the color histogram in appearance model of trajectory j and ψ^k is the observed histogram. The likelihoods of propagated particles, treated as weights, are normalized in such a manner that they sum to 1.

3. **Re-Sampling:** Over a period of time, the highest weighted particle may tend to a weight of one and the weights of other particles may tend to zero. To avoid this degeneracy in weights, the particles are re-sampled. In re-sampling many of the low weight particles are removed and higher-weight particles are replicated in order to obtain a new set of equally-weighted particles. We use the re-sampling technique as described by Brasnett et al. (2005).

Appearance Model

Color histograms are used in our appearance model. For every newly detected human object a color histogram ψ_j, is computed. The particle likelihoods, in the future frames, are calculated using these color histograms so we save all the computed histograms. A particle's likelihood is computed using the Bhattacharya similarity coefficient between the model histogram ψ_j and observed histogram $\psi^{(k)}$ assuming that there are 'n' bins in the histogram. The likelihood $\theta(\psi^k \alpha_{j,i}^{(k)}, \psi_j)$ of particle k is given as:

$$\theta(\psi^k \alpha_{j,i}^{(k)}, \psi_j) \propto e^{-d\left(\psi_j, \psi^{(k)}\right)}$$

$$d(\psi_j, \psi^{(k)}) = 1 - \sum_{b=1}^{n} \sqrt{\psi_{j,b} \psi_b^{(k)}} \qquad (5)$$

where $\psi_{j,b}$ and $\psi_b^{(k)}$ denote bin b of ψ_j and $\psi^{(k)}$, respectively.

The complete object tracking algorithm is given as below.

Algorithm for Multiple Human Detection and Tracking

Step 1: Let Z be the input video to the algorithm.

1. In first frame η_0 of Z, detect humans using the human detector. Let ω be the number of detected humans.
2. Initialize trajectories δ_j, $1 \leq j \leq \omega$ with initial positions $\alpha_{j,0}$ of the human beings detected by the detector and also set the occlusion count ϕ_j for each of these trajectories to 0.
3. Initialize the appearance model ψ_j for each trajectory from the region around $\alpha_{j,0}$.
4. Set the occlusion count.

Step 2: For each subsequent frame η_i of input vide Z,

1. For each existing trajectory δ_j,
   a. Use motion model to predict the distribution $\theta(\alpha_{j,i} \alpha_{j,i-1})$, over locations for human j in frame i, creating a set of candidate particles $\alpha_{j,i}^{(k)}$, $1 \leq k \leq K$.
   b. Use appearance model to compute the color histogram $\psi^{(k)}$ and likelihood $\theta(\psi^k \alpha_{j,i}^{(k)}, \psi_j)$ for each particle k.
   c. Acquire k*, the index of the most likely particle, after re-sampling the particles according to their likelihoods.
   d. Now run the human detector on the location $\alpha_{j,i}^{(k^*)}$. If the location is classified as a human, reset $\phi_j \leftarrow 0$; else increase $\phi_j \leftarrow \phi_j + 1$.

e.   If ϕ_j exceeds a threshold, remove trajectory j.

Step 3: Now for frame η_i, search the new human objects and compute the Euclidean distance $\Omega_{j,k}$ between each newly detected human k and each existing trajectory δ_j. When $\Omega_{j,k} > \tau$ for all j, initialize a new trajectory for detection k. where τ is a threshold in pixels whose value is less than the width of the tracking window.

Results of Automatic Real-Time Human Detection and Tracking for Visual Surveillance Using Machine Learning Approach

We have tested the proposed automatic human detection and tracking technique on a number of realistic videos. The human detection and tracking results with some of the representative videos are given in Figure 10 and Figure 11. Human detection and tracking using the proposed method starts automatically without providing any initialization parameters, unlike many other existing object tracking techniques in which operator intervention is required. In Figure 10 we have shown the human detection and tracking results with a realistic video consisting of three human objects walking towards the camera. The video was shot in evening time in dim lighting conditions at a resolution of 640×480 and a frame rate of 17 frames per second. The video consisted of total 500 frames. In Figure 10 the detection and tracking results for 16 frames, from frame 1 to 375, at a difference of 25 frames are given. One can observe from Figure 10 that the proposed method detects and tracks all the three human objects from one frame to another with accuracy.

One can observe from Figure 11 that the maximum centroid distance between the ground truth value and the calculated value is nearly 14 pixels(13.89) for the video of frame resolution

640×480, which is not too much with respect to the frame size. Most of the time the centroid distance is either 0 or is too small to cause any big deviation from ground truth values, showing algorithm's accuracy.

Human Detection and Tracking Results for Considering Different Human Poses

Figure 12 shows the human detection and tracking results where the human may appear in different poses. There are four human beings in the video frame sequence in different poses. The first one is walking, second one is standing. The third human is sitting and the fourth one is bending over. Results show that our proposed algorithm can detect and track all four human beings even in this complex video. The average detection and tracking accuracy of the proposed technique is 87.44% and the average execution speed is 18 frames per second.

HUMAN ACTIVITY RECOGNITION

An activity is a sequence of movements generated during performance of a task. Activity recognition is a difficult task because the shape of the different actors performing an activity can be different and the speed and style in which an activity is performed can vary from person to person. Activity recognition in video is an active area of research because of its useful applications in visual surveillance, human robot interaction, content based video retrieval, human computer interfaces etc.,.(Weinland et al., 2011). Although, the approaches to solve the activity recognition problem are few and far between, but the activity recognition methods available in literature can broadly be categorized into two groups: sensor based activity recognition and vision based activity recognition. In sensor based activity recognition methods some smart sensory device is used to

Figure 10. Detection and tracking results with the proposed method on a real-time video in outdoor environment

Figure 11. The distance between the object-centroid estimated using the proposed method and the ground truth; X-axis shows the video frame number and y-axis shows the distance between Centroids (in pixels) for three objects shown in Figure 10 video results.

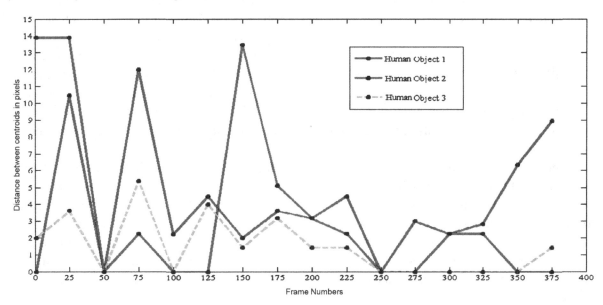

Figure 12. The human detection and tracking results with the proposed method when the humans appear in different poses

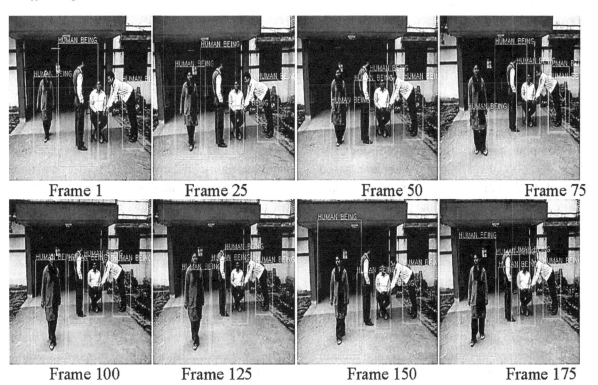

capture various activity signals for activity recognition. Vision based activity recognition methods use the spatial or temporal structure of an activity in order to recognize it.

Human Activity Recognition Techniques

A recent survey on vision-based action representation and recognition methods can be found by Weinland et al (2011). Machine learning based and template based methods are popular vision based approaches for human activity recognition in videos. The machine learning based approaches for activity recognition generally solve the problem of activity recognition as a classification problem and classify an activity into one of known activity classes. For training such classifiers a number of feature types (Losch et al., 2007) and methods are used, but the drawbacks of machine learning based methods are the long training time, slow operation, constrained accuracy and it is difficult to include a new activity as well. Template based methods are good options for activity recognition in video and can be easily used because of their simplicity and robustness

Template-Based Activity Recognition

Weinland et al. (2011) divide the template-based activity recognition methods into three groups: body template based methods (Gavrila & Davis, 1998; Yacoob, 1998), image template based methods and feature template based methods. Image models are simpler than the body models and can be computed efficiently. Motion energy images and motion history images can be used to compute 'where' and 'how' motion in the scene is taking place which helps in figuring out the location and type of activity in the scene. Chamfer distance or shape context descriptors are used in contexts where background segmentation is difficult. Motion energy images (MEI) and motion history images (MHI) can be used for describing

'where' and 'how' in a video scene. 'Where' represents the location of an action in image and MHI records the steps of action i.e., 'how'. Bobick et al. (2001), use motion templates for recognizing the activities in an aerobic exercise. They used only motion information for constructing the MHIs in a view-specific environment and for obtaining segmented foreground they used MEIs, which does not give good activity recognition accuracy in outdoor environment. Moreover, their technique is capable of only identifying one activity in the scene with one actor at a time. Our present work is an extension of the work of Bobick et al. This thesis presents a template based activity recognition approach which also considers the shape information along with the motion history in performing an activity. For obtaining the good foreground segmentation a robust statistical background model is constructed. The technique can recognize the activities of no motion such as standing and sleeping, along with those with motion such as walking, jumping etc.

Real-Time Human Activity Recognition in Videos

This section proposes a novel approach for human activity recognition in video. The proposed method is based on spatio-temporal template matching. First, the templates for various human activities are constructed using the shape and motion history information of the actors and then these templates are matched against the sequence of movements of the actors in video. The seven Hu moments and Mahalanobis distance are used for activity recognition. The experimental results given demonstrate that the technique can recognize various human activities like standing, jogging, walking, boxing, crawling, squat-moving, bend-moving etc., with speed and accuracy and can also tag the activities as 'normal' and 'abnormal'. The detailed description of the proposed method is given in the following section.

The Proposed Method for Human Activity Recognition

The proposed technique of activity recognition is based on the background modeling, motion history image creation and template matching. For background modeling we use a simple statistical background model. This model is used to subtract the background from the video frame in order to obtain the foreground. Using the motion history and pose information of these objects, templates for different activities are created. These templates are matched using seven Hu moment invariants and Mahalanobis distance. The confusion in recognizing the activities is also handled on the basis of the values of Mahalanobis distance calculated for each of them. The proposed technique has two basic steps as given below:

- Spatio-temporal template creation for different activities.
- Template matching and activity recognition.

The details of this method can be found in the work of Sharma et al. (2011).

Results of Human Activity Recognition Technique

From Figure 13, one can observe that there are three human objects, one is in walking position, second is in bending position, and third is in standing position. Results show that the method can determine the three activities walking, bending, and standing accurately.

The location of objects, in bending and standing activities, remains still whereas location of human object, in walking position, changes with respect to time from frame 1 to 275. But the proposed method accurately measures these activities. The facial direction of object in standing position also changes from frame 1 to 25. But this does not affect the accuracy of proposed method. Similarly

the frontal view of the human object in bending position does not remain same in frame 1 to 25. In this situation also the proposed method performs accurately. Therefore the proposed approach is good for static as well as dynamic activities.

From Figure 14 one can observe that the proposed approach performs accurately for four human objects involved in four activities jumping, standing, bending and sleeping. The direction of human object performing jumping activity changes in frame no. 25, 125 and 175. But the proposed method is able to recognize the activity performed by this object. The object in bending position is performing two activities simultaneously: bending and walking. In this situation the proposed method recognizes the object correctly and the change in position of the object does not affect the accuracy of the proposed method. In addition, the size of this object also increases as the object gets closer to the camera but the proposed method performs well. Therefore the proposed method gives accurate results for static as well as dynamic activities in this video also. We have achieved a frame speed of 25 frames per second for these real time videos and can achieve a higher processing speed for videos having low resolution.

One can observe from Figure 15 that the PSNR values for segmented videos in the proposed method are higher than Bobick's method for the realistic video. This means that the segmentation results using our method are better than the ones obtained from Bobick's method. In the proposed method, the video frames are segmented more accurately which leads to better activity template formation and eventually better activity recognition.

NORMAL AND ABNORMAL ACTIVITY RECOGNITION

The proposed activity recognition method can also tag the activities as 'normal' and 'abnormal'. Those activities, in which the deviation from the natural course of action is sought, are considered to be abnormal. The activities such as bend-moving, squat-moving,

Figure 13. Recognition of the three activities: walking, bending, and standing

crawling etc. are considered to be abnormal. Activities such as standing, walking, jogging, sleeping etc. are considered to normal. Based on this hypothesis, the activities are tagged as 'normal' and 'abnormal'. The results, for tagging the activities as normal or abnormal, are shown in Figure 16 and in Figure 17.

The video used for experiments in Figure 16 consists of a total of 150 frames. There are three human beings in the video performing three different activities. One is jogging, another one is standing and the third one is moving while bending and holding a wooden

Figure 14. Recognition of four activities: jumping, standing, bending, and sleeping

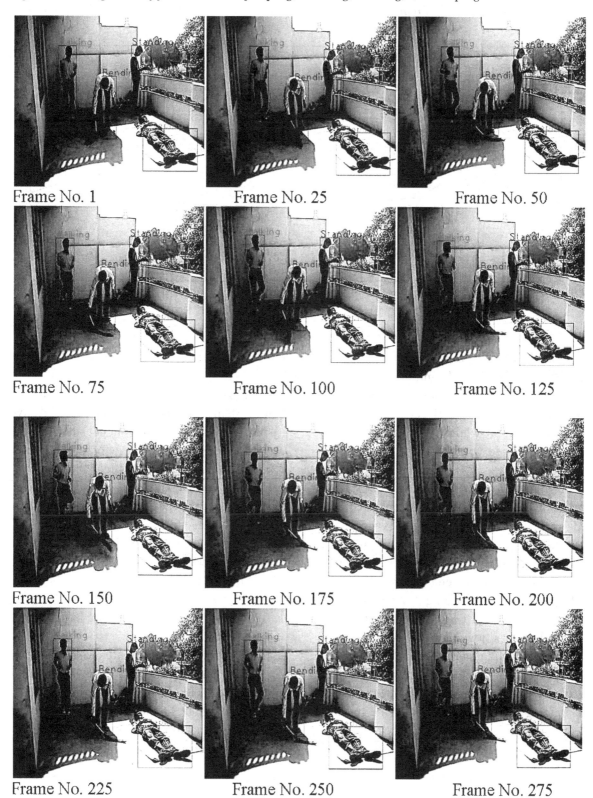

Figure 15. Plot for PSNR values for segmentation obtained using proposed method and Bobick's method for the video frames given in Figure 14

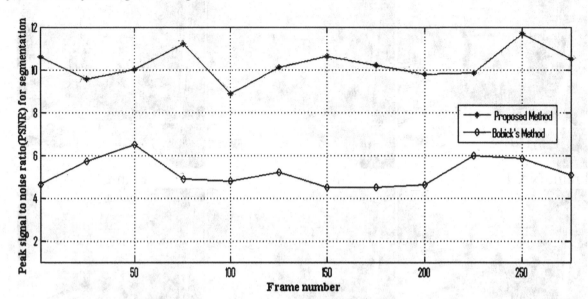

log in his hand. The proposed method tags the activities 'jogging' and 'standing' as 'normal' while the 'bend-moving' activity is tagged as 'abnormal'. The abnormal activity is tagged with the blue text while the normal activities have been tagged with the red text, as shown in Figure 16.

In Figure 17, activity tagging results, with another realistic video, have been presented. The video consists of a total of 110 frames and results have been given for all frames at a difference of 10 frames. It can be observed from Figure 17 that there are three human beings engaged in three different activities 'jogging', 'crawling', and 'squat-moving'. The proposed activity recognition method tags 'jogging' activity as 'normal' while the 'crawling' and 'squat-moving' activities are tagged as 'abnormal' activities. Normal activities have been tagged with blue text while for tagging the abnormal activity the red text has been used.

FUTURE RESEARCH DIRECTIONS

Our ultimate goal is to develop a video surveillance system for human behavior analysis. Activity recognition is necessary but not sufficient for accurately analyzing the behavior and intension of a human being. For accurately analyzing the behavior of a person other factors such as facial expression and the speed of performing a certain activity, also need to be taken into consideration. So the aim, henceforth, is to take the human facial expressions along with human action, into account. The future objectives are as follows:

1. Proposal of novel methods for human facial expression recognition.
2. Fusion of data using multiple vision cameras and other multi-modal sensors like infrared cameras, etc.
3. To integrate human activity information with the facial expressions in order to predict human behavior more accurately.

Figure 16. Tagging of normal and abnormal activities in video using the proposed activity recognition method

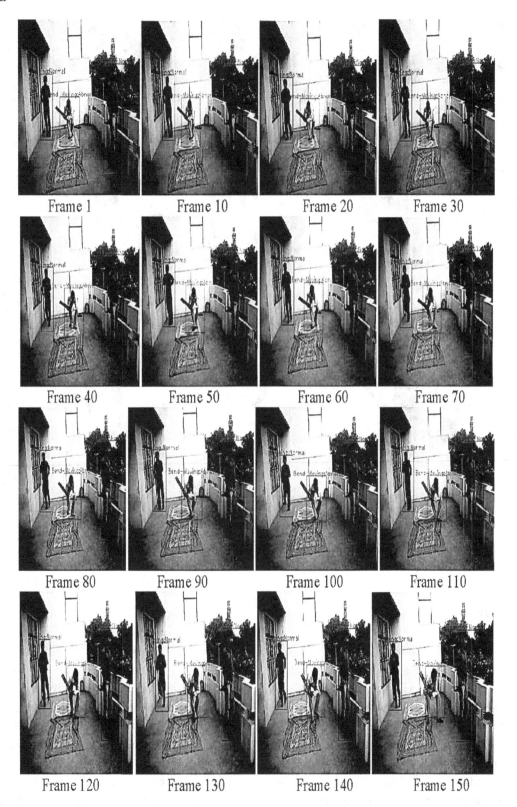

Figure 17. Tagging of normal and abnormal activities in video using the proposed activity recognition method

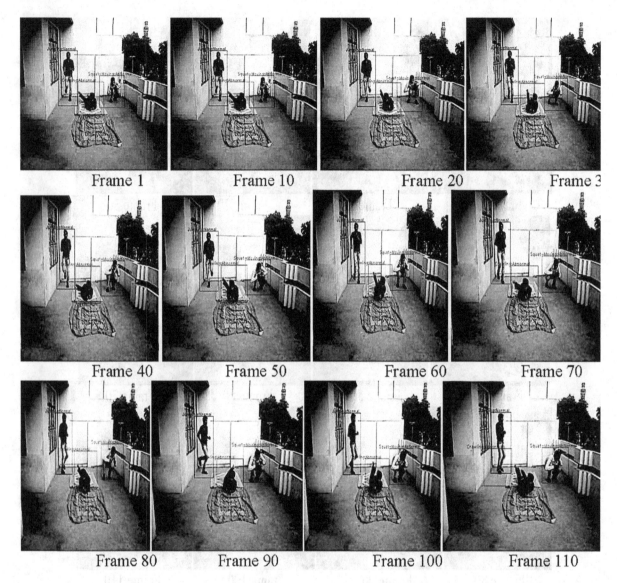

| Frame 1 | Frame 10 | Frame 20 | Frame 3 |

| Frame 40 | Frame 50 | Frame 60 | Frame 70 |

| Frame 80 | Frame 90 | Frame 100 | Frame 110 |

CONCLUSION

Smart cameras are becoming increasingly popular in surveillance systems for detecting humans, vehicles among others. The goal of research, in visual surveillance, is to push more intelligence and adaptability to the computer devices for autonomous analysis of the captured video data. The cloud based architecture for visual surveillance system has various advantages including less cost, effective command & control, real-time response, etc.

The chapter has reviewed state-of-art development and research in the field of visual surveillance and it discusses several efficient methods for motion segmentation, object classification, object tracking and human activity analysis. For motion segmentation, a novel computationally efficient and robust technique has been discussed. The proposed segmentation technique works on the formation of a robust statistical background model using the variance and covariance of the images, accumulated over a period of time. For object classification, a multiclass object classification technique based on Haar-like features and State-wise Additive Modeling using Multiclass Exponential Loss Function (SAMME), has been proposed. The problem of multiple object tracking has been solved using particle filtering. The objects are detected in the first frame of the video and then tracked in subsequent frames using particle filters. The proposed object tracking technique has the following advantages. A human activity recognition technique based on spatio-temporal template matching has been proposed which uses motion history images and spatial pose information to construct the activity templates. The chapter gives a detailed overview for implementing visual surveillance as a service (VSaaS). The framework can be easily implemented by a government on a private cloud (considering the sensitivity of defense data).

REFERENCES

Bobick, A. F., & Davis, J. W. (2001). The recognition of human movement using temporal templates. *IEEE Transactions on Pattern Analysis and Machine Intelligence*, *23*(3), 257–267. doi:10.1109/34.910878

Brasnett, P., Mihaylova, L., Canagarajah, N., & Bull, D. (2005). Particle filtering for multiple cues for object tracking in video sequences. In *Proceedings of 17th SPIE Annual Symposium on Electronic Imaging, Science and Technology* (vol. 5685, pp. 430–440).

Chang, V. (2014). The business intelligence as a service in the cloud. *International Journal of Future Generation Computer Systems*, *37*, 512–534. doi:10.1016/j.future.2013.12.028

Chang, V., Walters, R. J., & Wills, G. (2013). The development that leads to the cloud computing business framework. *International Journal of Information Management*, *33*(3), 524–538. doi:10.1016/j.ijinfomgt.2013.01.005

Gavrila, D., & Davis, L. (1995). Towards 3-d model-based tracking and recognition of human movement. In *Proceedings of the International Workshop on Face and Gesture Recognition* (pp. 272–277).

Gong, S. G., & Buxton, H. (2002). Editorial: Understanding visual behavior. *International Journal of Image and Vision Computing*, *20*(12), 825–826. doi:10.1016/S0262-8856(02)00092-6

Hu, W., Tan, T., Wang, L., & Maybank, S. (2004). A survey on visual surveillance of object motion and behaviors. *IEEE Transactions on Systems, Man and Cybernetics, Part C: Applications and Reviews*, *34*(3), 334–352. doi:10.1109/TSMCC.2004.829274

Kim, I. S., Choi, H. S., Yi, K. M., Choi, J. Y., & Kong, S. G. (2010). Intelligent visual surveillance— a survey. *International Journal of Control, Automation and Systems*, *8*(5), 926–939. doi:10.1007/s12555-010-0501-4

Kushwaha, A. K. S., Sharma, C. M., Khare, M., Prakash, O., & Khare, A. (2014). Adaptive real-time motion segmentation technique based on statistical background model. *The Imaging Science Journal*, *62*(5), 285–302. doi:10.1179/1743131X13Y.0000000056

Kushwaha, A. K. S., Sharma, C. M., Khare, M., Srivastava, R. K., & Khare, A. (2012). Automatic multiple human detection and tracking for visual surveillance system. In *Proceedings of the IEEE International Conference on Informatics, Electronics and Vision* (pp. 326-331).

Lanvin, P., Noyer, J.-C., & Benjelloun, M. (2003). Object detection and tracking using the particle filtering. In *Proceedings of the IEEE 37ᵗʰ Asilomar Conference on Signals, Systems and Computers* (Vol. 2, pp.1595-1599). doi:10.1109/ACSSC.2003.1292254

Lipton, A. J., Fujiyoshi, H., & Patil, R. S. (1998). Moving target classification and tracking from real-time video. In *Proceedings of the IEEE Workshop on Applications of Computer Vision* (pp. 8-14). doi:10.1109/ACV.1998.732851

Olson, T., & Brill, F. (1997). Moving object detection and event recognition algorithms for smart cameras. In *Proceedings of the DARPA Image Understanding Workshop* (pp. 159–175).

Shah, M., Javed, O., & Shafique, K. (2007). Automated visual surveillance in realistic scenarios. *IEEE MultiMedia, 14*(1), 30–39. doi:10.1109/MMUL.2007.3

Sharma, C. M., & Kumar, H. (2014). Architectural framework for implementing visual surveillance as a service. In *Proceedings of IEEE International Conference INDIACOM* (pp. 296-301). doi:10.1109/IndiaCom.2014.6828147

Sharma, C. M., Kushwaha, A. K. S., Nigam, S., & Khare, A. (2011). On human activity recognition in video sequences. In *Proceedings of IEEE 2nd International conference on Computer and Communication Technology* (pp. 152-158). doi:10.1109/ICCCT.2011.6075172

Sharma, C. M., Kushwaha, A. K. S., Nigam, S., & Khare, A. (2011). Automatic human activity recognition in video using background modeling and spatio-temporal template matching based technique. In *Proceedings of ACM International Conference on Advances in Computing and Artificial Intelligence* (pp. 97-101). doi:10.1145/2007052.2007072

Stockholm International Peace Research Institute. (2014). Trends in world military expenditure-2013 (pp. 1-8). SIPIRI.

Wang, W., Hu, W., & Tan, T. (2003). Recent developments in human motion Analysis. *International Journal of Pattern Recognition, 36*(3), 585–601. doi:10.1016/S0031-3203(02)00100-0

Weinland, D. & Ronfard, R.(2011). A survey of vision based methods for action representation, segmentation and recognition. *International Journal of Computer Vision and Image understanding, 115*(2), 221-241.

Wren, C. R., Azarbayejani, A., Darrell, T., & Pentland, A. P. (1997). Pfinder: Real-time tracking of the human body. *IEEE Transactions on Pattern Analysis and Machine Intelligence, 19*(7), 51–56. doi:10.1109/34.598236

Yacoob, Y., & Black, M. (1998). Parameterized modeling and recognition of activities. In *Proceedings of International Conference on Computer Vision* (pp.120-127). doi:10.1109/ICCV.1998.710709

Zhang, Y. (2006). *An overview of image and video segmentation in the last 40 years. Advances in Image and Video Segmentation* (pp. 1–16). IRM Press.

Section 5
Security

Chapter 16
Secure Deduplication with Encrypted Data for Cloud Storage

Pasquale Puzio
SecludIT, France & EURECOM, France

Melek Önen
EURECOM, France

Refik Molva
EURECOM, France

Sergio Loureiro
SecludIT, France

ABSTRACT

With the continuous increase of the number of users and the size of their data, data deduplication becomes a necessity for cloud storage providers. By storing a unique copy of duplicate data, cloud providers greatly reduce their storage and data transfer costs. The advantages of deduplication unfortunately come with a high cost in terms of new security and privacy challenges. In this chapter we propose ClouDedup, a secure and efficient storage service which assures block-level deduplication and data confidentiality at the same time. Although ClouDedup is based on convergent encryption, it remains secure thanks to the definition of a component that implements an additional encryption operation. Furthermore, as the requirement for deduplication at block-level raises an issue with respect to key management, we suggest to include a new component in order to implement the key management for each block together with the actual deduplication operation. In this chapter we show how we have implemented the proposed architecture, the challenges we have met and our solutions to these challenges.

CASE DESCRIPTION

Introduction

With the potentially infinite storage space offered by cloud providers, users tend to use as much space as they can and vendors constantly look for techniques aimed to minimize redundant data and maximize space savings. A technique which has been widely adopted is cross-user deduplication. The simple idea behind deduplication is to store duplicate data (either files or blocks) only once. Therefore, if a user wants to upload a file (block) which is already stored, the cloud provider will add the user to the owner list of that file (block) only. Deduplication has proved to achieve high

DOI: 10.4018/978-1-4666-8210-8.ch016

Copyright © 2015, IGI Global. Copying or distributing in print or electronic forms without written permission of IGI Global is prohibited.

space and cost savings and many cloud storage providers are currently adopting it. Deduplication can reduce storage needs by up to 90-95% for backup applications (Opendedup, 2014) and up to 68% in standard file systems (Meyer, 2012).

Along with low ownership costs and flexibility, users require the protection of their data and confidentiality guarantees through encryption.

Unfortunately, deduplication and encryption are two conflicting technologies. While the aim of deduplication is to detect identical data segments and store them only once, the result of encryption is to make two identical data segments indistinguishable after being encrypted. This means that if data are encrypted by users in a standard way, the cloud storage provider cannot apply deduplication since two identical data segments will be different after encryption. On the other hand, if data are not encrypted by users, confidentiality cannot be guaranteed and data are not protected against curious cloud storage providers.

A technique which has been proposed to meet these two conflicting requirements is convergent encryption (Douceur, Adya, Bolosky, Simon, & Theimer, 2002) whereby the encryption key is usually the result of the hash of the data segment. Although convergent encryption seems to be a good candidate to achieve confidentiality and deduplication at the same time, it unfortunately suffers from various well-known weaknesses (Bellare, Keelveedhi, & Ristenpart, 2013)(Perttula, 2008) including dictionary attacks: an attacker who is able to guess or predict a file, can easily derive the potential encryption key and verify whether the file is already stored at the cloud storage provider or not.

We cope with the inherent security exposures of convergent encryption and propose ClouDedup, which preserves the combined advantages of deduplication and convergent encryption. The security of ClouDedup relies on its new architecture whereby in addition to the basic storage provider, a metadata manager and an additional gateway are defined: the gateway adds an ad-

ditional encryption layer to prevent well-known attacks against convergent encryption and thus protect the confidentiality of the data; on the other hand, the metadata manager is responsible for the key management task since block-level deduplication requires the memorization of a huge number of keys: we define an efficient key management mechanism to avoid users to store one key per block.

To summarize the key features of ClouDedup:

- ClouDedup assures block-level deduplication and data confidentiality while coping with weaknesses raised by convergent encryption. Block-level deduplication renders the system more flexible and efficient;
- ClouDedup preserves confidentiality and privacy even against potentially malicious cloud storage providers thanks to an additional layer of encryption;
- ClouDedup offers an efficient key management solution through the metadata manager;
- The new architecture defines several different components and a single component cannot compromise the whole system without colluding with other components;
- ClouDedup works transparently with existing cloud storage providers. As a consequence, ClouDedup is fully compatible with standard storage APIs and any cloud storage provider can be easily integrated in our architecture.

BACKGROUND

Deduplication

According to the data granularity, deduplication (for a practical example see Figure 1) strategies can be classified into two main categories: file-level deduplication (Wilcox-O'Hearn & Warner, 2008) and block-level deduplication (Cox, Murray,

Figure 1. Block-level deduplication

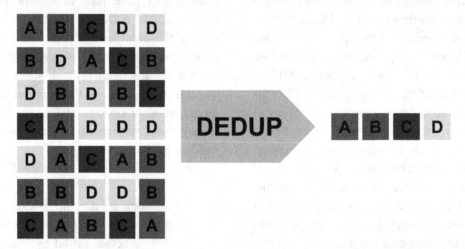

& Noble, 2002). In block-based deduplication (which is nowadays considered the most common strategy), the block size can either be fixed or variable (Rabin, 1981). Another categorization criterion is the location at which deduplication is performed: if data are deduplicated at the client, then it is called source-based deduplication, otherwise it is being defined as being target-based.

In source-based deduplication, the client first hashes each data segment he wishes to upload and sends the result to the storage provider to check whether that data segment already stored: thus, only unique data segments will be actually uploaded by the user. While deduplication at the client side can achieve bandwidth savings, it unfortunately can make the system vulnerable to side-channel attacks (Harnik, Pinkas, & Shulman-Peleg, 2010) whereby attackers can immediately discover whether a certain data is stored or not. On the other hand, while by deduplicating data at the storage provider the system is protected against side-channel attacks, such a solution does not decrease the communication overhead.

Convergent Encryption

The basic idea of convergent encryption (CE) is to derive the encryption key from the hash of the plaintext. The simplest implementation of con-

vergent encryption can be defined as follows: Alice derives the encryption key K from her message M such that $K = H(M)$, where H is a cryptographic hash function; she encrypts the message with this key, hence:

$$C = E(K, M) = E(H(M), M),$$

where E is a block cipher.

As shown in Figure 2, by applying this technique, two users with two identical plaintexts will obtain two identical ciphertexts since the encryption key is the same and the encryption algorithm is deterministic; hence the cloud storage provider will be able to perform deduplication on such ciphertexts. Furthermore, encryption keys are generated, retained and protected by users. As the encryption key is deterministically generated from the plaintext, users do not have to interact with each other for establishing an agreement on the key to encrypt a given plaintext. Therefore, convergent encryption seems to be a good candidate for the adoption of encryption and deduplication in the cloud storage domain.

Convergent encryption suffers from several weaknesses which have been widely discussed in the literature (Bellare, Keelveedhi, & Ristenpart, 2013) (Perttula, 2008)(Is Convergent Encryption

Figure 2. Convergent encryption as a solution to achieve confidentiality

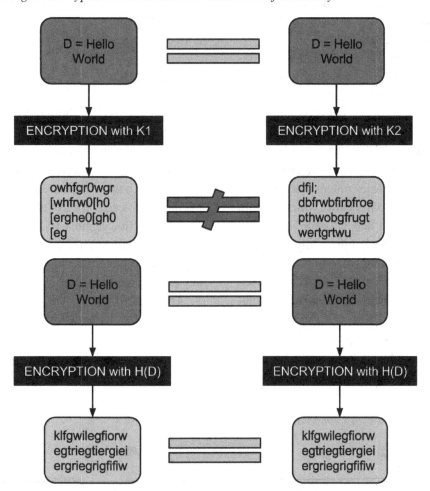

really secure?, 2011). As the encryption key depends on the value of the plaintext, an attacker who has gained access to the storage can perpetrate the so called "dictionary attacks" by comparing the cipher-texts resulting from the encryption of well-known plaintext values derived from a dictionary with the stored ciphertexts. Indeed, even if encryption keys are strongly protected, the potentially malicious cloud provider, who has no access to the encryption key but has access to the encrypted chunks (blocks), can easily perform offline dictionary attacks and discover predictable files. This issue arises in (Storer, Greenan, Long, & Miller, 2008) where chunks are stored at the storage provider after being encrypted with convergent encryption.

As shown in (Perttula, 2008), there are two known possible attacks against convergent encryption: confirmation of a file (COF) and learn-the-remaining-information (LRI). These attacks exploit the deterministic relationship between the plaintext and the encryption key in order to check if a given plaintext has already been stored or not. In COF, an attacker who already knows the full plaintext of a file, can check if a copy of that file has already been stored. If the attacker is the cloud provider or an insider, he might also learn which users are the owners of that file. Depending on the content of the file, this type of information leakage can be dangerous. For instance, while some users could not be worried about leaking such information, it is worth pointing out that by performing this attack, it is possible to find out if a user has stored a given file.

While COF might be considered as a non-critical problem, LRI can disclose highly sensitive information: in LRI, the attacker already knows a big part of a file and tries to guess the unknown parts by checking if the result of the encryption matches the observed ciphertext. This is the case of those documents that have a predefined template and a small part of variable content. For instance, if users store letters from a bank, which contain bank account numbers and passwords, then an attacker who knows the template might be able to learn the account number and password of selected users. The same mechanism can be used to guess passwords and other sensitive information contained in files such as configuration files, web browser cookies, etc. In general, the more the attacker knows about the victim's data, the more the attack can be effective and dangerous. Hence,

a strategy is needed to achieve a higher security degree while preserving combined advantages of both convergent encryption and deduplication.

ClouDedup

The design goal of ClouDedup is to provide deduplication at block-level while coping with the inherent security exposures of convergent encryption. As illustrated in Figure 3, the scheme defines two basic components: a gateway that is in charge of access control and that achieves the main protection against COF and LRI attacks; another component, named as metadata manager (MM), is in charge of the actual deduplication and key management operations.

The goal of the system is to guarantee data confidentiality without losing the advantage of deduplication. Confidentiality must be guaranteed for all files, including the predictable ones. The security of the whole system should not rely on

Figure 3. High-level view of ClouDedup

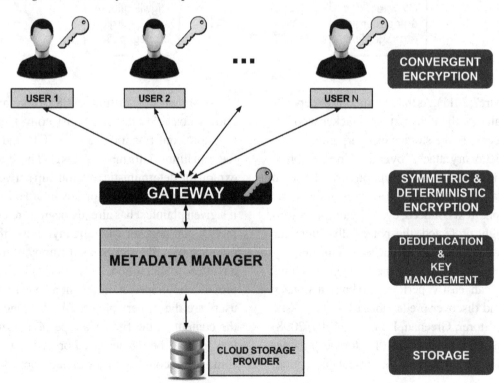

the security of a single component (single point of failure), and the security level should not collapse when a single component is compromised.

We consider the gateway as a trusted component with respect to user authentication, access control and additional encryption. The gateway is not trusted with respect to the confidentiality of the data stored at the cloud storage provider. Indeed, the gateway is not able to perform offline dictionary attacks since he does not possess the credentials required to have access to the stored data.

Anyone who has access to the storage environment is considered as a potential attacker, including employees at the cloud storage provider and the cloud storage provider itself. In our threat model, the cloud storage provider is honest but curious, meaning that it carries out its tasks but might attempt to decrypt data stored by users. We do not take cloud storage providers that can choose to delete or modify files into account.

Among the potential threats, we also identify external attackers. An external attacker does not have access to the storage and operates outside the system. Such an attacker attempts to compromise the system by eavesdropping messages between different components or by compromising a user's account. External attackers have a limited access to the system and can be effectively neutralized by adopting strong authentication mechanisms and secure communication channels.

In the proposed architecture, only one component, that is the gateway, is trusted with respect to a limited set of operations: therefore we call it semi-trusted. Once the gateway has applied the additional encryption, data are no longer vulnerable to CE weaknesses. Indeed, without possessing the keying material used for the additional encryption, an adversary can perform dictionary attacks on data stored at the cloud storage provider.

The gateway is a simple semi-trusted component that is deployed on the user's premises and is in charge of performing user authentication, access control and additional symmetric encryption.

The primary role of the gateway is to encrypt the received and securely retain the secret key used for the additional encryption. In a real scenario, this goal can be effectively accomplished by using a hardware security module (HSM) (SafeNet, 2014). When data are retrieved by a user, the gateway plays another important role. Before sending data to a given recipient, the gateway must verify whether those blocks actually belong to the requester by verifying the signature of each block with the received public key.

The metadata manager (MM) and the cloud storage provider are not trusted with respect to data confidentiality, indeed, they are not able to decrypt data stored at the cloud storage provider. We do not take into account components that can misbehave and hence do not accomplish the tasks they have been assigned.

The Gateway

A simple solution to prevent the attacks against convergent encryption (CE) consists of encrypting the ciphertexts resulting from CE with another encryption algorithm using the same keying material for all input. This solution is compatible with the deduplication requirement since identical ciphertexts resulting from CE would yield identical outputs even after the additional encryption operation. Yet, this solution will not anymore suffer from the attacks such as COF and LRI targeting CE.

The core component of ClouDedup is thus a gateway that implements the additional encryption operation to cope with the weaknesses of CE, together with a user authentication and an access control mechanism embedded in the data protection mechanism. Each data segment is thus encrypted by the gateway in addition to the convergent encryption operation performed by the user. Each encrypted data segment is linked with a signature generated by its owner and verified by the gateway upon data retrieval requests.

The gateway has three main roles: authenticating users during the storage/retrieval request, performing access control by verifying block signatures embedded in the data, encrypting/decrypting data traveling from users to the cloud and vice versa.

The gateway takes care of performing an additional layer of encryption to the data (blocks, keys and signatures) uploaded by users. Before being forwarded to MM, data are further encrypted in order to prevent MM and any other component from performing dictionary attacks and exploiting the well-known weaknesses of convergent encryption.

During file retrieval, blocks are decrypted and the gateway verifies the signature of each block with the user's public key. If the verification process fails, blocks are not delivered to the requesting user.

Metadata Manager (MM)

Even though the mechanisms of the gateway cope with the security weaknesses of CE, the requirement for deduplication at block-level further raises an issue with respect to key management. As an inherent feature of CE, the fact that encryption keys are derived from the data itself does not eliminate the need for the user to memorize the value of the key for each encrypted data segment. Unlike file-level deduplication, in case of block-level deduplication, the requirement to memorize and retrieve CE keys for each block in a secure way, calls for a fully-fledged key management solution.

We thus suggest to include a new component, the metadata manager (MM), in the new ClouDedup system in order to implement the key management for each block together with the actual deduplication operation.

MM is the component responsible for storing metadata, which include encrypted keys and block signatures, and handling deduplication (see Figure 4). Indeed, MM maintains a linked list and a small database in order to keep track of

file ownerships, file composition and avoid the storage of multiple copies of the same data segments. The tables used for this purpose are file, block pointer and signature tables. The linked list is structured as follows:

- Each node in the linked list represents a data block. The identifier of each node is obtained by hashing the encrypted data block received from the gateway.
- If there is a link between two nodes X and Y, it means that X is the predecessor of Y in a given file. A link between two nodes X and Y corresponds to the file identifier and the encryption of the key to decrypt the data block Y.

In addition to the access control mechanism performed by the gateway, when users ask to retrieve a file, MM further checks if the requesting user is authorized to retrieve that file. This way, MM makes sure that the user is not trying to access someone else's data. This operation can be considered as an additional access control mechanism, since an access control mechanism already takes place at the gateway.

Another important role of MM is to communicate with cloud storage provider (SP) in order to actually store and retrieve the data blocks and get a pointer to the actual location of each data block.

Cloud Storage Provider (SP)

SP is the most simple component of the system. The only role of SP is to physically store data blocks. SP is not aware of deduplication and ignores any existing relation between two or more blocks. Indeed, SP does not know which file(s) a block is part of or if two blocks are part of the same file. This means that even if SP is curious, it has no way to infer the original content of a data block to rebuild the files uploaded by the users.

Figure 4. Data and metadata protection in ClouDedup

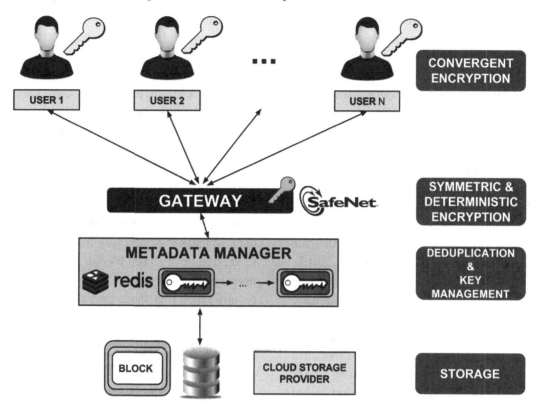

It is worth pointing out that any cloud storage provider would be able to operate as SP. Indeed, ClouDedup is completely transparent from SP's perspective, which does not collaborate with MM for deduplication. The only role of SP is to store data blocks coming from MM, which can be considered as files of small size. Therefore, it is possible to make use of well-known cloud storage providers such as Google Drive (Google, 2014), Amazon S3 (Amazon, 2014) and Dropbox (Dropbox, 2014).

Security Considerations

When designing solutions for secure cloud storage, it is important to take into account any potential attack scenarios and possible issues that might arise. We assume that an attacker, like the malicious storage provider, has full access to the storage. If the attacker has access to the storage only, he cannot get any information. Indeed, files are split into blocks and each block is first encrypted with convergent encryption and further encrypted with one or more secret keys. Moreover, metadata are not stored at the cloud storage provider. Clearly, thanks to this setup, such an attacker cannot perform any dictionary attack on predictable files.

A worse scenario is the one in which the attacker manages to compromise the metadata manager and thus has access to the data, metadata and encrypted keys. In this case, confidentiality would still be guaranteed since block keys are encrypted with users' secret keys and the gateway's secret key. The only information the attacker can get are data similarity and relationships between files, users and blocks. However, as file names are encrypted by users, these information would be of no use for the attacker, unless he manages to find a correspondence with a predictable file according to its size and popularity.

The system must guarantee confidentiality and privacy even in the unlikely event where the gateway is compromised. An additional encryption performed by the metadata manager before storing data in the cloud storage provider would enforce data protection against the malicious gateway; therefore confidentiality is still guaranteed and offline dictionary attacks are not successful. On the other hand, if the attacker compromises the gateway, only online attacks would be possible since this component directly communicates with users. The effect of such a breach is limited since data uploaded by users are encrypted with convergent encryption, which achieves confidentiality for unpredictable files (Bellare, Keelveedhi, & Ristenpart, 2013). Furthermore, a rate limiting strategy put in place by the metadata manager can limit online brute-force attacks performed by the gateway.

In the worst scenario, the attacker manages to compromise both the gateway and the metadata manager. In this case, the attacker will be able to remove the two additional layers of encryption and perform offline dictionary attacks on predictable files. However, confidentiality for unpredictable files is guaranteed.

Finally, we analyze the impact of an attacker who attempts to compromise users and have no access to the storage. If an attacker compromises one or more users, he can attempt to perform online dictionary attacks. As the gateway is not compromised, the attacker will only retrieve data belonging to the compromised user (access control mechanism). Furthermore, the gateway can limit such attacks by setting a maximum threshold for the rate with which users can send requests.

TECHNOLOGY CHALLENGES

Implementing such an architecture presents several technical challenges. Some of them become critical when dealing with huge amounts of data and users, which is a typical scenario in Cloud Computing.

The first challenge is strictly related to block-level deduplication. In order to deduplicate a single block, the metadata manager has to check if that block has already been stored in the past or not. This means that the metadata manager has to look for the block id over the entire system. This activity, if not properly optimized, can be very costly and represent an obstacle to the feasibility of our solution. Indeed, storing big datasets requires to handle millions of blocks.

The second challenge is scalability. In order to perform deduplication, the service provider needs to maintain a relatively small database for metadata. Metadata are all those information needed to keep track of stored blocks, file composition, users and file ownerships. Even though metadata require much less space than the actual data, in case of very large datasets a single server might not be sufficient. Therefore, the solution must take into account the possibility to scale up to multiple servers.

Since users cannot access their data without the help of the metadata manager, it is important to guarantee the availability of this component. Also, in order to protect users' data and avoid any risks related to data loss, it is crucial to put in place a strategy to backup metadata and easily recover the metadata manager in case of an unfortunate event such as a crash. Losing metadata would mean losing the entire data, even though the latter are still stored at the cloud storage provider. Indeed, without the information stored at the metadata manager, it would be extremely difficult and costly, if not impossible, for the user to recover his data.

However, MM is not the only potential bottleneck of our architecture. Indeed, the gateway, if not efficient, can represent an important bottleneck since it has to handle every upload/download operation in order to encrypt/decrypt content.

Performance and scalability are not the only aspects to take into account. Also security must be guaranteed. As we mentioned earlier, the gateway encrypts/decrypts users' data with the same secret key, in order to make deduplication possible over encrypted data. The protection of this key is fundamental. For instance, if this key is lost, users cannot recover their data. Even worse, if an attacker manages to steal the key, users' data are not confidential anymore.

Finally, the last technical challenge we face is related to the interaction with the cloud storage provider. As we mentioned, files are split into blocks (for a more effective deduplication) before being uploaded to the Cloud. Therefore, a single user request to store one single file, can generate up to thousands of requests (one for each block) which need to be handled in an efficient way in order to avoid performance degradation.

SOLUTIONS

We solved the first technical challenge by making use of hash tables. Each block corresponds to an entry in our hash table: the block id is the key and the value is the data structure containing the information on the block and the pointer to the location (the Cloud) where the block is actually stored. Thanks to our solution, any information on any block can be retrieved in a constant time, resulting in efficient and fast deduplication.

In order to be able to easily scale up in case of big datasets, the global hash table can be split into multiple hash tables. Therefore, the metadata, which is a set key-value pairs, can be stored in a distributed fashion among multiple servers, each storing a subset of the entire metadataset. Several strategies can be adopted for splitting the dataset. For instance, given a key, it is possible to decide on which server it is going to be stored by looking at the first bits. For example, let us suppose we use the first three bits of the key to determine the destination server: if the first three bits are 001, the key (and its associated value) will be stored on the server 1. More details on the data structures employed in our data layer are available in our previous work (Puzio, 2013).

As previously mentioned, any data loss or corruption at the metadata manager may compromise the integrity of users' data. In order to guarantee availability and prevent data loss, we propose to put in place a replication system. In other words, the metadata manager will be paired with an additional server which will be a replica of the metadata manager. Whenever the metadata manager becomes unavailable, the replica can take over and thus guarantee the continuity of the service. In REDIS, this goal can be achieved thanks to the built-in master-slave functionality.

However, in some cases it may not be necessary to replace the metadata manager with a replica. For instance, in case of a simple system reboot, it would not be convenient to replace the main metadata manager. Therefore, in addition to replication, REDIS provides periodic snapshots and journaling, which allow to rebuild the whole dataset and retrieve all metadata without any loss.

Also the gateway can represent a critical point for the performance of the whole system. In ClouDedup, the gateway works as a proxy and is responsible for encrypting/decrypting users' data. This operation is performed in a streaming fashion, meaning that the client sends chunked-encoded requests (Fielding e. a., 1999), where each chunk corresponds to a block-key pair. The gateway, instead of waiting for the reception of the entire request, encrypts/decrypts blocks and keys as soon as a chunk is received. This way the delay introduced by this intermediate component is minimal and does not negatively affect performance.

Also, security plays a crucial role in cloud storage systems. In order to guarantee data confidentiality, the unique secret key used by the gateway for encryption and decryption, must be well protected and any communication of the key with external entities must be forbidden. One of the many hardware security modules (HSM (SafeNet, 2014)) available in the market can be used to ensure the protection of the keying material.

Finally, as we mentioned earlier, the interaction with the cloud storage provider can be an important source of delay since in ClouDedup every file is split into many blocks, resulting in the generation of many storage requests. In order to optimize the performance, all operations on blocks (upload, download, delete) are performed in parallel. For instance, during the download of a file, depending on the capacity of the network and the physical host, hundreds of blocks can be downloaded at the same time.

TECHNOLOGICAL COMPONENTS

ClouDedup is composed by 4 components, as shown in Figure 5.

The first component is the client run by the cloud user. The role of the client is limited to splitting files into blocks (using the Rabin fin-

gerprinting scheme (Rabin, 1981)), encrypting them with the convergent encryption technique, signing the resulting encrypted blocks and creating the storage request. In addition, the user also encrypts each key derived from the corresponding block with the previous one and his secret key in order to outsource the keying material as well; the client thus only stores the key derived from the first block and the file identifier. For each file, this key will be used to decrypt and re-build the file when it will be retrieved. Instead, the file identifier is necessary to univocally identify a file over the whole system. Finally, the user also signs each block with a special signature scheme.

The client, which is currently available as command line script, has been implemented in Python and makes use of several open-source libraries. In particular, we used:

Figure 5. Components of ClouDedup

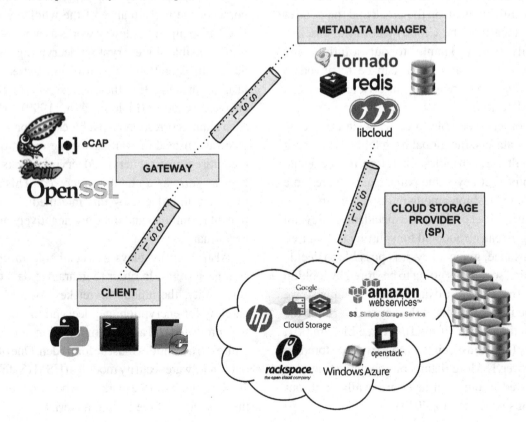

- Pyrabin (Huang, 2014) for the file chunking functionality;
- Py-convergent-encryption (Haardt, 2014) and pycrypto (Litzenberger, 2014) for the functionalities involving cryptography;
- Requests (Reitz, 2014) for the communication (HTTPS) with the gateway and the metadata manager;
- Python-gnupg (GNU, 2014) for the interaction with the gateway and the creation of signatures for the access control mechanism.

The second component is the encryption gateway, which works as a proxy between the client and the metadata manager. As we mentioned above, it is important to make the gateway able to handle several requests at the same time in order to avoid any bottleneck in the system. For this very reason, we decided to employ Squid (Squid, 2014), which is a scalable and high-performing HTTP(S) proxy with support for content adaptation, which is a feature required in order to encrypt/decrypt content. We use the eCAP (The Measurement Factory, 2014) scripts for modifying requests "on the fly" and forwarding them to the original destination. These scripts are written in C++ and make use of OpenSSL (OpenSSL, 2014) for encrypting and decrypting blocks. In addition to encryption and decryption, the gateway also performs access control by verifying signatures during the download operation. This is achieved by employing sks (GNU, 2014), an open-source PGP key server which securely stores users' public keys that are needed for the verification.

The third component is the metadata manager, which is responsible for the actual deduplication operation, maintaining all the information on blocks, files and users and the interaction with the cloud storage provider.

In order to make the deduplication operation as efficient as possible, we decided to use REDIS (Sanfilippo, 2014) as data layer, which is a lightweight, scalable, flexible and high-performing key-value store. REDIS allows us to easily and quickly store and retrieve high-level data structures, such as lists and hash tables, which are used to store metadata without handling costly and complex databases and indices. Also, the possibility to directly handle high-level data structures allows us to simplify the mapping between our internal logic and the underlying data layer.

The software layer which is actually responsible for the communication with clients is a HTTPS server exposing a REST (Fielding R. T., 2000) API. We implemented this server by using Tornado (Darnell, 2014), an open-source, powerful and high-performing web server developed at Facebook. The role of this server is to receive requests from users and forward them to the core module of the metadata manager, which directly communicates with the REDIS server, running on the same physical host, and the remote cloud storage provider. We used libcloud (Apache, 2014), which is an abstraction layer meant to unify the APIs of different providers, to handle the storage operations with the cloud storage provider. Parallel storage operations have been implemented by using threads and the gevent (Bilenko, 2014) library.

Finally, the last and simplest component of ClouDedup is the cloud storage provider. It is important to point out that ClouDedup is completely storage agnostic, meaning that any storage provider can be used for this functionality and integrated with our system. Indeed, the only role of the cloud storage provider is to physically store and eventually delete or return encrypted blocks. Also, the cloud storage provider does not have any knowledge on the structure of files or the relation between encrypted blocks, so it cannot extract any information from the sotred data. Also, users only interact with the gateway and the metadata manager, resulting in a high level of privacy since the cloud storage provider does not know which blocks belong to which users.

In our implementation, we have successfully integrated and tested Amazon S3 and other storage services such as Dropbox (Dropbox, 2014), Google Drive (Google, 2014) and OpenStack SWIFT (OpenStack, 2014).

PERFORMANCE ANALYSIS

As mentioned above, block-level deduplication requires to handle a certain amount of metadata. Indeed, the component responsible for deduplication has to perform several operations such as identifying those blocks that have already been stored in the past (in order to find duplicates), keeping track of the structure of each file, storing pointers to the actual location of each block, etc. A reasonable question that may arise is about the size of these metadata and whether it significantly reduces the gains achieved thanks to deduplication. Therefore, in this section we evaluate the overhead introduced by our system in terms of storage space. In order to refer to a realistic scenario, we use the same parameters of (Meyer, 2012).

We take into account a scenario in which there are 857 file systems. The mean number of files per file system is 225K and the mean size of a file is 318K, resulting in about 57T of data. In our design, we use SHA256 as hash function so the size of the key, which is the result of the hash of the block, of each block is 256 bits. Metadata storage space is estimated by taking into account the main data structures used by the metadata manager (Puzio, 2013).

According to the results of (Meyer, 2012), Rabin 8K (expected block size of 8K) has proved to be the best chunking algorithm, achieving 68% of space savings. In Figure 6 we show that the overhead introduced by the MM component is minimal and does not affect space savings of deduplication. In the best deduplication setup (Rabin 8K and deduplication rate of 68%) the total storage space required for metadata is equal to 2.22% of the size of non-deduplicated data. These results prove that the overhead for block-level deduplication is affordable despite the introduction of additional encryption and key management operations.

Figure 6. Overhead in terms of storage space of our solution compared to solutions with no metadata

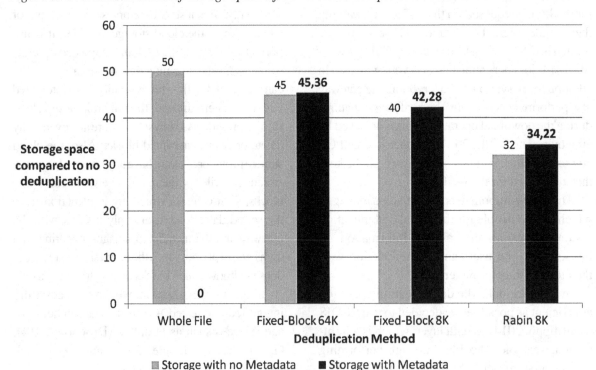

In cloud storage, performance and reliability are among the most important design goals (Chang et al., 2013). In particular, when talking about systems which involve several components, performance degradation is a serious risk which must be taken into account since the first phases of the design. In ClouDedup, every architectural decision has been made with performance in mind. Indeed, the goal was to minimize the overhead introduced by the additional components and provide performance as close as possible to simple cloud storage. However, it is obvious to expect a worse performance compared to cloud storage providers such as Amazon S3, since traditional cloud storage providers involve less components. Also, a little performance degradation is the price to pay to achieve high storage space savings and confidentiality.

It is worth explaining more in detail why we implemented upload/download requests in a streaming fashion by using chunked-encoded requests: this way, a single block can be processed (encrypted/decrypted) and stored in the Cloud as soon as it has been received without waiting for the entire request body to be received. Another potential threat for performance might be represented by the additional encryption/decryption operation performed in the middle by the gateway. However, we recall that the implemented encryption algorithm is symmetric and therefore efficient. Indeed, our tests showed that the cost of this additional encryption is negligible and does not represent a bottleneck for the whole system.

In Figure 7, we show the results of the preliminary performance results on our implementation of the ClouDedup architecture for upload, download and delete operations and we compare them with the performance Amazon S3, which is the de-facto reference for cloud storage.

Figure 7. Results of preliminary performance tests with no duplicate content (time is expressed in logarithmic scale)

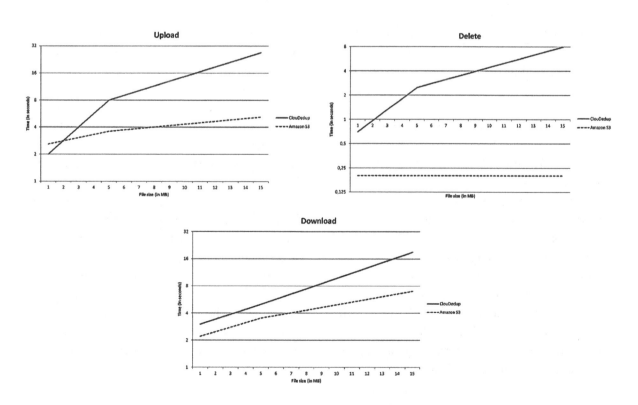

In order to measure the impact of the gateway and the additional encryption/decryption, we ran the same tests without the gateway but we did not notice any significant change. This proves that the gateway does not represent a bottleneck. We repeated each test 10 times and we computed the average of all the results.

During our experiments, the gateway was deployed within the same network of the client. The metadata manager was deployed on a m3.large instance on Amazon EC2 (2 vCPUs, 7.5 GB of RAM, Moderate network performance) and a bucket at Amazon S3 was used as actual storage for blocks. Of course, better results could be easily achieved by running the metadata manager on a more powerful machine with high network performance. The performance of Amazon S3 was measured by using the s3cmd client.

Observing the results, upload, download and delete operations have a linear cost with respect to the number of blocks of the file, which is not surprising. It is straightforward that performances of Amazon S3 are better than ours. However, this is not surprising either since there are several factors to take into account.

First, ClouDedup involves multiple components which, even if implemented as efficiently as possible, introduce an unavoidable delay in the communication.

Second, ClouDedup performs block-level deduplication over encrypted data, which requires to handle individual blocks and keys, resulting in a significant overhead. However, this overhead can be removed by deploying the gateway and the metadata manager in the same network (or perhaps on the same machine) and putting in place a local storage for blocks.

Moreover, it is straightforward that with no duplicate content the benefits of our solution are partially obfuscated by the performance overhead. In a real scenario, it is very likely to deal with duplicate files and blocks, therefore the performance overhead will be visible only during the first stages of ClouDedup's deployment. Despite of taking more time in presence of no duplicate data, ClouDedup provides an accurate and efficient solution for securely detecting duplicate content in files that will be uploaded in the future.

Third, in our experiments there was no duplicate content, which negatively affects the performance of upload and delete operations. For instance, if a file is a duplicate, no block will be uploaded to the Cloud since a copy of each block has already been stored in the past. On the other hand, if a file is original, every block will be uploaded to the Cloud. The same scenario occurs in the delete operation.

Fourth, in our tests we have been using an Amazon S3 bucket as final storage component. Despite to be easy to integrate and reliable, this solution did not prove to be the most efficient one. Indeed, every new data block has to be uploaded twice: first on the metadata manager and then to the bucket. Therefore, in order to improve performance and get much closer to Amazon S3, it is recommended to use a storage system with a lower latency than Amazon S3.

Finally, Amazon S3 and ClouDedup have been designed for two quite different scenarios. Indeed, the former is meant for simple and reliable cloud storage of large files, while the latter is mainly suitable for internal enterprise storage of documents, which have a limited size.

It is worth pointing out why the cost of the delete operation is linear on ClouDedup while it is constant on Amazon S3: this is due to the different nature of the two systems. Indeed, Amazon S3 provides an object storage in which every file is seen as a single object. On the other hand, ClouDedup treats every file as a set of blocks, which are deduplicated and stored in the Cloud by the metadata manager.

In order to measure the gains in terms of performance achieved thanks to deduplication and the actual overhead of the additional symmetric encryption and the block-level deduplication, we tested the upload and delete operations (deduplication does not affect download performance) on two different versions of a 15MB file, respectively with 50% and 100% of duplicate content. Once again, we compared the results with Amazon S3.

As it is shown in Figure 8, the presence of duplicate content significantly reduces the time required for uploading and deleting a file. In particular, when the entire file is a duplicate, the performance of ClouDedup is comparable to Amazon S3. This means that the overhead introduced by the gateway and the metadata manager is negligible. Indeed, the operation that represents a bottleneck is the interaction with the cloud storage provider. As we mentioned earlier, this overhead can be removed by deploying the storage provider locally (e.g. OpenStack SWIFT (OpenStack, 2014)) or executing the upload, download and delete operations in the background. Also, maintaining a local cache

with the most popular blocks at the metadata manager can be a great solution for improving the performance of download.

Therefore, block-level deduplication not only cuts down costs by reducing the required storage space, but also allows to improve performance.

We plan to repeat the same analysis on a real dataset and show how our proposed architecture can bring security together with good performance.

DEPLOYMENT AND USE-CASES

ClouDedup can be adopted for many different use-cases. The main use-case we took into account is the one called "big enterprise", which is illustrated in Figure 9.

Figure 8. Results of preliminary performance tests in case of duplicate content

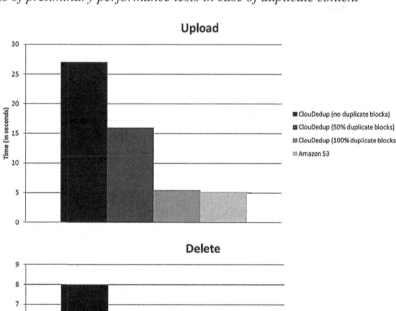

Figure 9. Deployment for the "big enterprise" use-case

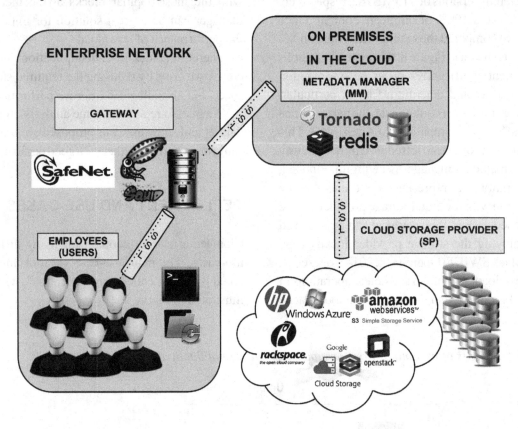

In this use-case, users belong to the same organization, a big enterprise, and want to store their data (documents, emails, etc.) in the Cloud. It is very likely that a big part of their data is duplicated. Also, users will probably want to share several files with each other. In such a context, deduplication can be very effective and can greatly decrease the total amount of required storage space.

Deploying ClouDedup in the above-mentioned context would be straightforward. Users will manage their files through a client running on their machine. This client can be directly used from the user through a command line, a graphical interface or a web interface, or provide a different kind of interface such as FTP, SMB, etc. The gateway can be deployed on premises and will only be accessible by authorized users within the same network. The metadata manager can be deployed either in the Cloud, being hosted by a service provider, or

on premises, for those companies that do not want to trust an external service provider. Finally, the cloud storage provider can be a public provider such as Amazon S3, Dropbox, Google Drive, etc. or a local storage service such as OpenStack SWIFT.

Even though ClouDedup has been originally designed for an enterprise use-case, it may also be used for personal cloud storage without any particular adaptation. Indeed, the gateway (proxy) is a very simple component which is lightweight enough to be run on a laptop, while the metadata manager can be hosted by an external service provider, which can take care of the actual storage as well. In the particular case of personal cloud storage, the gateway may even be replaced by a simple software layer, providing the same functionalities. This way, deploying ClouDedup on a personal device to provide personal cloud storage, would be as easy as installing an application and communicating with a remote service provider.

Furthermore, thanks to its generic structure, ClouDedup can be easily adapted to any storage use-case which can benefit from data deduplication. ClouDedup may also work as storage end-point for applications and more complex systems in two possible ways: either by directly using ClouDedup's client in order to perform storage operations; or by developing a software layer called connector responsible for receiving storage requests sent by the application and forwarding them to ClouDedup. Of course, the latter would make much easier to integrate any application with ClouDedup. By providing software connectors, ClouDedup may communicate with applications compatible with NFS file-system, FTP, SMB, Amazon S3's API, CDMI and many other protocols.

Finally, thanks to software connectors, ClouDedup may cooperate with a backup system with the aim to provide high storage space savings together with data confidentiality. Indeed, it is well known that data generated by backup systems have a high degree of redundancy and duplicate content. For instance, between two consecutive snapshots, it is very likely that only a small fraction of the whole data has been modified, while the rest of the data is intact. In this scenario, block-level deduplication can guarantee huge storage space savings by storing only the data blocks that have been actually modified and increasing a reference counter for each of the other blocks. It has been measured that deduplication can offer savings up to 90-95% in backup applications (Opendedup, 2014).

CONCLUSION

We explained our motivations to design ClouDedup, our design goals and the technologies we have employed in order to guarantee confidentiality and block-level deduplication at the same time. Our proposed solution is built on top of convergent encryption. We proposed three core components: the client, the gateway and the metadata manager. In particular, the gateway is the core component

which adds an additional layer of symmetric encryption. We showed that the overhead of metadata management is minimal despite the requirements of bock-level deduplication. We explained the weaknesses of existing approaches and demonstrated that our proposed approach can fully address CE vulnerabilities and prevent malicious providers from accessing users' data.

We performed a preliminary evaluation of our solution in order to show that it can efficiently reduce costs and storage space in the cloud. Indeed, the storage space required to store metadata and encrypted keys is minimal for both users and the metadata manager. It is worth pointing out that our proposed solution provides a robust security layer which provides confidentiality and privacy without having an impact on the underlying deduplication technique. Each file is split into blocks by the client who applies the best possible chunking algorithm. When encrypted data blocks are received by the metadata manager, a hash of each block is calculated in order to compare it to the ones already stored. This task is completely independent from the chunking technique (Rabin fingerprint) used by clients. Also, all the encryptions performed in the system do not affect the deduplication effectiveness since the encryption is deterministic. Therefore, ClouDedup provides additional security on top of convergent encryption without having an impact on the deduplication rate.

We also performed a preliminary performance analysis in order to measure the overhead introduced by the additional components. The results of this analysis show that the overhead due to encrypted/decrypted blocks, deduplication and interaction with the cloud provider does not represent an obstacle to the adoption of our solution.

We also described the implementation of our proposed architecture, explained the role of each component and discussed the reasons behind our technological choices. It is important to point out that our architecture has been implemented with open-source, widespread and well-known technologies.

We are currently developing our solution and we aim to provide a complete performance analysis in comparison with the most popular cloud storage services and we will analyze performance for both unique files and duplicate files. Furthermore, thanks to the results obtained from the performance analysis, we will work on finding possible optimizations in terms of bandwidth, storage space and computation.

Also, we are investigating how ClouDedup can be further extended with other security features such as search over encrypted data (Bellare M. a., 2007) and data integrity checking (Bowers K. D., 2009). However, integrating such a scheme with these functionalities is challenging. Indeed, the additional encryption performed by the gateway and the requirement for deduplication prevent the adoption of existing solutions proposed in the literature.

Last but not least, we aim to study and design a set of innovative and efficient solutions in order to provide valuable features such as file sharing with fine-grained access control, replication over different cloud storage providers, parallel usage of multiple cloud storage providers and data migration from one cloud storage provider to another.

DISCUSSION

The PERFORMANCE section has been extended and now includes a more detailed explanation on the reason behind the performance overhead with respect to Amazon S3. Also, a simple and feasible solution has been proposed to improve performances of upload, download and delete operations.

To summarize, the source of the performance overhead is due to the interaction with the final storage component, which in our tests was an Amazon S3 bucket. By using a storage component with lower latency, such as a local file-system or an OpenStack Swift installation

deployed in the same network of the metadata manager, performances comparable to Amazon S3 can be achieved.

Finally, it is important to point out that performances can benefit from duplicate content (as we show in Figure 9), which is very likely in real scenarios. Therefore, the initial overhead is the price to pay to achieve high storage space savings without sacrificing data confidentiality.

REFERENCES

Amazon. (2014). *Amazon S3*. Retrieved from http://aws.amazon.com/s3/

Apache. (2014). *Apache Libcloud*. Retrieved from https://libcloud.apache.org/

Ateniese, G. a. (2007). Provable data possession at untrusted stores. In *Proceedings of the 14th ACM Conference on Computer and Communications Security* (pp. 598--609). Alexandria, VA: ACM. doi:10.1145/1315245.1315318

Bellare, M. a. (2007). Deterministic and Efficiently Searchable Encryption. Proceedings of the 27th Annual International Cryptology Conference on Advances in Cryptology (pp. 535–552). Santa Barbara, CA, USA: Springer-Verlag; Retrieved from http://dl.acm.org/citation.cfm?id=1777777.1777820

Bellare, M., Keelveedhi, S., & Ristenpart, T. (2013). Message-locked encryption and secure deduplication. In Advances in Cryptology--EUROCRYPT 2013 (pp. 296-312). Springer. doi:10.1007/978-3-642-38348-9_18

Bilenko, D. (2014). *Gevent*. Retrieved from http://www.gevent.org/

Bowers, K. D. (2009). HAIL: A high-availability and integrity layer for cloud storage. *Proceedings of the 16th ACM Conference on Computer and Communications Security* (pp. 187--198). Chicago, IL: ACM. doi:10.1145/1653662.1653686

Bowers, K. D., Juels, A., & Oprea, A. (2009). HAIL: A high-availability and integrity layer for cloud storage. In Proceedings of the 16th ACM conference on Computer and communications security (pp. 187–198). New York: ACM. doi:10.1145/1653662.1653686

Chang, V., Walters, R. J., & Wills, G. (2013). Cloud Storage and Bioinformatics in a private cloud deployment: Lessons for Data Intensive research. In *Cloud Computing and Services Science* (pp. 245–264). Springer International Publishing.

Cox, L. P., Murray, C. D., & Noble, B. D. (2002). Pastiche: Making backup cheap and easy. *ACM SIGOPS Operating Systems Review, 36*, 285-298.

Darnell, B. (2014). *Tornado*. Retrieved from http://tornado.readthedocs.org/en/latest/index.html

Douceur, J. R., Adya, A., Bolosky, W. J., Simon, P., & Theimer, M. (2002). Reclaiming space from duplicate files in a serverless distributed file system. In *Proceedings of the 22nd International Conference on Distributed Computing Systems, 2002* (pp. 617-624).

Dropbox. (2014). *Dropbox*. Retrieved from https://www.dropbox.com

Fielding, A. (1999). *HTTP/1.1: Protocol parameters*. Retrieved from http://www.w3.org/Protocols/rfc2616/rfc2616-sec3.html

Fielding, R. T. (2000). *Representational State Transfer*. Retrieved from http://www.ics.uci.edu/~fielding/pubs/dissertation/rest_arch_style.htm

GNU. (2014). *Python-GnuPG*. Retrieved from https://bitbucket.org/vinay.sajip/python-gnupg

GNU. (2014). *SKS OpenPGP keyserver*. Retrieved from https://packages.debian.org/search?keywords=sks

Google. (2014). *Google Drive*. Retrieved from https://drive.google.com

Haardt, H. (2014). *Py-convergent-encryption*. Retrieved from https://github.com/HITGmbH/py-convergent-encryption

Harnik, D., Pinkas, B., & Shulman-Peleg, A. (2010). Side channels in cloud services: Deduplication in cloud storage. *Security & Privacy, IEEE, 8*(6), 40-47.

Huang, A. (2014). *PyRabin*. Retrieved from https://github.com/aitjcize/pyrabin

Is convergent encryption really secure? (2011). Retrieved from http://crypto.stackexchange.com/questions/729/is-convergent-encryption-really-secure

Juels, A., & Kaliski, J. B. (2007). Pors: Proofs of retrievability for large files. In Proceedings of the 14th ACM conference on Computer and communications security (pp. 584–597). New York: ACM. doi:10.1145/1315245.1315317

Litzenberger, D. C. (2014). *PyCrypto*. Retrieved from https://github.com/dlitz/pycrypto

Meyer, D. T., & Bolosky, W. J. (2012). A study of practical deduplication. [TOS]. *ACM Transactions on Storage, 7*(4), 14. doi:10.1145/2078861.2078864

Opendedup. (2014). *Opendedup*. Retrieved from http://opendedup.org

OpenSSL. (2014). *OpenSSL*. Retrieved from http://www.openssl.org/

OpenStack. (2014). *OpenStack SWIFT*. Retrieved from https://www.openstack.org/software/openstack-storage/

Perttula. (2008). Attacks on convergent encryption. *Attacks on Convergent Encryption*.

Puzio, P. a. (2013). *ClouDedup: Secure deduplication with encrypted data for cloud storage. In IEEE CloudCom 2013. 1* (pp. 363–370). Bristol, UK: IEEE; doi:10.1109/CloudCom.2013.54

Rabin, M. O. (1981). *Fingerprinting by random polynomials*. Center for Research in Computing Technology, Aiken Computation Laboratory.

Reitz, K. (2014). *Requests*. Retrieved from http://docs.python-requests.org/en/latest/

SafeNet. (2014). *Hardware security modules*. Retrieved from http://www.safenet-inc.com/data-encryption/hardware-security-modules-hsms/

SafeNet. (2014). *Luna SA HSM*. Retrieved from http://www.safenet-inc.com/data-encryption/hardware-security-modules-hsms/luna-hsms-key-management/luna-sa-network-hsm/

Sanfilippo, S. (2014). *REDIS*. Retrieved from http://redis.io

Squid. (2014). *Squid proxy*. Retrieved from http://www.squid-cache.org/

Storer, M. W., Greenan, K., Long, D. D., & Miller, E. L. (2008). Secure data deduplication. In *Proceedings of the 4th ACM international workshop on Storage security and survivability* (pp. 1-10). doi:10.1145/1456469.1456471

The Measurement Factory. (2014). *eCAP*. Retrieved from http://www.e-cap.org/Home

Wilcox-O'Hearn, Z., & Warner, B. (2008). Tahoe: The least-authority filesystem. In *Proceedings of the 4th ACM international workshop on Storage security and survivability* (pp. 21-26). doi:10.1145/1456469.1456474

KEY TERMS AND DEFINITIONS

Cloud Computing: Cloud computing is a type of computing that relies on sharing computing resources rather than having local servers or personal devices to handle applications.

Cryptographic Hash Function: A function impossible to invert that can be used to map data of arbitrary size to data of fixed size, with slight differences in input data producing very big differences in output data.

Cryptographic Key: Piece of information (a parameter) that determines the functional output of a cryptographic algorithm or cipher.

Cryptographic Signature: A mathematical scheme for demonstrating the authenticity of a digital message or document.

Data Storage: A technology consisting of computer components and recording media used to retain digital data.

Encryption: The process of encoding messages or information in such a way that only authorized parties can read it.

Enterprise Encryption Gateway: An encryption device that allows for strong authentication and encryption for data.

Proxy: A server (a computer system or an application) that acts as an intermediary for requests from clients seeking resources from other servers.

Chapter 17
Management of Privacy and Security in Cloud Computing:
Contractual Controls in Service Agreements

Deniz Tuncalp
Istanbul Technical University, Turkey

ABSTRACT

There are a number of risk domains that are relevant for information privacy and security in cloud-based scenarios and alternative deployment models, which require implementation of a number of controls. However, cloud service providers often take a one-size-fits-all approach and want all their customers to accept the same standardized contract, regardless of their particular information security and legal compliance needs. Taking ISO 27001 Information Security Management standard as a guide, we have employed the Delphi method with a group of cloud computing experts from around the world who are subscribed to the "Cloud Computing" group on LinkedIN to identify the most applicable controls in a generic cloud service provider – customer context. Based on these results, we use a sample of cloud computing customer service agreement as a case study to further discuss related contingencies. As a result, this chapter argues that a more balanced approach is needed in service contracts to ensure the maintenance of necessary service levels and the protection of cloud users.

INTRODUCTION

The widespread diffusion of information and communication technologies (ICTs) has significantly altered the way people live and work. People spend significant portion of their time on and around computers in their daily lives. Companies utilize ICTs to perform and support all their business processes. ICTs are critical for the performance of the immediate operations, and the long-term survival of the organizations. The worldwide diffusion of ICTs not only brings personal, social and commercial changes, but also carries new risks to contemporary society. Compared to the functioning of the society in the pre-computer era, both personal and business uses of ICTs involve: generating, storing, processing, and transferring much larger amounts of information. The

DOI: 10.4018/978-1-4666-8210-8.ch017

Copyright © 2015, IGI Global. Copying or distributing in print or electronic forms without written permission of IGI Global is prohibited.

development and expansion of ICTs, therefore, affects individuals' right to information privacy. It is necessary to balance the societal benefits promised by new technology infrastructures and related business models with individual rights to information privacy and organizations need for information security. Thus, an adequate level of information privacy and security control is essential to ensure public and commercial trust in online services. This is especially crucial for the success of new technologies when they are first launched for public use.

INFORMATION PRIVACY AND SECURITY

In this chapter, information security is discussed in the context of privacy protection or the general personal data protection. For the purpose of this study, personal data protection is used as personal information privacy protection that includes the protection of data privacy and data security.

Warren and Brandeis (1890) defined the right to privacy as the right "to be left alone". Burgoon et al. (1989) distinguished four types of privacy violations: physical, interactional, psychological/ informational, and impersonal. DeCew (1997) divided privacy into three dimensions: informational, accessibility and expressive privacy. More recently Braman (2006) differentiated four aspects of privacy as spatial (home and body), communicative (mediated communication), relational (communication with professionals and spouse), and data (disclosure and/or use of personal information) privacy. In all these categorizations, information (data) privacy is a key dimension of privacy, which is defined by Westin (1967) as the amount of control that individuals can have over the type of information, and the extent of that information revealed to others. In this study, the discussion of privacy is limited to information privacy, which is often referred to as personal data.

Regarding personal information, Smith, Milberg, and Burke (1996) identified four dimensions of concerns about organizational privacy practices:

1. Unauthorized secondary use of personal information,
2. Improper access of personal information (internal and external),
3. Collection of personal information, and
4. Errors in collected personal information.

These dimensions indicate that information privacy practices cover data collection, data use, data disclosure, and data quality. The dimension of external improper access of personal information and the other dimensions also contain the component of data security (Chang & Ramachandran, 2014).

The concept of information privacy emerged in the 1960s and 1970s, at about the same time as data protection (Bennett, 2002). Although debates on information privacy protection are not new, advances in ICT threaten individuals' privacy more easily and pervasively than ever before because of the increased ability to collect, assemble, and distribute personal information, particularly on the Internet. Personal information privacy in the digital age has increased in salience and has been discussed in various fields, such as public policy, law, and Internet study worldwide (e.g., Baumer, Earp, & Poindexter, 2004; Banisar & Davies, n.d.; Baumer, Earp, & Poindexter, 2004; Bennett, 2002; Buchanan, Paine, Joinson, & Reaps, 2007; Zwick, 1999).

Information Security is "the protection of information from a wide range of threats in order to ensure business continuity, minimize business risk, and maximize return on investments and business opportunities" (International Organization for Standardization [ISO], 2005). ISO has published ISO 27001 standard in 2005 to provide guidance to organizations that want to manage their information security with a management system with explicit controls and policies. The ISO 27001 standard not only specifies a management system for information security, but also lists a set of applicable controls for the protection of relevant information assets in an organizational scope. Organizations are advised to define the scope of their information security risk management system, to make an inventory of their information assets and to evaluate each asset against the set of controls to control the information security risks associated with each and every asset in their protection scope effectively. The list of controls in Annex A of the ISO 27001 standard stands for an industry standard that covers a wide range of possible information security control categories addressing specific objectives. We used these control categories to identify applicable control categories in our study, in addition to those controls identified during our Delphi rounds:

- **Control Category: Security Policy**
  - "**Information Security Policy:** To provide management direction and support for information security in accordance with business requirements and relevant laws and regulations." (ISO, 2005, p. 13)
- **Control Category: Organization of Information Security**
  - "**Internal Organization:** To manage information security within the organization." (ISO, 2005, p. 13)
  - "**External Parties:** To maintain the security of the organization's information and information processing facilities that are accessed, processed, communicated to, or managed by external parties." (ISO, 2005, p. 14)
- **Control Category: Asset Management**
  - "**Responsibility for Assets:** To achieve and maintain appropriate protection of organizational assets." (ISO, 2005, p. 15)
  - "**Information Classification:** To ensure that information receives an appropriate level of protection." (ISO, 2005, p. 15)

- **Control Category: Human Resources Security**
  - "**Prior to Employment:** To ensure that employees, contractors and third party users understand their responsibilities, and are suitable for the roles they are considered for, and to reduce the risk of theft, fraud or misuse of facilities." (ISO, 2005, p. 15)
  - "**During Employment:** To ensure that all employees, contractors and third party users are aware of information security threats and concerns, their responsibilities and liabilities, and are equipped to support organizational security policy in the course of their normal work, and to reduce the risk of human error." (ISO, 2005, p. 16)
  - "**Termination or Change of Employment:** To ensure that employees, contractors and third party users exit an organization or change employment in an orderly manner." (ISO, 2005, p. 16)
- **Control Category: Physical and Environmental Security**
  - "**Secure Areas:** To prevent unauthorized physical access, damage and interference to the organization's premises and information." (ISO, 2005, p. 17)
  - "**Equipment Security:** To prevent loss, damage, theft or compromise of assets and interruption to the organization's activities." (ISO, 2005, p. 17)
- **Control Category: Communication and Operational Management**
  - "**Operational Procedures and Responsibilities:** To ensure the correct and secure operation of information processing facilities." (ISO, 2005, p. 18)

- "**Third Party Service Delivery Management:** To implement and maintain the appropriate level of information security and service delivery in line with third party service delivery agreements." (ISO, 2005, p. 18)
- "**System Planning and Acceptance:** To implement and maintain the appropriate level of information security and service delivery in line with third party service delivery agreements." (ISO, 2005, p. 19)
- "**Protection Against Malicious and Mobile Code:** To protect the integrity of software and information." (ISO, 2005, p. 19)
- "**Back-Up:** To maintain the integrity and availability of information and information processing facilities." (ISO, 2005, p.19)
- "**Network Security Management:** To ensure the protection of information in networks and the protection of the supporting infrastructure." (ISO, 2005, p. 20)
- "**Media Handling:** To prevent unauthorized disclosure, modification, removal or destruction of assets, and interruption to business activities." (ISO, 2005, p. 20)
- "**Exchange of Information:** To maintain the security of information and software exchanged within an organization and with any external entity." (ISO, 2005, p. 20)
- "**Electronic Commerce Services:** To ensure the security of electronic commerce services, and their secure use." (ISO, 2005, p. 21)
- "**Monitoring:** To detect unauthorized information processing activities." (ISO, 2005, p. 21)

- **Control Category: Access Control**
  - "**Business Requirement for Access Control:** To control access to information." (ISO, 2005, p. 22)
  - "**User Access Management:** To ensure authorized user access and to prevent unauthorized access to information systems." (ISO, 2005, p. 22)
  - "**User Responsibilities:** To prevent unauthorized user access, and compromise or theft of information and information processing facilities." (ISO, 2005, p. 22)
  - "**Network Access Control:** To prevent unauthorized access to networked services." (ISO, 2005, p. 23)
  - "**Operating System Access Control:** To prevent unauthorized access to operating systems." (ISO, 2005, p. 23)
  - "**Application and Information Access Control:** To prevent unauthorized access to information held in application systems." (ISO, 2005, p. 24)
  - "**Mobile Computing and Teleworking:** To ensure information security when using mobile computing and teleworking facilities." (ISO, 2005, p. 24)
- **Control Category: Information Systems Acquisition, Development, and Maintenance**
  - "**Security Requirements of Information Systems:** To ensure that security is an integral part of information systems." (ISO, 2005, p. 24)
  - "**Correct Processing in Applications:** To prevent errors, loss, unauthorized modification or misuse of information in applications." (ISO, 2005, p. 25)
  - "**Cryptographic Controls:** To protect the confidentiality, authenticity or integrity of information by cryptographic means." (ISO, 2005, pp. 13-28)

- ○ **"Security of System Files:** To ensure the security of system files." (ISO, 2005, p. 25)
- ○ **"Security in Development and Support Processes:** To maintain the security of application system software and information." (ISO, 2005, p. 26)
- ○ **"Technical Vulnerability Management:** To reduce risks resulting from exploitation of published technical vulnerabilities." (ISO, 2005, p. 26)
- **Control Category: Incident Management**
  - ○ **"Reporting Information Security Events and Weaknesses:** To ensure information security events and weaknesses associated with information systems are communicated in a manner allowing timely corrective action to be taken." (ISO, 2005, p. 26)
  - ○ **"Management of Information Security Incidents and Improvements:** To ensure a consistent and effective approach is applied to the management of information security incidents." (ISO, 2005, p. 27)
- **Control Category: Business Continuity Planning**
  - ○ **"Information Security Aspects of Business Continuity Management:** To counteract interruptions to business activities and to protect critical business processes from the effects of major failures of information systems or disasters and to ensure their timely resumption." (ISO, 2005, p. 27)
- **Control Category: Compliance**
  - ○ **"Compliance with Legal Requirements:** To avoid breaches of any law, statutory, regulatory or contractual obligations, and of any security requirements." (ISO, 2005, p. 28)

- ○ **"Compliance with Security Policies and Standards, and Technical Compliance:** To ensure compliance of systems with organizational security policies and standards." (ISO, 2005, p. 28)
- ○ **"Information Systems Audit Considerations:** To maximize the effectiveness of and to minimize interference to/from the information systems audit process." (ISO, 2005, p. 29)
- **Control Category: Legal and Regulatory Disclosure**
  - ○ "Lawfully mandated disclosure of information to legal and/or regulatory parties." (Expert panel opinion in the round 1 of the study)
- **Control Category: Post Termination Assistance**
  - ○ "Ensuring clear description of responsibilities in the transition of the relevant services either back to the customer systems or to the replacement provider." (Expert panel opinion in the round 1 of the study)
- **Control Category: Privacy of Third Parties**
  - ○ "Privacy of personal information and data related to third parties that are expressively authorized without any withdrawal to be processed on the systems." (Expert panel opinion in the round 1 of the study)

The control categories and objectives given above are the most crucial, because they come from an internationally accepted information security best practice, known as the ISO 27001 standard or from our world-wide panel of cloud-computing experts. We have also supplemented the list with three specific control categories that are identified by our expert panel with diverse experience bases, specifically for cloud computing.

Cloud Computing

Cloud Computing is an advanced technological model to host and share software and hardware over the Internet. In this way, different organizations may pool their IT resources via large-scale providers but virtually use logically separate resources. Therefore, they may scale upwards or downwards when required, without purchasing and setting up those resources physically on their premises (Voorsluys, Brober, & Buyya, 2011).

The National Institute of Standards and Technology (NIST) of the United States, defines cloud computing as a "model for enabling convenient, on-demand network access to a shared pool of configurable computing resources (e.g., networks, servers, storage, applications, and services) that can be rapidly provisioned and released with minimal management effort or service provider interaction" (Mell & Grance, 2011). Cloud infrastructures have measured and on-demand self-service capabilities that are available via network access for different client devices. It also has the advantage of pooling and sharing of resources with elastic provisioning for sudden increases in demand. Since the introduction of the cloud model, various service providers have offered a wide range of services. NIST defines three basic types of service models for cloud computing:

- **Software as a Service (SaaS):** The capability provided is to use the provider's applications running on a cloud infrastructure. Customer has limited or no control, even on application configuration settings.
- **Platform as a Service (PaaS):** The capability provided is to deploy consumer-created or acquired applications onto the cloud infrastructure. Customer has control over the deployed applications and possibly over the application hosting environment configurations.

- **Infrastructure as a Service (IaaS):** The capability provided is to provision processing, storage, networks, and other fundamental computing resources where the consumer is able to deploy and run software of choice, which may include operating systems and applications. Customer has control over operating systems, storage, deployed applications, and possibly limited control of select networking components like host firewalls.

In all these models, customers do not manage or control the underlying cloud infrastructure including network, servers, operating systems, or storage. In addition to these models, NIST define four types of clouds according to its deployment: private, public, hybrid and community clouds, with different capabilities and requirements (Mell & Grance, 2009).

Cloud computing has brought new sets of opportunities for businesses, governments, and consumers. Gartner Group, a well-known and influential global strategic information technology (IT) consulting company, has listed cloud computing as one of the top10 issues that has the potential to reinvent and transform the IT industry (Pettey, 2011). Forrester Research, another famous IT consulting-house, has estimated the global cloud market to reach USD 241 billion by year 2020 (Ried, Kisker, Matzke, Bartels, & Lisserman, 2011). However, it also brought new risks and respective legal implications. These should be addressed effectively in service contracts to reap cloud benefits. It may give rise to new and significant information privacy and security questions, due to its complex and distributed service model. For example, due to nature of the service, client companies have limited control over the cloud infrastructure. This may give rise to privacy and security of business and customer data stored in the cloud (Voorsluys, Brober, & Buyya, 2011). There are business risks involved and thus a comprehensive solution such as business intelligence as a service should be used to identify risk and return for the investors and stakeholders (Chang, 2014). Furthermore, this lack of control may lead to concerns about integrity and availability of cloud services. Migration to cloud is a significant, and potentially one-way decision, as moving back to conventional IT structures may be very costly to implement once you are on the cloud. However, as strategic choices emerge, companies should be able to switch one provider to another.

As these examples illustrate, different roles and responsibilities exist in a cloud-computing scenario and due to the novelty of the related business models, there are significant questions to be answered in service agreements. For example, in a typical cloud-computing scenario, which technical and legal rights does a service provider need directly or indirectly for accessing personal data and what access rights should be granted to users? These are very relevant questions for data protection. In more complex business scenarios, questions become even more complicated. For example, in a multinational scenario, what data protection issues might be relevant as companies start using foreign cloud providers, where different forms of data and their processing might be scattered over different countries and jurisdictions? Therefore, methods of addressing issues of information privacy and security on corresponding service contracts are crucially important.

While this paper tries to identify major risk items and respective controls for information privacy and security, it does not try to be an exhaustive and detailed analysis of all relevant risks and controls involved. Our target is to pinpoint the most significant of those risks and assess how they might be controlled with different clauses on a typical service provider contract. For a detailed analysis of cloud computing risks and security issues, we recommend readers to visit Chang, Walters, and Wills (2014), Bisong and Rahman (2011), Onwubiko (2010), and Mather, Kumaraswamy and Latif (2009).

In the next section, we introduce our methodology. In the third section, we present results of our first round of results covering applicable controls for information privacy and security in cloud environment. In the fourth section, we analyze a sample cloud-computing contract as the case study and discuss what alternative clauses need to cover for different security controls. In the last section, we conclude with a discussion of how information security, privacy and data protection issues can be addressed in cloud computing service contracts.

METHODOLOGY

In our study, we have employed the Delphi method to a group of cloud computing experts to understand their consensus on the most applicable information security controls for cloud computing environment in a generic service provider – customer context. We have used ISO 27001: 2005 Information Security Management standard, as a comprehensive guide of available information security controls and supplemented that with initial views of cloud computing experts participating to our panel. We considered seeking expert opinion and consensus with the Delphi method as the most appropriate, as this is a new topical area that has not matured yet with extant literature.

The Delphi Method

The Delphi method was first developed and applied in the 1950's by the RAND Corporation, to address a specific military issue and forecast potential military needs of the United States Air Force (Dalkey & Helmer, 1951; Helmer, 1965). It sought future projections on the problem with participation of a panel of experts in a series of face-to-face group meetings and rounds of surveys with a feedback process (Linstone & Turoff, 1975).

Validity and reliability of the Delphi Method highly depends on the selection of the expert panel. In this method, panel participants are selected using reputational sampling, which does not seek for a representative sample, but looks for highly experienced practitioners based on their reputation. Tashakkori and Teddlie (2008) describe reputational sampling as a method of purposive sampling, where sampling is made "to achieve comparability across different types of cases on a dimension of interest" (p. 175). The method assumes that a small group of participants with high level of expertise, is more desirable than a large group of ordinary participants (e.g., random survey takers) and thus former alternative is more capable of understanding and indirectly discussing on a problem and reaching consensus. While this type of sampling may create some generalization problems (Tashakkori & Teddlie, 2008), the validity and reliability of the results is built into the Delphi process and collection of reliable data from experienced professionals (Dalkey & Helmer, 1951; Helmer, 1965; Linstone & Turoff, 1975; Scheibe, Skutsch, & Schofer, 1975). As Gray et al. (2007) noted, reputational sampling "will not produce a broadly representative sample" (p. 117) but will be an invaluable tool for "gaining access to informed and experienced people who may provide in-depth information available nowhere else" (p. 118). Landeta (2006) further discussed the general validity of the Delphi Method and noted that it "can be adapted to different social realities and requirements, making a positive contribution to social progress provided it is applied with the necessary methodological rigour" (p. 472). He considered that contacting the panel of experts during the Delphi process is very enlightening and methodologically it is widely accepted in the scientific community. He reports that the use of the Delphi Method in research has increased in the last 30 years with very significant proliferation after year 2000-2005. A brief search on literature databases also reveals that the trend has also been continuing in the last 10 years.

Mitroff and Turoff (1975) describe philosophical foundations of the Delphi Method as a constructed truth achieved by a group of experienced practitioners, as they suggest there is no absolute truth (Popper, 1963). Mitroff and Turoff (1975) suggest that truth is experiential and is entirely associated with the empirical content of communication. According to this perspective, truth is dependent on our ability to reduce complex propositions down to simple empirical referents (i.e., simple observations) and to ensure their validity by means of the widespread, freely obtained agreement between different human observers (Mitroff & Turoff, 1975, p. 45). In order to achieve this, we have selected experts on our panel using procedures outlined in Linstone and Turoff (1975). They recommend that panels can be of any size, however they recommend a small, experienced and diverse panel for most research.

In the original Delphi method, the objective is to develop forecasts and future projections on the topic of interest. Expert panel members meet directly in a conventional meeting setup. However, forecasts and future projections may not be created as the outcome of an expert panel consensus. Face-to-face meeting format may also create some social pressure for reaching a premature agreement or may create extended contestation due to group dynamics. Physically bringing people together is also costly and makes it impossible to cover a globally diverse team of experts. Due to its historical nature, novel communication capabilities are also not utilized in the regular Delphi process. In order to solve these problems and to tap mentioned potentials, the Delphi method is modified in this research.

Modifications in the Delphi Method

Modified Delphi Method has actually emerged during 1970s and 1980s to enhance consensus building on a particular research question (Custer, Scarcella, & Stewart, 1999). Turoff (1975) suggests that the modifications to the Delphi Method can be done depending on the specific research project. For example, he generated "the Policy Delphi" version, aiming to generate opposing opinions rather than consensus.

In our version of the modified Delphi method, we have deviated from the original Delphi Method by:

- Seeking consensus rather than forecasts and future projections,
- Introducing solely online and process mediated interaction with informant anonymity among experts, and
- Employing technology by online surveys and email notifications.

Avoiding face-to-face interaction among the panel members and enabling their anonymity helps us to collect opinions of panel members in a neutral environment, encouraging free expression and avoiding group pressures. Face-to-face interactions in a Delphi panel has been reported to create problems in collecting alternative views due to group dynamics, personality differences and even use of body language (Adler & Ziglio, 1996). Since participants face every comment and statement of every member, it may also limit idea generation. Face-to-face group meetings also create logistics problems and limit diversity of the expert panel involved. Above modifications helped us avoiding such problems, maximize expert panel diversity and the cumulative experience.

In our modified version of the Delphi method, experts' opinions are collected with an open-ended survey at the first stage, without any initial face-to-face, in-depth discussion. In a number of rounds, opinions are combined, organized and predicted to extract valid factors consistently. As more people participate in the process, wisdom of larger groups is expected to supplement missing knowledge more objectively, which is called quantitative objectivity (Gaukroger, 2012). In this method, experts participate in a survey to express their opinions without any restriction. These views are then organized as representative views and shown back to the participating experts. They are then asked to reconsider their earlier judgment. These rounds continue until the opinions converge to an acceptable degree, usually in two-to-five rounds (Linstone & Turoff, 1975).

Our Delphi Method Implementation

Since we wanted to identify relevant information security controls for cloud computing, using reputational sampling as a basis for panel selection, we had selected 30 cloud computing experts subscribed to the "Cloud Computing" group on LinkedIN, which has more than 250,000 expert members worldwide. We first randomly select a group of experts; prescreened their level of expertise on cloud computing from their LinkedIN profile, contacted them individually to describe the study, asking whether they would identify themselves as cloud experts, whether they are currently working for a client company rather than a cloud provider, and their acceptance to participate in this study. Screening continued until we reached 30 participants across the world, identifying themselves as cloud experts working in client companies other than cloud providers. We had purposefully avoided including cloud providers in our study, to avoid potential provider biasness towards security measures in protecting security and privacy of cloud users. While sampling, we had also employed a stratified sampling strategy according to geographical regions of the world and selected 10 from each of the following three geographical areas to ensure diversity: North America, Europe and elsewhere. Our resulting panel members represent a large variety of experience base, from cloud service planning, to vendor selection, cloud operation to cloud service transfer. Majority of our panel (96.7%) had more than five years of experience in information technology departments. Almost half of the members of this group (46.7%) had more than ten years of experience. 83.3% of our panel members were male, and almost 87% of the members were in their 30s. Also half of our panel was working in a managerial position in an IT department, whereas the other half was made up of team members. The demographic figures of our panel members are given in Table 1.

Table 1. Expert panel demographics

Age	n	%	Experience	n	%
20s	1	3.3	0-5 years	1	3.3
30s	26	86.6	5-10 years	15	50.0
40s	3	10	10+ years	14	46.7
Total	30	100%	Total	30	100%
Gender	**n**	**%**	**Role**	**n**	**%**
Male	25	83.3	Manager	15	50.0
Female	5	16.7	Member	15	50.0
Total	30	100%	Total	30	100%

Through collection of expert opinions with an open-ended survey in the first round, solicitation of collected declarative statements and subsequent rounds of Likert-scale questionnaires, we sought consensus of experienced practitioners on our panel systematically concerning information security management in cloud computing. We performed the Delphi process in three rounds and contacted the expert panel three times, asking them separate questions seeking their consensus without bringing them together in a meeting room:

1. In the first round, we asked panel members to generate their opinions freely with a brief open-ended questionnaire, asking what was important in terms of information security and privacy in cloud computing. In order not to limit or direct their comments, we did not present ISO 27001 standard items to them at this stage. Information security issues and controls suggested by each panel member were then organized and sorted, eliminating the repeated items. While processing and organizing panel opinions on our side, we started employing ISO 27001 standard for the second round, and mapped panel ideas to control categories mentioned in the standard.

2. In the second round, the panel members were provided with the grouped security controls for cloud computing, together with every other control categories listed in ISO

27001 standard. We had only delisted the "security policy" and "organization of information security" control categories, due to their general and encompassing nature. Panel members were then asked to rank their importance on a 5-point Likert scale. When questionnaires were returned, we calculated the mean, median and mode values for each security control and presented the values back to panel members for consideration in the next round.

3. In the third round, we asked our panel members to re-rate the importance of each factor on the same scale. Our target was to increase consensus among the panel members by reporting central tendency values of the entire panel and giving an opportunity to revise their earlier thoughts. Our Delphi procedure is summarized in Table 2. Our Delphi surveys, namely Round-0: Screening (see Table 7), Round-1: Opinion Gathering (see Table 8), Round-2: Initial Rating (see Table 9) and Round-3: Re-rating (see Table 10) are given in the Appendix.

Dedication and engagement of experts are critical for the results of any Delphi study. Since we had removed time and distance barriers with no face-to-face meetings and online anonymous interaction, the panel members stayed engaged through the three rounds. Since we had asked every panel

Table 2. Our Delphi procedure

Panel Formation	Select a panel of 30 experts, 10 from each of three areas: North America, Europe and Elsewhere.	
Round 1	• Collect opinions on information security controls that are necessary for cloud computing from each panel participant. • Sort and organize the derived controls, removing repeating controls/issues. • Design the questionnaire for Round 2.	3 weeks
Round 2	• Ask panel members to assess cloud information security controls on a 5-point Likert scale. • ISO 27001 controls presented together with panel opinions generated in the previous round.	3 weeks
Round 3	• Ask panel members to re-rate the importance of each security control identified. • Mean, median, and mode values for each control are presented back. • Verify the agreement level between panel members.	2 weeks

member to commit to the entire Delphi process with approximately three rounds, there was no change in the participant sample throughout the study.

Based on our results from the Modified Delphi Method, we used a cloud computing customer service agreement of a service provider as a case study, to discuss related contingencies further from a data protection perspective. Alternative clauses are designed based on the issues detected to provide guidance to different cloud customers with different information security needs.

RESULTS

Since the central aim in the Delphi Method is to seek consensus, descriptive statistics such as central tendency measures (mean, median, and mode) and dispersion measures (standard deviation and inter-quartile range) have been used to report information about the collective judgments and the level of consensus of the expert panel.

In the first stage of our Delphi study, the factors suggested by the experts were grouped into different categories. In the second stage, we had prepared a questionnaire, which combined the results of the first stage with all of the control categories of ISO 27001 standard. We presented all these categories with their descriptions and asked the panel input for each of them with a 5-point Likert scale. At this stage we had calculated the mean, median, mode, standard deviation and interquartile range for each item (See Table 3).

Results of the second round shows that there is a significant agreement over importance of most of the controls, the highest level of agreement is about the "Post Termination Assistance" with IQR = 0.00. The greatest discrepancy among the expert panel were on "Human Resources Security" and "Communication and Operational Management" specifically for cloud context. The other controls had relatively satisfying consensus level about their importance at the second round. Standard deviations with these items are also higher than 1, showing a significant level of divergence among the panel members. While there is some level of consensus on many of the items, we had presented every item in the third round to double-check the level of consensus and gave an opportunity to our panel members to reflect and possibly change their ideas in the third round.

In the third stage, the same questionnaire had been utilized, together with the results calculated. The panel was asked to reconsider their assessment in the previous round. This aimed to help panel members to think about their earlier considerations again, reflect other people's responses and therefore to help the assessment results to converge. As intended the level of standard deviation for almost every item had dropped and the ordering of some of the items had marginally changed. While the change of this ordering was not significant, the achieved convergence showed that the panel experts had reconsidered and revised their earlier responses. The results of this round are presented In Table 4.

Table 3. Information security control categories after Delphi round 2

Category	Mean Score	Median Score	Mode Score	Standard Deviation	Interquartile Range
Data Protection and Privacy	4.53	5	5	0.629	1
Information Leakage	4.27	4	5	0.785	1
Legal and Regulatory Disclosure	4.13	4	4	0.819	1
Post Termination Assistance	3.93	4	4	0.828	0
Access Control	3.63	4	4	0.89	1
Audit Logging	3.47	4	4	0.629	1
Privacy of Third Parties	3.33	3	3	0.661	1
Comm. & Oper. Management	2.73	3	3	1.258	1.75
Business Continuity Planning	2.67	3	2	0.959	1
Human Resources Security	2.07	2	1	1.172	2
Physical & Env. Security	1.8	2	2	0.714	1
IS Acq., Dev. & Maintenance	1.73	2	1	0.868	1
Asset Management	1.43	1	1	0.626	1

1: Strongly disagree - 5: strongly agree.

In the third round, all IQR values had dropped to 1 and below, showing sufficient level of consensus on the importance of control categories for security of cloud computing. The highest level of agreement with post termination assis- tance remained. Whereas, legal and regulatory disclosure also achieved highest consensus with IQR=0 compared to other control categories. All standard deviation results, regardless of their mean importance scores, also had dropped below

Table 4. Information security control categories after round 3

Category	Mean Score	Median Score	Mode Score	Standard Deviation	Interquartile Range
Data Protection and Privacy	4.63	5	5	0.49	1
Information Leakage	4.37	4	4	0.49	1
Post Termination Assistance	4.1	4	4	0.481	0
Legal and Regulatory Disclosure	4.07	4	4	0.45	0
Access Control	3.63	4	4	0.615	1
Audit Logging	3.33	3	3	0.479	1
Privacy of Third Parties	3.3	3	3	0.651	1
Comm. & Oper. Management	2.57	2	2	0.774	1
Business Continuity Planning	2.47	2	2	0.681	1
Human Resources Security	1.87	2	2	0.681	1
Physical & Env. Security	1.77	2	2	0.626	1
IS Acq., Dev. & Maintenance	1.53	2	2	0.507	1
Asset Management	1.37	1	1	0.556	1

1: Strongly disagree - 5: strongly agree.

1. Six control categories received a mean score higher than 3 in terms of its importance to cloud computing. These control categories are "Data Protection and Privacy", "Information Leakage", "Post Termination Assistance", "Legal and Regulatory Disclosure", "Access Control", "Audit Logging" and "Privacy of Third Parties". These items also have median and mode values are also higher than 3. 5 of those 7 items have a standard deviation less than 0.5, showing strong consensus among the panel members.

Parametric tests such as t-test are not applicable for Delphi studies employing interval scales like Likert. Because such test are normally applicable to continuous variables. Therefore, in addition to descriptive statistics, non-parametric tests may also be employed. The most common of those methods for Delphi studies are Friedman test of the changes in scores across the rounds, and Mann-Whitney 'U' test to differences between different sets of desirability scores. Since we reached a satisfactory level of consensus on almost all items, we chose to analyze the significance of differences between scores of control categories after Round 3 using Mann-Whitney 'U' test.

The Mann-Whitney test is a nonparametric test that allows two groups to be compared without assuming normal distribution. While using the test, a statistic called U score is calculated, indicating whether the test results can be used. The distribution of U under the null hypothesis is known and tabulated, in the case of small samples. We employed Mann-Whitney 'U' test, to compare desirability score of every control category with another category with adjacent mean score, to see whether their differences are significant. For example, we compared "Data Protection and Privacy" with "Information Leakage", "Information Leakage" with "Post Termination Assistance" and so on. Results of Mann-Whitney 'U' test, Z-scores and p-values, significance results and U-values are calculated and shown in Table 5. All U-values were found to be satisfactory and the results can be used.

According to Mann-Whitney 'U' test results, differences in scores between the following control categories are not significant:

- "Post Termination Assistance" and "Legal and Regulatory Disclosure",

Table 5. Differences between preceding control categories

Category	Z-Score	p-Value	Significance at p ≤ 0.05	U-Value
Data Protection and Privacy	1.7667	0.03836	significant	330
Information Leakage	1.8259	0.03362	significant	326
Post Termination Assistance	0.1996	0.42074	not significant	436
Legal and Regulatory Disclosure	2.5207	0.00587	significant	279
Access Control	1.6928	0.04551	significant	335
Audit Logging	0.0074	0.49601	not significant	450
Privacy of Third Parties	3.3413	0.00042	significant	223.5
Comm. & Oper. Management	0.3844	0.35197	not significant	423.5
Business Continuity Planning	2.7869	0.00264	significant	261
Human Resources Security	0.4879	0.31207	not significant	416.5
Physical & Env. Security	1.2345	0.10935	not significant	366
IS Acq., Dev. & Maintenance	1.2049	0.11507	not significant	368
Asset Management	-	-	-	-

- "Audit Logging" and "Privacy of Third Parties",
- "Communications & Operational Management" and "Business Continuity Planning",
- "Human Resources Security", "Physical and Environmental Security", "Information Systems Acquisition", "Development and Maintenance" and "Asset Management".

Our cut-off point, where the mean, median and mode scores drop below 3 over 5-point Likert scale, namely the difference between "Privacy of Third Parties" and "Communication and Operational Management" categories found to be significant. Using these results, we drew a hierarchy of relevant control categories for cloud computing at 7 levels, considering significant and not significant differences between control categories with adjacent mean scores from the Delphi study (See Figure 1).

Based on our results, we analyzed a cloud service contract and discussed the alternative issues that needed to be included in service contract clauses in the light of our results in the Delphi study in the next section.

SECURITY AND PRIVACY CLAUSES OF A CLOUD COMPUTING CONTRACT

In this section, we analyze, discuss and propose alternative clauses for a cloud computing service contract to address current state and the potential alternatives of the identified control categories. We have used the results of our Delphi study that as our focus area to identify what clauses are currently available and what alternative clauses might be applicable for information security and privacy in cloud computing.

Figure 1. Hierarchy of control categories for cloud computing

Level-1	**Data Protection and Privacy:** One sided or non-existent, warranties disclaimed.
Level-2	**Information Leakage:** Not mentioned.

Level-3	**Post Termination Assistance:** Not provided regularly and contractually. Arbitrary provision is possible at the service provider discretion.	**Legal and Regulatory Disclosure:** Ensured in a one sided manner without any customer notice.

Level-4	**Access Control:** Not mentioned.

Level-5	**Audit Logging:** Not mentioned.	**Privacy of Third Parties:** Only privacy of third parties that are in relationship to service provider. No mention for service provider's actions or privacy policy.

Disclaiming Data Protection Responsibility

The sample cloud computing service contract we analyzed is written to primarily protect the service provider. It actively disclaims any responsibility in information security and privacy in multiple points of the service contract, suggesting security breaches to sensitive data and applications are almost natural parts of the nature of the Internet. Instead of taking responsibilities and outlining the security controls implemented on the service provider side, it takes a consultative tone and suggests security controls like using encryption technology, routinely archiving and applying latest security patches or updates. The service provider also declares that it is not responsible of any unauthorized access or use, corruption, deletion, destruction or loss of applications or data.

Despite the security clause provided above, it also disclaims further potential responsibilities in a separate clause. In that clause, the service provider disclaims giving warranties of any kind about the cloud service, including merchantability, satisfactory quality, fitness for a particular purpose, non-infringement and any trade-related warranties.

The service provider does not give any warranty about the service offerings. It does not promise the service will function as described, run interruptedly or function in an error free manner. It also does not give any assurance that the service components or data are protected and secure. As cloud customers trust all their data and applications to cloud providers, we believe disclaiming any data privacy, security and integrity is a very strong contractual statement.

Disclosure to Government, Legal, and Regulatory Authorities

Potential disclosure and related notices to the customer have been mentioned once in the service contract, in a passing reference. The service provider takes no responsibility in giving a notice to the customer about related legal or regulatory demands when possible. Therefore, regardless of the jurisdiction of the customer, the service provider or related cloud infrastructures' physical location, legal disclosure is preserved as a right to all regulatory authorities, without even giving a notice to the data and/or application owner.

Data Preservation in the Event of Suspension or Termination

In the contract, the service provider lists several conditions where it can suspend or terminate the service unilaterally. The clause also describes the resulting consequences on private data and application of cloud customer. According to this term, the service provider will not erase any of customer data during suspension of customer, due to payment settlement problems etc., whereas in a termination event, the data and application is preserved for 30 days after the effective day of termination. Customers can only retrieve their data if they pay all incurred charges for the period following the termination of the agreement and the customers' compliance with any terms and conditions the service provider may establish about such data retrieval. Clearly, this clause is highly arbitrary and quite one sided, as relative terms and conditions that the service provider may impose for post-termination period is not defined or described in the contract. Other than these conditions, the service provider also disclaims any obligation about data storage and protection, or providing any permit to customer for data retrieval.

Post Termination Assistance

According to the service contract, the service provider does not take the liability for comprehensive post-termination assistance, but it only promises that it 'may elect to make that available'. If we consider how much the customer is tied to the cloud provider during service duration, this is also a highly one-sided and arbitrary statement. The service provider gives no promises and actively denies any obligation to provide post-suspension or post-termination assistance. These services, if they have been provided by the service provider at all, either generally or specifically and uniquely to a customer, will be subject to unspecified fees and conditions, at the time of the cloud service contract acceptance.

Privacy of Third Parties

Privacy of third parties is mentioned only in two passing references in the contract. One of them is about limiting potential spam attempts from one customer to other customers, business partners etc. whose information may be collected from the service provider sites and services, which shouldn't be disclosed on the service provider properties. Clearly this clause aims to protect third parties from the service provider side. It does not cover every third party and does not limit service provider's actions. It only tries to impose controls on the customer side. However, a symmetric clause prohibiting service providers' use of third party data entrusted to the cloud systems by the cloud customer is non-existent.

The second reference to third party privacy is specified in listing the responsibilities of the customer about its application. In this reference, service provider holds customer responsible for providing a privacy policy or explanation of how third party data is handled and used in its own application. The clause does not mention the service provider's own privacy policy reference.

Overall Assessment

After making an overall assessment of the cloud service contract, three of the seven control categories identified in our Delphi Study are not mentioned. These are: "Information Leakage", "Access Control" and "Audit Logging". This is a major deficiency from the cloud customer perspec-

tive. Rights and responsibilities of both parties in such cases need to be described. However, as the other issues have been considered in a very unbalanced way, the contract being silent on these issues may even be for the benefit of the cloud customer. Because, already mentioned control categories are handled in a one-sided, unbalanced manner. For example, "Data Protection and Privacy" related clauses do not give any assurance or warranties for any kind of suitable performance for the cloud user. "Post Termination Assistance" is not provided as a proper service and it is only promised as an arbitrary and conditional service that may be provided in the future, without any specific terms and conditions today. The service provider also declares its rights to disclose customer data to legal and regulatory bodies in its jurisdiction. However, it does not give any promise to acknowledge such disclosure to the owners of the data. Similarly, only privacy of third parties that are in relationship with the service provider is mentioned and customers required providing a privacy policy to their own customers. However, the service provider's own privacy policy is not mentioned (See Figure 2).

Since customer contracts need to define and regulate rights and responsibilities of respective parties, a more balanced approach is needed. In the next section, we will describe alternative ways to describe a number of control categories in cloud service contracts.

DISCUSSION

Based on the analysis above, this chapter argues that reasonable controls and provisions need to be included to protect information privacy and security of information assets that the customer may place on the cloud. Contracts should specify how the service provider safeguards the data stored and applications hosted on the cloud, including applications and their proper functioning. If the service provider promises to keep the customer's

Figure 2. Sample cloud contract - security controls assessment

Level-1	Data Protection and Privacy			
Level-2	Information Leakage			
Level-3	Post Termination Assistance		Legal and Regulatory Disclosure	
Level-4	Access Control			
Level-5	Audit Logging		Privacy of Third Parties	
Level-6	Comm. & Operational Management		Business Continuity Planning	
Level-7	Human Resources Security	Physical & Environmental Security	Information Systems Acquisition, Development & Maintenance	Asset Management

data logically separate from other data, it should be noted and defined in the contract. Based on the analysis in the previous section, we have mapped how those security controls selected in our Delphi study may be placed on a Cloud Service Contract (See Table 6). According to that, we propose placing of respective security controls in "Data Security and Protection", "Legal and Regulatory Disclosure" and "Post Termination Assistance" sections of a service contract. In this section, we describe the potential clauses to address those controls.

Auditing Rights in the customer agreement should be reviewed and confirmed that they are sufficient to cover the regulatory compliance needs of the customer. Especially for customers with extensive auditing needs, this could be a major source of disagreement with the service provider. Unlike traditional IT outsourcing contracts, cloud computing providers are not expected to agree to give audit rights easily to their customers due to potential disruptions and resource requirements created by such audits (Ryan & Loeffler, 2010; Erdman & Stark, 2010). Ryan and Loeffler (2010) suggest that customers in specific industries with higher data protection requirements may also need to obtain industry standard certifications to maintain the adequacy of the internal controls of the provider. Also, they may be required to insist on the ability of the regulators to conduct audits, if a regulator requires (Erdman & Stark, 2010).

Like any service provider, cloud providers may often reject being liable for the third party actions, particularly for security breaches or service interruptions. However, some sort of protection or indemnification is required in the case of a security breach or similar events where the customer incurs damages. Customers should not allow the new cloud paradigm to act as a vehicle to shift the balance of responsibilities in a subcontract relationship (Erdman & Stark, 2010). The contract should also define the process of the service provider that provides a notice to the customer if the provider suffers an information security breach.

In a multinational cloud-computing scenario, which jurisdiction's law governs the contract? What other jurisdictions may influence the contract relationship? What may be the legal and regulatory compliance issues and their implications in the cloud? Selection of the relevant jurisdiction is critical in multi-country scenarios. Cloud computing infrastructures often reside in servers in multiple countries, storing data and

Table 6. Mapping of security controls and contract sections

Security Control	ISO 27001 Section	Security Control Description	Contract Issue
Audit Logging	10.10.1.	Audit logs recording user activities, exceptions, and information security events should be produced and kept for an agreed period to assist in future investigations and access control monitoring.	Data Security and Protection
Access Control	11	Access to information, information processing facilities, and business processes should be controlled on the basis of business and security requirements.	Data Security and Protection
Data Protection and Privacy	15.1.4.	Data protection and privacy should be ensured as required in relevant legislation, regulations, and if applicable, contractual clauses.	Data Security and Protection
Information Leakage	12.5.4.	Opportunities for information leakage should be prevented.	Data Security and Protection
Legal and Regulatory Disclosure	-	Lawfully mandated disclosure of information to legal and/or regulatory parties.	Legal and Regulatory Disclosure
Post Termination Assistance	-	Ensuring clear description of responsibilities in the transition of the relevant services either back to the customer systems or to the replacement provider.	Post Termination Assistance
Privacy of Third Parties	-	Privacy of personal information and data related to third parties that are expressively authorized without any withdrawal to be processed on the systems.	Data Security and Protection

applications belonging to customers in various jurisdictions and is managed by a service provider in yet another jurisdiction. In some cases, law enforcement or other government actors in these jurisdictions may seek to assert jurisdiction and seek data disclosure from a cloud provider (Gellman, 2009).

The problem gets even more complicated when these multiple jurisdictions have different laws and regulations regarding privacy and data retention. When these rules conflict, a cloud provider's compliance to a lawful demand for user data in one jurisdiction may create risk of violating laws of another jurisdiction (Microsoft, 2010).

The compliance requirements may differ significantly, depending on the industry of the customer organization. For instance in the United States, the Gramm-Leach-Bliley Act regulates the privacy and information security practices of

financial institutions, whereas the Health Insurance Portability and Accountability Act (HIPAA) similarly address regulatory requirements with regard to protecting health information (Ryan & Loeffler, 2010). Furthermore, if a customer is utilizing payment cards on the cloud systems, it may be contractually bound to be compliant with the Payment Card Industry Data Security Standard (PCI DSS). In such cases, customer needs to ensure that its service providers, including the cloud provider, are PCI DSS compliant. Therefore, such issues may directly influence the contractual requirements that should be imposed on the cloud service provider.

In a multinational data processing scenario, the applicable legal framework will most probably be determined by principle of territoriality. National provision where the processing is carried out on the territory of the relevant state is applicable.

However, Cloud computing potentially involves worldwide transfer of data processing and may not be traceable. In a dispute, there is a risk of forum shopping to locate favorable legal environment.

Another major question on the cloud computing environment is about what rights and responsibilities do the parties have when a Cloud Computing Provider is initiated, replaced or terminated? Considering the criticality of the services assumed by the cloud infrastructure, the assistance services that the provider gives during initiation, termination and transfer process is a major issue to be clarified.

Rules and agreements should be introduced on how the provider should return all existing data to the customer (transmission, media, format, timing, cost, etc.) and destroy any leftover customer data on its systems, when a service is replaced or terminated. In the event of termination by either party, there should be an obligation to assist in the transition period with the migration of services and data. Migration of the services being provided is even more crucial where the service is businesses critical service otherwise the customer may become the hostage of the service provider. Post-termination assistance that might be relevant for the cloud-computing customer needs to be defined in the contract. For a detailed discussion of respective cloud computing clauses, see Erdman and Stark (2010).

A limitation of the study is the potential for generalizability. As we have developed our results based on a Delphi study, they cannot be generalized to all cloud computing scenarios in different types of cloud deployments. However, we think that our results could be used as a best-practice scenario to provide some guidance to other cloud computing environments. While we do some statistical analysis, our meta-theoretical stance in this research aligns with post-positivist and constructivist paradigms. We used a modified version of the Delphi method, as a participatory research method, where we looked for consensus rather than forecasts and future projections, introduced

online and process mediated interaction to ensure expert anonymity and employed online surveys and email notifications, unlike the original Delphi method. As there is no absolute truth according to our paradigm, the Delphi Method helps us to get a potentially truthful perspective with experiential accumulation of panel members' opinions, seeking validity by reaching consensus of different and diverse individuals with high level of expertise.

CONCLUSION

Despite a variety of cloud computing customers, service providers often take a one-size-fits-all approach and ask customers to be satisfied with the same set of controls, regardless of their particular data protection and compliance needs, in order to homogenize different types of customers and to keep their operational costs down. The main contribution of this chapter is providing a novel perspective on the cloud security and privacy issue, using controls in the ISO 27001 standard. ISO 27001 is an increasingly accepted international standard which thousands of companies deploy to establish their information security management system. Bringing a perspective to privacy and security of cloud computing that uses the same notation and reference may help those companies with an ISO 27001 certificate to assess related risks and possibly decide on adopting cloud-computing scenarios more easily. The Hierarchy of Control Categories model developed in this chapter may be used as a guide to assess applicable controls and to ensure all important risk categories are addressed with technical measures and contractual terms.

Limitations of this study may be overcome in future using alternative methodologies with analytical modeling, scenario-based quantification and simulation of cloud related risks in different implementations. As the number of cloud computing clients grow, empirical data can be directly collected from user organizations to address, the types of cloud computing risks that have been arising in different industries and cloud configurations. With increased competition among various cloud providers, analyzing available service agreement alternatives may also give us a contractual perspective on how relevant security and privacy risks can be managed, controlled and addressed in various cloud computing environments. In future, results of legal interpretations of cloud service contracts in various legal cases in different courts across the world, may act as a fruitful data source to develop more mature and balanced cloud computing service agreements.

This study represents an attempt towards developing a more balanced discussion regarding legality of data protection in the cloud environment. As more people around the world try to find out how best to use the cloud-computing model, such approaches may be used to assess existing gaps for better risk management and devise cloud computing service contracts based on particular requirements of different businesses, different governments and different consumers.

The cloud-computing model has potential to change fundamentally how information technologies are produced, employed and used in different business and individual settings. However, it is still an immature business model despite the major business and technology hype around the world. Considering the complicated nature of the relevant legal scrutiny, we can conclude that the cloud-computing model is still an immature business model, despite the major business and technology hype around the world.

There are also a great number of relevant controls and a greater number of alternative contractual clauses to be implemented for customers with different information security and compliance needs. This study represents an initial attempt that is limited only to data protection. However, in future more studies are needed to establish a foundation for a systematic source of reference for researchers, executives and other professionals to help them develop a more balanced and complete understanding of the cloud environment including its contractual implementation.

REFERENCES

Adler, M., & Ziglio, E. (1996). *Gazing into the oracle: The Delphi method and its application to social policy and public health.* London: Kingsley.

Banisar, D., & Davies, S. (n.d.). *Privacy and human rights—An international survey of privacy laws and practice.* Retrieved March 15, 2011, from http://www.gilc.org/privacy/survey/

Baumer, D. L., Earp, J. B., & Poindexter, J. C. (2004). Internet privacy law: A comparison between the United States and the European Union. *Computers & Security, 23*(5), 400–412. doi:10.1016/j.cose.2003.11.001

Bennett, C. J. (2002). Information policy and information privacy: International arenas of governance. *Journal of Law, Technology and Policy, 2*, 385–406.

Bisong, A., & Rahman, S. S. M. (2011). An overview of the security concerns in enterprise cloud computing. *International Journal of Network Security & Its Applications, 3*(1), 30–45. doi:10.5121/ijnsa.2011.3103

Braman, S. (2006). *Change of state – information, policy, and power.* Cambridge, Massachusetts: The MIT Press.

Buchanan, T., Paine, C., Joinson, A. N., & Reips, U. D. (2007). Development of measures of online privacy concern and protection for use on the Internet. *Journal of the American Society for Information Science and Technology, 58*(2), 157–165. doi:10.1002/asi.20459

Burgoon, J. K., Parrott, R., Poire, B. A. L., Kelley, D. L., Walther, J. B., & Perry, D. (1989). Maintaining and restoring privacy through communication in different types of relationship. *Journal of Social and Personal Relationships, 6*(2), 131–158. doi:10.1177/026540758900600201

Chang, V. (2014). The business intelligence as a service in the cloud. *Future Generation Computer Systems, 37*, 512–534. doi:10.1016/j.future.2013.12.028

Chang, V., & Ramachandran, M. (2014). *A proposed case for the cloud software engineering in security.* Paper presented at the first international workshop on Emerging Software as a Service, Spain, 3-5 Apr.

Chang, V., Walters, R. J., & Wills, G. (2014). Review of cloud computing and existing frameworks for cloud adoption. In *Advances in Cloud Computing Research.* Nova Publishers.

Custer, R., Scarcella, J., & Stewart, B. (1999). T*he modified Delphi technique – A rotational model.* Retrieved from http://scholar.lib.vt.edu/ejournals/JVTE/v15n2/custer.html

Dalkey, N., & Helmer, O. (1951). *The use of experts for the estimation of bombing requirements: A project Delphi experiment.* Santa Monica: RAND Corporation.

DeCew, J. W. (1997). *In pursuit of privacy: Law, ethics, and the rise of technology.* Ithaca, NY: Cornell University Press.

Electronic Privacy Information Center. (n.d.). *The census and privacy.* Retrieved March 4, 2013, from http://epic.org/privacy/census/

Erdman, K., & Stark, N. (2010). *Legal challenges for U.S. healthcare adopters of cloud computing.* Paper presented at the International Technology Law Association Annual European Conference, Berlin, Germany.

Gaukroger, S. (2012). *Objectivity: A very short introduction.* Oxford: Oxford University Press. doi:10.1093/actrade/9780199606696.001.0001

Gellman, R. (2009). *Privacy in the clouds: Risks to privacy and confidentiality from cloud computing.* World Privacy Forum. Retrieved February 4, 2014, from http://gato-docs.its.txstate.edu/vpit-security/policies/WPF_Cloud_Privacy_Report.pdf

Gray, P.S., Williamson, J.B., Karp, D.A., & Dalphin, J. (2007). *The research imagination: An introduction to qualitative and quantitative methods.* Cambridge University Press. doi:10.1017/CBO9780511819391

Helmer, O. (1965). *Social technology.* Santa Monica, CA: RAND Corporation.

ISO. (2005). *ISO IEC 27001: Information technology — Security techniques - Information security management systems – Requirements.* Geneva: ISO.

Landeta, J. (2006). Current validity of the Delphi method in social sciences. *Technological Forecasting and Social Change, 73*(5), 467–482. doi:10.1016/j.techfore.2005.09.002

Linstone, H. A., & Turoff, M. (Eds.). (1975) The Delphi Method: techniques and applications, Reading, MA: Addison Wesley.

Mather, T., Kumaraswamy, S., & Latif, S. (2009). *Cloud security and privacy: An enterprise perspective on risks and compliance.* Sebastopol: OReilly.

Mell, P., & Grance, T. (2011). *The NIST definition of cloud computing.* Retrieved March 5, 2014, from http://csrc.nist.gov/publications/nistpubs/800-145/SP800-145.pdf

Microsoft. (2010). *Building confidence in the cloud: A proposal for industry and government action to advance cloud computing.* Retrieved February 12, 2014 from http://www.microsoft.com/presspass/presskits/cloudpolicy/

Mitroff, I., & Turoff, M. (1975). Philosophical and methodological foundations of Delphi. In H. Linstone, & M. Turoff (Eds.), The Delphi method: Techniques and applications (pp. 17-34).

Onwubiko, C. (2010). Security issues to cloud computing. In N. Antonopoulos & L. Gilliam (Eds.), *Cloud computing principles, systems and applications*. London: Springer. doi:10.1007/978-1-84996-241-4_16

Pettey, C. (2010). *Gartner identified the top 10 strategic technologies for 2011*. Retrieved September 10, 2011 from http://www.gartner.com/it/page.jsp?id=1454221

Popper, K. (1963). *Conjectures and refutations: The growth of scientific knowledge*. New York: Routledge. doi:10.1063/1.3050617

Rechtsanwalt, M., & Kempermann, P. (2010). *Secrets of the cloud: Licensing and data protection – particularities and pitfalls*. Paper presented at the International Technology Law Association *Annual European Conference*, Berlin, Germany.

Ried, S., Kisker, H., Matzke, P., Bartels, A., & Lisserman, M. (2011). *Sizing the cloud – a BT futures report*. Retrieved December 21, 2013 from, http://www.forrester.com/Sizing+The+Cloud/fulltext/-/E-RES58161?objectid=RES58161

Ryan, W. M., & Loeffler, C. M. (2010). Insights into cloud computing. *Intellectual Property & Technology Law Journal*, 22(11), 22–27.

Scheibe, M., Skutsch, M., & Schofer, J. (1975). Experiments in Delphi methodology. In H. A. Linstone & M. Turoff (Eds.), *The Delphi method - Techniques and applications* (pp. 262–287). Reading: Addison-Wesley.

Smith, H. J., Milberg, S. J., & Burke, S. J. (1996). Information privacy: Measuring individuals' concerns about organizational practices. *Management Information Systems Quarterly*, 20(2), 167–196. doi:10.2307/249477

Tashakkori, A., & Teddlie, C. (2008). *Foundations of mixed methods research: Integrating quantitative and qualitative approaches in the social and behavioral sciences*. Thousand Oaks, CA: Sage Publications.

Tsilas, N. (2010). Moving responsibly to the cloud to ensure its full potential. *The Computer & Internet Lawyer*, 27(11), 16–24.

Turoff, M. (1975). The policy Delphi. In H. Linstone & M. Turoff (Eds.), *The Delphi method: Techniques and applications*. Reading, PA: Addison-Wesley.

United States Department of Justice (USDOJ). (2007). *Chapter 1: Computer fraud and abuse act*. Retrieved March 23, 2011, from http://www.cybercrime.gov/ccmanual/01ccma.pdf

Voorsluys, W., Brober, J., & Buyya, R. (2011). Introduction to cloud computing. In R. Buyya, J. Broberg, & A. Goscinski (Eds.), Cloud computing principles and paradigms. Hoboken, NJ: John Wiley & Sons Inc. doi:10.1002/9780470940105.ch1

Warren, S., & Brandeis, L. (1890). The right to privacy. *Harvard Law Review*, 4(5), 193–220. doi:10.2307/1321160

Westin, A. F. (1967). *Privacy and freedom*. New York: Atheneum Press.

Wittow, M. H., & Buller, D. J. (2010). Cloud computing: Emerging legal issues for access to data, anywhere, anytime. *Journal of Internet Law*, 14(1), 1–10.

Zwick, D. (1999). *Models of privacy in the digital age: Implications for marketing and ecommerce*. Retrieved May 26, 2011, from http://ritim.cba.uri.edu/Working%20Papers/Privacy-Models-Paper%5B1%5D.pdf

KEY TERMS AND DEFINITIONS

Access Control: Ability to control access to information to ensure correct people are able to access necessary data on a timely and systematic manner.

Information Leakage: Unintended or uncontrolled flow of personal or private data to third parties.

Information Privacy: Right to have control over personal information, and the extent of personal information or the underlying data are revealed to other parties.

Information Security: Protection of information assets and personal data from privacy, integrity and availability risks and threats.

Post Termination Assistance: Assistance services given by the service providers after the termination of the cloud computing services for data and business process migration, including data cleaning and sanitation at the cloud-based systems.

Privacy of Third Parties: Privacy of data belonging to non-contracting parties, such as customers, employees or business partners.

Service Contracts: Contractual agreements between the sides of the cloud computing services that defines rights of responsibilities of contracting parties.

APPENDIX: SURVEYS

Table 7. Round–0: screening

Name Surname:							
E-mail:							
Age:		Sex:	❑ Female ❑ Male	Location:	❑ Europe ❑ North America ❑ Other		
Would you identify yourself as a cloud-computing expert?						Yes	No
Are you currently working in a cloud-provider company?						Yes	No
Are you currently working for a cloud-user company?						Yes	No
Are you working at on IT or a similar department in your company?						Yes	No
For how many years you have been working on IT?						Yes	No
Are you working on a managerial position?						Yes	No
How would you best describe your experience with cloud computing?							
Would you attend a research project online as an informant to locate relevant security controls for cloud computing? (Workload estimation: 3-4 short online surveys in few months)						Yes	No

Table 8. Round-1: opinion gathering

Name, Surname:
What are the most important information security and privacy issues in a generic cloud service provider – customer context and how a company / user may control them? Please feel free to describe all your opinions:
Any additional comments?
Thank you for your participation in the Round 1.

Table 9. Round-2: initial rating

		Very unimportant			Very important	
Name, Surname:						
Please assess how important are the following control domains for information security and privacy in a generic cloud service provider – customer context. **Note:** Currently the following control domains are listed in the alphabetical order. **Note:** If you need descriptions of these controls, see the attached table below.						
	Don't Know	①	②	③	④	⑤
Access control	❑	①	②	③	④	⑤
Asset management	❑	①	②	③	④	⑤
Business continuity planning	❑	①	②	③	④	⑤
Communication and operational management	❑	①	②	③	④	⑤
Compliance	❑	①	②	③	④	⑤
Human resources security	❑	①	②	③	④	⑤
Participant identified domain 1	❑	①	②	③	④	⑤
Incident management	❑	①	②	③	④	⑤
IS acquisition, development and maintenance	❑	①	②	③	④	⑤
Organization of information security	❑	①	②	③	④	⑤
Participant identified domain 2	❑	①	②	③	④	⑤
Physical and environmental security	❑	①	②	③	④	⑤
Security policy	❑	①	②	③	④	⑤
...	❑	①	②	③	④	⑤
Participant identified domain n	❑	①	②	③	④	⑤
Any additional comments?						
				Thank you for your participation in the Round 2.		

Table 10. Round-3: re-rating

Name, Surname:								
You have previously reviewed how important are the following control domains for information security and privacy of cloud computing in a generic cloud service provider – customer context. Please find all of the assessments in the last round below. Do your ratings change after this review in the Round 3? **Note:** You don't need to change your position if you disagree with the rest of the expert panel.								
	Round 2 Results				**Round 3**			
	You	Panel Mean	Panel Median	Panel Mode	Very unimportant			Very important
Access control					①	②	③	④	⑤
Asset management					①	②	③	④	⑤
Business continuity planning					①	②	③	④	⑤
Communication and operational management					①	②	③	④	⑤
Compliance					①	②	③	④	⑤
Human resources security					①	②	③	④	⑤
Participant identified domain 1					①	②	③	④	⑤
Incident management					①	②	③	④	⑤
IS acquisition, development and maintenance					①	②	③	④	⑤
Organization of information security					①	②	③	④	⑤
Participant identified domain 2					①	②	③	④	⑤
Physical and environmental security					①	②	③	④	⑤
Security policy					①	②	③	④	⑤
…					①	②	③	④	⑤
Participant identified domain n					①	②	③	④	⑤
Any additional comments?								
					Thank you for your participation in the Round 3.			

Chapter 18
Enterprise Security Framework for Enterprise Cloud Data Centres

Muthu Ramachandran
Leeds Beckett University, UK

ABSTRACT

Enterprise security is the key to achieve global information security in business and organisations. Enterprise Cloud computing is a new paradigm for that enterprise where businesses need to be secured. However, this new trend needs to be more systematic with respect to Enterprise Cloud security. This chapter has developed a framework for enterprise security to analyze and model Enterprise Cloud organisational security of the Enterprise Cloud and its data. In particular, Enterprise Cloud data & Enterprise Cloud storage technologies (Amazon s3, Drop Box, Google Drive, etc.) have now become a normal practice for almost every computing user's. Therefore, building trust for Enterprise Cloud users should be the one of the main focuses of Enterprise Cloud computing research. This chapter has developed a framework for enterprises which comprises of two models of businesses: Enterprise Cloud provider enterprise model and Enterprise Cloud consumer enterprise model.

INTRODUCTION

Enterprise Cloud computing technology has emerged to provide a more cost effective solution to businesses and services while making use of inexpensive computing solutions which combines pervasive, internet, and virtualisation technologies. Enterprise Cloud computing has spread to catch up with another technological evolution as we have witnessed internet technology, which has revolutionised communication and informa-

tion superhighway. Enterprise Cloud computing is emerging rapidly and software as a service paradigm is increasing its demand for more services. However, this new trend needs to be more systematic with respect to software engineering and its related processes. For example, current challenges that are faced with cyber security and application security flaws, lessons learned and best practices can be adopted. Similarly, as the demand for Enterprise Cloud services increases and so increased importance sought for security

DOI: 10.4018/978-1-4666-8210-8.ch018

Copyright © 2015, IGI Global. Copying or distributing in print or electronic forms without written permission of IGI Global is prohibited.

and privacy. The business of Enterprise Cloud technology can only be sustained if we can maintain balance between demand for services in-line with improved Enterprise Cloud security and privacy. Popović & Hocenski (2010) have reported an analysis of results from an IDC ranking of security challenges that 87.5% responded to demand for Enterprise Cloud security against on-demand Enterprise Cloud services. This confirms the importance of Enterprise Cloud security against Enterprise Cloud services.

Enterprise Cloud service providers such as Microsoft, Google, Sales force.com, Amazon, GoGrid are able to leverage Enterprise Cloud technology with pay-per-use business model with on-demand elasticity by which resources can be expended or shortened based on service requirements. They often try to co-locate their servers in order to save cost. There every effort by several other enterprises to establish their Enterprise Cloud efforts to build their own Enterprise Cloud (private Enterprise Clouds) on their premises but can't afford to compromise security of their applications and data which is their major hurdle in their new effort. Most important of all, they need to develop a legitimate and controlled way of establishing service-level-agreements with their clients and to embed these rules to be built-in with services.

Standardisation has been active in software development and information technology to ensure systematic use of process, methods, and to that of client's requirements. Standards include on Quality, Quality of Services (QoS), Usability, and Process such as ISO, CMMI, and others to ensure product and service quality are adhered. The emergence and adherence of standardization such as Information Technology Infrastructure Library (ITIL), ISO/IEC 27001/27002, and Open Virtualization Format (OVF 2010) are critical in establishing expected Enterprise Cloud sustainability and trust in this new technological service business. Hence, it is highly recommended OVF standard as a vendor and platform independent,

open, secure, portable, efficient and extensible format for the packaging and distribution of software to be run in virtual machines (software stacks that incorporates the target applications, libraries, services, configuration, relevant data, and operating enterprise).

This paper proposes two tier enterprises for Enterprise Cloud computing: Enterprise Cloud provider as an enterprise and an Enterprise Cloud consumer as an enterprise. This will allow us to apply best practice security measures, principles, and frameworks. This chapter addresses some of the key research issues in this area such as how do we learn and adopt a decade of best practices on enterprise security to Enterprise Cloud technology transition? How we can also improve and sustain Enterprise Cloud enterprise security framework continuously?

BACKGROUND

Enterprises Engineering incorporates a systematic and comprehensive approach to modelling, designing, and developing enterprises includes software and service based enterprises. Caminao project (2013) provides a comprehensive framework for enterprises engineering methods and concepts. The internet technology has revolutionized the way we live on a daily basis. The use of internet is growing rapidly from devices, appliances and Enterprise Cloud computing, which has emerged to address a cost-effective solution for businesses. However, security is the most common security concerns of all. Therefore, security for Enterprise Cloud computing is the main aim of this chapter. The everyday Enterprise Cloud applications and apps can be protected using commonly available anti-security software packages. However, it is harder to protect us from security related attacks which emerges unexpectedly and are often hard to predict. This isn't sufficient for Enterprise Cloud service providers who offer three different types of services such as Software as a Service (SaaS),

Platform as a Service (PaaS), and Infrastructure as a Service (IaaS). Therefore, there is a need for going beyond boundaries of existing security techniques such as password protection, virus checks, secured financial transaction techniques, etc. The following are categories of the broad spectrum of security related research that are undertaken:

- Application software security deals with how we can build enterprises that can automatically protect itself.
- Network (LAN, MAN, GAN), Wireless network security, and Platform Security include Operating Enterprises, Virtualisation, and other enterprise software.
- VoIP security as the application is gaining popularity.
- Convergence network security where converging multi-network media infrastructures, social networks and technologies which is one of the emerging areas of research.
- Service-oriented security where issues related to enterprise services such as denial of service attacks, distributed denial of services, and web services.
- Enterprise Cloud security deals with services security, data security and privacy so that services delivered and assets are protected.
- Open-source software security deals with issues such as trust, certification and qualification models.
- Software components and architecture security deals with building components and architectures with security can be used as plug-ins.
- Web services security is essential to ensure secure services are delivered with integrity
- Enterprises &Software security engineering deals with building security in (BSI) right from requirements. This also considers developing software applications with BSI.

Security engineering deals with many aspects of protecting assets and delivering secured services including business services and building trust. Figure 1 shows a landscape of enterprise security related areas of research which will dominate most of Enterprise Cloud computing in the forthcoming areas.

Security research is emerging as we discover and learn new forms of threats. Therefore, the research landscape shown in Figure 1 will have to be expanded. Computer security can be classified into a number of general concepts and processes such as identification which identifies objects, functions, and actions, authentication, authorisation, privacy, integrity, and durability. This is categorized and presented in Figure 2 as basic security principles. We have so far well established basic security features with identification, authentication, authorisation, and digital security encryption and decryption techniques. However, there are number challenging issues that are undiscovered to be addressed when dealing with Enterprise Cloud services. Basic security features have also been defined briefly.

- **Identification:** A basic and the first process of establishing and distinguishing amongst person/user & admin ids, a program/process/another computer ids, and data connections and communications. Often we use alphanumerical string as user identification key and some may use your email itself as the user identification key and this can be checked against when a user login into the enterprise. Authentication and authorisation are two distinct forms of allowing users to access what they are not allowed to access any information in the enterprise.
- **Privacy:** The key to maintaining the success of Enterprise Cloud computing and its impact on sharing information for social networking and teamwork on a specific project. This can be maintained by allow-

Figure 1. Enterprise security research landscape

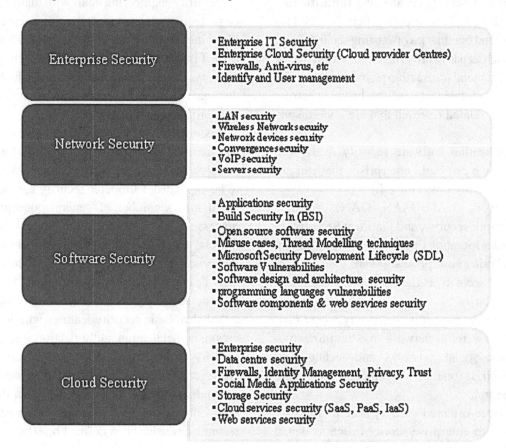

Figure 2. Basic security principles

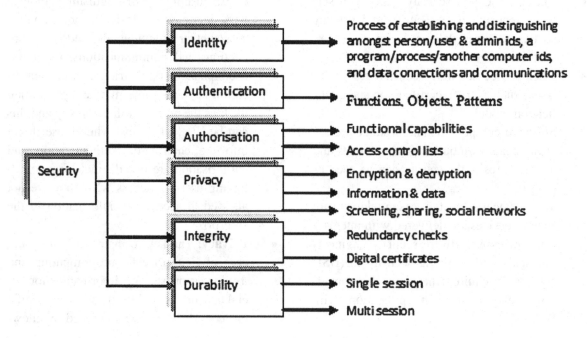

Figure 3. Cyclic security principles

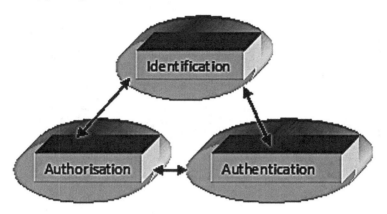

ing users to choose when and what they wish to share in addition to allowing encryption & decryption facilities when they need to protect specific information/data/media content.

- **Integrity:** Defined as the basic feature of the human being as a process of maintaining consistency of actions, communications, values, methods, measures, principles, expectations, and outcomes. Ethical values are important for Enterprise Cloud service providers to protect integrity of Enterprise Cloud user's data with honesty, truthfulness and accuracy at all time. In Enterprise Cloud computing terms, we can achieve integrity by maintaining regular redundancy checks and digital certification in addition to other basic security features of maintaining identification, authentication, and authorisation. *Durability* is also known as, persistency of user actions and services in use should include sessions and multiple sessions.

In general, we can emphasis on basic of security principle into three main categories as Identification, Authentication, and Authorisation (IAA). The basic process is a cyclic in nature as illustrated in Figure 3 and can be defined based on IAA steps. This is a recursive process which must be applied to every action, transactions, and service provisions.

Andress (2011) provides an excellent literature survey on the basics of information security techniques. The cyclic security principles known as IAA is not limited pattern of solution for developing secure enterprises. There are other security concepts that form a pattern of solution known as CIA (Confidentiality, Integrity, and Availability). The CIA considers more towards how well we should design supporting those three characteristics of enterprises including software and services. In addition, Andress (2011) stated the concept of *ParkerianHexad*, which consists of six principles CIA (3) + PAU (3) (Possession or control, Authenticity, and Utility).

Traditionally, security has been added and fixed by releasing security patches on a daily basis by major software vendors. This practice needs to change by systematically identifying and incorporating enterprise security right from requirements. This process is known as *Building In Security (BSI)*. Readers are urged to follow the work by McGraw (2004 & 2006) and Ramachandran (2011). This chapter contributes towards providing an enterprise engineering process for developing and deploying Enterprise Cloud services systematically. It also provides a classification system for enterprise Cloud security and Enterprise Cloud data security which are useful for developing and maintaining large scale enterprises with build in security. Finally, data security has

Figure 4. EC-SQUARE model

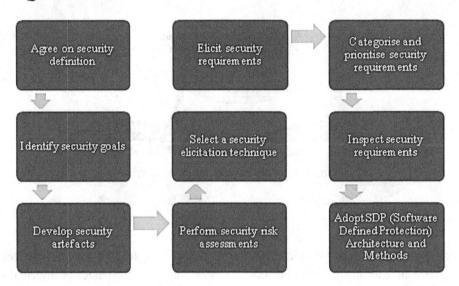

been modelled and simulated using the business process methodology. The results show effectiveness when we develop enterprises systematically with good enterprises engineering principles and tools. Therefore, our main recommendation towards building security in (BSI) strategy is to follow one of our guidelines/recommendations:

The aforementioned processes and classification (security principles diagrams shown in Figure 2 & 3) of security attributes can be used as a framework for capturing security specific requirements supporting BSI focus by Enterprises and Software Engineers. In other words, Security requirements = principles of CIA + PAU

The following section introduces a systematic approach to developing security specific enterprise requirements for building BSI right from requirements phase of the enterprise engineering life-cycle.

Enterprise Security Framework for Enterprise Cloud Services

Capturing and identifying requirements for security explicitly is one of challenges in software engineering. Often security is considered as one the non-

functional requirements which have been considered as constraints identified during and after software has been developed and deployed. However, it has an impact on the functionality of the enterprise. Therefore, we need to be able specify security requirements explicitly throughout the security-specific life-cycle phases as part of achieving BSI (security requirements, design for security, security testing & securability testing). Tondel et al. (2008) has provided an extensive survey on security requirements methods which help to identify security requirements systematically and structure them. For example, Mead (2005) for the SEI's (software Engineering Institute) has identified a method known as SQUARE (Secure Quality Requirements Engineering) and our earlier work on SysSQUARE (Ramachandran 2014) which has been extended to address Enterprise Cloud security EC-SQUARE (Enterprise Cloud security), is shown in Figure 4, towards enterprises security engineering method. Our extended method consists of nine steps as follow:

- **Agree on Security Definition:** To define a set of acronyms, definitions, and domain-specific knowledge needs to be agreed by stakeholders. This will help identify and validate security-specific requirements clearly by stakeholders.

- **Identify Security Goals:** To clearly define what is expected by the enterprise with respect to security by the business drivers, policies, and procedures.
- **Develop Security Artifacts:** To develop scenarios, examples, misuse cases, templates for specifications, and forms.
- **Perform Security Risk Assessments:** To conduct risk analysis for all security goals identified, conduct threat analysis.
- **Select a Security Elicitation Technique:** Includes enterprise identification and analysis of security requirements from stakeholders in the forms of interviews, business process modelling and simulations, prototypes, discussion and focus groups. As part of this phase, one has also to identify level of security, cost-benefits analysis, and organisational culture, structure, and style.
- **Elicit Security Requirements:** Includes activities such as producing security requirements document based security specific principle structure as part of our goal of developing BSI earlier, risk assessment results, and techniques, identifies for analysis such as business process modelling and simulations, threat modelling, and misuse cases, etc.
- **Categorise and Prioritise Security Requirements:** Includes activities such as classifying and categorising security requirements based on company-specific requirements specification templates and to use our recommended security principles as this will help Enterprises Engineers to apply BSI and track security-specific requirements for validation & verification at all stages of the enterprises engineering life-cycle.
- **Identify Enterprises Data Security Requirements:** Include activities on extracting and carefully identifying data security and relevant sub-enterprises such as data centres, servers, Enterprise Cloud VM, and software security, SQL security, and other types of security that are relevant to data. This separation of concerns allows enterprises engineers to integrate, track, design, and develop data security as part of enterprise wide enterprises development.
- **Prioritise Security Requirements:** Include activities of selecting and prioritising security requirements based on business goals as well as cost-benefit analysis.
- **Inspect Security Requirements:** To conduct requirements validation process using requirements inspection and review meetings.
- **Adopt SDP (Software Defined Protection):** Layers for building enterprise security blueprint.

According to our EC-SQUARE model, the first phase starts with identifying security requirements that are achievable and agreed by all stakeholders who are involved in the process. The second step focuses mainly on developing a list all possible security goals as part of the business and functional goals. Thirdly, to develop a list of artifacts that are needed to achieve those security goals. Fourthly, to conduct a detailed risk assessment for each security goal identified and assessed. Clear identification of the requirements of the whole enterprise applications and to extract security requirements for those applications. Interact with stakeholders to clarify security requirements and the technology they want to use, and cost implications. Categorisation and prioritisation of security requirements will help achieve realistic goals against business targets. For example, for a networked enterprise, we need to separate the enterprise system into two further categories of security requirements such wired and wireless security enterprises. The EC-SQUARE method elicitation of security requirements have been applied to study the behaviour of threat modelling for Enterprise Cloud data security which has been presented in the last section of this chapter.

The traditional software development life cycle (SDLC) process does not state security requirements explicitly. Software security is part of a quality requirements collection process and it consists of three different requirements subcategories: 'confidential and privacy' builds the trust (trust is one of the basic and backbone for establishing quality), 'integrity', and 'availability'. Therefore, security needs to be identified early, designed and to be tested as part of the SDLC process explicitly. Firstly, we need to identify all the attributes of software security so that we can assess and evaluate each requirement against a set of security attributes that will enable us to extract security related requirements. Security is an essential part of the enterprise in achieving and protecting enterprises and its users. Security has several attributes that are related to a simple email enterprise (where most of the attacks, such as virus, spam, intrusions, and identity fraud occur frequently); security baselines are standards that specify a minimum set of security controls that has to be met for most organisations under normal circumstances. They also include both technical and operational security concerns. Enterprise Cloud computing has emerged to address the needs of the IT cost-benefit analysis and also a revolution in technology in terms of reduced cost for internet data and speed. Therefore, the demand for securing our data in the Enterprise Cloud has also increased as a way of building trust for Enterprise Cloud migration and to benefit business confidence in the Enterprise Cloud technology by Enterprise Cloud providers such as Amazon, Microsoft, Google, etc. Therefore, we also want to make sure our BSI model and strategies are applicable to Enterprise Cloud services as well as traditional enterprises. Figure 5 shows a detailed technical model to structure enterprise Cloud security attributes to develop and integrate BSI across the enterprise development life-cycle. This model has evolved based on further research and gain knowledge and experience of our own enterprise and therefore the model will be expanded as and when we discover new attributes.

Most of the security attributes and principles identified earlier are clearly applicable to developing Enterprise Cloud services with enterprises engineering focus. However, there are some Enterprise Cloud-specific security related issues such as security in virtualisation and server environments. Enterprise Cloud security attributes can be found in many-fold as shown in Figure 5. They belong to broadly into the following categories:

- **Confidentiality, Privacy, and Trust:** These are well known basic attributes of digital security such as authentication and authorisation of information as well protecting privacy and trust
- **Enterprise Cloud Services Security:** This includes security on all its services such as SaaS, PaaS, and IaaS. This is the key area of attention needed for achieving Enterprise Cloud security
- **Data Security:** This category is again paramount for sustaining Enterprise Cloud technology. This includes protecting and recovering planning for Enterprise Cloud data and service centres. It is also important to secure data in transactions.
- **Physical Protection of Enterprise Cloud Assets:** This category belongs to protecting Enterprise Cloud centres and its assets.

The above Enterprise Cloud security attributes/ characteristics are essential and useful to understand non-functional aspects of services development and service provision. These attributes are also useful for building BSI and maintaining security. The following section will identify some of the challenges, issues, and opportunities for tackling security-specific enterprise development and how this can be applied to solve some of the key challenges that are facing Enterprise Cloud computing benefits. The following section will also use Enterprise Cloud security attributes and frameworks identified in this section as the main input for building security in (BSI) not developing security patches after Enterprise Cloud services has been delivered.

Figure 5. Enterprise cloud security attributes

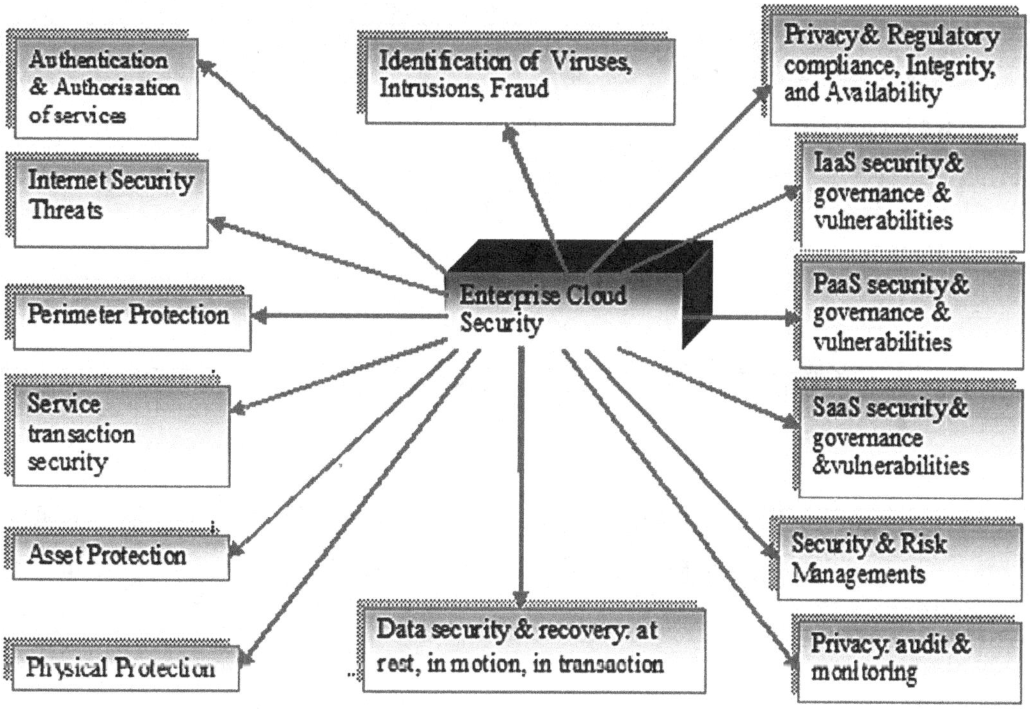

Checkpoint, a software technologies limited, more recently, has introduced the concept of a Software Defined Protection (SDP) for enterprise security blueprint by emphasising the need for a secured enterprise security for dynamic networks and infrastructures. The concept of SDP offers a pragmatic approach to building an enterprise security based on the enterprise architecture and agile methodology. The SDP architecture divides the security infrastructure into three interconnected layers (ESB 2014):

- An Enforcement Layer that is based on physical and virtual security enforcement points and that segments the network, as well as executes the protection logic in high demand environments.
- A Control Layer that analyzes different sources of threat information and generates protections and policies to be executed by the Enforcement Layer.

- A Management Layer that orchestrates the infrastructure and brings the highest degree of agility to the entire architecture.

The SDP, as shown in Figure 6, has been extended with our EC-SQUARE model as discussed in this chapter for a more systematic approach to building enterprise SDP.

In the context of our EC-QDUARE SDP framework, the management layer provides support for overall management of Enterprise Cloud security for clients as well as in-house. The various modules in this layer are componentised to provide flexibility for making changes and reuse. The control layer provides support for security policies for access control and data protection for the Enterprise Cloud data centres as well as client devices. This layer also supports with threat intelligence based a number of key BSI techniques including SDL. The Enforcement layer supports key enforcement points where a complete profile for each user can be created and analysed securely.

Figure 6. EC-SQUARE SDP framework

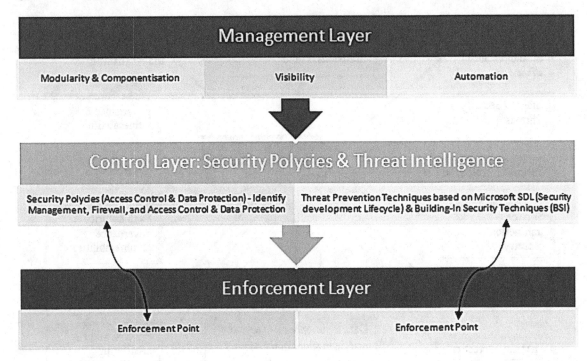

Enterprise Security Engineering for Enterprise Cloud Computing: Issues, Problems, Challenges, and Opportunities

So far we have seen in the past 20 years of unsecure applications and we have experienced the loss and recovery. We have also invented many security patches to protect against spam, viruses, id theft, and phishing. It is now time to build secure applications from start to delivery which will save cost and effort enormously. Figure 7 provides a framework for providing solution to software security challenges and provides a basic means of achieving software security: benefits such as increased trust, integrity and availability; means of achieving this are by using techniques such as requirements elicitation method for software security and by designing secured functions, objects, components, frameworks, and architectures; and its threats are lack of finding software security engineers, additional cost involved, and people's willingness to develop secured applications.

Software and Web based applications are growing fast and so the attacks such as virus, phishing, id theft, and spam. In order for us to build trust in web based application users, we need to therefore build software security (preventions) as opposed to protection (applying patches soon after attacks have happened in most cases so far in IT industry). Software security touchpoints (one of the software security methodology proposed by McGraw 2004) are a set of specific security specific activities to be applied during each software phase in the software development Lifecycle. This is discussed later in the section and also has shown in Figure 10 (identify security requirements and apply abuse cases during Requirements and use cases (phase 1), employ risk analysis during Architecture and design (phase 2), identify risk-based security tests during test plan, conduct tools-based code reviews during coding, conduct risk analysis and adopt penetration testing techniques during the test phase, and observe security operations during feedback/release phase. Risk analysis should be

Figure 7. Enterprise security challenges solution framework

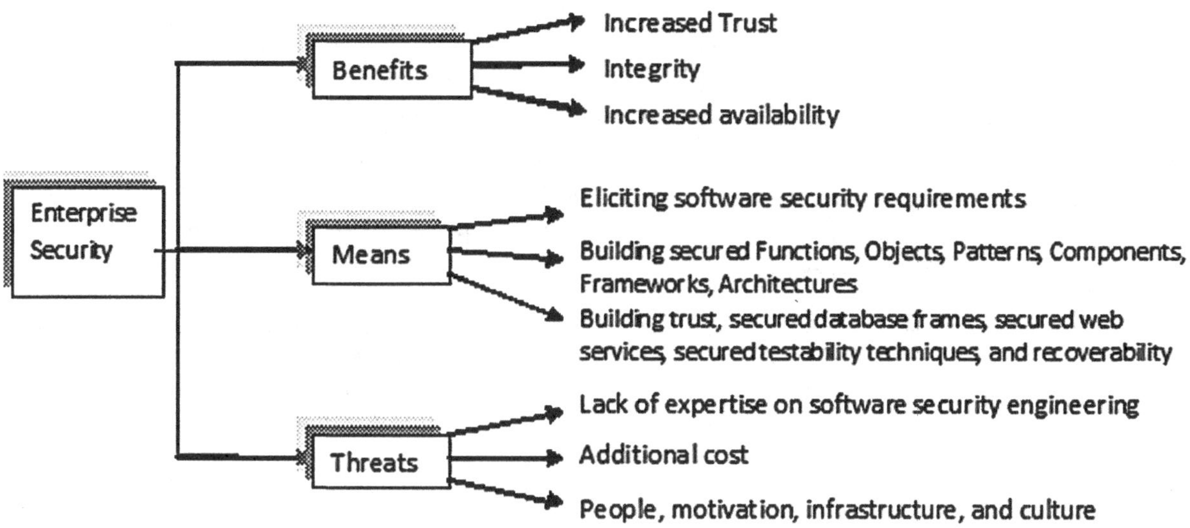

conducted across the phases and need to feedback knowledge gained from attacks and exploitations on a regular basis.

The notion of taxonomy is the practice and science of classification. Taxonomy helps to identify new categories to shelve and retrieve easily when needed. We know where to find. Gonzalez-Castillo (2004) defines security as a set of knowledge and tools obtained and developed by means of the observation and the reasoning, systematically structured and of which general principles and laws are deduced to protect the human life and the existing resources. Taxonomy of software security helps to classify techniques and methods, therefore the relevant technique can easily be identified for use. We can also develop a set of specific guidelines which can be used as a checklist for security validation. A kingdom of security considered as a highest group or a top group in the hierarchy. The parameters that affect the kingdom of security are:

- Economical;
- Political;
- Social;
- Functionality.

Gonzalez-Castillo (2004) defines further classify software security engineering and its implementation into two major groups: software acquisition security (includes the security specifications in all processes to buy, rent, or interchange software to use in an enterprise) and enterprises & software development security (includes the security specifications in all processes to develop information enterprises), as shown in Figure 8.

As shown in Figure 8, software acquisition deals with the COTs (component off-the-shelves), packages, and buy-in tools. Information enterprises development has been divided further into two main categories known as static and dynamic enterprises. Static enterprises security includes compilers (involves specification to develop compilers), assemblers, Programming Languages (PLs), and Operating Enterprises (OS). Dynamic enterprise security deals with enterprise business management (take control of business process information), enterprise administration (security specs to develop applications which objective is to provide control of administrative process information), Manufacturing enterprises, database enterprises, and end user enterprises which deal with developing applications for daily activity tools for end users.

Figure 8. Enterprises security taxonomy

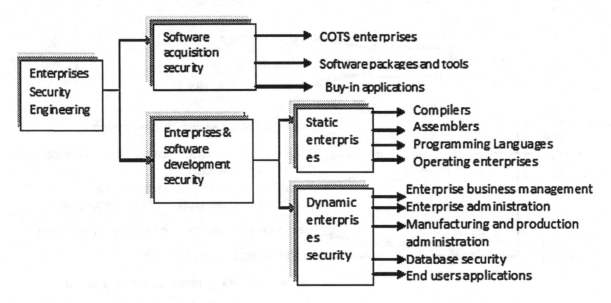

In this section we have seen a generic taxonomy and software security taxonomy, which will help us to identify and organise new security categories. It helps to organise information and contents for many useful purposes. The software security challenges framework (shown in Figure 7) and enterprise security taxonomy (shown in Figure 8) together provides a solution to identify security threats and applying security-specific development right from the upfront of the enterprise engineering development life-cycle for successfully completing our goal of BSI.

Information security is the overall security for the whole enterprise and its network environment. Network security is to make sure the secured transactions and communications take place. Whereas application security is to make sure software enterprises as a whole is secured in its environment. Figure 9 shows a distinction between classical software engineering (SE) Lifecycle vs. enterprises security engineering Lifecycle (SSE). The SSE extracts and specifies security requirements using specific methods in

Figure 9. Enterprises security engineering life cycle

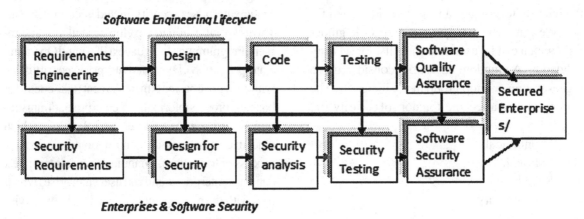

Figure 10. Software security techniques (build-in security)

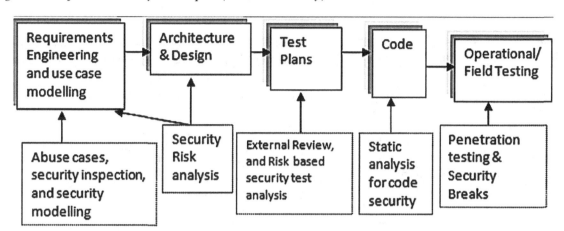

addition to the usual functional modelling conducted during requirements engineering phase of SE Lifecycle.

Design for security is part of a design phase where specific design artifacts are created for handling security requirements purposefully. Design for security calls for specific design rationale and features supporting security explicitly. We can also distinguish furthermore in defining security design where functional design artifacts are created as usual with security. McGraw (2004) has identified a number of security techniques against each stage in the software development Lifecycle (SDLC). Figure 10 illustrates a set of these techniques. For example, abuse cases, security inspection and security modelling should be conducted as part of the RE process, security risk analysis should be conducted during design phase, external review and risk based security test analysis should be done during test planning stage, static analysis for security at the code level (this may include code inspection or automated code analysis tools equipped with security), and penetration testing & security breaks should be conducted during operational and field testing.

The processes shown in Figure 9 & 10 illustrates how we can use security-specific techniques from analysis, modelling, integrating data security, designing, developing, and testing enterprises development with build in security. The techniques are applicable to traditional enterprises development as well as Enterprise Cloud services. There are also a number of methods have been developed for addressing security-specific enterprises development, such as Microsoft security development life-cycle (SDL), McGraw's security touchpoints (shown in Figure 10) and others (CLASP, UMLsec, VGCs, S2D-ProM).

Microsoft Security Development Lifecycle (SDL)

In 2004, Microsoft introduced its own security development Lifecycle as strategic based method to be adapted for all its product development. Therefore Windows Vista enterprise has been developed according to the SDL process. The process consists of a very specific set of activities to be followed for each stage in the software development Lifecycle as shown in Figure 11 (Howard & Lipner 2006). This illustration is based on SDL v4.1. The process consists of seven stages: Training, Requirements, Design, Implementation, Verification, Release, and Response. Each stage is focused on a specific set of activities that are tailor-made for software security.

Figure 11. Microsoft's Security Development Lifecycle (SDL)

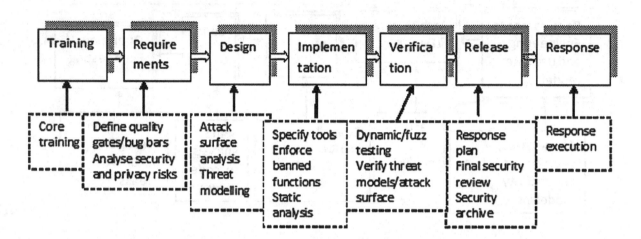

SDL has added value for security modelling as it comes with a threat modelling tool which is comprehensive for analysing requirements and generates threats and risks (Ramachandran 2011; Chang and Ramachandran, 2015). Some of the benefits of SDL are:

- Complete Lifecycle support for security based development;
- Have been used in Windows Vista and SQL server development;
- Reducing the number of software vulnerabilities;
- Reducing the total cost of development (it is possible to save 30 times if security vulnerabilities are fixed early).

Some of the terms used for activities are based on Microsoft in-house such as bug bars and quality gates. The idea is to start identifying and providing security-specific skills before even identifying security requirements. During the requirements phase start gathering quality goals and conduct risk analysis. Conduct threat modelling and attack analysis during the design phase. During implementation conducts static analysis and identify banned functions that are known. During verification phase conduct dynamic and threat analysis. During release phase conduct security review plan.

We conclude this section with a comparison table of security processes that are most popular such as Microsoft SDL the security development Lifecycle (Howard & Lipner 2006), McGraw's Touchpoints (McGraw 2004 & 2006), CLASP (Owasp 2006), VCGs (Byers & Shahmehri 2007), S2D-ProM (Essafi, Labed, & Ghezala 2007), and UMLsec (Jurgen 2005). The process methods feature comparison is shown in Table 1.

As we have seen, a number of software security specific processes have emerged and provide a systematic approach to developing and integrating security requirements right from business analysis to build security in. The following section focuses mainly on our approach on how do we apply and customise SSE specific process towards Enterprise Cloud computing.

Software Engineering has been well established for the past 30 years with high end methods, techniques, and tools. We have also seen a good number of well established guidelines and best practices ranging from management to software development. It is time to make use of it all for new emerging applications and technologies when delivering new services such as Enterprise Cloud paradigm. Ramachandran (2008) has captured such good practices in the form of software guidelines across software development, reuse, and component based software engineering (CBSE).

Table 1. Software security process comparison

Methods \ Features	Microsoft SDL(Howard and Lipner2006)	McGraw's Touchpoints (McGraw 2004 & 2006)	OWASP's CLASP (2006)	VCGs (Byers & Shahmehri2007)	S2D-ProM (Essafi, Labed, & Ghezala 2007)	UMLSec (Jurjen 2005)
Process Stages/ Activities	Full set of activities supported	Range of activities	A set of activities	VCG based	Risk based	UML based profiling and formalism
Risk Management	Part of	Aspect of	Aspect of	Not explicitly	Risk based	Aspect of
Security Techniques	Threat modelling	Threat modelling	Threat modelling	Process is based on specifically to Vulnerability Cause Graphs (VCGs)	Attack tree and labelled directed graph with goals/ intentions(state transitions diagrams)	UMLsec
Lifecycle Support	✓	✓	✓	✓	✓	✓
Iterative	✓	✓	✓	✓	✓	✓
Strengths	Applied to Windows Vista internal experience	Experience over years and other companies	consortium	evolving	evolving	evolving
Weaknesses	internal					

Software as a Service provides new abstraction for developing and delivering business application as part of the Enterprise Cloud. Service implementation is based on software component for implementing their core logics. Ramachandran (2012) has produced a number of service component models for implementing services with build in security. In this section, we need clearly to distinguish amongst general security principles discussed in the earlier section such as information security, business security, etc.; software security is a means of developing software with build in security (BSI) whereas Enterprise Cloud security, which is a process of developing Enterprise Cloud services with BSI.

Software engineering has established techniques, methods and technology over two decades. However, due to the lack of understanding of software security vulnerabilities, we have been not successful in applying software engineering principles when developing secure software enterprises. Therefore, software security can't be just added after a enterprise has been built as seen in today's software applications. SSE (software security engineering) has emerged to address various software security vulnerabilities right from requirements to testing.Security is a major concern for Enterprise Cloud service providers because both the program and customer data are residing on the Enterprise Cloud service provider's premises. Furthermore, Open Enterprises Architectures have higher levels of security vulnerabilities therefore security is an important factor to be addressed continuously by the Enterprise Cloud service providers.

Srinivasan, et al. (2012) discusses a number of key security taxonomies and challenges for Enterprise Cloud computing. They have divided Enterprise Cloud security into two broad areas:

1. Architectural and Technological Aspects were issues of logical storage segregation and multi-tenancy security issues, identity management, insider attacks, virtualisation and cryptography issues are highlighted; and

2. Process and Regulatory-related issues where governance, insures APIs, SLAs and Trust Management, and Enterprise Cloud Migration issues are identified.

These two categories are the key to Enterprise Cloud security challenges. This chapter has devoted to addressing Enterprise Cloud data security as the key factor for determining Enterprise Cloud technology. This chapter highlights most of the issues and have also provided a number of systematic approaches and solutions to address some of these issues. This section proposes a comprehensive framework for Enterprise Cloud security and discusses an important issue of Enterprise Cloud data security and some protection mechanisms.

Security-specific enterprises development process methods and techniques shown in this section helps to achieve BSI to traditional enterprises as well as Enterprise Cloud computing applications which needs to be engineered to reap benefits of Enterprise Cloud technology. The following section considers Amazon Enterprise Cloud services as an example for studying the performance of Enterprise Cloud data security. The main reason for choosing Enterprise Cloud data security is that there is little research on this very important issue and data is one of the main reason that hinders Enterprise Cloud users with respect to building trust.

A MODEL AND PROCESS FOR BUILD-IN ENTERPRISE CLOUD DATA SECURITY: PROPOSED SOLUTIONS AND RECOMMENDATIONS

This section emphasises a rule of thumb to categorise Enterprise Cloud design principles at the heart of Enterprise Cloud computing as a core principle of service design when dealing with developing Enterprise Cloud services. Figure 12 shows a model of the pillars of Enterprise Cloud computing with a triangular model. The central focus is Enterprise Cloud security and data security with corner one as scalability, availability, elasticity, and discoverability of Enterprise Cloud services, corner two for service reuse and integrity, and corner three for measuring and continuously improving security and performance assessments of Enterprise Cloud services.

This model provides a framework for integrating data security and developing build-in Enterprise Cloud security systematically. For example, how do we develop a continuous monitoring strategy for Enterprise Cloud identify management and how do improve from failures? This is one the key aim of this model to build on from experience and user feedback and trails in order for Enterprise Cloud providers to be in a sustainable business of Enterprise Cloud computing.

Figure 12. Pillars of enterprise cloud computing

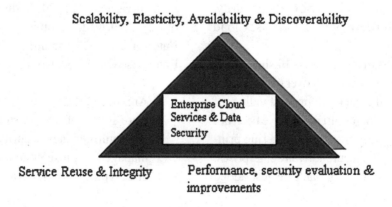

Figure 13. Enterprise cloud security-based service development and integrating data security process with build-in security

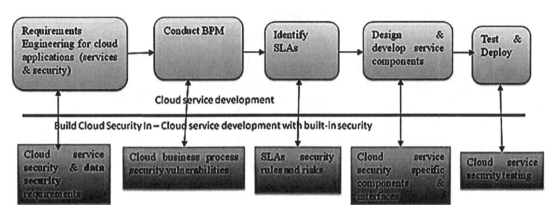

We also need a process by which this model can be established when developing and delivering Enterprise Cloud services. In particular, our aim is to build security in (BSI) right from beginning of service development. The Figure 13 shows a process model for developing Enterprise Cloud services with BSI simultaneously when developing Enterprise Cloud services.

As shown in Figure 13, Enterprise Cloud service development are classified into a number of phases:

1. Requirements engineering for Enterprise Cloud services during which time we can identify security related requirements from various stakeholders,
2. Conduct business process modelling and simulations (BPM) for each Enterprise Cloud services during which time we can also simulate security aspects and study performance related measures and also introduce a possible number of intrusion and conduct simulations before actual service implementation take place,
3. Identify SLAs identifies a number of service level agreements and regulatory and governance related compliances during this time we should be able to separate out security related SLAs and risks,

4. Design and develop services during this phase we can actually implement security related threads that have been carried continuously from all phases, and finally
5. Test and deploy services that are developed with BSIs.

Also, we can:

- Apply software security engineering techniques all identified Enterprise Cloud services. This includes using security analysis tree and various other techniques specified by Ramachandran (2011).
- The second step is on identifying BPM (Business Process Modelling) which should include software security analysis for each business process identified to allow us to identify potential security threats which start with service requirements and business requirements as the input to conduct service security analysis using techniques such as Enterprises Secure Quality Requirements Engineering (EC-SQUARE), and Microsoft Secure Development Lifecycle (SDL). The outcome of this process should yield a set of Enterprise Cloud services security requirements with clear indication of software security issues.

Figure 14. Enterprise cloud security framework

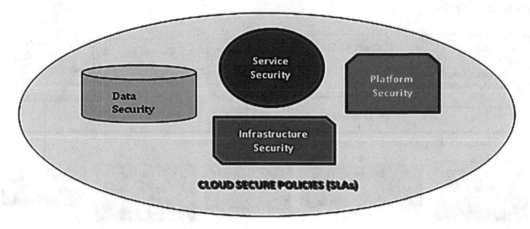

We also need to use a framework for classifying Enterprise Cloud securities and policies as shown in Figure 14. Enterprise Cloud security is the key to business sustainability and hence we need to structure security related aspects into a simple framework that helps us to evolve and improve over a time period.

The Enterprise Cloud framework is based on specifying securities into five classes such as data security, services security, infrastructure security, platform security, and security policies (SLAs). This provides a clear guidance and mechanisms for Enterprise Cloud providers to monitor and improve their Enterprise Cloud security related concerns.

Enterprise Cloud Data Security Classification

There is almost not much work found in the literature on Enterprise Cloud data security currently. This is a key issue for Enterprise Cloud computing for its sustainability. Data security address most of the Enterprise Cloud computing security challenges either you consider architectural and technological concerns nor process and regulatory security challenges; all of them comes down to data in many forms such as information (deals with identity management), data in transition

and transaction, data in modification, privacy of user's data, and data at rest on servers and storages. However, Oracle (2012) has identified about eight key data security issues that are:

- **Data Tampering:** Issues of unauthorised modification to a transaction. For example, if you add 100 times to a simple transaction of £/$1000.00 this equals to £/$100K. Oracle (2012) also says there 80% of security breaches caused by insider attacks than any other forms of security attacks.
- **Eavesdropping and Data Theft:** Stealing critical personal data (personal and financial information such as credit card, etc.) during data transmission. Network and packet sniffers can be used to steal such information.
- **Falsifying User Identities:** Identity theft by gaining access to data and can also threaten digital signatures with non-repudiation attacks
- **Password-Related Threats:** Stealing passwords
- **Authorised Access to Tables, Columns, and Rows:** Security at the database level
- **Lack of Accountability:** Enterprise administrators for monitoring and protecting data access and user account management

Figure 15. Enterprise cloud data security model

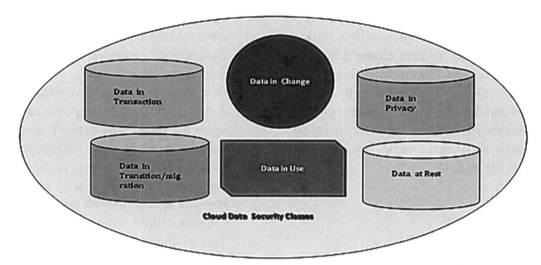

- **Complex User Management Requireme nts:** User account management strategies.
- **Multitier Enterprises:** Providing access to other services and application layers.
- Scaling the security administration of multiple Enterprises poses extra complexity for managing Enterprise Cloud security as it deals with providing multiple access to multiple applications.

Although these are primitive security loopholes that are well known and have been addressing on a daily basis. However, these issues provide important lessons for Enterprise Cloud data centres and servers and other forms of Enterprise Cloud security issues. CSA (2010) provides a clear and detailed guidance for Enterprise Cloud providers to manage and maintain Enterprise Cloud identity management.

For protecting Enterprise Cloud data, we need to distinguish different states of transitions that can occur in the Enterprise Cloud. This will allow us to employ appropriate data security techniques. An example model for different classes/states for Enterprise Cloud data is shown in Figure 15. Our notion of Enterprise Cloud data security concept is to "Divide Enterprise Cloud data transactions into six possible ways:

- **Data at Rest:** Enterprise Cloud storage servers and all types of storage on the Enterprise Cloud.
- **Data in Change:** All types of data creation and modification processes, from file creation/deletion of folders.
- **Data in Use:** A file or a program that has being used currently at this point in time for a single or a multiple session.
- **Data in Privacy:** Users' data that are protected which needs to be respected by Enterprise Cloud service providers.
- **Data in Transaction:** A process where a Enterprise Cloud service uses users data or applications.
- **Data in Transition or Migration:** A process where data have been physically relocated or moved to a different server or a storage which needs to transparent to Enterprise Cloud users and to make sure privacy is protected.

We have seen different states in the user's data which must be protected and managed logically and consistently. How do we achieve data security in these circumstances with different scenarios that exist? How do we ensure a business process will provide that expected return on investment (ROI) before actually investing in implementing an Enterprise Cloud business or a service process? Therefore, we have created a number of BPMN (Business Process Modelling Notation) models (BPMN2 2012) for each of those scenarios and run a number of possible simulations with various business variability using an open source simulation tool, known as Bonita Soft (2012) BOS 5.8.

BEST PRACTICE RECOMMENDATIONS

In the context of the work being carried out in the area of enterprise cloud security, this chapter summarises a key set of best practices on enterprise security:

- Always ensure to establish the basic security triad (The essential security principles of confidentiality, integrity, and availability applies to most systems).
- Always establish and allow a flexible provision for legal and regulatory constrains and governance, as these are likely to change internationally based on political policies and cultural constraints.
- Always ensure physical security. This includes protecting against natural disaster, preparedness, and recovery planning. This should also look at availability of services by building resiliency. The scope of issues in physical security is significant, and it involves a range of measures to avoid, prevent, detect, and respond to unauthorized access to the facility or to resources or information on the facility.
- Establish enterprise cloud security standards and policies which are consistent with appropriate standards, such as International Organization for Standardization (ISO) 27001 and ISO 27002.

- Develop and apply a set of guidelines for enabling security in the development of infrastructure software, infrastructure management processes, and operational procedures.
- Develop a set of security standards for access control, incident response and management, system and network configuration backups, security testing practices such as penetration testing, resilience testing, disaster recovery testing, emergency-response testing, firewall testing, data and communication encryption techniques such as encryption algorithms used, etc., password standards, and continuous monitoring.
- Establish enterprise architecture for security and its infrastructure services.
- Establish a consistent identify management, which is the key element of an enterprise security. Controls must be implemented to protect the confidentiality, integrity, and availability of identity information.
- Establish Access Management, where access controls use identity information to enable and constrain access to an operating cloud and its supporting infrastructure.
- Apply a consistent encryption and decryption key management requirements. In an enterprise cloud, encryption is a primary means to protect data at rest (storage) and between storage and processing phases.
- Establish a regular system for auditing system and networking practices in place, which should include presenting and reviewing all event logs for all devices and systems on the network and on the infrastructure, all virtual machines (VM), user logs, operational logs, security logs, reviewing archiving policies, etc.
- Establish a regular Security Monitoring process in place. Security monitoring is predicated on audit logs, network security

monitoring (using traffic inspection such as snort and so on), and environmental data. This service should be available on premises as well as remotely.

These are, as we believe, are a critical and essential set of best practices for all enterprises and in particular enterprise cloud services. These are not fixed and it is continue to grow as we learn from systematic literature and also in discussion with key experts in the area of enterprise security.

FUTURE RESEARCH DIRECTIONS

This chapter provided our approach to developing Enterprise Cloud services systematically with build in security. We have developed a number of security-specific components that can be reused and customised because they are components with message interfaces. We have also developed a number of business processes with simulation to pre-inform us about their performances and security measures that can be taken before service implementation and deployment. As we discussed in this chapter, to make Enterprise Cloud computing as a new technological business model that is highly successful, profitable, and sustainable, we need to ensure Enterprise Cloud security and privacy can be maintained and trusted. Therefore, most of the future research will focus mainly on Enterprise Cloud security related issues, in particular:

- Control of Enterprise Cloud resources where it is being used and shared and their physical security if this is a hardware resource. In other words, security concerned with sharing resources and services.
- Seizure of a company because it has violated the local legislative requirement. Concerns of client's data when it has also been violated. Therefore, forensic investigation of Enterprise Cloud services and

Enterprise Cloud data recovery and protection issues will dominate much of the future research.

- Consumer switching to price competition. Storage services provided by one Enterprise Cloud vendor may be incompatible with another vendor's service if user decides to move from one to the other (for example, Microsoft Enterprise Cloud is currently incompatible with Google Enterprise Cloud).
- Security key encryption/decryption keys and related issues. Which is suitable technique for a specific service request and for a specific customer data? Who should control? Consumers or providers?
- Enterprise Cloud service development paradigm. What is the suitable development paradigm for this type of business driven delivery model?
- Service security vs. Enterprise Cloud security vs. data security will dominate most of the future research.
- Privacy related issues. Who controls personal and transactional information?
- Audit and monitoring: How do we monitor and audit service provider organisations and how do we provide assurance to relevant stakeholders that privacy requirements are met when their Personally Identifiable Information (PII) is in the Enterprise Cloud?
- Engineering Enterprise Cloud services. How do we develop, test, and deploy Enterprise Cloud services? Can we continue to follow traditional methods and process?
- Business process modelling integrated with Enterprise Cloud service development will emerge and can address business related issues.
- Integrating data security as part of the enterprises, software, and service engineering processes.

- Improvement model for enterprise security.
- Software defined security framework.
- Resilient cloud architecture which is able to sustain all types of security attacks.

As we discussed in this chapter, there are a number of issues, problems, and challenges need to be addressed if want to create sustainable and successful business paradigm for Enterprise Cloud computing. We also discussed a number of research challenges and areas of research focus in the coming years on Enterprise Cloud security in section of this chapter. To summarise some of the research issues & challenges are:

- What can we learn from different paradigms of SDLC? How do we address Enterprise Cloud security? Security vs. Software security vs. Enterprise Cloud Services Security.
- How do we address service reuse as opposed to component reuse? Composability is the main characteristics of Enterprise Cloud computing (to build Enterprise Cloud applications with component parts). Here we want to compose Enterprise Cloud applications with built-in security.
- Are existing design principles can address service composition? Learning the autonomic nature of service-oriented computing when applying design principles.
- How do we customise and apply SE principles to Enterprise Cloud application development? Software component models vs. Service component models.
- How do we learn and reuse best practices? Service component characteristics to match Enterprise Cloud characteristics. Building large scale Enterprise Cloud architectures that are scalable.
- Two major challenges: applying SE principles and best practices; applying SSE principles and best practices.

- How do we address Enterprise Cloud data security and how do we protect Enterprise Cloud centres? Are there data recovery planning that has been continuously monitored and improved?

CONCLUSION

Enterprise Cloud computing has established its businesses and software as a service paradigm is increasing its demand for more services. However, this new trend needs to be more systematic with respect to software engineering and its related processes. For example, current challenges that are witnessed today with cyber security and application security flaws are important lessons to be learned. It also has provided best practices that can be adapted. Similarly, as the demand for Enterprise Cloud services increases and so increased importance sought for security and privacy. We can build Enterprise Cloud application security from the start of the Enterprise Cloud service development. Enterprise Cloud computing is a multidisciplinary that includes social engineering, software engineering, software security engineering, distributed computing, and service engineering. Therefore, a holistic approach is needed to build Enterprise Cloud services. Use Business process modelling and simulation to study service and business performances before implementation.

REFERENCES

Andress, J. (2011). *The basics of information security: Understanding the fundamentals of infosec in theory and practice, syngress*. USA: Elsevier.

BPMN2. (2012). *BPMN 2.0 handbook* (2nd ed.). Future Strategies Inc.

Bonita Soft. (2012) BOS 5.8, Open source BPMN simulation software. Retrieved from http://www.bonitasoft.com/resources/documentation/top-tutorials

Caminao Project. (2013) Caminao's way: Do enterprises know how symbolic they are? *Modelling Enterprises Engineering Project*. Retrieved June 21, 2014, from http://caminao.wordpress.com/overview/?goback=%2Egde_3731775_member_251475288

Chang, V. & Ramachandran, M., Towards achieving Big Data Security with the Cloud Computing Adoption Framework, IEEE Transactions on Services Computing.

CSA. (2010) Enterprise Cloud Security Alliance, domain 12: Guidance for identity & access management. Retrieved from https://Enterprise-Cloudsecurityalliance.org/guidance/csaguide-dom12-v2.10.pdf

ESB. (2014) Software defined protection – Enterprise security blueprint. Retreived April 18, 2014, from https://www.checkpoint.com/press/2014/check-point-introduces-software-defined-protection.html

Iaa, S. (2010), Enterprise Cloud computing world forum. Retreived from http://www.EnterpriseCloudwf.com/iaas.html

McGraw, G. (2004). *Software security: Building security in.* IEEE Security & Privacy.

McGraw, G. (2006). *Software security: building security in.* USA: Addison Wesley.

Mead, N. R., Hough, E., & Stehney, I. I. T. (2005). Security quality requirements engineering (SQUARE) methodology. TECHNICAL REPORT, CMU/SEI-2005-TR-009. Retrieved from http://www.sei.cmu.edu/library/abstracts/reports/05tr009.cfm

OVF. (2010) Open virtualization format (OVF). Distributed Management Task Force. Retrieved from http://dmtf.org/sites/default/files/standards/documents/DSP0243_1.1.0.pdf

Oracle. (2012) Data security challenges. Oracle9i security overview release number 2(9.2), retrieved November 4, 2012, from http://docs.oracle.com/cd/B10501_01/network.920/a96582/overview.htm

Popović, K., & Hocenski, Z. (2010) *Enterprise cloud computing security issues and challenges.* Paper presented at MIPRO 2010, May 24-28, Opatija, Croatia

Ramachandran, M. (2008). *Software components: Guidelines and applications.* NY: Nova Publishers.

Ramachandran, M. (2011). Component-based development for cloud computing architectures. In Z. Mahmmood & R. Hill (Eds.), *Cloud computing for enterprise architectures.* Springer.

Ramachandran, M. (2011). *Software security engineering: Design and applications,.* New York: *Nova Science Publishers.*

Ramachandran, M. (2012) Service component architecture for building enterprise cloud services. *Service Technology Magazine, 65.* Retrieved from http://www.servicetechmag.com/I65/0812-4

Ramachandran, M. (2014) Enterprises engineering processes for the development and deployment of secure enterprise cloud applications. In M. Khosrow-Pour (Ed.), Encyclopedia of Information Science and Technology. Hershey, PA: IGI Global.

Srinivasan, M. K., Sarukesi, K., Rodrigues, P., Manoj, M. S., & Revathy, P. (2012) *State-of-the-art enterprise cloud computing security taxonomies: A classification of security challenges in the present enterprise cloud computing environment.* Paper presented at ICACCI '12, August 03 - 05 2012, Chennai, India

Tondel, I. A., Jaatun, M. G., & Meland, P. H. (2008). *Security requirements for rest of us: A survey. IEEE Software,* 25(1).

KEY TERMS AND DEFINITIONS

Build Security in (BSI): A process of identifying service security requirements right from beginning of the service identification to the complete life cycle.

Business Process as a Service (BPaaS): A set of process related to managing process related activities of a service business.

Enterprise Cloud Data Security: Security of maintaining and preserving client's data that are kept in the Enterprise Cloud.

Security Attacks: Injected against normal working of software systems with the intention to destroy or collect data for misuse.

Service Reuse: A process of reusing services when composing new services.

Software Security Engineering (SSE): A new discipline of applying engineering principles to develop security requirements to engineer software applications including Enterprise Cloud services such as SaaS is essentially a software application which is delivered as a service.

Software Security: Resilience of software against security attacks.

Compilation of References

AAL-Europe. (2013). Ambient assisted living catalogue of projects 2013. Retrieved April 18, 2014, from http://www.aal-europe.eu/

Abawajy, J. H., & Dandamudi, S. P. (2003). Parallel job scheduling on multicluster computing system. In *Proceedings of the 2003 IEEE International Conference on Cluster Computing.*

Abbadi, I. M. (2013). A framework for establishing trust in cloud provenance. *International Journal of Information Security*, *12*(2), 111–128. doi:10.1007/s10207-012-0179-0

Abbass, I. M. (2012). Trends of rural-urban migration in Nigeria. *European Scientific Journal*, *8*(3), 97–125.

Abdelgadir, A. T., Pathan, A.-S. K., & Ahmed, M. (2011). *On the performance of MPI-OpenMP on a 12 nodes multicore cluster. Algorithms and architectures for parallel processing* (pp. 225–234). Springer.

Abdulaziz, A. E. (2012). Cloud Computing for Increased Business Value. *International Journal of Business and Social Science*, *3*(1), 235–238.

Abramowicz, W., Filipowska, A., Kaczmarek, M., Pedrinaci, C., Starzecka, M., & Walczak, A. (2014). *Organization Structure Description for the Needs of Semantic Business Process Management*. Retrieved from http://ceur-ws.org/Vol-472/paper3.pdf

ACCA. (2012). *Cloud readiness index 2012*. Asia Cloud Computing Association.

Accenture. (2014). Our cloud strategy approach. Retrieved from http://www.accenture.com/Microsites/cloudstrategy/documents/cloud_diagram/index.html

ACMA. (2010). Australia in the digital economy: The shift to the online environment. *Communication Reports*, 2009–2010.

Adeyemi, T. O. (2009). The effective management of primary schools in Ekiti State, Nigeria: An Analytical Assessment. *Educational Research Review*, *4*(2), 48–56.

Adler, M., & Ziglio, E. (1996). *Gazing into the oracle: The Delphi method and its application to social policy and public health*. London: Kingsley.

Admin. (2009). TOP500 Highlights - November 2009. Retrieved from http://www.top500.org/lists/2009/11/highlights

Admin. (2010). What is cluster computing. Retrieved from http://www.ccgrid.org/tag/cluster-computing

Admin. (2013). Top500 Supercomputer Sites.

Afgan, E., Baker, D., Coraor, N., Chapman, B., Nekrutenko, A., & Taylor, J. (2010). Galaxy CloudMan: Delivering cloud compute clusters. *BMC Bioinformatics*, *11*(Suppl 12), S4. doi:10.1186/1471-2105-11-S12-S4 PMID:21210983

Ahmed, A. U., Hill, R. V., Smith, L. C., Wiesmann, D. M., & Frankenberger, T. (2007). *The world's most deprived: characteristics and causes of extreme poverty and hunger*. Washington, DC: International Food Policy Research Institute.

Ahronovitz, M. (2009). *Cloud computing use cases white paper, version 4.0*. National Institute of Standards and Technology.

Ahuja, S. P., & Rolli, A. C. (2011). Survey of the state-of-the-art of cloud computing. *International Journal of Cloud Applications and Computing*, *1*(4), 34–43. doi:10.4018/ijcac.2011100103

Aitken, M., Backliwal, A., Chang, M., & Udeshi, A. (2013). *Understanding healthcare access in India: What is the current state?* Parsippany, NJ: IMS Institute for Healthcare Informatics.

Ajaero, C. K., & Onokala, P. C. (2013). The effects of rural-urban migration on rural communities of Southeastern Nigeria. *International Journal of Population Research*, *2013*, 1–10. doi:10.1155/2013/610193

Alemdar, H., & Ersoy, C. (2010). Wireless sensor networks for healthcare: A survey. *Computer Networks*, *54*(15), 2688–2710. doi:10.1016/j.comnet.2010.05.003

Alibaygi, A., Karamidehkordi, M., & Pouya, M. (2012). Using the Delphi technique to assess cost-effectiveness of rural information and communications technologies (ICT) centers in Iran. *Journal of Agricultural Extension and Rural Development*, *4*(20), 552–555.

Aljabre, A. (2012). Cloud computing for increased business value. *International Journal of Business and Social Science*, *3*(1), 234–240.

Al-Masud, S. M. R. (2012). Extended and granular classification of cloud's taxonomy and services. *International Journal of Soft Computing and Engineering*, *2*(2), 278–286.

Al-Qudah, H. S. (2011). Impacts of new recruited doctors refrain from working in rural remote areas at Jordan Southern Badia Region. *International Journal of Business and Social Science*, *2*(3), 186–194.

Alshamaila, Y., Papagiannidis, S., & Li, F. (2013). Cloud computing adoption by SMEs in the north east of England: A multi-perspective framework. *Journal of Enterprise Information Management*, *26*(3), 250–275. doi:10.1108/17410391311325225

Altman, E. J., Nagle, F., & Tushman, M. L. (2013). Innovating without Information Constraints: Organizations, communities, and innovation when information costs approach zero. *Harvard Business School Organizational Behavior Unit Working Paper* (14-043).

Amazon. (2014). *Amazon S3*. Retrieved from http://aws.amazon.com/s3/

Amies, A., Sluiman, H., Tong, Q. G., & Liu, G. N. (2012). *Developing and hosting applications on the cloud*. Indianapolis, IN: IBM Press.

Amirullah. (2014). Public private partnership in infrastructure development of rural areas: Opportunities and challenges in India. *The International Journal of Humanities & Social Studies*, *2*(2), 1-6.

Ammons, G., Bala, V., Mummert, T., Reimer, D., & Zhang, X. (2011). Virtual machine images as structured data: the Mirage image library. In *Proceedings of the 3rd USENIX conference on Hot topics in cloud computing. HotCloud 2011* (pp. 1–6).

Anastaya. (2011). *Data analysis for mobile industry, white paper*. Author.

Anderson, D. P., & Fedak, G. (2006). The computational and storage potential of volunteer computing. In *Proceedings of theSixth IEEE International Symposium on Cluster Computing and the Grid (CCGRID'06)* (pp. 73–80). doi:10.1109/CCGRID.2006.101

Anderson, J. E., Wiles, F. A., & Young, K. P. (2008). The Impact of Cloud Computing on IS/IT Academics. *Issues in Information Systems*, *9*(1), 203–206.

Andrei, T., & Jain, R. (2009). *Cloud computing challenges and related security issues: A survey paper*. Retrieved from http://www.cse.wustl.edu/~jain/cse571-09/ftp/cloud.pdf

Andress, J. (2011). *The basics of information security: Understanding the fundamentals of infosec in theory and practice, syngress*. USA: Elsevier.

Andrzejak, A., Kondo, D., & Anderson, D. P. (2010). Exploiting non-dedicated resources for cloud computing. In *Proceedings of the2010 IEEE Network Operations and Management Symposium - NOMS 2010* (341–348). doi:10.1109/NOMS.2010.5488488

Ango, A. K., Ibrahim, S. A., Yakubu, A. A., & Alhaji, A. S. (2014). Impact of youth rural-urban migration on household economy and crop production: A case study of Sokoto metropolitan areas, Sokoto State, North-Western Nigeria. *Journal of Agricultural Extension and Rural Development*, *6*(4), 122–131. doi:10.5897/JAERD2013.0547

Annukka, V. (2008). *Organisational factors affecting IT innovation adoption in the Finnish early childhood education.* Paper presented at the 16th European Conference on Information Systems (ECIS 2008), Galway, Ireland.

Anstett, T., Leymann, F., Mietzner, R., & Strauch, S. (2009). Towards BPEL in the Cloud: Exploiting Different Delivery Models for the Execution of Business Processes, 2009 World Congress on Services, I, 6-10 July, Los Angeles, CA, USA.

Anthes, G. (2010). Security in the cloud. *Communications of the ACM, 53*(11), 16–18. doi:10.1145/1839676.1839683

Anthony, B. (2012). *Forecast: Cloudy but fine: Privacy risks and potential benefits in the cloud.* Privacy Victoria - Office of the Victorian Privacy Commissioner.

Apache. (2014). *Apache Libcloud.* Retrieved from https://libcloud.apache.org/

Araújo, E. C., & Maeda, A. (2013). *How to recruit and retain health workers in rural and remote areas in developing countries: A guidance note.* Health, Nutrition and Population (HNP) Discussion Paper. Washington, DC: World Bank.

Armbrust, M., Fox, A., Griffith, R., Joseph, A. D., Katz, R. H., Konwinski, A., … Zaharia, M. (2009). *Above the clouds: A Berkeley view of cloud computing* (Technical Report, No. UCB/EECS-2009-28). UC Berkeley.

Armbrust, M., Fox, F., Griffith, R., Joseph, A. D., Katz, R., Konwinski, A., . . . Zaharia, M. (2009). Above the Clouds: A Berkeley View of Cloud Computing. Berketley, CA: UC Berkeley Reliable Adaptive Distributed Systems Laboratory.

Armbrust, M., Fox, A., Griffith, R., Joseph, A. D., Katz, R., Konwinski, A., & Zaharia, M. et al. (2010). A view of cloud computing. *Communications of the ACM, 53*(4), 50–58. doi:10.1145/1721654.1721672

Arnold, S. (2009). *Cloud computing and the issue of privacy* (pp. 14–22). KM World.

Arpaci, R. H., Dusseau, A. C., Vahdat, A. M., Liu, L. T., Anderson, T. E., & Patterson, D. A. (1995). The interaction of parallel and sequential workloads on a network of workstations. *Science* (Vol. 23). ACM. Retrieved from http://portal.acm.org/citation.cfm?id=223618

Article 29 Data Protection Working Party , June 2012, Press Release on Binding Corporate Rules for Processors. (2012). Retrieved February 4, 2014 http://ec.europa.eu/justice/data-protection/article-29/press-material/press-release/art29_press_material/20120619_pr_bcrwp_en.pdf

Arumugam, R., Enti, V. R., Liu, B., Wu, X., Baskaran, K., Kong, F. F., . . . Goh, W. K. (2010). A cloud computing framework for service robots. In *Proceedings of 2010 IEEE International Conference on Robotics and Automation* (ICRA). Singapore: IEEE. doi:10.1109/ROBOT.2010.5509469

Asik, O. (2014). *Location optimization to determine telecenter network in rural Turkey.* MS Thesis, Cornell University, Ithaka, NY.

ASMEA. (2012). *SME facts.* Retrieved from http://www.asmea.org.au/SMEFacts

Assuncao, M., Costanzo, A., & Buyya, R. (2009). *Evaluating the cost-benefit of using cloud computing to extend the capacity of clusters.* Paper presented at the 18th ACM International Symposium on High Performance Distributed Computing, Garching, Germany.

Assuncao, M. D. D., Costanzo, A. D., & Buyya, R. (2010). A cost-benefit analysis of using cloud computing to extend the capacity of clusters. *Journal of Cluster Compute, 13*(3), 335–347. doi:10.1007/s10586-010-0131-x

Ateniese, G. a. (2007). Provable data possession at untrusted stores. In *Proceedings of the 14th ACM Conference on Computer and Communications Security* (pp. 598--609). Alexandria, VA: ACM. doi:10.1145/1315245.1315318

Atwell, E., Arshad, J., Lai, C.-m., Nim, L., Asheghi, N. R., Wang, J., & Washtell, J. (2007). Which English dominates the World Wide Web, British or American? In *Proceedings of the Corpus Linguistics Conference* (pp. 1-13). Birmingham, UK.

Aubert, B. A., Patry, M., & Rivard, S. (2005). A framework for information technology outsourcing risk management. *ACM SIGMIS Database, 36*(Oct), 9–28. doi:10.1145/1104004.1104007

Avison, D., & Young, T. (2007). Time to rethink health care and ICT? *Communications of the ACM, 50*(6), 69–74. doi:10.1145/1247001.1247008

Avram, M. (2014) Advantages and challenges of adopting cloud computing from an enterprise perspective. In *Proceedings of the 7th International Conference Interdisciplinary in Engineering (INTER-ENG 2013).*

AWS. (2012). *Capacity vs Utilization Curve.* Retrieved May 15, 2013, from http://www.amazon.com/economics

Axelsson, K., Melin, U., & Söderström, F. (2011). *Analyzing best practice and critical success factors in a healthcare information systems case-Are there any shortcuts to succesfull IT implementation?* Paper presented at the 19th European Conference on Information Systems – ICT and Sustainable Service Development, Helsinki, Finland.

Aymerich, F. M., Fenu, G., & Surcis, S. (2008). *An approach to a cloud computing network.* Paper presented at the First International Conference on the Applications of Digital Information and Web Technologies, Ostrava, Czech Republic. doi:10.1109/ICADIWT.2008.4664329

Babcock, C. (2009). Ready for this? *Information Week, 1250,* 22–30.

Badger, L., Grance, T., Patt-Corner, R., & Voas, J. (2012). *Cloud computing synopsis and recommendations. Special Publication.* Gaithersburg, MD: U.S. Department of Commerce, National Institute of Standards and Technology.

Bai, X., Li, M., Chen, B., Tsai, W.-T., & Gao, J. (2011). Cloud testing tools. In *Proceedings of the IEEE 6th International Symposium on Service Oriented System Engineering. SOSE 2011* (pp. 1–12). doi:10.1109/SOSE.2011.6139087

Baier, C., & Katoen, J. P. (2008). *Principles of model checking* (p. 994). MIT Press.

Baker, M., & Buyya, R. (1999). Cluster computing: The commodity supercomputer. *Software–Practice and Experience, 29*(6), 551-576.

Baker, M., Apon, A., Buyya, R., & Jin, H. (2000). Cluster computing and applications. Retrieved from http://www.buyya.com/papers/encyclopedia.pdf

Baker, S. (2007). Google and the wisdom of clouds: A lofty new strategy aims to put incredible computing power in the hands of many. *Bloomberg Business Week.* Retrieved August 12, 2014, from http://www.businessweek.com/magazine/content/07_52/b4064048925836.htm

Baker, J. (2011). The technology-organization-environment framework. In Y. Dwivedi, M. Wade, & S. Schneberger (Eds.), *Information systems theory: Explaining and predicting our digital society* (pp. 231–246). New York, NY: Springer-Verlag.

Baldassari, J. D., Kopec, C. L., Leshay, E. S., Truszkowski, W., & Finkel, D. (2005, April4-7). *Autonomic cluster management system (ACMS): A demonstration of autonomic principles at work.* Paper presented at the 12th IEEE International Conference and Workshops on the Engineering of Computer-Based Systems, 2005. ECBS '05.

Bamiah, M. A., & Brohi, S. N. (2011). Exploring the cloud deployment and service delivery models. *International Journal of Research and Reviews in Information Sciences, 1*(3), 77–80.

Bandura, A. (1977). *Social learning theory.* New York, NY: Prentice-Hall.

Banerjee, P. (2009). *An intelligent IT infrastructure for the future.* Paper presented at the 15th International Symposium on High-performance Computer Architecture, Raleigh, NC. doi:10.1109/HPCA.2009.4798230

Banisar, D., & Davies, S. (n.d.). *Privacy and human rights—An international survey of privacy laws and practice.* Retrieved March 15, 2011, from http://www.gilc.org/privacy/survey/

Baqir, M. N., & Kathawala, Y. (2004). Ba for knowledge cities: A futuristic technology model. *Journal of Knowledge Management, 8*(5), 83–95. doi:10.1108/13673270410558828

Bargh, J. A., & McKenna, K. Y. (2004). The internet and social life. *Annual Review of Psychology, 55*(1), 573–590. doi:10.1146/annurev.psych.55.090902.141922 PMID:14744227

Barham, P., Dragovic, B., Fraser, K., Hand, S., Harris, T., Ho, A., & Warfield, A. et al. (2003). Xen and the art of virtualization. *Operating Systems Review, 37*(5), 164–177. doi:10.1145/1165389.945462

Barroso, L. A., & Hölzle, U. (2009). *The Datacenter as a computer: An introduction to the design of warehouse-scale machines* (Vol. 4, pp. 1–108). Synthesis Lectures on Computer Architecture. doi:10.2200/S00193ED1V01Y200905CAC006

Barry, D. K. (2012). *Web services, service-oriented architectures, and cloud computing: The savvy manager's guide*. Newnes.

Baumer, D. L., Earp, J. B., & Poindexter, J. C. (2004). Internet privacy law: A comparison between the United States and the European Union. *Computers & Security*, *23*(5), 400–412. doi:10.1016/j.cose.2003.11.001

Bayo-Moriones, A., & Lera-Lopez, F. (2007). A firm-level analysis of determinants of ICT adoption in Spain. *Technovation*, *27*(6-7), 352–366. doi:10.1016/j.technovation.2007.01.003

Becker, D. J., Sterling, T., Savarese, D., Dorband, J. E., Ranawak, U. A., & Packer, C. V. (1995). BEOWULF: A parallel workstation for scientific computation. In *Proceedings of the International Conference on Parallel Processing*.

Becker, S., Crandall, M. D., Fisher, K. E., Kinney, B., Landry, C., & Rocha, A. (2010). *Opportunity for all: How the American public benefits from internet access at U.S. libraries*. Washington, DC: Institute of Museum and Library Services.

Bégin, M. E., Jones, B., Casey, J., Laure, E., Grey, F., Loomis, C., & Kubli, R. (2008). An EGEE comparative study grids and clouds - Evolution or revolution? *EGEE III Project Report, 30*, 1–33. Retrieved from http://wr.informatik.uni-hamburg.de/_media/teaching/sommersemester_2009/egee-grid-cloud.pdf

Behl, A. (2011). *Emerging security challenges in cloud computing*. WICT.

Bellare, M. a. (2007). Deterministic and Efficiently Searchable Encryption. Proceedings of the 27th Annual International Cryptology Conference on Advances in Cryptology (pp. 535–552). Santa Barbara, CA, USA: Springer-Verlag; Retrieved from http://dl.acm.org/citation.cfm?id=1777777.1777820

Bellare, M., Keelveedhi, S., & Ristenpart, T. (2013). Message-locked encryption and secure deduplication. In Advances in Cryptology--EUROCRYPT 2013 (pp. 296-312). Springer. doi:10.1007/978-3-642-38348-9_18

Beloglazov, A., & Buyya, R. (2010). Energy efficient resource management in virtualized cloud data centers. In Proceedings of the 10th IEEE/ACM International Conference on Cluster, Cloud and Grid Computing (pp. 826–831). Washington, DC: IEEE Computer Society. Retrieved from http://dl.acm.org/citation.cfm?id=1845139

Beloglazov, A., Abawajy, J., & Buyya, R. (2012). Energy-aware resource allocation heuristics for efficient management of data centers for Cloud computing. *Future Generation Computer Systems*, *28*(5), 755–768. doi:10.1016/j.future.2011.04.017

Bennett, C. J. (2002). Information policy and information privacy: International arenas of governance. *Journal of Law, Technology and Policy*, *2*, 385–406.

Benson, T., Anand, A., Akella, A., & Zhang, M. (2010). Understanding data centre traffic characteristics. *Computer Communication Review*, *40*(1), 92–99. doi:10.1145/1672308.1672325

Bento, A., & Bento, R. (2011). Cloud computing: A new phase in information technology management. *Journal of Information Technology Management*, *22*(1), 39–46.

Benzadri, Z., Belala, F., & Bouanaka, C. (2013). Towards a formal model for cloud computing. In *Proceedings of the International Conference on Service Oriented Computing Workshops* (p. 381-393).

Benzadri, Z., Bouanaka, C., & Belala, F. (2014). *Verifying cloud systems using a bigraphical maude-based model checker*. Paper presented at the 4th International Conference on Cloud Computing and Services Science (ESaaSA 2014).

Berman, S. J., Kesterson-Townes, L., Marshall, A., & Srivathsa, R. (2012). How cloud computing enables process and business model innovation. *Strategy and Leadership*, *40*(4), 27–35. doi:10.1108/10878571211242920

Berry, R., & Reisman, M. (2012). *Policy challenges of cross-border cloud computing*. Retrieved February 4, 2014 http://www.usitc.gov/journals/policy_challenges_of_cross-border_cloud_computing.pdf, p. 13-14

Best, M. L., & Kumar, R. (2008). Sustainability failures of rural telecenters: Challenges from the Sustainable Access in Rural India (SARI) project. *Information Technologies & International Development*, *4*(4), 31–45. doi:10.1162/itid.2008.00025

Bethel, E. W., & Howison, M. (2012). Multi-core and many-core shared-memory parallel raycasting volume rendering optimization and tuning. *International Journal of High Performance Computing Applications*, *26*(4), 399–412. doi:10.1177/1094342012440466

Bezemer, C. P., Zaidman, A., Platzbeecker, B., Hurkmans, T., & Hart, A. (2010). *Enabling multi-tenancy: An industrial experience report.* Paper presented at the 2010 IEEE International Conference on Software Maintenance, Timisoara, Romania. doi:10.1109/ICSM.2010.5609735

Bhadauria, R., Chaki, R., Chaki, N., & Sanyal, S. (2012). *A Survey on Security Issues in Cloud Computing.* School of Electronics and Communications Engineering, Vellore Institute of Technology, Vellore, India.

Bharadwaj, S. S., & Lal, P. (2012). *Exploring the impact of cloud computing adoption on organizational flexibility: A client perspective.* Paper presented at the International Conference on Cloud Computing Technologies, Applications and Management (ICCCTAM 2012). doi:10.1109/ICCCTAM.2012.6488085

Bhatnagar, S. (2006). India's software industry. In V. Chandra (Ed.), *Technology, adaptation, and exports: How some developing countries got it right?* (pp. 95–124). Washington, DC: World Bank.

Bhayal, S. (2011). *A study of security in cloud computing.* (PhD. Dissertation). Retrieved from ProQuest Dissertations and Theses. (UMI No: 1504430).

Bilal, K., Saif Ur Rehman, M., Osman, K., Abdul, H., Enrique, A., Vidura, W., & Samee, K. et al. (2014). A taxonomy and survey on Green Data Centre Networks. *Future Generation Computer Systems*, *36*, 189–208. doi:10.1016/j.future.2013.07.006

Bilenko, D. (2014). *Gevent.* Retrieved from http://www.gevent.org/

Bisong, A., & Rahman, S. S. M. (2011). An overview of the security concerns in enterprise cloud computing. *International Journal of Network Security & Its Applications*, *3*(1), 30–45. doi:10.5121/ijnsa.2011.3103

Black, A. D., Car, J., Pagliari, C., Anandan, C., Cresswell, K., Bokun, T., & Sheikh, A. et al. (2011). The impact of eHealth on the quality and safety of health care: A Systematic overview. *PLoS Medicine*, *8*(1), e1000387. doi:10.1371/journal.pmed.1000387 PMID:21267058

Blagodurov, S., Gmach, D., Arlitt, M., Chen, Y., Hyser, C., & Fedorova, A. (2013). Maximizing server utilization while meeting critical SLAs via weight-based collocation management. In *Proceedings of the IFIP/IEEE International Symposium on Integrated Network Management* (pp. 277-285). Ghent, Belgium.

Blanquicet, F., & Christensen, K. (2008) Managing energy use in a network with a new snmp power state MIB. In *Proceedings of 33rd IEEE conference on Local Computer Networks, LCN 2008* (pp 509-511). doi:10.1109/LCN.2008.4664214

Bobick, A. F., & Davis, J. W. (2001). The recognition of human movement using temporal templates. *IEEE Transactions on Pattern Analysis and Machine Intelligence*, *23*(3), 257–267. doi:10.1109/34.910878

Bock, C., Reither, S., Mikeska, T., Paulsen, M., Walter, J., & Lengauer, T. (2005). BiQ Analyzer: Visualization and quality control for DNA methylation data from bisulfite sequencing. *Bioinformatics (Oxford, England)*, *21*(21), 4067–4068. doi:10.1093/bioinformatics/bti652 PMID:16141249

Boniface, M., Nasser, B., Papay, J., Phillips, S., Servin, A., Zlatev, Z., . . . Gogouvitis, S. (2010). *Platform-as-a-Service architecture for real-time quality of service management in clouds.* Paper presented at the 5th International Conference on Internet and Web Applications and Services (ICIW 2010), Barcelona, Spain. doi:10.1109/ICIW.2010.91

Bonita Soft. (2012) BOS 5.8, Open source BPMN simulation software. Retrieved from http://www.bonitasoft.com/resources/documentation/top-tutorials

Bootstrap. (2014). Bootstrap. Retrieved April 18 2014, from http://getbootstrap.com/

Borthakur, D. (2007). The Hadoop distributed file system: Architecture and design. *Hadoop Project Website, 11*, 21.

Boss, G., Malladi, P., Quan, D., Legregni, L., & Hall, H. (2007). *Cloud computing* (IBM white paper, Version 1.0). IBM.

Boulos, M. N., Wheeler, S., Tavares, C., & Jones, R. (2011). How smartphones are changing the face of mobile and participatory healthcare: An overview, with example from eCAALYX. *Biomedical Engineering Online, 10*(1), 24. doi:10.1186/1475-925X-10-24 PMID:21466669

Bowers, K. D. (2009). HAIL: A high-availability and integrity layer for cloud storage. *Proceedings of the 16th ACM Conference on Computer and Communications Security* (pp. 187--198). Chicago, IL: ACM. doi:10.1145/1653662.1653686

BPMN2. (2012). *BPMN 2.0 handbook* (2nd ed.). Future Strategies Inc.

Braman, S. (2006). *Change of state – information, policy, and power*. Cambridge, Massachusetts: The MIT Press.

Brandic, I., Music, D., Leitner, P., & Dustdar, S. (2009). *VieSLAF framework: Enabling adaptive and versatile SLA-management*. Paper presented at the 6th International Workshop on Grid Economics and Business Models, Delft, The Netherlands.

Brasnett, P., Mihaylova, L., Canagarajah, N., & Bull, D. (2005). Particle filtering for multiple cues for object tracking in video sequences. In *Proceedings of 17th SPIE Annual Symposium on Electronic Imaging, Science and Technology* (vol. 5685, pp. 430–440).

Breitenbücher, U., Binz, T., Kopp, O., Leymann, F., & Wettinger, J. (2013). Integrated cloud application provisioning: interconnecting service-centric and script-centric management technologies. In *Conferences on the move to meaningful internet systems* (pp. 130–148). OTM. doi:10.1007/978-3-642-41030-7_9

Briscoe, G., & Marinos, A. (2009). Digital ecosystems in the clouds: Towards community cloud computing. In *Proceedings of the 3rd IEEE International Conference on Digital Ecosystems and Technologies* (pp. 103-108). IEEE.

Brodkin, J. (2007). *IBM unveils cloud computing technologies for internet-scale computing on the way in spring. Network World.*

Brytting, T. (1999). *Organizing in the small growing firm: A grounded theory approach*. Stockholm School of Economics.

BSA. (2012). *Country reports*. Retrieved February 12, 2014, http://portal.bsa.org/cloudscorecard2012/countries.html

BSA. (n.d.). Retrieved from http://portal.bsa.org/cloudscorecard2012/countries.html

Buchanan, T., Paine, C., Joinson, A. N., & Reips, U. D. (2007). Development of measures of online privacy concern and protection for use on the Internet. *Journal of the American Society for Information Science and Technology, 58*(2), 157–165. doi:10.1002/asi.20459

Burger, T. W. (2005). Intel Multi-Core Processors: Quick Reference Guide.

Burgoon, J. K., Parrott, R., Poire, B. A. L., Kelley, D. L., Walther, J. B., & Perry, D. (1989). Maintaining and restoring privacy through communication in different types of relationship. *Journal of Social and Personal Relationships, 6*(2), 131–158. doi:10.1177/026540758900600201

Buyya, R., Beloglazov1, A., & Abawajy, J. (2010b). *Energy-efficient management of data center resources for cloud computing: A vision, architectural elements, and open challenges*. Paper presented at PDPTA'10 - The International Conference on Parallel and Distributed Processing Techniques and Applications, Las Vegas, NV.

Buyya, R., Broberg, J., & Goscinski, A. (2011). Cloud computing principles and paradigms. Hoboken, New Jersey: John Wiley & Sons, Inc. doi:10.1002/9780470940105

Buyya, R., Chee Shin, Y., & Venugopal, S. (2008). *High performance computing and communications*. Paper presented at the 10th IEEE International Conference, Dalian, China.

Buyya, R., Yeo, C. S., & Venugopal, S. (2009). *Market-oriented cloud computing: Vision, hype, and reality of delivering IT services as computing utilities*. Paper presented at the 10th IEEE International Conference on High Performance Computing and Communications.

Buyya, R., Hai, J., & Cortes, T. (2002).. . *Cluster Computing, 18*, 5–8.

Buyya, R., Ranjan, R., & Calheiros, R. N. (2010 a). *InterCloud: Utility-oriented federation of cloud computing environments for scaling of application services, algorithm and architectures for parallel processing.* Lecture Notes in Computer Science, 6081, 13–31.

Buyya, R., Yeo, C. S., Venugopal, S., Broberg, J., & Brandic, I. (2009). Cloud computing and emerging IT platforms: Vision, hype, and reality for delivering computing as the 5th utility. *Journal of Future Generation Computer Systems*, 25(6), 559–616. doi:10.1016/j.future.2008.12.001

Byrant, F. B., Yarnold, P. R., & Michelson, E. (1999). Statistical methodology: Using confirmatory factor analysis (CFA) in emergency medicine research. *Academic Emergency Medicine*, 6(1), 54–66. doi:10.1111/j.1553-2712.1999.tb00096.x PMID:9928978

Caldeira, M. M., & Ward, J. M. (2003). Using resource-based theory to interpret the successful adoption and use of information systems and technology in manufacturing small and medium-sized enterprises. *European Journal of Information Systems*, 12(2), 127–141. doi:10.1057/palgrave.ejis.3000454

Calheiros, R. N., Ranjan, R., De Rose, C. A. F., & Buyya, R. (2009). *CloudSim: A novel framework for modeling and simulation of cloud computing infrastructures and services, technical report.* Grid Computing and Distributed Systems Laboratory, The University of Melbourne.

Caminao Project. (2013) Caminao's way: Do enterprises know how symbolic they are? *Modelling Enterprises Engineering Project.* Retrieved June 21, 2014, from http://caminao.wordpress.com/overview/?goback=%2Egde_3731775_member_251475288

Cao, B. Q., Li, B., & Xia, Q. M. (2009). A service-oriented qos-assured and multi-agent cloud computing architecture. *Cloud Computing*, 644–649. Retrieved from http://www.springerlink.com/index/97H153M34UK4L000.pdf

Carey, V.A. (2010). *Questionnaire design for business research.* Academic Press.

Carlin, S., & Curran, K. (2011). Cloud computing security. *International Journal of Ambient Computing and Intelligence*, 3(1), 14–19. doi:10.4018/jaci.2011010102

Carr, P., & Madan, D. (1999). Option valuation using the fast Fourier transform. *Journal of Computational Finance*, 2(4), 61-73.

Carr, N. G. (2005). The end of corporate computing. *MIT Sloan Management Review*, 46(3), 67–73.

Carroll, M., Kotze, P., & van der Merwe, A. (2010). Securing virtual and cloud environments. In I. Ivanov, M. van Sinderen, & B. Shishkov (Eds.), *Cloud computing and services science* (pp. 73–90). Berlin, Germany: Springer-Verlag.

Catteddu, D., & Hogben, G. (2009). *Cloud computing: Benefits, risks and recommendations for information security.* Technical Report, European Network and Information Security Agency.

Cavailhes, J., Dessendre, C., Goffette-Nagot, F., Schmitt, B., & INRA-Dijon, . (1994). Change in the French countryside: Some analytical propositions. *European Review of Agriculture Economics*, 21(3-4), 429–449. doi:10.1093/erae/21.3-4.429

Cegielski, C. G., Jones-Farmer, L. A., Wu, Y., & Hazen, B. T. (2012). Adoption of cloud computing technologies in supply chains: An organizational information processing theory approach. *International Journal of Logistics Management*, 23(2), 184–211. doi:10.1108/09574091211265350

Celesti, A., Tusa, F., Villari, M., & Puliafito, A. (2010). How to enhance cloud architectures to enable cross-federation. In *Proceedings of the IEEE 3rd International Conference on Cloud Computing. CLOUD 2010* (pp. 337–345). doi:10.1109/CLOUD.2010.46

Celik, A., Holliday, J., & Hurst, Z. (2006). *Data dissemination to a large mobile network: Simulation of broadcast clouds.* Paper presented at the 7th International Conference on Mobile Data Management (MDM) 2006, Santa Clara, CA.

Cellary, W., & Strykowski, S. (2009). *E-government based on cloud computing and serviceoriented architecture.* Paper presented at the 3rd International Conference on Theory and Practice of Electronic Governance (ICEGOV '09), Bogota, Colombia. doi:10.1145/1693042.1693045

Cerbelaud, D., Garg, S., & Huylebroeck, J. (2009). Opening the clouds: qualitative overview of the state-of-the-art open source VM-based cloud management platforms. In *Proceedings of the 10th ACM/IFIP/USENIX International Conference on Middleware. Middleware 2009* (pp. 1–8).

Chai, L. (2009). *High performance and scalable MPI intra-node communication middleware for multi-core clusters. PhD.* The Ohio State University.

Chakraborty, R., Ramireddy, S., Raghu, T. S., & Rao, H. R. (2010). The information assurance practices of cloud computing vendors. *IT Professional, 12*(4), 29–37. doi:10.1109/MITP.2010.44

Chandra, A., & Weissman, J. (2009). Nebulas: Using distributed voluntary resources to build clouds. In Proceedings of the 2009 conference on hot topics in cloud computing (pp. 2–2). USENIX Association. Retrieved from http://citeseerx.ist.psu.edu/viewdoc/summary?doi=10.1.1.148.7267

Chandrakumar, T., & Parthasarathy, S. (2014). A framework for evaluating cloud enterprise resource planning (ERP). In Continued rise of the cloud: Advances and trends in cloud computing (pp. 161–175). doi:10.1007/978-1-4471-6452-4_7

Chang, V. (2013). *A proposed model to analyse risk and return for a large computing system adoption.* (PhD Thesis). University of Southampton.

Chang, V. (2013). Cloud bioinformatics in a private cloud deployment. Advancing medical practice through technology: Applications for healthcare delivery, management, and quality (p. 205). Hershey, PA: IGI Global.

Chang, V. (2013a). A case study for business integration as a service. Trends in e-business, e-services, and e-commerce: impact of technology on goods, services, and business transactions. Hershey, PA: IGI Global.

Chang, V. (2013b). Brain segmentation – A case study of biomedical cloud computing for education and research. In *Proceedings of Learning Technologies Workshop, Higher Education Academy* (HEA). University of Greenwich.

Chang, V. (2013b). *Cloud computing for brain segmentation technology.* Paper presented at the IEEE CloudCom 2013. http://eprints.soton.ac.uk/357188/

Chang, V. (2014a). *Introduction to the risk visualization as a service.* Paper presented at the First International Workshop on Emerging Software as a Service and Analytics, Barcelona, Spain.

Chang, V. (2014a). *The big data analysis for measuring popularity in the mobile cloud.* Paper presented at the First International Workshop on Emerging Software as a Service and Analytics, Barcelona, Spain.

Chang, V., & Ramachandran, M. (2014). A proposed case for the cloud software engineering in security. In *Proceedings of the First International Workshop on Emerging Software as a Service ESaaSA.* Academic Press.

Chang, V., Bacigalupo, D., Wills, G., De Roure, D. (2010a). *A categorisation of cloud computing business models.* Paper presented at the CCGrid 2010 IEEE Conference, Melbourne, Australia.

Chang, V., Li, C., De Roure, D., Wills, G., Walters, R. J., & Chee, C. (2012). The Financial Clouds Review. In Grid and Cloud Computing: Concepts, Methodologies, Tools and Applications (pp. 1062-1083). Hershey, PA: Information Science Reference. doi:10.4018/978-1-4666-0879-5.ch503

Chang, V., Mills, H., & Newhouse, S. (2007). *From open source to long-term sustainability: Review of business models and case studies.* Paper presented at the UK e-Science All Hands Meeting, Nottingham, UK.

Chang, V., Walters, R. J. & Wills, G. (2013a). Cloud storage and bioinformatics in a private cloud deployment: Lessons for data intensive research. In *Proceedings of Cloud Computing and Service Science* (LNCS). Berlin: Springer.

Chang, V., Walters, R. J. & Wills, G. (2013b). The development that leads to the cloud computing business framework. *International Journal of Information Management, 33*(3), 524-538.

Chang, V., Walters, R. J., & Wills, G. (2014). Review of cloud computing and existing frameworks for cloud adoption. In *Advances in cloud computing research.* Nova Publishers.

Chang, V., Walters, R., & Wills, G. (2014). Monte Carlo risk assessment as a service in the cloud. *International Journal of Business Integration and Management.*

Chang, V., Wills, G., & De Roure, D. (2010). *Towards financial cloud framework: Modelling and benchmarking of financial assets in public and private clouds*. Paper presented at IEEE Cloud 2010, the third International Conference on Cloud Computing, 5-10 July, Miami, Florida, USA.

Chang, V., Wills, G., & De Roure, D. (2010b). *A review of cloud business models and sustainability*. Paper presented at the IEEE Cloud 2010, the third International Conference on Cloud Computing, Miami, FL.

Chang, V., Wills, G., & Walters, R. (2011). *The positive impacts offered by Healthcare Cloud and 3D Bioinformatics*. Paper presented at the 10th e-Science All Hands Meeting 2011, York.

Chang, V., Wills, G., & Walters, R. J. (2011d). *Towards business integration as a service 2.0*. Paper presented at the IEEE International Conference on e-Business Engineering, the 3rd International Workshop on Cloud Services - Platform Accelerating e-Business, Beijing, China.

Chang, V. (2013a). Business integration as a service: Computational risk analysis for small and medium enterprises adopting SAP. *International Journal of Next-Generation Computing, 4*(3).

Chang, V. (2014c). Consulting as a service – Demonstrated by cloud computing consultancy projects in the greater China. In *Advances in cloud computing research*. Nova Publishers.

Chang, V. (2014d). The business intelligence as a service in the cloud. *Future Generation Computer Systems, 37*(1), 512–534. doi:10.1016/j.future.2013.12.028

Chang, V. (2014g). Measuring and analyzing German and Spanish customer satisfaction of using the iPhone 4S mobile cloud service. *Open Journal of Cloud Computing, 1*(1), 19–26.

Chang, V., De Roure, D., Walters, R. J., & Wills, G. (2011 b). Organisational sustainability modelling for return on investment: Case studies presented by a national health service (NHS) trust UK. *Journal of Computing and Information Technology, 19*(3). doi:10.2498/cit.1001951

Chang, V., De Roure, D., Wills, G., & Walters, R. (2011c). Case studies and organisational sustainability modelling presented by cloud computing business framework. *International Journal of Web Services Research, 8*(3), 26–53. doi:10.4018/JWSR.2011070102

Chang, V., Walters, R. J., & Wills, G. (2014). Monte Carlo risk assessment as a service in the cloud. *International Journal of Business Integration and Management, 7*(2), 1–16.

Chang, V., Wills, G., Walters, R., & Currie, W. (2012). (in press). Towards a structured cloud ROI. *Sustainable Green Computing: Practices Methodologies and Technologies.*

Chapman, C., Emmerich, W., Márquez, F. G., Clayman, S., & Galis, A. (2011). Software architecture definition for on-demand cloud provisioning. *Cluster Computing, 15*(2), 79–100. doi:10.1007/s10586-011-0152-0

Chard, K., Caton, S., Rana, O., & Bubendorfer, K. (2010). Social cloud: Cloud computing in social networks. In *Proceedings of 2010 IEEE 3rd International Conference on Cloud Computing* (pp. 99-106). IEEE.

Chatterjee, S., Chakraborty, S., Sarker, S., Sarker, S., & Lau, F. Y. (2009). Examining the success factors for mobile work in healthcare: A deductive study. *Decision Support Systems, 46*(3), 620–633. doi:10.1016/j.dss.2008.11.003

Chaudhry, I. S., Malik, S., & Ashraf, M. (2006). Rural poverty in Pakistan: Some related concepts, issues and empirical analysis. *Pakistan Economic and Social Review, 44*(2), 259–276.

Chellappa, R. K. (1997). Intermediaries in cloud-computing: A new computing paradigm. INFORMS. Cluster: Electronic Commerce.

Chen, X., Wills, G. B., Gilbert, L., & Bacigalupo, D. (2010). *Using cloud for research: A technical review*. TesciRes Report for JISC.

Chen, Z., Zhao, Y., Miao, X., Chen, Y., & Wang, Q. (2009). Rapid provisioning of cloud infrastructure leveraging peer-to-peer networks. In *Proceedings of the IEEE 26th Conference on Distributed Computing Systems. ICDCS 2009* (pp. 324–329). doi:10.1109/ICDCSW.2009.35

Chen, J., He, Y. B., & Jin, X. (2008). A study on the factors that influence the fitness between technology strategy and corporate strategy. *International Journal of Innovation and Technology Management*, 5(1), 81–103. doi:10.1142/S0219877008001308

Chen, K., Wallis, J. W., McLellan, M. D., Larson, D. E., Kalicki, J. M., Pohl, C. S., & Mardis, E. R. et al. (2009). BreakDancer: An algorithm for high-resolution mapping of genomic structural variation. *Nature Methods*, 6(9), 677–681. doi:10.1038/nmeth.1363 PMID:19668202

Chen, M., Zhang, D., & Zhou, L. (2007). Empowering collaborative commerce with web services enabled business process management systems. *Decision Support Systems*, 43(2), 530–546. doi:10.1016/j.dss.2005.05.014

Chen, X., Wills, G. B., Gilbert, L., & Bacigalupo, D. (2010). *Tecires report: Using cloud for research: A technical review*. University of Southampton.

Chesbrough, H. (2011). Bringing open innovation to services. *MIT Sloan Management Review*, 52(2), 85–90.

Chiaravigli, L., & Mellia, M. (2013). *Energy-efficient management of campus pcs. In Green communications: Theoretical fundamentals, algorithms, and applications*. CRC Press.

Ching, H. L., & Ellis, P. (2004). Marketing in cyberspace: What factors drive e-commerce adoption? *Journal of Marketing Management*, 20(3-4), 409–429. doi:10.1362/026725704323080470

Chopra, S., & Meindl, P. (2001). *E-business and the supply chain*. Upper Saddle River, NJ: Prentice-Hall.

Chou, T. (2009). Seven clear business models. Active Book Press.

Chow, R., Golle, P., Jakobsson, M., Shi, E., Staddon, J., Masuoka, R., & Molina, J. (2009). *Controlling data in the cloud: Outsourcing computation without outsourcing control*. Paper presented at the ACM workshop on Cloud Computing Security (CCSW '09), Chicago, IL. doi:10.1145/1655008.1655020

Chowdhury, G. (2012). Building environmentally sustainable information services: A green IS research agenda. *Journal of the American Society for Information Science and Technology*, 63(4), 633–647. doi:10.1002/asi.21703

Chowdhury, M., Krishnan, K., & Vishwanath, S. (2012). *Touching lives through mobile health: Assessment of the global market opportunity*. India: PricewaterhouseCoopers.

Christensen, K., Gunaratne, C., Nordman, B., & George, A. (2004). The next frontier for communications networks: Power management. *Computer Communications*, 27(18), 1758–1770. doi:10.1016/j.comcom.2004.06.012

Christudas, B. D. (2008). *Service oriented java business integration*. Packt.

Chute, C. G., Pathak, J., Savova, G. K., Bailey, K. R., Schor, M. I., Hart, L. A., . . . Huff, S. M. (2011). *The SHARPn project on secondary use of Electronic Medical Record data: Progress, plans, and possibilities*. Paper presented at the AMIA Annual Symposium Proceedings.

Cibulskis, K., Lawrence, M. S., Carter, S. L., Sivachenko, A., Jaffe, D., Sougnez, C., & Getz, G. et al. (2013). Sensitive detection of somatic point mutations in impure and heterogeneous cancer samples. *Nature Biotechnology*, 31(3), 213–219. doi:10.1038/nbt.2514 PMID:23396013

Cilesiz, S. (2004). Internet cafés: Bridges of the digital divide. *International Conference on Society for Information Technology & Teacher Education*, Atlanta, GA.

Cingolani, P., Platts, A., Wang, L. L., Coon, M., Nguyen, T., Wang, L., & Ruden, D. M. et al. (2012). A program for annotating and predicting the effects of single nucleotide polymorphisms, SnpEff: SNPs in the genome of Drosophila melanogaster strain w1118; iso-2; iso-3. *Fly*, 6(2), 80–92. doi:10.4161/fly.19695 PMID:22728672

Ciortea, L., Zamfir, C., Bucur, S., Chipounov, V., & Candea, G. (2009). Cloud9: A software testing service. *SIGOPS Oper.Syst.Rev.*, 43(4), 5–10. doi:10.1145/1713254.1713257

Clarke, E. M., Emerson, E. A., & Sistla, A. P. (1986). Automatic verification of finite-state concurrent systems using temporal logic specifications. *ACM Transactions on Programming Languages and Systems*, 8(2), 244–263. doi:10.1145/5397.5399

Clavel, M., Durán, F., Eker, S., Lincoln, P., Martí-Oliet, N., Meseguer, J., & Talcott, C. (2007). All about Maude - a high-performance logical framework: How to specify. Berlin, Heidelberg: Springer.

ClearHealth. (2013). ClearHealth smart. simple. sustainable. Retrieved April 15, 2014, from http://clear-health.com/

Clemensen, J., Rasmussen, J., Denning, A., & Craggs, M. (2011). *Patient empowerment and new citizen roles through telehealth technologies - The early stage.* Paper presented at the Third International Conference on eHealth, Telemedicine, and Social Medicine Gosier France.

Cloud Security Alliance. (2010). Top threats to cloud computing V1.0. Retrieved from http://www.cloudsecurityalliance.org/topthreats/csathreats.v1.0.pdf

CNIL. (2012). *Synthèse des réponses à la consultation publique sur le cloud computing lancée par la CNIL d'Octobre à Décembre 2011 et analyse de la CNIL.* Retrieved February 7, 2014, http://www.cnil.fr/fileadmin/images/la_cnil/actualite/Synthese_des_reponses_a_la_consultation_publique_sur_le_Cloud_et_analyse_de_la_CNIL.pdf, p. 10

Common Criteria, (2012). Common criteria for information technology security evaluation. CCMB-2012-09-003.

Corradi, A., Fanelli, M., & Foschini, L. (2014). VM consolidation: A real case based on OpenStack Cloud. *Future Generation Computer Systems, 32*, 118–127. doi:10.1016/j.future.2012.05.012

Cosmo, R., Zacchiroli, S., & Zavattaro, G. (2012). Towards a formal component model for the cloud. In G. Eleftherakis, M. Hinchey, & M. Holcombe (Eds.), Software engineering and formal methods (p.156-171). Berlin Heidelberg: Springer.

COUCHBASE. (2014). COUCHBASE NoSQL Database. Retrieved April 15, 2014, from http://www.couchbase.com

Cox, L. P., Murray, C. D., & Noble, B. D. (2002). Pastiche: Making backup cheap and easy. *ACM SIGOPS Operating Systems Review, 36*, 285-298.

Cragg, P., & King, M. (1993). Small-firm computing: Motivators and inhibitors. *Management Information Systems Quarterly, 17*(1), 47–59. doi:10.2307/249509

Creeger, M. (2009). CTO roundtable: Cloud computing, special article. *Communications of the ACM, 52*(8), 50. doi:10.1145/1536616.1536633

Creel, M., & Goffe, W. L. (2007). Multi-core CPUs, clusters, and grid computing: A tutorial. *Computational Economics, 32*(4).

Creese, S., Hopkins, P., Pearson, S., & Shen, Y. (2009). Data protection-aware design for cloud computing. Retrieved from http://www.hpl.hp.com/techreports/2009/HPL-2009-192.pdf

Crook, C., & Kumar, R. (1998). Electronic data interchange: A multi-industry investigation using grounded theory. *Information & Management, 34*(2), 75–89. doi:10.1016/S0378-7206(98)00040-8

Crystal, D. (2006). Language and the internet (2nd ed.). Cambridge: Cambridge University Press. doi:10.1017/CBO9780511487002

CSA. (2009). *Security guidance for critical areas of focus in cloud computing V2.1.* Cloud Security Alliance.

CSA. (2010) Enterprise Cloud Security Alliance, domain 12: Guidance for identity & access management. Retrieved from https://EnterpriseCloudsecurityalliance.org/guidance/csaguide-dom12-v2.10.pdf

Cunsolo, V. D., Distefano, S., Puliafito, A., & Scarpa, M. (2009). Volunteer computing and desktop cloud: The cloud@ home paradigm. In *Proceedings of the Eighth IEEE International Symposium on Network Computing and Applications, 2009 (NCA 2009)* (pp. 134–139). IEEE. doi:10.1109/NCA.2009.41

Cunsolo, V., Distefano, S., Puliafito, A., & Scarp, M. (2009). Cloud@ home: Bridging the gap between volunteer and cloud computing. In *Proceedings of the 5th international conference on Emerging intelligent computing technology and applications (ICIC'09).* doi:10.1007/978-3-642-04070-2_48

Curran, J., Blackburn, R. A., & Woods, A. (1991). *Exploring enterprise cultures: Small service sector enterprise owners and their views.* Kingston University.

Curtis, S. (2012). *CERN says EU data protection laws are hindering cloud adoption.* Retrieved February 24, 2014, http://www.computerworlduk.com/news/cloud computing/3364456/cern-says-eu-data-protection-laws-are-hindering-cloud-adoption/

Custer, R., Scarcella, J., & Stewart, B. (1999). *The modified Delphi technique – A rotational model*. Retrieved from http://scholar.lib.vt.edu/ejournals/JVTE/v15n2/custer.html

Cusumano, M. (2009). Technology strategy and management: The legacy of Bill Gates. *Communications of the ACM, 52*(1), 25–26. doi:10.1145/1435417.1435429

Cuzzocrea, A., Song, I.-Y., & Davis, K. C. (2011). Analytics over large-scale multidimensional data: the big data revolution! In *Proceedings of the ACM 14th international workshop on Data Warehousing and OLAP*. Glasgow, Scotland, UK. doi:10.1145/2064676.2064695

Dai, J., & Zhang, L. (2013). Trusted cloud platform oriented to knowledge management. *Journal of Computer Information Systems, 9*(12), 4997–5004.

Daitx, F., Esteves, R. P., & Granville, L. Z. (2011) *On the use of SNMP as a management interface for virtual networks*. In the *Proceedings of the IFIP/IEEE InternationalSymposium on Integrated Network Management* doi:10.1109/INM.2011.5990689

Dalal, P. (2006). *Use of ICT for women empowerment in India*. New York: United Nations.

Dalkey, N., & Helmer, O. (1951). *The use of experts for the estimation of bombing requirements: A project Delphi experiment*. Santa Monica: RAND Corporation.

Dally, W. J., & Towles, B. P. (2004). *Principles and practices of interconnection network*. Morgan Kaufmann.

Damanpour, F. (1991). Organizational innovation: A meta-analysis of effects of determinants and moderators. *Academy of Management Journal, 34*(3), 555–590. doi:10.2307/256406

Danet, B., & Herring, S. C. (Eds.). (2007). *The multilingual internet: Language, culture, and communication online*. Oxford: Oxford University Press. doi:10.1093/acprof:oso/9780195304794.001.0001

Daphne. (2013). Daphne data-as-a-service platform for healthy lifestyle and preventive medicine. Retrieved April 15, 2014, from http://www.daphne-fp7.eu/node/21

Darnell, B. (2014). *Tornado*. Retrieved from http://tornado.readthedocs.org/en/latest/index.html

Dave, A. (2012). The state of cloud computing security in Asia. *Trend Micro*, 1-5.

Dave, D., & Dave, R. (2012). Role of non-farm sector in rural development. *National Monthly Refereed Journal of Research in Arts & Education, 1*(7), 7–16.

Dave, M., Dave, M., & Shishodia, Y. S. (2013). Cloud computing and knowledge management as a service: A collaborative approach to harness and manage the plethora of knowledge. *International Journal of Information Technology, 5*(2), 619–622.

Davenport, T. (1992). *Process innovation: Reengineering work through information technology*. Harvard Business Review Press.

Davis, M. (2004). Planet of slum. *New Left Review, 26*, 5–34.

Daylami, N., Ryan, T., Olfman, L., & Shayo, C. (2005). *Determinants of a aaAAa pplication service provider (ASP) adoption as an innovation*. Paper presented at the 38th Annual Hawaii International Conference on System Sciences, Hawaii, HI. doi:10.1109/HICSS.2005.193

Deadalus. (2014). Interoperability Platform X1.V1. Retrieved April 17, 2014, from http://dedaluschina.com.cn/products-solutions/interoperability-platform-x1-v1/

DeCew, J. W. (1997). *In pursuit of privacy: Law, ethics, and the rise of technology*. Ithaca, NY: Cornell University Press.

Delahunty, S. (2009, January). *State of enterprise storage*. Paper presented by Byte & Switch. InformationWeek Analytics.com, Manhassett, NY.

Delaney, K. J., & Vara, V. (2007). Google plans services to store users' data. *Wall Street Journal*. Retrieved August 12, 2014, from http://online.wsj.com/article/SB119612660573504716.html?modhps_us_whats_news

Deloitte (2013). Moving to the Cloud? Engage internal audit upfront to manage risks. *Wall Street Journal*. Retrieved from http://deloitte.wsj.com/riskandcompliance/2013/12/11/moving-to-the-cloud-engage-internal-audit-upfront-to-manage-risks-2/?KEYWORDS=cloud

Deloitte. (2012). *Rethinking the role of IT for CPG companies using cloud computing to help escape the constraints of existing business economics.* Retrieved from https://www.deloitte.com/assets/Dcom-UnitedStates/Local%20Content/Articles/Consumer%20Business/Consumer%20Products/us_cp_rethinkingtheroleofIT_042512.pdf

DePietro, R., Wiarda, E., & Fleischer, M. (1990). The context for change: Organization, technology and environment. In L. G. Tornatzky & M. Fleischer (Eds.), *The process of technological innovation* (pp. 151–175). Lexington, MA: Lexington Books.

Despins, C., Labeau, F., Labelle, R., Cheriet, M., Leon-Garcia, A., & Cherkaoui, O. (2012). *Green communications for carbon emission reductions: Architectures and standards. Green communications: Theoretical fundamentals, algorithms, and applications.* CRC Press.

Detmer, D., Bloomrosen, M., Raymond, B., & Tang, P. (2008). Integrated personal health records: Transformative tools for consumer-centric care. *BMC Medical Informatics and Decision Making, 8*(1), 45. doi:10.1186/1472-6947-8-45 PMID:18837999

DFD. (2011a). *Opportunities and applicability for use by the Australian Government.* Cloud Computing strategic direction paper. DFD.

DFD. (2011b). *Better practice guide: Negotiating the cloud – Legal issues in cloud computing agreements.* DFD.

DFD. (2011c). *Better practice checklist: Privacy and cloud computing for Australian government agencies.* DFD.

Dhar, S. (2012). From outsourcing to cloud computing: Evolution of IT services. *Management Research Review, 35*(8), 664–675. doi:10.1108/01409171211247677

Dhar, S., & Balakrishnan, B. (2006). Risks, benefits and challenges in global IT outsourcing: Perspectives and practices. *Journal of Global Information Management, 14*(3), 59–89. doi:10.4018/jgim.2006070104

Diaz, J., von Laszewski, G., Wang, F., & Fox, G. (2012). Abstract image management and universal image registration for cloud and HPC infrastructures. In *Proceedings of the IEEE 5th International Conference on Cloud Computing. CLOUD 2012* (pp. 463–470). doi:10.1109/CLOUD.2012.94

Dibbern, J., Goles, T., Hirschheim, R., & Jayatilaka, B. (2004). Information systems outsourcing: A survey and analysis of the literature. *ACM SIGMIS Database, 35*(Nov), 6–102. doi:10.1145/1035233.1035236

Dihal, S., Bouwman, H., de Reuver, M., Warnier, M., & Carlsson, C. (2013). Mobile cloud computing: State of the art and outlook. *Info, 15*(1), 4–16. doi:10.1108/14636691311296174

DIISR. (2011). *Key statistics: Australian small business, Commonwealth of Australia 2011.* DIISR.

Dillon, T., Wu, C., & Chang, E. (2010). *Cloud computing: Issues and challenges.* Academic Press.

Dinh, H. T., Lee, C., Niyato, D., & Wang, P. (2011). A survey of mobile cloud computing: architecture, applications, and approaches. *Wireless Communications and Mobile Computing.*

Directive 95/46/EC of the European Parliament and of the Council of 24 October 1995 on the Protection of Individuals with Regard to the Processing of Personal Data and on the Free Movement of Such Data. (1995). Retrieved January 7, 2014, http://eur-lex.europa.eu/LexUriServ/LexUriServ.do?uri=CELEX:31995L0046:en:HTML

Doelitzscher, F., Sulistio, A., Reich, C., Kuijs, H., & Wolf, D. (2011). Private cloud for collaboration and e-learning services: From IaaS to SaaS. *Computing, 91*(1), 23–42. doi:10.1007/s00607-010-0106-z

Dong, H., Hao, Q., Zhang, T., & Zhang, B. (2010). Formal discussion on relationship between virtualization and cloud computing. In *Proceedings of the 2010 International Conference on Parallel and Distributed Computing, Applications and Technologies (PDCAT)* (pp. 448–453). doi:10.1109/PDCAT.2010.41

Dong, B., Zheng, Q., Qiao, M., Shu, J., & Yang, J. (2009). BlueSky cloud framework: An e-learning framework embracing cloud computing. *Lecture Notes in Computer Science, 5931*, 577–582. doi:10.1007/978-3-642-10665-1_55

Dong, L., Neufeld, D., & Higgins, C. (2009). Top management support of enterprise systems implementations. *Journal of Information Technology, 24*(1), 55–80. doi:10.1057/jit.2008.21

Douceur, J. R., Adya, A., Bolosky, W. J., Simon, P., & Theimer, M. (2002). Reclaiming space from duplicate files in a serverless distributed file system. In *Proceedings of the 22nd International Conference on Distributed Computing Systems, 2002* (pp. 617-624).

Dropbox. (2014). *Dropbox.* Retrieved from https://www. dropbox.com

Drupal. (2014). Drupal open source content management platform. Retrieved April 18, 2014, from https:// drupal.org/

Dunn, T. (2010). *Identity management: Cloud and virtualisation, keynote.* Munich Cloud.

Durbin, J., & Watson, G. S. (1950). Testing for serial correlation in least squares regression: I. *Biometrika, 37,* 409–428. PMID:14801065

Durkee, D. (2010). Why cloud computing will never be free. *Communications of the ACM, 53*(May), 62. doi:10.1145/1735223.1735242

Dwivedi, Y., Ravichandran, K., Williams, M., Miller, S., Lal, B., Antony, G., & Kartik, M. (2013). IS/IT project failures: A review of the extant literature for deriving a taxonomy of failure factors. In Y. Dwivedi, H. Henriksen, D. Wastell, & R. De' (Eds.), *Grand successes and failures in IT public and private sectors* (Vol. 402, pp. 73–88). Berlin Heidelberg: Springer. doi:10.1007/978-3-642-38862-0_5

Eberlein, E., & Keller, U. (1995). Hyperbolic distributions in finance. *Bernoulli, 1*(3), 281–299. doi:10.2307/3318481

Eder, L., & Igbaria, M. (2001). Determinants of intranet diffusion and infusion. *Omega, 29*(3), 233–242. doi:10.1016/S0305-0483(00)00044-X

Educause. (2008). *The tower and the cloud: Higher education in the age of cloud computing.* Author.

Eker, S., Meseguer, J., & Sridharanarayanan, A. (2002). The Maude LTL model checker. In *Proceedings of the 4th International Workshop on Rewriting Logic and its Applications (WRLA 2002). (Vol. 71, pp. 115-142).* Elsevier.

Eldred, M. E., Orangi, A., Al-Emadi, A. A., Ahmad, A. A., O'Reilly, T. J., & Barghouti, N. (2014). *Reservoir simulations in a high performance cloud computing environment.* Society of Petroleum Engineers. doi:10.2118/167877-MS

Electronic Privacy Information Center. (n.d.). *The census and privacy.* Retrieved March 4, 2013, from http://epic. org/privacy/census/

Elena, K., Detmar, W. S., & Norman, L. C. (1999). Information technology adoption across time: A cross sectional comparison of pre-adoption and post-adoption beliefs. *Management Information Systems Quarterly, 23*(2), 183–213. doi:10.2307/249751

EMC. (2014). Electronic health record infrastructure solutions. Retrieved April 17, 2014, from http://greece. emc.com/industry/public-sector/electronic-health-record-infrastructure.htm

ENISA. (2009). *Cloud computing, benefits, risks and recommendations for information security.* Retrieved January 21, 2014, http://www.enisa.europa.eu/act/rm/ files/deliverables/cloud-computing-risk-assessment/ at_download/fullReport

Ercan, T. (2010). Effective use of cloud computing in educational institutions. *Procedia: Social and Behavioral Sciences, 2*(2), 938–942. doi:10.1016/j.sbspro.2010.03.130

Erdman, K., & Stark, N. (2010). *Legal challenges for U.S. healthcare adopters of cloud computing.* Paper presented at the International Technology Law Association Annual European Conference, Berlin, Germany.

Erdogmus, H. (2009). Cloud computing: Does nirvana hide behind the nebula? *IEEE Software, 26*(2), 4–6. doi:10.1109/MS.2009.31

Eriksson, H.-E. & Penker, M. (1998). UML Toolkit. Wiley & Sons.

Eriksson, H.-E., & Penker, M. (1999). *Business Modeling with UML: Business patterns at work.* Wiley & Sons.

Ernst & Young and IE Foundation. (2013). Security solutions in consumer goods & retail. In Consumer Goods & Retail. Advanced series Foundation.

ESB. (2014) Software defined protection – Enterprise security blueprint. Retrieved April 18, 2014, from https://www.checkpoint.com/press/2014/check-point-introduces-software-defined-protection.html

Etro, F. (2011). The economics of cloud computing. *The IUP Journal of Managerial Economics, 9*(2), 7–22.

Europa. (n.d.). Retrieved from http://ec.europa.eu/avservices/video/player.cfm?ref=82655&sitelang=en

Europa.eu. (2012). *EU – US joint statement on data protection by European Commission Vice-President Viviane Reding and US Secretary of Commerce John Bryson*. Retrieved February 1, 2014, http://europa.eu/rapid/pressReleasesAction.do?reference=MEMO/12/192

European Comission. (2013). Glossary: Business functions - statistics explained. Retrieved from http://epp.eurostat.ec.europa.eu/statistics_explained/index.php/Glossary:Core_business_function

European Commission. (2011a). *Special Eurobarometer 359: Attitudes on data protection and electronic identity in the European Union*. Retrieved January 7, 2014, http://ec.europa.eu/public_opinion/archives/ebs/ebs_359_en.pdf

European Commission. (2011b). *Information society and media directorate-general, Cloud computing: Public consultation report*. Retrieved January 7, 2014, http://ec.europa.eu/information_society/activities/cloudcomputing/docs/ccconsultationfinalreport.pdf, p. 3-5

European Commission. (2011c). *Justice, commission decisions on the adequacy of the protection of personal data in third countries*. Retrieved January 9, 2014, http://ec.europa.eu/justice/policies/privacy/thridcountries/index_en.htm

European Commission. (2012a). *How will the EU's reform adapt data protection rules to new technological developments*. Retrieved January 9, 2014, http://ec.europa.eu/justice/data-protection/document/review2012/factsheets/8_en.pdf, p. 1

European Commission. (2012b). *Press release: Commission proposes a comprehensive reform of data protection rules to increase users' control of their data and to cut costs for businesses*. Retrieved February 3, 2014, http://europa.eu/rapid/pressReleasesAction.do?reference=IP/12/46&format=HTML&aged=0&language=EN&guiLanguage=en

European Commission. (2012c). *Proposal for a regulation of the european parliament and of the council on the protection of individuals with regard to the processing on personal data and on the free movement of such data*. Retrieved January 9, 2014, http://ec.europa.eu/justice/data-protection/document/review2012/com_2012_11_en.pdf

European Commission. (2014a). *Progress on EU data protection reform now irreversible following European Parliament vote*. Retrieved January 7, 2014, http://europa.eu/rapid/press-release_MEMO-14-186_en.htm

European Commission. (2014b). *Digital agenda: New strategy to drive European business and government productivity via cloud computing*. Retrieved January 21, 2014, http://europa.eu/rapid/press-release_IP-12-1025_en.htm

European Parliament. (2012). *Directorate-general for internal policies, cloud computing*. Retrieved January 9, 2014, http://ec.europa.eu/information_society/activities/cloudcomputing/docs/cc_study_parliament.pdf, p. 21

Evans, J. R., & Mathur, A. (2005). The value of online surveys. *Internet Research*, 15(2), 195–219. doi:10.1108/10662240510590360

Faithfull, A. J., Perrone, G. D., & Hildebrandt, T. (2013). *Big red: A development environment for bigraphs*. EASST Electronic Communications.

Fang, X., Wang, M., & Wu, S. (2013). A method for security evaluation in cloud computing based on petri behavioral profiles. In Z. Yin, L. Pan, & X. Fang (Eds.), *Proceedings of The Eighth International Conference on Bio-Inspired Computing: Theories and Applications (BIC-TA) (pp. 587-593)*. Berlin Heidelberg: Springer.

Farah, S. (2010). Cloud computing or software as a service-which makes the most sense for HR? Employment relations today. *ABI/INFORM Global, 36*(4), 31.

Farber, D. (2008). Oracle's Ellison nails cloud computing. *CNET News*. Received from http://news.cnet.com/8301-13953_10052188-80.html

Faye, M. L., McArthur, J. W., Sachs, J. D., & Snow, T. (2004). The challenges facing landlocked developing countries. *Journal of Human Development, 5*(1), 31–68. doi:10.1080/14649880310001660201

February, B. S. A. (2012). *Global patchwork of conflicting laws and regulations threatens fast growing cloud computing market.* Retrieved February 12, 2014, http://ww2.bsa.org/country/News%20and%20Events/News%20Archives/global/02222012-cloudscorecard.aspx

Fengguang, S., Moore, S., & Dongarra, J. (2009). *Analytical modeling and optimization for affinity based thread scheduling on multicore systems.* Paper presented at the IEEE International Conference on Cluster Computing and Workshops, 2009. CLUSTER '09.

Feng, W., Jiang, Z., Maoxiang, C., & Shoulin, S. (2012). An ontology cloud-shadow model based knowledge service framework. In *Proceedings of the 2012 International Conference on Communication, Electronics and Automation Engineering.*

Fielding, A. (1999). *HTTP/1.1:Protocol parameters.* Retrieved from http://www.w3.org/Protocols/rfc2616/rfc2616-sec3.html

Fielding, R. T. (2000). *Representational State Transfer.* Retrieved from http://www.ics.uci.edu/~fielding/pubs/dissertation/rest_arch_style.htm

Filipowska, A., Hepp, M., Kaczmarek, M., & Markovic, I. (2014.). Organisational ontology framework for semantic business prcoess management. Retrieved from http://www.heppnetz.de/files/OrganizationalOntologyFrameworkSBPM.pdf

Financial Times Book. (2009). Managing in a downturn: Leading business thinkers on how to grow when markets don't. *Financial Times.*

Fitch, D. F., & Xu, H. (2012). A Petri net model for secure and fault-tolerant cloud-based information storage. In *SEKE* (pp. 333–339). Knowledge Systems Institute Graduate School.

Flick, U. (2009). *An introduction to qualitative research* (4th ed.). Los Angeles, CA: SAGE Publications.

Foley & Lardner LLP. (2013). *Cloud computing: A practical framework for managing cloud computing risk.* Retrieved February 5, 2014, http://www.foley.com/files/Publication/493fc6cc-aa03-4974-a874-022e36d12184/Presentation/PublicationAttachment/c9bd65f3-a6fd-4acb-96de-d1c0434f1eb7/CloudComputingPractical-FrameworkforManagingCloudComputingRisk.pdf

Forster, S. C., Finkel, A. M., Gould, J. A., & Hertzog, P. J. (2013). RNA-eXpress annotates novel transcript features in RNA-seq data. *Bioinformatics (Oxford, England), 29*(6), 810–812. doi:10.1093/bioinformatics/btt034 PMID:23396121

Fortino, G., Mastroianni, C., Pathan, M., & Vakali, A. (2009). *Next generation content networks: Trends and challenges.* Paper presented at the 4th Edition of the UPGRADE-CN Workshop on use of P2P, GRID and Agents for the Development of Content Networks (UPGRADE-CN '09), Garching, Germany. doi:10.1145/1552486.1552516

Foster, H., & Spanoudakis, G. (2010). Formal methods in model-driven development for service- oriented and cloud computing. Retrieved from http://citeseerx.ist.psu.edu/viewdoc/download?doi=10.1.1.232.8422&rep=rep1&type=pdf

Foster, I., Zhao, Y., Raicu, I., & Lu, S. (2008). *Cloud computing and grid computing 360-degree compared.* Paper presented at the Grid Computing Environments Workshop. doi:10.1109/GCE.2008.4738445

Foster, I., Kesselman, C., & Tuecke, S. (2001). The anatomy of the grid: Enabling scalable virtual organizations. *International Journal of High Performance Computing Applications, 15*(3), 200–222. doi:10.1177/109434200101500302

Frambach, R., Barkema, H., Nooteboom, B., & Wedel, M. (1998). Adoption of a service innovation in the business market: An empirical test of supply-side variables. *Journal of Business Research, 41*(2), 161–174. doi:10.1016/S0148-2963(97)00005-2

Freitas, L., & Watson, P. (2012). Formalizing workflows partitioning over federated clouds: Multi-level security and costs. In *Proceedings of the IEEE Eighth World Congress on Services (SERVICES)* (pp. 219–226).

Friedman, A. A., & West, D. M. (2010). Privacy and security in cloud computing. *Issues in Technology Innovation, 3.*

Furhad, H., Haque, M., Kim, C.-H., & Kim, J.-M. (2013). An analysis of reducing communication delay in network-on-chip interconnect architecture. *Wireless Personal Communications,* 1–17. doi:10.1007/s11277-013-1257-y

Furuholt, B., & Kristiansen, S. (2007). Internet cafés in Asia and Africa – Venues for education and learning? *The Journal of Community Informatics, 3*(2).

Fu, T. M. (2005). Unequal primary education opportunities in rural and urban China. *China Perspectives, 60*, 2–8.

Gamage, P., & Halpin, E. F. (2007). E-Sri Lanka: Bridging the digital divide. *The Electronic Library, 25*(6), 693–710. doi:10.1108/02640470710837128

Ganti, R. K., Ye, F., & Lei, H. (2011). Mobile crowdsensing: Current state and future challenges. *Communications Magazine, IEEE, 49*(11), 32–39. doi:10.1109/MCOM.2011.6069707

Gao, J., Bai, X., & Tsai, W.-T. (2011). Cloud testing-issues, challenges, needs and practice. *Software Engineering, 1*(1), 9–23.

Garey, M., & Johnson, D. (1985). A 71/60 theorem for bin packing. *Journal of Complexity, 106*, 65–106. doi:10.1016/0885-064X(85)90022-6

Gartner. (2009). *Cloud computing inquiries at Gartner.* Retrieved August 12, 2014, from http://blogs.gartner.com/thomas_bittman/2009/10/29/cloud-computing-inquiries-at-gartner

Gartner. (2011a). *Gartner reveals top predictions for IT organisations and users for 2012 and beyond.* Retrieved January 20, 2014, http://www.gartner.com/it/page.jsp?id=1862714

Gartner. (2011b). *Forecast: Public cloud services, worldwide and regions, industry sectors, 2010–2015.* Retrieved January 20, 2014, http://www.vertical.ch/fileadmin/News/Forecast_Public_Cloud_Services__Worldwide_and_Regions__Industry_Sectors__2010-2015__2011_Update.pdf

Gartner. (2013). Gartner says cloud computing will become the bulk of new it spend by 2016. Retrieved from http://www.gartner.com/newsroom/id/2613015

Gaukroger, S. (2012). *Objectivity: A very short introduction.* Oxford: Oxford University Press. doi:10.1093/actrade/9780199606696.001.0001

Gavrila, D., & Davis, L. (1995). Towards 3-d model-based tracking and recognition of human movement. In *Proceedings of the International Workshop on Face and Gesture Recognition* (pp. 272–277).

Geer, D. (2005). Industry trends. *Chip Makers Turn to Multicore Processors, 38*, 11–13.

Geer, D. (2007). For programmers, multicore chips mean multiple challenges. *Computer, 40*(9), 17–19. doi:10.1109/MC.2007.311

Gellman, R. (2009). *Privacy in the clouds: Risks to privacy and confidentiality from cloud computing.* World Privacy Forum. Retrieved February 4, 2014, from http://gato-docs.its.txstate.edu/vpit-security/policies/WPF_Cloud_Privacy_Report.pdf

Gentzoglanis, A. (2011). EVA and the cloud: An integrated approach to modelling of cloud computing. *International Journal of Modellling and Optimization, 1*, 322–327.

George, F., & Shyam, G. (2010). Impact of cloud computing: Beyond a technology trend. *Systems Integration*, 262–269.

Ghazali, O., Osman, B., Ahmad, A., Abas, A., Rahmat, A. R., & Firdhous, M. (2013). Cloud powered rural telecenters – A model for sustainable telecenters. In *Proceedings of the 4th International Conference on Rural ICT Development* (pp. 136–142). Malacca, Malaysia.

Ghemawat, S., Gobioff, H., & Leung, S.-T. (2003). *The Google file system.* Paper presented at the ACM SIGOPS Operating Systems Review. doi:10.1145/945449.945450

Gibbs, J., & Kraemer, K. (2004). A cross-country investigation of the determinants of scope of e-commerce use: An institutional approach. *Electronic Markets, 14*(2), 124–137. doi:10.1080/10196780410001675077

Gillen, A., Grieser, T., & Perry, R. (2008). *Business value of virtualization: Realizing the benefits of integrated solutions* (White Paper). IDC.

Gillett, F. E. (2009). *The personal cloud – How individual computing will shift from being device-centric to information-centric.* Forrester Research White Paper.

Glenstrup, A.J., Damgaard, T.C., Birkedal, L., and Højsgaard, E. (2008). An implementation of bigraph matching. Retrieved from http://cs.au.dk/~birke/papers/implmatch.pdf

Global Netoptex Incorporated. (2009). Demystifying the cloud: Important opportunities, crucial choices (pp. 4-14). Retrieved from http://www.gni.com

GNU. (2014). *Python-GnuPG*. Retrieved from https://bitbucket.org/vinay.sajip/python-gnupg

GNU. (2014). *SKS OpenPGP keyserver*. Retrieved from https://packages.debian.org/search?keywords=sks

Goddard, A., Wilson, N., Cryer, P., & Yamashita, G. (2011). Data hosting infrastructure for primary biodiversity data. *BMC Bioinformatics*, *12*(Suppl 15), S5. doi:10.1186/1471-2105-12-S15-S5 PMID:22373257

Goldberg, R. P. (1974). Survey of Virtual Machine Research. *IEEE Computer*, *7*(6), 34–45. doi:10.1109/MC.1974.6323581

Gong, S. G., & Buxton, H. (2002). Editorial: Understanding visual behavior. *International Journal of Image and Vision Computing*, *20*(12), 825–826. doi:10.1016/S0262-8856(02)00092-6

Goo, J., & Nam, K. (2007). *Contract as a source of trust – Commitment in successful IT outsourcing relationship: An empirical study*. Paper presented at the 40th Annual Hawaii International Conference on System Sciences (HICSS 2007), Waikoloa, HI. doi:10.1109/HICSS.2007.148

Goode, S., & Stevens, K. (2000). An analysis of the business characteristics of adopters and non-adopters of world wide web technology. *Information Technology Management*, *11*(2), 129–154. doi:10.1023/A:1019112722593

Google. (2014). Angularjs. Retrieved April 15, 2014, from https://angularjs.org/

Google. (2014). *Google Drive*. Retrieved from https://drive.google.com

Gorniak, S. (2009). *Cloud computing European network and information security agency (ENISA)*. Retrieved from http://www.enisa.europa.eu/act/res/technologies/tech/dnssec/dnssec

Goscinski, A., & Brock, M. (2010). Toward dynamic and attribute based publication, discovery and selection for cloud computing. *Future Generation Computer Systems*, *26*(7), 947–970. doi:10.1016/j.future.2010.03.009

Governatori, G., Indulska, M., & zu Muehlen, M. (2009). *Formal models of business process compliance*. JURIX.

Gramsamer, F. (2003). *Scalable flow control for interconnection networks*. *Doctor of Tecnical Sciences thesis*, Swiss Federal Institute of Technology Zurich.

Grance, T. (2010). The NIST cloud definition framework. National Institute of Standards and Technology.

Grandison, T., Maximilien, E., Thorpe, S., & Alba, A. (2010). Towards a formal definition of a computing cloud. In *Proceedings of the 6th World Congress on Services (SERVICES-1), 2010* (pp. 191–192).

Grandon, E., & Pearson, M. (2004). Electronic commerce adoption: An empirical study of small and medium US businesses. *Information & Management*, *42*(1), 197–216. doi:10.1016/j.im.2003.12.010

Graubner, P., Schmidt, M., & Freisleben, B. (2011). Energy-efficient management of virtual machines in Eucalyptus. In Proceedings of the 2011 IEEE 4th International Conference on Cloud Computing (pp. 243–250). IEEE Computer Society. Retrieved from http://ieeexplore.ieee.org/xpls/abs_all.jsp?arnumber=6008716

Gray, A. (2013). Conflict of laws and the cloud. *Computer Law & Security Report*, *29*(1), 58–65. doi:10.1016/j.clsr.2012.11.004

Gray, P. S., Williamson, J. B., Karp, D. A., & Dalphin, J. (2007). *The research imagination: An introduction to qualitative and quantitative methods*. Cambridge University Press. doi:10.1017/CBO9780511819391

Greenberg, A., Hamilton, J., Maltz, D. A., & Patel, P. (2008). The cost of a cloud: Research problems in data center networks. *Computer Communication Review*, *39*(1), 68–73. doi:10.1145/1496091.1496103

Grobauer, B., Walloschek, T., & Stocker, E. (2011). Understanding cloud computing vulnerabilities. *Security & Privacy, IEEE*, *9*(2), 50–57. doi:10.1109/MSP.2010.115

Guazzelli, A., Zeller, M., Lin, W. C., & Williams, G. (2009). PMML: An open standard for sharing models. *The R Journal, 1*(1), 60–65.

Guelzim, T., & Obaidat, M. (2013). *Green computing and communication architecture. Handbook of green information and communication systems* (pp. 209–227). Elsvier.

Gulati, S. (2008). Technology-enhanced learning in developing nations: A review. *International Review of Research in Open and Distance Learning, 9*(1), 1–16.

Guo, Z., Song, M., & Song, J. (2010). *A governance model for cloud computing*. Paper presented at the Management and Service Science (MASS).

Gupta, A., & Awasthi, L. K. L. (2009). Peer enterprises: A viable alternative to Cloud computing? In Proceedings of the 2009 IEEE International Conference on Internet Multimedia Services Architecture and Applications (IMSAA) (Vol. 2, pp. 1–6). IEEE. Retrieved from http://ieeexplore.ieee.org/xpls/abs_all.jsp?arnumber=5439456

Gupta, P., Seetharaman, A., & Raj, J. R. (2013). The usage and adoption of cloud computing by small and medium businesses. *International Journal of Information Management, 33*(5), 861–874. doi:10.1016/j.ijinfomgt.2013.07.001

Haag, S., & Cummings, M. (2010). *Management information systems for the information age (8th ed.)*. New York: McGraw-Hill/Irwin.

Haardt, H. (2014). *Py-convergent-encryption*. Retrieved from https://github.com/HITGmbH/py-convergent-encryption

Habib, S. M., Hauke, S., Ries, S., Mühlhäuser, M., Antonopoulos, N., Anjum, A., & Rong, C. (2012). Trust as a facilitator in cloud computing: a survey. *Journal of Cloud Computing: Advances, Systems, and Applications, 1*(1), 19.

Haddad, I. (2006). *The HAS architecture: A highly available and scalable cluster architecture for web servers*. PhD thesis, Concordia University, Library and Archives Canada.

Hailu, A. (2012). *Factors influencing cloud-computing technology adoption in developing countries*. (PhD. Thesis), Retrieved from ProQuest Dissertations and Theses. (UMI No: 3549131).

Halamka, J., Mandl, K., & Tang, P. (2008). Early experiences with personal health records. *Journal of the American Medical Informatics Association, 15*(1), 1–7. doi:10.1197/jamia.M2562 PMID:17947615

Hall, J. A., & Liedtka, S. L. (2007). The Sarbanes-Oxley Act: Implications for large-scale IT outsourcing. *Communications of the ACM, 50*(3), 95–100. doi:10.1145/1226736.1226742

Hallowell, R. (1996). The relationships of customer satisfaction, customer loyalty, and profitability: An empirical study. *International Journal of Service Industry Management, 7*(4), 27–42. doi:10.1108/09564239610129931

Hamdaqa, M., Livogiannisand, T., & Tahvildari, L. (2011). *A reference model for developing cloud applications*. Paper presented at the 1st International Conference on Cloud Computing and Services Science, Noordwijkerhout, The Netherlands.

Hamdaqa, M., & Tahvildari, L. (2012). Cloud computing uncovered: A research landscape. *Advances in Computers, 86*, 41–85. doi:10.1016/B978-0-12-396535-6.00002-8

Hameed, M. A., Counsell, S., & Swift, S. (2012). A conceptual model for the process of IT innovation adoption in organizations. *Journal of Engineering and Technology Management, 29*(3), 358–390. doi:10.1016/j.jengtecman.2012.03.007

Hammond, L. D., & Post, L. (2000). Inequality in teaching and schooling: Supporting high-quality teaching and leadership in low-income schools. In R. D. Kahlenberg (Ed.), *A Notion at Risk: Preserving Public Education as an Engine for Social Mobility* (pp. 127–167). New York: The Century Foundation.

Handler, D.P., Barbier, J., & Schottmiller. (2012). *SMB public cloud adoption: Opening a hidden market*. Cisco Internet Business Solutions Group.

Hargraves, M. (2002). Elevating the voices of rural minority women. *American Journal of Public Health, 92*(4), 514–515. doi:10.2105/AJPH.92.4.514 PMID:11919041

Harnik, D., Pinkas, B., & Shulman-Peleg, A. (2010). Side channels in cloud services: Deduplication in cloud storage. *Security & Privacy, IEEE, 8*(6), 40-47.

Harris, T. D., Buzby, P. R., Babcock, H., Beer, E., Bowers, J., Braslavsky, I., . . . Efcavitch, J. W. (2008). Single-molecule DNA sequencing of a viral genome. *Science, 320*(5872), 106-109.

Harris, B., Goudge, J., Ataguba, J. E., McIntyre, D., Nxumalo, N., Jikwana, S., & Chersich, M. (2011). Inequities in access to health care in South Africa. *Journal of Public Health Policy, 32*, 102–123. doi:10.1057/jphp.2011.35 PMID:21730985

Harrison, D., Mykytyn, P. Jr, & Riemenschneider, C. (1997). Executive decision about adoption of information technology in small business: Theory and empirical tests. *Information Systems Research, 8*(2), 171–195. doi:10.1287/isre.8.2.171

Harutyunyan, A., Blomer, J., Buncic, P., Charalampidis, I., Grey, F., Karneyeu, A., & Skands, P. et al. (2012). CernVM co-pilot: An extensible framework for building scalable computing infrastructures on the cloud. *Journal of Physics: Conference Series, 396*(3), 032054. doi:10.1088/1742-6596/396/3/032054

Hayes, B. (2008). Cloud computing. *Communications of the ACM, 51*(7), 9–11. doi:10.1145/1364782.1364786

Heilig, L., & Voß, S. (2014b). A scientometric analysis of cloud computing literature. *IEEE Transactions on Cloud Computing. DOI:(preprint version)*.10.1109/TCC.2014.2321168

Heilig, L., & Voß, S. (2014a). (to appear). Decision analytics for cloud computing: A classification and literature review. *Tutorials in Operations Research*. doi:10.1287/educ.2014.0124

Heininger, R. (2012). *IT service management in a cloud environment: A literature review* (working paper). Social Science Research Network.

Helmer, K. G., Ambite, J. L., Ames, J., Ananthakrishnan, R., Burns, G., Chervenak, A. L., & Macciardi, F. et al. (2011). Enabling collaborative research using the biomedical informatics research network (BIRN). *Journal of the American Medical Informatics Association, 18*(4), 416–422. doi:10.1136/amiajnl-2010-000032 PMID:21515543

Helmer, O. (1965). *Social technology*. Santa Monica, CA: RAND Corporation.

Hendry, L. B., & Kloep, M. (2004). To stay or not to stay? – that is the question: Rural youths' views on living in Scandinavia. *Barn, 22*(4), 33–52.

Herbert, L., & Erickson, J. (2011). The ROI of cloud apps. In *A total economic impact™ analysis uncovers long-term value in cloud apps*. Forrester.

Herhalt, J., & Cochrane, K. (2012). Exploring the cloud. *KPMG*, 1–46.

Heskett, J. L., & Schlesinger, L. A. (1994). Putting the service-profit chain to work. *Harvard Business Review, 72*(2), 164–174.

Hillbrecht, R., & de Bona, L. C. E. (2012) A SNMP-based virtual machines management interface. In *Proceedings of the IEEE fifth International conference on Utility and Cloud Computing UCC-2012* (pp 279-286).

Hillson, D., & Murray-Webster, R. (2007). *Understanding and managing risk attitude*. Aldershot: Gower Publishing Co Ltd.

Hobona, G., Fairbairn, D., & James, P. (2010). Orchestration of grid-enabled geospatial web services in geoscientific workflows. *IEEE Transactions on Automation Science and Engineering, 7*(2), 407-411.

Hofer, C. W., & Schendel, D. (1978). *Strategy formulation: analytical concepts*. West Pub. Company.

Hogarty, K., Hines, C., Kromrey, J., Ferron, J., & Mumford, K. (2005). The quality of factor solutions in exploratory factor analysis: The influence of sample size, communality, and overdetermination. *Educational and Psychological Measurement, 65*(2), 202–226. doi:10.1177/0013164404267287

Holden, E. P., Kang, J. W., Bills, D. P., & Ilyassov, M. (2009). *Databases in the cloud: A work in progress*. Paper presented at the 10th ACM Conference on SIG-Information Technology Education (SIGITE '09), Fairfax, VA. doi:10.1145/1631728.1631765

Hope, L., & Lam, E. (n.d.). A review of applications of cluster computing. *World*, 1-10.

Hosman, L., & Fife, E. (2012). The use of mobile phones for development in {Africa}: Top-down-meets-bottom-up partnering. *The Journal of Community Informatics, 8*(3).

Hosono, S., Kuno, A., Hasegawa, M., Hara, T., Shimomura, Y., & Arai, T. (2009). A framework of co-creating business values for IT services. In *Proceedings of 2009 IEEE International Conference on Cloud Computing.* Bangalore, India: IEEE. doi:10.1109/CLOUD.2009.57

Hsbollah, H. M., & Idris, M. (2009). E-learning adoption: The role of relative advantages, trialability and academic specialization. *Campus-Wide Information Systems, 26*(1), 54–70. doi:10.1108/10650740910921564

HSSP. (2013). Healthcare services specification program. Retrieved January 19, 2013, from http://hssp.wikispaces.com/

Huang, A. (2014). *PyRabin.* Retrieved from https://github.com/aitjcize/pyrabin

Huang, D., Zhang, X., Kang, M., & Luo, J. (2010). MobiCloud: Building secure cloud framework for mobile computing and communication. In *Proceedings of the Fifth IEEE International Symposium on Service Oriented System Engineering (SOSE), 27*(34), 4-5. doi:10.1109/SOSE.2010.20

Hudson, P., & Hudson, S. (2008). Changing preservice teachers' attitudes for teaching in rural schools. *Australian Journal of Teacher Education, 33*(4), 67–77. doi:10.14221/ajte.2008v33n4.6

Huebscher, M. C., & McCann, J. A. (2008). A survey of autonomic computing degrees, models, and applications. *ACM Computing Surveys, 40*(3), 1–28. doi:10.1145/1380584.1380585

Hugos, M. H., & Hulitzky, D. (2010). *Business in the cloud: What every business needs to know about cloud computing.* Wiley Publishing.

Huie, M. C., Laribee, S. F., & Hogan, S. D. (2002). The right to privacy in personal data: The EU prods the US and controversy continues. *9 TULSA J. COMP. &. INT'L L, 391,* 441.

Hu, L., Ying, S., Jia, X., & Zhao, K. (2009). Towards an approach of semantic access control for cloud computing. In M. Jaatun, G. Zhao, & C. Rong (Eds.), *Lecture notes in computer science* (Vol. 5931, pp. 145–156). Berlin Heidelberg: Springer.

Hull, J. C. (2009). Options, futures, and other derivatives (7th ed.). Pearson, Prentice Hall.

Humble, J., & Farley, D. (2011). *Continuous delivery: Reliable software releases through build, test, and deployment automation.* Upper Saddle River, NJ: Addison-Wesley.

Hunter, J., Little, S., & Schroeter, R. (2008). The application of semantic web technologies to multimedia data fusion within e-science. In Semantic multimedia and ontologies (pp. 207-226). Academic Press.

Hutley, N. (2012). Modelling the economic impact of cloud computing. *KPMG,* 1–52.

Hüttermann, M. (2012). *DevOps for developers.* New York: Apress.

Huttlinger, K., Ayers, J. S., Lawson, T., & Ayers, J. (2003). Suffering it out: Meeting the needs of health care delivery in a rural area. *Online Journal of Rural Nursing and Health Care, 3*(2), 17–28.

Hu, W., Tan, T., Wang, L., & Maybank, S. (2004). A survey on visual surveillance of object motion and behaviors. *IEEE Transactions on Systems, Man and Cybernetics, Part C: Applications and Reviews, 34*(3), 334–352. doi:10.1109/TSMCC.2004.829274

Hwang, K., Kulkarni, S., & Hu, Y. (2009). *Cloud security with virtualized defense and reputation-based trust management.* Paper presented at the 2009 Eighth IEEE International Conference on Dependable, Autonomic and Secure Computing, Chengdu, China.

Iaa, S. (2010), Enterprise Cloud computing world forum. Retreived from http://www.EnterpriseCloudwf.com/iaas.html

Iacovou, C., Benbasat, I., & Dexter, A. (1995). Electronic data interchange and small organizations: Adoption and impact of technology. *Management Information Systems Quarterly, 19*(4), 465–485. doi:10.2307/249629

IBM Global Technology Services. (2010). *Getting cloud computing right.* Retrieved August 12, 2014, from http://public.dhe.ibm.com/common/ssi/ecm/en/ciw03078usen/CIW03078USEN.PDF

IBM Global Technology Services. (2011). *Strategies for assessing cloud security.* Retrieved August 12, 2014, from http://public.dhe.ibm.com/common/ssi/ecm/en/sew03022usen/SEW03022USEN.PDF

IBM. (2008). *IT service management to enable the fulfilment of your SOA strategy*. White paper. IBM Global Services.

IBM. (2009). *The benefits of cloud computing*. Retrieved August 12, 2014 from http://public.dhe.ibm.com/common/ssi/ecm/en/diw03004usen/DIW03004USEN.PDF

IBM. (2010). *Defining a framework for cloud adoption* (technical paper). IBM.

Ichikawa, S., & Takagi, S. (2009). *Estimating the optimal configuration of a multi-core cluster: a preliminary study*. Paper presented at the 2009 International Conference on Complex, Intelligent and Software Intensive Systems. CISIS '09.

IDC. (2012). *IDC releases market predictions for 2013: CIO agenda*. Retrieved from http://www.idc.com/getdoc.jsp?containerId=prUS24482213

IDC. (2013). *IDC predictions 2013: Competing on the 3rd platform*. Retrieved from http://www.idc.com/research/Predictions13/downloadable/238044.pdf

Idongesit, W., & Skouby, K. E. (Eds.). (2014). *The African mobile story*. River Publishers.

IETF. (1991) RFC 1213 Management Information Base. Retrieved June 7, 2014, from http://www.ietf.org/rfc/rfc1213.txt

IHE. (2012). Integrating the healthcare enterprise. Retrieved March 1, 2011, from http://www.ihe.net/

Ilavarasan, V. P., & Parthasarathy, B. (2012). Limited growth opportunities amidst opportunities for growth: An empirical study of the inter-firm linkages of small software firms in India. *Journal of Innovation and Entrepreneurship*, *1*(4), 1–12.

IMO. (2013). Better practice guide: Privacy and cloud computing for Australian government agencies. Australian Government.

Information Week Survey. (2009). *Why do you use SaaS and private clouds, results based on interview and surveys 250 managers and directors*. Author.

Intel. (1997). Moore's law and Intel innovation. Retrieved from http://www.intel.com/about/companyinfo/museum/exhibits/moore.htm?wapkw=moore+laws

International Business Machines Corp. (2006). *An architectural blueprint for autonomic computing*. White Paper Fourth Edition.

International Journal of Business Integration and Management Cloud Industry Forum. (2012). *USA cloud adoption & trends 2012*. Retrieved February 15, 2014, http://docs.media.bitpipe.com/io_10x/io_103375/item_496686/CIF%20white%20paper%20US%20Cloud_FINAL.pdf, p.12, 14

Is convergent encryption really secure? (2011). Retrieved from http://crypto.stackexchange.com/questions/729/is-convergent-encryption-really-secure

ISO. (2005). *ISO IEC 27001: Information technology — Security techniques - Information security management systems – Requirements*. Geneva: ISO.

ITIIC. (2011). Cloud computing: Opportunities and challenges. Information Technology Industry Innovation Council.

ITU-T Technology Watch Report. (2012). *Privacy in cloud computing*. ITU-T.

Jahangir, N., & Begum, N. (2007). Effect of perceived usefulness, ease of use, security and privacy on customer attitude and adaptation in the context of e-banking. *Journal of Management Research*, *7*(3), 147–157.

Jalonen, H., & Lehtonen, A. (2011). *Uncertainty in the innovation process*. Paper presented at the European Conference on Innovation and Entrepreneurship, Aberdeen, Scotland.

Jampani, R., Xu, F., Wu, M., Perez, L. L., Jermaine, C., & Haas, P. J. (2008, June). MCDB: A Monte Carlo approach to managing uncertain data. In *Proceedings of the 2008 ACM SIGMOD International Conference on Management of Data* (pp. 687-700). ACM. doi:10.1145/1376616.1376686

Jamwal, D., Sambyal, A., & Sambyal, G. S. (2011). Cloud computing: Its security & privacy aspects. *International Journal of Latest Trends in Computing*, *2*(1), 25–28.

Jarraya, Y., Eghtesadi, A., Debbabi, M., Zhang, Y., & Pourzandi, M. (2012). Cloud calculus: Security verification in elastic cloud computing platform. In *Proceedings of theInternational Symposium on Security in Collaboration Technologies and Systems (SECOTS 2012)* (pp. 447-454). IEEE Press.

Javadi, B., Akbari, M. K., Abawajy, J. H., & Nahavandi, S. (2006). *Multi-cluster computing interconnection network performance modeling and analysis.* Paper presented at the 2006 International Conference on Advanced Computing and Communications. ADCOM 2006.

Javadi, B., Abawajy, J. H., & Akbari, M. K. (2006). *Modeling and analysis of heterogeneous loosely-coupled distributed systems Technical Report TR C06/1.* Australia: School of Information Technology, Deakin University.

Javadi, B., Abawajy, J. H., & Akbari, M. K. (2008a). A comprehensive analytical model of interconnection networks in large-scale cluster systems. *Concurrency and Computation, 20*(1), 75–97. doi:10.1002/cpe.1222

Javadi, B., Abawajy, J. H., & Akbari, M. K. (2008b). Performance modeling and analysis of heterogeneous meta-computing systems interconnection networks. *Computers & Electrical Engineering, 34*(6), 488–502. doi:10.1016/j.compeleceng.2007.09.007

Javadi, B., Abawajy, J., & Buyya, R. (2012). Failure-aware resource provisioning for hybrid Cloud infrastructure. *Journal of Parallel and Distributed Computing, 72*(10), 1318–1331. doi:10.1016/j.jpdc.2012.06.012

Javadi, B., Kondo, D., Iosup, A., & Epema, D. (2013). The Failure trace archive: Enabling the comparison of failure measurements and models of distributed systems. *Journal of Parallel and Distributed Computing, 73*(8), 1208–1223. doi:10.1016/j.jpdc.2013.04.002

Jennett, P., & Watanabe, M. (2006). Healthcare and telemedicine: Ongoing and evolving challenges. *Disease Management & Health Outcomes, 14*(1).

Jensen, M., Schwenk, J. O., Gruschka, N., & Lo Iacono, L. (2009). *On technical security issues in cloud computing.* Paper presented at the 2009 IEEE International Conference on Cloud Computing, Los Angeles, CA. doi:10.1109/CLOUD.2009.60

Jeyaraj, A., Rottman, J. W., & Lacity, M. C. (2006). A review of the predictors, linkages, and biases in IT innovation adoption research. *Journal of Information Technology, 21*(1), 1–23. doi:10.1057/palgrave.jit.2000056

Jiang, D., Huang, P., Lin, P., & Jiang, J. (2012). Energy efficient VM placement heuristic algorithms comparison for cloud with multidimensional resources. *Information Computing and Applications,* 413–420. Retrieved from http://www.springerlink.com/index/K08740211M1W7834.pdf

Jingjing, W., Ponomarev, D., & Abu-Ghazaleh, N. (2012). *Performance analysis of a multithreaded PDES simulator on multicore clusters.* Paper presented at the 26th Workshop on Principles of Advanced and Distributed Simulation (PADS), 2012 ACM/IEEE/SCS.

Joanna, G., & Chiemi, H. (2010). *Exploring the future of cloud computing: Riding the next wave of technology driven transformation.* Paper presented at the World Economic Forum 2010.

Johnson, B. (2008). *Cloud computing is a trap, warns GNU founder Richard Stallman.* Retrieved from http://www.guardian.co.uk/technology/2008/sep/29/cloud.computing.richard.stallman

Joint, A., Baker, E., & Eccles, E. (2009). Hey, you, get off of that Cloud? *Computer Law & Security Report, 25*(3), 270–274. doi:10.1016/j.clsr.2009.03.001

Jones, I., Carr, D. L., & Dalal, P. (2011). Responding to rural health disparities in the United States: The geography of emergency care and telemedical technology. *Networks and Communication Studies, 25*(3-4), 273–290.

Juels, A., & Kaliski, J. B. (2007). Pors: Proofs of retrievability for large files. In Proceedings of the 14th ACM conference on Computer and communications security (pp. 584–597). New York: ACM; Retrieved from http://doi.acm.org/10.1145/1315245.1315317 doi:10.1145/1315245.1315317

June, I. D. C. (2011). *European enterprises will spend $8.2 billion on cloud professional services in 2015.* Retrieved January 21, 2014, http://www.idc.com/getdoc.jsp?containerId=prUK22881811

June, I. D. C. (2012). *Third of western European retailers expect to increase spending on cloud computing by up to 25%.* Retrieved January 21, 2014, http://www.idc-ri.com/getdoc.jsp?containerId=prUK23533512&pageType=PRINTFRIENDLY

Jung, J. J., Chang, Y. S., & Chao-Chinwu, Y. L. (2012). Advances in intelligent grid and cloud computing. *Information Systems Frontiers*, *14*(4), 823–825. doi:10.1007/s10796-012-9349-x

Jurison, J. (1995). The role of risk and return in information technology outsourcing decisions. *Journal of Information Technology*, *10*(Dec), 239–247. doi:10.1057/jit.1995.27

Juve, G., & Deelman, E. (2011). Automating application deployment in infrastructure clouds. In *Proceedings of the IEEE 3rd International Conference on Cloud Computing Technology and Science. CloudCom 2011* (pp. 658–665). doi:10.1109/CloudCom.2011.102

Kagermann, H., Österle, H., & Jordan, J. M. (2011). *IT-driven business models: Global case studies in trans formation.* John Wiley & Sons.

Kaliski, B. (2008). Multi-tenant cloud computing: From cruise liners to container ships. In *Proceedings of Third Asia-Pacific Trusted Infrastructure Technologies Conference.* Academic Press. doi:10.1109/APTC.2008.16

Kamaludeen, P., & Thamodaran, V. (2014). Role of information technology in unit linked insurance plans marketing. *Tactful Management Research Journal*, *2*(4), 1–3.

Kambil, A. (2009). Obliterate knowledge management: Everyone is a knowledge manager. *The Journal of Business Strategy*, *30*(6), 66–68. doi:10.1108/02756660911003149

Kangasharju, J., Lindholm, T., & Tarkoma, S. (2008). XML security with binary XML for mobile web services. *International Journal of Web Services Research, 5*(3), 1-19.

Kannan, P. K., Chang, A. M., & Whinston, A. B. (1998). Marketing information on the i-way: Data junkyard or information gold mine? *Communications of the ACM*, *41*(3), 35–43. doi:10.1145/272287.272295

Kantar Worldpanel ComTech. (2011). *Kantar worldpanel ComTech global consumer, white paper and VIP report.* Author.

Karakas, F., & Manisaligil, A. (2012). Reorienting self-directed learning for the creative digital era. *European Journal of Training and Development*, *36*(7), 712–731. doi:10.1108/03090591211255557

Karmakar, N. (2011). *Multi-core architecture. The new trend in processor making* (p. 44). India: North Maharashrta University.

Karunakaran, S. (2013). Impact of cloud adoption on agile software development. In Z. Mahmood & S. Saeed (Eds.), *Software Engineering Frameworks for the Cloud Computing Paradigm* (pp. 213–234). London: Springer. doi:10.1007/978-1-4471-5031-2_10

Kasemsap, K. (2013a). Innovative framework: Formation of causal model of organizational culture, organizational climate, knowledge management, and job performance. *Journal of International Business Management & Research*, *4*(12), 21–32.

Kasemsap, K. (2013b). Strategic business management: A practical framework and causal model of empowering leadership, team cohesion, knowledge-sharing behavior, and team performance. *Journal of Social and Development Sciences*, *4*(3), 100–106.

Kasemsap, K. (2013c). Unified framework: Constructing a causal model of Six Sigma, organizational learning, organizational innovation, and organizational performance. *The Journal of Interdisciplinary Networks*, *2*(1), 268–273.

Kasemsap, K. (2013d). Innovative human resource practices: An integrative framework and causal model of human resource practices, innovation, customer value, and workgroup performance. *International Journal of Business, Management &. Social Sciences*, *2*(7), 44–48.

Kasemsap, K. (2014a). The role of knowledge sharing on organisational innovation: An integrated framework. In L. Al-Hakim & C. Jin (Eds.), *Quality innovation: Knowledge, theory, and practices* (pp. 247–271). Hershey, PA: IGI Global. doi:10.4018/978-1-4666-4769-5.ch012

Kasemsap, K. (2014b). Strategic innovation management: An integrative framework and causal model of knowledge management, strategic orientation, organizational innovation, and organizational performance. In P. Ordóñez de Pablos & R. D. Tennyson (Eds.), *Strategic approaches for human capital management and development in a turbulent economy* (pp. 102–116). Hershey, PA: IGI Global. doi:10.4018/978-1-4666-4530-1.ch007

Katzan, H. (2010). On the privacy of cloud computing. *International Journal of Management & Information Systems, 14*(2), 1–12.

Katzan, H. J. (2009). Cloud computing economics: Democratization and monetization of services. *Journal of Business & Economics Research, 7*(6), 1–12.

Kazandjieva, M., Heller, B., Gnawali, O., Levis, P. & Kozyrakis, C. (2013) Measuring and analyzing the energy use of enterprise computing systems. *Sustainable Computing: Informatics and Systems, 3*, 218-229.

Kellis, M., Wold, B., Snyder, M. P., Bernstein, B. E., Kundaje, A., Marinov, G. K., & Hardison, R. C. et al. (2014). Defining functional DNA elements in the human genome. In *Proceedings of the National Academy of Sciences of the United States of America, 111*(17), 6131–6138. doi:10.1073/pnas.1318948111 PMID:24753594

Kelly, L. (2011). The security threats facing SMEs. *Computer Weekly*, 11-12.

Keniston, K. (2004). Introduction: The four digital divides. In K. Keniston & D. Kumar (Eds.), *IT Experience in India: Bridging the Digital Divide* (pp. 11–36). Delhi: Sage Publishers.

Keung, J., & Kwok, F. (2012). Cloud deployment model selection assessment for SMEs: Renting or buying a cloud. In *Proceedings of the 5th International Conference on Utility and Cloud Computing.* IEEE/ACM. doi:10.1109/UCC.2012.29

Khajeh-Hosseini, A., Greenwood, D., & Sommerville, I. (2010a). *Cloud migration: A case study of migrating an enterprise IT system to IaaS.* Paper presented at the 3rd IEEE International conference on Cloud Computing, Miami, FL.

Khajeh-Hosseini, A., Sommerville, I., & Sriram, I. (2010b). *Research challenges for enterprise cloud computing* (LSCITS Technical Report). Academic Press.

Khajeh-Hosseini, A., Sommerville, I., Bogaerts, J., & Teregowda, P. (2011). *Decision support tools for cloud migration in the enterprise.* Paper presented at the IEEE 4th Int. Conf. on Cloud Computing (CLOUD 2011), Washington, DC. doi:10.1109/CLOUD.2011.59

Khajeh-Hosseini, A., Greenwood, D., Smith, J. W., & Sommerville, I. (2011 b). The cloud adoption toolkit: Supporting cloud adoption decisions in the enterprise, software. *Practice.*

Khalif, A., & Nur, A. (2013). The African farmer and the challenge of food security in Africa. *Development, 56*(2), 257–265. doi:10.1057/dev.2013.25

Khosravi, A., Khorsandi, S., & Akbari, M. K. (2011). *Hyper node torus: A new interconnection network for high speed packet processors.* Paper presented at the 2011 International Symposium on Computer Networks and Distributed Systems (CNDS).

Kim, I. S., Choi, H. S., Yi, K. M., Choi, J. Y., & Kong, S. G. (2010). Intelligent visual surveillance— a survey. *International Journal of Control, Automation and Systems, 8*(5), 926–939. doi:10.1007/s12555-010-0501-4

Kirby, G., Dearle, A., Macdonald, A., & Fernandes, A. (2010). An approach to ad hoc cloud computing. *Arxiv preprint arXiv:1002.4738.* Retrieved from http://arxiv.org/abs/1002.4738v1

Kirto, M. J. (2003). *Adaption-innovation: In the context of diversity and change.* London, UK: Routledge.

Kiruthika, J., & Khaddaj, S. (2013). System performance in cloud services: Stability and resource allocation. In *Proceedings of the 12th International Symposium on Distributed Computing and Applications to Business, Engineering & Science* (pp. 127-131). Los Alamitos, CA. doi:10.1109/DCABES.2013.30

Klems, M., Nimis, J., & Tai, S. (2009). Do clouds compute? A framework for estimating the value of cloud computing. In Designing e-business systems: Markets, services, and networks (pp. 110-123). Springer.

Klems, M., Nimis, J., & Tai, S. (2009). Do cloud compute? A framework for estimating the value of cloud computing. *Journal of Designing E-Business Systems – Market Services and Network*, *22*(4), 110–123.

Ko, C. (2012). *Chinese government official: Is cloud HK's next advantage?* Retrieved January 9, 2014, http://www.asiacloudforum.com/content/chinese-government-official-cloud-hks-next-advantage

Koboldt, D. C., Zhang, Q., Larson, D. E., Shen, D., McLellan, M. D., Lin, L., & Wilson, R. K. et al. (2012). VarScan 2: Somatic mutation and copy number alteration discovery in cancer by exome sequencing. *Genome Research*, *22*(3), 568–576. doi:10.1101/gr.129684.111 PMID:22300766

Koibuchi, M., Akiya, J., Watanabe, K., & Amano, H. (2003). Descending layers routing: A deadlock-free deterministic routing using virtual channels in system area networks with irregular topologies. In *Proceedings of the 2003 International Conference on Parallel Processing*.

Koibuchi, M., Watanabe, K., Kono, K., Akiya, J., & Amano, H. (2003). Performance evaluation of routing algorithms in RHiNET-2 cluster. In *Proceedings of the 2003 IEEE International Conference on Cluster Computing*.

Koibuchi, M., Watanabe, T., Minamihata, A., Nakao, M., Hiroyasu, T., Matsutani, H., & Amano, H. (2011). *Performance evaluation of power-aware multi-tree ethernet for HPC interconnects*. Paper presented at the 2011 Second International Conference on Networking and Computing (ICNC).

Koibuchi, M., Jouraku, A., & Amano, H. (2002). *The impact of path selection algorithm of adaptive routing for implementing deterministic routing* (pp. 1431–1437).

Kondo, D., Taufer, M., & Brooks, C. (2004). Characterizing and evaluating desktop grids: An empirical study. *International Parallel and Distributed Processing Symposium 2004*, *00*(C). Retrieved from http://ieeexplore.ieee.org/xpls/abs_all.jsp?arnumber=1302936

Konstantinou, A. V., Eilam, T., Kalantar, M., Totok, A. A., Arnold, W., & Snible, E. (2009). An architecture for virtual solution composition and deployment in infrastructure clouds. In *Proceedings of the 3rd International Workshop on Virtualization Technologies in Distributed Computing. VTDC 2009* (pp. 9–18). doi:10.1145/1555336.1555339

Kosinska, J., Kosinski, J., & Zielinski, K. (2010). *The concept of application clustering in cloud computing environments: The need for extending the capabilities of virtual networks*. Paper presented at the Fifth International Multi-Conference on Computing in the Global Information Technology (ICCGI).

Koufi, V., Malamateniou, F., & Vassilacopoulos, G. (2013). An Android-enabled PHR-based system for the provision of homecare services. *International Journal of Measurement Technologies and Instrumentation Engineering*, *3*(2), 1–18. doi:10.4018/ijmtie.2013040101

Koumaditis, K., Themistocleous, M., Vassilacopoulos, G., Prentza, A., Kyriazis, D., Malamateniou, F., Mourouzis, A. (2014). *Patient-centered e-health record over the cloud*. Paper presented at the International Conference on Informatics, Management and Technology in Healthcare, Attica, Greece.

Kraska, T., Hentschel, M., Alonso, G., & Kossmann, D. (2009). Consistency rationing in the cloud: Pay only when it matters. *Proc. VLDB Endow*, *2*(1), 253–264. doi:10.14778/1687627.1687657

Krautheim, F. J. (2010). *Building trust into utility cloud computing*. (PhD. Dissertation). Retrieved from ProQuest Dissertations and Theses. (UMI No: 3422891)

Kridan, A. B., & Goulding, J. S. (2006). A case study on knowledge management implementation in the banking sector. *VINE: The Journal of Information and Knowledge Management Systems*, *36*(2), 211–222. doi:10.1108/03055720610683013

Kroes, N. (2012). *EU data protection reform and cloud computing*. Retrieved February 6, 2014, http://europa.eu/rapid/pressReleasesAction.do?reference=SPEECH/12/40&format=HTML&aged=0&language=EN&guiLanguage=en

Kshetri, N. (2010). Cloud computing in developing economies. *IEEE Computer*, *43*(10), 47–55. doi:10.1109/MC.2010.212

Kuan Hon, W., & Millard, C. (2012). *Data export in cloud computing – How can personal data be transferred outside the EEA*. Retrieved February 5, 2014, http://www.cloudlegal.ccls.qmul.ac.uk/Research/researchpapers/55649.html

Kumar, V., Grama, A., Gupta, A., & Karypis, G. (1994). *Introduction to parallel computing*. Canada: The Benjamin/Cummings Publishing Company, Inc.

Kuo, A. M.-H. (2011). Opportunities and challenges of cloud computing to improve health care services. *Journal of Medical Internet Research, 13*(3), e67. doi:10.2196/jmir.1867 PMID:21937354

Kuriyan, R., & Kitner, K. R. (2009). Constructing class boundaries: Gender, aspirations, and shared computing. *Information Technologies and International Development, 5*(1), 17–29.

Kushida, K. E., Murray, J., & Zysman, J. (2011). Diffusing the cloud: Cloud computing and implications for public policy. *Journal of Industry, Competition and Trade, 11*(3), 209–237. doi:10.1007/s10842-011-0106-5

Kushwaha, A. K. S., Sharma, C. M., Khare, M., Prakash, O., & Khare, A. (2014). Adaptive real-time motion segmentation technique based on statistical background model. *The Imaging Science Journal, 62*(5), 285–302. doi:10.1179/1743131X13Y.0000000056

Kushwaha, A. K. S., Sharma, C. M., Khare, M., Srivastava, R. K., & Khare, A. (2012). Automatic multiple human detection and tracking for visual surveillance system. In *Proceedings of the IEEE International Conference on Informatics, Electronics and Vision* (pp. 326-331).

Kusic, D., Kephart, J. O., Hanson, J. E., Kandasamy, N., & Jiang, G. (2008). Power and performance management of virtualized computing environments via lookahead control. *Cluster Computing, 12*(1), 1–15. doi:10.1007/s10586-008-0070-y

Lab of Medical Informatics. (2014). Providing integrated eHealth services for personalized medicine utilizing cloud infrastructure. Retrieved April, 17, 2014, from http://pincloud.med.auth.gr/en

Lacity, M. C., & Willcocks, L. P. (1998). An empirical investigation of information technology sourcing practices: Lessons from experience. *Management Information Systems Quarterly, 22*(3), 363–408. doi:10.2307/249670

Lagar-Cavilla, H. A., Whitney, J. A., Scannell, A. M., Patchin, P., Rumble, S. M., De Lara, E., & Satyanarayanan, M. et al. (2009). SnowFlock: Rapid virtual machine cloning for cloud computing. In *Proceedings of the 4th ACM European Conference on Computer systems. EuroSys 2009* (pp. 1–12). doi:10.1145/1519065.1519067

Lambo, T. (2012). Why you need a cloud rating score. *CloudSecurityAlliance*. Retrieved January 23, 2014, https://cloudsecurityalliance.org/wp-content/uploads/2012/02/Taiye_Lambo_CloudScore.pdf

Landeta, J. (2006). Current validity of the Delphi method in social sciences. *Technological Forecasting and Social Change, 73*(5), 467–482. doi:10.1016/j.techfore.2005.09.002

Langenberg, D., & Welker, M. (2011). Knowledge management in virtual communities. *Open Journal of Knowledge Management, 16*(3), 13–19.

Langmead, B., Hansen, K. D., & Leek, J. T. (2010). Cloud-scale RNA-sequencing differential expression analysis with Myrna. *Genome Biology, 11*(8), R83. doi:10.1186/gb-2010-11-8-r83 PMID:20701754

Langmead, B., Schatz, M. C., Lin, J., Pop, M., & Salzberg, S. L. (2009). Searching for SNPs with cloud computing. *Genome Biology, 10*(11), R134. doi:10.1186/gb-2009-10-11-r134 PMID:19930550

Langmead, B., Trapnell, C., Pop, M., & Salzberg, S. L. (2009). Ultrafast and memory-efficient alignment of short DNA sequences to the human genome. *Genome Biology, 10*(3), R25. doi:10.1186/gb-2009-10-3-r25 PMID:19261174

Lanvin, P., Noyer, J.-C., & Benjelloun, M. (2003). Object detection and tracking using the particle filtering. In *Proceedings of the IEEE 37th Asilomar Conference on Signals, Systems and Computers* (Vol. 2, pp.1595-1599). doi:10.1109/ACSSC.2003.1292254

Lausanne, É. P. F. d. (2014). Scala. Retrieved April 18, 2014, from http://www.scala-lang.org/

Lawrence, M.W.L., Brad, D.C.C., Chris, C., & Denna, M. (2010). Cloud computing business models for the channel. *A CompTIA Cloud/SaaS Community Resource*, 1–12.

Lease, D. R. (2005). *Factors influencing the adoption of biometric security technologies by decision making information technology and security managers.* Retrieved from ProQuest Digital Dissertations. (AAT 3185680).

Leavitt, N. (2009). Is cloud computing really ready for prime time? *Computer, 42*(1), 15–20. doi:10.1109/MC.2009.20

Lee, C. F., Lee, A. C., & Lee, J. (2010). *Handbook of quantitative finance and risk management.* Springer. doi:10.1007/978-0-387-77117-5

Lee, G., & Xia, W. (2006). Organizational size and IT innovation adoption: A meta-analysis. *Information & Management, 43*(8), 975–985. doi:10.1016/j.im.2006.09.003

Lee, J. (2004). Discriminant analysis of technology adoption behavior: A case of Internet technologies in small businesses. *Journal of Computer Information Systems, 44*(4), 57–66.

Lee, J., Huynh, M. Q., Kwok, R. C., & Pi, S. (2003). IT outsourcing evolution: Past, present, and future. *Communications of the ACM, 46*(5), 84–89. doi:10.1145/769800.769807

Lee, M. K. O., & Cheung, C. M. K. (2004). Internet retailing adoption by small-to-medium sized enterprises (SMEs): A multiple-case study. *Information Systems Frontiers, 6*(4), 385–397. doi:10.1023/B:ISFI.0000046379.58029.54

Lei, C., Hartono, A., & Panda, D. K. (2006). *Designing high performance and scalable MPI Intra-node communication support for clusters.* Paper presented at the 2006 IEEE International Conference on Cluster Computing.

Lei, C., Qi, G., & Panda, D. K. (2007). *Understanding the impact of multi-core architecture in cluster computing: A case study with intel dual-core system.* Paper presented at the Seventh IEEE International Symposium on Cluster Computing and the Grid. CCGRID 2007.

Leinwand, A., & Conroy, F. K. (1996). *Network management – A practical perspective* (2nd ed.). Addison-Wesley.

Levenburg, N., Magal, S. R., & Kosalge, P. (2006). An exploratory investigation of organizational factors and e-business motivations among SMFOEs in the US. *Electronic Markets, 16*(1), 70–84. doi:10.1080/10196780500491402

Leventhal, T., Taliaferro, P., Wong, K., Hughes, C., & Mun, S. (2012). The patient-centered medical home and health information technology. *Telemedicine Journal and e-Health, 18*(2), 145–149. doi:10.1089/tmj.2011.0130 PMID:22304440

Lewin, K. (2009). *Federal cloud computing initiative overview.* Retrieved from http://www.usaservices.gov/intergovt/ documents/StateWebPres6-18.ppt

Li, C. S. (2010). Cloud computing in an outcome centric world. Paper presented at IEEE Cloud 2010. Miami, FL.

Li, X., Li, Y., Liu, T., Qiu, J., & Wang, F. (2009). *The method and tool of cost analysis for cloud computing.* Paper presented at the 2009 IEEE International Conference on Cloud Computing, Bangalore, India. doi:10.1109/CLOUD.2009.84

Li, Z., Wang, Y., Olivier, K. K. S., Chen, J., & Li, K. (2009). *The cloud-based framework for ant colony optimization.* Paper presented at the First ACM/SIGEVO Summit on Genetic and Evolutionary Computation (GEC '09), Shanghai, China. doi:10.1145/1543834.1543872

Liao, X., Jin, H., & Liu, H. (2012). Towards a green cluster through dynamic remapping of virtual machines. *Future Generation Computer Systems, 28*(2), 469–477. doi:10.1016/j.future.2011.04.013

Liebenau, J., Karrberg, P., Grous, A., & Castro, D. (2012). *Modeling the cloud: Employment effects in two exemplary sectors in the United States, the United Kingdom, Germany and Italy.* Retrieved February 9, 2014, http://www2.lse.ac.uk/management/documents/LSE-Cloud-report.pdf, p. 24

Liferay. (2014). Liferay. Retrieved April 18, 2014, from http://www.liferay.com/

Li, H., & Durbin, R. (2009). Fast and accurate short read alignment with Burrows-Wheeler transform. *Bioinformatics (Oxford, England), 25*(14), 1754–1760. doi:10.1093/bioinformatics/btp324 PMID:19451168

Li, H., Handsaker, B., Wysoker, A., Fennell, T., Ruan, J., Homer, N., & Durbin, R. et al. (2009). The Sequence Alignment/Map format and SAMtools. *Bioinformatics (Oxford, England), 25*(16), 2078–2079. doi:10.1093/bioinformatics/btp352 PMID:19505943

Lim, A. (2012). *Cloud computing data protection – Two considerations*. Retrieved January 22, 2014, http://event. idsirtii.or.id/wp-content/uploads/2011/10/Cloud-Data-Security-Two-Considerations-Anthony-Lim-Secure-Age-email.pdf

Lim, H., Babu, S., Chase, J., & Parekh, S. (2009). *Automated control in cloud computing: challenges and opportunities*. Paper presented at the 1st workshop on Automated control for datacenters and clouds (ACDC '09). Barcelona, Spain. doi:10.1145/1555271.1555275

Lin, G., Fu, D., Zhu, J., & Dasmalchi, G. (2009, March/April). Cloud computing: IT as a service. IT Pro.

Lin, A., & Chen, N. C. (2012). Cloud computing as an innovation: Perception, attitude, and adoption. *International Journal of Information Management*, 32(6), 533–540. doi:10.1016/j.ijinfomgt.2012.04.001

Linstone, H. A., & Turoff, M. (Eds.). (1975) The Delphi Method: techniques and applications, Reading, MA: Addison Wesley.

Linthicum, D. (2009, January). Defining the cloud computing framework. *Cloud Computing Journal*.

Linthicum, D. S. (2009). Cloud Computing and SOA convergence in your enterprise: A step-by-step guide (1st edition). Addison-Wesley Professional.

Lin, X. (2003). *An efficient communication scheme for fat-tree topology on infiniband networks*. M.Sc thesis, Feng Chia University Taiwan.

Lippert, S., & Forman, H. (2005). Utilization of information technology: Examining cognitive and experiential factors of post-adoption behavior. *IEEE Transactions on Engineering Management*, 52(3), 363–381. doi:10.1109/TEM.2005.851273

Lipton, A. J., Fujiyoshi, H., & Patil, R. S. (1998). Moving target classification and tracking from real-time video. In *Proceedings of the IEEE Workshop on Applications of Computer Vision* (pp. 8-14). doi:10.1109/ACV.1998.732851

Litzenberger, D. C. (2014). *PyCrypto*. Retrieved from https://github.com/dlitz/pycrypto

Liu, F. et al. (2011). NIST cloud computing reference architecture. *NIST Special Publication 500-292*.

Liu, H., & Orban, D. (2008). *GridBatch: Cloud computing for large-scale data-intensive batch applications*. Paper presented at the 8th IEEE International Symposium on Cluster Computing and the Grid, Lyon, France. doi:10.1109/CCGRID.2008.30

Liu, W., & Cai, H. (2013). Embracing the shift to cloud computing: Knowledge and skills for systems librarians. *Perspectives*, 29(1), 22–29.

Li, X., Troutt, M. D., Brandyberry, A., & Wang, T. (2011). Decision factors for the adoption and continued use of online direct sales channels among SMEs. *Journal of the Association for Information Systems*, 12(1), 1–31.

Lloyd, A. D., & Sloan, T. M. (2011). Intercontinental grids: An infrastructure for demand-driven innovation. *Journal of Grid Computing*, 9(2), 185–200. doi:10.1007/s10723-011-9190-3

Lodi, G., Querzoni, L., Baldoni, R., Marchetti, M., Colajanni, M., Bortnikov, V., & Roytman, A. (2009). *Defending financial infrastructures through early warning systems: The intelligence cloud approach*. Paper presented at the 5th Annual Workshop on Cyber Security and Information Intelligence Research (CSIIRW '09), Oak Ridge, Tennessee. doi:10.1145/1558607.1558628

Lohr, S. (2007). Google and I.B.M. join in "cloud computing" research. *New York Times*. Retrieved August 12, 2014, from http://www.csun.edu/pubrels/clips/Oct07/10-08-07E.pdf

Lokhande, T. N., & Kale, V. P. (2014). Spatial distribution of health care facilities in Nanded District (Maharashtra) India. *Online International Interdisciplinary Research Journal*, 4(I), 316–325.

Longstaff, F. A., & Schwartz, E. S. (2001). Valuing American options by simulation: A simple least-squares approach. *Review of Financial Studies*, 14(1), 113–147. doi:10.1093/rfs/14.1.113

Loshin, D. (2012). *Business intelligence: The savvy manager's guide*. Newnes.

Low, C., Chen, Y., & Wu, M. (2011). Understanding the determinants of cloud computing adoption. *Industrial Management & Data Systems*, 111(7), 1006–1023. doi:10.1108/02635571111161262

Lowe, J. M. (2006). Rural education: Attracting and retaining teachers in small schools. *Rural Educator, 27*, 28–32.

Luis, M. V., Luis, R. M., Juan, C., & Maik, L. (2009). A break in the clouds: Towards a cloud definition. *SIGCOMM Comput. Commun. Rev, 39*(1), 50–55.

Luo, S. X., Liu, F. M., & Ren, C. L. (2011). A hierarchy attribute-based access control model for cloud storage. In *Proceedings of the International Conference on Machine Learning and Cybernetics (ICMLC)* (Vol. 3, pp. 1146–1150). doi:10.1109/ICMLC.2011.6016897

Lupse, O. S., Vida, M. M., & Stoicu-Tivadar, L. (2012). *Cloud computing and interoperability in healthcare information systems*. Paper presented at the The First International Conference on Intelligent Systems and Applications, INTELLI 2012.

Lutfiyya, M. N., Bhat, D. K., Gandhi, S. R., Nguyen, C., Weidenbacher-Hoper, V. L., & Lipsky, M. S. (2007). A comparison of quality of care indicators in urban acute care hospitals and rural critical access hospitals in the United States. *International Journal for Quality in Health Care, 19*(3), 141–149. doi:10.1093/intqhc/mzm010 PMID:17442745

Lyer, B., & Henderson, J. (2010). Preparing for the future: Understanding the seven capabilities of cloud computing. *Management Information Systems Quarterly Executive, 9*(2), 117–131.

MacGregor, R., & Kartiwi, M. (2010). Perception of barriers to e-commerce adoption in SMEs in developing and developed country: A comparison between Australia and Indonesia. *Journal of Electronic Commerce in Organizations, 8*(1), 61–82. doi:10.4018/jeco.2010103004

Mahmood, Z. (2011). Data location and security issues in cloud computing. In *Proceedings of IEEE International Conference on Emerging intelligent Data and Web Technologies*. IEEE. doi:10.1109/EIDWT.2011.16

Malhotra, N. (2010). *Marketing research: An applied orientation*. Pearson Education.

Malkowski, S., Kanemasa, Y., Chen, H., Yamamoto, M., Wang, Q., Jayasinghe, D., . . . Kawaba, M. (2012). Challenges and opportunities in consolidation at high resource utilization: non-monotonic response time variations in n-tier applications. In *Proceedings of the Fifth IEEE International Conference on Cloud Computing* (pp. 162-169). Honolulu, HI. doi:10.1109/CLOUD.2012.99

Marcati, A., Guido, G., & Peluso, A. (2008). The role of SME entrepreneurs' innovativeness and personality in the adoption of innovations. *Research Policy, 37*(9), 1579–1590. doi:10.1016/j.respol.2008.06.004

Marcotte, E. (2011). *Responsive web design*. Editions Eyrolles.

Marian, M., & Hamburg, I. (2012). *Guidelines for increasing the adoption of cloud computing within SMEs*. Paper presented at the 3rd International Conference on Cloud Computing, GRIDs, and Virtualization.

Mark, D. R. (2011). Cloud computing privacy concerns on our doorstep. *Communications of the ACM, 54*(1).

Marks, E. A., & Lozano, B. (2010). *Executive's guide to cloud computing*. Wiley.

Marks, E., & Lozano, B. (2010). *Executive's guide to cloud computing*. Wiley Publishing.

Marosi, A., Kovács, J., & Kacsuk, P. (2012). Towards a volunteer cloud system. *Future Generation Computer Systems*. doi:10.1016/j.future.2012.03.013

Marshall, P. (2008). City in the cloud. *Government Computer News, 27*(28), 29–29.

Marston, S., Li, Z., Bandyopadhyay, S., Zhang, J., & Ghalsasi, A. (2011). Cloud computing - The business perspective. *Decision Support Systems, 51*(1), 176-189.

Marston, S., Li, Z., Bandyopadhyay, S., Zhang, J., & Ghalsasi, A. (2011). Cloud computing—The business perspective. *Decision Support Systems, 51*(1), 176–189. doi:10.1016/j.dss.2010.12.006

Martin, L. (2010). *Awareness, trust and security to shape government cloud adoption*. Academic Press.

Martino, L.D., & Bertino, E. (2009). Security for web services: Standards and research issues. *International Journal of Web Services Research, 6*(4), 48-74.

Martin, S. M., Lorenzen, K., & Bunnefeld, N. (2013). Fishing farmers: Fishing, livelihood diversification and poverty in rural Laos. *Human Ecology, 41*(5), 737–747. doi:10.1007/s10745-013-9567-y

Martins, C., Steil, A., & Todesco, J. (2004). Factors influencing the adoption of the internet as a teaching tool at foreign language schools. *Computers & Education, 42*(4), 353–374. doi:10.1016/j.compedu.2003.08.007

Mather, T., Kumaraswamy, S., & Latif, S. (2009). *Cloud security and privacy: An enterprise perspective on risks and compliance.* Sebastopol: OReilly.

Mayer, R. (1998). Prozesskostenmanagement – State of the Ar (pp. 3-28). Horváth & Partners (Hrsg.).

McCabe, B., & Hancook, I. (2009). Cloud computing: Australian lessons and experiences. *KPMG*, 1–20.

McCombs, T. (2003). Maude 2.0 Primer. Retrieved from http://maude.cs.uiuc.edu/primer/maude-primer.pdf

McGraw, G. (2006). *Software security: building security in.* USA: Addison Wesley.

McKenna, A., Hanna, M., Banks, E., Sivachenko, A., Cibulskis, K., Kernytsky, A., & DePristo, M. A. et al. (2010). The genome analysis toolkit: A MapReduce framework for analyzing next-generation DNA sequencing data. *Genome Research, 20*(9), 1297–1303. doi:10.1101/gr.107524.110 PMID:20644199

Mead, N. R., Hough, E., & Stehney, I. I. T. (2005). Security quality requirements engineering (SQUARE) methodology. TECHNICAL REPORT, CMU/SEI-2005-TR-009. Retrieved from http://www.sei.cmu.edu/library/abstracts/reports/05tr009.cfm

Mechanic, D., & Tanner, J. (2007). Vulnerable people, groups, and populations: Societal view. *Health Affairs, 26*(5), 1220–1230. doi:10.1377/hlthaff.26.5.1220 PMID:17848429

Medscribbler. (2014). Medscribbler. Retrieved April 16, 2014, from http://www.medscribbler.com/

Mell, P., & Grance, T. (2009). *The NIST definition of cloud computing.* Retrieved from http://csrc.nist.gov/groups/SNS/cloud-computing/cloud-def-v15.doc

Mell, P., & Grance, T. (2011). *The NIST definition of cloud computing.* Retrieved March 5, 2014, from http://csrc.nist.gov/publications/nistpubs/800-145/SP800-145.pdf

Merriam, S. B. (1998). *Case study research in education: A qualitative approach.* San Francisco, CA: Jossey-Bass Publications.

Merritt, R. (2009). Vendors call for cloud computing standards. *EE Times.* Retrieved from http://www.eetimes.com/electronics-news/4081939/Vendors-call-for-cloud-computing-standards

Mett, P., & Tomothy, G. (2011). *The NIST definition of cloud computing.* Retrieved from http://www.csrc.nist.gov/publications/nistpubs/800-145/SP800-145.pdf

Metzker, M. L. (2010). Sequencing technologies—the next generation. *Nature Reviews. Genetics, 11*(1), 31–46. doi:10.1038/nrg2626 PMID:19997069

Meyer, D. T., & Bolosky, W. J. (2012). A study of practical deduplication.[TOS]. *ACM Transactions on Storage, 7*(4), 14. doi:10.1145/2078861.2078864

Meyer, S., Healy, P., Lynn, T., & Morrison, J. (2013). Quality assurance for open source software configuration management. In *Management of resources and services in cloud and sky computing* (pp. 1–8). MICAS. doi:10.1109/SYNASC.2013.66

Microsoft. (2010). *Building confidence in the cloud: A proposal for industry and government action to advance cloud computing.* Retrieved February 12, 2014 from http://www.microsoft.com/presspass/presskits/cloudpolicy/

Microsoft. (2011). *Protecting consumers and promoting innovation and growth in cloud computing.* Retrieved January 9, 2014, http://www.microsoft.eu/Portals/0/Document/Technology%20Policy/MicrosoftGrowthinCloudWP_LV.pdf, p. 3

Microsoft. (2014). HealthVault. Retrieved April 15, 2014, from https://www.healthvault.com

Microsoft. (n.d.a). *Cloud computing: A catalyst for European competitiveness.* Retrieved January 9, 2014, http://www.microsoft.eu/Portals/0/Document/Technology%20Policy/Cloud%20computing%20-%20a%20catalyst%20for%20European%20competitiveness.pdf

Microsoft. (n.d.b). *What is cloud computing.* Retrieved January 20, 2014, http://www.microsoft.eu/cloudcomputing/factsheets/whatiscloudcomputing.aspx

Miller, M. (2008). *Cloud computing: Web-based applications that change the way you work and collaborate online.* Indianapolis, IN: Que Publishers.

Mills, K., Filliben, J., & Dabrowski, C. (2011). Comparing VM-placement algorithms for on-demand clouds. In *Proceedings of the 2011 IEEE Third International Conference on Cloud Computing Technology and Science* (pp. 91–98). doi:10.1109/CloudCom.2011.22

Milner, R. (2009). *The space and motion of communicating agents.* Cambridge University Press. doi:10.1017/CBO9780511626661

Mirashe, S. P., & Kalyankar, N. V. (2010). Cloud computing. *Journal of Computing, 2*(3), 78–82.

Misra, S. C., & Mondal, A. (2010). Identification of a company's suitability for the adoption of cloud computing and modelling its corresponding return on investment. *Mathematical and Computer Modelling, 53*(3-4), 504–521. doi:10.1016/j.mcm.2010.03.037

Mitroff, I., & Turoff, M. (1975). Philosophical and methodological foundations of Delphi. In H. Linstone, & M. Turoff (Eds.), The Delphi method: Techniques and applications (pp. 17-34).

Mitroff, I. I., & Linstone, H. A. (2012). *The unbounded mind: Breaking the chains of traditional business thinking.* New York: OxFord University Press.

Moghavvemi, S., Hakimian, F., & Feissal, T. M. F. T. (2012). Competitive advantages through it innovation adoption by SMEs. *Social Technologies, 2.*

Mohamed, M. S., Ribie`Re, V. M., O'sullivan, K. J., & Mohamed, M. A. (2008). The re-structuring of the information technology infrastructure library (ITIL) implementation using knowledge management framework. *VINE: The Journal of Information and Knowledge Management Systems, 38*(3), 315–333. doi:10.1108/03055720810904835

Molawa, S. (2009). The "first" and "third world" in Africa: Knowledge access, challenges and current technological innovations in Africa. In *Proceedings of the First International Conference on African Digital Libraries and Archives*, (pp. 1-14). Addis Ababa, Ethiopia.

Mongo, D. B. I. (2013). MongoDB (from "humongous") is an open-source document database, and the leading NoSQL database. Retrieved April 15, 2014, from http://www.mongodb.org/

Monika, S., Ashwani, M., Haresh, J., Anand, K., Madhvendra, M., & Vijayshri, T. (2010). Scope of cloud computing for SMEs in India. *Journal of Computing, 2*(5), 144–149.

Moran, D., Vaquero, L. M., & Galan, F. (2011). *Elastically ruling the cloud: Specifying application's behavior in federated clouds.* Paper presented at the 2011 IEEE International Conference on Cloud Computing, Washington DC.

Moreno-Vozmediano, R., Montero, R. S., & Llorente, I. M. (2011). Multicloud deployment of computing clusters for loosely coupled MTC applications. *IEEE Transactions on Parallel and Distributed Systems, 22*(6), 924–930. doi:10.1109/TPDS.2010.186

Mouftah, H., & Kantarci, B. (2013). *Energy-efficient cloud computing: A green migration of traditional IT. Handbook of Green Information and Communication Systems* (pp. 295–329). Elsevier.

Mtega, W. P., & Malekani, A. W. (2009). Analyzing the usage patterns and challenges of telecenters among rural communities: Experience from four selected telecenters in Tanzania. *International Journal of Education and Development Using Information and Communication Technology, 5*(2), 68-87.

Mudge, J. C. (2010). *Cloud computing opportunities and challenges for Australia.* Melbourne, Australia: ATSE.

Musiyandaka, D., Ranga, G., & Kiwa, J. F. (2013). An analysis of factors influencing success of ICT4D projects: A case study of the schools computerisation programme in Mashonaland West Province, Zimbabwe. *The Journal of Community Informatics, 9*(4).

Mvelase, P., Dlodlo, N., Williams, Q., & Adigun, M. O. (2011). Custom-made cloud enterprise architecture for small medium and micro enterprises. *International Journal of Cloud Applications and Computing, 1*(3), 52–63.

Myers, G. J. Badgett, T., & Sandler, C. (2004). The art of software testing. Hoboken, NJ: John Wiley & Sons.

Myers, M. D., & Avison, D. (2002). *An introduction to qualitative research in information systems, a reader.* London: Sage.

Myhre, D. L., & Hohman, S. (2012). Going the distance: Early results of a distributed medical education initiative for royal college residencies in Canada. *Rural and Remote Health, 25*(12), 1–7. PMID:23110637

Nag, B. (2011). Mass media and ICT in development communication: Comparison & convergence. *Global Media Journal, 2*(2), 1–29.

Nam, K., Rajagopalan, S., Rao, H. R., & Chaudhury, A. (1996). A two-level investigation of information systems outsourcing. *Communications of the ACM, 39*(7), 37–44. doi:10.1145/233977.233989

Naone, E. (2007). Computer in the cloud. *Technology Review*. Retrieved August 12, 2014, from http://www.technologyreview.com/Infotech/19397/?af

Narayanan, H. A. J., & Giine, M. (2011). *Ensuring access control in cloud provisioned healthcare systems.* Paper presented at the Consumer Communications and Networking Conference (CCNC), 2011. IEEE. doi:10.1109/CCNC.2011.5766466

Narula, S. A., & Arora, S. (2010). Identifying stakeholders' needs and constraints in adoption of ICT services in rural areas: The case of india. *Social Responsibility Journal, 6*(2), 222–236. doi:10.1108/17471111011051739

Nattakarn, P., Xiaofeng, W., & Pekka, A. (2013). Towards a conceptual framework for assessing the benefits of cloud computing. In *Proceedings of the4th International Conference, ICSOB 2013*. Potsdam, Germany.

Ndubisi, N. O., & Jantan, M. (2003). Evaluating IS usage in Malaysian small and medium-sized firms using the technology acceptance model. *Logistics Information Management, 16*(6), 440–450. doi:10.1108/09576050310503411

Ning, X. (2013). *Personal health management system in cloud and adoption by older Australians: A conceptual research model.* Paper presented at the 21st Century Science Health, Agency, and Well-Being, Sydney, Australia.

Nir, K. (2010). Cloud computing in developing economies: Drivers, effects and policy measures. In *Proceedings of PTC'10*. PTC.

Nodejs. (2014). Node.js platform. Retrieved April 15, 2014, from http://nodejs.org/

Obiora, C. J. (2014). Agriculture and rural development versus youth rural-urban migration: The menace. *Journal of Agriculture Economics and Rural Development, 2*(2), 58–61. doi:10.12966/jaerd.05.05.2014

Ogbomo, M. O., & Ogbomo, E. F. (2008). *Importance of information and communication technologies (ICTs) in making a heathy information society: A case study of Ethiope East Local Government Area of Delta State* (pp. 1–8). Nigeria: Library Philosophy and Practice.

Okiy, R. B., & Ogbomo, E. F. (2011). Supporting rural women's use of information and communication technologies for sustainable economic development in Ethiope-East Local Government Area of Delta State, Nigeria. *Journal of Information Technology Impact, 11*(1), 71–84.

Oliner, A., Rudolph, L., & Sahoo, R. (2006). Cooperative checkpointing: A robust approach to large-scale systems reliability. In *Proceedings of the 20th annual international conference on Supercomputing (ICS '06)* (pp. 14–23). Retrieved from http://dl.acm.org/citation.cfm?id=1183406

Oliveira, T., & Martins, M. (2011). Literature review of information technology adoption models at firm level. *The Electronic Journal Information Systems Evaluation, 14*(1), 110–121.

Olson, T., & Brill, F. (1997). Moving object detection and event recognition algorithms for smart cameras. In *Proceedings of the DARPA Image Understanding Workshop* (pp. 159–175).

Onestopclick. (2012). *Over 70% CIOs confirm cloud computing benefits for UK business.* Retrieved January 21, 2014, http://hosting.onestopclick.com/technology_news/over-70-cios-confirm-cloud computing-benefits-for-uk-business_133.htm

Onwubiko, C. (2010). Security issues to cloud computing. In N. Antonopoulos & L. Gilliam (Eds.), *Cloud computing principles, systems and applications*. London: Springer. doi:10.1007/978-1-84996-241-4_16

Opala, O. J. (2012). *An analysis of security, cost-effectiveness, and IT compliance factors influencing cloud adoption by IT managers.* (PhD. Dissertation). Retrieved from ProQuest Dissertations and Theses. (UMI No: 3527699)

Opendedup. (2014). *Opendedup*. Retrieved from http://opendedup.org

OpenEMR. (2014). OpenEMR a free and open source electronic health records. Retrieved April 15, 2014, from http://www.open-emr.org

OpenSSL. (2014). *OpenSSL*. Retrieved from http://www.openssl.org/

OpenStack. (2014). *OpenStack SWIFT*. Retrieved from https://www.openstack.org/software/openstack-storage/

Oracle White Paper. (2009a). *Architectural strategies for cloud computing*. Oracle.

Oracle White Paper. (2009b). *Platform-as-a-service private cloud with Oracle fusion middleware*. Oracle.

Oracle White Paper. (2010). *Oracle cloud computing*. Oracle.

Oracle White Paper. (2011). *Oracle consulting cloud services framework*. Oracle.

Oracle. (2012) Data security challenges. Oracle9i security overview release number 2(9.2), retrieved November 4, 2012, from http://docs.oracle.com/cd/B10501_01/network.920/a96582/overview.htm

Orr, B. (2008). Will IT of the future have its feet firmly planted in the "cloud"? *ABI/INFORM Global, 100*(9), 50.

Overby, S. (2003). *The hidden costs of offshore outsourcing, keynote and technical report*. CIO.com.

OVF. (2010) Open virtualization format (OVF). Distributed Management Task Force. Retrieved from http://dmtf.org/sites/default/files/standards/documents/DSP0243_1.1.0.pdf

Ovwigho, B. O. (2014). Factors influencing involvement in nonfarm income generating activities among local farmers: The case of Ughelli South Local Government Area of Delta State, Nigeria. *Sustainable Agriculture Research, 3*(1), 76–84. doi:10.5539/sar.v3n1p76

Owojori, A. A., & Asaolu, T. O. (2010). Critical evaluation of personnel management problems in the Nigerian school system. *International Journal of Educational Sciences, 2*(1), 1–11.

Ozdemir, V., Rosenblatt, D. S., Warnich, L., Srivastava, S., Tadmouri, G. O., Aziz, R. K., . . . Joly, Y. (2011). Towards an ecology of collective innovation: Human variome project (HVP), rare disease consortium for autosomal loci (RADical) and data-enabled life sciences alliance (DELSA). *Current pharmacogenomics and personalized medicine, 9*(4), 243.

Pachouri, A., Sharma, M., Tewari, T., & Kaushik, P. (2010). Green operating system: Future low power operating system. *International Journal of Computers and Applications, 1*(21), 77–80. Foundation of Computer Science.

Paci, F., Bertino, E., & Crampton, J. (2008). An access-control framework for WS-BPEL. *International Journal of Web Services Research, 5*(3), 20-43.

Packer. (2014). Packer. [Online] Retrieved March 20, 2014, from: http://www.packer.io

Pade, C., Mallinson, B., & Sewry, D. (2011). Sustainable rural ICT project management practice for developing countries: Investigating the Dwesa and RUMEP projects. *Information Technology for Development, 17*(3), 187–212. doi:10.1080/02681102.2011.568222

Papazoglou, M. P., & Georgakopoulos, D. (2003). Service oriented computing. *Communications of the ACM, 46*, 25–28.

Papazoglou, M. P., & Van den Heuvel, W. J. (2007). Service oriented architecture: Approaches, technologies and research issues. *The VLDB Journal, 16*(3), 389–415. doi:10.1007/s00778-007-0044-3

Papazoglou, M. P., & van den Heuvel, W.-J. (2011). Blueprinting the cloud. *IEEE Internet Computing, 15*(6), 74–79. doi:10.1109/MIC.2011.147

Parkhill, D. (1966). The challenge of the computer utility. Boston, MA: Addison-Wesley Educational Publishers Inc.

Parthasarathy, M., & Bhattacherjee, A. (1998). Understanding post-adoption behavior in the context of online services. *Information Systems Research, 9*(4), 362–379. doi:10.1287/isre.9.4.362

Pase, D. M., & Eckl, M. A. (2005). A comparison of single-core and dual-core opteron processor performance for HPC I. IBM.

Patel, A., Seyfi, A., Tew, Y., & Jaradat, A. (2011). Comparative study and review of grid, cloud, utility computing and software as a service for use by libraries. *Library Hi Tech News, 3*(3), 25–32. doi:10.1108/07419051111145145

Patil, D. A., Dhere, A. M., & Pawar, C. B. (2009). ICT and empowerment of rural and deprived women in Asia. *Asia-Pacific Journal of Rural Development, 19*(1), 1–22.

Pearson, S. (2009). *Taking account of privacy when designing cloud computing services.* Paper presented at the ICSE Workshop on Software Engineering Challenges of Cloud Computing (CLOUD'09). doi:10.1109/CLOUD.2009.5071532

Pearson, S. (2012). *Privacy, security and trust in cloud computing.* Springer.

Peh, L. S. (2001). *Flow control and microarchitectural mechanism for extending the performance of interconnection networks.* PhD Thesis, Stanford University.

Peng, C., Kim, M., Zhang, Z., & Lei, H. (2012). VDN: Virtual machine image distribution network for cloud data centers. In *Proceedings of the IEEE 31st International Conference on Computer Communications. INFOCOM 2012* (pp. 181–189). doi:10.1109/INFCOM.2012.6195556

Peoples, C., Parr, G., McClean, S., Scotney, B. W., & Morrow, P. J. (2013). Performance evaluation of green data centre management supporting sustainable growth of the internet of things. *Simulation Modelling Practice and Theory, 34*, 221–242. doi:10.1016/j.simpat.2012.12.008

Perrine, D. (2007). *What is a scoring model?* Retrieved from http://www.scoringmodels.com/scoring%20models/what-is-a-scoring-model/

Perrone, G., Debois, S., & Hildebrandt, T. T. (2012). A model checker for bigraphs. In S. Ossowski & P. Lecca (Eds.), *SAC, ACM 1320–1325.* doi:10.1145/2245276.2231985

Perttula. (2008). Attacks on convergent encryption. *Attacks on Convergent Encryption.*

Petrini, F., Frachtenberg, E., Hoisie, A., & Coll, S. (2003). Performance evaluation of the quadrics interconnection network. *Cluster Computing, 6*(2), 125–142. doi:10.1023/A:1022852505633

Pettey, C. (2010). *Gartner identified the top 10 strategic technologies for 2011.* Retrieved September 10, 2011 from http://www.gartner.com/it/page.jsp?id=1454221

Pfister, G. F. (2001). An introduction to the infiniband architecture. *High Performance Mass Storage and Parallel I/O, 42*, 617-632.

Pilgrim, M. (2010). *HTML5: up and running.* O'Reilly Media, Inc.

Platform Computing. (2010). Enterprise cloud computing: transforming IT. *A Platform Computing Whitepaper* (p. 6).

Plummer, D.C., Smith, D.M., Bittman, T.J., Cearley, D.W., Cappuccio, D.J., Scott, D., Robertson, B. (2009). *Five refining attributes of public and private cloud computing.* Gartner.

Plummer, D., Bittman, T., Austin, T., Cearley, D., & Smith, D. (2008). *Cloud computing: Defining and describing an emerging phenomenon.* Stamford, CT: Gartner.

Pocatilu, P., Alecu, F., & Vetrici, M. (2009). Using cloud computing for e-learning systems. In *Proceedings of the 8th WSEAS International Conference on Data Networks, Communications and Computers* (pp. 54-59). Baltimore, MD.

Polonsky, M. J., & Waller, D. S. (2011). *Designing and managing a research project: A business student's guide.* Thousand Oaks, CA: Sage Publications.

Popović, K., & Hocenski, Z. (2010) *Enterprise cloud computing security issues and challenges.* Paper presented at MIPRO 2010, May 24-28, Opatija, Croatia

Popper, K. (1963). *Conjectures and refutations: The growth of scientific knowledge.* New York: Routledge. doi:10.1063/1.3050617

Poscher, R., & Miller, R. (2013). *Surveillance and data protection in the conflict between European American legal cultures, security and defense.* John Hopkins University.

Poulymenopoulou, M., Malamateniou, F., & Vassilacopoulos, G. (2012). Emergency healthcare process automation using mobile computing and cloud services. *Journal of Medical Systems, 36*(5), 3233–3241. doi:10.1007/s10916-011-9814-y PMID:22205383

Prasad, M. R., Gyani, J., & Murti, P. R. K. (2012). Mobile cloud computing: Implications and challenges. *Journal of Information Engineering and Applications*, *2*(7), 7–16.

Premkumar, P. (2003). Meta-analysis of research on information technology implementation in small business. *Journal of Organizational Computing and Electronic Commerce*, *13*(2), 91–121. doi:10.1207/S15327744JOCE1302_2

Preuveneers, D., Berbers, Y., & Joosen, W. (2013). The future of mobile e-health application development: exploring HTML5 for context-aware diabetes monitoring. *Procedia Computer Science*, *21*, 351–359. doi:10.1016/j.procs.2013.09.046

Puzio, P. a. (2013). *ClouDedup: Secure deduplication with encrypted data for cloud storage. In IEEE CloudCom 2013. 1* (pp. 363–370). Bristol, UK: IEEE; doi:10.1109/CloudCom.2013.54

Pyke, J. (2009). *Now is the time to take the cloud seriously*. Retrieved August 12, 2014, from http://www.cordys.com/cordyscms_sites/objects/bb1a0bd7f47b1c91ddf-36ba7db88241d/time_to_take_the_cloud_seroiusly_online_1_.pdf

Qian, Y. (2010). *Design and evaluation of effiecient collective communications on modern interconnects and multicore clusters*. PhD thesis, Queen's University, Canada.

Qiang, C. Z., Yamamichi, M., Hausman, V., Altman, D., & Unit, I. S. (2011). *Mobile applications for the health sector*. Washington, DC: World Bank.

Rabin, M. O. (1981). *Fingerprinting by random polynomials*. Center for Research in Computing Technology, Aiken Computation Laboratory.

Rader, D. (2012). Case - How cloud computing maximizes growth opportunities for a firm challenging established rivals. *Strategy and Leadership*, *40*(3), 36–43. doi:10.1108/10878571211221202

Ragan, C. T., & Lipsey, R. G. (2011). Challenges facing the developing countries. In C. T. Ragan, & R. G. Lipsey (Eds.), Macroeconomics (13th ed.). Don Mills, ON: Pearson.

Rahimli, A. (2013). Factors influencing organization adoption decision on cloud computing. *International Journal of Cloud Computing and Services Science*, *2*(2), 141–147.

Ramachandran, M. (2012) Service component architecture for building enterprise cloud services. *Service Technology Magazine*, *65*. Retrieved from http://www.servicetechmag.com/I65/0812-4

Ramachandran, M. (2014) Enterprises engineering processes for the development and deployment of secure enterprise cloud applications. In M. Khosrow-Pour (Ed.), Encyclopedia of Information Science and Technology. Hershey, PA: IGI Global.

Ramachandran, M., & Chang, V. (2014a). *Cloud security proposed and demonstrated by cloud computing adoption framework*. Paper presented at the first international workshop on Emerging Software as a Service and Analytics, Barcelona, Spain.

Ramachandran, M., & Chang, V. (2014b). *Modelling financial SaaS as service components*. Paper presented at the First International Workshop on Emerging Software as a Service and Analytics, Barcelona, Spain.

Ramachandran, M. (2008). *Software components: Guidelines and applications*. NY: Nova Publishers.

Ramachandran, M. (2011). Component-based development for cloud computing architectures. In Z. Mahmmood & R. Hill (Eds.), *Cloud computing for enterprise architectures*. Springer.

Ramachandran, M. (2011). *Software security engineering: Design and applications,*. New York: *Nova Science Publishers*.

Ramdani, B., & Kawalek, P. (2008). SMEs & IS innovations adoption: A review & assessment of previous research. *Academia Revista Latinoamericana de Administracioen*, *39*(1), 47–70.

Ranadive, A., Kesavan, M., Gavrilovska, A., & Schwan, K. (2008). Performance implications of virtualizing multicore cluster machines. In *Proceedings of the 2nd workshop on System-level virtualization for high performance computing*. Glasgow, Scotland. doi:10.1145/1435452.1435453

Rao, T. P. (2004). ICT and e-governance for rural development. In *Proceedings of theSymposium on Governance in Development: Issues, Challenges and Strategies* (pp. 1-13). Anand, Gujarat, India.

Rao, S. S. (2009). Role of ICTS in India rural communities. *The Journal of Community Informatics*, *5*(1).

Rasmussen, N. (2007). Calculating total cooling requirements for data centers. *American Power Conversion, White Paper #25*. Retrieved from http://68.170.159.58/Portals/0/CalculatingTotalCoolingRequirements.pdf

Rath, A., Mohapatra, S., Kumar, S., & Thakurta, R. (2012). *Decision point for adopting cloud computing for SMEs*. Paper presented at the The 7th International Conference for Internet Technology and Secured Transactions.

Ratten, V. (2012). Does the sky have to be the limit? Utilizing cloud-based learning in the workplace. *Development and Learning in Organizations*, 26(5), 21–23. doi:10.1108/14777281211258662

Ratten, V. (2014). Indian and US consumer purchase intentions of cloud computing services. *Journal of Indian Business Research*, 6(2), 170–188. doi:10.1108/JIBR-07-2013-0068

Rauber, T., & Runger, G. (2010). *Parallel Programming for Multicore and Cluster Systems*. Springer.

Rechtsanwalt, M., & Kempermann, P. (2010). *Secrets of the cloud: Licensing and data protection – particularities and pitfalls*. Paper presented at the International Technology Law Association*Annual European Conference*, Berlin, Germany.

Reding, V. (2012). *Webpage*. Retrieved January 3, 2014, http://ec.europa.eu/avservices/video/player.cfm?ref=82655&sitelang=en

Redolfi, A., McClatchey, R., Anjum, A., Zijdenbos, A., Manset, D., Barkhof, F., & Frisoni, G. B. et al. (2009). Grid infrastructures for computational neuroscience: The neuGRID example. *Future Neurology*, 4(6), 703–722. doi:10.2217/fnl.09.53

Reeve, R. (2011). Building a 21st century communications economy: Technical report, carbon disclosure project in support with AT&T.

Reitz, K. (2014). *Requests*. Retrieved from http://docs.python-requests.org/en/latest/

Research2guidance. (2014). *mHealth application developer economics 2014: The state of the art of m-health app publishing* (pp. 43). Retrieved from http://mhealtheconomics.com/mhealth-developer-economics-report/

Reti, S. R., Feldman, H. J., & Safran, C. (2009). Governance for personal health records. *Journal of the American Medical Informatics Association*, 16(1), 14–17. doi:10.1197/jamia.M2854 PMID:18952939

Ricardo J., Adina C., Carlos C, Moisés D., Parisa G. (2013) Ontology enriched framework for cloud-based enterprise interoperability. *Concurrent engineering approaches for sustainable product development in a multi-disciplinary environment*. Springer.

Ried, S., Kisker, H., Matzke, P., Bartels, A., & Lisserman, M. (2011). *Sizing the cloud – a BT futures report*. Retrieved December 21, 2013 from, http://www.forrester.com/Sizing+The+Cloud/fulltext/-/E-RES58161?objectid=RES58161

Rimal, B. P., Jukan, A., Katsaros, D., & Goeleven, Y. (2011). Architectural requirements for cloud computing systems: An enterprise cloud approach. *Journal of Grid Computing*, 9(1), 3–26. doi:10.1007/s10723-010-9171-y

Ristenpart, T., Tromer, E., Savage, S., & Shacham, H. (2009). Hey, you, get off of my cloud: Exploring information leakage in third-party compute clouds. In Proceedings of the 16th ACM conference on computer and communications security (pp. 199–212). ACM; Retrieved from http://portal.acm.org/citation.cfm?id=1653687 doi:10.1145/1653662.1653687

Rittinghouse, J. W., & Ransome, J. F. (2009). *Cloud computing: Implementation, management, and security*. New York: CRC Press.

Rochwerger, B., Breitgand, D., Levy, E., Galis, A., Nagin, K., Llorente, I. M., & Galan, F. (2009). The reservoir model and architecture for open federated cloud computing. *IBM Journal of Research and Development*, 53(4), 4–1. doi:10.1147/JRD.2009.5429058

Rodero-Merino, L., Vaquero, L. M., Gil, V., Galán, F., Fontán, J., Montero, R. S., & Llorente, I. M. (2010). From infrastructure delivery to service management in clouds. *Future Generation Computer Systems*, 26(8), 1226–1240. doi:10.1016/j.future.2010.02.013

Rogers, E. (2003). *Diffusion of innovations*. New York, NY: Free Press.

Rosenblum, M. (2004). The reincarnation of virtual machines. *Queue*, 2(5), 34. doi:10.1145/1016998.1017000

Rosenthal, A., Mork, P., Li, M. H., Stanford, J., Koester, D., & Reynolds, P. (2010). Cloud computing: A new business paradigm for biomedical information sharing. *Journal of Biomedical Informatics*, 43(2), 342–353. doi:10.1016/j.jbi.2009.08.014 PMID:19715773

Ross, V. W. (2010). *Factors influencing the adoption of cloud computing by decision making managers*. (PhD. Dissertation). Retrieved from ProQuest Dissertations and Theses. (UMI No: 3391308)

Ross, P., & Blumenstein, M. (2013). Cloud computing: The nexus of strategy and technology. *The Journal of Business Strategy*, 34(4), 39–47. doi:10.1108/JBS-10-2012-0061

Rouse, M. (2006). Node. Retrieved from http://search-networking.techtarget.com/definition/node

Rouse, M. (2006). Processor. Retrieved August 2, 2012, from http://whatis.techtarget.com/definition/processor

Roy, P. V. (2008). The challenges and opportunities of multiple processors: Why multi-core processors are easy and internet is hard. Retrieved from http://www.ist-selfman.org/wiki/images/5/54/Vanroy-mc-panel.pdf

Roy, N. K. (2012). ICT–enabled rural education in India. *International Journal of Information and Education Technology*, 2(5), 525–529. doi:10.7763/IJIET.2012.V2.196

Rui, G. (2007). *Information systems innovation adoption among organizations a match-based framework and empirical studies*. Singapore: National University of Singapore.

Ruiz-Zafra, Á., Benghazi, K., Noguera, M., & Garrido, J. L. (2013). *Zappa: An open mobile platform to build cloud-based m-health systems. Ambient Intelligence-Software and Applications* (pp. 87–94). Springer.

Ryan, W. M., & Loeffler, C. M. (2010). Insights into cloud computing. *Intellectual Property & Technology Law Journal*, 22(11), 22–27.

Sadashiv, N., & Kumar, S. M. D. (2011). Cluster, grid and cloud computing: A detailed comparison. In *Proceedings of the 6th International Conference on Computer Science & Education (ICCSE)* (pp. 477-482). doi:10.1109/ICCSE.2011.6028683

Saeed, A., & Ibrahim, H. (2005). Reasons for the problems faced by patients in government hospitals: Results of a survey in a government hospital in Karachi, Pakistan. *JPMA. The Journal of the Pakistan Medical Association*, 55(1), 1–3. PMID:15816698

Safawat, A., Hassanein, H., & Moufta, H. (2002) A MAC-based performance study of energy aware routing schemes in wireless ad-hoc networks. In *Proceedings of the Global Telecommunications Conference, 2002. GLOBECOM '02*. IEEE.

SafeNet. (2014). *Hardware security modules*. Retrieved from http://www.safenet-inc.com/data-encryption/hardware-security-modules-hsms/

SafeNet. (2014). *Luna SA HSM*. Retrieved from http://www.safenet-inc.com/data-encryption/hardware-security-modules-hsms/luna-hsms-key-management/luna-sa-network-hsm/

Sahandi, R., Alkhalil, A., & Opara-Martins, J. (2012). SMEs' perception of cloud computing: Potential and security. In Collaborative networks in the internet of services. Springer.

Salleh, S. M., Teoh, S. Y., & Chan, C. (2012). *Cloud enterprise systems: A review of literature and its adoption*. Paper presented at the PASIS 2012.

Sampaio, A., & Mendonça, N. (2011). Uni4Cloud: An approach based on open standards for deployment and management of multi-cloud applications. In *Proceedings of the 2nd International Workshop on Software Engineering for Cloud Computing. ICSE 2011* (pp. 15–21). doi:10.1145/1985500.1985504

San Lucas, F. A., Wang, G., Scheet, P., & Peng, B. (2012). Integrated annotation and analysis of genetic variants from next-generation sequencing studies with variant tools. *Bioinformatics (Oxford, England)*, 28(3), 421–422. doi:10.1093/bioinformatics/btr667 PMID:22138362

Sancho, J. C., Robles, A., & Duato, J. (2004). An effective methodology to improve the performance of the up*/down* routing algorithm. *IEEE Transactions on Parallel and Distributed Systems*, 15(8), 740–754. doi:10.1109/tpds.2004.28

Sanfilippo, S. (2014). *REDIS*. Retrieved from http://redis.io

Sanger, F., & Coulson, A. (1978). The use of thin acrylamide gels for DNA sequencing. *FEBS Letters*, *87*(1), 107–110. doi:10.1016/0014-5793(78)80145-8 PMID:631324

SAP AG. (2013). *SAP - The world's leading business software company*. Investor Presentation.

Sarasohn-Kahn, J. (2010). *How smartphones are changing health care for consumers and providers* (1st ed., pp. 23). California HealthCare Foundation. Retrieved from http://www.chcf.org/

Sarwar, A., & Khan, M.N. (2013). A review of trust aspects in cloud computing security. *International Journal of Cloud Computing and Services Science, 2*(2), 116–122.

Sasikala, P. (2011). Cloud computing in higher education. *International Journal of Cloud Applications and Computing, 1*(2), 1–13. doi:10.4018/ijcac.2011040101

Saunders, R. & Praw, J. (2013). *Small and midsize businesses cloud trust study: U.S. study results*. Mircosoft Study.

Saxena, S. (2012). Problems faced by rural entrepreneurs and remedies to solve it. *IOSR Journal of Business and Management, 3*(1), 23–29. doi:10.9790/487X-0312329

Saya, S., Pee, L., & Kankanhalli, A. (2010). *The impact of institutional influences on perceived technological characteristics and real options in cloud computing adoption*. Paper presented at the 31st International Conference on Information Systems (ICIS 2010), St. Louis, MO.

Sboner, A., Mu, X. J., Greenbaum, D., Auerbach, R. K., & Gerstein, M. B. (2011). The real cost of sequencing: Higher than you think! *Genome Biology, 12*(8), 125. doi:10.1186/gb-2011-12-8-125 PMID:21867570

Schauer, B. (2008). Multicore processors-A necessity. *ProQuest*. Retrieved from http://www.techrepublic.com/resource-library/whitepapers/multicore-processors-a-necessity/

Scheibe, M., Skutsch, M., & Schofer, J. (1975). Experiments in Delphi methodology. In H. A. Linstone & M. Turoff (Eds.), *The Delphi method - Techniques and applications* (pp. 262–287). Reading: Addison-Wesley.

Schroeder, M. D., Birrell, A. D., Burrows, M., Murray, H., Needham, R. M., Rodeheffer, T. L., & Thacker, C. P. et al. (1991). Autonet: A high-speed, self-configuring local area network using point-to-point links. *IEEE Journal on Selected Areas in Communications, 9*(8), 1318–1335. doi:10.1109/49.105178

Schubert, L., Jeffery, K., & Neidecker-Lutz, B. (2010). The future of cloud computing: opportunities for european cloud computing beyond 2010 (p. 66). European Commission, Information Society and Media.

Schulze, B. (2014). *SAP cloud strategy* [Interview]. Walldorf: SAP AG.

Schulze, B., Wemme, D., Schmidt, N., & Nelz, J. (2013). *Cloud 101 - Demystifying Cloud*. Cloud Week SAP.

Sclater, N. (2009). *Cloudworks: eLearning in the cloud*. Retrieved August 12, 2014, from http://cloudworks.ac.uk/cloud/view/2430

Scott, A., Gilbert, A., & Gelan, A. (2007). The urban rural divide: Myth or reality? SERG Policy Brief 2. London, UK: The Macaulay Institute, Socio-Economic Research Group.

Sewchurran, E., & Brown, I. (2011). Successful ICT service delivery: Enablers, inhibitors and hygiene factors - A service provider perspective. In *Proceedings of the Institute of Computer Scientists and Information Technologists Conference* (pp. 195-204). Cape Town, South Africa.

Shahhoseini, H. S., Naderi, M., & Buyya, R. (2000). Shared memory multistage clustering structure, an efficient structure for massively parallel processing systems. In *Proceedings of the Fourth International Conference/Exhibition on High Performance Computing in the Asia-Pacific Region, 2000*.

Shah, M., Javed, O., & Shafique, K. (2007). Automated visual surveillance in realistic scenarios. *IEEE MultiMedia, 14*(1), 30–39. doi:10.1109/MMUL.2007.3

Shainer, G., Lui, P., Hilgeman, M., Layton, J., Stevens, C., Stemple, W., & Kresse, G. (2013). Maximizing application performance in a multi-core, NUMA-aware compute cluster by multi-level tuning. In J. Kunkel, T. Ludwig, & H. Meuer (Eds.), *Supercomputing* (Vol. 7905, pp. 226–238). Berlin Heidelberg: Springer. doi:10.1007/978-3-642-38750-0_17

Shareef, M. A., Kumar, V., Kumar, U., & Dwivedi, Y. K. (2011). e-Government adoption model (GAM): Differing service maturity levels. *Government Information Quarterly*, *28*(1), 17–35. doi:10.1016/j.giq.2010.05.006

Sharif, A. M. (2010). It's written in the cloud: The hype and promise of cloud computing. *Journal of Enterprise Information Management*, *23*(2), 131–134. doi:10.1108/17410391011019732

Sharma, B., Thulasiram, R. K., Thulasiraman, P., Garg, S. K., & Buyya, R. (2012). Pricing cloud compute commodities: A novel financial economic model. In *Proceedings of the 2012 12th IEEE/ACM International Symposium on Cluster, Cloud and Grid Computing* (ccgrid 2012) (pp. 451-457). IEEE Computer Society. doi:10.1109/CCGrid.2012.126

Sharma, M. (2005). Information and communication technology for poverty reduction. *Turkish Online Journal of Distance Education, 6*(2).

Sharma, C. M., & Kumar, H. (2014). Architectural framework for implementing visual surveillance as a service. In *Proceedings of IEEE International Conference INDIACOM* (pp. 296-301). doi:10.1109/IndiaCom.2014.6828147

Sharma, C. M., Kushwaha, A. K. S., Nigam, S., & Khare, A. (2011). Automatic human activity recognition in video using background modeling and spatio-temporal template matching based technique. In *Proceedings of ACM International Conference on Advances in Computing and Artificial Intelligence* (pp. 97-101). doi:10.1145/2007052.2007072

Sharma, C. M., Kushwaha, A. K. S., Nigam, S., & Khare, A. (2011). On human activity recognition in video sequences. In *Proceedings of IEEE 2nd International conference on Computer and Communication Technology* (pp. 152-158). doi:10.1109/ICCCT.2011.6075172

Sharma, R. S., Hui, P. T. Y., & Tan, M. W. (2007). Value-added knowledge management for financial performance: The case of an East Asian conglomerate. *VINE: The Journal of Information and Knowledge Management Systems*, *37*(4), 484–501. doi:10.1108/03055720710838542

Sharpe, W. F. (1990). *Capital asset prices with and without negative holdings*. Nobel-Prize Economics Lecture.

Shawish, A., & Salama, M. (2014). Cloud computing: Paradigms and technologies. In F. Xhafa & N. Bessis (Eds.), *Inter-cooperative collective intelligence: Techniques and applications* (pp. 39–67). Heidelberg: Springer. doi:10.1007/978-3-642-35016-0_2

Shendure, J., & Ji, H. (2008). Next-generation DNA sequencing. *Nature Biotechnology*, *26*(10), 1135–1145. doi:10.1038/nbt1486 PMID:18846087

Sianipar, C. P., Yudoko, G., Adhiutama, A., & Dowaki, K. (2013). Community empowerment through appropriate technology: Sustaining the sustainable development. *Procedia Environmental Sciences, 17*, 1007–1016. doi:10.1016/j.proenv.2013.02.120

Sibley, L. M., & Weiner, J. P. (2011). An evaluation of access to health care services along the rural-urban continuum in Canada. *BMC Health Services Research*, *11*(20), 1–11. PMID:21281470

Silva, J. M. N., Drummond, L., & Boeres, C. (2010). *On modelling multicore clusters*. Paper presented at the 22nd International Symposium on Computer Architecture and High Performance Computing Workshops (SBAC-PADW), 2010.

Sim, K. M. (2012). Agent-based cloud computing. *IEEE Transactions on* Services Computing, *5*, 564–577.

Singer, S., Burgers, J., Friedberg, M., Rosenthal, M., Leape, L., & Schneider, E. (2011). Defining and measuring integrated patient care: Promoting the next frontier in health care delivery. *Medical Care Research and Review*, *68*(1), 112–127. doi:10.1177/1077558710371485 PMID:20555018

Singh, H. P., Bhisikar, A., & Singh, J. (2013). Innovative ICT through cloud computing. *IUP Journal of Computer Sciences, 7*(1), 37–52.

Skilton, M. (2010). *Building return on investment from cloud computing* (White Paper). The Open Group.

Sloman, J. (2006). Economics (6th ed.). Upper Saddle River, NJ: Prentice Hall.

Smith, H. J., Milberg, S. J., & Burke, S. J. (1996). Information privacy: Measuring individuals' concerns about organizational practices. *Management Information Systems Quarterly*, *20*(2), 167–196. doi:10.2307/249477

Smith, R. (2009). Computing in the cloud. *Research Technology Management*, *52*(5), 65–68.

SOASTA. (2014). CloudTest – cloud based load and performance testing. Retrieved July 21, 2014, from http://www.soasta.com/products/cloudtest

Sobel, W., Subramanyam, S., Sucharitakul, A., Nguyen, J., Wong, H., Klepchukov, A., . . . Patterson, D. (2008). Cloudstone: Multi-platform, multi-language benchmark and measurement tools for web 2.0. In Proceeding of Cloud Computing and its Applications (CCA 2008). Academic Press.

Sommerville, I. (2011). *Software engineering* (9th ed.). Boston, MA: Pearson.

Son, I., & Lee, D. (2011). *Assessing a new IT service model, cloud computing*. Paper presented at the PACIS 2011, Queensland, Australia.

Songan, P., Hamid, K. A., Yeo, A., Gnaniah, J., & Zen, H. (2008). Challenges to community informatics to bridging the digital divide. In F. B. Tan (Ed.), *Global information technologies: Concepts, methodologies, tools, and applications* (pp. 2121–2133). Hershey, PA: Information Science Reference. doi:10.4018/978-1-59904-939-7.ch152

Soryani, M., Analoui, M., & Zarrinchian, G. (2013). Improving inter-node communications in multi-core clusters using a contention-free process mapping algorithm. *The Journal of Supercomputing*, 1–26. doi:10.1007/s11227-013-0918-7

Sosonsky, B. (2011). *Cloud computing bible*. Indianapolis: Wiley Publishing.

Sotomayor, B., Montero, R. S., Llorente, I. M., & Foster, I. (2009). Virtual infrastructure management in private and hybrid clouds. *IEEE Internet Computing*, *13*(5), 14–22. doi:10.1109/MIC.2009.119

Squid. (2014). *Squid proxy*. Retrieved from http://www.squid-cache.org/

Srikantaiah, S., Kansal, A., & Zhao, F. (2008). Energy aware consolidation for cloud computing. In HotPower'08: Proceedings of the 2008 conference on Power aware computing and systems. Berkeley, CA: USENIX Association. Retrieved from http://www.usenix.org/event/hotpower08/tech/full_papers/srikantaiah/srikantaiah_html/

Srinivasan, M. K., Sarukesi, K., Rodrigues, P., Manoj, M. S., & Revathy, P. (2012) *State-of-the-art enterprise cloud computing security taxonomies: A classification of security challenges in the present enterprise cloud computing environment*. Paper presented at ICACCI '12, August 03 - 05 2012, Chennai, India

Srinivasan, S., & Getov, V. (2011). Navigating the cloud computing landscape: Technologies, services, and adopters. *Computer*, *44*(3), 22–23. doi:10.1109/MC.2011.91

Srinivasu, B., & Rao, P. S. (2013). Infrastructure development and economic growth: Prospects and perspective. *Journal of Business Management & Social Sciences Research*, *2*(1), 81–91.

Stein, L. D. (2010). The case for cloud computing in genome informatics. *Genome Biology*, *11*(5), 207. doi:10.1186/gb-2010-11-5-207 PMID:20441614

Stein, S., Ware, J., Laboy, J., & Schaffer, H. E. (2013). Improving K-12 pedagogy via a cloud designed for education. *International Journal of Information Management*, *33*(1), 235–241. doi:10.1016/j.ijinfomgt.2012.07.009

Sterling, T., Apon, A., & Baker, M. (2000). Cluster computing white paper. Cluster Computing.

Sterling, T. L. (2002). *Beowulf cluster computing with Windows computers* (p. 445). MIT Press.

Stevens, R. (1986). *Understanding Computers*. Oxford: Oxford University Press.

Stockholm International Peace Research Institute. (2014). Trends in world military expenditure-2013 (pp. 1-8). SIPIRI.

Storer, M. W., Greenan, K., Long, D. D., & Miller, E. L. (2008). Secure data deduplication. In *Proceedings of the 4th ACM international workshop on Storage security and survivability* (pp. 1-10). doi:10.1145/1456469.1456471

Subashini, S., & Kavitha, V. (2011). A survey on security issues in service delivery models of cloud computing. *Journal of Network and Computer Applications, 34*(1), 1–11. doi:10.1016/j.jnca.2010.07.006

SuccessFactors. (2013). *Employee central.* Retrieved December 8, 2013, from http://www.successfactors.com/content/dam/successfactors/en_us/resources/brochures-product/employee-central.pdf

SUCRE. (2014). Sucre state of the art report. Retrieved April 13, 2014, from http://www.sucreproject.eu

Suess, J., & Morooney, K. (2009). Identity management & trust services: Foundations for cloud computing. *ABI/INFORM Global, 44*(5), 24.

Sullivan, D. (2010). The definitive guide to cloud computing. Realtime Publishers.

Sullivan, D. R., Lewis, T. G., & Cook, C. R. (1988). *Computing today: Microcomputer concepts and application.* USA: Houghton Mifflin Company.

Sultan, N. (2010). Cloud computing for education: A new dawn? *International Journal of Information Management, 30*(2), 109–116. doi:10.1016/j.ijinfomgt.2009.09.004

Sultan, N. (2013). Knowledge management in the age of cloud computing and Web 2.0: Experiencing the power of disruptive innovations. *International Journal of Information Management, 33*(1), 160–165. doi:10.1016/j.ijinfomgt.2012.08.006

Sultan, N. (2014). Making use of cloud computing for healthcare provision: Opportunities and challenges. *International Journal of Information Management, 34*(2), 177–184. doi:10.1016/j.ijinfomgt.2013.12.011

Sultan, N. A. (2011). Reaching for the "cloud": How SMEs can manage. *International Journal of Information Management, 31*(3), 272–278. doi:10.1016/j.ijinfomgt.2010.08.001

Summit, E. U.-U. S.Joint Statement. (2014). Retrieved March 14, 2014, http://eeas.europa.eu/statements/docs/2014/140326_02_en.pdf

Sundar, K., & Srinivasan, T. (2009). Rural industrialisation: Challenges and proposition. *Journal of Social Science, 20*(1), 23–29.

Surendro, K., & Fardani, A. (2012). *Identification of SME readiness to implement cloud computing.* Paper presented at the International Conference on Cloud Computing and Social Networking (ICCCSN, 2012). doi:10.1109/ICCCSN.2012.6215757

Svantesson, D., & Clarke, R. (2010). Privacy and consumer risks in cloud computing. *Computer Law & Security Report, 26*(4), 391–397. doi:10.1016/j.clsr.2010.05.005

Swanson, R. A., & Holton, E. F. (2005). *Research in organizations: Foundations and methods of inquiry* (3rd ed.). San Francisco, CA: Berrett-Koehler Publishers.

Swisher, L. L., Beckstead, J. W., & Bebeau, M. J. (2004). Factor analysis as a tool for survey analysis. *Physical Therapy, 84*(9), 784–799. PMID:15330692

Tabachnick, B. G., & Fidell, L. S. (2007). *Using multivariate statistics.* Boston: Pearson Education Inc.

Talvitie, J. (2004). Incorporating the impact of ICT into urban and regional planning. *European Journal of Spatial Development*, 1-32.

Tan, C. et al.. (2013). An evaluation framework for migrating application to the cloud: Software as a service. In *Proceedings of 2nd International Conference on Logistics, Informatics and Service Science* (pp 967-972). doi:10.1007/978-3-642-32054-5_135

Tancock, D., Pearson, S., & Charlesworth, A. (2013). A privacy impact assessment tool for cloud computing. In Privacy and security for cloud computing. Springer.

Taneri, P. O., & Engin-Demir, C. (2011). Quality of education in rural schools: A needs assessment study. *International Online Journal of Educational Sciences, 3*(1), 91–112.

Tang, C. P., Wong, T. Y., & Lee, P. P. (2012). CloudVS: Enabling version control for virtual machines in an open-source cloud under commodity settings. In *IEEE Network Operations and Management Symposium. NOMS 2012* (pp. 188–195). doi:10.1109/NOMS.2012.6211898

Tang, P., Ash, J., Bates, D., Overhage, J., & Sands, D. (2006). Personal health records: Definitions, benefits, and strategies for overcoming barriers to adoption. *Journal of the American Medical Informatics Association, 13*(2), 121–126. doi:10.1197/jamia.M2025 PMID:16357345

Tashakkori, A., & Teddlie, C. (2008). *Foundations of mixed methods research: Integrating quantitative and qualitative approaches in the social and behavioral sciences.* Thousand Oaks, CA: Sage Publications.

Tayyaba, S. (2012). Rural-urban gaps in achievement, schooling conditions, student, and teachers' characteristics in Pakistan. *International Journal of Educational Management, 26*(1), 6–26. doi:10.1108/09513541211194356

Tclouds. (2014). TClouds - Trustworthy clouds healthcare scenario. Retrieved April 15, 2014, from http://www.tclouds-project.eu/downloads/factsheets/tclouds-factsheet-15-healthcare.pdf

Teunis, P. F. M., & Havelaar, A. H. (2000). The beta poisson dose-response model is not a single-hit model. *Risk Analysis, 20*(4), 513–520. doi:10.1111/0272-4332.204048 PMID:11051074

The Department of Commerce Internet Task Force. (2010). *Commercial data privacy and innovation in the internet economy: A dynamic policy framework.* Retrieved January 20, 2014, http://www.commerce.gov/sites/default/files/documents/2010/december/iptf-privacy-green-paper.pdf

The Measurement Factory. (2014). *eCAP.* Retrieved from http://www.e-cap.org/Home

Thinkstrategies. (2002). *Solving the IT challenges of small and mid-size organizations via "utility computing".* Retrieved August 12, 2014, from http://www.thinkstrategies.com/images/CBE_Whitepaper_110602.pdf

Thomas, P. Y. (2011). Cloud computing: A potential paradigm for practicing the scholarship of teaching and learning. *The Electronic Library, 29*(2), 214–224. doi:10.1108/02640471111125177

Thong, J. (1999). An integrated model of information systems adoption in small businesses. *Journal of Management Information Systems, 15*(4), 187–214.

Thong, J., Yap, C., & Raman, K. (1994). Engagement of external expertise in information systems implementation. *Journal of Management Information Systems, 11*(2), 209–231.

Thorlakson, T., & Neufeldt, H. (2012). Reducing subsistence farmers' vulnerability to climate change: Evaluating the potential contributions of agroforestry in western Kenya. *Agriculture & Food Security, 1*(15), 1–13.

Thorvaldsdottir, H., Robinson, J. T., & Mesirov, J. P. (2013). Integrative Genomics Viewer (IGV): High-performance genomics data visualization and exploration. *Briefings in Bioinformatics, 14*(2), 178–192. doi:10.1093/bib/bbs017 PMID:22517427

Tian, Y., Song, B., & Huh, E. N. (2011). *Towards the development of personal cloud computing for mobile thin-clients.* Paper presented at the IEEE International Conference on Information Science and Applications (ICISA), Jeju Island, South Korea.

Tilde. (2014). Emberjs. Retrieved April 15, 2014, from http://emberjs.com/

Tondel, I. A., Jaatun, M. G., & Meland, P. H. (2008). *Security requirements for rest of us: A survey. IEEE Software,25*(1).

Tornatzky, L., & Fleischer, M. (1990). *The process of technology innovation.* Lexington, MA: Lexington Books.

Trapnell, C., Pachter, L., & Salzberg, S. L. (2009). TopHat: Discovering splice junctions with RNA-Seq. *Bioinformatics (Oxford, England), 25*(9), 1105–1111. doi:10.1093/bioinformatics/btp120 PMID:19289445

Trapnell, C., Williams, B. A., Pertea, G., Mortazavi, A., Kwan, G., van Baren, M. J., & Pachter, L. et al. (2010). Transcript assembly and quantification by RNA-Seq reveals unannotated transcripts and isoform switching during cell differentiation. *Nature Biotechnology, 28*(5), 511–515. doi:10.1038/nbt.1621 PMID:20436464

Treese, W. (2008). Movin' to the cloud. *NetWorker, 12*(4), 13–15. doi:10.1145/1461981.1461985

Tsilas, N. (2010). Moving responsibly to the cloud to ensure its full potential. *The Computer & Internet Lawyer, 27*(11), 16–24.

Turetken, O., Elgammal, A., van den Heuvel W.-J., & Papazoglou, M. (2004). *Enforcing compliance on business processes.* Tilburg: European Research Institute in Service Science (ERISS).

Turoff, M. (1975). The policy Delphi. In H. Linstone & M. Turoff (Eds.), *The Delphi method: Techniques and applications.* Reading, PA: Addison-Wesley.

Tweel, A. (2012). *Examining the relationship between technological, organizational, and environment factors and cloud computing adoption.* (Doctoral Dissertation). Retrieved from ProQuest Dissertations and Theses. (UMI No: 3529668)

U.K. Information Commissioner's Office. (2010). *Data protection regulatory action policy.* Retrieved January 28, 2014, http://www.ico.org.uk/what_we_cover/taking_action/~/media/documents/library/Data_Protection/Detailed_specialist_guides/DATA_PROTECTION_REGULATORY_ACTION_POLICY.ashx

UN. (2011). *World urbanization prospects: The 2011 revision.* New York, NY: United Nations, Department of Economic and Social Affairs, Population Division.

United States Department of Justice (USDOJ). (2007). *Chapter 1: Computer fraud and abuse act.* Retrieved March 23, 2011, from http://www.cybercrime.gov/ccmanual/01ccma.pdf

Usman, A., Dutta, D., Habeeb, O., & Jean, A. (2013) Sustainable energy in rural communities of Bongouanou: Utilizing solar energy as a source for electricity. In *Proceedings of theIEEE Global Humanitarian Technology Conference: South Asia Satellite* (pp. 15-20). Trivandrum, India. doi:10.1109/GHTC-SAS.2013.6629881

USwitch Survey. (2011). *USwitch's guide to mobile phones.* Author.

Uusitalo, I., Karppinen, K., Juhola, A., & Savola, R. (2010). *Trust and cloud services-an interview study.* Paper presented at the 2nd International Conference on Cloud Computing Technology and Science (CloudCom). doi:10.1109/CloudCom.2010.41

van der Geest, K. (2010). *Rural youth employment in developing countries: A global view.* Rome, Italy: United Nations Food and Agriculture Organization.

van Dijk, J. (2008). One Europe, digitally divided. In A. Chadwick & P. N. Howard (Eds.), *The Routledge handbook of internet politics* (pp. 288–304). London: Routledge.

Van Hoorn, T. P. (1979). Strategic planning in small and medium-sized companies. *Long Range Planning, 12*(2), 84–91. doi:10.1016/0024-6301(79)90076-1

Vaquero, L. M., Rodero-Merino, L., Caceres, J., & Lindner, M. (2008). A break in the clouds: Towards a cloud definition. *Computer Communication Review, 39*(1), 50–55. doi:10.1145/1496091.1496100

Varga, A., & Hornig, R. (2008). An overview of the OMNeT++ simulation environment. In *Proceedings of the 1st international conference on Simulation tools and techniques for communications, networks and systems & workshops.* Marseille, France.

Vazirani, V. (2003). Approximation algorithms (2nd ed., p. 380). New York: Springer.

Velev, D., & Zlateva, P. (2012). *Enterprise 2.0 knowledge management development trends.* Paper presented at the International Conference on Economics, Business Innovation (ICEBI 2012), Singapore.

Venter, J. C., Adams, M. D., Myers, E. W., Li, P. W., Mural, R. J., Sutton, G. G., . . . Holt, R. A. (2001). The sequence of the human genome. *Science, 291*(5507), 1304-1351.

Verma, A., Ahuja, P., & Neogi, A. (2008). pMapper: Power and migration cost aware application placement in virtualized systems. In *Proceedings of the 9th ACM/IFIP/USENIX International Conference on Middleware (Middleware '08)* (pp. 243–264). New York: Springer-Verlag. Retrieved from http://dl.acm.org/citation.cfm?id=1496966

Vodera. (2014). VIGOR++ virtual gastrointestinal tract. Retrieved April 15, 2014, from http://www.vigorpp.eu/

Vogel, T. (2012). *Storms threaten storage in the clouds.* Retrieved January 3, 2014, http://www.europeanvoice.com/page/3323.aspx?LG=1&ArtID=74223&SecName=Special%20reports&SectionID=5

Voona, S., & Venkantaratna, R. (2009). *Cloud computing for banks.* Infosys Technologies Ltd.

Voorsluys, W., Brober, J., & Buyya, R. (2011). Introduction to cloud computing. In R. Buyya, J. Broberg, & A. Goscinski (Eds.), Cloud computing principles and paradigms. Hoboken, NJ: John Wiley & Sons Inc. doi:10.1002/9780470940105.ch1

Vouk, M. A. (2008). Cloud computing-issues, research and implementations. *Journal of Computing and Information Technology, 16*(4), 235–246.

Waltz, E. (2012). 1000 genomes on Amazon's cloud. *Nature Biotechnology*, *30*(5), 376–376. doi:10.1038/nbt0512-376

Wang, L., & Laszewski, G. V. (2008). *Scientific cloud computing: early definition and experience*. Paper presented at the IEEE International Conference on High Performance Computing and Communications, Dalian, China. doi:10.1109/HPCC.2008.38

Wang, D. (2013). Influences of cloud computing on e-commerce businesses and industry. *Journal of Software Engineering and Applications*, *6*(06), 313–318. doi:10.4236/jsea.2013.66039

Wang, K., Li, M., & Hakonarson, H. (2010). ANNOVAR: Functional annotation of genetic variants from high-throughput sequencing data. *Nucleic Acids Research*, *38*(16), e164. doi:10.1093/nar/gkq603 PMID:20601685

Wang, L., von Laszewski, G., Kunze, M., & Tao, J. (2008). *Cloud computing: A perspective study*. Eggenstein-Leopoldshafen, Germany: *Steinbuch Centre for Computing, Karlsruhe Institute of Technology*.

Wang, W. Y. C., Rashi, A., & Chuang, H. (2011). Toward the trend of cloud computing. *Journal of Electronic Commerce Research*, *12*(4), 238–242.

Wang, W., Hu, W., & Tan, T. (2003). Recent developments in human motion Analysis. *International Journal of Pattern Recognition*, *36*(3), 585–601. doi:10.1016/S0031-3203(02)00100-0

Warren, S., & Brandeis, L. (1890). The right to privacy. *Harvard Law Review*, *4*(5), 193–220. doi:10.2307/1321160

Wei, J., Zhang, X., Ammons, G., Bala, V., & Ning, P. (2009). *Managing security of virtual machine images in a cloud environment*. Paper presented at the 2009 ACM Workshop on Cloud Computing Security, CCSW '09. New York, NY. doi:10.1145/1655008.1655021

Wei, D. (2010). The impact of emerging technologies on small and medium enterprises (SMEs). *Journal of Business Systems, Governance, & Ethics*, *4*(4), 53–60.

Weinhardt, C., Anandasivam, A., Blau, B., & Stoßer, J. (2009). *Business models in the service world*. IEEE Computer Society.

Weinhardt, C., Anandasivam, A., Blau, B., Borissov, N., Meinl, T., Michalk, W., & Stoßer, J. (2009). Cloud computing: A classification, business models, and research directions. *Business & Information Systems Engineering*, *1*(5), 391–399. doi:10.1007/s12599-009-0071-2

Weinland, D. & Ronfard, R.(2011). A survey of vision based methods for action representation, segmentation and recognition. *International Journal of Computer Vision and Image understanding*, *115*(2), 221-241.

Weiss, A. (2007). Computing in the clouds. *netWorker*, *11*(4), 16–25. doi:10.1145/1327512.1327513

Weissman, J. B., Sundarrajan, P., Gupta, A., Ryden, M., Nair, R., & Chandra, A. (2011). Early experience with the distributed nebula cloud. In Proceedings of the fourth international workshop on Data-intensive distributed computing (pp. 17–26). ACM. Retrieved from http://portal.acm.org/citation.cfm?id=1996019

Wessing, T. (2010). Cloud computing. Retrieved from http://www.taylorwessing.com/fileadmin/files/docs/Cloud_computing.pdf

Westin, A. F. (1967). *Privacy and freedom*. New York: Atheneum Press.

Wheeler, B., & Waggener, S. (2009). Above campus services: Shaping the promise of cloud computing for higher education. *ABI/INFORM Global*, *44*(6), 52.

White Paper, I. B. M. (2008). *IT service management to enable the fulfilment of your SOA strategy*. IBM Global Services.

Wijesiri, S. (2010). *Cloud computing - A new wave in IT*. Retrieved from http://www.dailynews.lk/2010/07/22/fea15.asp

Wilcox-O'Hearn, Z., & Warner, B. (2008). Tahoe: The least-authority filesystem. In *Proceedings of the 4th ACM international workshop on Storage security and survivability* (pp. 21-26). doi:10.1145/1456469.1456474

Wilson, V., & Strong, D. (2014). Editors' introduction to the special section on patient-centered e-health: Research opportunities and challenges. *Communications of the Association for Information Systems*, *34*(15).

WinterGreen Research. (2010). *Worldwide cloud computing market opportunities and segment forecasts 2009 to 2015*. WinterGreen Research Inc. Retrieved from http://www.wintergreenresearch.com/reports/CloudOpportunities.htm

Wittow, M. H., & Buller, D. J. (2010). Cloud computing: Emerging legal issues for access to data, anywhere, anytime. *Journal of Internet Law*, *14*(1), 1–10.

Wolk, R. M. (2004). The effects of English language dominance of the internet and the digital divide. In *Proceedings of theInternational Symposium on Technology and Society* (pp. 174-178). Worcester, MA, USA. doi:10.1109/ISTAS.2004.1314348

Wong, Y. C., Fung, J. Y., Law, C. K., Lam, J. C., & Lee, V. W. (2009). Tackling the digital divide. *British Journal of Social Work*, *39*(4), 754–767. doi:10.1093/bjsw/bcp026

Wood, T., Ramakrishnan, K. K., Shenoy, P., & Van der Merwe, J. (2011). CloudNet: Dynamic pooling of cloud resources by live WAN migration of virtual machines. In ACM SIGPLAN Notices (vol. 46, pp. 121–132). doi:10.1145/1952682.1952699

Woodside, A. G., & Biemans, W. G. (2005). Modeling innovation, manufacturing, diffusion and adoption/rejection processes. *Journal of Business and Industrial Marketing*, *20*(7), 380–393. doi:10.1108/08858620510628614

World Economic Forum. (2010). *Exploring the future of cloud computing: Riding the next wave of technology-driven transformation*. Author.

Wren, C. R., Azarbayejani, A., Darrell, T., & Pentland, A. P. (1997). Pfinder: Real-time tracking of the human body. *IEEE Transactions on Pattern Analysis and Machine Intelligence*, *19*(7), 51–56. doi:10.1109/34.598236

Wunderlich, J. P. (2013). *SAP cloud applications portfolio*. SAP AG.

Wu, W. (2011). Developing an explorative model for SaaS adoption. *Expert Systems with Applications*, *38*(12), 15057–15064. doi:10.1016/j.eswa.2011.05.039

Wu, W. W. (2011). Mining significant factors affecting the adoption of SaaS using the rough set approach. *Journal of Systems and Software*, *84*(3), 435–441. doi:10.1016/j.jss.2010.11.890

Wu, X., & Taylor, V. (2013). Performance modeling of hybrid MPI/OpenMP scientific applications on large-scale multicore supercomputers. *Journal of Computer and System Sciences*, *79*(8). doi:10.1016/j.jcss.2013.02.005

Xu, M., Shang, Y., Li, D., & Wang, X. (2013). Greening data centre networks with throughput guaranteed power aware routing. *Computer Networks*, *57*(15), 2880–2899. doi:10.1016/j.comnet.2012.12.012

Yacoob, Y., & Black, M. (1998). Parameterized modeling and recognition of activities. In *Proceedings of International Conference on Computer Vision* (pp.120-127). doi:10.1109/ICCV.1998.710709

Yang, C., Liu, J., Huang, K., & Jiang, F. (2014). A method for managing green power of a virtual machine cluster in cloud. *Future Generation Computer Systems*, *37*, 26–36. doi:10.1016/j.future.2014.03.001

Yan, H. (2010). On the clouds: A new way of computing. *Information Technology & Libraries*, *29*(2), 87–92.

Yeboah-Boateng, E. O., & Essandoh, K. A. (2013). Cloud computing: The level of awareness amongst small & medium-sized enterprises (SMEs) in developing economies. *Journal of Emerging Trends in Computing and Information Sciences*, *4*(11), 832–839.

Yee, G. O. M., & Korba, L. (2008). Security personalization for internet and web services. *International Journal of Web Services Research*, *5*(1), 1-22.

Ye, K., Schulz, M. H., Long, Q., Apweiler, R., & Ning, Z. (2009). Pindel: A pattern growth approach to detect break points of large deletions and medium sized insertions from paired-end short reads. *Bioinformatics (Oxford, England)*, *25*(21), 2865–2871. doi:10.1093/bioinformatics/btp394 PMID:19561018

Yeo, C., Buyya, R., Pourreza, H., Eskicioglu, R., Graham, P., & Sommers, F. (2006). In A. Zomaya (Ed.), *Cluster computing: High-performance, high-availability, and high-throughput processing on a network of computers handbook of nature-inspired and innovative computing* (pp. 521–551). US: Springer.

Yoo, C. S. (2011). Cloud computing: Architectural and policy implications. *Review of Industrial Organization*, *38*(4), 405–421. doi:10.1007/s11151-011-9295-7

Younis, M. Z. (2003). A comparison study of urban and small rural hospitals financial and economic performance. *Online Journal of Rural Nursing and Health Care, 3*(1), 38–48.

Youseff, L., Butrico, M., & Da Silva, D. (2008). *Toward a unified ontology of cloud computing.* Paper presented at the Grid Computing Environments Workshop, Austin, TX.

Yulei, W., Geyong, M., Keqiu, L., & Javadi, B. (2012). Modeling and analysis of communication networks in multicluster systems under spatio-temporal bursty traffic. *IEEE Transactions on Parallel and Distributed Systems, 23*(5), 902–912. doi:10.1109/tpds.2011.198

Zeller, M., Grossman, R., Lingenfelder, C., Berthold, M. R., Marcade, E., Pechter, R., & Holada, R. (2009). *Open standards and cloud computing: KDD-2009 panel report.* Paper presented at the KDD '09: Proceedings of the 15th ACM SIGKDD International Conference on Knowledge Discovery and Data Mining, Paris, France. doi:10.1145/1557019.1557027

Zhang, Q., Cheng, L., & Boutaba, R. (2010). Cloud computing: State-of-the-art and research challenges. *Journal of Internet Services and Applications, 1*(1), 7-18.

Zhang, S., Chen, X., & Huo, X. (2010). The comparison between cloud computing and grid computing. In Proceedings of the 2010 International Conference on Computer Application and System Modeling (ICCASM) (Vol. 11, pp. V11–V72). IEEE. Retrieved from http://ieeexplore.ieee.org/xpls/abs_all.jsp?arnumber=5623257

Zhang, L. J., Zhang, J., Fiaidhi, J., & Chang, J. M. (2010). Hot topics in cloud computing. *Computer, 12*(5), 17–19.

Zhang, Q., Cheng, L., & Boutaba, R. (2010). Cloud computing: State-of-the-art and research challenges. *Journal of Internet Services and Applications, 1*(1), 7–18. doi:10.1007/s13174-010-0007-6

Zhang, Y. (2006). *An overview of image and video segmentation in the last 40 years. Advances in Image and Video Segmentation* (pp. 1–16). IRM Press.

Zhang, Y., Liu, T., Meyer, C. A., Eeckhoute, J., Johnson, D. S., Bernstein, B. E., & Liu, X. S. et al. (2008). Model-based analysis of ChIP-Seq (MACS). *Genome Biology, 9*(9), R137. doi:10.1186/gb-2008-9-9-r137 PMID:18798982

Zhou, F., Yang, H., Álamo, J., Wong, J., & Chang, C. (2010). Mobile Personal Health Care System for Patients with Diabetes. In Y. Lee, Z. Z. Bien, M. Mokhtari, J. Kim, M. Park, J. Kim, & I. Khalil et al. (Eds.), *Aging friendly technology for health and independence* (Vol. 6159, pp. 94–101). Berlin Heidelberg: Springer. doi:10.1007/978-3-642-13778-5_12

Zhu, H., Hall, P. A., & May, J. H. (1997). Software unit test coverage and adequacy. *ACM Computing Surveys, 29*(4), 366–427. doi:10.1145/267580.267590

Zhu, K., Dong, S., Xu, S., & Kraemer, K. (2006). Innovation diffusion in global contexts: Determinants of post-adoption digital transformation of European companies. *European Journal of Information Systems, 15*(6), 601–616. doi:10.1057/palgrave.ejis.3000650

Zhu, K., Kraemer, K., & Xu, S. (2003). Electronic business adoption by European firms: A cross-country assessment of the facilitators and inhibitors. *European Journal of Information Systems, 12*(4), 251–268. doi:10.1057/palgrave.ejis.3000475

Zikmund, W. G. (1994). *Exploring market research.* Dryden Press.

Zwick, D. (1999). *Models of privacy in the digital age: Implications for marketing and ecommerce.* Retrieved May 26, 2011, from http://ritim.cba.uri.edu/Working%20Papers/Privacy-Models-Paper%5B1%5D.pdf

About the Contributors

Victor Chang is a Senior Lecturer in Computing at Leeds Beckett University and a Visiting Researcher at University of Southampton. He has been a technical lead in web applications, web services, database, grid, cloud, storage/backup, bioinformatics, financial computing which subsequently have become his research interests. Victor has also successfully delivered many IT projects in Taiwan, Singapore, Australia, and the UK since 1998. Victor is experienced in a number of different IT subjects and has 27 certifications with 97% on average. He completed PGCert (Higher Education, University Greenwich, 2012) and PhD (C.S, University of Southampton, 2013) within four years part-time while working full-time, whereby the distance between his work and research is about 400 miles away. He has over 70 peer-reviewed published papers, including several high-quality journals up-to-date. Victor received BSc and BEng from University of Sydney in 2000, research MPhil from University of Cambridge in 2002. He won Â£20,000 funding in 2001 and Â£81,000 funding in 2009. He was involved in part of the Â£6.5 million project in 2004, part of the Â£5.6 million project in 2006 and part of a Â£300,000 project in 2013. Victor is a winner in 2011 European Identity Award in On Premise to Cloud Migration. He was selected to present his research in the House of Commons, UK, in 2011. He won the best student paper in CLOSER 2012. Victor has demonstrated Storage as a Service, Health Informatics as a Service, Financial Software as a Service, Education as a Service, Big Data Processing as a Service, Integration as a Service, Security as a Service, Social Network as a Service and Data Visualization as a Service (Weather Science) in Cloud Computing and Big Data services in both of his practitioner and academic experience. His proposed frameworks have been adopted by numerous organizations. In April 2014 he received 5 certificates in a single international conference. He is the chair of international workshops in Emerging Clouds and Enterprise Security. He is an editor of the Cloud Computing adoption book with IGI Global. He is a reviewer of *International Journal of Information Management, Expert Systems with Applications, IEEE Transactions on Cloud Computing, IEEE Transactions on Services Computing, Journal of Internet Services and Applications*, and *Journal of Computing and Information Technology*. He is also a founding Editor-in-Chief in *Open Journal of Big Data*. He is the Editor of a highly prestigious journal, *Future Generation Computer Systems* (FGCS). He is a keynote speaker of a few conferences and workshops including the combined CLOSER/WEBIST/ICT4AgeingWell 2015.

Robert J. Walters worked for almost 15 years in commercial banking before leaving to study Mathematics with Computer Science at University of Southampton. After completing his degree, he worked for several years as a software developer before returning to Southampton in 1996. Since then, he has completed his PhD in 2003 and is currently employed as a lecturer in Electronics and Computer Science at University of Southampton

Gary Wills graduated from the University of Southampton with an Honours degree in Electromechanical Engineering and then a PhD in Industrial Hypermedia systems. He is a Chartered Engineer, a member of the Institute of Engineering Technology, and a Principal Fellow of the Higher Educational Academy. He is also an adjunct professor at the Cape Peninsular University of Technology and a research professor at RLabs. Gary's main research projects revolve around providing people with relevant information in order for them to carry out a task. Gary's research projects focus on System Engineering and applications for industry, medicine and education.

* * *

Carl Adams is a researcher and academic in the digital economy, specializing in mobile technology, electronic money, Information Systems and impact of technology on people, organizations and society. Has over 100 publications in journals, conferences, book chapters and books.

Abdulelah Alwabel is a PhD student at the ECS school, University of Southampton, UK. He received his BSc degree in Computer Science from King Saud University, KSA. Abdulelah obtained his MSc degree in Computer Science in 2010 from the University of Bristol, UK. His research focuses on the fault-tolerance mechanisms for Cloud computing and Desktop Cloud.

Christopher Amos's focus has been in the development and application of novel methods for understanding the basis of inherited predisposition to cancer and other complex diseases. He developed design criteria for the conduct of genetics studies and subsequently applied these for studying families and for population based analysis. He colead the international Genetic Associations and Mechanisms in Oncology (GAME-ON) consortium which brings together population-based researchers studying genetic and environmental causes of lung, breast, prostate, colon and ovarian cancers. Through application of genome-wide association study methods, he has discovered novel variants that influence lung cancer risk. He identified a cluster of nicotinic receptor genes on chromosome 15q25.1 that commonly increase risk for lung cancer development and associate with increased nicotine dependence. Comparative studies showed an increase in risk of 30% per allele in Caucasians but a much higher risk of 80% per allele in African Americans. More recently, he identified a variant of BRCA2 that is associated with a 2.5 fold higher risk for squamous lung cancer. He is also a coleader of the Genetic Epidemiology of Lung Cancer Consortium that has targeted families that include multiple relatives affected with lung cancer and identified a locus on chromosome 6q, that predisposes individuals to have a high risk for lung cancer. He found that even light smoking greatly increases risk for lung cancer in these high-risk families. Currently, his lab is heavily involved in the development and support of next-generation sequencing and other genomic applications at Dartmouth. He has worked closely with the Department of Pathology to assist in the development of clinical sequencing, which is now being routinely applied for most sites presenting at Dartmouth. He is also very involved in sequencing for exploratory analyses to identify causes of a variety of cancers including lung, adrenal, breast, and colon cancers. He has also given assistance to Cancer Control initiatives including the New Hampshire Colonoscopy Registry. Finally, he has lead family studies of Peutz-Jeghers syndrome and Hereditary Nonpolyposis Coli.

Faiza Belala is Professor in the Department of software technology and information system at the University of Constantine 2. She also currently serves as Chief of the GLSD team at the LIRE Laboratory of the same University. She received her PhD in computer science from Constantine University in 2002. Her research interests lie in the general field of theoretical computer science, with special focuses on formal methods (based on Petri nets, rewriting logic, bigraphs), applied to several domains as, service web computing and architecture description language. Pr. Faiza BELALA research has been published in various international journals and conferences. She frequently serves as a program committee member for various international conferences and workshops.

Zakaria Benzadri is a second year PhD student at the University of Constantine 2, working under the supervision of Professor Faiza Belala in the Department of software technology and information system. His thesis title is "A FORMAL MODEL FOR CLOUD SYSTEMS SPECIFICATION AND ANALYSIS". His research will address key question in relation to cloud computing and the role of formal methods in response to the complexity of cloud architecture. His doctoral work might be able to support major cloud computing concepts specification and allows formal analysis of high level services provided over the cloud computing. Currently, he is a Graduate Teaching Assistant and has spoken at a number of conferences on Cloud Computing. His research is supported by the University of Constantine 2 and the LIRE laboratory.

Chafia Bouanaka received her PhD in Computer Science from the University Mentouri of Constantine in 2010. She is actually lecturer at the university of Constantine 2 and member of the LIRE Laboratory. Her research interests include formal specification and refinement of mobile and context-aware software systems, complex and hierarchical systems verification using strategies and reflection in declarative languages. She is actually also interested with specifying and verifying cloud systems.

Wei Chen has an MS in Molecular Biology, MS in Computer Science/Computer Information System. Over 15 years of experience in bioinformatics field.

Morgan Eldred is currently undertaking his PhD in Computing from the University of Portsmouth and holds a Legal Law Masters in IT Law from the University of Edinburgh, an Executive Masters in Business Administration from IE Business School and a M.Sc. in Strategic Business IT from the University of Portsmouth. He is currently employed as a Research Director, has written several industry publications and has over 10 years experience having worked in IT strategy development and transformational program delivery.

Mohamed Fazil Mohamed Firdhous is a Senior Lecturer and the Director of Postgraduate Studies at the Faculty of Information Technology, University of Moratwua, Sri Lanka. He is engaged in undergraduate and postgraduate teaching along with cutting edge research in the areas of trust and trust management for cloud computing, Internet of Things, mobile adhoc networks, vehicular networks, computer security and rural ICT development. He has teaching, research and industry experience in many countries including Sri Lanka, Singapore, United States of America and Malaysia. In addition to his teaching and research activities at the University, he is a highly sought after ICT consultant to the government and private institutions in Sri Lanka.

Alice Good is a senior lecturer and researcher at the University of Portsmouth, supervising PhD students in the area of information technology and its application to particular user groups. Expertise in areas relating to human computer interaction and applications for well-being. Member of various conference and journal committee and editorial boards.

Norhazlina Hamid received a Bachelor in Information Technology (Hons) from Northern University of Malaysia (UUM) in 2000 and an MSc in Information Technology from MARA University of Technology (UiTM) in 2003. She is now a final year PhD student in the School of Electronics and Computer Science of University of Southampton.

Leonard Heilig holds a B.Sc. (University of MÃ¼nster, Germany) and an M.Sc. (University of Hamburg, Germany) in Information Systems. Currently he holds a position at the Institute of Information Systems at the University of Hamburg. He spent some time at the University of St Andrews (Scotland, UK) focusing on security management, web technologies and software engineering. Practical experiences include work at companies like Adobe Systems, Airbus Group Innovations and Beiersdorf Shared Services. His current interest focuses on cloud computing and virtualization. Related applications incorporate mobile workforce management systems and maritime logistics.

Kijpokin Kasemsap received his BEng degree in Mechanical Engineering from King Mongkut's University of Technology Thonburi, his MBA degree from Ramkhamhaeng University, and his DBA degree in Human Resource Management from Suan Sunandha Rajabhat University. He is a Special Lecturer at Faculty of Management Sciences, Suan Sunandha Rajabhat University based in Bangkok, Thailand. He is a Member of International Association of Engineers (IAENG), International Association of Engineers and Scientists (IAEST), International Economics Development and Research Center (IEDRC), International Association of Computer Science and Information Technology (IACSIT), International Foundation for Research and Development (IFRD), and International Innovative Scientific and Research Organization (IISRO). He also serves on the International Advisory Committee (IAC) for International Association of Academicians and Researchers (INAAR). He has numerous original research articles in top international journals, conference proceedings, and book chapters on business management, human resource management, and knowledge management published internationally.

Konstantinos Koumaditis is a Research Associate at University of Piraeus in the Department of Digital Systems with research focus on Service Oriented Architecture (SOA) and especially SOA Governance in Healthcare Information Systems (HIS). Holds a bachelor degree on Electrical/Electronic Engineering from the University of Portsmouth UK, Masters degree with specialization in Electronics, Digital Systems, University of Hertfordshire UK, Masters degree on Engineering Management with honors from Brunel University, UK and a PhD from University of Piraeus, Greece. In the past he has worked as an educator of new technologies/ICT in: (a) primary education and (b) public colleges (IEK). Furthermore, he has been a seminar trainer in various management/IS/HIS subjects. Also, he participated as a researcher in European research projects. He has published research articles in international scientific conferences/journals and chapters in books with focus on: IS, SOA, SOA Governance, HIS. His research interests include amongst other: digital health services, HIS, EHR, SOA, SOA & Cloud Computing Governance, IS and IS management.

Harish Kumar received his Ph.D from Indian Institute of Technology Roorkie and PDF from INRIA France. He is working as Director-IT at Institute of Technology and Science, Ghaziabad. Earlier, he worked with Samsung Electronics in the capacity of chief engineer. He has deep interest in the field of image & video processing, machine learning and cloud computing.

Dimosthenis Kyriazis is a faculty member at University of Piraeus and a research engineer at the National Technical University of Athens (NTUA). He received his Electrical and Computer Engineering diploma in 2001 and his MSc degree in "Techno-economics" in 2004, while since 2007 he holds a PhD in the area of Service Oriented Architectures with a focus on quality aspects and workflow management. His expertise lies with service-based, distributed and heterogeneous systems, software and service engineering. He has participated in several EU and National funded projects (e.g. VISION Cloud, IRMOS, 4CaaSt, BEinGRID, NextGRID, AkoGRIMO, EchoGRID) addressing issues related to quality of service provisioning, workflow management, performance modeling and prediction in service oriented environments and application domains such as multimedia, finance, e-health and others. He is currently focusing on virtualization technologies for high-availability in clouds and socially-enhanced techniques for IoT management – coordinating EU funded projects that target these areas, while also analyzing topics related to big data management and content syndication.

Sergio Loureiro, CEO and Co-Founder, has worked in network security for more than 15 years. He has occupied top management positions in 2 startups where he was responsible for email security products and services, and security gateways. Before he was the lead architect for a number of security products such as SSL VPNs, log management, web security and SSL crypto accelerators. His career started in several research labs, where he participated in European projects focusing on security. Sergio holds a Ph.D. in computer science from the ENST Paris and MSc and BSc degrees from the University of Porto (Portugal). He is the holder of 3 patents.

Flora Malamateniou is Associate Professor at the Department of Digital Systems of the University of Piraeus, Greece. She has previously worked as a consultant and senior researcher in research centers and has published many papers in international scientific journals, conference proceedings and books on various subjects regarding digital healthcare services. She has been a referee in international scientific journals, conferences and books and has been involved in many Greek and EU-funded R&TD projects. She is a member of national and international scientific associations. Her current research interests include web-based digital healthcare services, pervasive healthcare systems, (personal) electronic health records, health information security and workflow systems.

Refik Molva is a full professor and the head of the Networking and Security Department at EURECOM in Sophia Antipolis, France. His current research interests are the design and evaluation of protocols for security and privacy in cloud computing. He previously worked on several research projects dealing with security and privacy in social networks, RFID systems, self-organizing systems, and mobile networks. He was program chair or general chair for security conferences such as ESORICS, RAID, SecureComm, IEEE ICC and various security related workshops. He has been an area editor for various journals such as Computer Networks, Pervasive and Mobile Computing, Computer Communications, and the International Journal of Information Security. Beside security, he worked on distributed multimedia applications over high speed networks and on network interconnection. Prior to joining EurÃ©com, he worked in the Zurich Research Laboratory of IBM where he was one of the key designers of the KryptoKnight security system. He also worked as a consultant in security for the IBM Consulting Group. Refik Molva has a Ph.D. in Computer Science from the Paul Sabatier University in Toulouse (1986) and a B.Sc. in Computer Science (1981) from Joseph Fourier University, Grenoble, France.

Bo Peng possesses strong programming skills and a background in applied mathematics, biostatistics, and bioinformatics, and is interested in applying advanced computational techniques (parallel computation, large-scale simulations) to research topics in population genetics, genetic epidemiology and bioinformatics. In particular, he has developed unique skills in the design and implementation of large-scale individual-based simulations and have developed novel simulation methods for the simulation of realistic samples for genome wide association studies, and recently next-gen sequencing studies. The simulation program that he has developed and maintained in the past few years (simuPOP) is currently one of the leading population genetics simulators, with more than 10,000 downloads and many applications in diverse research areas such as conservation biology and public health genomics. Collaborating with groups in MD Anderson Cancer Center and Baylor College of Medicine, he is developing software tools (Variant Tools, Variant Association Tools, Variant Simulation Tools) for the integrated annotation, manipulation and analysis of genetic variants from whole exome and whole genome sequencing studies.

George Pittas is a PhD candidate at University of Piraeus. He has bachelor degree of Department of Digital Systems and Master degree of Techno-economic Management of Digital System. Currently, he is working as researcher on PINCLOUD project at University of Piraeus.

Andriana Prentza is an Associate Professor at the Department of Digital Systems of the University of Piraeus, Greece. She received her Diploma in Computer Engineering and Information Sciences and her M.Sc. in Biomedical Engineering from the University of Patras, Greece, and her Ph.D. degree in Biomedical Engineering from the Eindhoven University of Technology, Eindhoven, the Netherlands. She has been a teaching/research assistant at the Department of Electrical Engineering of Eindhoven University of Technology and a senior Research Scientist at the Biomedical Engineering Laboratory of the Institute of Communication and Computer Systems of National Technical University of Athens (ICCS-NTUA), Athens, Greece. She has been very actively involved in a number of European (FP4, FP5, FP6, FP7) and National R&D programs focusing on Information Communication Technologies (ICT) projects and she serves as expert evaluator and reviewer for the European Commission and national research and development programmes. She has published more than 70 scientific papers in peer-reviewed international journals, book chapters and conference proceedings. She is Associate Editor for the IEEE Transactions on the Information Technology in Biomedicine and IEEE Journal of Biomedical and Health Informatics and serves as a reviewer for several other scientific journals. Her current research interests include Software Engineering techniques and methodologies for the development and evaluation of software systems and services in the areas of e-government, e-health and biomedicine. She is a Senior Member of the Institute of Electrical and Electronics Engineers (IEEE) and a member of the Technical Chamber of Greece. Since 2013, she is a member of the Horizon 2020, Advisory Group for Health, demographic change and wellbeing of the European Commission.

Pasquale Puzio is a CIFRE PhD Student at SecludIT and EURECOM, under the supervision of Sergio Loureiro and Refik Molva. He got a Master's Degree in Computer Science from University of Bologna and a Master's Degree in Ubiquitous Computing from University of Nice-Sophia Antipolis. The topic of his PhD thesis is DataStorage Security in Cloud Computing but his research interests include also infrastructure security in cloud computing. In 2013, his paper "ClouDedup: Secure Deduplication with Encrypted Data for Cloud Storage" was accepted in IEEE CloudCom.

Muthu Ramachandran is currently a Principal Lecturer in the Computing, Creative Technologies, and Engineering School as part of the Faculty of Arts, Environment and Technology at Leeds Metropolitan University in the UK. Previously, he spent nearly eight years in industrial research (Philips Research Labs and Volantis Systems Ltd, Surrey, UK) where he worked on software architecture, reuse, and testing. Prior to that he was teaching at Liverpool John Moores University and received his PhD from Lancaster University. His first career started as a research scientist from India Space Research Labs where he worked on real-time systems development projects. Muthu is an author of two books: Software Components: Guidelines and Applications (Nova Publishers, NY, USA, 2008) and Software Security Engineering: Design and Applications (Nova Publishers, NY, USA, 2011). He is also an edited co-author of a book, Handbook of Research in Software Engineering (IGI, 2010) and has edited books KE for SDLC (2011) and Advances in Cloud Computing Research (2014, Nova Scientific). He has also widely authored published journal articles, book chapters and conferences materials on various advanced topics in software engineering and education. He received his Master's from Indian Institute of Technology, Madras and from Madurai Kamaraj University, Madurai, India. He is a member of various professional organizations and computer societies: IEEE, ACM, Fellow of BCS, and Fellow of HEA. He is also invited speaker on several international conferences. Muthu's research projects can be accessed on www.se.moonfruit.com and books publications on www.soft-research.com.

Melek Önen is a senior researcher at EURECOM. Her current research interests are the design of security and privacy protocols for various systems and communication networks such as cloud computing, ad hoc networks, sensor networks, opportunistic networks and social networks. She was involved in many European and national French research projects. She holds a PhD in Computer Science from ENST (EURECOM, 2005); her thesis was focusing on securing multicast communications in satellite networks.

Ute Riemann was born and grew up in Dortmund, gained a Master in Computer Science and an MBA. She started her career as a consultant for IT systems. Before she joined SAP she worked for companies such as T-Systems, Kurt Salmon Associates and Giesecke & Devrient where she headed focused on the process optimization and implementation into the organization. Ute Riemann published various articles in the area of business process management and process controlling. With her expertise in business process development and her background in project and process management she teaches change management at the university of applied science in Villingen-Schwenningen.

Scott Salzman is a numerical modeller with a diverse multidisciplinary background and more than 50 peer reviewed publications in a diversity of fields of research endeavour. His work has been cited more than 250 times.

Ishan Senarathna is a Research Candidate in School of Information and Business Analytics at Deakin University, Australia. He is a Lecturer in Department of Industrial Management at Wayamba University, Sri Lanka. He has published few journal papers and conference papers. He has taught in Sri Lanka and Australia.

Deepika Sharma holds Masters degree in Computer Applications and Bachelors degree in Science. She is working with Govindam Business School as a lecturer since 2011. Earlier, she worked in the department of computer applications, SPRC, Baghpat and had a small industrial stint with Innovative Analytical Solutions as a Dot Net developer. She writes articles and research papers in the field of cloud computing, software engineering and visual surveillance.

Chandra Mani Sharma is working as an assistant professor in Department of IT, Institute of Technology & Science, Ghaziabad, India. He holds Master of Technology degree in Computer Science from University of Indore, India. He has more than 25 research papers/articles/ book chapters published in various journals, conferences, and books of repute. In past, he had worked on research project - Development of an Intelligent Video Surveillance System for Human Behavior Recognition sponsored by University Grants Commission of India. He received MHRD Scholarship during 2009-2011, ITS- Star Performer Award in 2013, and ITS- Meritorious Scholarship in 2008. His areas of interest include cloud computing, image processing, algorithms, soft computing and software testing.

Marinos Themistocleous is an Associate Professor at the Department of Digital Systems at University of Piraeus, Greece. He holds a B.Sc. in Computer Science, a Postgraduate Degree in Teaching and Learning in Higher Education, a M.Sc. in Information Systems Management and Ph.D. in Informatics. Before joining University of Piraeus, he worked as a Lecturer and a Senior Lecturer at Brunel University, UK. He has close relationships with industry and has worked as a consultant for the Greek Ministry of Finance, the Greek Standardization body, the Greek Federation of SMEs, the Bank of Greece, ORACLE UK, Havering Council, etc. He has authored several teaching textbooks, internationally refereed journal papers and conference articles and has received many citations and awards of excellence. His research has attracted funding from various funding bodies. He acts as an international reviewer for research proposals submitted to the European Union and other funding bodies. His current research interests include Information Systems, Information Systems Management, Service-Oriented Architectures, e-business and Net-Centric Information Systems.

Deniz Tuncalp is Assistant Professor of Management at the Department of Management Engineering, Istanbul Technical University, Turkey. He has contributed to journals such as Operations Research and Journal of Organizational Ethnography, as well as various edited collections. His research interests are in organization theory and he specifically focuses on how organizations, industries and markets adapt to new technologies.

George Vassilacopoulos received his PhD from the University of London. He is currently Professor in the Department of Digital Systems; Director of the "Health Informatics laboratory"; Director of the Post-graduate Programme "Digital Systems and Services" and Director of the International Certificate Programme in "Health Informatics" at the University of Piraeus, Greece, where he served as Chairman of the Department of Digital Systems for over ten years, and served the university administration as

Vice Rector of Academic Affairs. He is currently Deputy President of the University of Piraeus Council. He has worked in both the private and public sectors in various administrative and advisory capacities. He has served as Health Informatics advisor to the Greek Ministry of Health, as a member of the board of several large Greek hospitals, as advisor of informatics to the National Emergency Medical Service of Greece and as member of various informatics committees in the public and private sectors. He has participated in several national and EU-funded research and development projects, mainly in the area of health informatics. He has authored many publications in peer-reviewed international journals, has written four books and several book chapters and has taken part either as a contributor or committee member in numerous conferences and workshops. He has also served as editor or associate editor for several published conference proceedings and books. His research interests include electronic patient records, healthcare workflow systems, service-oriented healthcare systems and healthcare systems security. He is a Fellow of the British Computer Society.

Stefan Voß is professor and director of the Institute of Information Systems at the University of Hamburg. Previous positions include full professor and head of the department of Business Administration, Information Systems and Information Management at the University of Technology Braunschweig (Germany) from 1995 up to 2002. He holds degrees in Mathematics (diploma) and Economics from the University of Hamburg and a Ph.D. and the habilitation from the University of Technology Darmstadt. His current research interests are in quantitative / information systems approaches to supply chain management and logistics including public mass transit and telecommunications. He is author and co-author of several books and numerous papers in various journals. Stefan Voß serves on the editorial board of some journals including being Editor of Netnomics and Editor of Public Transport. He is frequently organizing workshops and conferences. Furthermore, he is consulting with several companies.

Kiran Voderhobli is a Senior Lecturer at Leeds Beckett University specialising in teaching Network Management and Network Security among other areas related to networking systems. He is the course leader for Masters in Networking and Masters in Computer Science at Leeds Beckett. Before joining as an academic, Kiran also worked in industry developing secure commercial VoIP solutions. His research areas include network security and sustainable computing. He received the M.Phil degree from Leeds Beckett University after undertaking research into ubiquitous paradigms for network security. He is currently working towards a PhD in the area of sustainable networks and Green ICT. He is an active researcher in the sustainability research group at Leeds Beckett University.

Yun Wan is an Associate Professor of Computer Information Systems at the University of Houston at Victoria. He is also the Directors of MS-CIS and BAAS Program. He received his Ph.D. from the University of Illinois at Chicago in 2005. Wan's current research focuses are B2C electronic commerce, enterprise information system integration, and the design of comparison-shopping and recommendation agents. His previous research includes the design of Web-based intelligent agents and decision support systems to better serve online shoppers, the impact of policy and regulations on intelligent agents' evolution, and knowledge management. Wan's research has appeared at CACM (Communications of the ACM), IEEE Computer, EM (Electronic Markets), IEEE-IC (IEEE Internet Computing), JSIS(Journal of Strategic Information Systems), ISeBM (Information Systems and e-Business Management) and JASIST (Journal of the American Society for Information Science and Technology), etc.

Matthew Warren is a Professor of Information Systems at Deakin University, Australia. Professor Warren is a researcher in the areas of Information Security, Computer Ethics and Cyber Security. He has authored and co-authored over 300 books, book chapters, journal papers and conference papers. He has received numerous grants and awards from national and international funding bodies, such as: Australian Research Council (ARC); Engineering Physical Sciences Research Council (EPSRC) in the United Kingdom; National Research Foundation (NRF) in South Africa and the European Union. Professor Warren gained his PhD in Information Security Risk Analysis from the University of Plymouth, United Kingdom and he has taught in Australia, Finland, Hong Kong and the United Kingdom.

Lars Wulfken is a Senior Product Manager heading cloud technologies at Adobe in Hamburg, Germany. He is driving the development of a company wide, globally deployed Platform as a Service (PaaS). He has an MBA from HHL - Leipzig Graduate School of Management and holds a degree in Engineering (diploma) from the University of Technology Ilmenau. Besides that, he is an advisory board member of a publishing house. His current interest focuses on cloud computing and modern deployment systems.

William Yeoh is a Lecturer in School of Information and Business Analytics at Deakin University. He received his PhD from the University of South Australia and he has taught within Australia, Malaysia and Hong Kong. He has published numerous research papers in peer-reviewed journals and conference proceedings. He is also a frequent speaker in practitioners' conferences.

Index

Printed in the United States
By Bookmasters